“The most beautiful pastel ever seen.”

Staatliche
Kunstsammlungen
Dresden

“The most beautiful pastel ever seen.”

The *Chocolate Girl* by Jean-Étienne Liotard

HIRMER

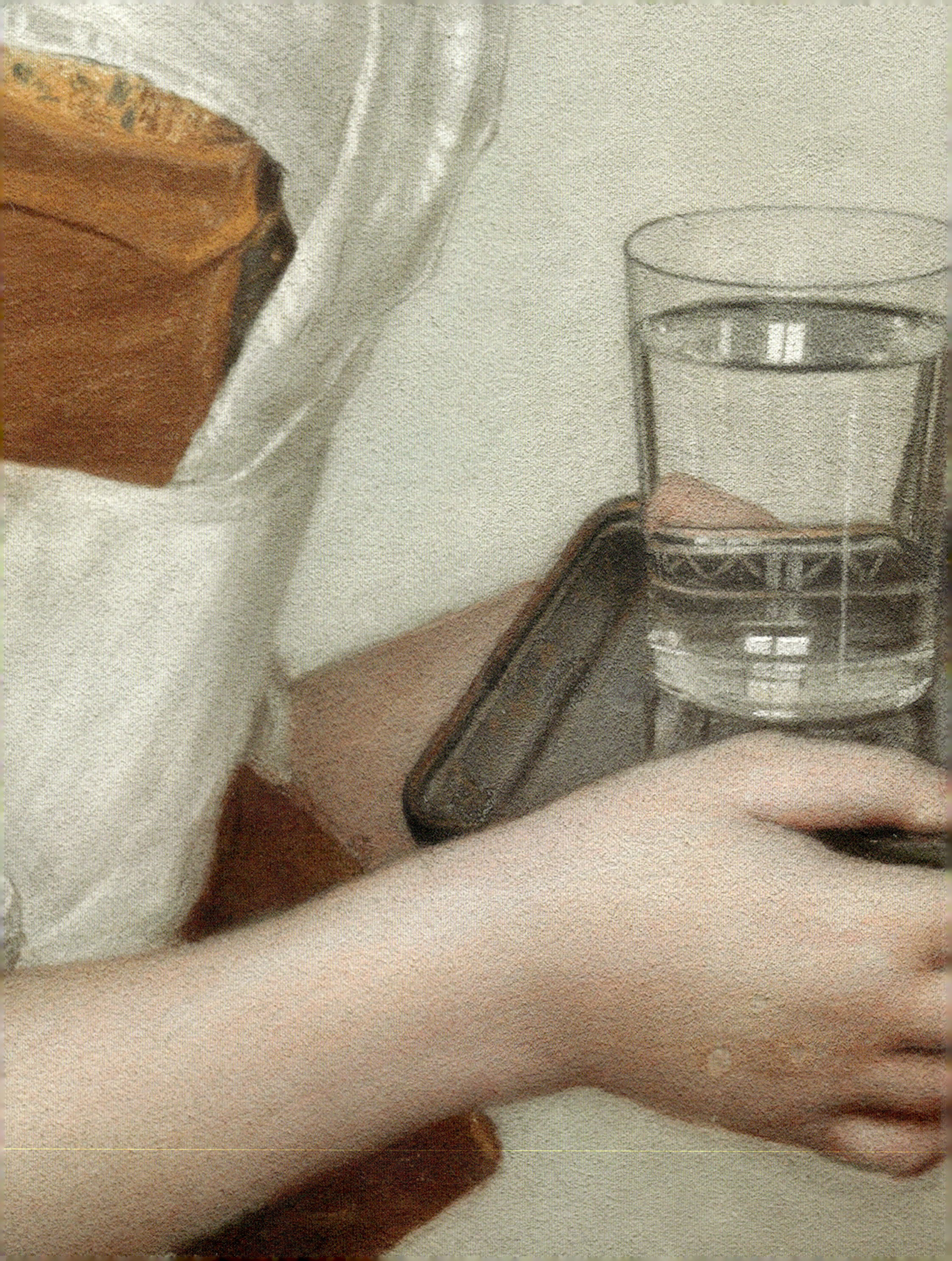

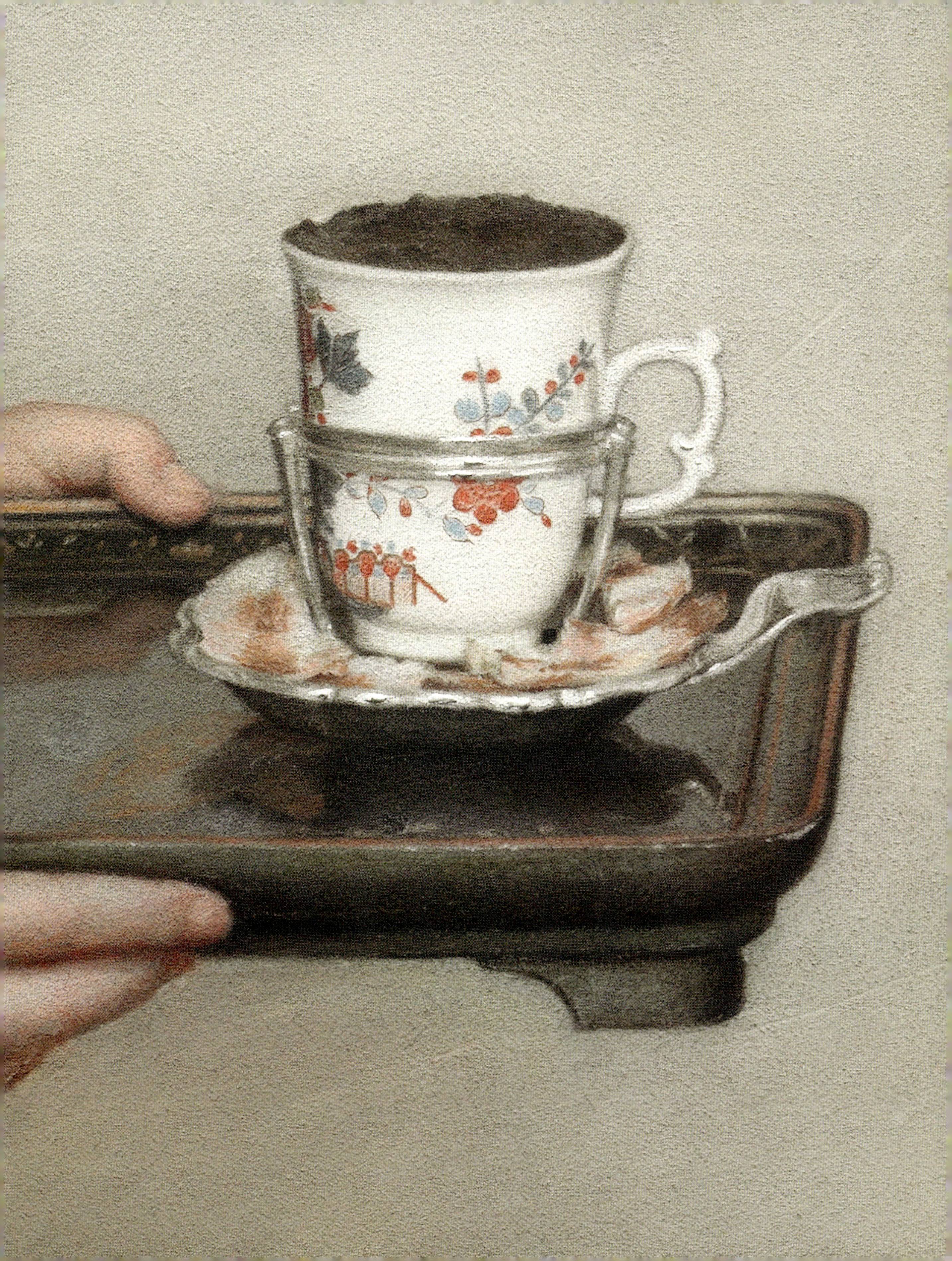

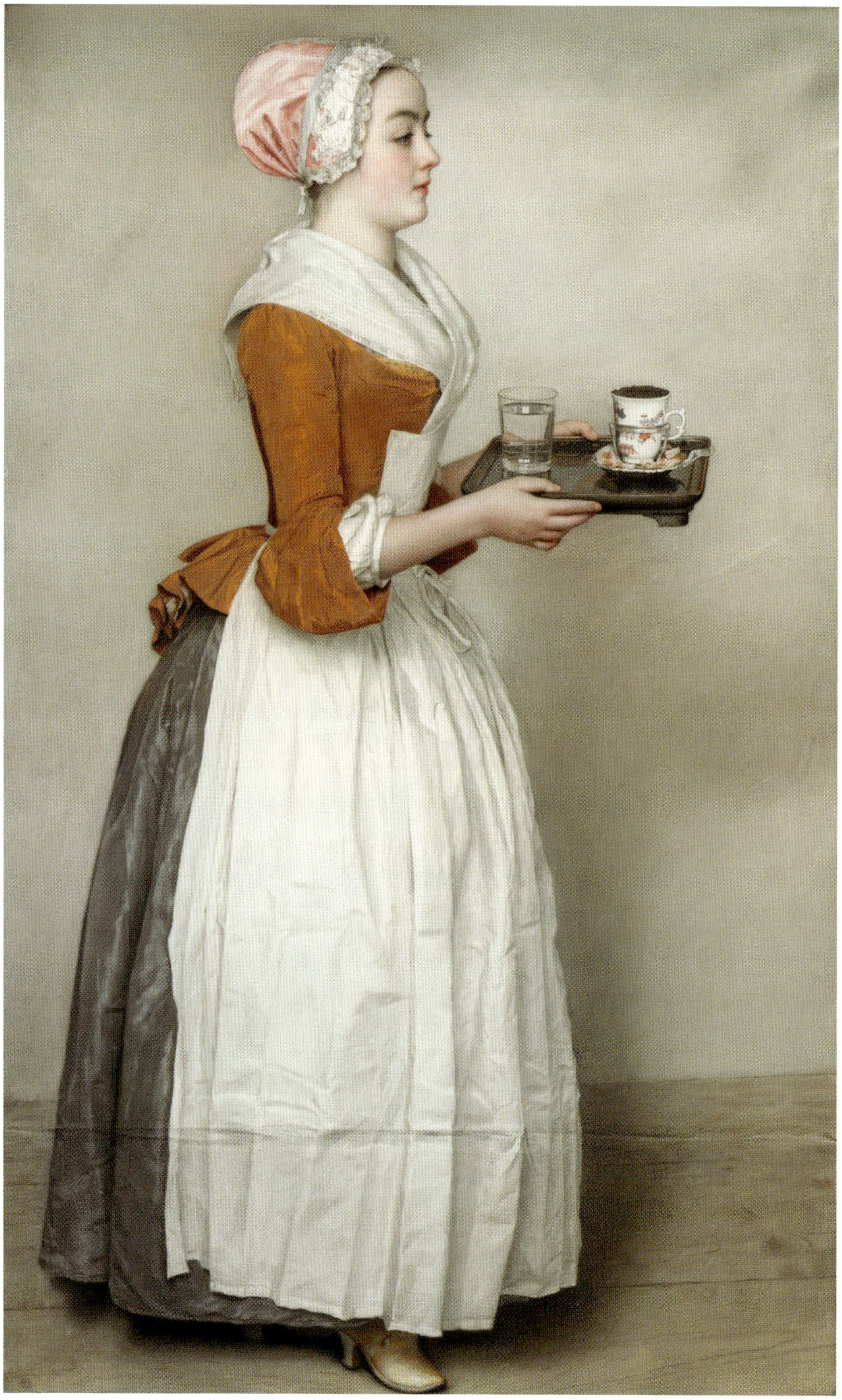

CONTENTS

FOREWORD

Marion Ackermann
Director General
Staatliche Kunstsammlungen Dresden

Jean-Étienne Liotard was a truly European artist. Born in Calvinist Geneva, he was an indefatigable traveler, especially in the first few decades of his life, journeying to Paris, Italy, and, by way of the Greek islands, to Constantinople, where he stayed for four years. His tour continued to Jassy, capital of the Principality of Moldavia (now in Romania), and to Vienna, which he would visit three times. Well into his advanced age he would continue to travel from Geneva to the Netherlands, England, and France. His life and career spanned nearly the whole of the eighteenth century: when he was born, the absolutist Louis XIV ruled in Versailles, and he died in 1789, shortly before the French Revolution began with the Storming of the Bastille.

Liotard left behind more than five hundred works—mostly paintings in pastel, but also in oil, as well as miniatures, enamels, drawings, and prints—among them countless portraits of Europe's royal and princely families, a few genre scenes, still lifes, and trompe-l'oeils. But none of these pictures is remotely as famous as his *Chocolate Girl* in Dresden. One might even say that this masterpiece is better known than the artist himself. At least today, for in his time Liotard was an artist in great demand internationally, not least because, following his stay in the Ottoman Empire, he had styled himself as a "peintre turc," with caftan, fur hat, and a long beard. For this reason he was very much "talk of the town" everywhere he went, and this was also part of the secret to his artistic and financial success.

In 1745, when the *Chocolate Girl*, painted in Vienna, found its way from Venice to Dresden and into the unique Pastellkabinett of the Saxon elector and Polish king Augustus III, the unknown serving girl stood out among the ethereal Rococo portraits, the allegories and Muses, because of its frame, its size, and its motif, but even more because of its precise rendering of details and its porcelain-like surface. It became a gallery icon and a visitors' favorite.

The aim of this wonderful exhibition by the Gemäldegalerie Alte Meister is to shine a new light on the artist and his Dresden masterpiece. In the context of his work, and especially of his oriental travels and his time in Vienna, the unique position of the *Chocolatière* becomes apparent. Such insights are made possible thanks to the numerous loans from international museums, above all the Musée d'art et d'histoire in Liotard's hometown of Geneva. We are sincerely grateful to all the lenders, public and private.

The exhibition project was reliably financed in large part with generous support from the Sparkassen-Finanzgruppe, for which we are greatly indebted to the president of the Deutscher Sparkassen- und Giroverband, Helmut Schleweis. We also thank the Swiss Kulturstiftung Pro Helvetia and Alfred Ritter GmbH & Co. KG for their continued assistance.

WELCOME

Helmut Schleweis
President
Deutscher Sparkassen- und Giroverband

"The most beautiful pastel ever seen." This assertion by the Venetian artist Rosalba Carriera, the best-known pastel painter of the first half of the eighteenth century, marks the beginning of a true success story—the story of the *Chocolate Girl*, the most famous work by the Genevan artist Jean-Étienne Liotard.

Carriera's judgement would hold up. From the outset, the *Chocolate Girl* was highly celebrated and a main attraction of Dresden's Gemäldegalerie. With its arrival in 1745, the gallery was able to present its first contemporary work—unquestionably one of the reasons for its immediate fame. But it was—and is—above all the motif itself that attracts visitors. Inspired by his stay in Vienna, with the *Chocolate Girl* Liotard chose a subject rarely seen in painting before: an unknown domestic servant. At the same time the artist captured on parchment a motif that anticipated the art of the Enlightenment, a figure of identification and a bridge between the museum and the everyday world—even today. Whether as a poster, on cups and napkins, or as a fridge magnet, the *Chocolate Girl* is now seen everywhere and in all kinds of forms. But it has been copied, adapted, and reproduced for much longer. As early as 1858, the writer Józef Ignacy Kraszewski stated that "on average at least fifty thousand copies of the 'Chocolate Girl' appear each year."

With every reproduction, the story of the *Chocolate Girl* is told again, its role as a figure of identification further reinforced, not just for the residents of Dresden and Saxony. She reminds us that art conveys both stories and history, creates memories, prompts narratives, and can shed light on previously unfamiliar figures and events.

Expanding perspectives and establishing new connections—these are essential features of the power of art, and at the same time the motivation behind museum work in general and behind the sponsorship by the Sparkassen-Finanzgruppe, not only of the present exhibition, but of the Staatliche Kunstsammlungen Dresden as a whole, as one of Germany's most important museum groups.

Since 2006, the Sparkassen-Finanzgruppe, as part of a network consisting of the Ostsächsische Sparkasse Dresden, the Ostdeutscher Sparkassenverband with all of Saxony's Sparkassen, LBS Ostdeutsche Landesbausparkasse AG and Sachsen Bank, Sparkassen-Versicherung Sachsen, DekaBank Deutsche Girozentrale, and the Deutscher Sparkassen- und Giroverband's Sparkassen-Kulturfond, has helped support the Staatliche Kunstsammlungen Dresden, and since 2011 as its primary sponsor.

The Dresden *Chocolate Girl*—who, on her lacquer tray, delivers the message that, happily, art and enjoyment are closely intertwined—is inviting you to indulge. It is in this sense that we wish you an enjoyable and stimulating journey through this catalogue and the associated exhibition.

FOREWORD

Stephan Koja
Director, Gemäldegalerie Alte Meister
Sculpture Collection (up until 1800)

In his *Traité des principes et des règles de la peinture*, published in Geneva in 1781, Jean-Étienne Liotard wrote: "You should never paint what you don't see." But it was not only because of these written instructions that Liotard came to be known as a "peintre de la vérité." Responsible for this descriptor were above all his true-to-life depictions in pastel and miniature portraits, with their flawless painted surfaces. Although stylistically assigned to French pastel painting, Liotard's work, in its painterly treatment, the absence of hatching or visible brush or chalk strokes, and his extremely soft, blurred transitions, is clearly distinct from that of such contemporaries as Maurice Quentin de La Tour or Jean-Baptiste Peronneau. The differences are particularly striking in the treatment of skin tones. In addition, Liotard cultivated a preference for bright, luminous colors that give his works their unique radiance.

Liotard was born in Geneva on December 22, 1702, as son of French Huguenots who in 1685 had emigrated from Montélimar near Lyon to Geneva and attained citizenship there in 1701. If his language and family background had already provided close ties with France, these were further strengthened by his training under Jean-Baptiste Massé in Paris. He worked here from 1723 to 1735, and was clearly influenced by French art, where pastel painting enjoyed a special flowering in the eighteenth century, especially in portraiture. The portraitist Joseph Vivien, a pupil of Charles Le Brun and member of the Académie royale de peinture et de sculpture, was the first to employ pastel crayons in painting. And, as early as 1720/2, the Venetian Rosalba Carriera had stayed in Paris and left a lasting impression as a pastel painter. The young Liotard intensively studied her works as well as those of Maurice Quentin de La Tour.

Dresden's Pastellkabinett offers a wonderful opportunity to study the different painting styles of these artists, as, in addition to the abundance of pastels by Rosalba Carriera, it permits direct comparison between works on the same subject: in the late 1740s both La Tour and Liotard portrayed the famous "Maréchal de Saxe," Maurice Count of Saxony, one of France's seven marshals general and illegitimate son of the elector of Saxony Frederick Augustus I, better known as Augustus II the Strong.

A constant characteristic of Liotard's art was its true-to-life rendering. Accordingly, he often inscribed his etchings and engravings with the phrase "d'après nature." In this, Liotard anticipated nineteenth-century Realism and, to a certain extent, Gustave Courbet's famous maxim that only what could be seen was worthy of depiction and his call for "Réalisme": "Painting is an essentially concrete art and can only consist of the representation of real and existing things." To Courbet, Realism was inherently a democratic art as well. And here, too, Liotard proved to be a precursor, when, with the *Chocolate Girl*, he took up a subject that, at the time, was not normally considered worthy of depiction, inasmuch as the maidservant belonged to a lower social class.

Liotard's realistic approach can be noticed, for example, in his rendering of the water glass in the

Fig. 1 **Jean-Étienne Liotard, Maurice de Saxe, Marshal General of France,** ca. 1746/49, pastel on parchment, 64 x 53 cm, Gemäldegalerie Alte Meister, Staatliche Kunstsammlungen Dresden

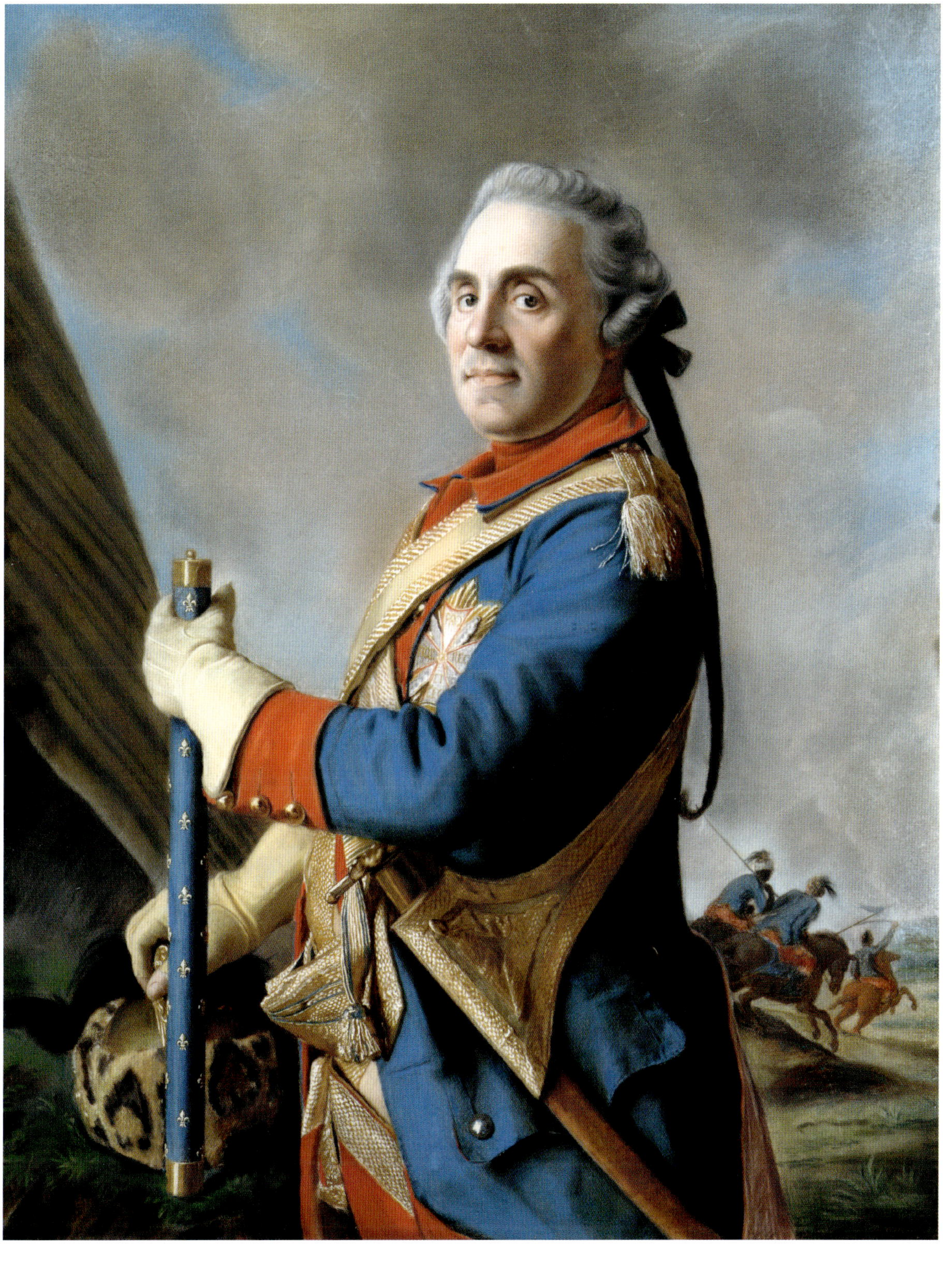

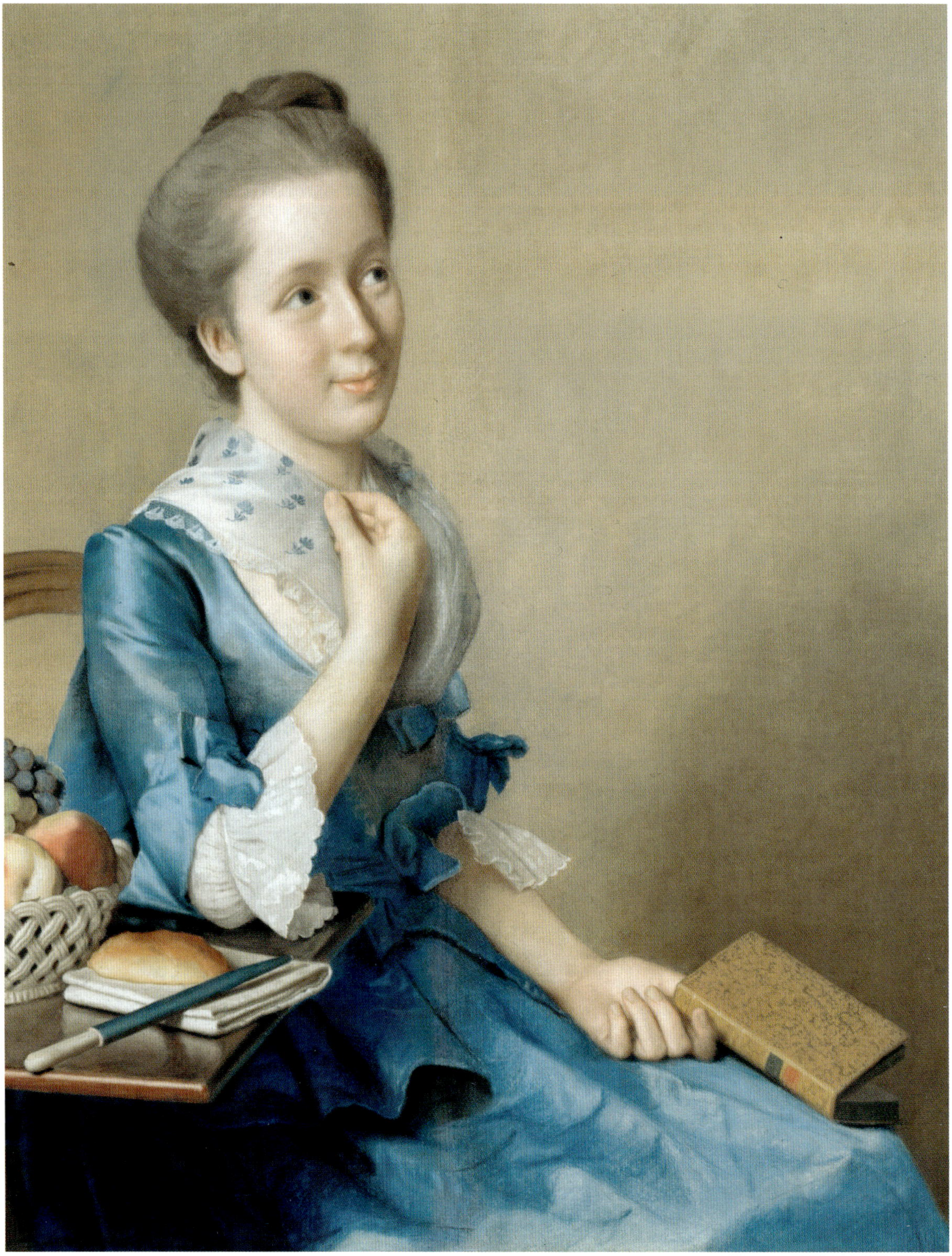

Chocolate Girl, but also in his later still lifes, which in their simplicity go beyond even those of Jean Siméon Chardin. Altogether, the restrained, clear compositions of his works have an extremely modern quality.

With the exhibition *The Most Beautiful Pastel Ever Seen*, the Gemäldegalerie Alte Meister presents its own holdings, supplemented with loans from elsewhere in Germany and abroad, thus placing the works of the Genevan master both in their wider art-historical context and that of the history of the Dresden collection. The exhibition format aims to explore the distinctive features of the Dresden Gemäldegalerie. At the same time, the show is the first in a series of special exhibitions to be held on the ground floor of the Semperbau's west wing.

I would like to thank all lenders for their generous support of this exhibition project. I am also extremely grateful to all the staff at the Staatliche Kunstsammlungen Dresden, whose expertise and dedication contributed to the exhibition's success. I am particularly indebted to the management and restoration teams of the Gemäldegalerie Alte Meister, especially Roland Enke as the exhibition's curator and curator of German painting, who developed the project with extraordinary vigor and sagacity, and his assistant Susanne Drexler, who supported him with great competence and commitment. I am also grateful to the restorer Christoph Schölzel and to Michael Mäder and Wolfgang Kreische for investigating the painterly technique of the pastel *The Chocolate Girl*. Responsible for the design and implementation of the exhibition and the felicitous display of the works was KKS Architektur + Gestaltung under the leadership of Daniel Kunze. Finally, the Hirmer Verlag and the designer Peter Baldinger have created a beautiful catalogue, for which I also wish to express my gratitude.

Fig. 2 **Jean-Étienne Liotard, Mademoiselle Suzanne Curchod, the Future Madame Jacques Necker** (detail) ca. 1760, pastel on parchment, mounted on canvas and cardboard 87.5 x 106 cm, Bundesmobilienverwaltung, Schönbrunn Palace, Vienna

ACKNOWLEDGEMENTS

For their kind support and helpful advice we would like to thank:
Annette Ahrens, Vienna
Dr. Hans Boekh, Geneva
Dr. Duncan Bull, Amsterdam
Ulrike Fischer, Munich
Caroline Guignard, Geneva
Dr. Elisabeth Hipp, Munich
Dr. Bodo Hofstetter, Berlin
Dr. Elfriede Iby, Vienna
Neil Jeffares, London
Prof. Dr. Monika Kopplin, Münster
Petra Landsberg, Dresden
Dr. Georg Lechner, Vienna
Marcus Lilge, Dresden
Prof. Dr. Harald Marx, Dresden
Dr. Christof Metzger, Vienna
Prof. Ivo Mohrmann, Dresden
Dr. Paulus Rainer, Vienna
Isabelle Roché, Paris
Prof. Dr. Marcel Roethlisberger, Geneva
Dr. Christian Rümelin, Geneva
Leila Sauvage, Amsterdam
Margaret Zayer, Paris

A further special thanks goes to our colleagues at the Staatliche Kunstsammlungen Dresden:
Dr. Stephan Adam, Ines Beyer, Tulga Beyerle, Anne Böttger, Jenny Brückner, Dr. Andreas Dehmer, Steffen Dietrich, Valerie Eckl, Clara von Engelhardt, Christiane Ernek-van der Goes, Elke Estel, Andrea Feistl, Bettina Forger, Andreas Frauendorf, Tilo Frenzel, Dirk Gedlich, Maria Geppert, Prof. Marlies Giebe, Jan-Markus Göttsch, Dr. Andreas Henning, Dr. Wilhelm Hollstein, Elisabeth Horschik, Dr. Igor Jenzen, Michael John, Heike Kauffenstein, Hans-Peter Klut, Wolfgang Kreische, Gunhild Krüger, Peter Kubsch, Dr. Petra Kuhlmann-Hodick, Heidrun Lange, Dr. Birgit Langhanke, Marina Langner, Katrin Lauterbach, Anette Loesch, Annelie Lorenz, Dr. Michael Mäder, Melanie Meier, Dr. Gudula Metze, Kai-Uwe Metzler, Martina Miesler, Ulla Paul, Dr. Peter Plassmeyer, Juliana Polte, Anja Priewe, Steffi Reh, Rainer Richter, Angela Rietschel, Annabell Rink, Thomas Rossig, Doreen Scherfke, Elisabeth Schlesinger, Claudia Schmidt, Elke Schmieder, Dr. Christoph Schölzel, Holger Schuckelt, Olaf Simon, Kerstin Stöver, Heike Ulbricht, Michael Wagner, Dr. Julia Weber, Dr. Ulrike Weinhold, Anna-Pauline Weinke, Vera Wobad, Dr. Martin Zavesky

LENDERS

Rijksmuseum Amsterdam
Staatliche Museen zu Berlin, Kupferstichkabinett
Museum für angewandte Kunst Cologne
Schokoladenmuseum Cologne GmbH
Museum Huis Doorn
Dieter Härtel, Dresden
Hochschule für Bildende Künste Dresden
Petra Landsberg, Dresden
Antje Roesner, Dresden
Sächsische Landesbibliothek – Staats- und Universitätsbibliothek Dresden
Staatliche Kunstsammlungen Dresden
- Albertinum/Galerie Neue Meister
- Grünes Gewölbe
- Kunstgewerbemuseum
- Kupferstich-Kabinett
- Mathematisch-Physikalischer Salon
- Münzkabinett
- Porzellansammlung
- Rüstkammer
- SES – GRASSI Museum für Völkerkunde zu Leipzig

Städtische Galerie Dresden – Kunstsammlung, Museen der Stadt Dresden
Musée d'art et d'histoire, Geneva
Stiftung Schloss Friedenstein Gotha
Staatliche Porzellan-Manufaktur Meissen GmbH
Brigitte und Jochen Mütze, Moritzburg
The British Museum, London
Lowell Libson & Jonny Yarker Ltd, London
The J. Paul Getty Museum, Los Angeles
Bibliothèque Nationale de France, Paris
Musée du Louvre, Paris
Bundesmobilienverwaltung, Vienna
Kunsthistorisches Museum, Vienna
Oesterreichische Nationalbank, Vienna
Schloß Schönbrunn Kultur- und Betriebsges.m.b.H., Vienna
Royal Łazienki Museum, Warsaw
Kunst Museum Winterthur, Foundation Oskar Reinhart
as well as private lenders who wished to remain anonymous.

ON JEAN-ÉTIENNE LIOTARD: LIFE AND WORK

Marcel Roethlisberger

Liotard Today

There are artists whose names are automatically associated with a particular masterpiece—Leonardo da Vinci and the *Mona Lisa*, Michelangelo and *David*, Diego Velázquez and *Las Meninas*, Rembrandt and *The Night Watch*, Théodore Géricault and *The Raft of the Medusa*, Edvard Munch and *The Scream*, Pablo Picasso and *Guernica*, to name but a few examples. One such picture with a unique standing in art history is Jean-Étienne Liotard's *Chocolate Girl* from 1744: a young woman pauses, her right foot demurely placed at an angle, attentatively waiting for something not shown in the tall, narrow format of the painting.

For nearly 275 years the picture has been among the holdings of Dresden's Gemäldegalerie, accessible to the public from the outset and widely disseminated through countless copies, engravings, and reproductions, so it is hardly a new discovery. The subject, a domestic servant, dressed with extreme care and courteously reserved, is a figure long absent from our everyday lives. But what, aside from its historical value, makes this picture so special for the present-day viewer? It is the simplicity of the composition, the severe profile, the figure's immediate presence, the light-filled radiance, the clear separation of colors, the utter minimalism of the scene. Much of this conforms to a sensibility expressed in the art of our own time. At the same time, the picture is the opposite of what one would expect from a work of its period: there is no staged setting, no idealized Venus or Diana in a classical pose, no noblewoman in courtly finery, no literary narrative, no display of coquettishness or frivolity.

What still fascinates in this picture today was seen as fascinating from the very beginning. Count Algarotti, who purchased it for the Dresden art collections in Venice in 1745, described at the time the almost shadowless light ground, the remarkable relief, the extreme delicacy of execution, as "a nature in no way mannered."[1] The highly sensitive art connoisseur, along with, in his own words, "all the painters in Venice, and Rosalba Carriera herself, who judged the work to be the most beautiful pastel ever seen,"[2] praised its style not as a negation of the prevailing aesthetic, but as innovation, and, in his role as agent of the Saxon elector Friedrich Augustus II, promptly substantiated his verdict by acquiring the work.

The Exhibition

The present exhibition in Dresden is a logical continuation and expansion, chronologically and thematically, of recent engagement with the artist Liotard (fig. 1). Among the expressions of this new interest have been: a survey of Liotard's drawings exhibited in Geneva and the Louvre in 1992,[3] a dissertation on Liotard's artistic aims by Andreas Holleczek from 2002,[4] the encyclopedia of pastel painters published by Neil Jeffares in 2006,[5] the catalogue raisonné by Marcel Roethlisberger and Renée Loche from 2008,[6] Marianne Koos's 2014 book on the artistic treatment of skin and surfaces in Liotard's work,[7] a series of short essays, and, finally, the Liotard exhibition in Edinburgh and London in 2015/16.[8] This com-

Fig. 1 Jean-Étienne Liotard, **Self-Portrait with Beard and Cap**, ca. 1746, pastel on blue paper, 60.5 x 46.5 cm, Gemäldegalerie Alte Meister, Staatliche Kunstsammlungen Dresden

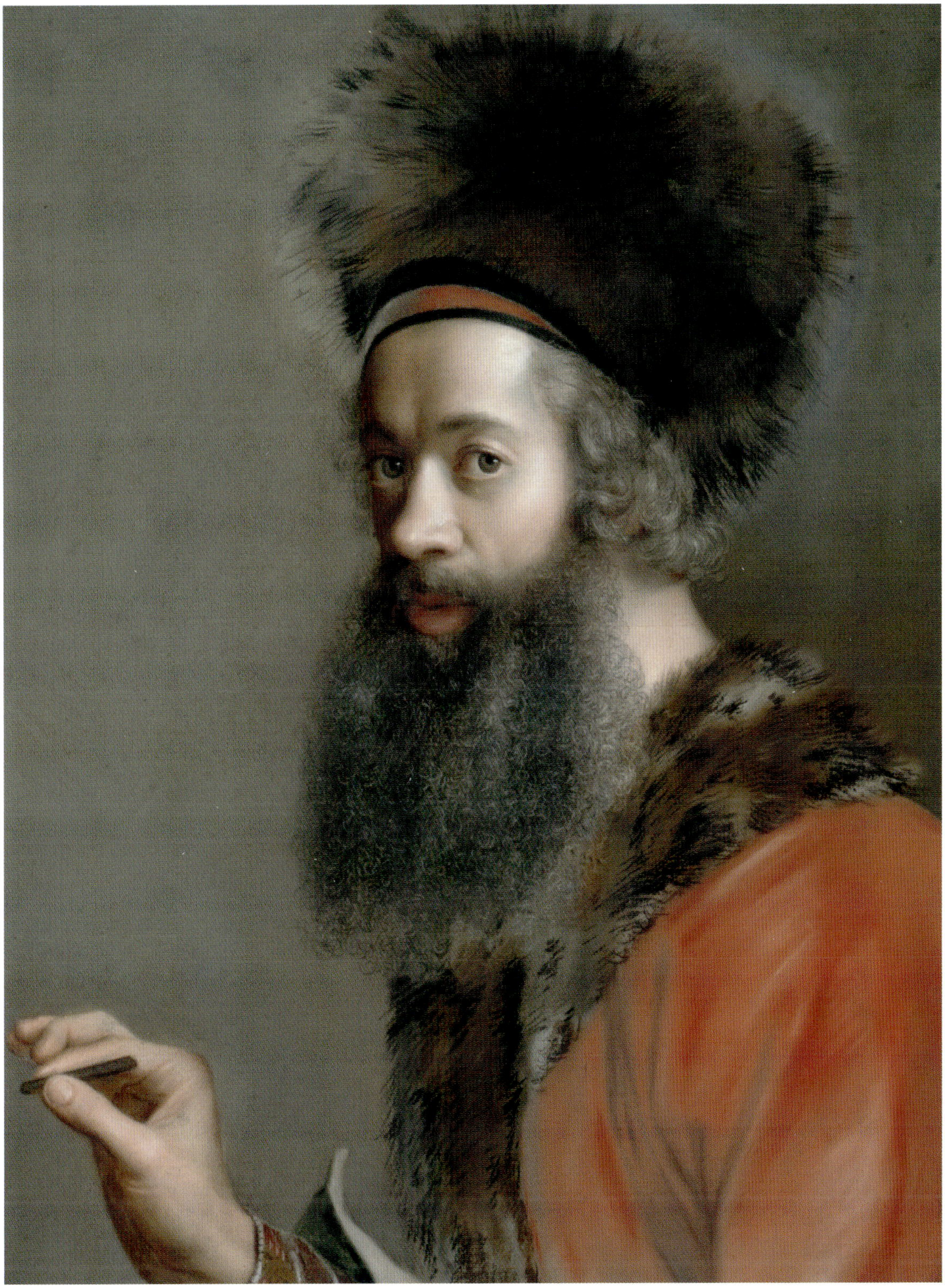

mendable and successful show was the first attempt to present an overview of Liotard's entire oeuvre—a difficult undertaking, given the sensitivity of the pastels, which do not take kindly to being moved about. And, consequently, a large contingent of his major works were missing in London. The Dresden exhibition, by contrast, places the *Chocolate Girl* at its center. The four Liotard pastels in the Dresden collection, combined with the unprecedented number of masterworks by Rosalba Carriera and the pastels by Anton Raphael Mengs, provide an exceptional foundation for the show. The following pages intend to give a brief chronological background for it.

Jean-Étienne Liotard, born in 1702 in Geneva, grew up during the era of Louis XIV and died in his hometown in 1789, one month before the Storming of the Bastille. His life thus spanned from the Late Baroque through the Rococo and up into the Age of Enlightenment. An itinerant portraitist without permanent position, he remained an outsider, unassociated with any school, famous but isolated, without pupils, enthusiastically lavished with commissions by his clients, viewed with hostiliy by his French and English rivals.

Liotard was a pastellist, an enamel painter, a miniaturist, portraitist, draftsman, and printmaker, painter of oriental subjects, genre scenes, and still lifes, and lastly the author of a treatise on painting. Some three hundred pastels, thirty oil paintings, thirty enamels, one hundred and fifty drawings, and fifteen of his graphic works are known today, widely distributed among museums and private collections. The most extensive holdings are in Geneva's Musée d'art et d'histoire and Amsterdam's Rijksmuseum. The known losses are immense: the first four decades of his life are only very sporadically represented. Self-assured, fully aware of his artistic mastery, enterprising, successful, professionally envied and embattled, an art dealer on the side, Liotard knew how to ingratiate himself into the highest social circles. As a portraitist he naturally had a more immediate relationship with his models; and in the more than twenty surviving self-portraits he also placed himself on display with perfect candor.

Liotard in His Time

Liotard was a contemporary of François Boucher, Maurice Quentin de La Tour, Jean Siméon Chardin, Giovanni Battista Tiepolo, and Pompeo Batoni. In Paris, Nicolas de Largillière and Hyacinthe Rigaud represented the traditional portrait up until the middle of the century; and Rosalba Carriera, another member of their generation, also lived until 1757. Jean-Marc Nattier and Jean-Baptiste Pater were continuing the legacy of Antoine Watteau, only recently deceased. A generation younger than Liotard were Jean-Baptiste Greuze, Jean-Honoré Fragonard, Anton Raphael Mengs, and Anton Graff, appointed court painter in Dresden in 1766. Francisco de Goya was born in 1746, Angelika Kauffmann in 1741, Jacques-Louis David in 1748, Elisabeth Vigée-Lebrun in 1755, and in England Joshua Reynolds in 1723 and Thomas Gainsborough in 1727. Within this artistic range between tradition and the future, Liotard stands essentially alone, but a towering figure thanks to the mastery of his works.

Pastel Painting

Trained as an enamel painter, Liotard is known above all as one of the most important pastellists of his century, along with Maurice Quentin de La Tour, who was equally famous throughout Europe. The venerable medium of pastel suddenly burst into a new flowering in the eighteenth century, especially in France.[9] Pastel painting was almost exclusively devoted to portraiture, predominantly portraits of women. One practical reason for this was that the artist could interrupt his work at any time and take it up again, unlike when working with oils, which simplified the problem of sittings—half a dozen of which were often required for a portrait. The standard picture support was paper, though Liotard occasionally preferred smooth parchment or vellum. Fixing and preservation behind glass were essential.

Liotard's picture surfaces are flat and vivid, his colors intense. He avoided the arbitrary hatching that most pastellists liberally applied to enliven their surfaces, and argued against the practice in his treatise, although in rare instances he employed it himself. The result of his technical skill are seamless surfaces, perfected down to the most delicate nuances, comparable to a Holbein in pastel, as Algarotti noted,[10] or akin to the glossy surfaces of oil paintings by Jean-Auguste-Dominique Ingres and many classical and Romantic portrait painters. All contemporary commentators saw the startling likenesses he produced of his models as one of his most outstanding accomplishments. In almost shadowless light, his figures stand before us motionless, dispassionate, with enduring presence. In bust portraits, without arms and hands, the body plays no part. Affect, expression of feeling, or any intimate glimpses of personality traits are very rarely recorded. Painters like Reynolds or Graff, bound to the Baroque tradition, were far more expressive in their portraits, using light, shadow, movement, or gaze to capture profound sensations or momentary emotions.

Geneva

Geneva, the artist's home in his youth and old age, was at the time a small, independent municipal republic and a stronghold of Calvinism (religion had no relevance for Liotard). As such it attracted migrants from far away with its religion, its liberal, enlightened outlook, and its system of public education. However, Liotard spent forty creative years in other European centers. His parents had emigrated to Geneva in 1685 from Montélimar, near Lyon, along with countless other expelled Huguenots, and attained citizenship in 1701. His father was a well-established tailor and textile dealer, Jean-Étienne and his twin brother Jean-Michel the youngest of fourteen children. Geneva's economy flourished thanks to its textile and luxury watch and jewelry industry, though, paradoxically, its watches and jewelry were destined exclusively for export, owing to restrictive local legislation. Watch cases and boxes were adorned with enamel. The Arlaud, Gardelle, Huaud, and other families were well-known miniaturists and enamel specialists. It was in this milieu that Liotard matured, but only very little is known about his training. His autobiography makes not the slightest mention of teachers or other masters. Yet a technically perfect enamel by the twenty-year-old artist attests to the fact that he must have spent several years in a Geneva workshop—there was no art school—acquiring this difficult skill.[11]

Paris and Rome

In cultural matters, then as now, Geneva looked to Paris. In 1723, the elder Liotard apprenticed his son—at the late age of twenty-one—to the Paris miniaturist and engraver Jean-Baptiste Massé. To the young man from Geneva, the flourishing metropolis was a whole new world. Shortly before, during a year's stay, the Venetian Rosalba Carriera had introduced the pastel portrait to the city. Liotard copied and studied little, but with interruptions would remain there for another nine years, becoming increasingly active as a portraitist in pastel. Aside from a few engravings and a first small self-portrait in oil,[12] almost nothing from this period survives.
Without prospects of success in Paris, he took the opportunity in 1735 to journey to Rome—again rather late for an artist—with the new ambassador Louis Philogène Brulart, Marquis de Puysieux. With his first princely patrons he found entrée into Rome's upper echelons of society, right up to the Pope, and produced a number of miniatures on enamel, parchment, and paper for the exiled Jacobite Stuarts in Rome, of which but few are preserved. He knew Naples; a sojourn in Florence is only documented through a signed pastel self-portrait dated 1737.[13] He admired the portraitist Pier Leone Ghezzi. However, he did not become involved in Rome's artistic scene: he neither became a member of the Accademia di San Luca, nor received commissions from prominent patrons of the time or had contact with any of the leading painters. Except for two pastels in which he copied an antique sculpture of *The Three Graces* and Bernini's *Apollo and Daphne* group[14]—but in a lifelike form with skin tones—his work shows no sign of any reception of classical or contemporary Italian art.

Constantinople

After two years in Rome, again without a breakthrough, an opportunity arose to take part in an expedition to the Near East as an illustrator, as was

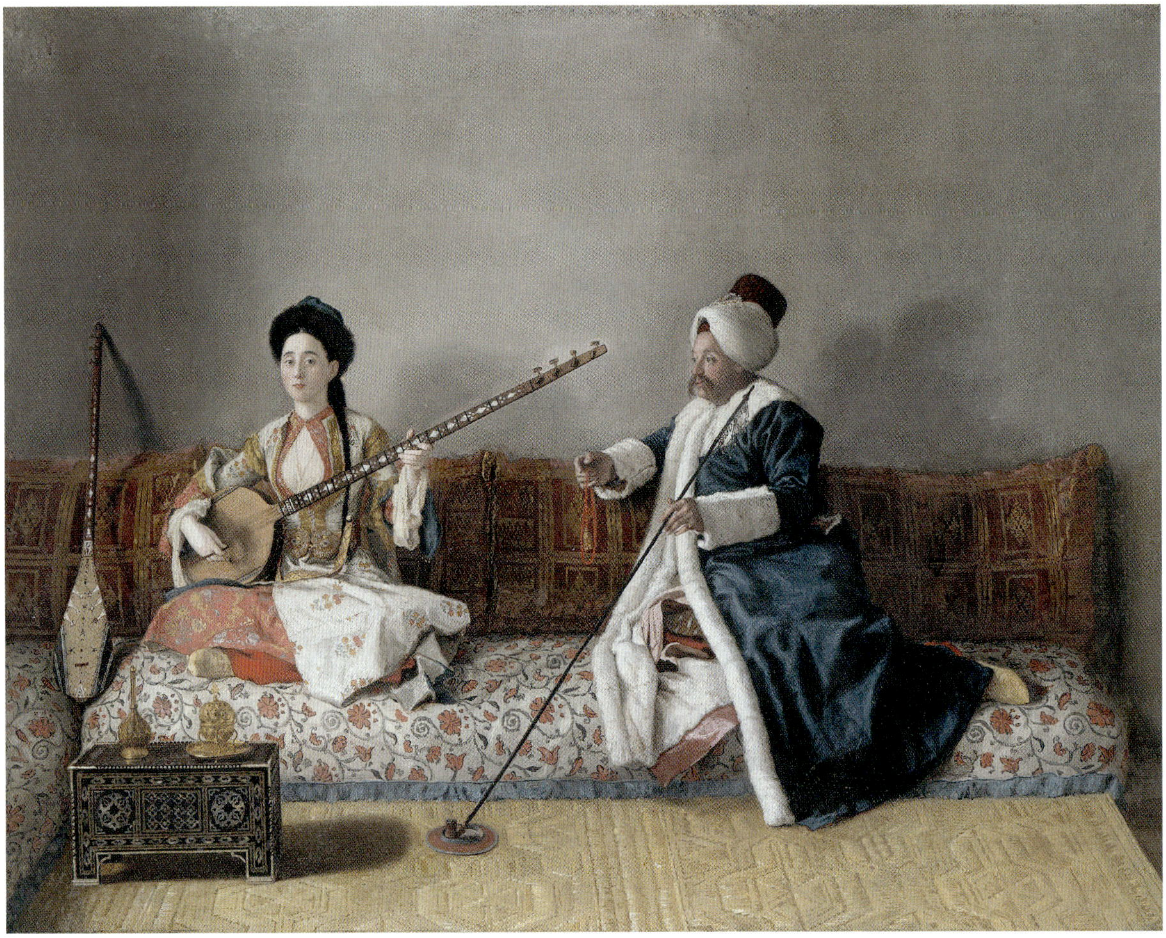

Fig. 2 **Jean-Étienne Liotard**, **Helene Glavany and Mr. Levett**, 1738/40, oil on carton, 27 x 37 cm, Musée du Louvre, Paris

customary at the time. The expedition was led by John Montagu, Earl of Sandwich, and William Ponsonby (later 2nd Earl of Bessborough) and took him by way of Sicily, Malta, various Greek islands, and Smyrna to Constantinople in 1738. The French painter Jean Baptiste van Mour, who had died the year before, had been painting Turkish subjects there since the beginning of the century; his compendium of engravings of Turkish figures from 1712–15 was widely exploited, by Liotard too, as motifs to copy or for inspiration. Liotard spent four years in the Ottoman capital, finding work primarily among Western diplomats and merchants. He declined the opportunity of continuing on to Egypt with Sandwich and Ponsonby. His Turkish sojourn was an unexpected stage in his life that would be full of consequence, leading to his self-presentation in Turkish costume and leaving an enduring mark on his art and his legacy to this day. Best known are drawings of Western women in Turkish dress and in local settings, to which he would later return again and again, as well as a number of pastel portraits and a few miniatures, including enamels, which suggests that he had the technical facilities for firing his enamel colors.

The intimacy of Turkish homes was inaccessible to Liotard. The highlight from his Turkish years is a small oil painting picturing Helene Galvany and the Englishman Levett on a sofa, documented as having been painted in Constantinople (fig. 2).[15] Helene is wearing the Tatar costume of the Crimea, where her father served as the French consul; Levett, an English merchant, is dressed in Turkish clothing. The picture was painted with great delicacy in oil on cardboard in the style of a miniature.

Moldavia

In Constantinople, the enlightened Prince of Moldavia, Constantine Mavrocordatos, invited Liotard to come to his court in Jassy. Apparently the artist saw insufficient professional prospects in the Western society of the Turkish metropolis and accepted the invitation. In October 1742 a three-week overland journey took him to Jassy, the capital of Moldavia, a province visited by no other Western painter. He spent ten months there, until the reigning prince was replaced by his brother; for the only time in his life, Liotard was appointed painter to a court.[16] There are virtually no documents telling us what Jassy—now Iaşi, an important city in Romania—was like at the time; nor are there any further records of Liotard's stay there. He produced portraits of the princely family and all the Moldavian and Wallachian princes. Except for one drawing of the princess, no confirmed work from this time has survived. His stay there did change his appearance, however, for in keeping with the local custom he grew a beard and took to wearing a fur hat. Beards were highly unfashionable in European society at the time, yet it became his trademark and he continued to wear it until his marriage fourteen years later.

Vienna

There was no professional future for Liotard in Moldavia either. After a long journey through Transylvania and Hungary, he arrived in Vienna in September 1743 and would stay there for nearly two years. He immediately met with success, and found it easy to adapt to his completely new surroundings. He made pastel portraits of the young and beautiful Maria Theresa and her consort Francis Stephen, as well as of other Habsburg family members. These half-figure pieces, all of them very much focused on the face, are impressive court portraits, yet more approachable than the formal, full-figure works by the court painters Martin van Meytens and Johann Gottfried Auerbach, who were still indebted to the international courtly style of France. The iconic portrait of Maria Theresa, which would immediately and for posterity become the enduring image of the queen, is a Liotard creation. Disseminated throughout the Habsburg territories—in the War of the Austrian Succession there was a particular need for Maria Theresa's far-reaching presence to stabilize the existing balance of power—the many workshop versions of the ruling couple present without exception the same unchanged visage.

For the only time in his life, and much to his displeasure, Liotard was forced to employ assistants: the Genevans Jean-Adam Serre and Peter Kobler; for this reason it is occasionally difficult to determine the authenticity of Liotard's works from this period. According to his autobiography, dozens of Viennese aristocrats sought to have their portraits painted by him, yet none of these works have survived. There are, however, two extraordinary works that date from this time: the *Florentine Self-Portrait* (fig. p. 48), commissioned by Francis Stephen, and the *Chocolate Girl*, painted on his own initiative.

Venice, Vienna, Frankfurt, Geneva

During his stay in Vienna, in early 1745, for reasons that are not fully known, Liotard undertook a brief journey to Venice. He took with him the pastel *Chocolate Girl*, which had failed to sell in Vienna, perhaps in anticipation of an encounter with the Venetian pastellist Rosalba Carriera or a possible purchase by Count Algarotti, known to be working as an agent for the Saxon elector. And the count did indeed buy the work for Dresden.

After his return to Vienna, in September 1745, he accompanied the court to Frankfurt for the Emperor's coronation, most likely with the intention of using the occasion to secure new patrons. There (or in Bayreuth) he painted the Margravine of Bayreuth and her daughter, and there he also got to know the young Princess of Hesse, Caroline Louise, later Margravine of Baden, who, for a period of six weeks, became the only student he had in his entire career. He made a portrait of her engaged in painting, in a composition inspired by Pietro Longhi. He then moved on to Geneva, where he spent one year, then to Lyon, where he visited relatives and stayed slightly longer. In this period, from 1746 to 1748, he produced such masterpieces as the portrait of the young Genevan woman Madame Boissier,[17] the *Self-Portrait with Beard and Cap*, which was acquired by the Duc de Richelieu and taken to Dresden (fig. 1), the first of several versions of Liotard's Lyonnese niece *Marianne Lavergne Reading* (see cat. 69), and the enamel portrait of Maria Theresa, at 62 x 51 cm the largest ever made and a technical tour de force that he kept with him for the rest of his life and which is now in Amsterdam.[18]

The pastel of a woman in Maltese dress is one of Liotard's few full-figure portraits (fig. 3).[19] A drawing of his, inscribed "Maltaise Avril 1738,"[20] is not identical, but shows the same costume, which is also seen in several pictures by Antoine de Favray, who worked in Malta.[21] Liotard had stopped in Malta on his travels in 1738; however, the style of the work suggests a later date. A comparison with the *Chocolate Girl* is tempting: the use of parchment, the same format, the figure reversed, and this time a distinguished lady dressed in black. The painting's creation and provenance are unknown, but it may well be the as yet unidentified portrait of this format recorded in Liotard's "List of My Best Paintings" as showing a Venetian woman.[22] In all likelihood it was painted in either Vienna or Venice in 1745, though the precise circumstances and its relation to the *Chocolate Girl* escape us.

Paris

Fully conscious of his mastery, Liotard spent the next four years—until 1752—in Paris, where at the time François Boucher was the leading painter and Maurice Quentin de La Tour the most admired pastellist. According to Liotard's own testimony, this second Paris sojourn was the most successful period in his life. The Académie Royale was denied to him; however, he was able to exhibit his work in the Académie de Saint-Luc from 1751 to 1753. His *Portrait of Maurice, Comte de Saxe* was willed by the subject to the Dresden collection (cat. 71). It was he who, as an uncle of the crown princess Maria Josepha (see cat. 76), introduced Liotard at the French court, whereupon he was able to produce portraits of the entire royal family, a distinct mark of prestige for the newly arrived foreigner. His greatest works from these years are the *Self-Portrait in a Red Jacket with a Long Beard*, which he retained for himself and bequeathed to the Geneva Library,[23] the Munich genre piece showing a lady in half-figure with a cup of chocolate,[24] a series of Turkish motifs—a pensive woman seated on a sofa, a woman reclining on a sofa reading,[25] miniatures of the portrait known as "Laura Tarsi" (cat. 44)—and the large painting done in Lyon in 1752, showing his nephew Antoine Lavergne at his writing table conversing with a young boy.[26]

London

In early 1753, having had repeated contacts with English aristocrats in Rome, Constantinople, and Paris, Liotard set out to spend two years in London, another period of great success. In English art, the portrait was especially highly valued. As previously in Vienna and Paris, Liotard began at the very highest social level with the portraits of Crown Prince Frederick, the Dowager Princess of Wales, Augusta, and her nine children.[27] In contrast to the French princesses, these children appear in simple close-ups without courtly attributes. Aristocratic men and women, Lord Duncannon, the later 2nd Earl of Bessborough, in an imitation cameo, and politicians like Henry Fox commissioned portraits of themselves, some in Turkish costume or seated with a book, a popular pose at the time. On request he also created replicas of genre pieces from his Turkish years.

During a stay in Lyon in 1754 he painted the *Lavergne Breakfast* (fig. 4)[28] as a pendant to the painting of his nephew at his writing table from 1752. It pictures two of his relatives, a young woman and a girl, at table drinking coffee. He himself referred to it as one of his masterpieces and sold it in London to his most important collector there, Lord Duncannon, for 200 guineas, the highest price he ever received in his life. He recreated it in oil in 1773.[29]

Holland

In early 1755 Liotard moved to Holland, where he would stay for two years, first with his nephew, a pastor in Delft, then in The Hague and Amsterdam. He painted some fifty portraits of the leading families, the Regent's two children, Count Bentinck, the van Tuyll family—mostly half-figure portraits of identical format without the inclusion of hands. In Amsterdam, in the summer of 1756, he married the 26-years-younger Marie Fargues, daughter of a French Huguenot family that had settled there—and to mark this change he sacrificed his beard.[30] On the art market in The Hague he bought on speculation the majority of his collection of Old Masters, mainly lesser Dutch and Flemish works from the seventeenth century,[31] which he later tried to sell with small profit, but which also inspired him to paint the small oil of the *Dutch Girl at Breakfast* (fig. 5).

Geneva, with Vienna, Paris, Holland, and London

At the age of fifty-five Liotard returned to Geneva a wealthy man and would remain active there for a further thirty years, interrupted by several extended journeys that he undertook alone. He bought a house with a garden and in the following years raised five children and a daughter from before his marriage. He formed a close friendship with the councilman and collector François Tronchin, who appears in a Liotard pastel next to a Rembrandt painting he owned.[32] Numerous members of Geneva's oligarchy and prominent visitors to the city commissioned portraits, among them the famous physician Théodore Tronchin[33] and his patients Madame d'Epinay[34] and Madame de Vermenoux,[35] as well as the latter's helpmate Suzanne Curchod, who would later marry Jacques Necker in Paris (cat. 72).

A second stay in Vienna followed in 1762, this time for seven months, with multiple portraits of the imperial couple and the well-known group of drawings of eleven of their children.[36] Liotard had done a number of portraits of the Habsburg rulers during his first Viennese sojourn between 1743 and 1745. Now, nearly twenty years later, he portrayed them again, thus producing the actual court portrait, reusing his earlier versions virtually unchanged (fig. 6). In the portrait of Emperor Francis I the picture space is expanded, monumentalized, and imitative of the representational portraits by Meytens, even down to the clothing, yet focused on the figure, without staged accessories like crowns and furnishings. But the real marvel of the work is its vibrant coloring in blues and yellows. Maria Theresa, in a dress and with draperies, is pictured somewhat more daintily in the pendant portrait. Among all of Liotard's royal portraits, none pictures such opulence without any of the accustomed courtly accessories.

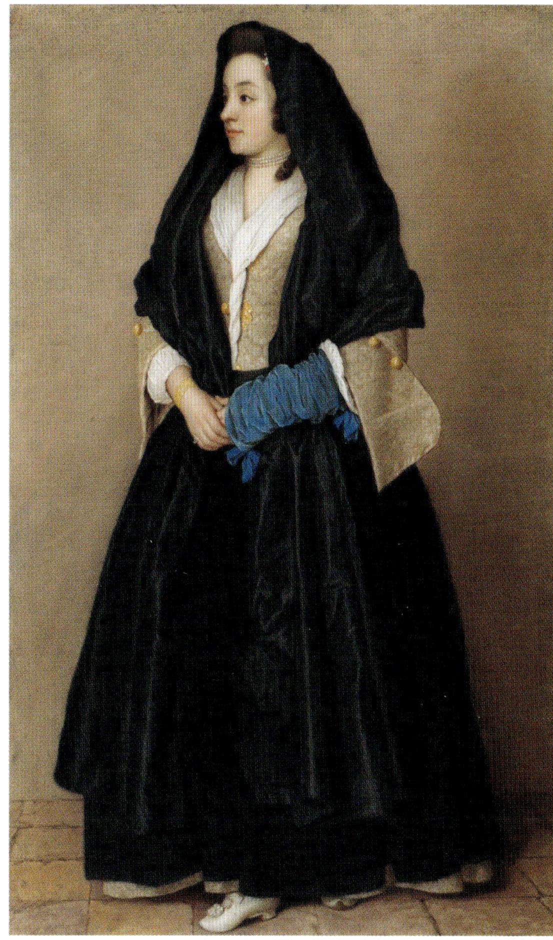

Fig. 3 **Jean-Étienne Liotard, An Elegant Young Woman in Maltese Costume**, ca. 1745, pastel on parchment, 82.5 x 53.5 cm, National Gallery of Art, Washington

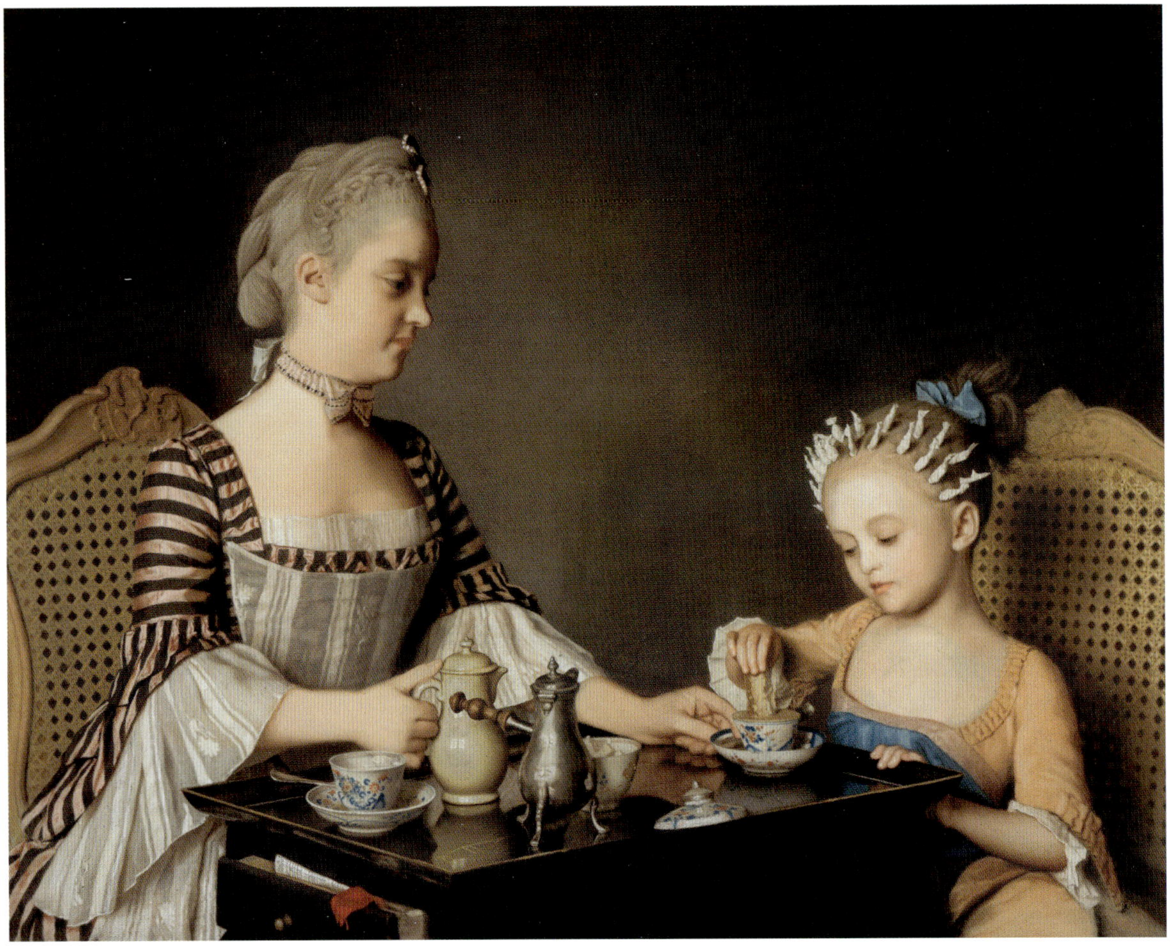

Fig. 4 **Jean-Étienne Liotard**, **Lavergne Breakfast**, 1754, pastel on paper, 80 x 100 cm, European private collection

In Geneva over the following years, he produced such inimitable works as the pastel of Lord Mount Stuart in a rare full-figure portrait,[37] his pose inspired by a portrait of his father by Allan Ramsay, and *Madame de Vermenoux Giving Thanks to Apollo*, Liotard's sole allegorical depiction in the taste of the time.[38] Less overwhelmed by commissions, he again occupied himself with self-portraits—among them the large oil painting showing him with a pointing index finger[39]—as well as still lifes, the trompe-l'oeils so treasured in France, a few transparencies painted on glass, and his only landscape, picturing the view from his house toward the mountains.[40]

On commission from Maria Theresa, he was in Paris in 1770 to paint her daughter Marie-Antoinette (pastel, now lost), and a year later in Holland, where he produced the portrait of Frederica of Orange-Nassau as a child.[41] Then he once again spent a year in London. While there he produced an astonishing variety of portraits of English aristocrats. His last journey, now together with his son Jean-Étienne, took him for a third time to Vienna in 1777, where he stayed for seven months and drew Joseph II and Archduke Maximilian.[42] Always open to experiment with new techniques, he then made eight mezzotints, a medium practiced above all in England. These then became illustrations for his treatise on the principles and rules of painting, which appeared in a small edition in Geneva in 1781, but remained virtually unnoticed.[43] His last group of works com-

prises a dozen small still lifes with fruits and two flower pieces.
In his last years his strength declined. He received only few commissions, younger painters like Alexander Roslin were given preference over him. The art market stagnated. Given the tense political situation, and as a representative of the old guard, he felt insecure and for a while sought safety away from Geneva, for example in 1781 in Lyon, in 1782 at his country house in Confignon, and in 1786/87 in Begnins and Nyon. He died in Geneva on June 12, 1789.

Résumé

Liotard grew up a citizen of the independent Republic of Geneva. In the local luxury industry he learned the art of enameling, which he later, along with miniature painting in gouache, practiced exclusively as a portraitist. Work in the tiniest of formats, both executed and to be admired with a magnifying glass, was a starting point that would significantly influence his work. The art of the miniature had flourished in book illumination since the early Middle Ages, in goldsmithing, printmaking, and painting—the Flemish painter Joris Hoefnagel, the German Hans Hoffmann, the landscape, flower, and still life painters in the circle of Pieter Brueghel the Younger come to mind, among others. Enamel painting was highly prized at the leading northern European courts. Famous Genevan enamel artists had preceded Liotard, most notably Jean Petitot and Jacques-Antoine Arlaud, both of whom were active at the royal courts of England and France, as well as many who practiced as itinerant artists, a career forced upon any number of portrait painters.
The roughly thirty surviving Liotard enamel portraits comprise only a fraction of his work in this medium, most of them from the decade around 1750. After that there are only a few isolated examples. The portrait, both in large and the tiniest format, had been a staple of European painting since the Renaissance. The popularity of the miniature portrait is explained by its diminutiveness and portability: without accessories like draperies or furniture it solely focused on the subject's head. In Liotard's time the earlier elaborate perukes and robes were abandoned; with almost voyeuristic intimacy the viewer is beholding the face, fascinated by the accuracy of the likeness so often praised in Liotard's portraits. Needless to say, these works are ill-suited for exhibitions. Only with the invention of photography did the popularity of the portrait miniature end.

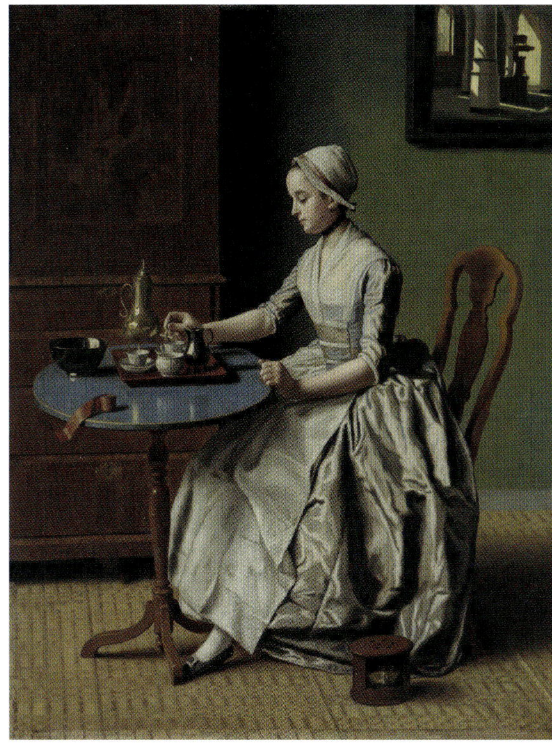

Fig. 5 **Jean-Étienne Liotard**, **A Dutch Girl at Breakfast**, ca. 1756, oil on canvas, 46.8 x 39 cm, Rijksmuseum Amsterdam

In Paris, under his teacher Jean-Baptiste Massé, from whom he learned very little, he turned to engraving, then primarily to the pastel portrait, which soon became the main focus of his work and for which there were no precedents in Geneva. The medium of pastel—old, yet rarely practiced until then, related to drawing through its use of crayons, and to painting through the use of color—experienced a sudden flourishing among his Paris contemporaries. Liotard's work has nothing in common with the airy, painterly style of the Venetian Rosalba Carriera, who had worked in Paris a short time before. In his autobiography he shows himself to be fully conscious of his mastery: “His way of painting in pastel is unique, his coloring very beautiful, of a perfection and vibrancy that no one is likely to advance further in this kind of painting.”[44]

At every stage of his career he had to prove himself in his uniqueness against the masters of the prevailing school. His awareness of his independence may have been one of the reasons behind his creation of the series of self-portraits. In many of these, his Turkish dress serves as an outward sign of his individuality. Only at the Viennese court did the potential of his art suddenly unfold. Much as he managed to adapt to the demands of the courtly style there, he would later find the informality of the English aristocracy more congenial. In his half-figure portraits, often without arms in front of a neutral background, the head dominates above the torso, painted in radiant colors and with sculptural clarity, which brings Liotard close to our modern sensibilities. By comparison, the portraits by his contemporaries La Tour and Perronneau are embedded in an emphatically painterly mood, often with subtle body language. In addition—and also in contrast to those masters—there is the variety of Liotard's subjects, aside from portraits: the Turkish genre scenes that were in such demand during his lifetime, causing him to be called “le peintre turc,” the late still lifes, trompe-l'oeils, mezzotints, and such individual pieces as the *Chocolate Girl*.

In his time, Liotard was famous in the places where he worked. Most of the contemporary copies of his works, as one might expect, picture the Habsburg rulers. Among the many engravers who immediately disseminated his work, Johann Christoph von Reinsperger in Vienna stands out. On the other hand, many of the artist's masterpieces are to this day found in inaccessible private collections, especially in Great Britain. He also had no notable students. Around 1800, the French Revolution led to social and artistic upheavals that, by the time of Liotard's death, extended across the entire continent, bringing with it a pusuit of new ideals. In the art of portraiture, the traditional norms of the eighteenth century were first replaced by a Neoclassical image of man and shortly afterward by Romanticism. Liotard continued to be known locally, and certain works, along with his Turkish motifs, kept his memory alive. Literature on him has proliferated in the past hundred years and now surpasses in quantity that relating to all other pastellists. The present exhibition is a most telling testament to Liotard's enduring legacy.

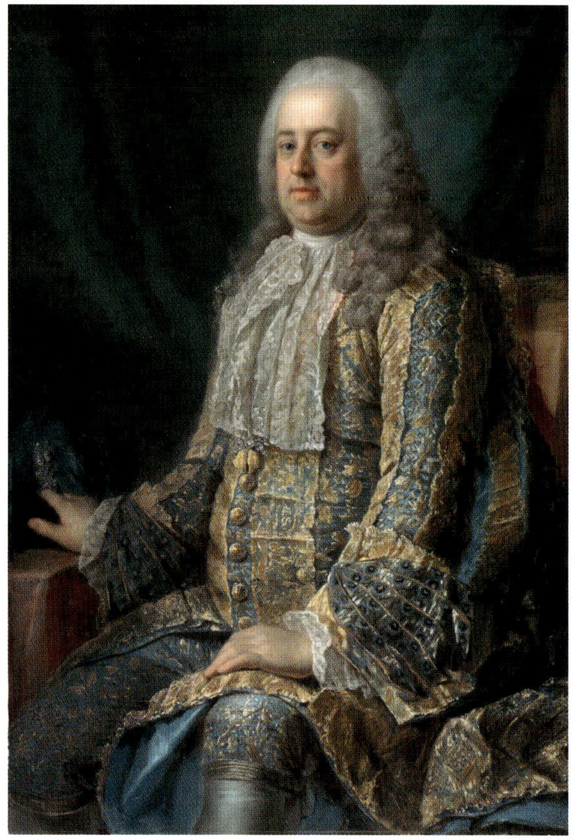

Fig. 6 **Jean-Étienne Liotard**, **Emperor Francis I Stephen**, 1762, pastel on parchment, 111 x 79.5 cm, Albertina, Vienna

1 Quoted from Marcel Roethlisberger and Renée Loche, *Liotard: Catalogue, Sources et Correspondance*, 2 vols. Doornspijk 2008, vol. 1, p. 324.

2 Letter from Algarotti to Brühl from April 23, 1746, quoted from Hans Posse, "Die Briefe des Grafen Francesco Algarotti an den sächsischen Hof und seine Bilderkäufe für die Dresdner Gemäldegalerie 1743–1747," in: *Jahrbuch der Preußischen Kunstsammlungen* 52 (1931), supplement, p. 70.

3 *Dessins de Liotard: Suivi du catalogue de l'œuvre dessiné*, exh. cat. Musée d'art et d'histoire, Geneva; Musée du Louvre, Paris, ed. Anne de Herdt, Geneva 1992.

4 Andreas Holleczek, *Jean-Étienne Liotard. Erkenntnisvermögen und künstlerischer Anspruch*, diss. Freie Universität Berlin, Frankfurt am Main 2002.

5 Neil Jeffares, *Dictionary of Pastellists before 1800*, London 2006; see also www.pastellists.com/.

6 R/L 2008.

7 Marianne Koos, *Haut, Farbe und Medialität: Oberfläche im Werk von Jean-Étienne Liotard (1702–1789)*, habilitation thesis Universität Fribourg 2009, Paderborn 2014.

8 *Jean-Étienne Liotard, 1702–1789*, exh. cat. Scottish National Gallery, Edinburgh; Royal Academy of Arts, London, ed. Christopher Baker et al., London 2015.

9 See Jeffares 2006, and www.pastellists.com

10 Francesco Algarotti, *Opere, Edizione novissima*, vol. 8, Venice 1792, p. 32.

11 *Selene and Endymion*, 1722, enamel, 5.2 x 7 cm, Geneva, Musée de l'horlogerie et de l'émaillerie; see R/L 2008, no. 6.

12 *Self-Portrait*, oil, n.d., 46 x 37 cm, private collection; see R/L 2008, no. 17.

13 The so-called *Florentine Self-Portrait*, 1737, pastel, 38 x 24.7 cm, Geneva, Musée d'art et d'histoire; see R/L 2008, no. 36.

14 *Apollo and Daphne*, 1736, pastel, 66.2 x 51.2 cm; *The Three Graces*, 1737, pastel, 59.4 x 45.4 cm, both Rijksmuseum, Amsterdam; see R/L 2008, nos. 32, 33.

15 *Helene Glavany and M. Levett*, 1738/40, oil, 27 x 37 cm, Paris, Louvre; see R/L 2008, no. 64.

16 Remus Niculescu, "Jean-Étienne Liotard à Jassy, 1742–1743," in: *Genava* 30 (1982), p. 140.

17 *Mme. Jean-Jacques Boissier, née Marie Charlotte Lullin*, pastel, 61 x 47.5 cm, private collection; see R/L 2008, no. 157.

18 *Maria Theresia*, 1747, enamel, 62 x 51 cm, Amsterdam, Rijksmuseum; see R/L 2008, no. 162.

19 *An Elegant Young Woman in Maltese Costume*, ca. 1745, pastel, 82.5 x 53.5 cm, Washington, National Gallery of Art; see R/L 2008, no. 140.

20 *Lady from Malta*, drawing in black and red chalk, 19.7 x 14.8 cm, private collection; see exh. cat. Geneva/Paris 1992, cat. 8; R/L 2008, no. 93, fig. 140.

21 Stephen Degiorgio and Emmanuel Fiorentino, *Antoine de Fabray (1706–1798), A French Artist in Rome, Malta and Constantinople*, Valletta 2004, pp. 22–23, figs. 2.3 and 2.5.

22 R/L 2008, vol. 1, p. 145.

23 *Self-Portrait with Long Beard*, 1751/52, pastel, 97 x 71 cm, Geneva, Musée d'art et d'histoire; see R/L 2008, no. 196.

24 *Lady with Cup of Chocolate (The Breakfast)*, pastel, 66.5 x 53.7 cm, Munich, Bayerische Staatsgemäldesammlungen, Alte Pinakothek; see R/L 2008, no. 205.

25 See R/L 2008, nos. 190, 191.

26 *Writing*, 1752, pastel, 81 x 107 cm, Vienna, Schloss Schönbrunn; see R/L 2008, no. 200.

27 All in the Royal Collection, London; see R/L 2008, no. 247–257. The portrait of Prince Frederick, who had died in 1751, was the only time Liotard ever painted a subject posthumously.

28 *The Lavergne Breakfast*, 1754, pastel, 80 x 100 cm, European private collection; see R/L 2008, no. 299.

29 *The Lavergne Breakfast*, 1773, oil, 81 x 103 cm, private collection; see R/L 2008, no. 495.

30 Marianne Koos, "La jouissance du détail: Liotards Bartlocke," in: *Kritische Berichte* 36 (2008), pp. 19–27.

31 R/L 2008, vol. 1, p. 123; see the inventory of his collection, ibid, pp. 133–155.

32 *François Tronchin*, 1757, pastel, 37.5 x 46 cm, Cleveland Museum of Art; see R/L 2008, no. 349.

33 *Théodore Tronchin*, 1763, pastel, 66.8 x 54.6 cm, private collection; see R/L 2008, no. 416.

34 *Madame Denis-Joseph la Live d'Epinay*, 1759, pastel, 68 x 54 cm, Geneva, Musée d'art et d'histoire; see R/L 2008, no. 365.

35 *Madame Paul Girardo de Vermenoux*, pastel, 76 x 60.5 cm, private collection; see R/L 2008, no. 366.

36 All in Geneva, Musée d'art et d'histoire; see R/L 2008, nos. 401–411.

37 *Lord Mount Stuart*, 1763, pastel, 111.5 x 87.5 cm, Los Angeles, Getty Museum; see R/L 2008, no. 421.

38 *Madame de Vermenoux Giving Thanks to Apollo*, 1764, pastel, 120 x 95 cm, Staatliche Kunsthalle Karlsruhe; see R/L 2008, no. 427.

39 *Self-Portrait, Laughing*, ca. 1768, oil, 84 x 74 cm, Geneva, Musée d'art et d'histoire; see R/L 2008, no. 446.

40 *Genevan Landscape*, ca. 1768, pastel, 46 x 59.7 cm, Amsterdam, Rijksmuseum; see R/L 2008, no. 438.

41 *Frederica Louise Wilhelmina of Orange-Nassau*, 1772, pastel, 68 x 58 cm, Moscow, Pushkin Museum; see R/L 2008, no. 481.

42 *Joseph II*, 1777, drawing and pastel, 67 x 49.3 cm; *Archduke Maximilian Francis*, 1777, drawing and pastel, 67 x 49.5 cm, both Amsterdam, Rijksmuseum; see R/L 2008, nos. 515, 516.

43 Jean-Étienne Liotard, *Traité des Principes et des règles de la Peinture*, Geneva 1781.

44 Quoted from the 1760 autobiography; see R/L 2008, p. 61.

“In all things related to comfort, pleasure, and the sensual enjoyment of life its inhabitants are far in advance . . .”

Jean-Étienne Liotard and Maria Theresa's Vienna

Stephan Koja and Verena Perlhefter

When, on September 2, 1743, Jean-Étienne Liotard first set foot in Vienna, the artist arriving fresh from the Orient attracted such great attention that he was duly invited to the Viennese court. Maria Theresa was impressed by his works and let him paint her portrait—the first of many portraits Liotard made of the ruler, and a masterpiece that would open him many doors in Vienna (fig. 1). Austria was at war with Prussia; every victory was celebrated, every defeat lamented. Yet Vienna was thriving, its population growing steadily, splendid new buildings were being erected, theater and opera were flourishing, and the Viennese were taking life in their stride, enjoying exotic hot drinks in the city's increasingly popular coffeehouses.

The Political and Economic Situation

Emperor Charles VI had done everything he could to safeguard his succession by his daughter Maria Theresa, born to him and his wife Elisabeth Christine of Brunswick-Wolfenbüttel on May 13, 1717. As early as 1713, with the “Pragmatic Sanction,” he had tried to address succession disputes between the various archduchesses and prevent a division of the empire by decreeing that, in the absence of a male heir to the throne, his daughters would succeed him. In 1735 Maria Theresa married the man she had loved since childhood, Francis Stephen, Duke of Lorraine, her “caro viso,” or, as she later called him, “mon cher Alter” (“my dear old man”).[1]

When Maria Theresa took the throne after Charles's death in 1740, her authority nevertheless stood on very shaky ground, for, despite her father's far-reaching precautions to ensure her succession, she was forced to fight for her acceptance as the new sovereign. Prince Eugene of Savoy had pertinently commented about the “Pragmatic Sanction” that a strong army would be more effective than such a decree,[2] and he was proven right. Before the year was up, Frederick II of Prussia saw an opportunity to expand his territory and, supported by Saxony and France, invaded Silesia.

In 1743, after reconquering Prague, which had been occupied by the French and Bavarians, Maria Theresa organized a celebration in Vienna's Winter Riding School, the highlight of which was a “Ladies' Carousel.” In this, the Empress led the first mounted quadrille. The carriages were driven by cavaliers, while the ladies were charging with swords at wooden or papier mâché models of Turks' heads. Following the festivity, the Empress and some of her ladies rode through the city in their carousel carriages for the entertainment of the general public. Maria Theresa deemed the event one of the high points of her reign and commissioned the artist Martin van Meytens to paint a picture of the carousel (fig. 2).

After eight years of war, Frederick II had achieved his aim and won Silesia. However, Maria Theresa was able to uphold the greater part of the Habsburg Monarchy and retain the imperial crown of the Holy Roman

Fig. 1 **Jean-Étienne Liotard, Maria Theresa in a Fur-Trimmed Gown**, 1743, pastel on vellum, 62 x 49.4 cm, Sammlung Oesterreichische Nationalbank, on permanent loan to Schloss Schönbrunn, Vienna

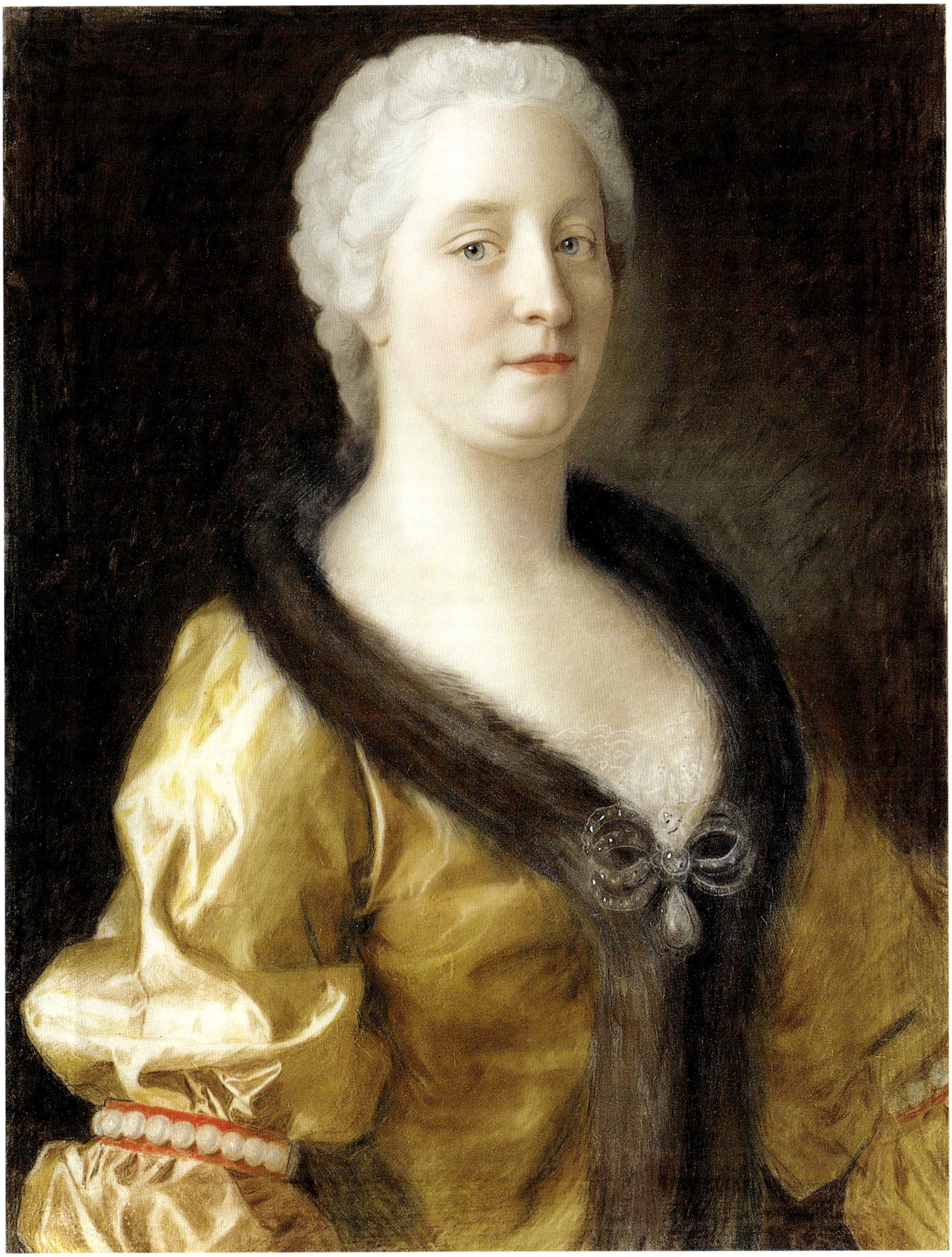

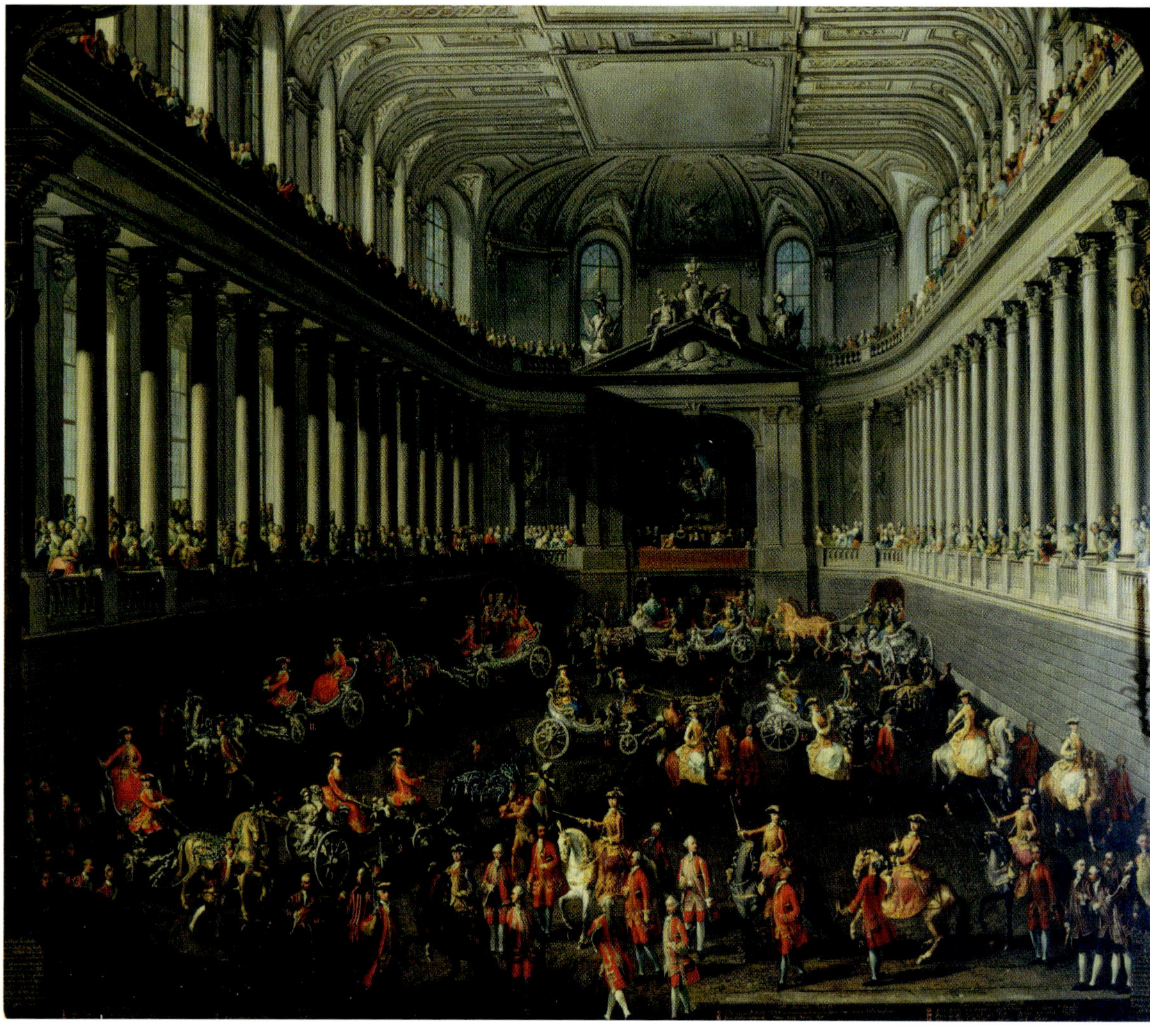

Fig. 2 **Martin van Meytens** (workshop), **The Ladies' Carousel in the Winter Riding School of the Hofburg in Vienna, on January 2, 1743**, after 1764, oil on canvas, 350 x 420 cm, Bundesmobilienverwaltung, Schönbrunn Palace, Vienna

Empire for her husband, who reigned as Francis I from 1745 to 1765. Having been crowned Queen of Bohemia and Hungary in the meantime, Maria Theresa found the loss of the Silesian territories hard to accept and attempted to regain her lost lands during the Seven Years' War (1756–1763), fighting together with her new ally France against Prussia and England—but to no avail.

Francis Stephen died quite unexpectedly in 1765, and from that time onward Maria Theresa would dress in mourning and wear her hair short, having lost "the only object of her love."[3] Her son Joseph II, having already been crowned "King of the Romans" (i.e. the Roman-German King) in 1764, succeeded his father as Holy Roman Emperor. Around that time, Austria gained the territories of Galicia and Lodomeria, Bukovina, and the so-called Innviertel, partly as a result of victories and partly through negotiations and treaties. Along with these outward challenges, the Empress sought to reform the financially strapped empire and its antiquated administration. Standing on the threshold of the Enlightenment, Maria Theresa understood that as a ruler she had a responsibility for her subjects' welfare. To her daughter Marie-Antoinette she wrote: "We live in this world in order to do good for our fellow men. Your task is of the greatest responsibility, for we are not here for ourselves or simply for our own amusement."[4] And she also related this kind of "maternal concern" to her lands and their inhabitants (fig. 3).[5]

With ever more comprehensive centralization measures she set out to reform Austria's administration. Revenues had to be increased and the powers of the nobility were much reduced; she also aimed to introduce a general tax liability for both the nobility and the clergy. A prerequisite for this was a general survey of the Habsburg Empire with all its lands, assets, and its entire population, regardless of class and status, in a land register that came to be known as the "Theresian Cadaster." In addition to newly created offices such as the "Directorium in publicis et cameralibus" and the Supreme Judiciary, which had extensive political and financial powers, the establishment of a uniform legal code brought greater clarity to jurisprudence. The *Constitutio Criminalis Theresiana*, published in 1769, still included witchcraft and sorcery as a punishable offence—showing little regard to Enlightenment concepts—as well as stipulating the use of torture to determine the truth. Yet, on the other hand, it did introduce legal safeguards to protect peasants from the whims of oppressive landlords and relaxed some of the rules on serfdom. Steps to abolish it altogether were later undertaken by Maria Theresa's son Joseph II.

Universal education was introduced in an attempt to raise standards of literacy in the Habsburg Empire. Vienna's university was restructured and brought up to contemporary standards with the appointment of experts of European stature in the fields of science and medicine. For training and education in specific fields, Maria Theresa created the Military Academy and an Academy for Oriental Languages, a precursor to today's Diplomatic Academy. Also established around that time were a merchants' academy, an early version of the College of Veterinary Medicine, and a specialist college for the mining industry. The Imperial and Royal Engraving Academy opened in 1766, which, in a union with several other art academies, would later become the Vienna Academy of Fine Arts. These numerous reforms and foundations were first steps in the spirit of the Enlightenment.

Such innovations with the aim of raising standards of living and improving public education as crucial cornerstones of the economy were of considerable urgency: In 1790, for example, around sixty-five percent of Vienna's population died penniless, i.e. owning nothing but the shirt on their back. Especially poor were day laborers and coachmen, horse grooms, and carters, but a good eighty percent of those employed in domestic service, too, were unable to build up any savings over the course of their working lives.[6] In the waning eighteenth century servants made up roughly fifteen percent of the population of Vienna and its suburbs, amounting to some 40,000 people.[7]

Under Maria Theresa's reign, Vienna's population rose from 130,000 on her accession to 192,972 in the year 1772.[8] This rapid population growth notwithstanding, the Viennese were still very much partial to the good life, as Friedrich Nicolai, an Enlightenment author from Berlin, observed with a certain inner

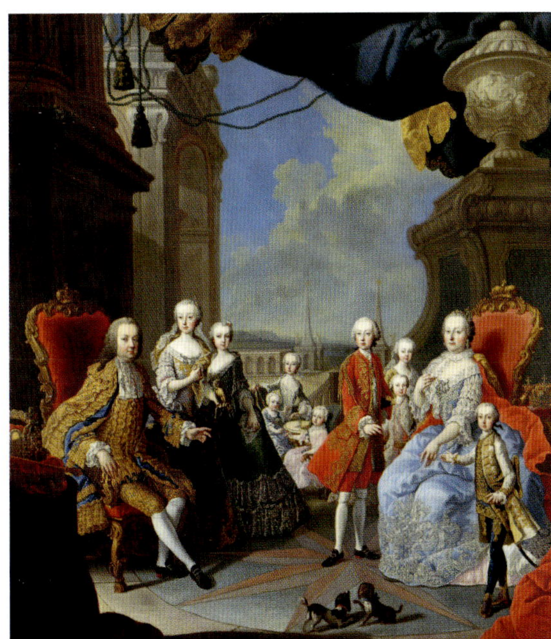

Fig. 3 **Martin van Meytens**, **Group Portrait of the Imperial Family with Nine Children**, 1752, oil on canvas, 204 x 189 cm, Kunsthistorisches Museum, Gemäldegalerie, Vienna

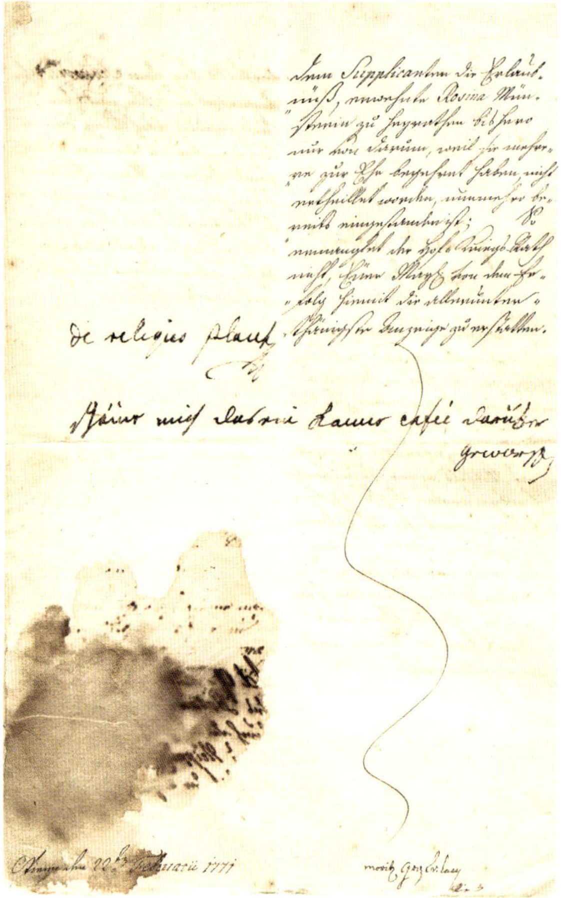

Fig. 4 **File with coffee stain and handwritten note by Maria Theresa**, 1771, Österreichisches Staatsarchiv, Kriegsarchiv, Vienna

detachment in 1781: "In all things related to comfort, pleasure, and the sensual enjoyment of life its inhabitants are far in advance of the inhabitants of any other German city."[9]

Life at Court

At court, Maria Theresa continued the Baroque tradition of ostentation and pomp, albeit to a slightly lesser degree than her father. It all served the greater good by providing an opportunity for artisans and craftspeople to show off their skills as clothmakers, silk embroiderers, clockmakers, clock tenders, armorers, bladesmiths, instrument makers, beadworkers, feather-arrangers, leatherworkers, gem cutters, gilders, wig makers, tailors and dressmakers, furriers, jewelers, and silversmiths. Only under her more puritanical son Joseph II was this lavish lifestyle reined in. Privately, however, the Empress lived quite modestly, adopting an almost middle-class lifestyle, and also expected the same from those around her.[10] Yet she was generous with gifts to friends and subordinates. For example, when one of her maidservants got married and therefore lost her pension, the Empress added the difference to the salary of the woman's husband, who was employed as a paperhanger at court.[11]

The Empress worked extremely long hours. She had her ministers submit any problems to be dealt with in writing and responded in the same way—she loathed unnecessary chatter.[12] A coffee stain on a file—with the Empress's handwritten apology (fig. 4)—is a telling testament to her industry.[13]

Life at court followed strict daily and annual schedules. The regularly published *Kayser-Königlicher Hof- und Ehren-Calender* reported on forthcoming gala days, court festivities, and church visits. Birthdays and name days of all members of the imperial family were gala occasions on which the court had to appear in festive attire. On "Toison Days," the Knights of the Golden Fleece (French: *Toison d'or*) attended dedicated church services in the costume of the order. The entire court celebrated feast days for the Virgin Mary and on special occasions traveled to the Marian shrine at Mariazell. For the Habsburgs, daily life was governed by ceremony, with its etiquette, its dress codes, its hierarchies of people and even objects, all of which must have placed a great strain on the members of the imperial family, and early signs of a gradual retreat into the private sphere were already in evidence.[14]

Maria Theresa liked to stay at Schönbrunn and in Laxenburg, where she undertook major construction projects to improve her residences. Her preferred architect was Nikolaus Pacassi—"he builds fast and cheap,"[15] she noted. By 1749 he had remodeled Schönbrunn palace, extended the imperial apartments, and built the Great and Small Galleries. The Prussian ambassador Count Podewils was unimpressed by the result: "She delights in building, without understanding anything about it, to which the

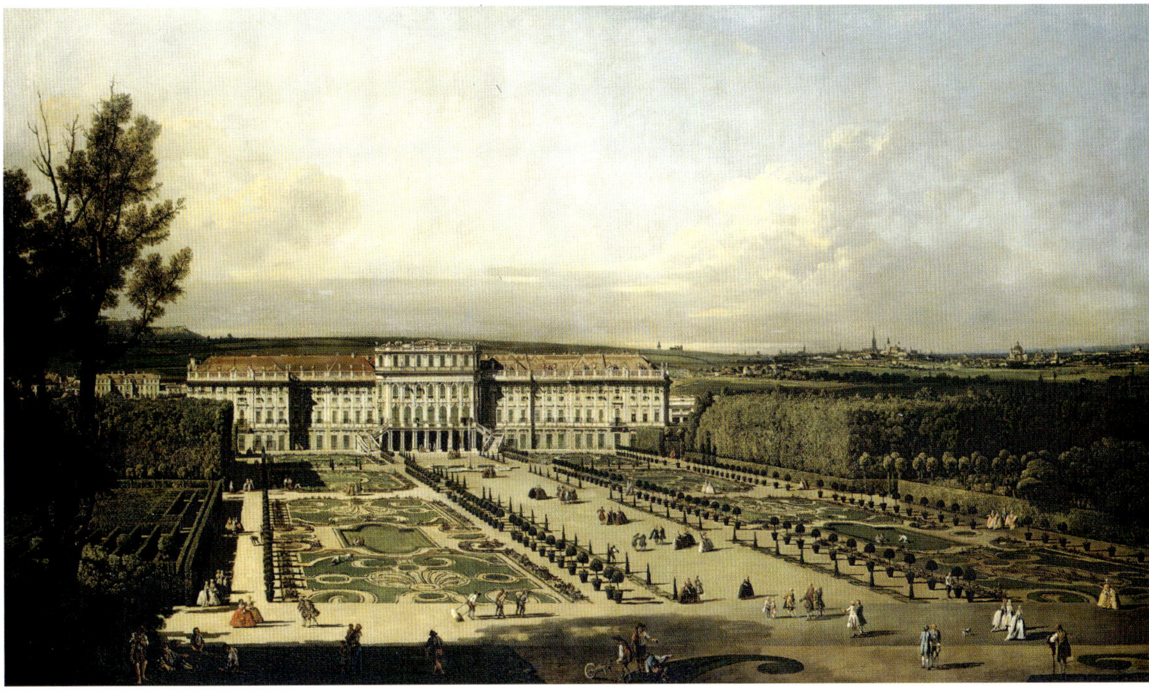

Fig. 5 **Bernardo Bellotto, The Imperial Summer Palace Schönbrunn, Garden Side**, 1759–60, oil on canvas, 134 x 238 cm, Kunsthistorisches Museum, Gemäldegalerie, Vienna

house she has had built to her taste at Schönbrunn testifies."[16] In matters of interior decoration, her guiding principle was thrift, and she frequently reused existing elements in new contexts. At major festivities chandeliers were either collected from all over the palace or borrowed, likewise the porcelain for the tables. The palace gardens at Schönbrunn (fig. 5) were redesigned in 1750 by Nicolas Jadot and again in 1765 by Ferdinand von Hohenberg; in addition to rare plants and elaborate fountains, a menagerie was added in 1752, initially just with "tame" animals, to be followed in 1781 by beasts of prey. The animals were kept in small cages—initially with only a few species: lions, apes, and colorful "Indian" birds.[17] Francis I was especially interested in natural history and followed the Enlightenment practice of systematic collection and classification. For example, he purchased Giovanni de Baillou's collection of curiosities with 30,000 objects, in particular minerals—the largest collection of its kind at the time—which would provide the basis for today's Natural History Museum in Vienna.

Music, Theater, and Musical Theater

In the mid eighteenth century, the Habsburgs, like other dynasties elsewhere, withdrew as the primary patrons of music—a result of the general belt-tightening after various wars, but also of a more relaxed court ceremonial—so the aristocracy and the emerging middle classes took over that role. And, just as in the bourgeois homes, music-making became more of a domestic entertainment for the family, even at court. Maria Theresa had been instructed in singing and dance but, unlike her father Charles VI, she did not compose music of her own. In her youth she often appeared in modest performances at court (although she had to give this up once she had become the Empress) and was said to have a pleasant soprano voice.[18] Her son Joseph II played the piano, viola, and cello, and regularly performed with chamber players. Leopold II, however, showed little interest in music, and his wife Maria Luisa of Spain famously referred to Mozart's *La clemenza di Tito* as "una porcheria tedesca" ("a German muck").[19]

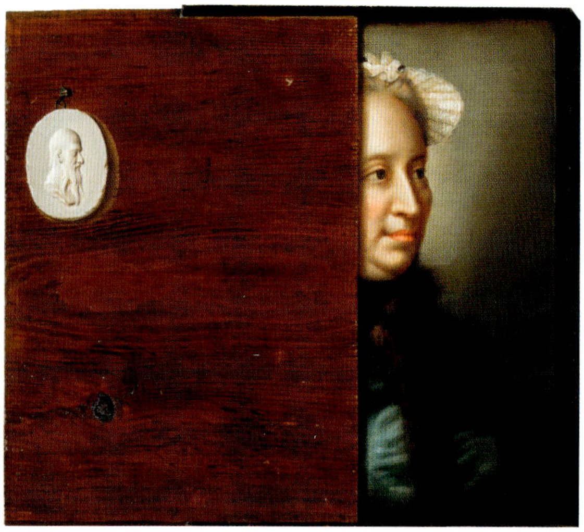

Fig. 6 **Jean-Étienne Liotard, Trompe-l'Oeil with Portrait of Maria Theresa**, 1762/63, oil on wood, 36.2 x 43.4 cm, private collection

Italian operas, French comedies, and German plays and ballets were highly popular at court—occasionally all mixed together. Particularly admired was *opera seria*, based on subjects from classical mythology, with noble virtues and heroic emotions, *affetti generosi*. Often commissioned in celebration of marriages, these were internationally noted events. The last Baroque court opera was performed in 1744 on the occasion of the marriage of Francis's brother Prince Charles of Lorraine to Maria Theresa's sister Maria Anna. This was court Kapellmeister Johann Adolph Hasse's *Ipermestra*, with a libretto by Pietro Metastasio, who for more than fifty-two years served as court poet, first under Charles VI and then, until Francis I's death, under Maria Theresa, whose children he tutored.

Christoph Willibald Gluck's *Orfeo ed Euridice* was premiered in Vienna in 1762, but Maria Theresa favored Italian opera: "Gluck and the others . . . can occasionally make one or two good pieces, but all in all I still prefer the Italians. In instrumental music there is a certain Haydn, who has remarkable ideas, but that is only a beginning."[20]

Maria Theresa liked drama and had an unused building next to the palace converted into a theater, the Burgtheater, which was ceremoniously inaugurated in 1748. When the imperial balcony was not being used the theater was also open to the general public. Italian and French comedies and operas were performed here, while German plays were shown at the Theater am Kärntnertor. Both theaters were overseen by the court, since extempore German comedies, in particular, were considered difficult to monitor, as, unlike for books, censorship was not easily enforceable for them. For that reason, in 1752, it was decreed that in public performances "no innuendo or obscene words are permitted, also comedians are not allowed to use such language without penalty."[21]

Artists engaged at the theaters were called upon to lead respectable lives, and the "chastity commission," as it was mockingly called, was charged to enforce this. The commission, established by edict from Maria Theresa on February 12, 1752, was tasked with combating prostitution, sexual relations outside marriage, licentious behavior, and homosexuality; to that end its commissioners were entitled to gain access to private homes and apartments, usually having been tipped off by snitches and informers. Prostitution was most severely punished: starting with having their hair cut off, to tarring of heads and whipping—to the deportation of persistent offenders to the Banat, specifically to Timișoara, as part of a resettlement program known as the "Temeswarer Wasserschübe." Adulterers, sodomites, and homosexuals were subject to fines and even death sentences, and unmarried couples caught having sex were forced to marry. One especially famous victim of the commission was Giacomo Casanova, who was twice banished from Vienna for such crimes.

Johann Pezzl, the sardonic chronicler of eighteenth-century Vienna, thus ascribed a very special function to maidservants: "Under the Empress's strict rule regarding the Sixth Commandment, chambermaids were a highly important commodity. As everyone knows, they are altogether respectable girls, and live only in respectable houses: so when a young gentleman went to a society event at the residence of Frau von X or the widow von Y, then the police could not be so inquisitive as to sneak in after him to see whether the young gentleman had not perhaps arrived by mistake at the chambermaid's door. . . . But since, for very wise reasons, such secret trysts are no longer quite so diligent-

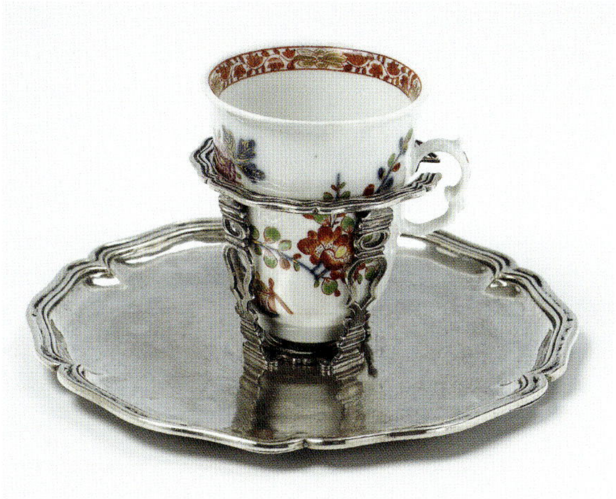

fig. 7 **Meissen Porcelain Manufactory, chocolate cup with *trembleuse* (mancerina)**, Meissen porcelain, eighteenth century, holder: South America, eighteenth century, silver, chased, private collection

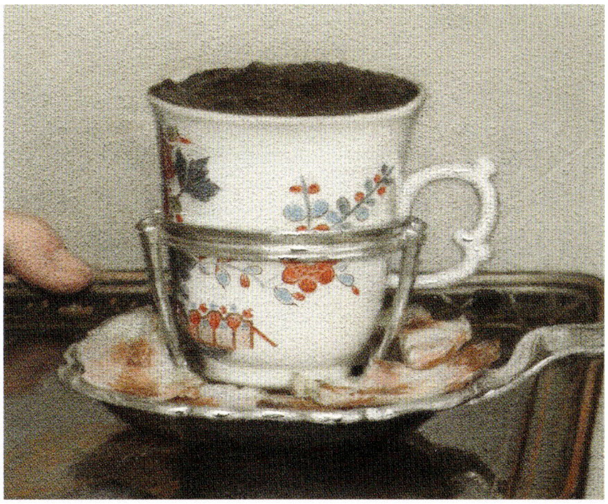

fig. 8 **Jean-Étienne Liotard, The Chocolate Girl**, ca. 1744, pastel on vellum, detail, Gemäldegalerie Alte Meister, Staatliche Kunstsammlungen Dresden

ly investigated, the value of these chambermaids has fallen greatly, and, with but a few exceptions, they are now once more back among the circles in which they belong: as the mistresses of hunters, messengers, footmen, cavalrymen, and, especially, sales clerks in silk and fashion accessories stores."[22] Emperor Joseph II later rescinded the majority of his mother's strict morality laws.

By way of evening entertainment at court—and this also included Maria Theresa—card games like faro or piquet were popular. Depending on the season, sleigh rides, hunts, and garden parties were organized. Social inequalities and class hierarchies were seen as the will of God and not to be questioned. The theatrical depiction of characters representing the lower classes was considered amusing, while scenes from the lives of the aristocracy were the stuff of classical drama. When the court paid a visit to the countryside, the host would provide entertainment in the form of carefully staged presentations of the colorful rustic lives of the peasantry. Members of the nobility also enjoyed playing such roles themselves, by dressing up as farm workers and picking grapes into dainty baskets or churning butter in precious porcelain vessels.[23] The head chamberlain Prince Johann Joseph Khevenhüller-Metsch, whose diaries provide illuminating insights into life at court, once organized a peasant dance for his imperial guests, a very popular entertainment: "It was danced by four quadrilles, three of which were dressed in the respective local costumes of our territories, namely of Bohemian, Austrian, and Carinthian peasants, the fourth as Transylvanian Saxons." After the dance, the party was served "hot dishes and other treats, pies, pastries, cakes, etc., for which forty places were set."[24] Not all of these arranged festivities were a success—Khevenhüller gloatingly tells of a visit to the Prince of Kaunitz-Rietberg's residence in Austerlitz: the palace was unfinished, the trees had been pruned in the French fashion and looked like "shorn and bobtailed poodles."[25] Rain foiled the planned illuminations of the garden, so all that remained was the visit to the Maierhof farmstead, where "a few dogged peasant men and women were dancing barefoot to a bagpipe wearing their everyday rags, rendered sodden and muddy by the rain."[26]

Dance in all forms was the order of the day, which was reflected in countless balls and costume parties, children's dances and ballet performances (also often involving members of the imperial family). As a child, Maria Theresa had performed together with her sister in the opera *Eurystheus* composed by Antonio Caldara, and even as late as 1730 she appeared at a costume party dressed as a peasant girl from Lower Austria. She had also intended to perform in the opera *L'Iper-*

mestra at the wedding of her sister Maria Anna, but had to abstain from this, since it was considered inappropriate—as Prince Khevenhüller-Metsch reports: "This plan was thwarted, however, by certain reservations, the fact that it would offend against decorum were a reigning queen to appear in such a spectacle."[27]

Official Portraits and More Private Paintings

As part of the consolidation of state finances, the royal household was reduced and previously salaried court artists were instead employed on a fee basis. The title "painter to the court," which Maria Theresa conferred on artists she personally admired, was now merely a badge of honor and did no longer guarantee a stable income. The artist she valued in particular for official court paintings was Martin van Meytens, who, born in Stockholm, had arrived in Vienna via England and Paris in 1730. His clearly arranged family and group portraits, elegant gestures and precisely rendered accessories obviously appealed to her. Van Meytens also painted several portraits of the Empress (cat. 38).[28]

Along with Van Meytens, Jean-Étienne Liotard, who lived in Vienna from 1743 to 1745, became one of her favorite painters: "the epitome of enlightened proto-bourgeoisie in his unerring ability as a practitioner of Western portraiture."[29] Not least on account of his striking appearance—since his stay at the court of Jassy in Moldavia he had taken to dressing in a "Turkish" style—the artist was an immediate sensation in Vienna. In the ensuing years he enjoyed the particular patronage of Maria Theresa and her husband. In his function as Grand Duke of Tuscany, Francis I commissioned him to paint a self-portrait for the collection of artist portraits at the Uffizi in Florence—Liotard's first self-portrait in Turkish attire and with his impressively tall fur hat (fig. p. 48). Once he had also painted Maria Theresa and her daughter Maria Anna in Turkish costume, the practice was eagerly taken up in fashionable circles and, along with the consumption of Turkish tobacco and Turkish fruits, people were adorning themselves and their surroundings with Turkish fabrics and oriental rugs. To really belong to the high avant-garde, it was *de rigueur* to have Turkish coffee served by a little African page boy.

With his half-figure portraits, Liotard set himself apart from the more formal, courtly style of Martin van Meytens and Johann Gottfried Auerbach. The precision and the soft, porcelain-like transitions of his pastel paintings were in distinct contrast to the bold brush strokes and animated compositions of Austrian painting at the time. Becoming acquainted with the Venetian Giuseppe Camerata, who had been active in Vienna since 1742, also gave Liotard an opportunity to produce engravings of several of his oriental motifs, whereby Camerata usually produced the figures and Liotard the heads.

In September 1745 Liotard accompanied the court to Frankfurt am Main for the coronation of Francis I as Holy Roman Emperor. He continued to enjoy close ties to the imperial couple, especially Maria Theresa, throughout the following years (fig. 6). The Empress even served as godmother to Liotard's daughter Marie-Thérèse, born in 1763.

As he became more familiar with Viennese conventions, Liotard also noted the customs surrounding another fashionable stimulant, alongside coffee and tea, namely hot chocolate, usually served by a pretty young chambermaid. To present this beverage, new types of cups had been especially designed (figs. 7 and 8).[30] With his *Chocolate Girl* from 1744, Liotard translated a motif he had developed while living in Constantinople—that of a lady-in-waiting presenting a cup of tea or coffee (see cat. 3)—into a central European context.

Chocolate was preferably consumed at breakfast, as the contemporary Vienna chronicler Johanna Theresia Harrach noted in her diary: "Today I read in *The Lives of Saints* for a time until 7 a.m., then I took a cup of chocolate, as I do every day, then got dressed and went to mass."[31] Since chocolate was often enjoyed before rising, the *trembleuse*—a saucer with a ring of porcelain and, usually, silver to stabilize the cup—made it easier to stir the drink

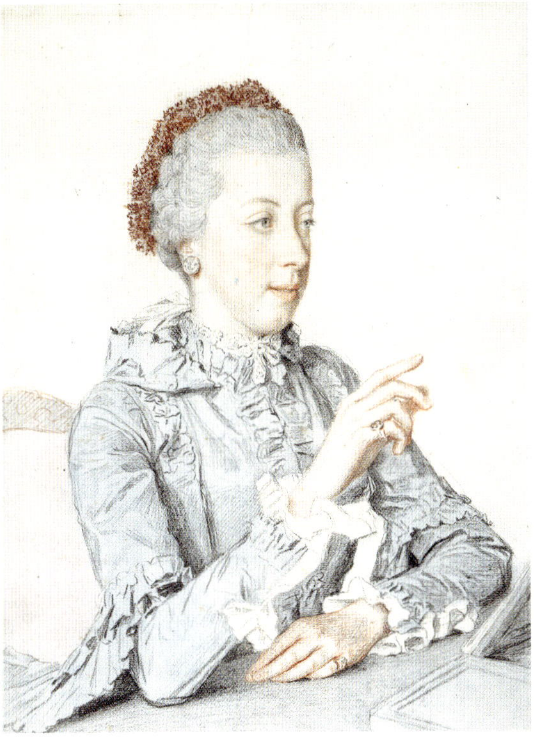

fig. 9 **Jean-Étienne Liotard, Portrait of Archduchess Maria Elisabeth, Future Abbess in Innsbruck**, 1762, red chalk, black crayon, and watercolor, 32.1 x 24.6 cm, Cabinet d'arts graphiques des Musées d'art et d'histoire, Geneva, on permanent loan from the Schweizerische Eidgenossenschaft, Gottfried-Keller-Stiftung

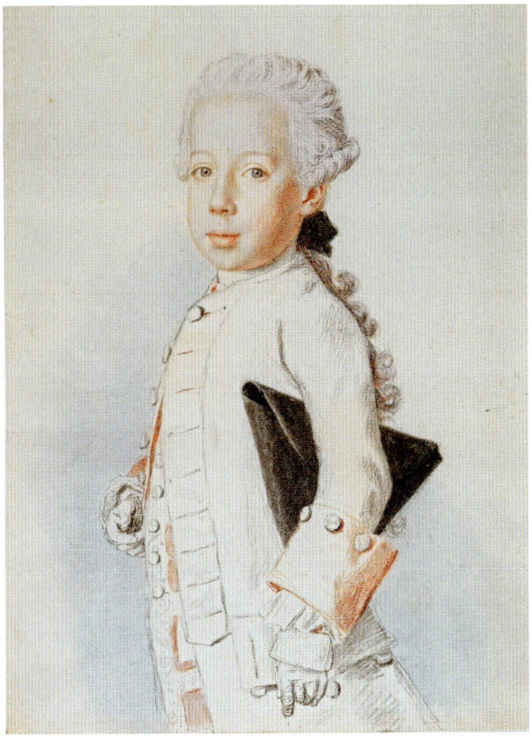

Fig. 10 **Jean-Étienne Liotard, Portrait of Maximilian Franz, Archduke of Austria, at the age of six**, 1762, red chalk, black crayon, lead, and pastel, 32.2 x 24.8 cm, Cabinet d'arts graphiques des Musées d'art et d'histoire, Geneva, on permanent loan from the Schweizerische Eidgenossenschaft, Gottfried-Keller-Stiftung

while lying down.[32] The 1740 inventory of Maria Theresa's silverware lists six chocolate cups of silver and wood.[33] Eight years later, the inventory already lists twelve chocolate cups with saucers, two chocolate pots, six silver chocolate cups, and a chocolate cup on two silver saucers.[34]

The exclusivity of chocolate at the time is reflected in contemporary coffeehouse price lists: in Vienna at around 1770 a cup of chocolate cost between 7 and 10 kreuzer, a cup of coffee only 3 kreuzer—at a time when an average day's pay was 15 kreuzer.[35] To underscore the high regard for chocolate, not only were serving vessels especially elaborate, where possible, chocolate also had to be served by well-presented servant girls. Johann Pezzl described the duties of a chambermaid in Vienna as follows: "To make coffee and chocolate, to warm a shirt, to polish a table, to make the bed, to iron a neckerchief—these are the arts of the Viennese chambermaids. They dress with the utmost neatness, choosing their garments with taste and generally adhering to the costume already established among them, which is made especially appealing by the Bohemian bonnet and close-fitting bodice. . . . Their annual salaries are between 25 and 40 guldens; this is just sufficient to allow them to pay for their shoes and their hair powder."[36] A household handbook from the eighteenth century admonishes that, if the "kitchen maid . . . wipes the plates with a greasy apron or perhaps even waits at the table with flying hair and a sweaty face,"[37] this does not do credit to the lady of the house. And there is even guidance on their outer appearance in verse form:

"Like the deer a model of poise and grace,
A spotless hand and fresh-scrubbed face,
With snow-white apron and tucked-in hair,
Lend spice even to the blandest fare.[38]

Philipp Hafner, a successful writer of comedies during Maria Theresa's reign, published short "dream essays" under the title *Songes Hannswurstiques*. In *Hannswurst* the hero of the story is transformed into a chambermaid who is forced to bear the abuse and insults of Baroness Wunderlich; when her breakfast (i.e. her chocolate) is not served promptly the lady berates her as a "common slut" and a "dancing bear."[39] In another dream, Hafner becomes the chocolate cup that a pretty chambermaid presents to her mistress every day at breakfast, but sadly it develops a crack and has to be discarded.[40]

In 1745, Liotard left Vienna for Venice, where, on behalf of Augustus III, Elector of Saxony and King of Poland, Count Algarotti purchased the *Chocolate Girl* pastel, which was soon to rise to such great fame. By way of Frankfurt and Bayreuth, Liotard then returned to Geneva, only to proceed to Paris and London soon after, before finally settling down in his hometown. It was 1762 before he returned to Vienna, and during that second stay (probably from April to November) he produced his splendid portraits of Maria Theresa and Francis I (Albertina, Vienna, see fig. p. 26), as well as eleven color drawings of their children (see figs. 9 and 10). He also painted the portrait of Suzanne Curchod (cat. 72), which Maria Theresa purchased from him to display in her private apartments. Liotard would make a copy of it during his third stay in Vienna a decade later.

The Empress recommended the artist in a letter to her daughter Marie-Antoinette: "I hope, however, that someone will send me a good portrait, and especially one from the hand of Liotard, who is heading to Paris expressly so as to paint it for me. I pray that you may give him the time to paint it."[41]

In 1777, three years before Maria Theresa's death, Liotard and his son Jean-Étienne arrived in Vienna for one last time. He was there at the invitation of Joseph II, who had previously visited him incognito at his studio in Geneva, traveling under the pseudonym Count Falkenstein. Liotard arrived on October 14 and left on June 5 of the following year, during which time he was also allowed to reside in the imperial palace for a while. He made drawings of Joseph II and the archdukes Maximilian and Ferdinand Karl, and painted a portrait of his son Jean-Étienne in Austrian uniform. Anticipated commissions for portraits of the imperial daughters never materialized, however. Liotard suspected that this was due to the ladies' vanity: "It is said that Herr Roslin, a Swedish painter, has painted a very nice portrait of the archduchess Christine. The Empress and her daughters fear that I do not make them look pretty enough, and for that reason I will not be portraying any of them this time."[42] Perhaps in part to ease his disappointment, Maria Theresa gave him as a parting gift a coffee service from Vienna's porcelain manufactory, which is now in Amsterdam's Rijksmuseum.[43]

1 Quoted from Michael Krapf, "Das Zeitalter Maria Theresias: Eine erfolgreiche Spurensuche," in: Michael Krapf and Cornelia Reiter, eds., *Das Zeitalter Maria Theresias: Meisterwerke des Barock,* Österreichische Galerie Belvedere, Akademie der bildenden Künste Vienna, exh. cat. Musée national d'histoire et d'art de Luxembourg, Vienna 2006, p. 14.

2 Quoted from Karl Vocelka, *Geschichte Österreichs: Kultur-Gesellschaft-Politik*, Graz etc. 2002, p. 154.

3 Quoted from Krapf 2006, p. 15.

4 Quoted from Vocelka 2002, p. 157.

5 Karl Vocelka, "Aufbruch in neue Zeiten. Der Reformeifer Maria Theresias," in: *Maria Theresia 1717–1780: Strategin – Mutter – Reformerin*, exh. cat. Schloss Hof, Schloss Niederweiden, Hofmobiliendepot – Möbel Museum Wien, Kaiserliche Wagenburg Wien, eds. Elfriede Iby etc., Vienna 2017, p. 45.

6 See Hannes Stekl, "Unterschichten und Obrigkeit im Wien des ausgehenden 18. Jahrhunderts," in: *Österreich im Europa der Aufklärung: Kontinuität und Zäsur in Europa zur Zeit Maria Theresias und Josephs II., Internationales Symposium Wien 20.–23. Oktober 1980*, Vienna 1985, p. 295.

7 See Hannes Stekl, "Hausrechtliche Abhängigkeit in der industriellen Gesellschaft," in: *Wiener Geschichtsblätter, Verein für Geschichte der Stadt Wien* 30 (1975), pp. 301–02.

8 See Günter Düriegl, "Wien – eine Residenzstadt im Übergang von der adeligen Metropole zur bürgerlichen Urbanität," in: *Österreich im Europa der Aufklärung. Kontinuität und Zäsur in Europa zur Zeit Maria Theresias und Josephs II., Internationales Symposium Wien 20.–23. Oktober 1980*, Vienna 1985, p. 306.

9 Friedrich Nicolai, *Beschreibung einer Reise durch Deutschland und die Schweiz im Jahre 1781*, Berlin and Stettin 1783, vol. 3, p. 190.

10 See Roger Bauer, "'Luxus' in *Österreich: Joseph von Sonnenfels zwischen Jean-Jacques Rousseau und Adam Smith," in: Österreich im Europa der Aufklärung. Kontinuität und Zäsur in Europa zur Zeit Maria Theresias und Josephs II., Internationales Symposium Wien 20.–23. Oktober 1980*, Vienna 1985, p. 321.

11 See Gerda and Gottfried Mraz, *Maria Theresia: Ihr Leben und ihre Zeit in Bildern und Dokumenten*, Munich 1979, p. 134.

12 Barbara Stollberg-Rilinger, *Maria Theresia: Die Kaiserin in ihrer Zeit*, Munich 2017, p. 226.

13 1771, Österreichisches Staatsarchiv Wien, Kriegsarchiv, HKR 1771, 98-136, fol. 8v. Inscribed on top: "de reliquo placet," center: "Schäme mich das eine Kanne cafée darüber geworffen," ("I am ashamed that I've spilled a pot of coffee on this.").

14 See Karl Vocelka and Lynne Heller, *Die Lebenswelt der Habsburger. Kultur- und Mentalitätsgeschichte einer Familie*, Graz etc. 1997, p. 249.

15 Christian Witt-Dörring, "Die Möbel am Hofe Maria Theresias," in: Pierre Béhar, Marie-Thérèse Mourey, and Herbert Schneider, eds., *Maria Theresias Kulturwelt*, Hildesheim etc. 2011, p. 247.

16 Ibid., p. 248.

17 See Vocelka/Heller 1997, p. 89.

18 See Elisabeth Theresia Hilscher, *Mit Leier und Schwert: Die Habsburger und die Musik*, Graz etc. 2000, p. 165.

19 Vocelka/Heller 1997, p. 65.

20 Quoted from Mraz 1979, p. 162.

21 Edict of February 17, 1752; quoted from Otto Teuber, *Die Theater Wiens*, Vienna 1896, vol. II/I, p. 63.

22 Johann Pezzl, *Skizze von Wien,* no. 4, Vienna and Leipzig 1787, p. 513.

23 See Stollberg-Rilinger 2017, p. 347.

24 Khevenhüller, June 14, 1756, in: Elisabeth Grossegger, *Theater, Feste und Feiern zur Zeit Maria Theresias 1742–1776: Nach den Tagebucheintragungen des Fürsten Johann Joseph Khevenhüller-Metsch, Obersthofmeister der Kaiserin*, Vienna 1987, p. 176.

25 Quoted from Mraz 1979, p. 168.

26 Ibid.

27 Quoted from Marie-Thérèse Mourey, "Tanz und Ballettkultur unter Maria Theresia," in: Pierre Béhar, Marie-Thérèse Mourey, and Herbert Schneider, eds., *Maria Theresias Kulturwelt*, Hildesheim etc. 2011, p. 173.

28 See Krapf 2006, p. 19.

29 Gerhard Heinz, "Bemerkungen zur Geschichte der Malerei zur Zeit Maria Theresias," in: Walter Koschatzky, ed., *Maria Theresia und ihre Zeit*, Salzburg and Vienna 1979, p. 277.

30 Our thanks to Marcus Lilge for identifying the cup as a product of the Meissen porcelain manufactory.

31 Österreichisches Staatsarchiv Wien – Allgemeines Verwaltungsarchiv, FA Harrach, Karton 350, 3.9.1677.

32 Annerose Menninger, *Genuss im kulturellen Wandel: Tabak, Kaffee, Tee und Schokolade in Europa (16.–19. Jahrhundert)*, Stuttgart 2004, p. 357.

33 Ingrid Haslinger, "Die Wiener Silberkammer zur Zeit Maria Theresias," in: Ilsebill Barta-Fliedl, Andreas Gugler, and Peter Parenzan, eds., *Tafeln bei Hofe: Zur Geschichte der fürstlichen Tafelkultur*, Hamburg 1998, p. 88.

34 Ibid., pp. 89–90.

35 Menninger 2004, p. 337.

36 Pezzl 1787, pp. 510–511.

37 Euphemia von Kudriaffsky, *Die historische Küche: Ein Culturbild*, Vienna etc. 1880, p. 246.

38 Ibid.

39 Philipp Hafner, *Songes Hannswurstiques oder auf gut Chinesisch: Es könnte einem nicht närrischer träumen*, Vienna 1700, pp. 7–8.

40 Ibid., pp. 50–54.

41 Letter from Maria Theresa to Marie-Antoinette, November 1, 1770, in: Paul Christoph, ed., *Marie Theresia: Geheimer Briefwechsel mit Marie Antoinette*, Vienna and Munich 1908, pp. 29–30.

42 Quoted from Frieda Beerli, *Jean-Étienne Liotard: Die Kinder der Kaiserin—Zwölf farbige Bildnisse der Kinder Maria Theresias*, Wiesbaden 1955, p. 45.

43 Marcel Roethlisberger and Renée Loche, *Liotard:Catalogue, Sources et Correspondance*, 2 vols., Doornspijk 2008, vol. 1, p. 164, fig. 838.

FROM "STOUBMENCHE" TO *CHOCOLATE GIRL*

On Jean-Étienne Liotard's Iconic Pastel Painting in Dresden's Gemäldegalerie

Roland Enke

"What is it about Liotard's Chocolate Girl in the Dresden Galerie that delights most visitors? You need only ask any viewer, and without hesitation they will answer: 'Because everything in it is painted so inimitably true to nature, beginning with her lovely face and down to the cup and glass on her tray.'"[1] This verdict by Michail Alpatow captures in a few brief words the fascination that this pastel picture, painted by Jean-Étienne Liotard in Vienna in 1744, has always held for visitors to Dresden's Gemäldegalerie—and that remains unbroken to this day (fig. 1 and p. 6). The painting pictures a young woman in profile view, passing through a room from left to right. She wears a pink Bohemian bonnet. The shawl that covers her décolletage reveals a glimpse of corsage beneath her lustrous ocher jacket. The freshly unfolded apron over her gray skirt is tied at the waist. The flesh tone of her delicate face is rendered with palpable realism. Her pink skin and red mouth are all part of the girl's immaculate appearance. Her blue eyes are fixed on her task: to serve the cup of hot chocolate and glass of water on her tray.

Despite its so frequently mentioned realism, the "almost photographic accuracy" on the grounds of which Alpatow numbered the *Chocolate Girl* among the "marvels of optical illusion,"[2] on many levels the pastel eludes ready interpretation and raises more questions than it answers. But it is precisely this ambiguity that is the real reason the picture arouses such interest and allows for such varied—even personal—possible interpretations. Liotard took care to avoid any suggestion of a narrative involving time or people; he declined to depict a specific activity: only a motionless object allowed him to observe so precisely what he wished to paint. Movement presupposes a more penetrating understanding of the figure and demands its placement in a given context.[3] Liotard, however, pictured the *Chocolate Girl* from without, almost as though she were an object, and as a result the picture meets the criteria of a genre scene more than those of a portrait. The ambivalence of the situation is even implied in the position of her feet, which provides no indication as to whether the girl is walking slowly or has momentarily paused. Nor does she display any specific emotion—as Alpatow criticized: "Moreover, as compared to Vermeer, Liotard seems cold and empty. The mere fact that he extracts the girl from life and poses her in such a way that one can study her as if through a magnifying glass is evidence of his soullessness and hard-heartedness."[4] Liotard took a different approach in his Munich pastel *The Breakfast*,[5] which—almost like a sequel to the *Chocolate Girl*—is now indeed telling a story (fig. 2): an unidentified young woman in a puckered, blue-green dress is seated in an armchair, a brown blanket drawn over her knees, about to receive her morn-

Fig. 1 **Jean-Étienne Liotard, The Chocolate Girl** (detail), ca.1744, pastel on vellum, 82.5 x 52.5 cm, Gemäldegalerie Alte Meister, Staatliche Kunstsammlungen Dresden

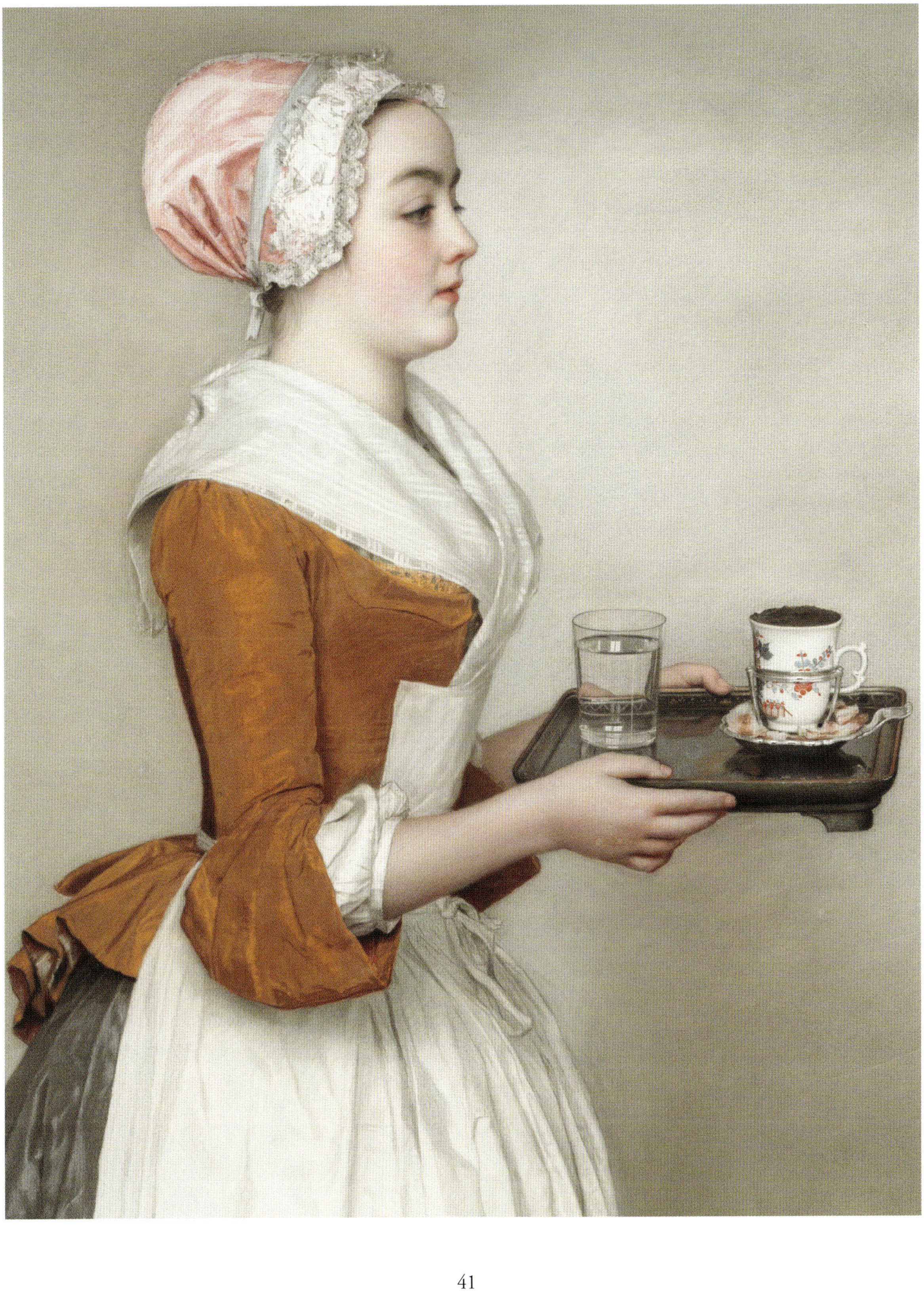

ing cup of chocolate. Her maid is just visible at the left edge of the picture by her face in profile, her décolletage, and her right hand. Her gaze is focused on the lacquer tray on which she is presenting a gold-rimmed water glass and a porcelain cup. As so often with Liotard, the space around the *Chocolate Girl* is barely defined. Simple floorboards and a blank wall create a minimum of spatial depth. The diagonal line between floor and wall lends the picture a certain dynamic, similar to his late self-portrait in Geneva (p. 77), but without providing any further visual context. The much-quoted criticism by Jean Bernard abbé Le Blanc from 1751—"It is flat, flat, flat, three times flat, and the flattest thing there ever was"[6]—although referring to the depiction of physical objects in Liotard's painting, could equally be applied to the spatial arrangement of the entire picture.

The *Chocolate Girl* must have stood out from all the other paintings in the Pastellkabinett simply on account of its size and its brightness alone (in contrast to most of the other pastels, for example those by Rosalba Carriera, it has a light background). Equally, the motif of a serving girl—especially in full figure—assured the painting considerable attention among the portraits, allegories, and Muses. In Liotard's oeuvre there are several other depictions of servants, but always in a secondary role to their masters and mistresses (see cat. 3). Yet to picture them, in combination with the exotic stimulants coffee, chocolate, and tea, and with precious china, exerted a particular charm, as shown by the *Portrait of a Young Woman, Possibly Hannah, the Artist's Maid, Holding a Tea Tray* by the Berlin-born Huguenot painter Philippe Mercier, who was active in London (fig. 3).[7] The young woman is presenting a tray with a painted Chinese teapot, three cups, and a black canister. The fact, however, that she is looking toward the viewer makes the picture too much of an ordinary genre scene.

Unlike so many other works of his with successful and sought-after motifs, the *Chocolate Girl* was not followed up with further versions by Liotard's own hand. Geneva's Musée d'art et d'histoire holds a drawing on four combined sheets of paper that has the precise dimensions of the Dresden original (fig. 4). Placing same-scale photographs of the two works on top of each other confirms the complete agreement in their contours and details, suggesting that a direct relationship between the drawing and the Dresden pastel is likely. Presumably the drawing would have been made shortly before the painting was sold, for in early 1745 Liotard sent the pastel to Dresden. Our assumption here is that it is a copy of the pastel, for example a tracing from the original, the paper having been placed on the protective glass and the pastel lit from behind to then trace the lines and contours in ink. On studying the drawing's lines more closely, it is noticeable that some of the horizontals, for example the underside of the tray, consist of tiny, almost identical strokes, suggesting the use of some kind of mechanical tracing or copying device. Other lines, like the vertical that marks the position of the shadow, were clearly drawn by hand. It is also theoretically conceivable that the drawing was made later, provided that the artist was able to refer to his preliminary sketches from which the motif was transferred to the parchment. Some of the preliminary stages, which Liotard used to develop and refine his subjects, have survived—especially for his Turkish motifs—but not for the *Chocolate Girl*. Even so, it can be assumed that Liotard developed the picture by way of several preliminary drawings on paper, as there is hardly any evidence of underdrawings or alterations on the parchment to suggest that he developed the motif directly on the picture support.[8] Since the Geneva drawing exhibits no pricking marks, obviously retraced outlines, or any coloring on the back, it cannot have been used as a transfer medium, as De Herdt surmised in 1992.[9] The drawing came to the Geneva collection from Liotard's estate in 1934 by way of his descendants.[10] As a pure working draw-

Fig. 2 **Jean-Étienne Liotard**, **The Breakfast**, ca. 1752, pastel on parchment, 66.5 x 53.7 cm, Bayerische Staatsgemäldesammlungen – Alte Pinakothek Munich, on permanent loan from the Hypo-Vereinsbank, Member of UniCredit

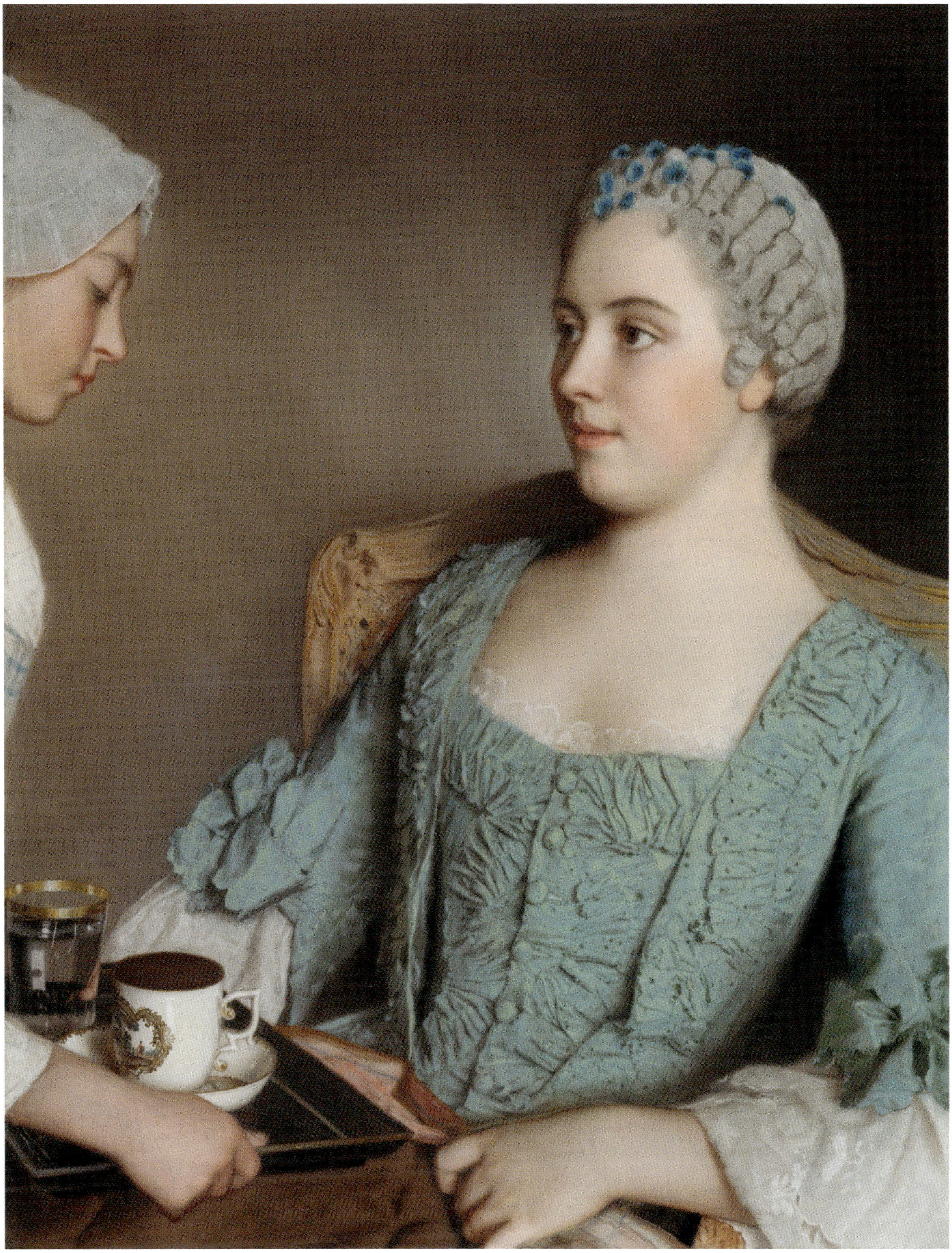

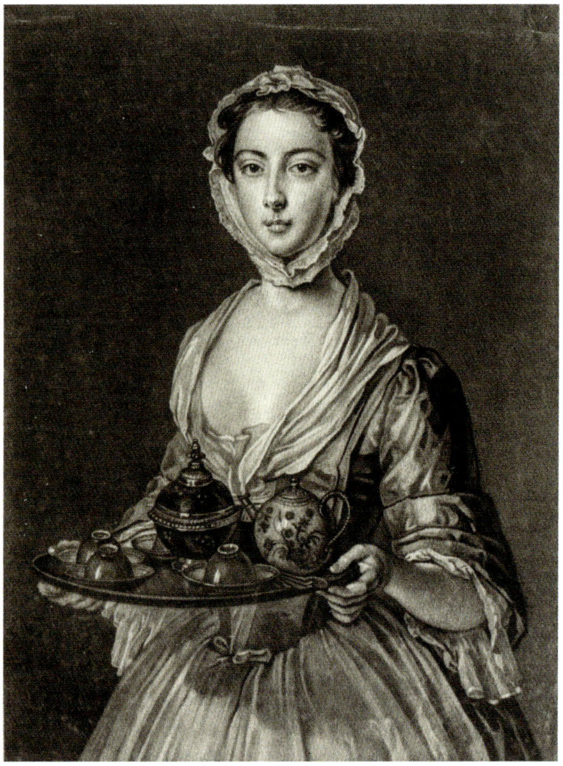

Fig. 3 **John Faber**, after **Philippe Mercier**, **Portrait of a Young Woman Holding a Tea Tray**, 1744, mezzotint, 32. 7 x 22.8 cm, The British Museum, London

ing, in this case a record or model for potential copies, it gave Liotard the option to produce a later repeat of the *Chocolate Girl.*

The Purchase

The purchase of the painting is well documented. By a stroke of luck the receipt survives on which Liotard confirmed in writing the payment in Venice on February 3, 1745, of 120 sequins from Count Francesco Algarotti (fig. 5). The enterprising art agent was in Italy to purchase works of art for Augustus III's Dresden painting collection, then being formed. Algarotti had arrived in early 1742 at the Saxon court from Berlin, where he had already advised Frederick the Great on art purchases.[11] In Dresden he was hoping for a prestigious position in the royal collections. In October 1742 he submitted to King Augustus at Schloss Hubertusburg his *Proposal for the completion of the Royal Museum in Dresden*, in which he devoted particular attention to paintings.[12] As part of it, he suggested a small but select collection of modern works that might successfully compete with the art of the Old Masters. Algarotti drew up a detailed program of pictorial themes, which he then commissioned from the Venetian painters Giovanni Battista Tiepolo, Giovanni Battista Piazzetta, Giovanni Battista Pittoni, Jacopo Amigoni, and Francesco Zuccarelli.[13] Between 1743 and 1753, Schloss Hubertusburg had been expanded into a hunting lodge by Johann Christoph Knöffel. Its showpiece was the painting gallery in the west wing, where some two hundred paintings from the

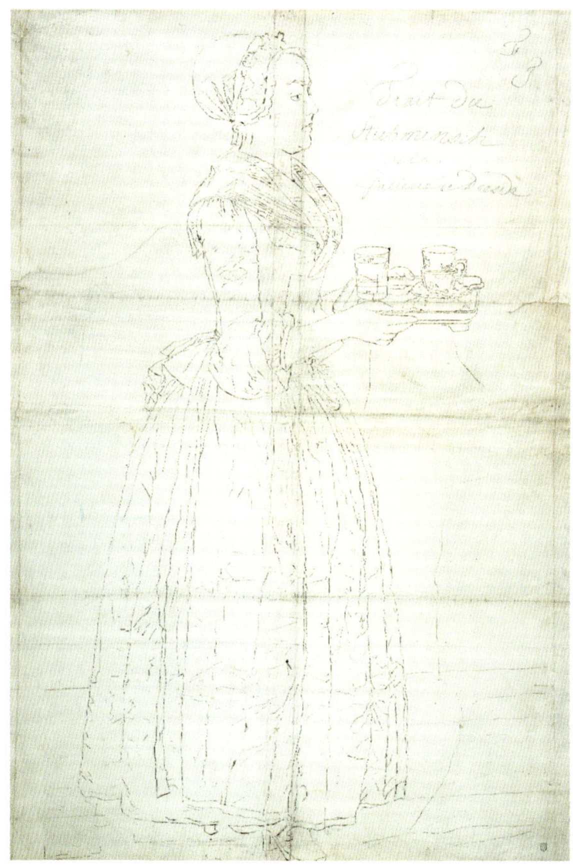

Fig. 4 **Jean-Étienne Liotard**, **The Chocolate Girl**, ca. 1744, black ink on paper, 83.8 x 58.5 cm, Cabinet d'arts graphiques des Musées d'art et d'histoire, Geneva

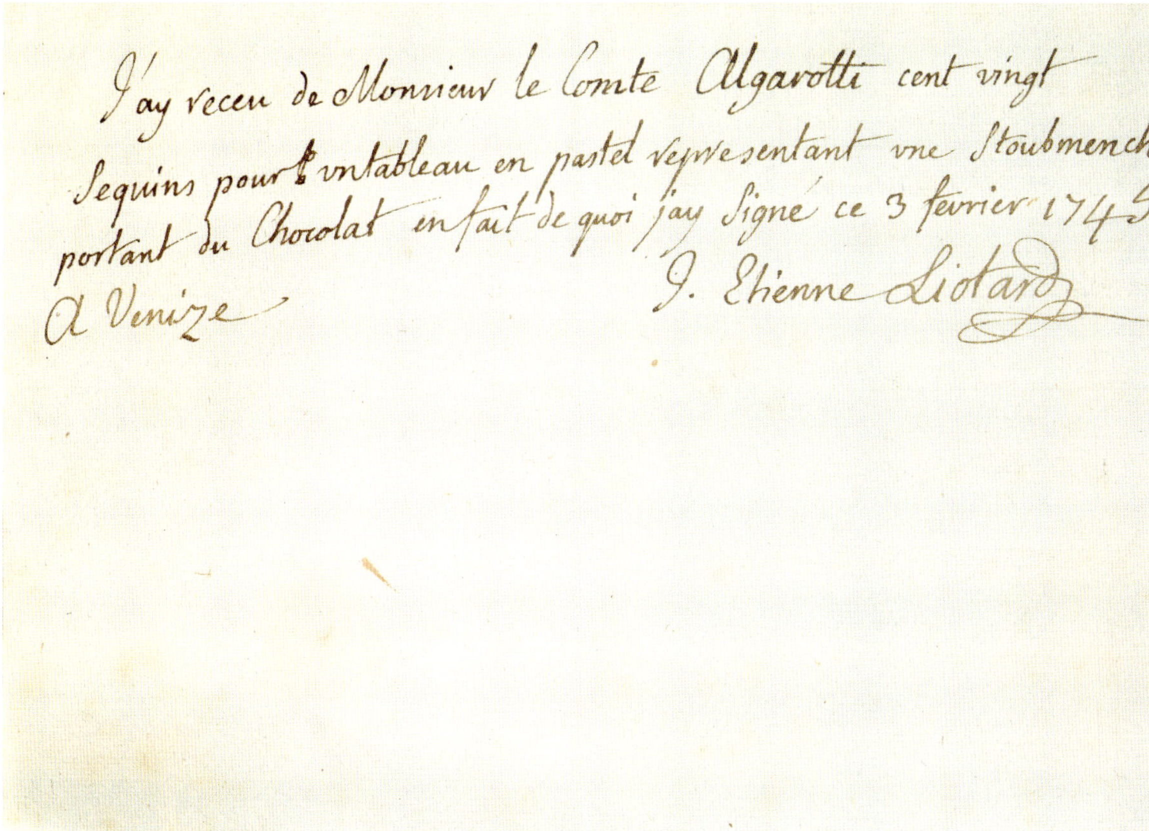
J'ay receu de Monsieur le Comte Algarotti cent vingt
Sequins pour un tableau en pastel representant une Stoubmenche
portant du Chocolat en fait de quoi jay Signé ce 3 fevrier 1745
J. Etienne Liotard
A Venize

Fig. 5 **Jean-Étienne Liotard, receipt for the payment of 120 sequins from Count Francesco Algarotti**, 1745, handwritten on paper, Lowell Libson & Jonny Yarker Ltd., London

sixteenth to eighteenth centuries were displayed. These were joined, in 1754, by the newly commissioned contemporary works. The display would not last long, however: in 1761, in the course of the Seven Years' War, the palace was plundered by Prussian troops and the majority of its picture holdings ended up being auctioned in Amsterdam in 1765.[14]

Algarotti's other major achievement on behalf of the Dresden Gemäldegalerie were the purchases he made in Italy between 1743 and 1746. The extensive correspondence, in which he reported all his acquisitions in detail, including prices, to Minister Heinrich von Brühl has been preserved at the Saxon Main State Archive in Dresden.[15] In the *Instruction pour Le Comte Algarotti au sujet de sa Commission d'acheter des Tableaux en Italie*, issued in February 1743, it was established precisely which artists' works he was to acquire; almost without exception the list named Italian masters of the sixteenth and early seventeenth centuries, among them Leonardo da Vinci, Michelangelo, Raphael, Correggio, Titian, Veronese, Tintoretto, the Carracci, and Caravaggio.[16] The Count was able to send a total of thirty-four works to Dresden, twenty-eight of which are still in the gallery's holdings today, for example works by Bernardo Strozzi, Palma Vecchio, Jacques Courtois (Le Bourguignon), and Carlo Maratta.

Algarotti also occasionally sent pictures to Saxony by contemporary artists whose names were not included in the *Instruction*: works by Sebastiano Ricci or the above-named Piazzetta, also by Bartolomeo Nazari and Giuseppe Nogari (cat. 11), whom Algarotti personally championed. The name Liotard was also not explicitly mentioned on his shopping list, but the Count was perfectly familiar with the Saxon elector's taste in art and knew that he was particularly fond of pastel paintings. By way of his extensive network he doubtless learned of Liotard's arrival in Venice in early 1745, perhaps from the artist's twin brother Jean-Michel, who was living there at the time. As an engraver, Jean-Michel sometimes worked for the British consul Joseph Smith,[17] who in turn was an important patron of Rosalba Carriera. It is likely that Algarotti was also well acquainted with both of these figures, as they would have been important contacts for him. Liotard and Carriera may even have been in direct contact at the time, since Liotard owned a small *Diana* by Rosalba, which he may have bought directly from the artist.[18] It is known for certain that he painted a portrait of Count Algarotti (fig. 6) during his stay in Venice.

One of Algarotti's important tasks was to assure that paintings were genuine and ascertain their provenance; in addition, before each purchase he had to obtain the king's permission and solicit appraisals from the finest painters who were active in the locality where the piece was being sold.[19] Although as yet no authorization from the king or his intermediary Brühl has been found for the purchase of the *Chocolate Girl*, Algarotti was eager to request Rosalba Carriera's opinion. In a draft letter to Brühl from May 26, 1745, he wrote: "I am taking the opportunity to inform Your Excellency that I have just purchased a painting in pastel, as precise and rare in its kind as only a Holbein. The picture of a whole figure is of such perfection, such realism, and such beauty, that Rosalba, the day she was able to see the picture, said that, based on the high praise she had already heard from other painters, her expectations had been exceptional, but her impression of the work itself had exceeded even those, and she would not have believed that pastel painting could ever be taken to such heights, and that she should no longer dare to paint in pastel after seeing this work. I am mainly conveying this judgment to Your Excellency because it is the purest truth that can be said of this work, and because it comes from the person who has the highest authority on pastel painting—and moreover an authority so greatly admired by Your Excellency, also, because this verdict from Madame Rosalba is free from any trace of the envy and profound jealousy with which artists of all kinds are not uncommonly affected; it does as much credit to Madame Rosalba as the most beautiful of her works. . . . This verdict, together with the exquisiteness of the work, permits me to believe that His Majesty might consider it worthy of his collection and the most beautiful pastel cabinet in the world."[20] In this draft letter, Algarotti not only refers specifically to the Pastellkabinett just then being created, he also suggests the descriptors, which would only gradually take root. He never sent this letter; however, almost a year later, on April 23, 1746, he addressed a long correspondence to Brühl, in which he also briefly mentions Liotard's *Chocolate Girl* and Carriera's verdict—which also provided the title of the present exhibition: "I will not speak here of Rosalba's *Magdalena*, which she herself considers her masterpiece, nor of the 'Stoubmenche,' which is judged by all the painters in Venice and by Rosalba herself as the most beautiful pastel ever seen."[21] With his reference to Holbein the Younger, he did, of course, allude to his own most prestigious acquisition for Dresden, which he purchased in 1743: the "Madonna di Ca' Dolfin," considered one of the masterpieces by the famous Renaissance artist. Not until 1871/72, after considerable controversy, did it transpire that the so-called *Darmstadt Madonna* (now in the Würth Collection, Schwäbisch Hall) was the original Holbein, while the Dresden version was a deliberate forgery by Bartolomäus Sarburgh from 1635/37.[22] In his 1751 *Briefe über die Malerei* (Letters on painting), Algarotti declared publicly: the Liotard picture "represents nature in bright light entirely without affectation and, although it is a European painting, it would be highly regard-

Fig. 6 **Jean-Étienne Liotard, Il Conte Francesco Algarotti**, ca. 1745, pastel on parchment, 40.5 x 31.5 cm, Museum Huis Doorn

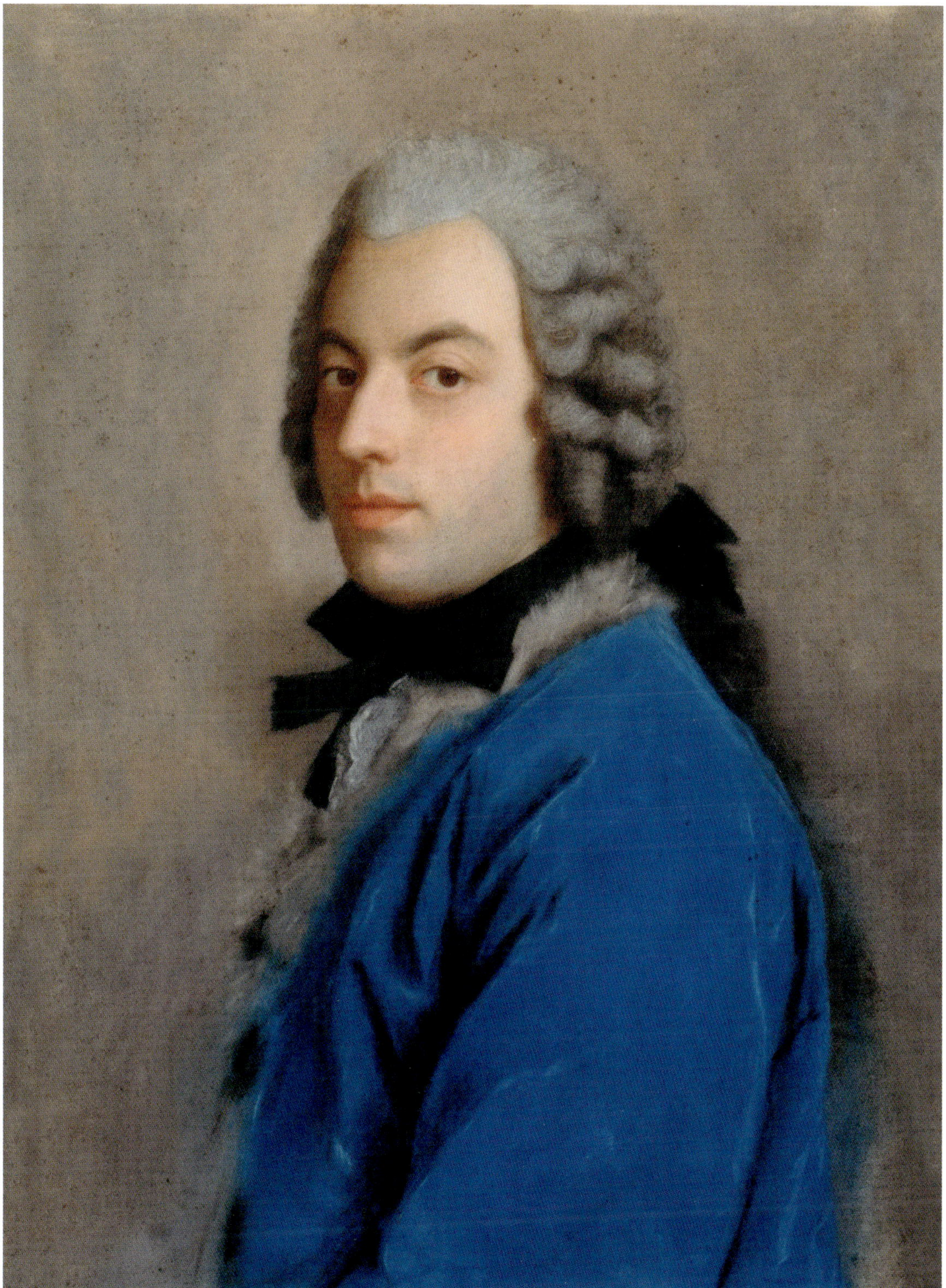

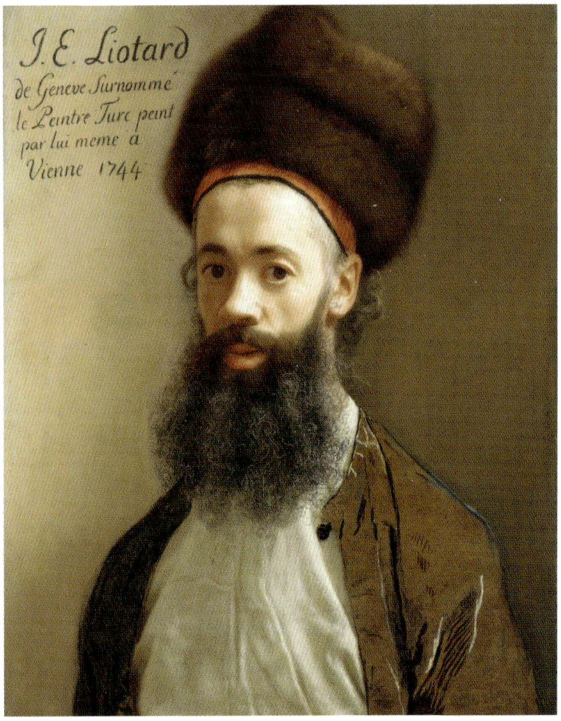

Fig. 7 **Jean-Étienne Liotard, Self-Portrait**, 1744, pastel on paper, 61 x 49 cm, Galleria degli Uffizi, Florence

ed even by the Chinese, who are sworn enemies of any kind of shadow. It is a Holbein in pastel."[23]

That the savvy art agent broadcast these two assessments himself can be thought of as a classic sales pitch. They also served to justify the high price of 120 sequins (see cat. 10, 11) Liotard received for his *Chocolate Girl*. It accords with the artist's pricing policy, which he used to position himself in the market. References to his high prices, often seen as inflated, are frequent in contemporary writing about Liotard's life and work. For example, in 1763, Johann Rudolf Füssli wrote in his *Allgemeines Künstler-Lexicon*: "In 1744 he again arrived in Venice and sold a pastel painting for 130 sequins, also charging very dearly for his portraits."[24] Pierre Clément in Paris also mentions the "extravagant prices"[25] Liotard demanded there, and Horace Walpole said much the same thing: "Liotard, the painter, has arrived. He is from Geneva, but from having lived in Constantinople he wears a Turkish habit and a beard down to his girdle: this and his extravagant prices, which he has raised even beyond what he asked at Paris, will probably get him as much money as he covets for he is avaricious beyond imagination."[26]

It is easy to recognize the remarkably modern—even from today's perspective—marketing strategy Liotard had developed for himself and which he successfully implemented all his life. It was based on three interrelated strands: building a brand, i.e. by styling himself as "peintre turc," then disseminating this through his self-portraits, and, finally, differentiating himself by charging high prices, a fact that was always mentioned in connection with his outer appearance.[27] Of central importance was his Florentine self-portrait, painted in Vienna in 1744, on which the name "peintre turc" is inscribed in large letters, thus firmly establishing this personal brand (fig. 7). Furthermore, the picture was on public display in the Uffizi collection and was widely disseminated in the form of prints (cat. 16). His Dresden self-portrait was likewise not hidden away in a private salon, but on show in the largest museum collection of pastels, where it also attracted considerable attention (fig. p. 17). Although in Paris he applied in vain for acceptance into the Académie Royale, his disappointment was offset by gaining membership in the Académie de Saint-Luc, which in 1751 began organizing its own exhibitions, akin to the Académie Royale. Liotard used this to present his Geneva self-portrait to the public,[28] and soon everybody was talking about the "Turkish painter." Unmistakable proof of his great notoriety is provided in a small silhouette from 1754 by the Genevan painter Jean Huber, in which Liotard, with his fur hat and long beard, is immediately recognizable, even though pictured only in outline.[29] The reason for Liotard's distinctly mercantile behavior may have been his father's bankruptcy, while his French-Huguenot heritage may also have accounted for greater adherance to the Protestant work ethic. His confident approach paid off: Liotard achieved a healthy income for many years, enabling him to purchase property in Geneva and support his family.[30]

The "Stoubmenche"

It is tempting to see in the *Chocolate Girl* the handmaid of some high aristocrat or even one of the Empress's servants.[31] In the archival sources, however, the young woman pictured is referred to as "Stoubmenche" (which literally translates as "room person").[32] This was the term used in eighteenth-century Vienna for a domestic servant, a person at the very bottom of the social hierarchy. Disparagement was also implied by the use of the neuter form "*das* Mensch"—instead of the usual "*der* Mensch"—referring to a female employee, who was moreover never addressed by name. Along with the unspoken conventions of how such personnel were to behave, there were strict clothing regulations that clearly betrayed their social status. Although these were formally repealed in 1766, there were repeated attempts to establish new rules. For example, the 1781 *Gedanken über die Kleidertracht in Wien* (Thoughts on clothing conventions in Vienna)[33] stipulated that a maid should "not be coiffed, but her hair tucked neatly beneath her bonnet, not a stitched one, but a Bohemian bonnet of gold, . . . not rouged, a linen scarf around her neck, no earrings, but a neckband of velvet, no watch at her waist, no ring on her finger, in the summer a blouse and skirt of cotton, but no brooch, in winter of woolen fabric of whichever color, a linen apron, shoes of black leather, cotton stockings, composition buckles; required to pay a 10 fl. fine [if she fails to follow these rules]."[34] Serving girls must have been very visible at the time, however (fig. 8), for they appear in numerous operettas and stage plays, albeit somewhat later, from the second half of the eighteenth century. Here they are represented in a number of different types, as for example in *Die versoffenen Köche und die verliebten Stubenmädel* (The boozy cooks and the love-struck maidservants) from 1770,[35] full of love, intrigue, and jealousy, or, slightly later, the anonymously published *Die Stubenmägdchen—Eine Satyre* (The maidservants—a satirical play),[36] in which two domestic servants discuss the positive and negative aspects of their profession. Finally, in 1781, likewise anonymously, though attributed to Johann Rautenstrauch, the pamphlet *Über die Stubenmädchen in Wien* (On Vienna's maidservants) was published.[37] Concerned to uphold social hierarchies, it describes the alleged negative character traits of serving girls in detail, blaming them for the general moral decline: "For some years now our Viennese young ladies, our fledgling and fully-fledged Fräuleins, and even married women of all classes have been complaining mightily about their maids, as these are luring away their lovers, or causing their husbands to waver and, not uncommonly, to be unfaithful."[38] Admittedly, so the pamphlet's male author adds, the ladies of society are in part to blame: "These wenches are not quite as stubborn, and permit

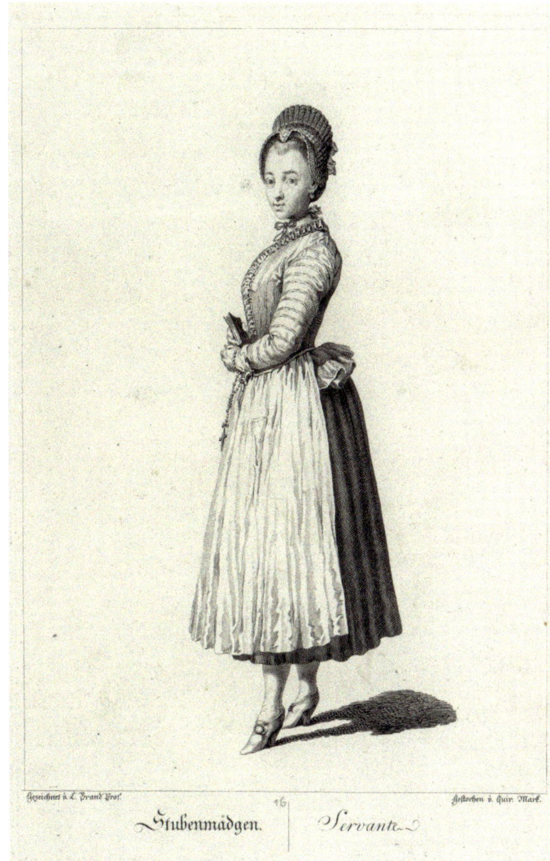

Fig. 8 **Johann Christian Brand, Chambermaid**, ca. 1775, engraving, from *Zeichnungen nach dem gemeinen Volke besonders der Kaufruf in Wien*, 1775, Wien Museum, Vienna

more without making such high demands. It is therefore no wonder that many lovers . . . owing to the primness and prudery of their goddesses, seek to compensate themselves with more compliant chamber nymphs."[39] Finally, Rautenstrauch gets to the apparent heart of the problem, which he sees solely in these maidservants' outward appearance: "The reason for their attractiveness clearly lies in their costume. It is the most flattering, the most attractive one for the female body: it places the forms of all their limbs in the truest light; it admirably emphasizes the waist and hips—in short, it tantalizes the eye. . . . Herein lies the reason why ladies and Fräuleins have every cause to consider these serving maids their greatest enemies, their most dangerous rivals."[40]

As a reaction against this publication, two refutations appeared in the same year: the *Schutzschrift der gekränkten Stubenmächen in Wien* (Defense of the maligned maidservants in Vienna)[41] takes the precise opposite position, so that some contemporaries suspected that it, too, was written by Rautenstrauch.[42] The other was published by a Theresia M., herself purportedly a maid in Vienna, under the title *Dem Verfasser des Büchels über die Stubenmädchen: Etwas auf die Nase* (To the author of the little book about chambermaids: a rebuke).[43] In this she explains that she herself had been poor and shabbily dressed, and only out of the goodness of her employers had been furnished with fine clothing, so that one might infer from this their own good taste and wealth. That through reading she had been able to gain knowledge, with which she could now—as a maidservant and writer—vehemently challenge the "Herr fashion writer" and his prejudices: "In order to be loved one has to please, and to please one has to be pleasant, clean, white, in a word, well groomed, ergo one has to be well groomed in order to be loved. . . . But why do you deny us poor girls the hope of making our fortune through an advantageous marriage?"[44]

Thus the role of serving maids and the effect they had—in particular on men—was publicly debated, probably even before this was reflected in performances at the popular theater. Was Liotard aware of this? Is his picture perhaps a response to this discussion, a social stand even, a criticism of the hierarchical structures? The number of people working in domestic service was often enormous, depending on a country's political and economic situation, and with vast differences in terms of employers and duties. Whereas paintings showing servants as a way of emphasizing the superior rank of the picture's primary subject were relatively common—such as in seventeenth-century Dutch genre painting by Johannes Vermeer, David Teniers the Younger, and Caspar Netscher, or in the court portraits from the early eighteenth century—depictions of servants as the main subject, or even as portraits, were extremely rare.[45] One notable exception is William Hogarth's painting *Heads of Six of Hogarth's Servants*, in which he not only depicts the most varied characters, but also the wide range in their ages (fig. 9). In his unusual arrangement of the portraits in two rows, they are all gazing in different directions and, although they are not all identifiable by name, Hogarth has captured them as individuals.[46]

The Title

Liotard's pastel did not go by the name so well known today, *The Chocolate Girl*, from the beginning. From the Dresden gallery catalogues it is easy to see that, from the picture's arrival in 1745, it took roughly one hundred years for this name to become established.[47] As is the case with many other paintings, there is a clear trend away from longer, descriptive titles toward more succinct ones. In the first German-language edition of the gallery catalogue from 1771 it is listed as "Wienerisches Cammermädchen, welche Chocolade serviert" (Viennese Chambermaid Serving Chocolate).[48] In 1801 the designation originally chosen by Liotard turns up again: "Ein Wiener Stubenmädchen mit Chocolade" (A Viennese Stoubmenche with Chocolate).[49] An exception is its listing in the 1817 catalogue: "La limonadière de Vienne."[50] In 1833 the subject is for the last time named as "Viennese Chambermaid,"[51] before, in 1835, the title was changed to "The So-

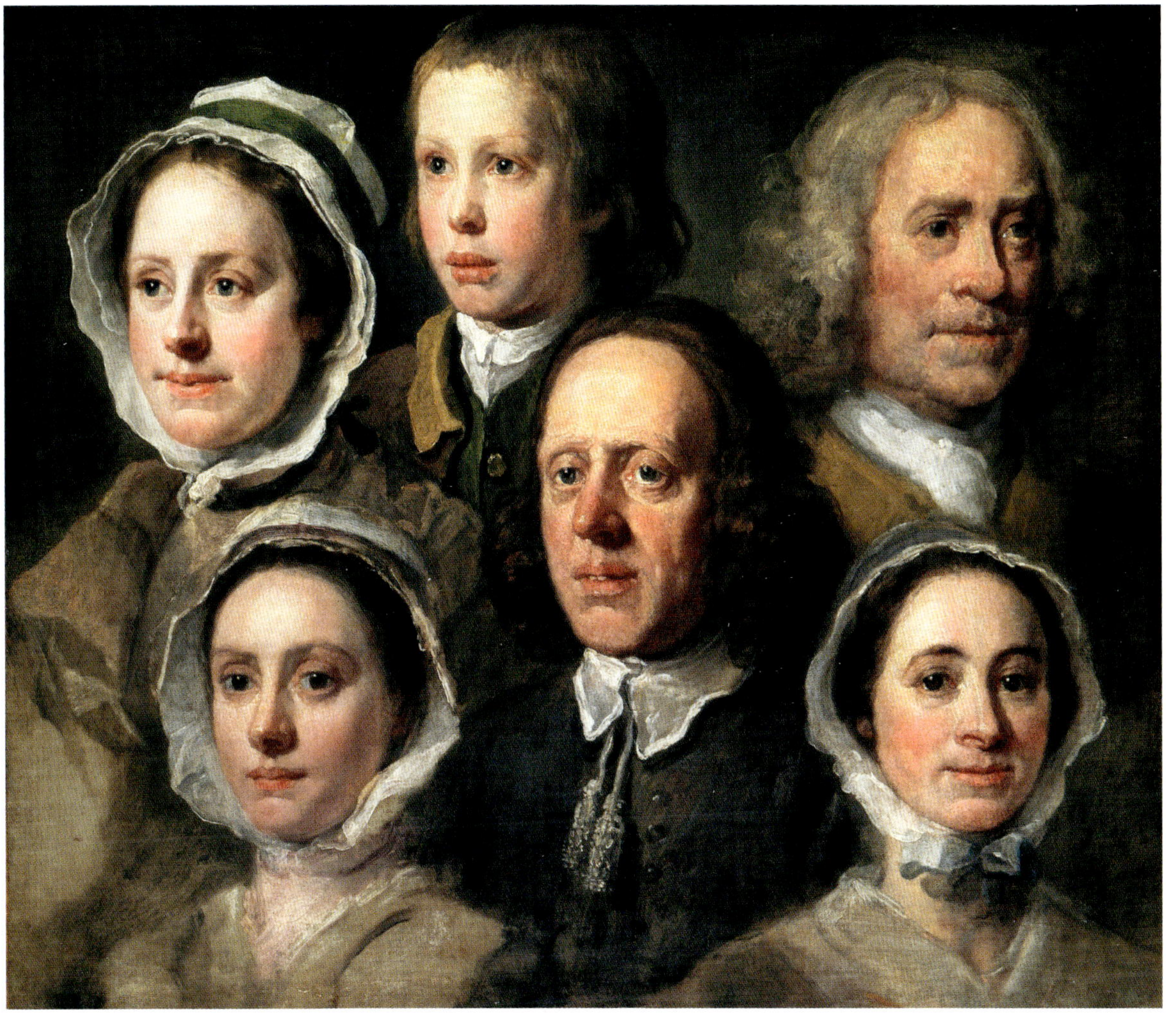

Fig. 9 **William Hogarth, Heads of Six of Hogarth's Servants**, ca. 1750–55, oil on canvas, 63.0 x 75.5 cm, Tate London

called Viennese Chocolate Girl," with the description: "She is dressed in the style of the time and carries a serving tray on which are a cup of chocolate and a glass of water. Full figure, half lifesize."[52] The focus had shifted from the girl's serving function to the enjoyment of the chocolate drink. The extent to which the picture also served as a projection medium for nineteenth-century romantic imagination is apparent from the attempts to provide the heretofore anonymous girl with a name and biography. Whereas Racknitz had still mused: "Whether the Viennese chocolate girl was intended as a portrait or an ideal image is unknown, but most probably the former,"[53] catalogues from 1846 onward list the picture as "The So-called Viennese Chocolate Girl with the Name Baldauf."[54] It was thus believed, in Dresden too, that the serving maid portrayed by Liotard had been identified as a young Viennese woman by the name of Anna Baldauf. She herself had joined the aristocracy, so the story went, when on July 23, 1802, she married a prince. It was further related that, overjoyed at her elevation in rank, on the day of her marriage she had invited her former fellow servants and told them: "See, now I'm a countess, you may kiss my hand!"[55] Only later was it noted that, although an actual Anna Bald(t)auf did indeed marry a Johann Baptista Karl Walther von Dietrichstein in 1802, she was born in 1757 and could therefore be ruled out as Liotard's model.[56] In another anecdote—which is also a reflection of contemporary life and the connection between the *Chocolate Girl* and the emerging coffeehouse culture—the "Stubenmensch" was transformed into a waitress at a coffeehouse.[57] Such descriptors can still be found right up until the beginning of the twentieth century.

Even more puzzling and altogether invented was the attempt in 1872 to move the creation of the painting to Dresden at the time of the Prussian occupation during the Seven Years' War.[58] Fact was colorfully mixed with fictitious events and generalizations: Liotard supposedly wished to paint the lovely serving girl Zili in a coffeehouse across from Count von Brühl's Palace, run by a Pole by the name of Monsieur Cacao. However, her jealous fiancé, Herr von Kötteritz, Brühl's majordomo, tried to prevent the portrait being painted. When Kötteritz is arrested as a spy, Zili begs Liotard to intercede for him with King Frederick the Great. Frederick agrees to pardon the man, on the condition that the painter adopts French clothing and parts with his beard. Liotard finally paints the portrait of Zili "in barely an hour . . . as she scurried about the room with her serving tray and chocolate cup." Frederick pronounces the work "Trés charmant! In highly accomplished taste, full of lightness and most life-like. Is he selling the picture?"[59] This, however, the story continues, remained at Monsieur Cacao's in Dresden, finding new admirers every day.

The Copies

An artwork's popularity can be gauged by the number of copies made from it; they simultaneously satisfy demand and further stimulate it. By the middle of the nineteenth century it was matter-of-factly reported that "*La belle Chocolatière* is widely known through copies."[60] In his comprehensive collection of material on eighteenth-century pastel painters, Neil Jeffares lists thirty-seven copies, both in pastel and oil, just of the *Chocolatière* [61]—most of these on the art market, only a few in museums.[62] It is well known that, as long as the Dresden gallery has been in existence, works from its holdings have been copied; to do so, painters were required to submit a written request to the director.[63] The so-called "Kopistenbuch" (book of copiers), covering the period from 1912 to 1930—a register the artists were required to sign with their name, address, target artwork, and date—shows that over the course of those eighteen years more than thirty people applied to copy the *Chocolate Girl* (some of them several times). Hence it can be assumed that far more versions exist, or at least existed, than those documented to date.

The first and oldest copy is probably the one Matthias Oesterreich made for the Saxon minister Heinrich Count von Brühl in 1756—only eleven years after the picture arrived in Dresden. In 1752, he had produced the *Recueil de quelques desseins de plusieurs habiles maîtres*, a collection of forty etchings after drawings, mostly from Brühl's collection, also under commission from the Count (see cat. 5). Brühl had been de-facto prime minister of Saxony since 1738, and from 1746 also by title. One of his roles was supervisor of the royal collections. He was not only intimately familiar with the existing painting collection, but also employed art agents to expand it through purchases of additional pictures. Oesterreich, an engraver and writer on art, had come to Dresden to join his uncle Carl Heinrich von Heineken. As director of the collection of prints and drawings (today's Kupferstich-Kabinett), Heineken was initially able to employ him as assistant curator there in 1752/53, before, in 1753, Oesterreich transferred to the paintings gallery, where he would have become familiar with Liotard's original, which he copied in pastel at around 1756. That work is known only from Oesterreich's correspondence after Brühl's death with the Count's heirs and the administrators of his estate in 1765/67.[64] According to the surviving letters, Oesterreich demanded either the still-outstanding payment or the work's return. Unfortunately it is unclear from the documents what the outcome was.

Another early copy was in the possession of the officer and writer on military subjects Karl Theophil Guichard. He entered Prussian service in 1758 and a year later was ennobled under the name Quintus Icilius by Frederick II. Guichard was close to the king and in charge of his library. He owned an extensive collection of paintings as well as coins and medals, which was sold off after his death.[65] In his collection was a copy after Liotard: "A Viennese girl about to serve chocolate, painted with pastels. The original is in the Dresden Gallery."[66] The dimensions given are very close to those of the original. Whereas a large part of his coin collection and his books were bought by Frederick the Great, the whereabouts of the pastel are unknown. It can only be speculated whether this copy was the one Oesterreich had made for Brühl. Since it was Oesterreich who compiled the inventory of Icilius's painting collection, it is at least theoretically possible that he advised Guichard on his purchases and may even have sold him his own version—if it was indeed returned to him by the heirs and adminstrators of Brühl's estate in Dresden.

With the exception of Princess Caroline Louise of Hesse-Darmstadt, who received personal tuition from him for several weeks in 1745/46, Liotard had no pupils. Nor is there any evidence of a workshop with assistants. Apart from the engravers Giuseppe Camerata and Johann Christoph von Reinsperger, who produced prints after Liotard's drawings, the only other men known to have worked with him were the artist and miniaturist Jean-Adam Serre,[67] also from Geneva, who is considered the best copyist of Liotard's miniatures, and Peter Kobler, who helped him with his pastels. Liotard worked with both of them in Vienna. However, as yet it has not been possible to attribute any work to them that could justify the designation "Liotard workshop."

Reproductions in Print

Along with the many copies in pastel and oil, the *Chocolate Girl* is so well known thanks to the extremely large number of prints produced from it. A first overview from 1897 already listed twenty-one different versions,[68] and it included by no means all of them. Every one of their authors, starting from the first etching by Carl von Pechwell in 1782 (cat. 79), had to produce their preliminary drawing in front of the original at the gallery, which they then transferred to their respective printing plates. It is also astonishing how many artists from other European countries chose to copy this pastel, and as a result the *Chocolate Girl* became widely known beyond Saxony's borders too. The Parisian Alphonse Léon Noël deserves special mention here, who, with his black-and-white lithograph from around 1837, was able to imitate the pastel's soft, powdery surface (cat. 81). The French publisher Rose-Joseph Lemercier, who also published the picture in London and New York as licensed editions, worked closely with contemporary artists while also relying on industrial production methods, which enabled him to produce inexpensive prints in large numbers. And in 1842 the British engraver James Posselwhite rose to the challenge of capturing the pastel surface of the *Chocolate Girl* in print by using the stipple engraving technique developed in England by William Wynne Ryland (cat. 82).

The concise gallery catalogues, which were published regularly from 1801, were still without illustrations. The first two volumes of the ambitious *Recueil d'Estampes d'après les plus célébres tableaux de la Galerie Royale de Dresde*, published in 1753 and 1756 by Carl Heinrich von Heineken, included large-format engravings, thereby establishing the genre of illustrated catalogues featuring a collection's masterworks. In 1835, the Royal Picture Gallery commissioned the innovative Bavarian lithographer Franz Seraph Hanfstaengl to reproduce its best-known paintings in lithographs. He transferred the paintings directly onto the limestone without intermediary drawings. At forty folios of three prints each, one hundred and twenty paintings had been reproduced by 1845, after ten years. Following the great success of *Die Vorzüglichsten Gemälde der Königlichen Galerie in Dresden*, another seventy-five were published, bringing the total

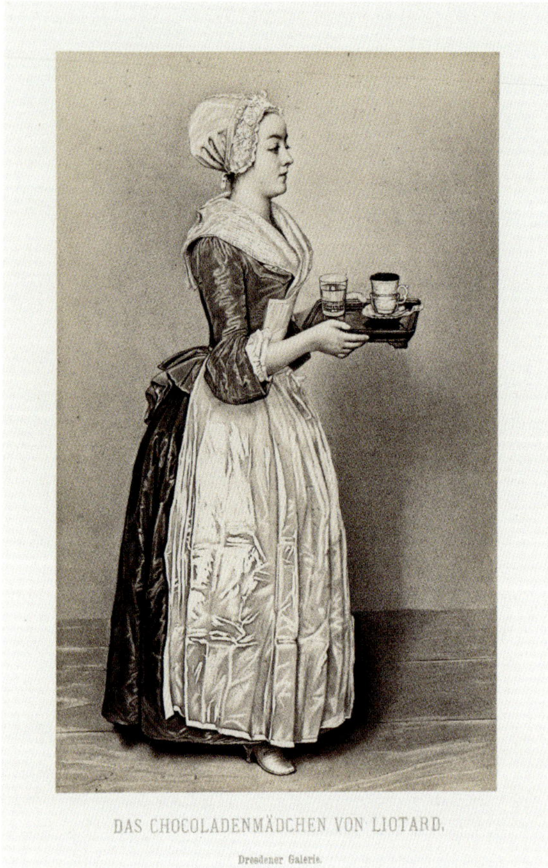

Fig. 10 **The Chocolate Girl after Jean-Étienne Liotard**, from: *Dresdner Galerie*, photographs and publication by F. & O. Brockmann's Nachfolger R. Tamme, Dresden 1887, Gemäldegalerie Alte Meister, Library, Staatliche Kunstsammlungen Dresden

number to one hundred and ninety-five in the complete edition, which appeared in three large-format volumes until 1852.[69] Needless to say, the *Chocolate Girl* was included.

Among the countless technological innovations of the second half of the nineteenth century, photography was the medium most important for the reproduction of paintings in print—and remains so to this day. Hanfstaengl also successfully turned to this new method and issued portfolios with photographs of the Dresden paintings, once again including the *Chocolate Girl*.[70] A major competitor appeared in the French photographer Adolphe Braun, who began producing photographs of artworks in 1864. When, in 1866, he acquired a franchise for the newly developed carbon printing process, he paved the way for industrialized production of photographic art prints.[71] His "main objective was always to replicate the color values of the original as precisely as possible. He also discovered that, by carbon-printing directly onto Dutch laid and sized paper, a far greater delicacy of tones and depth of shadows could be achieved."[72]

In Dresden, beginning in 1883, photographic reproductions were made in a special studio on the roof of the Zwinger, between the French and Wall Pavilions. After initial deliveries with forty reproductions each, in May 1886, the complete edition with 575 pictures and descriptive texts by gallery director Karl Woermann was published.[73] The *Chocolate Girl* was presented in two different formats, a small variant of 30 x 24 centimeters, and one at 80 x 60 centimeters, nearly the size of the original.[74] Since the Photographische Gesellschaft Berlin[75] and the Dresden photographers Brockmann and Tamme (fig. 10) were also offering prints, sales figures of the modern gallery works by Braun and Hanfstaengl were modest.

Conclusion

The extent to which Liotard was aware of the fact that, with the *Chocolate Girl*, he had created his most enduring work cannot be verified; there is no record of his own assessment of the picture. In his autobiography he does mention a comment ("un mot") by Maria Theresa, but without divulging what precisely she had to say about this particular picture.[76] It can only be a matter of speculation why he later, once it became apparent how greatly this work was admired, failed to produce further versions, as he routinely did of other successful compositions. It was left to other artists to respond to and disseminate the motif, for example Matthias Oesterreich in 1756, with his pastel copy for Count Brühl, or Bernardo Bellotto, who in one of his large-format *vedute* of Sonnenstein Fortress in Pirna (fig. 11) seems to cite the *Chocolate Girl*.[77] Copyists in the nineteenth and well into the twen-

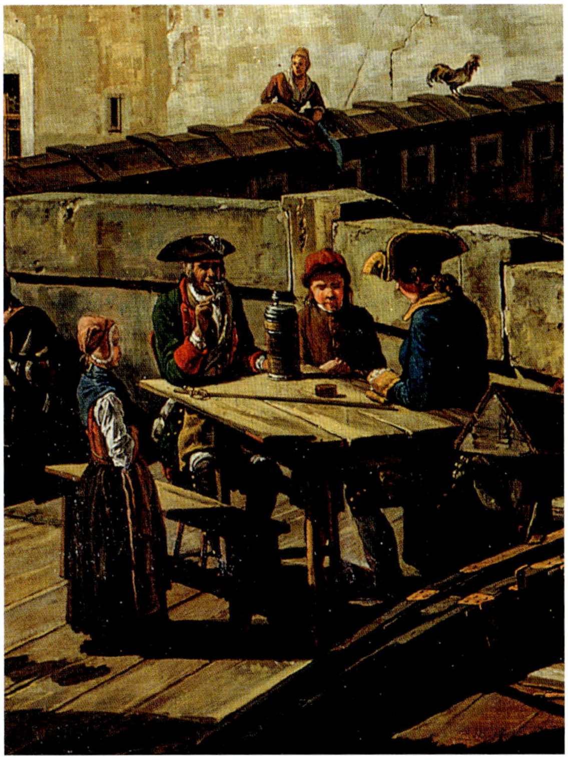

Fig. 11 **Bernardo Bellotto, called Canaletto, Fortress of Sonnenstein above Pirna** (detail), 1754/56, oil on canvas, Gemäldegalerie Alte Meister, Staatliche Kunstsammlungen Dresden

tieth century created countless variants, though greatly surpassed in quantity by reproductions in print. It is truly astounding that, despite all the intervening changes in taste, Liotard's "Stoubmenche" still, even after 273 years, remains what it was when it first came to Dresden: "The most beautiful pastel ever seen."

1 Michail W. Alpatow, *Die Dresdner Galerie Alte Meister*, Dresden 1966, p. 109.
2 Ibid.
3 Andreas Holleczek, *Jean-Étienne Liotard: Erkenntnisvermögen und künstlerischer Anspruch*, diss. Freie Universität Berlin 2000, Frankfurt am Main 2002, pp. 18–20.
4 Alpatow 1966, p. 110.
5 Marcel Roethlisberger and Renée Loche, *Liotard: Catalogue, Sources et Correspondance*, 2 vols., Doornspijk 2008, no. 205.
6 Le Blanc directed this critique at Liotard's self-portrait in the Uffizi; quoted from R/L 2008, p. 321.
7 Christie's London, auction 2003, no. 6730, lot 33, oil, 91.6 x 71.1 cm, before 1744. www.christies.com/lotfinder/Lot/philip-mercier-c1689–1760-portrait-of-a-4112714-details.aspx (accessed July 6, 2018). For the reproduction by John Faber from 1744, see R/L 2008, p. 333 (no. 130), fig. 226.
8 See the essay by Christoph Schölzel in this volume, pp. 100–01.
9 See *Dessins de Liotard: Suivi du catalogue de l'œuvre dessiné*, exh. cat. Musée d'art et d'histoire, Geneva, Musée du Louvre, Paris, ed. Anne de Herdt, Geneva 1992, p. 282, no. 98.
10 Ibid.
11 Heiner Krellig, "Francesco Algarotti as an agent acquiring works of art for the German courts at Berlin, Dresden and Kassel," in: Andreas Tacke et al., eds., *Kunstmärkte zwischen Stadt und Hof: Prozesse der Preisbildung in der europäischen Vormoderne*, Petersberg 2017, pp. 263–78.
12 Francesco Algarotti, *Opere: Edizione novissima*, vol. 8, Venice 1792, pp. 351–88. Hans Posse, "Die Briefe des Grafen Francesco Algarotti an den sächsischen Hof und seine Bilderkäufe für die Dresdener Gemäldegalerie 1743–1747," in: *Jahrbuch der Preußischen Kunstsammlungen* 52 (1931), supplement, pp. 6–9; Valentina Ciancio, "Francesco Algarotti und die Galerie der modernen Maler am Hof von Dresden (1742–1746)," in: Hans Schumacher and Brunhilde Wehinger, eds., *Francesco Algarotti: Ein philosophischer Hofmann im Jahrhundert der Aufklärung*, Hannover 2009, pp. 151–60.
13 Thomas Liebsch, "'. . . una picciola e scelta raccolta di quadri moderni' – Francesco Algarottis Gemäldeauftrag für Dresden an zeitgenössische Maler in Venedig," in: Barbara Marx and Andreas Henning, eds., *Venedig – Dresden: Begegnung zweier Kulturstädte*, Italien-Zentrum of the TU Dresden, Staatliche Kunstsammlungen Dresden, Leipzig 2010, pp. 226–39.
14 Thomas Liebsch, "Das Schicksal der Gemäldegalerie König Augusts III. von Polen im Jagdschloss Hubertusburg im Siebenjährigen Krieg," in: *Jahrbuch der Staatlichen Kunstsammlungen Dresden* 33 (2006/07), pp. 42–57.
15 See Posse 1931.
16 Ibid., pp. 10–11.
17 Francis Vivian, *Il console Smith – mercante e collezionista*, Vicenza 1971, pp. 109, 155, 174, 184.
18 R/L 2008, p. 137.
19 Posse 1931, p. 11.
20 Barbara Marx, "Diplomaten, Agenten, Abenteuer im Dienst der Künste – Kunstbeziehungen zwischen Dresden und Venedig," in: Barbara Marx and Andreas Henning, eds., *Venedig – Dresden: Begegnung zweier*

Kulturstädte, Italien-Zentrum of the TU Dresden, Staatliche Kunstsammlungen Dresden, Leipzig 2010, pp. 54, 64–65, doc. 5.

21 Posse 1931, p. 70, letter 28.

22 Of the extensive literature I would mention only Lena Bader, *Bild-Prozesse im 19 Jahrhundert: Der Holbein-Streit und die Ursprünge der Kunstgeschichte*, diss. Humboldt-Universität Berlin 2010, Paderborn 2013.

23 Algarotti 1792, pp. 32–33; Posse 1931, p. 29.

24 Quoted from R/L 2008, p. 77.

25 Ibid., p. 92.

26 Ibid., p. 94.

27 Claudia Denk, "At any Price! Jean-Étienne Liotard's Self-Marketing Strategy and the *extravangce de son prix*," in: Andreas Tacke et al., eds., *Kunstmärkte zwischen Stadt und Hof: Prozesse der Preisbildung in der europäischen Vormoderne*, Petersberg 2017, p. 123.

28 R/L 2008, no. 196; Denk 2017, ibid.

29 Denk 2017, p. 127.

30 R/L 2008, pp. 48–50.

31 Rulers and the higher nobility were not only served according to strict protocol, but the ladies-in-waiting who provided service in the apartments of female rulers often came from the nobility themselves; see Ingrid Haslinger, *Küche und Tafelkultur am kaiserlichen Hofe zu Wien: Zur Geschichte von Hofküche, Hofzuckerbäckerei und Hofsilber- und Tafelkammer*, Bern 1993, pp. 82–83; also Fredrich Carl von Moser, *Deutsches Hofrecht*, vol. 2, Frankfurt and Leipzig 1755, pp. 160–61.

32 See cat. 2, 9.

33 R-u-ff, *Gedanken über die Kleidertracht in Wien, und mir gutscheinende Kleiderordnung*, Vienna 1781.

34 Ibid., pp. 10–11.

35 [Joseph von Kurz], *Ein Neues Pantomimisches Singspiel . . . oder Die versoffenen Köche und die verliebten Stubenmädel*, Vienna 1770.

36 *Die Stubenmägdchen – Eine Satyre in drey Gesprächen*, [Munich, ca. 1778].

37 [Johann Rautenstrauch], *Über die Stubenmädchen in Wien* (1st ed. Vienna 1781), 4th ed. Vienna 1781.

38 Ibid., p. 4.

39 Ibid., p. 5.

40 Ibid., pp. 6–7.

41 *Schutzschrift der gekränkten Stubenmädchen in Wien*, 2nd ed. Vienna 1781.

42 Kai Kauffmann, *"Es ist nur ein Wien!" – Stadtbeschreibungen von Wien 1700 bis 1873: Geschichte eines literarischen Genres*, Vienna etc. 1994, p. 179.

43 *Dem Verfasser des Büchels über die Stubenmädchen: Etwas auf die Nase, von Theresia M., einem Stubenmädchen in Wien*, Vienna 1781. The name of the purported author could be understood as an ironical reference to Empress Maria Theresa, who on assuming the throne saw herself subject to male prejudice.

44 Ibid., pp. 10, 14.

45 *Below stairs: 400 years of servants' portraits*, ed. Giles Waterhouse et al., exh. cat. National Portrait Gallery London, London 2003, pp. 7–19.

46 Ibid., pp. 108–10.

47 The picture is not listed in the inventory from 1754; but only appears in the 1809 inventory, p. 159 a, no. 1230: "The Vienna chambermaid in her costume, with a bonnet on her head, a yellow corset, white neck cloth and similar apron. She carries a coffee tray on which are a cup of chocolate and a glass of water. Full figure, on parchment."

48 Johann Anton Riedel and Christian Friedrich Wenzel, *Verzeichniß der Gemälde in der Churfürstl. Gallerie in Dresden*, Leipzig 1771, p. 215. In the French-language first edition it was "Une Fille de Chambre Viennoise, qui sert le Chocolat, figure entiere"; see Jean Antoine Riedel and Chrêtien Frédéric Wenzel, *Catalogue des tableaux de la galerie electorale a Dresde*, Dresden 1765, p. 243.

49 [Johann Anton Riedel], *Verzeichnis der Gemälde welche in der Churfürstl. Gallerie zu Dresden befindlich sind*, Dresden 1801, p. 178.

50 [Karl Friedrich Demiani], *Catalogue explicatif des tableaux de la Galerie Royale de Dresde*, Dresden 1817, p. 269. Apparently this was an effort to establish a connection to the "belle Limonadière" then living in Paris: Madame Romain, the wife of a restaurant owner and lemonade producer, was idolized for her beauty in the 1810s.

51 [Friedrich Matthäi], *Neues Sach- und Ortsverzeichniss der Königlich Sächsischen Gemälde-Gallerie zu Dresden*, Dresden 1833, p. 255.

52 Friedrich Matthäi, *Verzeichnis der Königlich Sächsischen Gemälde-Galerie zu Dresden*, vol. 2, Dresden 1835, p. 121, no. 19.

53 [Joseph Friedrich zu Racknitz], *Versuche zur Beurtheilung einiger Gemälde der Königl. Sächs. Gemähldesammlung und deren Meister*, Dresden 1811, p. 5.

54 [Friedrich Matthäi], *Catalog der königlichen Gemälde-Galerie zu Dresden*, Dresden 1848, p. 204.

55 Julius Hübner, *Die Dresdener Galerie: Photographien nach den Original-Gemälden*, vol. 2, Berlin [1900], no. 29.

56 Wilhelm Schäfer, *Führer in der königlichen Gemälde-Gallerie zu Dresden*, Dresden 1864, p. 289.

57 Ibid.

58 Adolph Görling, *Deutschlands Kunstschätze, eine Sammlung der hervorragendsten der Berliner, Dresdener, Münchener, Wiener, Casseler und Braunschweiger Galerien*, vol. 4, Leipzig 1872, pp. 19–39.

59 Ibid., p. 36.

60 Friedrich Faber, *Conversations-Lexicon für Bildende Kunst*, vol. 3, Leipzig 1846, p. 370.

61 http://www.pastellists.com/Articles/LIOTARD1.pdf, pp. 11–13 (accessed June 25, 2018).

62 For example, in Warsaw's Muzeum Narodowe, second half of the eighteenth century, inv. MNW 210856, and Staatliche Museen zu Berlin, Alte Nationalgalerie, attributed to Nikolaus Lauer, ca. 1800, inv. A I 100.

63 The archive of the Staatliche Kunstsammlungen Dresden holds copying applications from 1847 to 1930. A sampling of the unresearched documents produced six requests for the *Chocolate Girl* between the years 1847 and 1849 alone.

64 Sächsisches Hauptstaatsarchiv Dresden, 10047 Amt Dresden, Nr. 3471, 1865–67, unpaginated.

65 Matthias Oesterreich, *Verzeichnis der Gemäldesammlung des verstorbenen Obristen Quintus Icilius*, Potsdam 1784; *Verzeichniß der zum Nachlaß des verstorbenen Königl. Preuß. Obristen Herrn von Quintus gehörigen und zum Verkauf stehenden Gemälde, Antiquen alten Münzen*, Berlin 1790; *Catalogue Des Médailles Et Monnoies Antiques Du Cabinet De Feu Monsieur Quintus Icilius*, Potsdam 1790.

66 Oesterreich 1784, p. 13, no. 113.

67 R/L 2008, pp. 709–10; see also Marcel Roethlisberger, "Liotard mis à jour," in: *Zeitschrift für schweizerische Archäologie und Kunstgeschichte* 71, nos. 2–3 (2014), pp. 194–95, fig. 14.

68 Edouard Humbert, Alphonse Revilliod, and Jan Willem Reinier Tilanus, *La vie et les œuvres de Jean-Étienne Liotard (1702–1789), Étude Biographique et Iconographique*, Amsterdam 1897, pp. 193–95.

69 Heinz Gebhardt, *Franz Hanfstaengl: Von der Lithographie zur Photographie*, exh. cat. Münchner Stadtmuseum, Munich 1984, pp. 52–66.

70 Helmut Heß, *Der Kunstverlag Franz Hanfstaengl und die frühe fotographische Kunstreproduktion: Das Kunstwerk und sein Abbild*, diss. Ludwig-Maximilians-Universität München 1993, Munich 1999.

71 Paul Mellenthin and Dorothea Peters, "Das photographsiche Museum," in: *Adolphe Braun: Ein europäisches Photographie-Unternehmen und die Bildkünste im 19. Jahrhundert*, ed. Ulrich Pohlmann and Paul Mellenthin, exh. cat. Münchner Stadtmuseum, Munich 2017, pp. 297–310.

72 A.S., "Ad. Brauns Photographien nach Gemälden der Dresdener Galerie," in: *Kunstchronik* 19 (1884), cols. 331–32.

73 *Königliche Gemäldegalerie zu Dresden, Photographien von Ad. Braun & Co.*, Dornach and Paris, from 1884.

74 Ad. Braun & Cie, *Catalogue général des photographies inaltérables au charbon et héliogravures*, Paris and Dornach 1887, p. 36, nos. 19 and 20.

75 Hübner 1900, vol. 2, no. 29.

76 Quoted from R/L 2008, p. 68.

77 Harald Marx, "'Das ganze Colorit ist belebt und verschmolzen.' Jean-Étienne Liotard zum 300. Geburtstag," in: *Dresdener Kunstblätter* 46, no. 6 (2002), pp. 194–95.

THE TURKISH FASHION IN SAXONY

Holger Schuckelt

Courtly festivities in early modern times were largely influenced by what interested and affected people in their historical situation. Beginning in the late fifteenth century, the Turkish motif was virtually omnipresent for more than three hundred years, exemplified in costumed tournaments, masquerades, ballets, masked balls, theater plays, and operas. The craze for things Turkish spread throughout Europe, not only as a major element in courtly festivities but even in everyday life at court. A common element of the Turkish fashion was the establishment in many European cities of collections of oriental art that could serve as prop rooms for Turkish festivals, processions, tournaments, and operas. One of the most important such collections is the "Turkish Chamber" created by the electors of Saxony in Dresden, which dates from the early sixteenth century.

Over the centuries, Europe's view of the Turks varied, depending on current events. The Turk was either a cruel, barbaric enemy of Christendom or an admirable warrior, a cultured exotic or an erotic Oriental. The Turkish fashion reached a first peak at the time of Sultan Süleyman I, during whose reign the Ottoman Empire was at the height of its power. In his campaigns, especially at the beginning of his reign, Süleyman concentrated on Europe. Within only a few years his troops conquered large portions of the Balkans and in 1529 they stood for the first time before the gates of Vienna. At that time, a blend of fear of a militarily powerful foe and admiration for a culturally and economically highly developed nation gave rise to the fashion for all things Turkish. Festivities with a predominant Turkish theme served as effective propaganda for princes and were a way of dealing psychologically with the perceived menace. Featured at most European courts were enactments of actual or fictional victories over the Ottomans. In these, Hungarians, or the Hussars equated with them, symbolized the heroic, universally celebrated defenders of Christendom, and the Hussar became the personification of the ruler per se. Examples of such festivities, in which the high nobility portrayed themselves as victors over the Eastern barbarians, are found as early as the reign of the elector Maurice of Saxony. On October 7, 1548, his younger brother and the later elector Duke Augustus of Saxony married Anna of Denmark. As part of the wedding celebrations in Torgau there was a mock siege of a "Turkish" water fortress. A wooden structure erected on the Elbe for the occasion was shelled by cannons, attacked from ships, and finally set on fire. Five years later, Maurice staged a skirmish intended to recall his personal participation in the Turkish wars (1542 and 1552). During carnival in 1553, a structure occupied by "Turks" that Maurice had had erected on Dresden's Altmarkt was stormed by "Hussars." Maurice himself had been given command—supposedly by lot—over the attacking and ultimately victorious Hussars, while his brother, Duke Augustus, had to play the role of the defeated Turkish commander. Maurice and his "Hussars" fought in black and shining armor, and over theirs Augustus and his "Turks" wore oriental costumes. Their horses were also provided with Turkish saddle cloths, and the defenders' arquebusiers were dressed as Ottoman janissaries.[1]

In the second half of the sixteenth century, other types of entertainment came to be favored. Tourna-

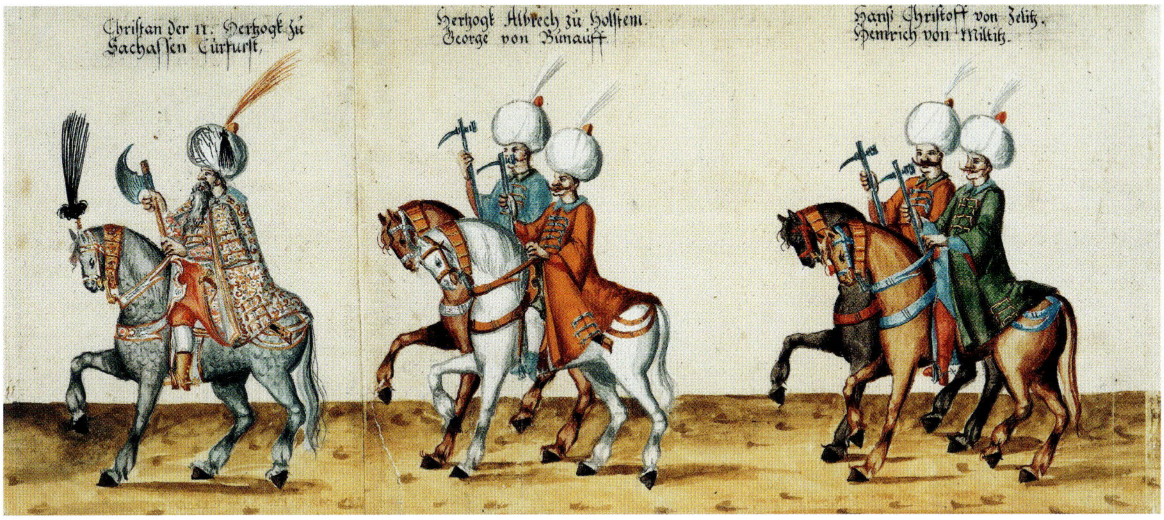

Fig. 1 **Eigengliche abkondrafagttur des Rinckrennen welches Christian der Ander Hertzogk zu Sachssen . . . gehalden hatt . . . fastnacht Anno 1607 den 24. 25. vnd 26. Februarius** (Actual Rendering of the Races Staged by Christian II, Duke of Saxony, at Shrovetide 1607, February 24, 25, and 26) gouache, 15 x 11 cm and 15 x 25.2 cm, SLUB Dresden

ments with ring or quinte jousting, in which the rider no longer faced a human opponent but a fixed target, became increasingly popular. Accordingly, armor was no longer required for protection, and splendid costumes became the main feature of competitions and the processions associated with them. Opposing notions of the Orient were more clearly evident in these events than in the previous mock battles and skirmishes. To determine whether these were perceived as a contradiction or to what extent they are to be seen simply as two equally valid European views of the Ottomans, one has to consider regional peculiarities and differences.

In many parts of Europe, the dominant theme in Turkish entertainments was the celebration of a defeat of the barbaric enemy in the form of triumphal processions, in which genuine or imitation oriental goods were carried as trophies and men dressed as Turkish captives were paraded to the glory of the highest-ranking prince and his followers. An early example of such an event was the tournament pageant of 1613.[2] Prince August of Saxony, the Administrator of Naumburg, served as host, assuming the role of an ancient Roman hero victorious over evil. In chains behind his horse he led wild men and giants—as a symbol of the threat to Christendom—as well as a "captive" Turkish couple. Up into the early eighteenth century, such processions, along with quintain games, in which the targets took the form of Turks, were typical elements of such pageants.

By contrast, processions in which participants appeared at tournaments dressed in expensive caftans and with horses in oriental trappings, reveal a wholly different perspective. Members of the high nobility routinely presented themselves in the role of sultan. He was no longer primarily the foe, but rather came to be considered a model, and esteem for him was publicly expressed. By far the most examples of such "Turkish worship" come from Saxony. For example, in the parade to the ring joust during carnival in 1607, Elector Christian II of Saxony, dressed as the sultan, rode through Dresden to the stable yard at the head of the Turkish contingent accompanied by a janissary band (fig. 1).[3] Christian II deliberately chose the role of the sultan, even though the "Turks" were immediately preceded by a contingent of Hungarians or Hussars. Prince August, who in 1613 still presented himself as the victor over the Turks, also adopted the guise of sultan.[4] In the procession to one tournament, unfortunately undated, August now

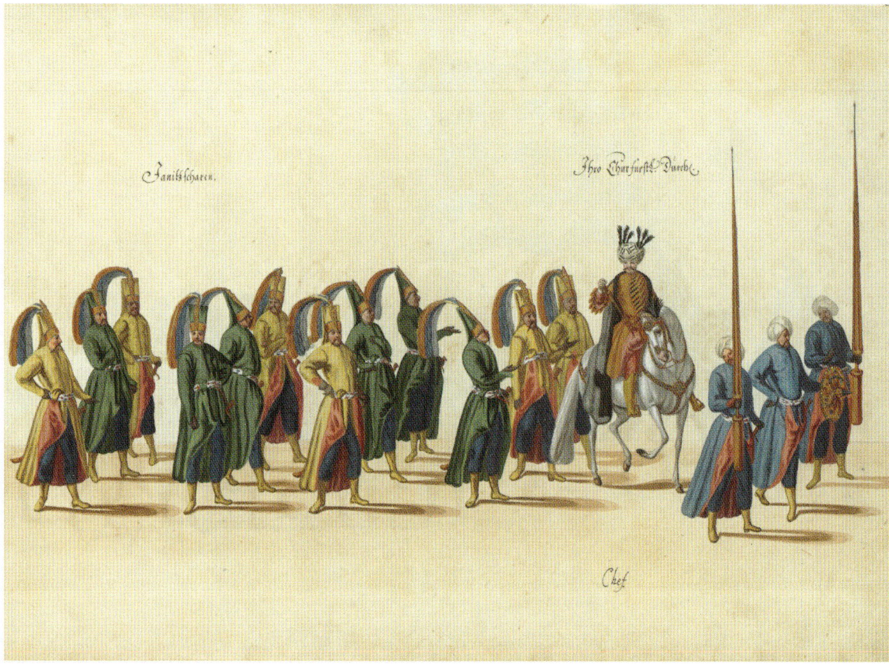

Fig. 2 **Johann Samuel Mock, Parade for the Cartel Race in Dresden in 1697, probably Augustus the Strong as the Turkish Sultan**, presumably Dresden, after 1697, gouache, 40.7 x 59.5 cm, Kupferstich-Kabinett, Staatliche Kunstsammlungen Dresden

appeared as leader of the Turkish contingent, which included numerous members of the court, also in oriental costume, serving as Turkish horsemen and janissaries. As before, in 1607, a janissary band marched at the head of the parade.

After the Turkish army was annihilated before the gates of Vienna on September 12, 1683, Turkish-themed entertainments were little by little divested of their earlier frisson, and, over the course of the eighteenth century, they changed everywhere in Europe. The traditional Ottoman enemy was eliminated from court entertainments and replaced by the "civilized Oriental" in the form of costumed divertissements. Even so, the Saxon court retained its special status with respect to the Turkish fashion for another few decades. The Turkish motif was pervasive in festivities at the Dresden court, and Augustus the Strong again and again presented himself in the role of sultan. Even the few entertainments in which he assumed a different role were prominently Turkish in theme. Two such festivities might serve as examples here. Of particular importance was the cartel race in Dresden in 1697. In the previous two years, Augustus the Strong had held supreme command over the imperial army in Hungary, and, on August 26, 1696, at the Battle of Ólas, he had faced, at the Bega River in present-day Romania, an army under the personal command of Sultan Mustafa II. After changing fortunes over the course of the battle, in the evening the two agreed to a standoff, and the combatants returned to their winter quarters. Augustus returned to Dresden only a few weeks before the race. On February 9, 1697, in a wooden amphitheater erected specially for the occasion, four quadrilles competed in knightly games. Augustus the Strong appeared as sultan at the head of the Turkish quadrille with a large number of attendants in exotic costumes (fig. 2). An additional attraction was a mock battle, but now it was not Christians triumphing over Muslims, as might have been expected at other courts. Instead, in Dresden, it was "Turks" against "Turks." There has been much debate about the background to this anomaly, and just what it was that led Au-

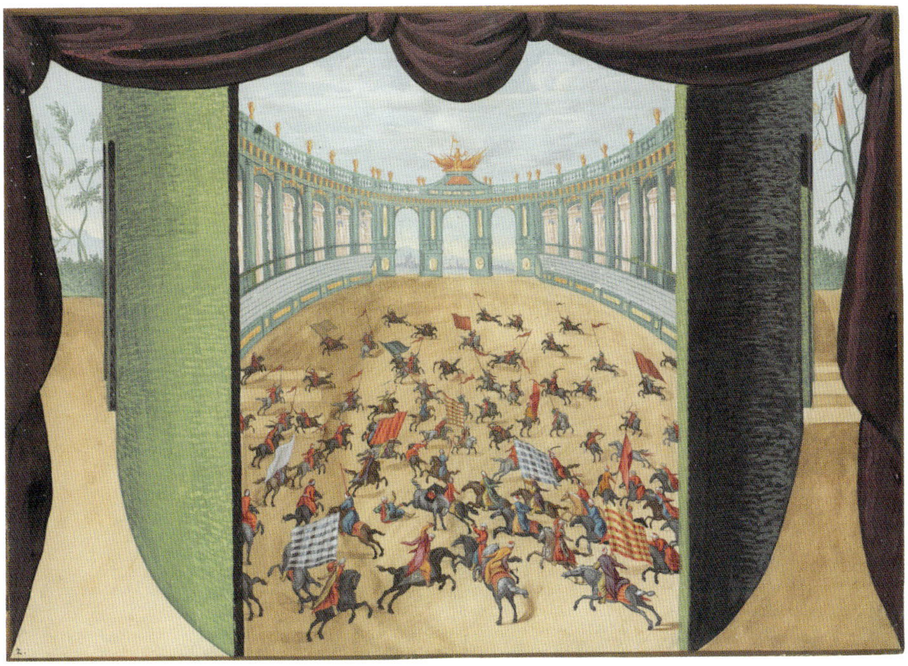

Fig. 3 **Johann Samuel Mock, Mock Battle at the Cartel Race in Dresden in 1697**, probably Dresden, 1701, gouache, 42 x 60 cm, Kupferstich-Kabinett, Staatliche Kunstsammlungen Dresden

gustus the Strong to conceive of this unusual idea is a mystery to this day. Normally such mock battles served to glorify actual or fictitious Christian victories over Muslim foes, with the host prince assuming the role of victorious commander defending the Christian faith against barbarian attack. The skirmish in Dresden was altogether different. Campaigns of the previous years had apparently had a great influence on Augustus. In those battles he had been able to experience firsthand the excellence of the Turkish troops, and was clearly fascinated by their strength. He had not suffered any direct defeat, to be sure, but he had also failed to capture a victory and at the end of the campaign withdrawn in a standoff. Instead of whitewashing his own role in actual warfare for propaganda purposes, staging a mock battle with a fictional victory, Augustus presented the Ottomans as equals, culturally and militarily, at the head of which he could see himself properly represented as sultan. On the other hand, even in the framework of a fictional battle it would have been hardly possible for his "Turks" to triumph over the Christian nations, so Augustus arrived at an unconventional solution: the skirmish was performed by men in exclusively oriental garb, and "Sultan" Augustus the Strong could leave the field as victor without a guilty conscience (fig. 3). But the absolute culmination of the Turkish craze in Saxony were the celebrations in Dresden in 1719 on the occasion of the marriage of Prince Frederick Augustus (II) of Saxony to Archduchess Maria Josepha. The wedding itself and a ceremonial banquet had taken place on August 20 in Vienna, in the presence of the Ottoman ambassador Ibrahim Pasha. The young couple subsequently traveled to Dresden, where they arrived on September 2. Augustus the Strong, who associated with this union the hope of capturing the imperial crown for Saxony, received his son and daughter-in-law with oriental splendor, he himself dressed as sultan. On the bank of the river Elbe, where the newlyweds' ship docked, nine Ottoman tents had been erected, some of them guarded by native Turks in their national costumes. On the procession to the palace, a

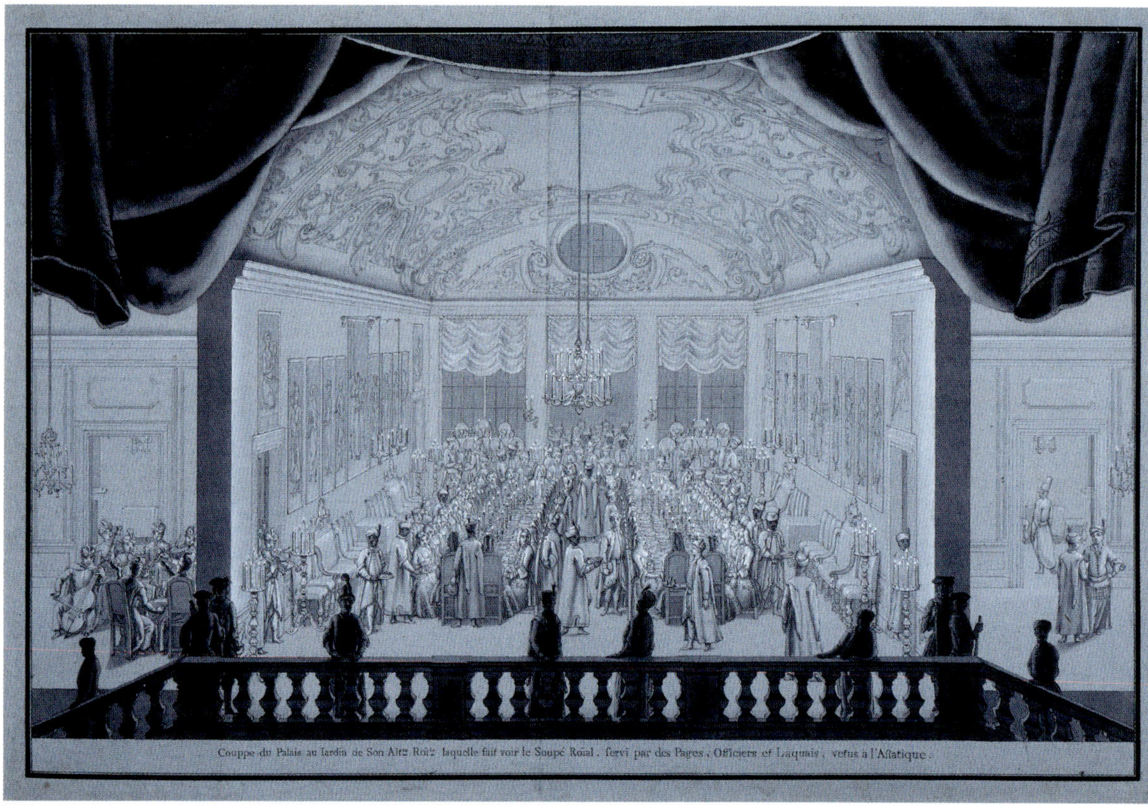

Fig. 4 **Carl Heinrich Jacob Fehling, Banquet at the Turkish Palace in Dresden, 1719**, Dresden, after 1729, gray and black ink, applied with quill and brush, heightened in white, on blue paper, 57 x 88.2 cm, Kupferstich-Kabinett, Staatliche Kunstsammlungen Dresden

knight in armor, accompanied by twenty-four led horses in Turkish ceremonial trappings, carried before the king an Ottoman *tugh*.[5] In late 1718, Augustus had already ordered the creation of a corps of janissaries, 341 men strong. Each of the selected infantrymen was obliged to grow a "moustache à la Turque." Originally they were meant to lead the procession into the city with their music, but this menacing scenario was rejected, so that the janissaries came to be involved only in the following festivities (a Turkish feast in the former Italian Garden, a Mercury celebration in the Zwinger Garden, a ladies ring race in the Grosser Garten, and a Saturn festival in the Plauenscher Grund). Whereas only serving people were dressed in oriental costume at the Turkish feast on 17 September, at the large fair ("Mercerie") three days later, as part of the Mercury celebration, the guests also appeared in costume.

Perhaps the most exotic picture awaited the wedding guests at the Turkish feast. The palais in "Ihro Hoheit Garten" (Your Majesty's Garden)[6] was decorated in oriental style, and its banquet room had been hung with large paintings of figures in oriental dress. The waiters at the crescent-shaped table were dressed as Turks, and the Polish court orchestra—needless to say also in Turkish costumes—played throughout the evening (fig. 4). An even more spectacular highlight of the wedding festivities was the "Serail" or "Circle Ottman," a wax figure cabinet with sixteen lifesize figures, created by the sculptor Jean Joseph Vinache. Dressed in oriental garb and some armed with Ottoman weapons, these figures represented the sultan, women of his harem, and a number of high dignitaries (fig. 5).[7] Like the models for the large paintings just mentioned,[8] the inspiration for the collection of wax figures could have come from Marquis Charles de Ferriol's *Recueil de cent estampes representant différentes nations du Levant*, with engravings after Jean-Baptiste van Mour (fig. 6).[9] In this period, costume entertainments with an oriental theme took place elsewhere too; for example, one at the court of the margraves of Baden-Baden in Rastatt, which is impressively documented by the fifty-six surviving illustrations in Schloss Favorite. They depict Ludwig Wilhelm, Margrave of Baden-Baden—called the "Turkish Louis"—and his wife in various guises, the Margrave as Grand Vizier, for example, both as oriental conjurers and even as a pair of Turkish slaves. In their thematic juxtaposition, these gouaches, presumably painted in the first decade of the eighteenth century, reveal that here the Turkish theme was employed somewhat arbitrarily. There was no distinction between various nations, and even Far Eastern and American Indian motifs found their way into the pictures. With these pictures and the festivities on which they were based, no specific statement seemed to have been intended. The Dresden wedding of 1719 was a wholly different matter. All the festivities were thematically thought out and their effect planned in detail. That Augustus the Strong presented himself as sultan, that a portion of his guard detail were not Saxons, in Turkish costume but native-born Turks, and that among the harem women in the wax figure cabinet there was one that, though officially labeled as Saxon, was covertly interpreted to represent Maria Josepha, were obviously elements that were meant to communicate a clear message. Augustus the Strong wished to portray himself as an absolutist ruler, at least the equal of the emperor, symbolically adopting the role of the still-exotic, magnificent sultan with whom the emperor had shortly before made peace.

Manifestations of the Turkish fashion had meanwhile taken new forms. Courtly festivities no longer merely called for orientally clad servants or guests. Indispensable components were now such hot drinks as coffee, tea, and chocolate. On April 30, 1713, Augustus the Strong made out a shopping list for Johann Georg Spiegel,[10] then already resident in Adrianople (Edirne),

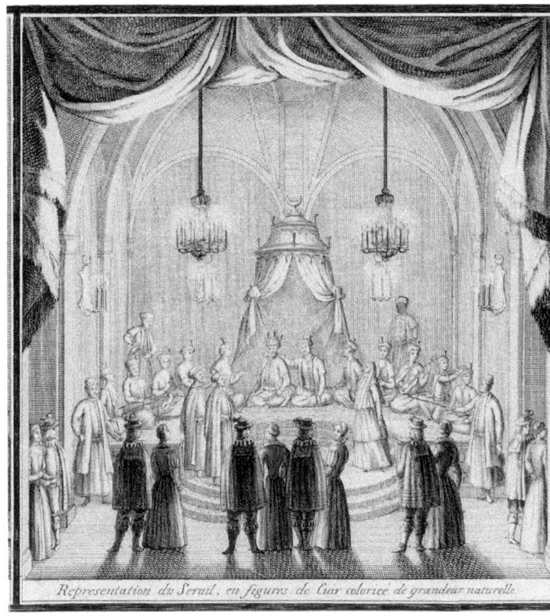

Fig. 5 **Johann August Corvinus, The Royal Table and Stalls at the Mercury Celebration in the Dresden Zwinger, Serail, 1719,** Dresden, after 1725, engraving, Kupferstich-Kabinett, Staatliche Kunstsammlungen Dresden

which, in addition to weapons, garments, and arious other objects, listed slaves (including eunuchs), tent makers, musicians and their instruments, Persian wine from Shiraz, exotic fruits (such as melons), coffee, sorbet, and other oriental drinks. Unfortunately, it is not known whether among Spiegel's purchases were indeed human beings or any of the above-mentioned delicacies, yet a description of the Turkish entertainment held in Warsaw on January 6, 1715, provides a few hints. In the afternoon of that day, Augustus the Strong, with 140 men of his guard, dressed as janissaries and accompanied by a janissary band, made his way to the "Bojaslowski Palais,"[11] decorated in Turkish style. Guests were received by servants in Turkish costume and led up the steps. Ahead of them, also in "Turkish habit," strode Adam Dorengowski, who as legation secretary had lived in Adrianople and Constantinople (Istanbul) from 1712 to 1714 and had since adopted a "wholly Turkish" demeanor.[12] Following a comedy performance, guests were ushered to table, which was was built in the shape of a crescent moon and sur-

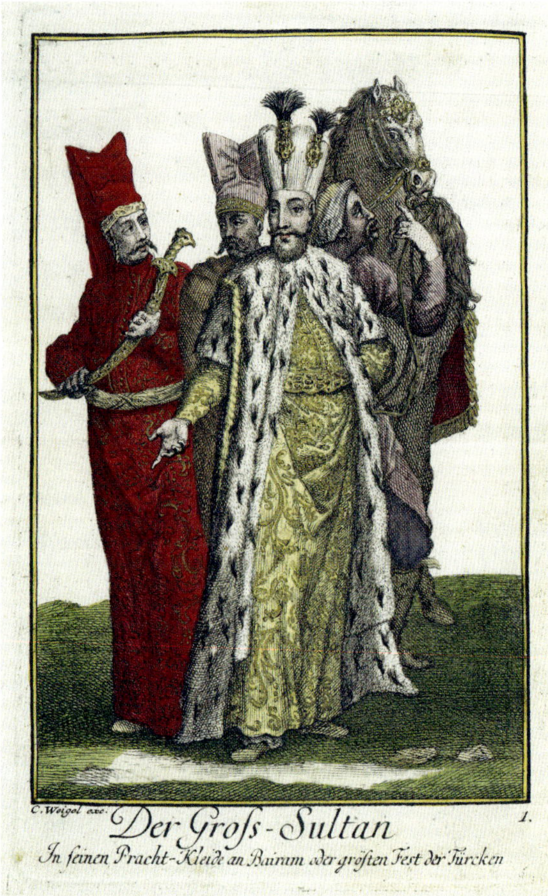

Fig. 6 **Wahreste und neueste Abbildung des Türckischen Hofes, welche nach denen Gemälde, so Monsr. de Ferriol 1707 und 1708 nach dem Leben hat verfertigen lassen** (Truest and Newest Illustration of the Turkish Court after the Painting Done from Nature by M. de Feriol in 1707 and 1708), Nuremberg 1719, copper engraving, colored, 18.5 x 15 cm, plate 1, SLUB Dresden

rounded by orange trees. Afterward there was gaming and dancing until five in the morning, with costumed waiters passing around "at various times chocolate, tea, coffee, and other things."[13]

The Turkish fashion had long since made its way into everyday court life as well. Drinking coffee was part of it, as were orientalizing room decors, splendid garments, and exotically clad staff. Particular mention must be made of the office of the "Chamber Turks." Although these frequently made an appearance at the Dresden court, it is still unclear what nationality they were. It is known that large numbers of Ottomans who had converted and been baptized Christians were living in Saxony. The inventory of the Turkish Chamber of 1683, in which it is noted that, on April 30, 1684, a Hungarian saddle had been given to the "Chamber Turk Soliman for his use,"[14] suggests that at least one of the Chamber Turks was indeed a native-born Ottoman. Yet they were also dispatched to the Ottoman Empire to purchase luxury goods, and one has to wonder whether a captive, even one who had risen to rank and honor in Dresden, would have been sent back to his homeland to run errands.

With the death of Augustus the Strong on February 1, 1733, the Turkish craze more or less subsided in Saxony, although in other European residences it was only now that celebrations "alla turca" came to be held in grand style.[15] In any case, Elector Frederick Augustus II of Saxony (King Augustus III of Poland) appears to have had no interest in continuing his father's Turkish celebrations. Instead, influenced by his long stay in Venice in the course of his six-year-long Grand Tour, he showed a preference for Italian opera and painting. Although everything military was alien to him, he was an enthusiastic hunter and had numerous Ottoman gun barrels rebored and adapted for hunting purposes in the taste of the time. Frederick Augustus II had obviously not inherited is father's interest in oriental culture and the Turkish Chamber. Only at the beginning of his reign did he reprise the Turkish celebrations of his father for one last time: when he was crowned King of Poland on January 17, 1734, he had a number of oriental objects from the holdings of the Turkish Chamber brought to Kraków to be used during the coronation ceremony.

Otherwise, Turkish entertainments played no role in the life of Frederick Augustus II, but he fully indulged his partiality to Italian opera. Beginning in 1734, Johann Adolf Hasse, as Royal and Electoral Kapellmeister, composed numerous operas and other pieces of music for special occasions. The high point of his artistic career was the opera *Solimano*, which premiered in Dresden on Feburary 5, 1753. In expense and decor it topped all that had come before—with more than six hundred singers, extras, as well as horses and camels, in colorful costumes and trappings, some of them genuinely oriental. The Turkish Chamber provided a large number of props and costumes. The armory inventories are filled with notes about the use of its holdings during *Solimano* performances, including damage and occasional losses of items. For example, there is this entry about an Ottoman harness given to the collection by Count Brühl in 1744 (cat. 67): "a brass pendant lost at the opera Solimann, February 28, 1754."[16] We get a sense of the splendor of these stagings from twenty-three pen and watercolor illustrations by Francesco Ponte in the graphic arts collection of the Albertina in Vienna[17] and from the stage directions by Giovanni Ambrogio Migliavacca, Dresden's court poet and Johann Adolf Hasse's librettist (fig. 7).[18]

On the diplomatic front, Augustus III maintained his father's neighborly relations with the Ottomans and Tatars. A number of Ottoman-Tatar embassies were received during his reign, either in Warsaw or in Wschowa in western Poland, and Saxon-Polish delegations were dispatched to the Ottoman Empire. For example, in July 1737, Augustus III met with the Ottoman ambassador Muchurdar Mustapha Effendi in Wschowa. In September 1744 and July 1750, he received gifts in Warsaw from the ambassador of the Tatar khans Selim II Girai and Arslan Girai (cat. 68). And in 1755 he again received in Wschowa the representative of the Ottoman Sultan Osman III. Some of the gifts he received on these occasions, and also a magnificent saddle cloth made in May 1755 for the reception of the Ottoman ambassador, have been preserved in the Turkish Chamber to this day.

Whereas in Saxony the Turkish fashion was stagnating or in some respects even declining, in other states it was only just taking off—gradually morphing into a general fascination with all things oriental—especially in the fields of music and painting. It was greatly fostered by Lady Mary Wortley Montagu (1689–1762), whose husband served as English ambassador in Constantinople and with whom she lived there from 1716 to 1718. Lady

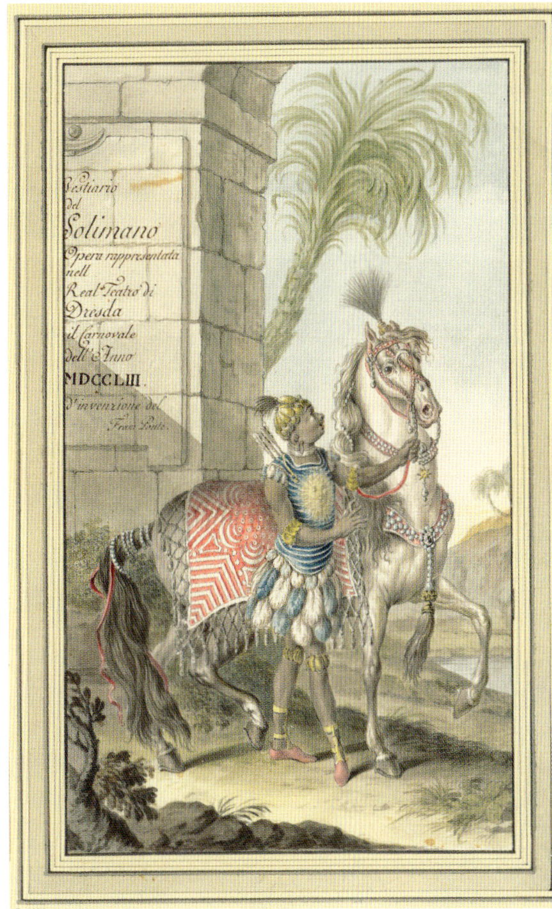

Fig. 7 **Francesco Ponte, Vestiario del Solimano Opera rappresentata nell Real Teatro di Dresda il Carnovale dell' Anno MDCCLIII. D' invenzione del Fran: Ponte** (Costume from the Opera *Solimano* presented at Dresden's Royal Theater at Carnival 1753, design by Fran. Ponte), Gray and brown ink, gray wash, watercolor, 33.8 x 20.5 cm, Albertina, Vienna

Montagu became famous for her *Turkish Embassy Letters* and the introduction of smallpox inoculation in Great Britain. Having contracted smallpox herself, shortly before her departure, she had her children—her son Edward born in London in 1713 and daughter Mary born in Pera in 1718—inoculated in Turkey, and made the precautionary treatment known among her contemporaries. While in Turkey in 1717, she was painted by Jean-Baptiste van Mour (1671–1737). The picture shows her wearing the typical local dress and holding her son by the hand, with a view of Constantinople in the background.[19] After her return home, and during her years in France and Italy, additional portraits followed, again picturing her in oriental costume, which by that time had become highly fashionable. In addition to paintings by unknown artists, there are portraits of Lady Montagu by Charles Jervas, by Jonathan Richardson the Younger, and by Jean-Étienne Liotard.

In 1737, Liotard had become acquainted in Florence with Lord William Ponsonby, 2nd Earl of Bessborough, and with him journeyed to the Ottoman Empire, where he then lived and worked from 1738 to 1743, first in Constantinople and later in Jassy in the northeast of present-day Romania.[20] After his return to Europe, Liotard worked in various cities, including Vienna, Venice, Paris, London, Amsterdam, and Geneva, producing a large number of portraits with an oriental flair. Everywhere in these years, he cultivated his oriental image and continued to dress, like Adam Dorengowski at the court of Augustus the Strong in Warsaw and Dresden, "alla turca." He even wore Turkish costume for his meeting with Empress Maria Theresa in 1744. With his works and his extravagant appearance he gave new impetus to the enthusiasm for things oriental that had evolved out of the Turkish craze.

1 See Claudia Schnitzer, "Zwischen Kampf und Spiel – Orientrezeption im höfischen Fest," in: *Im Lichte des Halbmonds: Das Abendland und der türkische Orient*, exh. cat. Staatliche Kunstsammlungen Dresden, Albertinum; Kunst- und Ausstellungshalle der Bundesrepublik Deutschland, Bonn, Dresden 1995, pp. 230–31.

2 Sächsisches Hauptstaatsarchiv Dresden, (HStADD), OHMA Pläne und Zeichnungen, no. 4; exh. cat. Dresden/Bonn 1995, p. 249, cat. no. 295.

3 Sächsische Landesbibliothek – Staats- und Universitätsbibliothek Dresden (SLUB), Sign. Mscr. Dresd. J 10; exh. cat. Dresden/Bonn 1995, p. 248, cat. no. 294.

4 HStADD, OHMA Pläne und Zeichnungen, no. 6; exh. cat. Dresden/Bonn 1995, p. 249, cat. no. 296.

5 An Ottoman battle standard of tufts and braids of horsehair on a wooden pole.

6 The setting for the Turkish Festival was the garden and palace first known as the Italian Garden or Italian Palais and then as "His Majesty's Garden." Only after the celebration was the name "Turkish Garden" or "Turkish Palais" used in reference to its interior decor. On the day of the celebration, Augustus the Strong presented the garden and palace to his daughter-in-law as a wedding present. In 1760, during the Seven Years' War, the complex was almost completely destroyed by Prussian shelling.

7 Extensive description of the Serail in the inventory of the Turkish Chamber from 1783, pp. 275–87 and in Holger Schuckelt, "'Folget Das Türckische Serail'—Das Wachsfigurenkabinett Augusts des Starken, Kammertürken und Türkenkammer am Dresdner Hof," in: *Eine gute Figur machen: Kostüm und Fest am Dresdner Hof*, ed. Claudia Schnitzer and Petra Hölscher, exh. cat. Kupferstich-Kabinett Dresden, Dresden 2000, pp. 69–83.

8 See Gregor J. M. Weber, "Alles getürkt: Die lebensgrossen Figurenbilder im Türkischen Palais Dresdens," in: *Eine gute Figur machen: Kostüm und Fest am Dresdner Hof*, ed. Claudia Schnitzer and Petra Hölscher, exh. cat. Kupferstich-Kabinett Dresden, Dresden 2000, pp. 85–99.

9 After the festivity, the figures were preserved in the Turkish Chamber, where they could still be seen until 1783.

10 Johann Georg Spiegel, whose origins are unknown, had been a personal page and close confidant of Augustus the Strong's since 1685. He was repeatedly entrusted with delicate assignments. For example, in 1706, he was married to Fatima, Augustus the Strong's former Turkish mistress. Spiegel was a valet and excise councillor and, after 1709, lived in Lviv. From 1712 to 1714 he traveled on behalf of Augustus to Edirne and Istanbul. He died in the spring of 1715 under as yet unexplained circumstances.

11 Doubtless what was meant was the former Bokumowski Palace of the Polish magnate Jerzy Ignacy Lubomirski, which stood on the grounds of Augustus III's later orangery in Warsaw, and, according to the Warsaw professor Jakub Sito, was furnished in the Turkish style.

12 HStADD, Oberhofmarschallamt II.1.1. 1564–1920, Akte G 15, Film 0908, Einheit 0197ff., fol. 181–185, "Türckisches Festin so den 6. Jannua: in Warschau gehalten worden 1715," fol. 182.

13 Ibid., fol. 184.

14 Inventory of the Turkish Chamber from 1683, p. 34, no. 49.

15 There has been much speculation about the abrupt decline in the Turkish fashion at the Saxon court, and it is conceivable that Maria Josepha, as the new Electress of Saxony, played an important role in it. She may well have perceived her reception in Dresden shortly after her marriage as demeaning, which would make her distaste for such festivities perfectly understandable.

16 Inventory of the Gute Sattelkammer from 1716, Blatt 86, no. 187 (addendum).

17 Francesco Ponte, "Vestiario del Solimano Opera rappresentata nell Real Teatro di Dresda il Carnovale dell'Anno MDCCLIII. D' invenzione del Fran: Ponte," Graphic Arts Collection of the Albertina, Vienna, inv. nos. 4580–4603.

18 "Solimano, ein Singespiel, welches auf dem Königl. Pohln. und Churfürstl. Sächß. Hof-Theater in Dresden, zur Carnevals-Zeit ist aufgeführet worden. Im Jahr 1753. Die poesie ist von hrn. Giannambrogio Migliavacca, sr. Königl. Majest Poeten., u. Legations-rathe, die Musick ist von Herrn Johann Adolph Haßen, Königl. Ober-Capell-Meister. Dreßden, gedruckt bey der verwittw. Königl. Hof-Buchdr. Stößelin," Schuckelt 2010a, p. 325.

19 The Flemish painter Jean-Baptiste van Mour traveled in 1699 with the French ambassador Marquis Charles de Ferriol to Constantinople, where he remained until his death in 1737. He created countless city views and portraits. His pictures served as models for the engravings in Ferriol's *Recueil de cent estampes représentant différentes nations du Levant*, first published in 1714.

20 Jassy belonged to the Principality of Moldavia, which was founded in the mid fourteenth century in the territory between the khanate of the Crimean Tatars, the Grand Duchy of Lithuania, the kingdoms of Poland and Hungary, and the Ottoman Empire. Originally dependent on Hungary and Poland, since 1512 the principality had been a vassal of the Sultan, preserving internal autonomy. Beginning in the second half of the eighteenth century, the Principality of Moldavia came into the Russian and Austrian spheres of interest.

WHAT STRUCK ALGAROTTI AS CHINESE IN LIOTARD'S *CHOCOLATE GIRL*

Julia Weber

In a letter to the art critic Pierre-Jean Mariette from February 1751, Count Francesco Algarotti described the *Chocolate Girl*, which he had bought from the artist five years earlier, as a picture that—though European through and through—would appeal in particular to the Chinese. Algarotti expressly emphasized that Liotard's work stood squarely in the European tradition, yet spoke of its hybrid quality, which also had something "Chinese" about it. Struck by certain painterly details, which will be discussed later on, Algarotti stepped out of his cultural context and adopted the—assumed—perspective of a non-European viewer. Inspired by this contemporary view of the famous *Chocolate Girl*, this essay attempts to define more closely the oscillation between West and East in both the painting and its subject matter. In the mid eighteenth century, the "opening up of the world" (from a European viewpoint) had become a tangible reality, with the discovery of new sea lanes and countries, and the colonization of overseas territories. Whereas attempts at global hegemony on the part of individual states increasingly threatened the balance of power and thus the peace, rapidly expanding international trade was bringing to Europe ever greater quantities of new consumer goods such as tobaccco, tea, coffee, chocolate, porcelain, lacquers, and silk. Their wholesale import both disrupted and stimulated existing markets, and brought fundamental changes to European material culture.[1] The growing presence of these luxury goods from faraway countries forced people, even those outside the higher social circles, to recognize that their own culture was but one among many.[2] It was upon this recognition that Algarotti's change of perspective in his consideration of the *Chocolate Girl* was based.

In his pastel, Liotard devoted as much attention to the material evidence of these foreign cultures as to the main figure. He "portrayed" objects and items of clothing so precisely that they can be positively identified (fig. 1): with its bracket feet, inset curved edges, and landscape depiction in gold, the lacquer tray the Viennese maid is carrying so carefully resembles surviving Japanese originals (fig. 2).[3] Contemporaries also associated with the Far East the material and decor of the porcelain cup filled to the brim with hot chocolate, whereas its tall shape and delicately curved handle identify it as a European substitute from Meissen, Europe's oldest porcelain manufactory. The Meissen decor, with "Indian" flowers in the typical colors blue, red, and gold, repeated in countless variants, was based on East Asian wares in the Imari style.[4] In Empress Maria Theresa's breakfast service, Meissen chocolate cups with the popular *Tischchenmuster* ("little table pattern") design were combined with Japanese tea and coffee bowls as equivalent substitutes (fig. 3). In material and form, the Meissen cup Liotard "portrayed" has the same hybrid quality as do the girl's silk garments of a European cut.[5] In their very materials alone, cup and clothing led contemporary viewers to think of the Far East.

Like very few other artists, Liotard was able to render the different materials and surface qualities that constituted the charm of the novel import goods

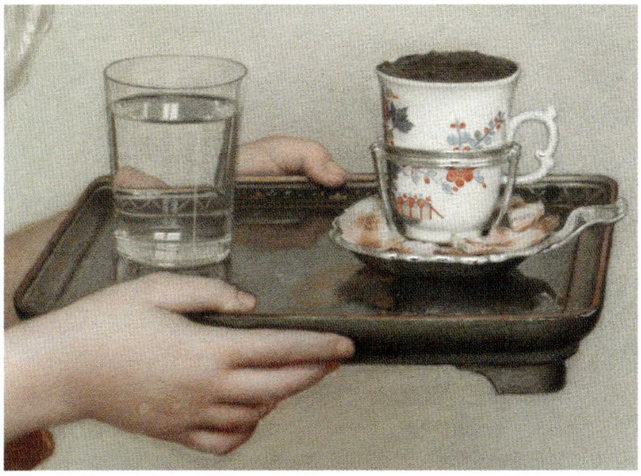

Fig. 1 **Jean-Étienne Liotard**, **The Chocolate Girl**, ca. 1744, Gemäldegalerie Alte Meister, Staatliche Kunstsammlungen Dresden, detail showing cup and tray

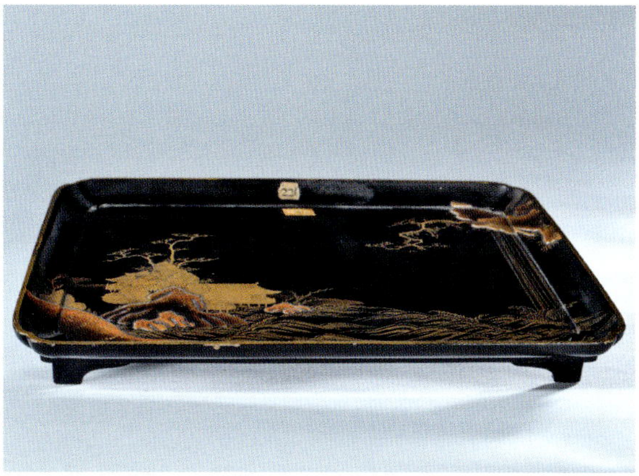

Fig. 2 **Japanese lacquer tray**, late eighteenth century, wood, black lacquer, gold decor, long side, Stiftung Schloss Friedenstein Gotha

from Asia. Lacquer, porcelain, and silk enchanted Europeans with their sheen, which they sought to imitate in a variety of other mediums. Liotard's skill at emulating in painting the brilliance of shimmering surfaces and the depth and radiance of the colors of lacquer and porcelain is evident in the late *Still Life: Tea Set* (fig. 4): on an imitation Asian lacquer tray a porcelain tea service is arranged, a set of uniformly decorated crockery in the European manner. Details, for example the slightly curved lip of the teapot, suggest that Liotard was looking at English Staffordshire porcelain painted in a reduced palette after Chinese export porcelain.[6] But in the still life it is not only the European copies that imitate with deceptive accuracy East Asian luxury goods. The rich dark ground itself, against which, in Liotard's painting, the highlights of the porcelain and silver gleam like the sparkling inlays in Japanese lacquerwork, appears to compete with the coveted exotic material.[7]

Inspired by East Asian imports, the question of the kind and degree of sheen and the brilliance of colors became part of a lively artistic discourse that also extended to painting.[8] In this it was held that pastels were superior to oil paintings in the rendering of fabrics and flesh.[9] The popularity of pastel portraits was owing precisely to their ability to reproduce velvety soft and both matte and reflecting surfaces, thanks to the high concentration—up to 90 percent—of pigment. Not only was the intensity of pastels vaunted, but also the durability and brilliance of their colors, compared to oil paintings[10]—qualities that were also admired in East Asian porcelains and Indian and Persian miniatures.[11] Liotard's characteristic technique of painting on parchment lent his pastels yet further luster and radiance.[12] Like the craftsmen who sought to replicate Far Eastern luxury wares, Liotard also competed with non-European materials and techniques.[13]

He boasted himself of his skill in reproducing with astonishing naturalism the most varied surface qualities with pastel crayons,[14] encountering vehement criticism from many of his artist colleagues. His mimetic representation of motifs and restrained painterly expression went against the prevailing Rococo style, and Liotard was accused of dryness and lack of imagination.[15] Algarotti, on the other hand, in his above-mentioned letter to Mariette, praised the lack of affectation in the *Chocolate Girl* and the accuracy of its painterly execution, flatteringly comparing Liotard's work to that of Holbein. But it was not the perfection in the representation of Far Eastern materials that led Algarotti to think of China when contemplating the pastel, it was rather the way of painting with virtually no shadows, as described by Liotard himself, and with a much reduced chiaroscuro in the subtle tone-in-

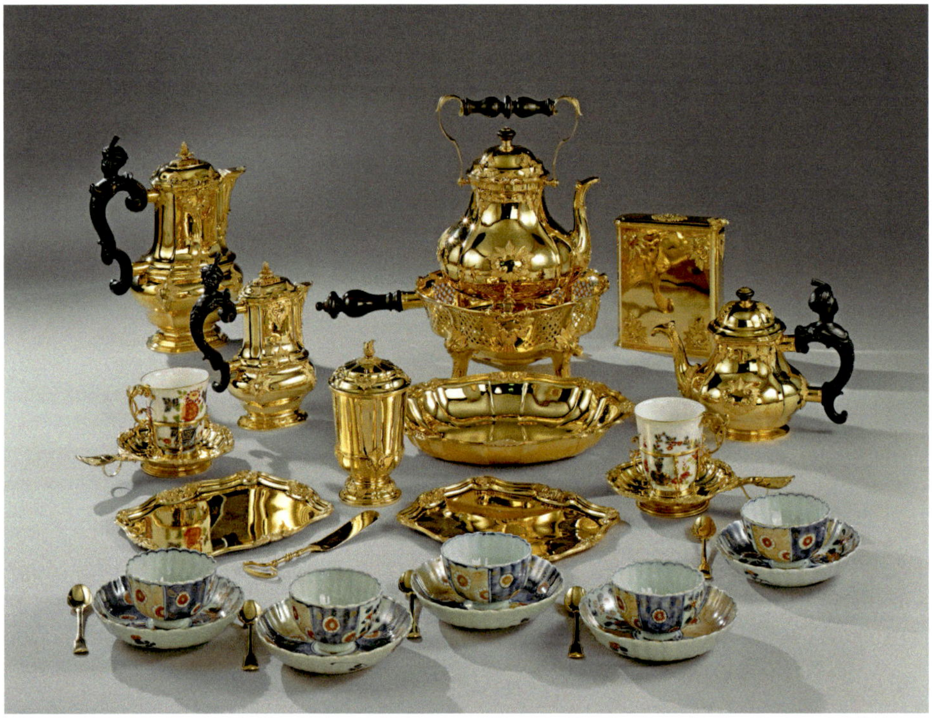

Fig. 3 **Anton Matthias Domanek, Empress Maria Theresa's Breakfast Service**, ca. 1750, Kunsthistorisches Museum, Kunstkammer, Vienna

tone modeling of volumes[16] that led Algarotti to assume the picture would appeal to the Chinese, who, as he claimed, were sworn enemies of shadows.[17] Indeed, uniform lighting and absence of shadows were generally considered to be characteristics of Chinese and Eastern painting.[18]

Liotard had come across Turkish and Persian book illustrations and miniatures during his several-years stay in Constantinople.[19] His encounter with oriental art and—in contrast to Algarotti—personal experience of standing outside the prevailing artistic conventions, had a lasting effect on his concept of art.[20] In the capital of the Ottoman Empire, Liotard not only developed his characteristic way of painting, with precise observation and description, which he would later field against the extravagance and affectation of the French Rococo;[21] in his Turkish drawings he also for the first time adapted stylistic devices from Ottoman painting that in Europe were necessarily considered in defiance of academic rules. Among them were the uniform lighting and reduced shadows, but also his light, monochrome backgrounds and flat, barely defined and perspectively irregular picture spaces. Without being direct copies of Ottoman miniatures, Liotard's Turkish drawings attest to a receptivity to their charms and a readiness to integrate foreign aesthetic principles in his own work.[22] The *Chocolate Girl*, which he painted in Vienna shortly after his return from Constantinople—without a commission or buyer, simply as a demonstration of his art—illustrates the new pictorial conception he had acquired abroad. This was altogether apparent to contemporaries, as attested by Algarotti's comment that the pastel seemed somehow "Chinese." He was probably taken aback not only by the absence of shadows, but also by the undefined spatial situation and the inconsistent perspective. While the viewer's gaze is roughly eye level with the girl, the floorboards and

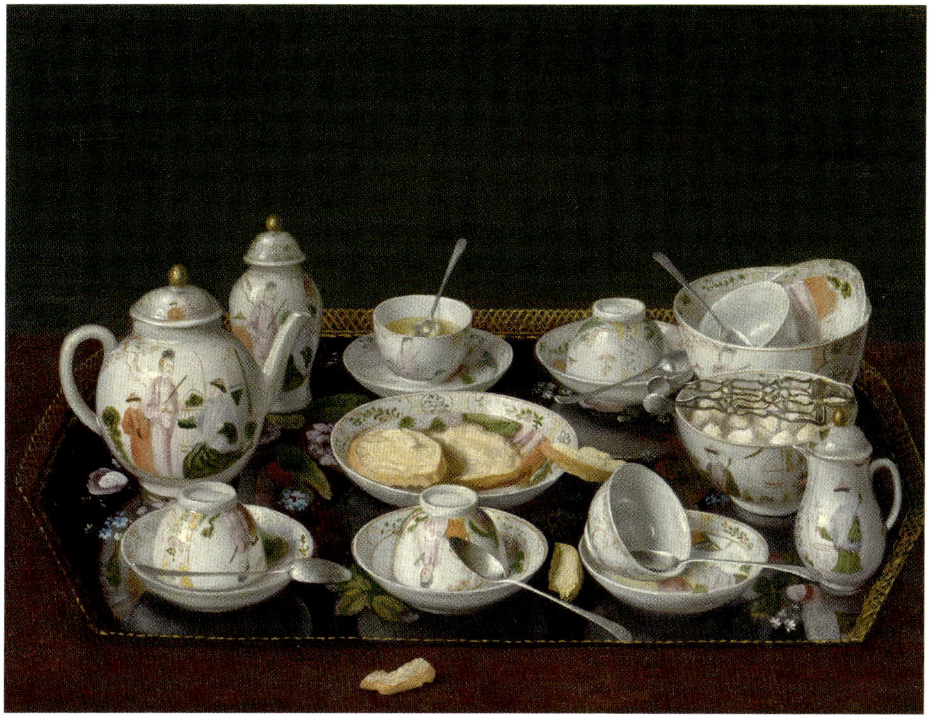

Fig. 4 **Jean-Étienne Liotard**, **Still Life: Tea Set**, ca. 1781–83, oil on canvas mounted on cardboard, 37.8 x 51.6 cm, J. Paul Getty Museum, Los Angeles

the lacquer tray are seen to varying degrees from above. The monochrome wall also mitigates against any sense of spatial depth. Finally, the maid's stiff, upright posture must also have struck Algarotti as unusual, her motionless silhouette so clearly set off against the pale background. The iconic depiction of the young woman in full figure is anticipated in one of Liotard's chalk drawings from Constantinople (cat. 3) Both the motif of the attendant serving tea and the pose of the seated mistress of the house were based on illustrations in the highly popular book of Ottoman costumes, published by the previous French ambassador to the Sublime Porte, Charles de Ferriol, in 1714.[23] Yet the housemaid in the analogous scene in the *Recueil Ferriol* is pictured from the back (fig. 5). Liotard's choice of the profile view must have other roots. Contemporaries associated portrait depictions in profile or three-quarter view with Persian and Indian miniatures.[24] And indeed, the girl's upright pose, the way her head is rendered in strong profile view while her upper body is turned slightly toward the viewer, as well as the barely defined picture space with a small section of floor and monochrome background, recall portraits of Indian Mughal emperors (fig. 6). Indian miniatures produced for export were coveted collectors' items not only among European princes and aristocrats, but also the wealthy bourgeoisie and affluent artists.[25] In the posthumous inventory of Liotard's estate, no non-European works are listed, but he could have seen plenty of Indian miniatures during his stay in Vienna. Empress Maria Theresa, who received him warmly, described herself as a passionate collector of Asian art.[26] Beginning in the 1750s she had various chinoiserie cabinets installed at Schönbrunn Palace, including the so-called "Millionenzimmer" with sixty collages made from Indian Mughal miniatures set into its wood paneling.[27] Given the large number of portrait se-

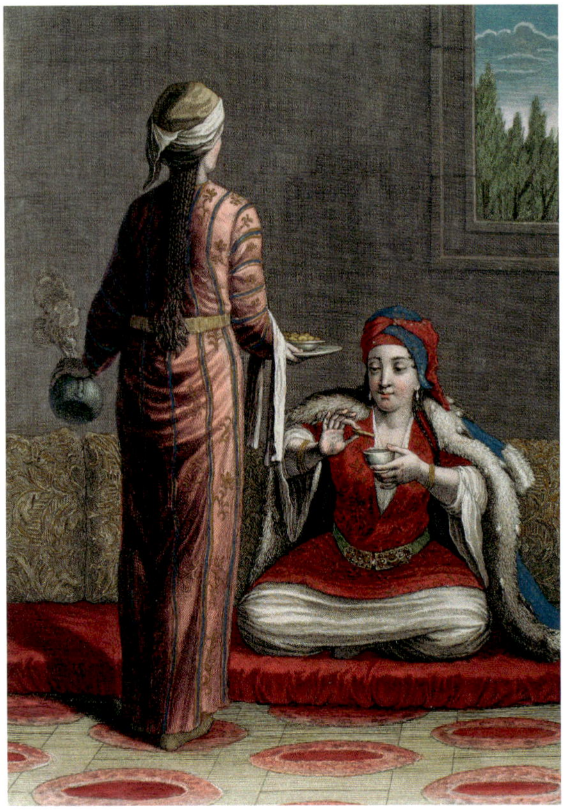

Fig. 5 **Recueil Ferriol** (*Recueil de cents estampes répresentant différentes nations du Levant),* Paris 1714, sheet 48, *Fille turque prenant le Caffé sur le Sopha*, engraving, colored, 49. 6 x 34. 8 cm, Kupferstich-Kabinett, Staatliche Kunstsammlungen Dresden

ries that found their way to Europe, a general familiarity can be assumed with the conventions of Indian ruler portraits, which were moreover disseminated as engraved reproductions in richly illustrated compendiums on Indian culture (fig. 7).[28] The formal similarity between Liotard's *Chocolate Girl* and Indian Mughal miniatures can therefore be interpreted as a further recourse to foreign pictorial conventions.[29]

Algarotti's description of Liotard's *Chocolate Girl* indicates that he recognized the pastel's hybrid nature, oscillating between East and West, one that can be credited to a conscious integration of non-European painting styles and that Algarotti explicitly identified, based on its virtual absence of shadows. He seems not to have considered this a detriment or flaw, since he simultaneously praised Liotard's ability to subtly model volumes in halftones.[30] By contrast, in another text, Algarotti expressed himself most dismissively about Chinese painting.[31] The reception of Chinese art in general combined admiration and a fascination with its foreignness with rejection and scorn. The English politician and scholar James Marriot even went so far as to declare that Chinese paintings "continually revolt against the truth of things . . . . False lights, false shadows, false perspective and proportions, gay colours . . . in short every incoherent combination of forms in nature, without expression and without meaning, are the essentials of Chinese painting."[32]

Similarly severe were the reactions of fellow artists and art critics to Liotard's openness to non-European styles and conventions, which was even more apparent in his physical transformation into a "peintre turc" with a long beard, caftan, and fur hat (fig. p. 17).[33] Mariette condemned his deliberate break with European academic rules and conventions as incompetence, based on his being self-taught, and the English painter Joshua Reynolds considered him to be an artist with little genius or none at all.[34] Jean-Bernard Le Blanc even described Liotard's painting as scandalous, and called him an imposter in carnivalesque masquerade.[35] In these assertions, scholars have rightly recognized a fundamentally skeptical to dismissive attitude toward cultural hybridization, combined with a negative moral judgment as a reaction to the political and social changes that accompanied the "opening up of the world."[36]

Even Liotard, who in his 1781 *Traité des principes et des règles de la peinture* praised the painting of the Chinese as consistent, unadulterated, and pristine, simultaneously denied them any kind of artistic understanding, and thus affirmed European superiority.[37] Yet, although he refused to recognize Chinese painters as equals, Liotard admitted that their art held a special aesthetic charm for the untrained European viewer. The instinctive judgment of the "ignorart" (unschooled in art) served him as a legitimation to ignore, like the Chinese,

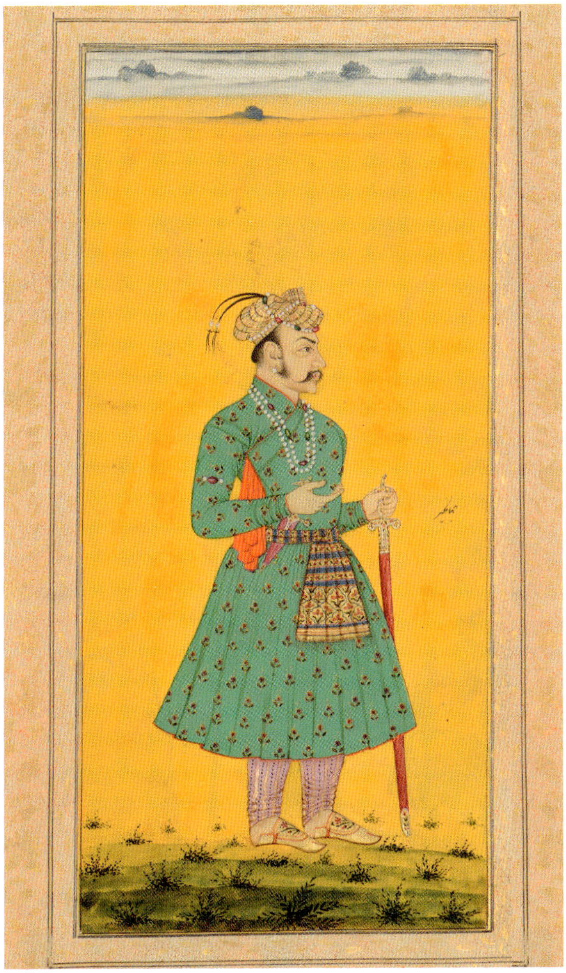

Fig. 6 **Jahāngīr**, from an album of forty-six portraits of kings and nobles from Persia, Mughal, and Deccan, Golkonda (Deccan), 1668–89, watercolor and gold, 24.5 x 11.8 cm (sheet), Kupferstich-Kabinett, Staatliche Kunstsammlungen Dresden

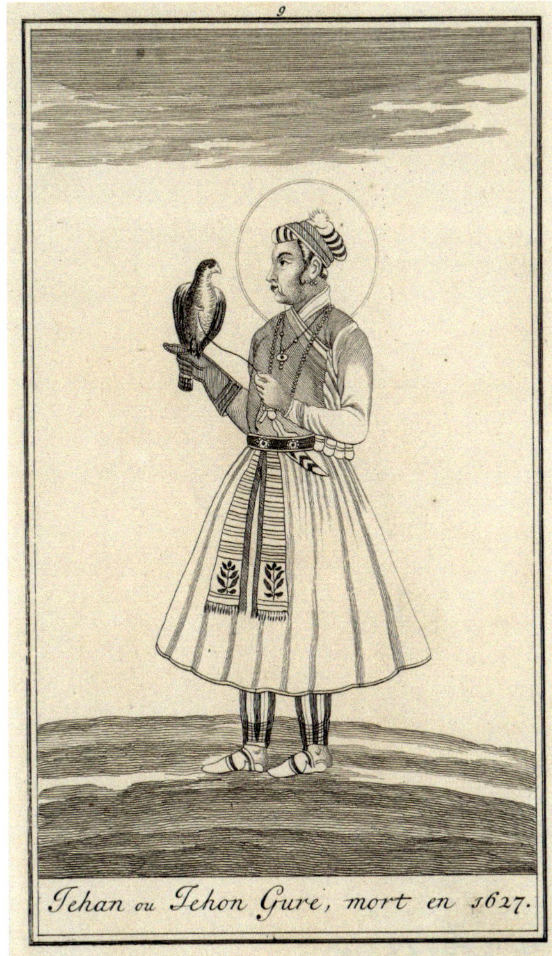

Fig. 7 **Bernard Picart**, **Tehan**, engraving and etching, from: Henri Chatelain, Atlas Historique, Amsterdam 1719, vol. 5, no. 38, p. 110, Kupferstich-Kabinett, Staatliche Kunstsammlungen Dresden

certain academic rules.[38] In response to the predominantly scathing criticism by contemporary art critics, Liotard pointed to his great success with the art-buying public, which appeared to prove him right. The "Chinese" aspect of his art—as detected by Algarotti—that caused him to be repudiated by the art world, was clearly valued by his buyers and provoked the interest of such lovers of Asian art as Augustus the Strong and Maria Theresa. Liotard's readiness to be influenced by its culture during his long stay in the East made him and his art authentic testaments to an equally fascinating and frightening foreign world.

1 See Stacey Sloboda, *Chinoiserie: Commerce and Critical Ornament in Eighteenth-Century Britain*, Manchester and New York 2014, pp. 3–4, 65–67; Noémie Etienne and Chonja Lee, "Lüster, Lack und Liotard: Techniken und Texturen zwischen Asien und Europa," in: *Kunst + Archiektur in der Schweiz* 69, no. 1 (2018), pp. 4–5.

2 See Kristel Smentek, "Looking East. Jean-Étienne Liotard, the Turkish Painter," in: *Ars Orientalis* 39 (2010), p. 97.

3 See Oliver Impey and Christiaan Jörg, *Japanese export lacquer, 1580–1850*, Amsterdam 2004, p. 328. I am grateful to Christiaan Jörg for his detailed assessment of the depicted lacquer tray.

4 See Julia Weber, *Meißener Porzellane mit Dekoren nach ostasiatischen Vorbildern*, Munich 2013, vol. 2, cat. 75–90. For the shape of the cup and its handle, see ibid., cat. 91.

5 For the garments pictured, see Marcel Roethlisberger and Renée Loche, *Liotard. Catalogue, Sources et Correspondance*, Doornspijk 2008, vol. 1, p. 325.

6 I am grateful to Christiaan Jörg for identifying the European substitutes pictured.

7 Such is the theory of Noémie Etienne and Chonja Lee in Etienne/Lee 2018, p. 7. I am grateful to Noémie Etienne for a critical reading of the present manuscript.

8 See Noémie Etienne, *The Restoration of Paintings in Paris, 1750–1815*, Los Angeles 2017, pp. 95, 104; Etienne/Lee 2018, p. 5.

9 "This kind of painting [pastel] is used almost exclusively for portraits; the kind of velvety nap produced by this powder is better suited than any other medium for the depiction of fabrics and the softness and freshness of skin; the color seems truer; but to fully realize it one has to be extremely skillful." Antoine-Joseph Pernety, *Dictionnaire portatif de peinture, sculpture et gravure*, Paris 1757, pp. cxxvii–cxxviii, quoted from R/L 2008, vol. 1, p. 106.

10 "I rashly venture to say that the pastel portraits of M. de la Tour have one major virtue as compared to those painted with oil—namely that they will not change. Oil darkens over time, and dulls the radiance of the most beautiful colors. . . . The glass-covered pastel is changeless, protected from the corruption of air." Jean-Bernard Le Blanc, *Lettre sur l'exposition des ouvrages de peinture, sculpture, etc. de l'Année 1747. Et en général sur l'utilité de ces sortes d'Expositions*, Paris 1747, pp. 89–90, quoted from R/L 2008, vol. 1, p. 106. See also Etienne 2017, p. 97.

11 See note 24; Smentek 2010, p. 103; Corinna Forberg, *Die Rezeption indischer Miniaturen in der europäischen Kunst des 17. und 18. Jahrhunderts*, Petersberg 2015, p. 175.

12 See in detail Neil Jeffares, "Liotard and the Medium of Pastel," in: *Jean-Étienne Liotard, 1702–1789*, exh. cat. Scottish National Gallery, Edinburgh; Royal Academy of Arts, London 2015, pp. 31–32; William Hauptmann, "Painting in Dry Colours," in: ibid., p. 23. For the reception of Indian miniatures, see Forberg 2015, p. 175.

13 See Etienne/Lee 2018, p. 5.

14 See R/L 2008, vol. 1, p. 33.

15 See R/L 2008, vol. 1, p. 35; Smentek 2010, p. 86.

16 See R/L 2008, vol. 1, pp. 33–34, 169.

17 "A pastel painting roughly three feet tall by the famous Herr Liotard that pictures a young German chambermaid in profile carrying a tray with a glass of water and a cup of chocolate. This painting is virtually without shadows against a light background; and the light sources are two windows reflected in the glass: all done in half-tones and with imperceptible gradations of light, and with astonishing relief. It pictures nature with no hint of mannerism; and although it is a European painting it would be most pleasing to the Chinese, who as you know are arch-enemies of shadows. As for its extremely high level of execution, to put it briefly it is a Holbein in pastels." Francesco Algarotti, *Opere*, vol. 8, Venice 1792, pp. 32–33; quoted from R/L 2008, vol. 1, p. 324. For the reception of European perspective and the formation of shadows in Chinese painting of the eighteenth century, see Christina Kleuthgen, "From Science to Art: The Evolution of Linear Perspective in Eighteenth-Century Chinese Art," in: Petra ten-Doesschate Chu and Ding Ning, eds., *Qing Encounters: Artistic Exchanges between China and the West*, Los Angeles 2015, pp. 173–89; also Lihong Liu, "Shadows in Chinese Art: An Intercultural Perspective," in: ibid., pp. 190–213.

18 See Smentek 2010, pp. 86, 101; Sloboda 2014, p. 24; Forberg 2015, p. 175.

19 See Smentek 2010, pp. 91–93.

20 For an extensive discussion, see Smentek 2010; Nebahat Avcıoğlu, *Turquerie and the Politics of Representation, 1728–1876*, Farnham 2011, pp. 20–23; Mary D. Sheriff, "The Dislocations of Jean-Étienne Liotard, Called the Turkish Painter," in: idem, ed., *Cultural Contact and the Making of European Art since the Age of Exploration*, Chapel Hill 2010, pp. 97, 121.

21 See Smentek 2010, p. 100.

22 Ibid., pp. 87–88, 93–95.

23 See Charles de Ferriol, ed., *Recueil de cent estampes représentant les diverses nations du Levant, tirées d'après nature en 1707 et 1708 par les ordres de M de Ferriol, ambassadeur du Roy à la Porte et gravées en 1712 et 1713 par les soins de Le Hay*, Paris 1714, plates 45, 48; Smentek 2010, pp. 93, 97.

24 "The Persians . . . are less scrupulous in all things than the Turks, and paint faces and figures. . . . Their portraits are all in profile or three-quarter profile, as they know nothing about assigning shadows when depicting a face frontally. However ,they excel in Moorish ornaments and flowers, which they rarely paint in oil but rather as miniatures. . . . Their brush is fine, their colors are bright and long-lasting. . . . Perspective would not be so disregarded were they to study their compatriots who have written about it." Jean-Baptiste Bourguignon d'Anville, "Mémoire où il est question de la Peinture des Turcs & des Persans, de la façon dont les Turcs meublent leur apartemens, & principalement de la richesse des apartemens du Sérail du grand-Seigneur," in: *Le Nouveau Mércure*, April 1721, pp. 27–28.

25 See Forberg 2015, pp. 137–43; Avcıoğlu 2011, pp. 18–19; Petra Kuhlmann-Hodick, "Introduction," in: idem, ed., *Indian Paintings: The Collection of the Dresden Kupferstich-Kabinett*, Dresden 2017, pp. 22–23. I am grateful to Petra Kuhlmann-Hodick for her helpful suggestions and critical reading of my manuscript.

26 "Nothing in the world, no diamonds mean anything to me, only what comes from India, . . . that is the one thing that gives me pleasure." Quoted from *Maria Theresia 1717–1780: Strategin – Mutter – Refor-*

merin, exh. cat. Schloss Hof, Schloss Niederweiden, Hofmobiliendepot – Imperial Furniture Collection Vienna, Kaiserliche Wagenburg, ed. Elfriede Iby et al., Vienna 2017, p. 300.

27 See exh. cat. Vienna 2017, pp. 301–02: *Miniatur-Geschichten: Die Sammlung indischer Malerei im Dresdner Kupferstich-Kabinett*, exh. cat. Kupferstich-Kabinett, Staatliche Kunstsammlungen Dresden, ed. Monica Juneja and Petra Kuhlmann-Hodick, Dresden 2017.

28 See Forberg 2015, pp. 137, 152.

29 A further parallel in Liotard's work suggests as much, namely the formal similarity between the seated woman in the oil painting A *Dutch Girl at Breakfast* from 1756/57 (cat. 21) and the typical seated pose in Indian Mughal miniatures, see, for example, exh. cat. Dresden 2017, p. 129, fig. 1. I am grateful to Corinna Forberg for this suggestion.

30 See note 17.

31 "The mediocrity of the Chinese can also be clearly seen in painting, as in many other things. It would be incorrect to speak of a diversity of Chinese schools or manners. All their little figures and pagodas belong to a single family: and one could suspect that this multitudinous nation had always had but a single eye to see things with and a single hand for their representation." Francesco Algarotti, *Opere*, vol. 7, Venice 1792, p. 235.

32 See Sloboda 2014, p. 24.

33 See Sheriff 2010, pp. 110–17.

34 See Jeffares 2015, p. 30.

35 See Sheriff 2010, pp. 101f.; Smentek 2010, p. 101.

36 See Avcıoğlu 2011, p. 22.

37 "What lends Chinese paintings their appeal is that they are uniform, unfalsified, and pure, although created by a people with no understanding of art." Quoted from R/L 2008, vol. 1, p. 324, note 10.

38 See Smentek 2010, pp. 102–03.

THE DRAWINGS OF JEAN-ÉTIENNE LIOTARD

Christian Rümelin

The last self-portrait (fig. 1) is one of the few in which Jean-Étienne Liotard pictures himself at work.[1] It belongs to the group of his rare full-figure portraits, but here he has depicted himself seated, with a drawing board on his knee, a crayon in his hand, gazing frontally at his own reflection and thus at the viewer. Turned at a slight angle to the mirror, he suggests a three-dimensional space, thereby heightening the impression of an actual observation. This drawing was in fact made in preparation for a now-lost painting, yet by presenting himself as a draftsman, the artist not only reveals his essential view of himself but also his confrontation with his own work.

Over the course of his long career, Liotard produced seventeen different self-portrait compositions, representing all his various media.[2] The first one was made during his stay in Paris around 1731; the last was executed in 1783. They become more numerous in the 1740s, then again around 1768/1770 and 1780, after his last stay in Vienna and the preparations for the publication of his treatise.[3] In the correspondence with his wife during his stay in Vienna it becomes apparent how much Liotard thought of himself first and foremost as a draftsman all his life, and what enormous importance drawing had in his working process.[4] He also speaks of this in several letters to François Tronchin and later to his son Jean-Étienne Liotard.[5] The steps involved in his working process, however, were so obvious to him that he only mentions them sketchily. For Liotard, as for the eighteenth century in general, drawing was both an art form, and thus a physical manifestation, and a category of art theory referring mainly to accuracy in representation, the right distribution of light and shadow, and precision of forms.[6] Yet for him, drawing was not merely about observation or preparatory work for a painting; its status and function could vary. This was independent of physical characteristics or chosen technique, what mattered was the context in which a drawing was produced. During his last stay in Vienna, for example, Liotard made several two-color drawings, in part in the hope that they would bring him commissions for pastels. It appears that he had long since perfected this technique, creating such works not only as preparation for works in other mediums, but also as autonomous drawings, in the event that there was no prospect of a more involved commission. One such instance is the portrait of an Englishman who happened to be passing through Geneva, which Liotard let the man have for a relatively modest sum.[7] It would ultimately remain a precisely observed stand-alone work. This raises the question as to the importance drawing had for Liotard, what kinds of drawings are found in his oeuvre, and what conclusions might be drawn from them, relating to his working process and his understanding of himself.

Types of Drawings in Liotard's Work

In Liotard's drawings it is possible to distinguish various functions; some are autonomous works,

Fig. 1 Jean-Étienne Liotard, **Self-Portrait Drawing "With the New Beard,"** 1783, black chalk, smudged, heightened in white, on three sheets of blue paper pasted onto canvas, 54 x 43 cm, Cabinet d'arts graphiques des Musées d'art et d'histoire, Geneva

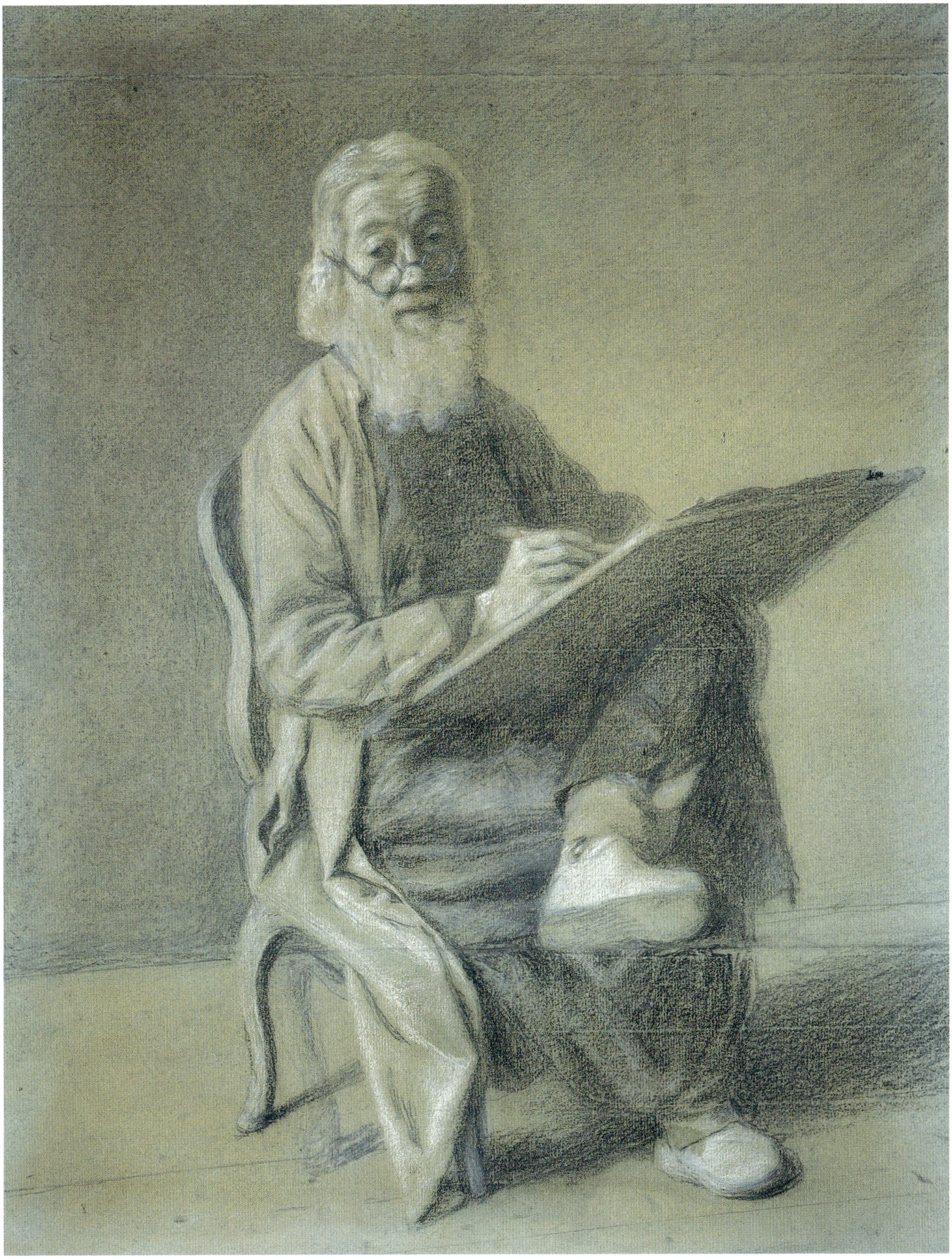

others simple preliminary or transfer drawings, still others are artist's replicas or counterproofs. The boundaries between these functions are fluid. Fundamentally, however, preliminary drawings clearly refer to another work, usually a pastel or a miniature, at most a painting. In addition, there are a large number of autonomous drawings, which in his particular case can be grouped together as portraits and documentary, genre-like scenes. These are primarily from his early years, roughly until the 1740s, that is, until his return from Constantinople and arrival in Vienna.

One special difficulty in the study of Liotard's work is the apparent loss of a large number of his early drawings. At the beginning of his artistic career he certainly must have drawn a great deal.[8] Only thirty-one works are known from before his departure for Italy in 1735, among them a mere four drawings. But it is hard to imagine that the miniatures and paintings were created without preparatory studies. The same can be said of the works he produced during his stay in Italy.[9] In any case, his surviving drawings from Rome reveal an indebtedness to a figure type borrowed from Antoine Watteau. In Paris, Liotard had produced an engraving after a Watteau painting, and he owned the *Figures de différents charactères*, a book of engravings after Watteau drawings, including depictions of individual figures on a white ground; he was thus fully familiar with the practice of isolating a figure in front of a neutral background.[10]

Just like Watteau, Liotard, too, followed the tradition of first outlining his drawings in red and black chalk; only in the profile portrait *Young Roman Woman* (fig. 2) did he add pastel and watercolor on the reverse to heighten the drawing's coloring and vibrancy.[11] His lines, meanwhile, were freed from a painstaking fidelity to nature, especially in the flesh tones. This shows that by this time Liotard had already gained considerable experience in his craft; nothing suggests any hesitation or need for correction. It was precisely this practical competence that led to his engagement as a travel companion to William Ponsonby, the future Lord Bessborough, and John Montagu, Earl of Sandwich, as a recorder of costumes and places of interest.[12] Unfortunately, only few of those drawings have survived: a group of figure studies, mainly of people the group encountered on their journey, for example in Malta, Milo, and Paros. The basic composition of the drawings is always the same: a standing, usually female figure, turning slightly away from the picture plane and gazing at the viewer. They are all executed in red and black chalk; only in one case did Liotard add a little additional color in a second step.[13]

With the group's arrival in Smyrna in May 1738, his drawing technique began to change slightly. The *Portrait of Madame Gaspard de Péleran*, wife of the French chargé d'affaires, exhibits a new range of draftsmanly possibilities. Whereas the folds in her skirt and the shadow on the right are formed with swift, summary, broad hatchings, certain details of the lace and especially her face are drawn with extreme delicacy. Liotard continues to limit himself to red and black chalk, but so balanced and differentiated in thickness of line that it almost seems as though additional mediums have been employed.[14] This effect is largely owing to his special feel for the paper. In two-color drawings it serves not only as picture support or neutral background, but within the pattern of lines it comes to represent light itself. The white of the paper takes on a twofold function, and the small white spaces between the lines create transparency, lending the drawing a special lightness. Liotard increasingly varied the thickness of his strokes and his speed in drawing these lines, and, depending on function or necessity, was able to distinguish between greater precision or the depiction of an underlying mood, aiming at either faithful detail or spontaneity.

For the drawing itself it was immaterial whether it would end up later in another work or remain autonomous. After 1738 in particular, a new approach becomes evident in Liotard's work. He pictures people standing, slightly turned, in a space not further defined. Individual elements like facial features, pose, and size are worked out in detail, also the specifics of clothing. Everything

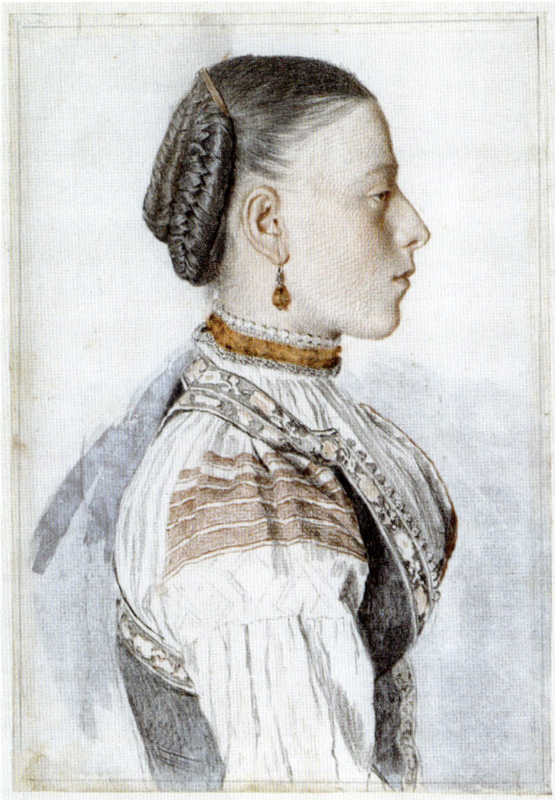

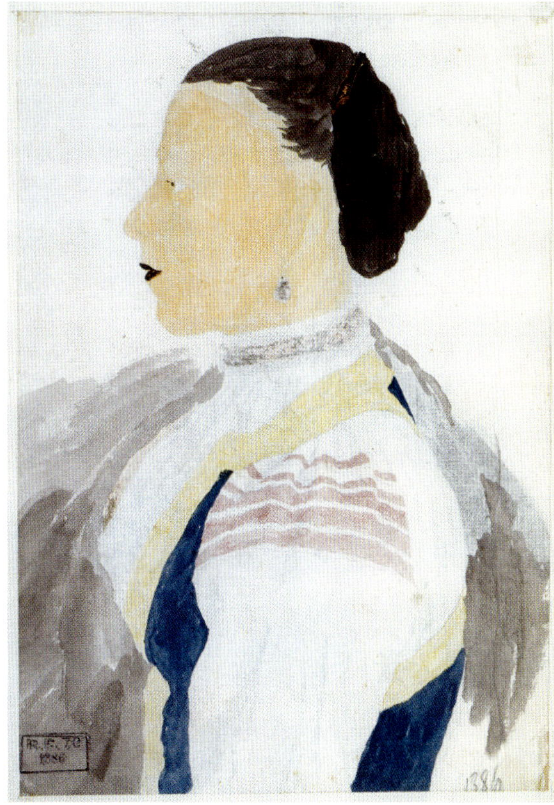

Fig. 2 **Jean-Étienne Liotard, Profile Portrait of a Roman Woman**, ca. 1737, recto and verso, red and black chalk, and watercolor, 20 x 14.5 cm, Musée du Louvre, Paris

contributes to making these drawings seem especially lifelike. They are precise enough to be further refined later if necessary, but preserve their spontaneity, so they could also stand as autonomous drawings. For Liotard these were not primarily precise preliminary drawings that he might then slavishly follow; they offered the possibility of later creating a pastel or oil painting from a relatively free drawing. An outstanding example is the *Portrait of Madame James Fremeaux, née Margaret Cooke*, drawn in May 1738 and subsequently executed as a pastel.[15] It is the first concrete instance in Liotard's work of a drawing serving as the starting point for a pastel. It pictures a full figure, isolated like numerous others, standing in an undefined space, with strong light entering from the left. What predominates are the distribution of light and shadow and the richness of the fabrics. Nothing points to the intention to transfer it later on; it is swiftly sketched and was not the product of a lengthy and tiring portrait sitting. In the pastel later developed from it there is also no indication of a setting, but because of the colored background, the distinctly closer cropping and resulting closer view, this is less apparent. However, it also already shows that Liotard distinguished precisely between the function of a drawing and the work possibly derived from it. A second example is the portrait of the archaeologist and theologian Richard Pococke.[16] The differences between the preliminary drawing and the painting are striking. The drawing is wholly characterized by a strict vertical linearity, one that particularly emphasizes the most important folds of the caftan and thus the view from below; the painting, on the other hand, with its landscape backdrop and horizontal clouds, exhibits an almost unaccustomed balance (fig. 3).

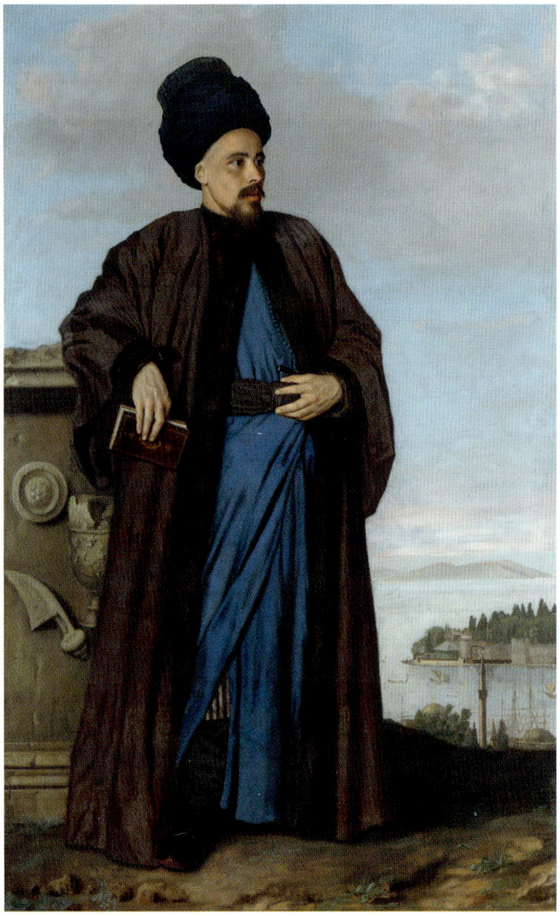

Fig. 3 **Jean-Étienne Liotard, Portrait of Richard Pococke**, 1740, oil on canvas, 202.5 x 134 cm, Musée d'art et d'histoire, Geneva

It is striking that the majority of Liotard's figures from this time are pictured at an angle from below (fig. 4)—not only standing subjects, but also seated ones. This is more than a psychological effect; rather, it allowed Liotard, especially in his drawings, to get closer to his models. In none of his drawings from this time does he overstep an intimate boundary, but he remains close enough to be able to capture precise observations. It is a pictorial strategy that he was working out at this point and would employ again and again in his portraits.

A second consequence of his stay in Constantinople was a new subject matter, to some extent a combination of portraits with a type of genre scene. Liotard was uninterested in seemingly rustic subjects, but instead documented embroiderers, young serving women, and musicians. Only some of these are identified by name, but they are all treated with the same precision as his aristocratic Western European models. He makes no distinction between social standing; rather, in his extremely swift observations he appears to be primarily interested in psychological phenomena: their focus on their work, pleasure in what they are doing, or control over their own appearance. Further qualities are added here, namely the spatial situation or the indication of an architectural context. Only in one case does Liotard picture a concrete interior, that is his room in Constantinople (fig. 5). Even more reduced in its hatching and linearity, it is Liotard's only attempt from this time to picture a space without people.[17] There are in fact a few works, again usually drawings, showing subjects seated on a similar sofa, but the primary focus here is immediately shifted from the surrounding space to the figure (cat. 51, 52). Always there is one element, either the figure, the sofa, or the room itself, that is placed at a slight angle, thus preventing any too palpable rigidity.[18] The relevance of the subject's activity is only indirectly suggested, but then becomes all the more tangible. The *Chocolate Girl* (cat. 1) is an outstanding example, and the Karlsruhe portrait of *Princess Caroline Louise of Hesse-Darmstadt* takes up the theme again in a different context,[19] before Liotard again occupied himself in occasional further works with the positioning of his subjects in the picture space.[20] This is a consequence of his drawings from the Constantinople period. These deliberations would also make it possible for Liotard to later include more detailed backing walls or colored surfaces, at least during his stay in England in 1773/74, and thus develop new ways of positioning his subjects.

Fig. 4 **Jean-Étienne Liotard, Dame franque de Péra**, 1738, pastel on paper pasted onto canvas, 63.5 x 48 cm, Cabinet d'arts graphiques des Musées d'art et d'histoire, Geneva

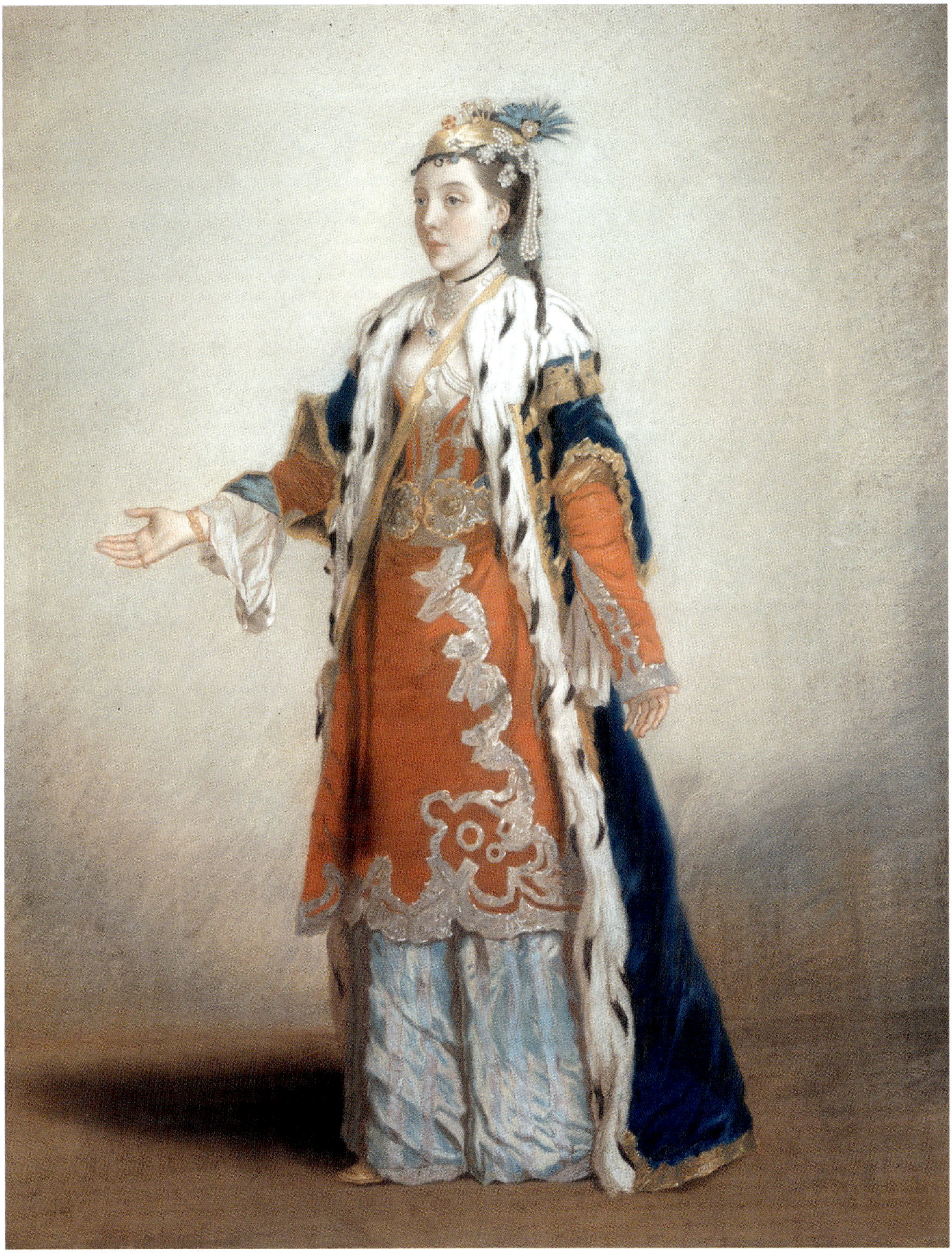

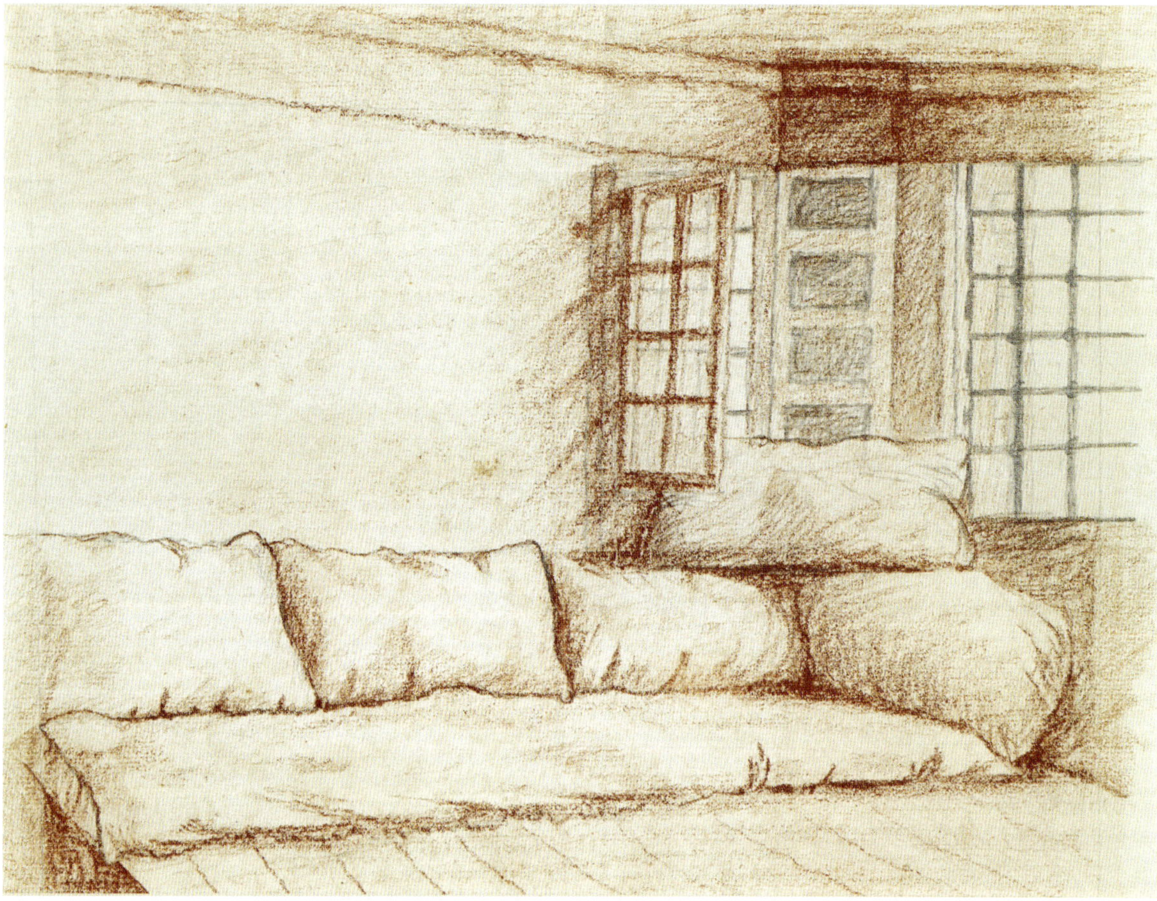

Fig. 5 **Jean-Étienne Liotard, The Divan (Liotard's Room in Constantinople)**, ca. 1740, red chalk and graphite on white paper, 18.6 x 22.8 cm, Cabinet d'arts graphiques des Musées d'art et d'histoire, Geneva, gift of the Société auxilière du Musée

Drawing in the Working Process

Even though the majority of the drawings produced in Constantinople and Jassy were not further developed into other works, it was not automatically ruled out that some drawings might lend themselves to translation into pastels or—less frequently—miniatures or paintings.[21] With his return to Western Europe, and the resulting renewed access to a much larger market, Liotard had new opportunities to profit from the pictorial strategies he had developed, and to exploit his draftsmanly competence and speed accordingly. By this point he had clearly developed an outstanding mastery and sophistication in drawing; however, aside from autonomous drawings, his opportunities to apply it had been limited. With his return to Vienna and then to northern Italy and Paris, this very rapidly changed. He was obviously under pressure to reassert himself professionally as fast as possible. To achieve this, Liotard used a twofold approach: firstly, fleshing out drawings or ideas in pastel in the late 1740s and 1750s and, secondly, using prints as a way of making his works known to a wider audience.[22] In 1744, in collaboration with Giuseppe Camerata, he engraved four motifs from previous compositions (cat. 49, 50). These were later followed by additional engravings by Reinsperger and Tardieu.

At the beginning of his stay in Vienna, Liotard had an opportunity to produce several portraits of the imperial family. However, only one drawing relating to this commission is known, a profile of Francis I, probably some time before his accession and quite clearly created during a portrait sitting.[23] The sheet's directness, the absolute focus on the face and the modeling, the omission of unimportant elements like the peruke or clothing make it clear that Liotard was still influenced by his experiences in Constantinople, but was now preparing to produce his pastels in a different way. He had little time at his disposal—especially at the imperial court—and he compensated for this by working faster. Many of these sheets seem not to have been destined for further use, and perhaps this is why they were preserved. Yet they mostly reveal a still relatively complex approach that sought to capture his subject from a psychological point of view as well. In this, Liotard remained true to his former drawing technique, that is to say, he continued to use red and black chalk, occasionally combined with white chalk or graphite, in lines of varied thickness. He worked the same way even in some of his more personal and private drawings.[24] To enhance them, beginning in 1758, he repeatedly resorted to a method he had already used during his stay in Rome, treating the reverse of relatively thin paper in a technique known from miniature painting.[25] Adding colors to the back of portions of a composition heightens the intensity of those on the front, owing to the slight transparency of the paper. He did not employ this technique systematically, but only in autonomous drawings. It ultimately produced a hybrid form between a more elaborate execution—despite a noticeable difference to his pastels—and the more sketchlike drawings, even those with two or more colors. Liotard already seems to have applied this technique, at least occasionally, in the 1730s, the first known example of it being the drawing of a *Young Roman Woman* from 1737. It is later found in a variant of the painting known as *La Sultane Lisant*, mainly reinforcing the shadowed areas. From around 1758 to 1762, Liotard used it several times, in both versions of the portrait of Jean-Robert Tronchin,[26] the portrait of Baron de Lubières,[27] and one of an unknown man.[28] With the drawings of the Empress's children he produced a larger group of such works. Here their function was obviously important (fig. 6): although considerably larger than miniatures, they were still easier to carry than pastels, making it possible for Maria Theresa to take them with her on her travels. In addition, they had a more spontaneous, less official and thus more intimate character.

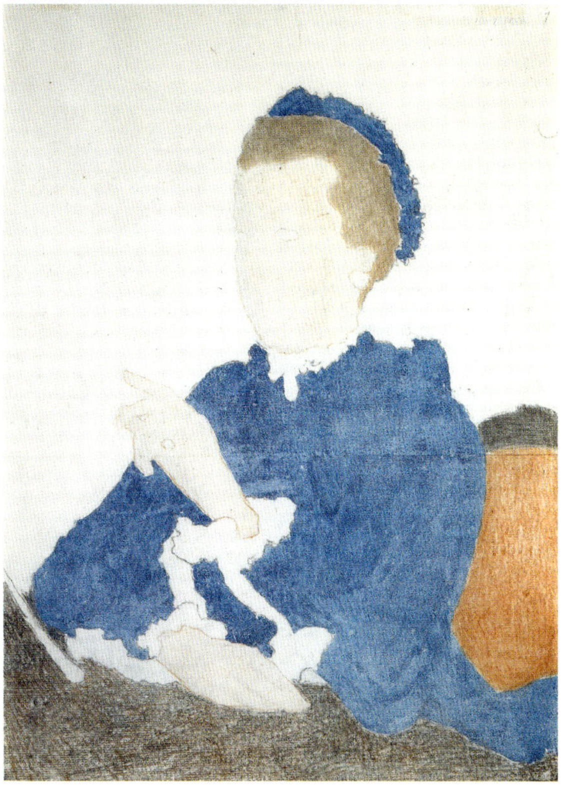

Fig. 6 Jean-Étienne Liotard, **Portrait of Archduchess Maria Elisabeth, Future Abbess in Innsbruck**, 1762, verso, red and black chalk, watercolor, 32.1 x 24.6 cm, Cabinet d'arts graphiques des Musées d'art et d'histoire, Geneva, on permanent loan from the Schweizerische Eidgenossenschaft, Gottfried-Keller-Stiftung

Apparently owing to increasing demand in the 1750s, he turned to yet another technique, one that he would employ until the 1780s: for preliminary drawings he abandoned white paper and replaced it with blue. Although this cannot convey the light values so important to Liotard in his drawings from Constantinople and some of his autonomous drawings, and, moreover, lacks the transparency of the two-color drawings, the blue paper had the advantage of enabling a much clearer representation of mid tones. This meant that for portraits it was enough to define the contours, the most important facial features and characteristics, while the rest could be fleshed out without the model.[29] Especially in the case of high-ranking figures, who could invest but little time in portrait sittings, this was a great advantage. Liotard could thus continue to produce his portraits from direct observation and stay true to his demand for absolute fidelity, but the execution was much more efficient. Ultimately, these highly condensed drawings served him to work up his paintings, and for that reason he was unwilling to part with them. One of the earliest examples in this mode, the *Portrait of Jean-Jacques Cottin de la Thuilerie* from 1757, already shows all the characteristics of this type of drawing.[30] The composition could be outlined with great speed, with just a few cursory lines, some of them straight, or double contours defining the subject. Interestingly, Liotard produced these drawings on blue paper in two steps: first he drew a thin line, which he then retraced in the step immediately following. We see this approach both in the drawing of Cottin de la Thuilerie and in that of Lord Mount Stuart (fig. 7).[31] If corrections were necessary, as in the positioning of Mount Stuart's right hand and a few smaller corrections to the face, the hip, and the free leg, these were integrated into the working process and applied directly in the second step. It were these thicker and darker lines, reinforcing the contours and modeling, that were decisive for the next stage. To transfer the drawing, Liotard used two well-known techniques: either small needle pricks that gave him reference points or a backing in red chalk that enabled him to duplicate a contour through light pressure with a stylus or a stump (fig. 8). These were transfer techniques adopted from printmaking, efficient ways to transfer an existing drawing in the same size. They do, however, require sufficiently large sheets of paper—if necessary pieced together. Transfer by stylus has the advantage, as opposed to counter-proofing, that the figure's orientation remains the same, which is particularly important here because of the subject's decorations and the placement of the dagger. Another technique that Liotard occasionally used was

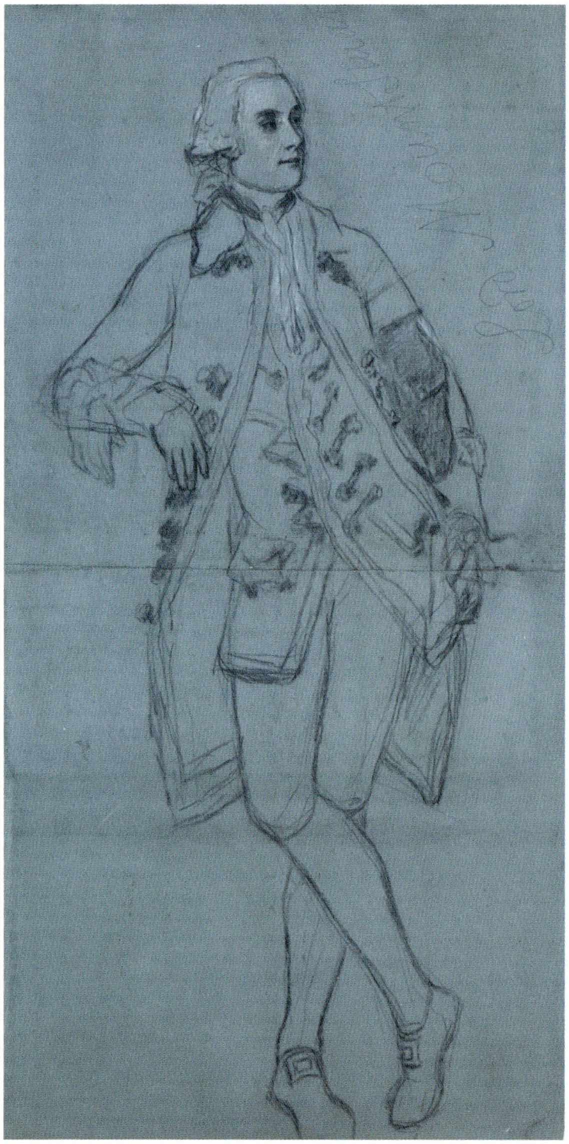

Fig. 7 **Jean-Étienne Liotard, Portrait of Lord Mount Stuart, Future Fourth Count of Bute and First Marquess of Bute**, 1763, black and white chalk, heightened in red chalk, on two sheets of blue paper, 90.7 x 48.1 cm, Cabinet d'arts graphiques des Musées d'art et d'histoire, Geneva

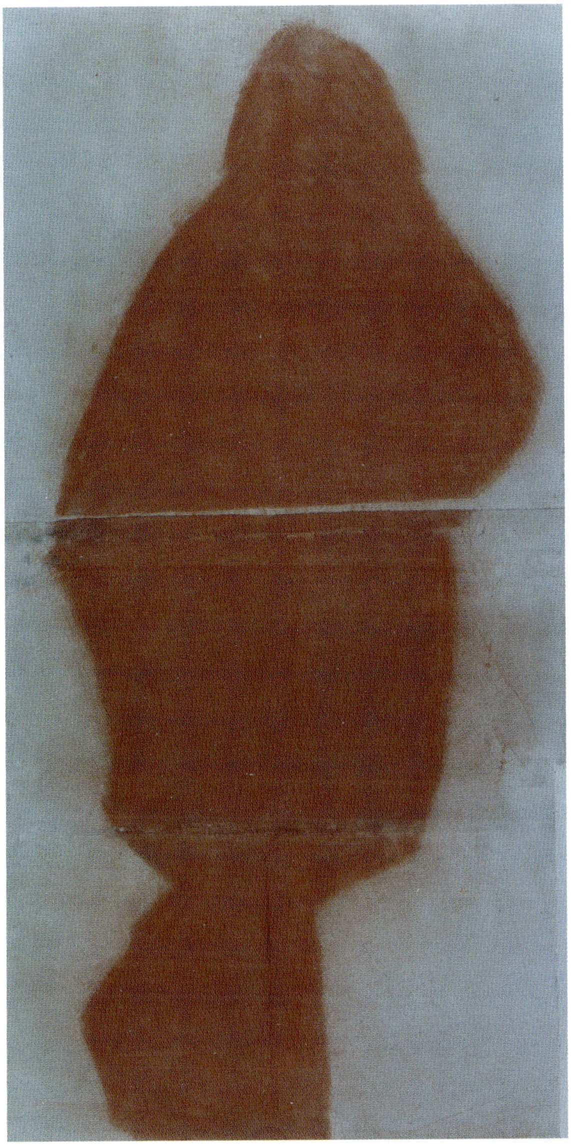

Fig. 8 Jean-Étienne Liotard, **Portrait of Lord Mount Stuart, Future Fourth Count of Bute and First Marquess of Bute**, 1763, verso, red chalk, 90.7 x 48.1 cm, Cabinet d'arts graphiques des Musées d'art et d'histoire, Geneva

covering an outline drawing with a grid of squares, as in *Effendi, Smoking* (cat. 64). This made it possible to easily produce an enlargement or reduction. However, these squared sheets must necessarily have been preceded by another drawing like his two-color drawings from this period. Only on the basis of such a preliminary work was an outline drawing possible; for Liotard, however, this was merely a step in the process of transferring the image and had no intrinsic artistic value to him. Even though the transfer itself posed a challenge, since, apparently, only the two-color or blue-paper drawings were produced in the presence of the subject, whereas the transfer and further elaboration had to be accomplished without the model.

Liotard's last self-portrait was more than merely another depiction of himself. Perhaps he was not aware that with it he had almost completely encapsulated his own biography and laid open important key elements of his work. Ever since his first stay in Paris, drawing had been crucial to him, the only way to capture his immediate impressions, to make a first step toward a work of art—and to earn his living with it. It was so natural for him that he scarcely spoke of it, only a few references to it appear in his letters. He developed his own, highly individual approach, generally employing red and black chalk. In his draftsmanship he was not academically tied to a strict sequence of steps—a consistent progression from first considerations to transfer drawings or, perhaps, copies—but, depending on the situation, was able to alternate between an extremely precise but nevertheless atmospheric, sketchlike drawing and an actual preliminary drawing for a pastel or painting. Whereas the majority of his pastels exhibit careful elaboration, in his drawings we can clearly see his spontaneity and speed, his delight in observation.

I am most grateful to Caroline Guignard for numerous stimulating discussions relating to the Geneva Liotard holdings, and to Victor Lopes, Roland Enke, and Marcel Roethlisberger for helpful communications.

1 Geneva, Musée d'art et d'histoire, Cabinet d'arts graphiques, inv. no. 1984-129; for extensive discussion of this portrait, see *Dessins de Liotard. Suivi du catalogue de l'œuvre dessiné*, exh. cat. Musée d'art et d'histoire, Geneva; Musée du Louvre, Paris 1992, ed. Anne de Herdt, Geneva 1992, cat. 139; Cësar Menz, "Zu Jean-Étienne Liotards Selbstbildnissen," in: *Liber Veritatis. Mélanges en l'honneur du Professeur Marcel G. Roethlisberger*, eds. Leila el-Wakil, Patrick-André Guerratta, Paul Lang, et al., Milan 2007, p. 197; Marcel Roethlisberger and Renée Loche, *Liotard: Catalogue, Sources et Correspondance* (in the following abbreviated to "R/L 2008"), 2 vols., Doornspijk 2008, no. 546; Hannah Williams, "A Phenomenology of Vision: the Self-Portraits of Jean-Étienne Liotard," in: *RIHA Journal* 34 (2012), URN: urn:nbn:de:101:I-201202207526, http://www.riha-journal.org/articles/2012/2012-jan-mar/williams-phenomenology-of-vision (accessed May 19, 2018).

2 Effectively there are twenty-six different works, including drawings, pastels, oil paintings, prints, miniatures, and enamel miniatures, as well as one self-portrait known only from a copy by Favray. In some cases they are repeats of compositions. For the self-portraits, see R/L 2008, nos. 16–18, 36, 106, 128–29, 158, 164, 196–98, 262, 440–47, 522, 523, 546; also the detailed comments in Claude Reichler, "Liotard avec Variations: Les autoportraits de Jean-Étienne Liotard," in: *Genava* 16 (1978), pp. 221–228; Menz 2007; R/L 2008, pp. 37–39; and Huigen Leeflang, "A Self-Portrait by Jean-Étienne Liotard from the Artist's Family Holdings," in: *The Rijksmuseum Bulletin* 59 (2011), pp. 204–207.

3 Jean-Étienne Liotard, *Traité des principes et des règles de la peinture*, Geneva 1781, p. 17 ("dessin") and pp. 19–20 ("invention"). For recent writing on this text in detail, see exh. cat. Geneva/Paris 1992, pp. 7–8; Marcel G. Roethlisberger, "Le 'Traité' de Liotard," in: Jürg Albrecht and Michael Egli, eds., *Horizonte: Beiträge zu Kunst und Kunstwissenschaft: 50 Jahre Schweizerisches Institut für Kunstwissenschaft*, Ostfildern-Ruit 2001, pp. 65–72; Andreas Holleczek, *Jean-Étienne Liotard: Erkenntnisvermögen und künstlerischer Anspruch*, Frankfurt am Main 2002, pp. 134–138; also R/L 2008, pp. 165–179.

4 On May 2, 1778, Liotard wrote to his wife from Vienna: "j'ay vendu 3 portraits dessinez et colorez a l'Imperatrice qui en a été contente, je lui fais actuellement un pastel avec 2 mains de l'Archiduc Ferdinand et encor un dessin de l'Empereur qui n'aura aucune couleur a l'habillement." On his drawings, see the notes in R/L 2008, pp. 118–119, and under the relevant catalogue numbers, also the seminal work by Edouard Humbert, Alphonse Revilliod, and Jan Willem Reinier Tilanus, *La vie et les œuvres de Jean Étienne Liotard (1702–1789): étude biographique et iconographique*, Amsterdam and Geneva 1897; N. S. Trivas, "Les portraits de Liotard par lui-même," in: *Revue de l'art ancien et moderne* 70 (1936), pp. 153–62; and Anne de Herdt (exh. cat. Geneva/Paris 1992).

5 See the letter to his son Jean-Étienne Liotard from May 27, 1783, reprinted in R/L 2008, pp. 766–67: "Je contois envoyer a Mr Vaute le portrait de ma femme avec les autres desseins de mes filles m'ont prié de n'en rien faire parce que c'étoit le portrait le plus ressemblant qu'ily a it de ma defunte leur Mere je le copie en pastel et en 15 jours il sera prêt pour envoyer a Mr Voute et il lui fera plus de plaisir de l'avoir en pastel qu'en dessein le blanc a joni dans le dessein; tu me marques l'excessif plaisir d'avoir tous ces desseins, ce grand plaisir que tu t'aurois fait ces desseins n'indiquent ils pas que tu est tres content de rester en hollande."

6 The discussions on drawing were sheer endless in the eighteenth century. It is enough to point to Claude-Henri Watelet, "Dessein," in: Denis Diderot, Jean-Baptiste le Rond d'Alembert, *Encyclopédie ou Dictionnaire raisonné des Sciences, des Arts et des Métiers, par une société de gens de lettres. Mis en ordre et publié par Diderot, et, quant à la partie mathématique, par d'Alembert*, vol. 4, Paris 1754, pp. 889–91.

7 Liotard mentions an example of this in a letter to his son from May 5, 1779, referring to the portrait of M. Jacson that he had drawn at M. Tissot's (possibly François-Léonard-Pierre-Auguste Tissot). On this, most recently, R/L 2008, no. 532 and p. 754.

8 For this, see both his autobiography and the version expanded by his son; both in R/L 2008, especially pp. 60 and 62–63.

9 See exh. cat. Geneva/Paris 1992, p. 276, nos. 5–10. For the pastels and paintings before he set out toward Constantinople, see R/L 2008, nos. 32–55.

10 R/L 2008, p. 159, transcription of the inventory of Liotard's estate, which lists under no. 51 a "portefeuille des dessins de Wateau. 100." In view of the relatively modest price of 100 guldens, and the fact that it was listed under prints, this is likely to refer to the volumes published in Paris between 1726 and 1728 of the *Figures de différents caractères, de paysages, d'études dessinées d'après nature par Antoine Watteau*.

11 On this portrait, most recently R/L 2008, no. 578, and exh. cat. Geneva/Paris 1992, cat. 6 and 7. See also the review by Alastair Laing, "Review Dessins de Liotard. Suivi du catalogue de l'œuvre dessiné, Genf, Paris 1992, ed. Anne de Herdt, Geneva 1992," in: *The Burlington Magazine* 134 (1992), pp. 749–750.

12 See R/L 2008, p. 261.

13 This refers to the portrait of *Signora Leneta Shepri à Paros*, May 1738. See exh. cat. Geneva/Paris 1992, cat. no. 11.

14 For this sheet and its pendant, the portrait of her husband, see exh. cat. Geneva/Paris 1992, cat. 16 and 17. It also refers to the counterproof in the Bibliotèque Nationale, Paris.

15 For the drawing, see exh. cat. Geneva/Paris 1992, cat. 18; for the pastel, R/L 2008, no. 56.

16 Exh. cat. Geneva/Paris 1992, cat. 33 and 34; R/L 2008, no. 33.

17 The second example is the drawing of an exterior space, the village of Cumaragikien; see exh. cat. Geneva/Paris 1992, cat. 35, and R/L 2008, p. 261; For Liotard's room in Constantinople, see also exh. cat. Geneva/Paris 1992, cat. 66, and R/L 2008, p. 261.

18 Examples of this are in exh. cat. Geneva/Paris 1992, cat. 18, 25–28, 30, 36a, 40, 40a, 41, 43, 44a, 50, 51, 61, 62a, 63, 69, 71, 72.

19 R/L 2008, no. 147. For Caroline Louise of Hesse-Darmstadt, later Margravine of Baden, see *Die Meistersammlerin Karoline Luise von Baden*, exh. cat. Staatliche Kunsthalle Karlsruhe, ed. Holger Jacob-Friesen and Pia Müller-Tamm, Berlin and Munich 2015.

20 These are *L'Écriture* (R/L 2008, no. 200), *Dame à la tasse de chocolat* (R/L 2008, no. 205), *Lavergne Breakfast* (R/L 2008, no. 299), *Dutch Girl at Breakfast* (R/L 2008, no. 342), *François Tronchin*

(R/L 2008, no. 349), *Suzanne Curchod* (R/L 2008, no. 380), *Lord Mount Stuart* (R/L 2008, no. 421), *Madame de Vermenoux Giving Thanks to Appollo* (R/L 2008, no. 427), and some of his still lifes or English portraits from 1773–74.

21 Only a few pastels or works that were clearly produced in Constantinople are known, among them the *Dame franque de Péra* (drawing in exh. cat. Geneva/Paris 1992, cat. no. 42; pastel in R/L 2008, no. 70). Roethlisberger and Loche have rightly pointed out that, in terms of its technique, the pastel falls between the *Portrait of Mme Fremeaux* and the *Chocolate Girl*, which suggests that it dates from the second half of his stay in Constantinople. However, they were unable to provide definite proof of this.

22 Examples are portraits of Maria Theresia in Turkish costume, or the engraving in Dresden *A Lady from Pera Receives a Visitor*, which bear an inscription with a reference to Maria Theresia and her daughter Maria Christina (cat. 49). It is true that a certain similarity cannot be dismissed, but neither the drawing (cat. 47) nor the engraving or the pastel (R/L 2008, no. 70) is a recognizable portrait of the Empress. Liotard's work as a graphic artist has so far received little notice; see, most recently, Christian Rümelin, "Jean-Étienne Liotard als Radierer," in: *Von der Genauigkeit des Sehens: Festschrift zum 75. Geburtstag von Anne Röver-Kann*, eds. Rebecca Duckwitz and Christien Melzer, Bremen 2018, pp. 83–88.

23 The sheet is reproduced in exh. cat. Geneva/Paris 1992, cat. 76.

24 Liotard refers to a two-color drawing of the Emperor, which is now lost (possibly a preliminary drawing for the portrait in Amsterdam, R/L 2008, no. 515), produced during his last stay in Vienna. See his letter of November 19, 1777, to François Tronchin (R/L 2008, p. 744) and the one to his wife from November 29, 1777 (ibid., pp. 744–45).

25 For the versos, see exh. cat. Geneva/Paris 1992; Laing 1992; R/L 2008, nos. 401–411 and nos. 578–585.

26 Exh. cat. Geneva/Paris 1992, pp. 285–86, nos. 125 and 126; R/L 2008, nos. 580–581.

27 Exh. cat. Geneva/Paris 1992, p. 286, no. 132; R/L 2008, no. 583.

28 Exh. cat. Geneva/Paris 1992, p. 286, no. 133; R/L 2008, no. 579.

29 Mention of this technique is found in Liotard's letter to his wife from December 10, 1777 (R/L 2008, p. 745): "J'ay enfin commené hier et aujourd'huy 2 Archiducs frères de l'Empereur l'un s'appelle Maximilien et l'autre Fertinant qui est duc de Milan je les ay dessinez sur du papier bleu pour en [suite?] les copier de telle façon qu'on voudra soit en pastel huile au 2 crayons comme j'ay fait la famille Impériale il y a 16 années, avec une autre Seance je finirai chaque portrait l'Imperatrice fut presente pendant plus de demi heure."

30 Exh. cat. Geneva/Paris 1992, cat. 101; R/L 2008, no. 346.

31 Exh. cat. Geneva/Paris 1992, cat. 127; R/L 2008, no. 421.

THE "KABINETT DER ROSALBA"

On the History of the Pastel Cabinet in Dresden's Gemäldegalerie

Roland Enke

In 1711, the young Frederick Augustus, son of Augustus II the Strong, King of Poland, set out on his Grand Tour of Germany, Switzerland, France, and Italy, which would extend until 1719. In February 1712 it took him to Venice for the first time. Beyond enjoying the boisterous goings-on of the Carnival—and in addition to receptions in his honor—he would also have come into contact with artists. Perhaps even already in that year, but certainly during his second stay in the city in 1713, he met the famous pastellist Rosalba Carriera.[1] The artist, born in 1673, was known for her miniature paintings, with which she had successfully applied at Rome's Accademia di San Luca in 1705. She was supported in this by Christian Cole, secretary to the British ambassador in Venice, who also helped her secure commissions from aristocratic English travelers. She then shifted to pastel painting, probably in part because the technique allowed portraits to be completed and passed on to their buyers in a very short time. This also enabled fixed prices, graduated according to size, which would have been financially advantageous. Her fame far beyond Venice's city limits is further confirmed by her acceptance into Paris's Académie Royale in 1720, where she was greatly admired for her pastel paintings (fig. 1).

The heir to the Saxon throne, just like his father, developed a great liking for Venetian art and soon became the most passionate admirer of Carriera's work. It is, however, surprising that no pastel but only an oil painting of the youthful Frederick Augustus survives from their meeting. Although Carriera is known to have employed this technique, no other oils of hers are known aside from this portrait, probably painted in 1714.[2] It came from the collection of Girolamo Ravagnan, Carriera's biographer, who in 1836 described the Saxon's admiration for the artist at length: "The portrait most treasured by the artist herself was that of the Venetian Marina Capitano. Augustus III, King of Poland, could not resist the desire to purchase this picture at any price, as he was wont to do with every admired work of Rosalba's, wherever it might be. After long negotiations he obtained it and, having had a carriage made for its transport, he sent this to Venice to fetch the work and commissioned the messenger to present its owner with a purse with 150 ducats and a table service of the finest porcelain. So great was the passion he bestowed on the works of this artist that she sold him more than forty portraits of noblemen that adorned her rooms and for which she was generously remunerated."[3] It is likely that the forty pastels mentioned were the pictures acquired by Augustus III's son, Prince Frederick Christian, during his stay in Venice in 1739 while on his own Grand Tour.[4] Purchases of whole groups of pictures are repeatedly documented: at the behest of Augustus III, Count Francesco Algarotti commissioned from Carriera the cycle of the Four Elements, which she produced between 1744 and

Fig. 1 Rosalba Carriera, **Self-Portrait as "Winter,"** 1730/31, pastel on paper, 46.5 x 34 cm, Gemäldegalerie Alte Meister, Staatliche Kunstsammlungen Dresden

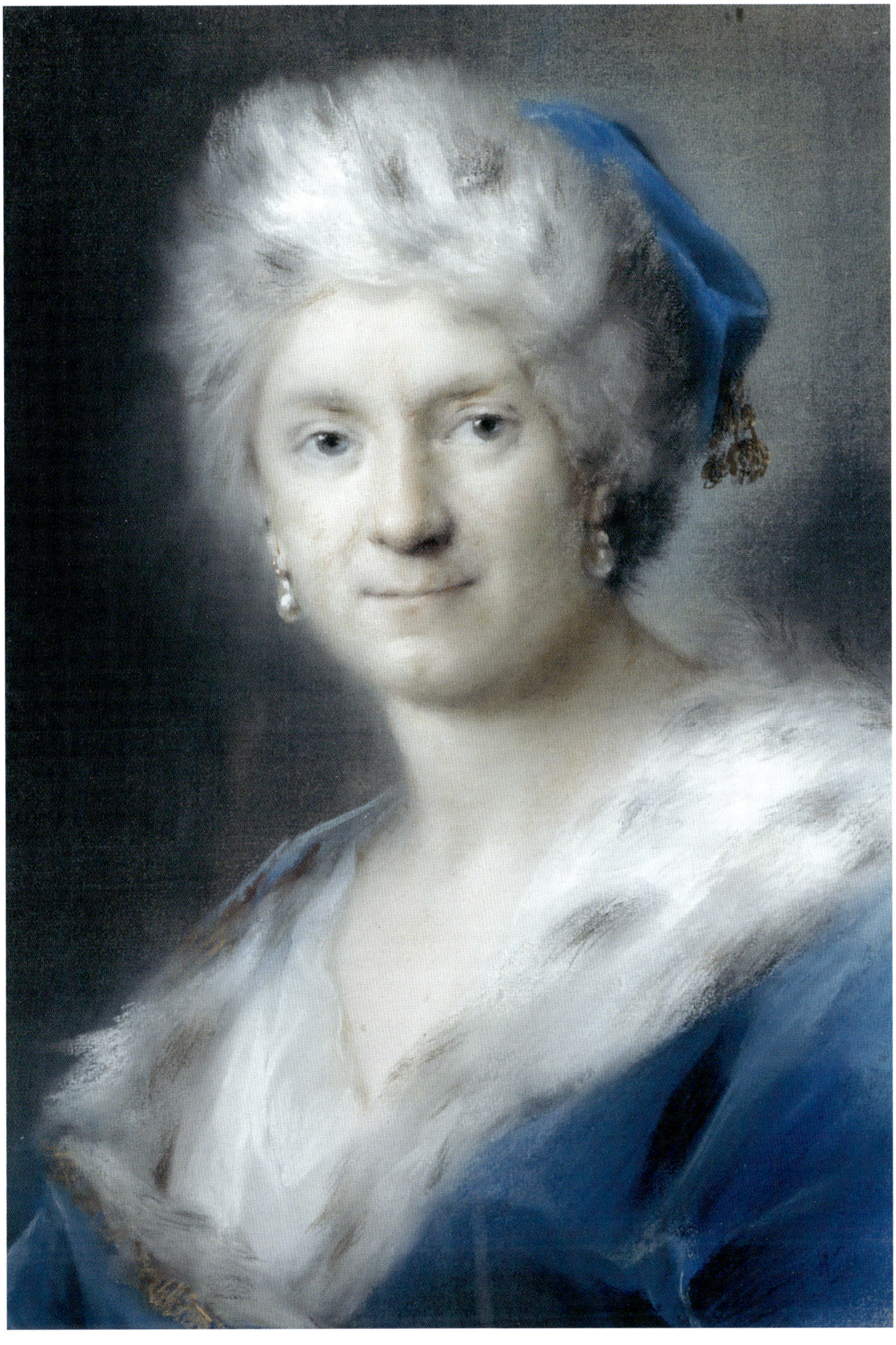

1746 (see p. 225–26).[5] In 1750, twelve pastels made their way to Dresden from the estate of the scholar Giambattista Recanati, which were sold by his widow Fioravanza Ravagnani and for which she received a Meissen porcelain service.[6] Likewise, the Cavaliere Andrea Diedo, who delivered five Carriera pastels in 1753, was remunerated with a chocolate and a coffee service for six.[7] Finally, it is reported that in August 1757, following Rosalba's death, Augustus bought all the works that had remained in her studio.[8] The collection of the British consul Joseph Smith (c. 1674–1770) also deserves to be mentioned, which he assembled in his house in Venice from around 1720. The merchant was a noted art patron and a close friend of Carriera's. He owned a total of thirty-eight of her works, among them several miniatures. He was forced to sell the latter in the early 1760s, at which point twenty-three works were offered to the Dresden collection for 2,000 gold ducats.[9] Owing to the Seven Years' War, Augustus was unable to accept the offer and the pictures ended up in England in the collection of George III. Nevertheless, with a total of 157 works, Dresden had been able to acquire the largest collection of Rosalba's pastels ever assembled. Even today, after some reduction through exchange or sale in the nineteenth and twentieth century and the loss of twenty-seven works in the Second World War, the holdings of Dresden's Gemäldegalerie, with seventy-three pastels, are still the most comprehensive in the world.[10] This rich collection of pastels by Rosalba Carriera alone may well have inspired the plan to present them together, and apart from the oil paintings.

The use of dry chalk and pastel colors as a draftsmanly medium can be traced back to the fifteenth century. It was used to sketch out motifs in their outlines and study light reflections with white on dark papers. But it was Carriera who developed the technique into full-scale painting. Her softly blurred, light tones imitating the surfaces of skin and fabrics capture the spirit and taste of the Rococo. Her delicately rouged and powdered ladies dressed in shimmering silks and filmy laces and adorned with flowers, pearls, and gems are apt expressions not only of eighteenth-century fashion but also of the century's art. Needless to say, the individual portrait likeness was subordinate to the prevailing ideal of beauty in courtly society.

With the conversion of the former court stables into a painting gallery through Johann Christoph Knöffel in the years 1745–46, a special room was created for the exclusive display of the pastels. In the first volume of the gallery work *Recueil d'Estampes d'après les plus célèbres Tableaux de la Galerie Royale de Dresde*, published by Carl Heinrich von Heineken in 1753, the appended floor plan by Michael Keyl shows the space labeled "C" as the "Cabinet de Pastel" (fig. 2). It was in the northeast corner of the building, accessed from the Outer Gallery. Behind the Cabinet was the so-called Long Corridor, which circled the stable courtyard and connected the stables with the palace. After the corridor's completion in 1588 it first housed the ancestral gallery, with portraits of Saxon rulers and depictions of tournaments painted by Heinrich Göding in the late sixteenth century.[11] Approaching the Cabinet from the palace, the last painting in that gallery to be seen before entering the Pastel Cabinet was the splendid portrait of King Augustus II by Louis de Silvestre.

The Cabinet itself was an elongated space on the second floor, some fifty-five square meters in area, with a height of just under nine meters. Light was provided from the northeast through two large windows; the wall on the courtyard side was closed. The first description of the interior decor is provided by Giovanni Ludovico Bianconi, originally from Bologna, who was active in Germany for many years and in Dresden functioned not only as medical advisor, but also as an art agent and writer. Johann Joachim Winckelmann wrote about him: "If you have any kind of intention at the Dresden court, you must seek to gain favor with Bianconi, who is everything in one."[12] In his text on Anton Raphael Mengs from 1781, Bianconi wrote: "The Cabinet of Rosalba is a large, bright room with green wall covering, looking out onto a wide and attractive street. The long wall opposite the windows is covered floor to ceiling with the most beautiful pastel paintings by the hand of this talented painter, and there may be more than a hundred of them. In the midst of them, as in her residence, one sees the self-portrait of this immortal Venetian lady, which stands out from everything else. On the two end walls, with two gilded doors on either side through which one enters, one finds all the pastels by Mengs, those by Liotard, by Mr. de La Tour, and several others by the very best pastel painters of our century. The fourth and long wall, opposite the Rosalba one, has just windows with large panes of polished glass, and on the intervening wall spaces (negl'interfenestri) large French mirrors have been installed from the ceiling down to the floor, which, in that they duplicate such delightful objects, enchant the visitor. The pastel paintings, along with their gleaming glass and gilt frames, are all of the same size. The floor is inlaid with all manner of exotic woods; the ceiling vault is white, but ornamented and gilded in the Arabic taste."[13] It is important to note that Bianconi's description was based on impressions from the early 1760s. He left Dresden in 1764 and wrote, or at least published, his historical encomium some fifteen years later, or more than twenty-five years after the museum's opening. Its primary aim was to exalt the work of the new hero of Neoclassical painting—including his pastels—who was also represented with ten works in the Dresden Cabinet: Anton Raphael Mengs.[14]

In his *Umständliche Beschreibung*, the Dresden chronicler Johann Christian Hasche somewhat modified Bianconi's elaborate description with the words: "When printed sources rave about a painted room, about statues, groups in marble and metal, about porphyry and serpentine, that's certain proof that they have never seen them. The ceiling is white, unpainted, the walls dressed in green damask with gilded moldings, and similar foliage above, and thereon hang the pictures in exquisitely carved gold frames. The bottom molding of each frame displays the royal coat of arms, the top one a crown, in gold. . . . One wall is hung with pictures under the finest plate-glass: the op-

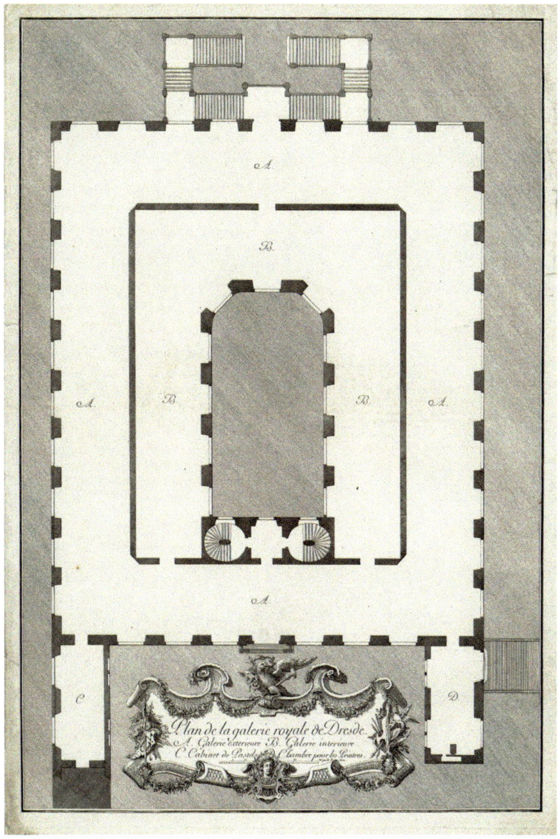

Fig. 2 **Michael Keyl**, **Plan de la galérie royale de Dresde**, before 1753, engraving, 75 x 35 cm, Kupferstich-Kabinett, Staatliche Kunstsammlungen Dresden

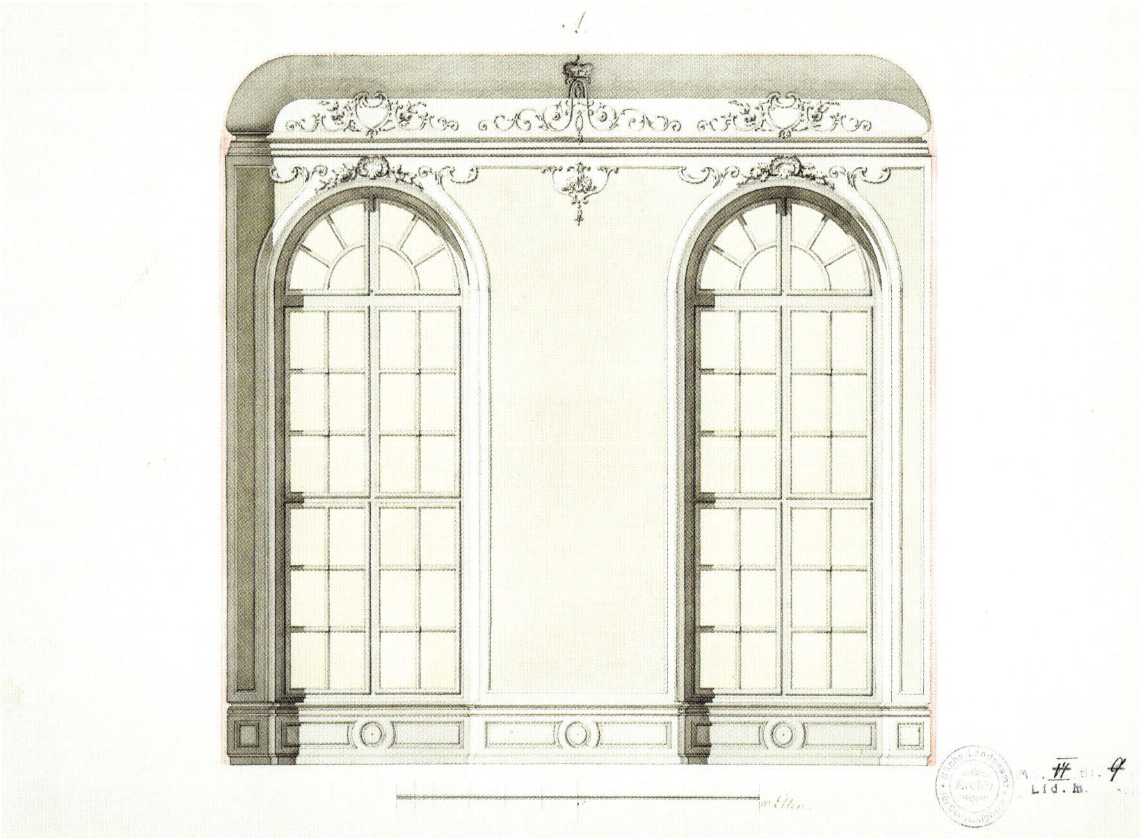

Fig. 3 UNKNOWN DRAFTSMAN, after JOHANN CHRISTOPH KNÖFFEL, **Kurfürstliches Stallgebäude, Pastellkabinett, longitudinal section**, 1745/46, pen and ink, wash, 36.5 x 52.5 cm, Landesamt für Denkmalpflege Sachsen (LfDS)

posite one is adorned with splendid tall mirrors that create a unlimited view."[15]

Two design drawings from the conversion phase in 1745/46 have been preserved in the Landesamt für Denkmalpflege Sachsen (Saxon State Office for Conservation and Monuments), and are published here for the first time.[16] The longitudinal section with elevation (fig. 3) shows two tall round-arch windows. The base of the wall is clad with wood wainscoting. The cornice above the windows is decorated with a long garland of gilt rocailles, which blends into the vaulted ceiling, forming a crowned "A" for Augustus at the center of each of the long walls. The cross section also shows this ornament (fig. 4), which, together with the carved and gilded frames of the pastel paintings must have dominated the overall impression of the room.[17] Added to this was the multiplication of the artworks in the aforementioned mirrors, which are, however, not shown in these drawings. Thus, despite the essential agreement between the Bianconi and Hasche descriptions, it is unclear whether the surviving drawings are designs created before the work was completed or documentation of the finished ensemble. Furthermore, it is equally uncertain whether the green wash on the end wall in the cross-section drawing reflects the actual color used in the Cabinet. Nothing has survived from this decor; the building was heavily damaged in the Second World War, and when it was rebuilt between 1965 and 1968, a false ceiling was installed in the room.

Although far smaller, the Pastellkabinett's architectural decor still echoes the example of Versailles: here too, in the famous Galerie des Glaces, begun in 1678, the room was dominated by tall mirrors that were installed opposite equally tall windows. Well into the eighteenth century, galleries in countless palaces were furnished with expensive mirror glass. Several direct precursors come to mind, such as, for example, the Green Gallery in the Munich Residence, created between 1733 and 1737 after plans by François Cuvilliés, where the green walls were also covered with closely hung paintings.[18] In Dresden, the picture gallery of the Saxon minister Heinrich, Count von Brühl should be mentioned, sporting a similarly splendid design, as described by the English traveler Jonas Hanway in 1756: "156 ells long, which is 18 ells longer than [the Mirror Gallery] of Versailles. The pictures are set off to great advantage, being ranged only on one side; the windows fronting them are very lofty . . . The pannels between the casements are of looking-glass."[19]

The unparalleled collection of choice pastels undoubtedly reflected the elector-king's personal taste, and it was the first of its kind to be displayed for visitors anywhere in a museum. Just who exactly made the decision to present them separately in a room of their own is unknown. One theory has it that it was Algarotti, wishing to shift the emphasis of a future royal museum away from older art to that of contemporaries, and this cannot be wholly discounted.[20] Yet in a letter to Brühl from 1745 the same Algarotti conveys Carriera's opinion that, with the recently acquired *Chocolate Girl* by Liotard, a stylistic shift had occured and that pastel painting in general was now outdated, including her own work.[21] This is also an indication of the limits to his project: within the shortest time, contemporary art, too, becomes "old art." As for the installation of the Pastellkabinett in the stable building, it is tempting to think of the Venetian Pietro Maria Guarienti as its initiator. He was instrumental in the purchase of the ducal collection in Modena in 1745, and a year later was appointed curator of the Dresden gallery, responsible for the arrangement of the new display of Italian oils in the remodeled stable building's Inner Gallery.[22]

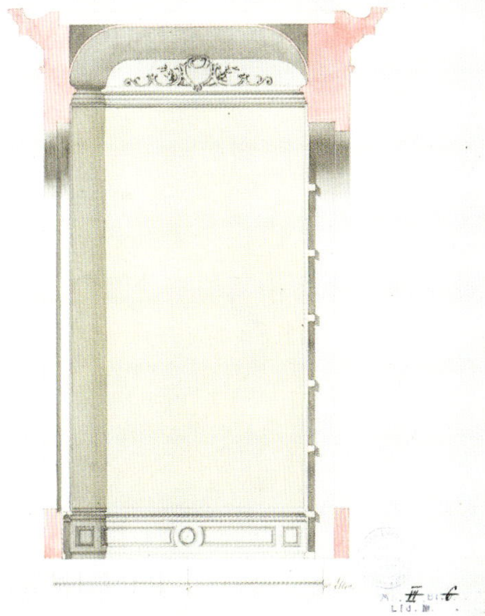

Fig. 4 **Unknown draftsman**, after **Johann Christoph Knöffel**, **Kurfürstliches Stallgebäude, Pastellkabinett, cross section**, 1745/46, pen and ink, wash, 52.5 x 36.2 cm, Landesamt für Denkmalpflege Sachsen (LfDS)

After the gallery's opening in 1748 there must have been frequent rehangings in the Pastellkabinett so as to integrate later acquisitions, by Liotard and La Tour, for example. There are no sources relating to this: the first two editions of the gallery catalogue by Johann Anton Riedel and Christian Friedrich Wenzel appeared much later, in 1765 and 1771. And they only list the exhibited works by artist, so it is impossible to know where they were placed on the wall.[23] This would gradually change in the catalogues that appeared regularly after 1801, which list the pastels in groups according to the way they were hung—yet even here the arrangement cannot always be clearly reconstructed.[24] Over the course of the decades, the earlier works were joined by new pastels by Therese Mengs, Anton Raphael's sister, by Johann Heinrich Schmidt, Felicitas Robert (Henriette Félicité Tassaert), and Daniel Caffé, as well as iso-

lated watercolors (David Friedrich Weller), paintings on glass (Madame Weidmüller), and an oil still life (Caroline Friederike Friedrich).
It is possible that one source of inspiration for the Pastellkabinett was the Finsteres Kabinett, or Dark Cabinet, that Augustus the Strong had established in the Dresden palace in 1707.[25] His rooms were on the second floor of the Georgenbau, from where he could easily reach his cabinet on the floor above by way of a flight of stairs. Not much is known about the (windowless or heavily curtained?) space. It contained 195 small-format oil paintings, hung closely together, among them ribald-realistic and burlesque genre scenes of mainly Dutch and Flemish origin—also a reflection of the king's personal taste, but in this case not accessible to the public and therefore lacking the aspect of princely self-representation. Presumably, however, the young heir to the throne would have been permitted entrance.
Just as there were no specific precedents for the Pastellkabinett, it did not become a model for later collections or museums either; it remained unique. In Dresden there was also the collection of the Saxon minister Brühl, which was quite extensive and comparable to the royal one, even though it had to defer to it.[26] This is evident from the fact that Brühl could only have a copy made of the *Chocolate Girl*.[27] Whether he also had as many pastels as Augustus III is difficult to determine; his cabinet, at least, was "furnished with enamels and crayons."[28] It is also reported that the Dresden artist Johann Alexander Thiele painted a whole cabinet full of pastels for Brühl: "Many consider him to be the first artist in Germany to paint landscapes in pastels."[29] Yet no works of his in this technique are known. Two works by Angelica Perotti from the Brühl collection, presumably pastels, were auctioned at Christie's in London in 1770.[30] And in 1926 the two pastel portraits of Louis XV and Marie Leszczyńska Queen of France by Maurice Quentin de La Tour from the Brühl family collection were consigned to Cassirer and Helbing in Berlin.[31] It seems that Brühl did not own any pictures by Rosalba Carriera. During the course of Czarina Catherine II's purchase of Brühl's art collection, the negotiator Count Belosselski is said to have acquired a pastel by a famous painter, which alone was appraised at 400 ducats.[32] Unfortunately neither painter nor picture were named.
A possible response to the presentation of the Dresden pastels could be the so-called "Cabinet of Muses and Graces" at Peterhof Palace in Russia: the painter Pietro Rotari left Dresden in 1756 for the court of the Russian czars, where he stayed until his death in 1762, producing countless works that Catherine II purchased. Beginning in 1764, a total of 368 works by Rotari came to be exhibited in one of the rooms of the residence—oil paintings, not pastels—completely covering the walls of the entire room, with only a slender strip of gilt molding separating the paintings from each other (fig. 5). Rotari had moved to Dresden from Vienna in 1752/53. In both cities he was able to admire works by Liotard, which would leave a lasting impression on him. Although his portraiture was highly admired in Saxony, he was not given a long-term appointment. And his attempt to gain entrée into the French court through Marie-Maximilienne de Silvestre, daughter of the Dresden court painter Louis de Silvestre and reader to Maria Josepha, Dauphine of France, was also without success. On the contrary, the dauphine cooly observed: "his [Rotari's] painting strikes me as too smooth . . . I prefer a bolder brush stroke."[33]
In Dresden, Rotari left sixty-two small-format portrayals of heads "which represent human facial expressions in countless different physiognomies, affects, and poses."[34] The tightly crowded display of this collection[35] anticipated the presentation of his paintings in the palace in Saint Petersburg.
After Dresden's Gemäldegalerie was moved into the Semper Building, completed in 1855, the pastel paintings were housed in two ground-floor rooms oriented toward Theaterplatz to the north.[36] Adjacent to them was a cabinet for the works of Christian Wilhelm Ernst Dietrich, followed by four rooms reserved for paintings by Antonio Canaletto and Bernardo Bellotto. Accord-

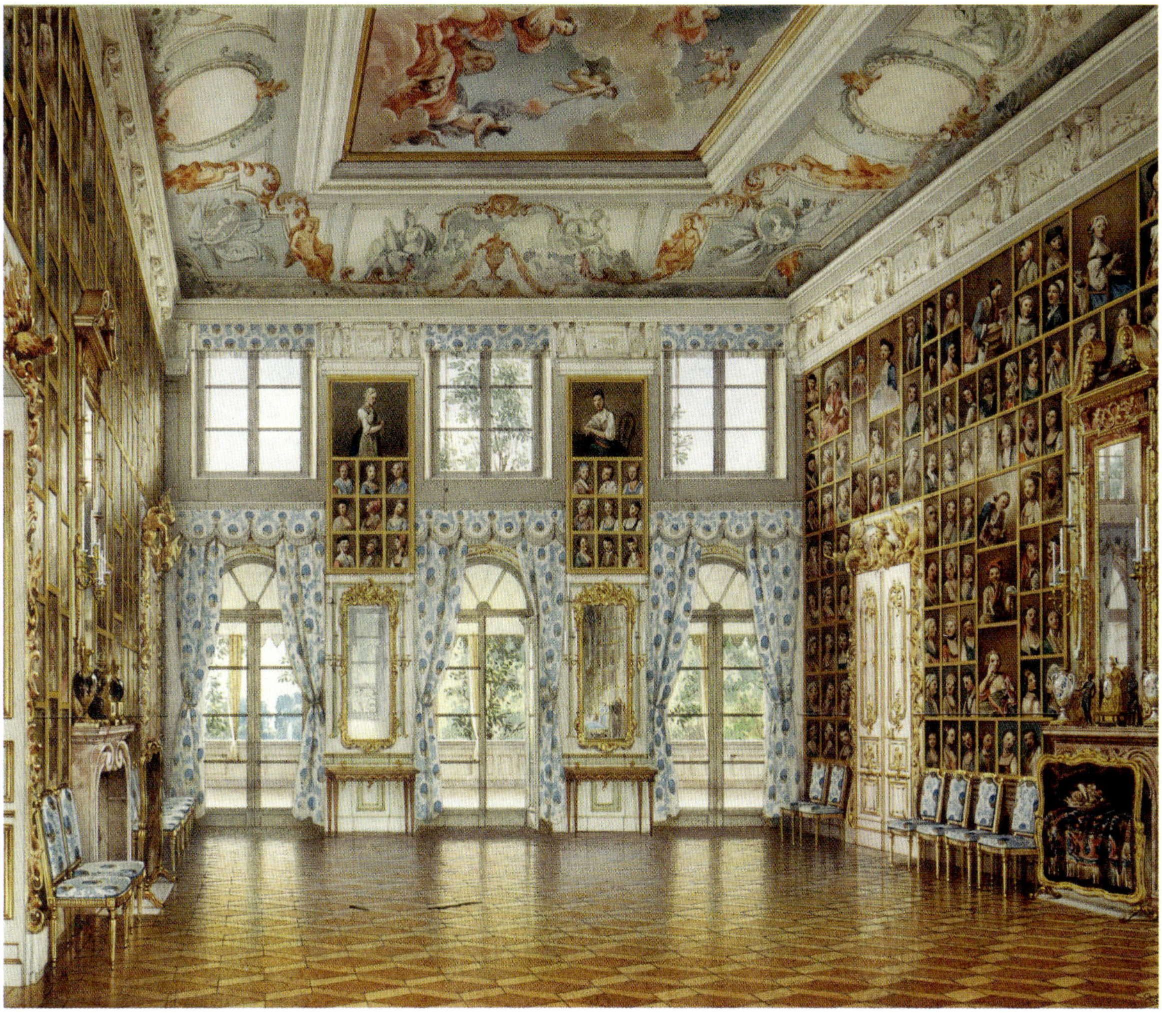

Fig. 5 LUIGI PREMAZZI, **Portrait Gallery (or Rotari Gallery)**, 1855, watercolor, Peterhof Palace

ing to the first catalogue of the gallery, which appeared after the remodeling in the Zwinger in 1856, a total of 178 pastels were displayed there.[37] No major changes were made in the following decades.

In 1889, when the plaster casts were moved from the East Hall of the Semper Building to the Albertinum, "these new rooms were wholly dedicated to the eighteenth century, its paintings, so important for Dresden's art history, thereby being united for the first time as a self-contained collection."[38] Included in this concept were the pastels, which were now displayed in the oval ground-floor room connecting the Semper Building with the Zwinger. There they stayed until 1924, when they were replaced by art from the late nineteenth century and the present; the pastels were now allocated to their different schools. Shortly before the start of the Second World War, on August 28, 1939, it was decreed that all museums, and this included the Gemäldegalerie, were to be closed and their works stored in safety. A large group of sixty-four pastels was taken to Schloss Weesenstein,[39] others were sent to the Königstein fortress. When, in 1945/46, Soviet trophy brigades raided the various storage depots in Saxony, a number of pastels were taken to Moscow and were only returned to Dresden in 1956. Since that time they have been on display, in reduced numbers, on the third floor of the Sempergalerie. The present exhibition, centered on the *Chocolate Girl*, attempts—at least partially—to invoke the former "Kabinett der Rosalba." A true reconstruction is out of the question. It was, and remains, unique.

1 Andreas Henning and Harald Marx, *"Das Kabinett der Rosalba" – Rosalba Carriera und die Pastelle der Dresdener Gemäldegalerie Alte Meister,* Staatliche Kunstsammlungen Dresden, Munich and Berlin 2007, p. 20.

2 *Sehnsucht und Wirklichkeit—Wunschbilder: Malerei für Dresden im 18. Jahrhundert*, exh. cat. Gemäldegalerie Alte Meister, Staatliche Kunstsammlungen Dresden 2009, ed. Harald Marx, Dresden 2009, pp. 157–59.

3 Girolamo Ravagnan, "Carriera (Rosalba)," in: *Biografia degli italiani illustri nelle scienze lettere ed arti del secolo XXVIII, e de' contemporanei*, ed. Emilio de Tipaldo, vol. 3, Venice 1836, p. 362.

4 Angelo Walther, "Zu den Werken der Rosalba Carriera in der Dresdener Gemäldegalerie," in: *Beiträge und Berichte der Staatlichen Kunstsammlungen Dresden* (1972–75), p. 66.

5 Ibid., p. 67.

6 Henning/Marx 2007, pp. 46–53; also Barbara Marx, "Diplomaten, Agenten, Abenteuer im Dienst der Künste – Kunstbeziehungen zwischen Dresden und Venedig," in: Barbara Marx and Andreas Henning, eds., *Venedig – Dresden: Begegnung zweier Kulturstädte*, Italien-Zentrum of the TU Dresden, Staatliche Kunstsammlungen Dresden, Leipzig 2010, p. 35.

7 Marx 2010, p. 35.

8 Bernardina Sani, "Il Gabinetto della Rosalba della Gemäldegalerie di Dresda florilegio della pittura a pastello europea tra Rococo e Illuminismo," in: Marx/Henning 2010, p. 206.

9 Frances Vivian, *Il console Smith – mercante e collezionista*, Vicenza 1971, pp. 172–173.

10 Henning/Marx 2007, p. 11. See also Walther 1975, p. 86, note 3.

11 Heinz-Werner Lewerken, "Zur Geschichte der Dresdner Gewehrgalerie," in: *Jahrbuch der Staatlichen Kunstsammlungen Dresden* 27 (1998/99), pp. 93–94.

12 Quoted from Giovanna Perini, "Giovanni Ludovico Bianconi: un bolognese in Germania," in: *Giovanni Ludovico Bianconi, Scritti tedeschi*, ed. Giovanna Perini, Bologna 1998, p. 37.

13 Giovanni Lodovico Bianconi, *Historische Lobschrift auf den Ritter Anton Raphael Mengs*, Zürich 1781, pp. 17–19.

14 Jean Antoine Riedel and Chrêtien Frederic Wenzel, *Catalogue des Tableaux de la Galerie Electorale a Dresde*, Dresden 1765, p. 242.

15 Johann Christian Hasche, *Umständliche Beschreibung Dresdens mit allen seinen inneren und äußeren Merkwürdigkeiten historisch und architektonisch*, vol. 2, Leipzig 1783, pp. 77, 90.

16 I am grateful to Martin Schuster, Landesamt für Denkmalpflege Sachsen, Plansammlung, for making these drawings available: wall elevation: inv. no. M 6. VI. Bl. 6; cross section: inv. no. M 6. VI. Bl. 9.

17 See the essay by Elisabeth Schlesinger in this volume.

18 Wolfgang Braunfels, *François Cuvilliés: Der Baumeister der galanten Architektur des Rokoko*, Munich 1986, pp. 73–77.

19 Jonas Hanway, *An Historical Account of the British Trade Over the Caspian Sea: With a Journal of Travels*, vol. 2, London 1753, p. 231.

20 Sani 2010, p. 207.

21 Marx 2010, pp. 54, 64–65.

22 Tristan Weddigen, "Der visuelle Diskurs des Inventars – Geschmackliche und kunstgeschichtliche Argumentationsmuster in der Dresdener Gemäldegalerie im 18. Jahrhundert," in: *Jahrbuch der Staatlichen Kunstsammlungen Dresden* 31 (2004), pp. 97–98.

23 Riedel/Wenzel 1765, pp. 239–243; Johann Anton Riedel and Christian Friedrich Wenzel, *Verzeichniß der Gemälde in der Churfürstl. Gallerie in Dresden*, Leipzig 1771, pp. 211–215.

24 [Johann Anton Riedel], *Verzeichnis der Gemälde welche in der churfürstl. Gallerie zu Dresden befindlich sind*, Dresden 1801, pp. 178–84.

25 Marx 2010, p. 11.

26 Ute Christina Koch, *Maecenas in Sachsen: Höfische Repräsentationsmechanismen von Favoriten am Beispiel von Heinrich Graf von Brühl*, diss. TU Dresden 2010, pp. 188–97; http://nbn-resolving.de/urn:nbn:de:bsz:14-qucosa-193760 (accessed May 25, 2016).

27 See the essay on the *Chocolate Girl* by Roland Enke in this volume, see pp. 52–53.

28 Hanway 1753, p. 230.

29 [Johann Friedrich von Racknitz], *Skizze einer Geschichte der Künste*, Dresden 1811, pp. 77–78.

30 Koch 2010, vol. 2, p. 11, lots 2.79 and 2.80.

31 Erwin Hensler, Ludwig Schnorr von Carolsfeld, ed., *Auktionskatalog Paul Cassirer und Hugo Helbing: Aus Königlich Sächsischem Besitz im Auftrag des Hauses Wettin Albertinische Linie e.V. Mit einem Anhang von Kunstgegenständen aus Gräflich Brühlschem Besitz und anderem Besitz*, Berlin 1926, p. 63, plate 25.

32 Jean Gustave de Sacken, "Korrespondenzen zum Ankauf der Bildergalerie der Grafen Brühl," in: *Sbornik imperatorskago russkago istoričeskago obščestva* 17 (1876), p. 392.

33 Valentina Ciancio, "'Signor Conte Rotari, dilettante di pittura' am Dresdener Hof – Archiv-Nachforschungen," in: Gregor J. M. Weber, *Pietro Graf Rotari in Dresden: Ein italienischer Maler am Hof König Augusts III.*, exh. and coll. cat., Gemäldegalerie Alte Meister, Staatliche Kunstsammlungen Dresden, Emsdetten and Dresden 1999, pp. 8–10.

34 Gregor J. M. Weber, "Die Gemälde Pietro Graf Rotaris für den sächsischen Hof, in: ibid., pp. 40–41.

35 At the beginning of the nineteenth century, the portraits of the Saxon ruling family were presented right next to the Pastellkabinett; see Johann Anton Riedel, *Catalogue des tableaux de la Galerie électorale à Dresde*, Dresden 1804, pp. 321–22.

36 Wilhelm Schäfer, *Die Königliche Gemälde-Gallerie im Neuen Museum zu Dresden*, vol. 1, Dresden 1860, plan between pp. 144 and 145: rooms 40/41.

37 Julius Hübner, *Verzeichniss der königlichen Gemälde-Gallerie zu Dresden*, Dresden 1856, pp. 336–40.

38 Karl Woermann, *Katalog der Königlichen Gemäldegalerie zu Dresden, Große Ausgabe*, Dresden 1892, p. VII.

39 See Roland Enke, "Schloss Weesenstein als Auslagerungsort für die Werke der Dresdner Gemäldegalerie," in: Birgit Finger and Robert Hänel, eds., *Bombensicher! Kunstversteck Weesenstein 1945*, exh. cat. Schloss Weesenstein, Staatliche Schlösser, Burgen und Gärten Sachsen GmbH, Dresden 2018, pp. 64–66.

“UN TABLEAU EN PASTEL”

Observations on Painting Techniques in Jean-Étienne Liotard’s *Chocolate Girl*

Christoph Schölzel

The following discussion on painting techniques used by Jean-Étienne Liotard to depict the *Chocolate Girl* is based on studies of the painting under various types of lighting and with the aid of a microscope (fig. 1). In addition, it relies on the findings from a series of special investigations performed with X-ray, X-ray fluorescence, and infrared reflectography[1] as well as material analysis of the picture support.[2] Along with comparison with the comprehensive studies on Liotard’s painting technique by Leila Sauvage and Cécile Gombaud,[3] it was particularly helpful to consult the copious literature on painting technique that accompanied the fashion for pastels in the eighteenth century.[4] Of particular interest here is the manuscript by the margravine Caroline Louise of Baden, inasmuch as her comments were based on her lessons with Liotard[5] and, in contrast to Liotard’s own treatise from as late as 1781,[6] contain a number of details specifically related to painting technique. Also, comparisons have been drawn with the other three Liotard paintings in Dresden (cat. 14, 69, 71), which have already been thoroughly investigated.[7]

The Supports

Whereas Liotard used blue paper as support for his *Self-Portrait in Turkish Costume* (cat. 14), he chose to use parchment for the three portraits in the Dresden collection (P 161, P 162, P 160), painted not much later,[8] a more expensive option.[9] Under a microscope the felt-like, roughened texture of the animal skin, so important for the pastel technique—also described as “tooth”[10]—is readily visible. At the same time, painters had to accept the organic irregularities of the material, although these could also be due to the methods employed by the parchment maker. Examples are the tiny craters in the background of the *Portrait of Maurice of Saxony* or on the right side of the background of the *Chocolate Girl*. Small, thin, speck-like spots, particularly concentrated in the areas of the torso and tray in the *Chocolate Girl*, are doubtless features of the parchment itself.[11] Both the *Chocolate Girl* and the *Girl Reading a Letter*, unlike the Maurice portrait, were executed on several pieces of parchment mounted together. The pieces were not joined in the same manner, so presumably the formats were extended at different stages in the works’ creation. Liotard probably enlarged the support for the *Girl Reading a Letter* during the painting process by attaching strips of parchment to the right side and the top, while, to create the large format he required for the *Chocolate Girl*, he combined one large piece of parchment with a smaller one (fig. 2). It is possible was unable to obtain a skin that was large enough, and that he had to assemble pieces together. His call for clean, smooth surfaces for pastel paintings, as formulated in his treatise, could suggest that he had to adapt to circumstances, and that the montage of the parchment pieces was not the result of artistic preference.[12]

He first stretched the two skins on separate wooden frames. With their slot-mortise-and-tenon

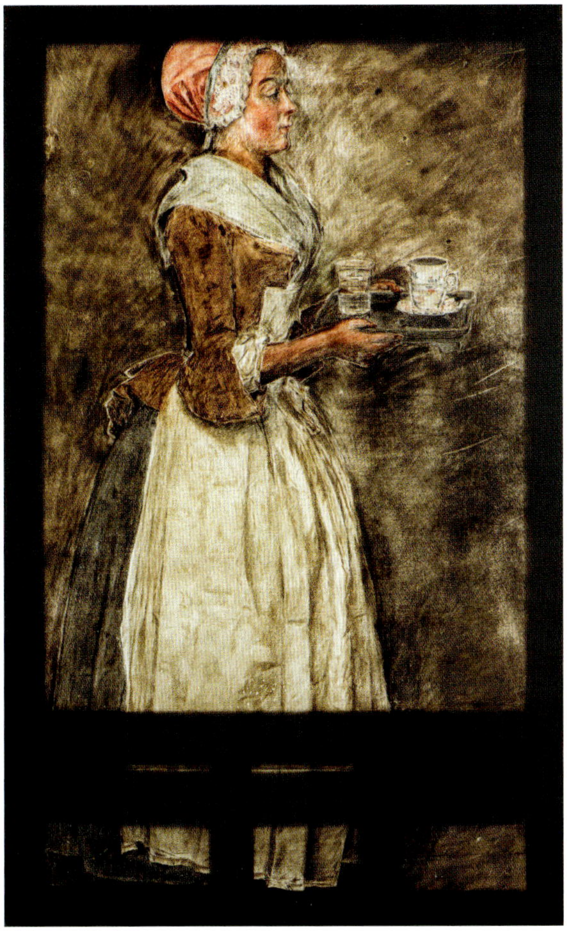

Fig. 1 **Jean-Étienne Liotard, The Chocolate Girl**, ca. 1744, Gemäldegalerie Alte Meister, Staatliche Kunstsammlungen Dresden: entire painting in backlight

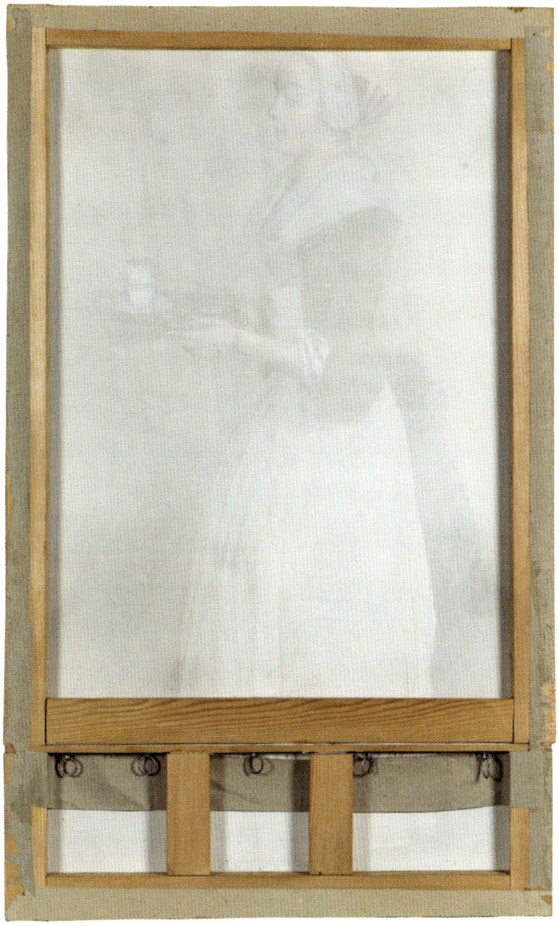

Fig. 2 Verso

joints, evident from the characteristic gauge marks in the corners, these differ somewhat in their construction from the frames for the self-portrait and the Maurice portrait. In cross section the frame moldings measure 1.9 x 4 cm. The corner joints were glued and additionally stabilized with wooden pins. To achieve the desired height of 83 cm, the top bar of the smaller frame was planed down to a thickness of 1.8 cm. Because of this, the ends of the canvas tacks, which pass clear through the wood, are visible on the back. To stabilize the frame, it was therefore necessary to insert two cross braces, which are simply secured with nails. Small printed papers have been glued in, probably to compensate for fluctuations in width. The two parchment pieces, stretched with slightly wider intervals between the nails, were joined using five long screws with eyes instead of screw heads. The paper backing was presumably inserted to prevent contact between the screw eyes and the parchment. On the recto, a strip of parchment between 2 and 2.3 cm wide was glued across the gap between the two sections of the picture support.

This somewhat complicated construction, created to obtain a relatively large picture format, has survived unchanged and in good condition to this day. It must have been completely finished before the artist started his painting. Various treatments to the picture support had to be undertaken as

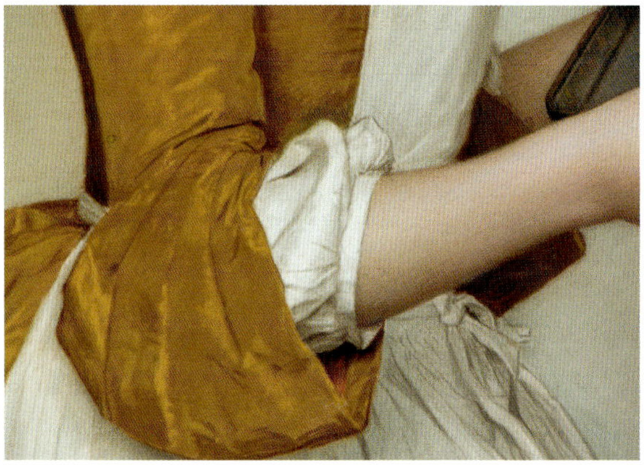

Fig. 3a Detail of the elbow

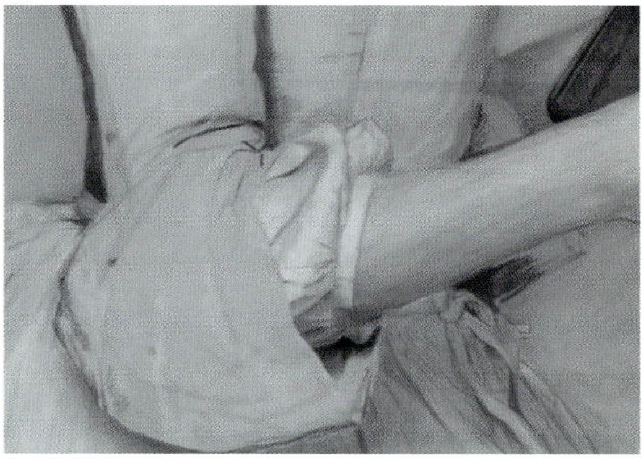

Fig. 3b Detail of the elbow in infrared reflectography

well. One of them was infilling the speck-like irregularities in the larger of the two vellum skins. These somewhat darker and transparent spots were masked on the verso of the picture with lead white pigment.

Our investigations found no evidence of a preparatory layer on the parchment as described, for example, by Peter Nathanael Sprengel in 1772.[13] It remains uncertain whether Liotard actually dispensed with any sort of surface preparation beyond merely roughening the skins. Furthermore, high radiation intensitives were necessary to produce X-ray images. The X-ray photo of the *Chocolate Girl* reveals a lighter zone in the center, a somewhat cloudy area extending vertically through the entire picture including the added-on piece. Could this be an indication that the recto was prepared with lead white to increase the radiance of the support? Lead was indeed detected everywhere in the picture with the aid of X-ray fluorescence. However, there is no evidence of the use of pumice powder, as Sprengel also suggests as a means of further roughening the parchment surface.[14]

The Underdrawings

A glance at three unfinished Liotard pastel paintings housed at the Rijksmuseum Amsterdam[15] reveals a consistent approach in organizing his first layers: he first established the figures' outlines with a brown or black chalk. Often these lines were reiterated several times, and one senses the concentration with which the painter sought the best contour. This was followed either by the placement of large areas of color in the garments or the background, or the artist would attend to the distribution of light and shadow in the faces. In our three examples, the three-dimensional modeling is largely established through clear indications of surfaces. It appears that Liotard, who was an accomplished draftsman, rarely resorted to scaled drawings as starting points for his pastel paintings. Far more frequently he seems to have developed his pastel pictures directly on the support, gradually proceeding in the course of the painting process from the more draftsmanly steps to colored planar elements.[16] The experienced painter was clearly able to do without such didactic sequences of steps as recommended, for example, by Günther in his introduction to pastel painting from 1762.[17]

Repeated swift chalk lines in search for the best arrangement of figures, as shown in the infrared reflectograph of the Munich *Breakfast* (fig. p. 43),[18] appear to be an exception.[19] In most of the Liotard pastels investigated so far—including the four Dresden pictures—it is possible to make out only very few lines, and it cannot be certain that these are in fact to be ascribed to the underdrawing phase. Studying the *Chocolate Girl* by means of infrared reflectography, one can see delicate lines on the upper arm and the puffed folds at the elbow that do not conform to the painted forms and possibly belong to underdrawings (figs. 3 a, b). In this picture we can see a search for the right contours in the face, the apron tie, and the bottom hem of the skirt. The few lines visible here, however, could also have been produced during the painting process itself (see fig. 4).

The sparse evidence of underdrawing allows only speculation on whether the artist used dry media that cannot be made visible with infrared reflectography, whether he followed Günther's recommendation and sketched out his picture with several different crayons, or whether he executed the underdrawing in red chalk,[20] which cannot be detected by this investigative method. Caroline Louise records in her notes that the initial sketch design was usually wiped off with bread.[21]

The Painting

Recent studies revealed that, in 1753, Liotard's student Caroline Louise of Baden purchased from the Paris dealer Moulle [Moule] a box of pastels containing 202 crayons.[22] Liotard's pastel box was likely no less comprehensive. Pastellists in the eighteenth century could already obtain professionally made crayons (as can also be seen from the margravine's contact with the famous Swiss pastel manufacturer Bernard-Augustin Stoupan[23]), but they could also make their own pastels, although Günther advises against this.[24] Pastels are composed of a mixture of pigments or dyestuffs with a filler (chalk, plaster, or clay, for example) and a binder (possibly gum arabic, tragacanth, or milk). After mixing, the paste was usually rolled into sticks and then dried. The number of different materials employed in this is vast,[25] and considerable expertise was required to produce pastel crayons in their various color blends, nuances of brightness, and degrees of hardness. Of the substances described in the literature, the inorganic pigments naturally stand out, as they are generally more stable than others and less susceptible to the bleaching effect of light.

In our examination of the Dresden Liotard pastels, we were able to determine by X-ray fluorescence

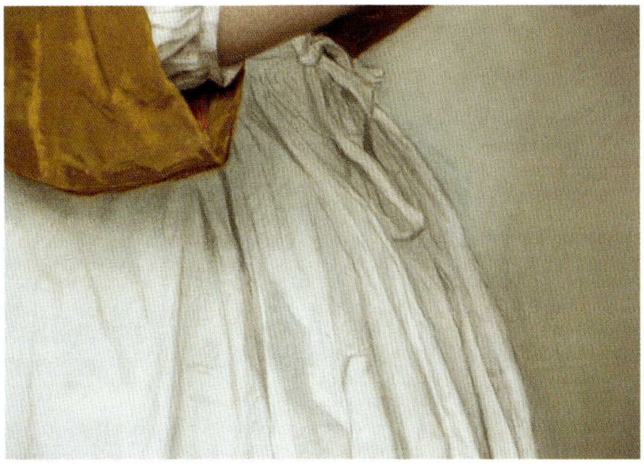

Fig. 4 Detail of the apron ties

the chemical elements present and draw conclusions about the color pigments used (see the table in the appendix). What cannot be determined by this method, however, are the quantities of the individual substances, nor the entire range of organic pigments and binders. So, while this research represents an important step in the study of the pastels Liotard used, the findings cannot be seen as a complete analysis of the artist's color palette. When painting with pastels, the artist needed to have a clear vision of the end result and final effects. He had to master the application of the crayon but also to anticipate the effect of multiple superimposed layers of color, the impact of the lower ones onto the layers above and the clean separation of color surfaces. Of course, corrections and changes could still be made by removing individual layers, perhaps with bread, but this always posed the risk of smudging and spoiling the adjacent colors, as can be seen on the back of the chair in *Girl Reading a Book*. For that reason it appears to have been typical of Liotard to get by with few corrections, thereby preserving the pristine radiance of his colors. A minor correction to the size of the bonnet in the *Chocolate Girl* was possibly made at an early stage and is therefore just barely visible in the transmitted light image.

Given Liotard's masterly skill, it is only with difficulty that his painting process can be broken down into individual steps, as is common in oil painting.

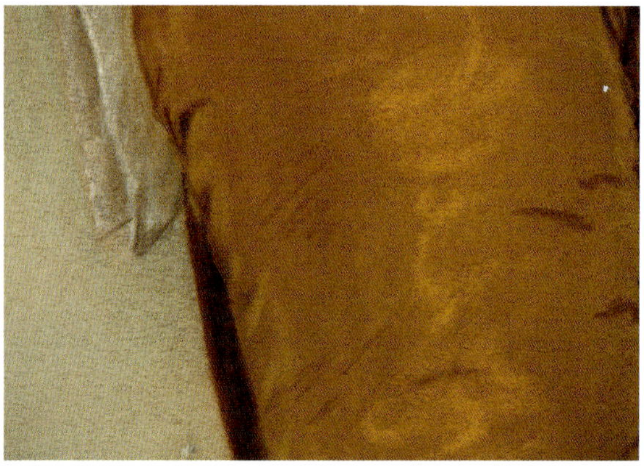

Fig. 5a Detail of the yellow jacket

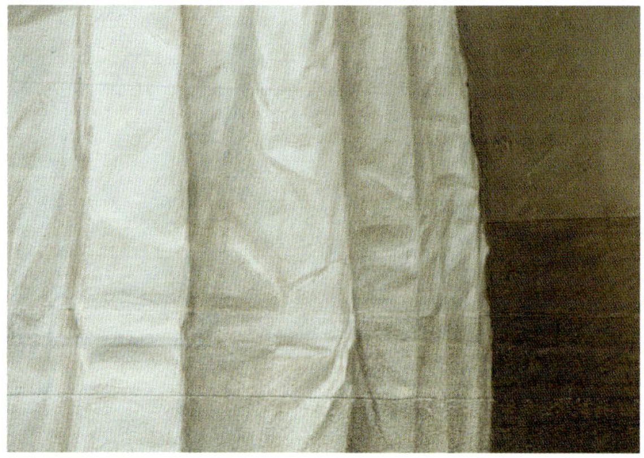

Fig. 5b Detail of the white apron

If, in his instructions to Caroline Louise, Liotard suggested a certain sequence—especially in the painting of faces—this probably reflects a fundamental notion of a picture's development. An important feature of Liotard's technique appears to have been to treat the areas of color separately, so that the isolation of color planes and a special sharpness of the outlines were guaranteed. For the underpainting of garments Caroline Louise formulated as a "general rule": "garments [are] sketched out thin, flat; afterward the folds [have to] be added in."[26] She was referring precisely to the respective garment colors, leaving small details for a later step, as we see in the blue garment of the unfinished portrait *Joseph II of Austria* in Amsterdam.[27] Just as blue was applied on the areas that would later become a blue coat, we can see applications of larger areas of color in the Dresden pictures. In the *Chocolate Girl*, for example, the bonnet was underlaid with pink, the jacket with a light ocher to reddish tone that is clearly set apart from the light gray undercoat of the shawl and the one in warm gray shades for the skirt.

The mostly monochrome backgrounds were produced relatively early in the painting process. Caroline Louise's "General Rule No. 11" reads: "for profiles, the grounds are made first, for others right after the first shading."[28] This was only logical, for, firstly, if the background was painted later it would have to respect the complex contours already established and, secondly, it also made for cleaner work, for when applying the background color—usually with the broad side of the crayon—any dust flaking off could easily spoil the adjacent areas of color. The transmitted light images of the *Chocolate Girl* reveal broad, animated strokes of color in the background, suggesting that the pastel was first vigorously applied and then smudged to produce a relatively homogeneous surface. Caroline Louise's "General Rule No. 2" warns against using fingers for this.[29] In contrast to the creation of flesh tones, which was accomplished, using rather similar steps, the modeling of garments, once they had been underpainted, could be highly variable. It was not only a matter of capturing the different colors of fabrics in their shadings of light and dark, but also suggesting their different textures. Only paragraphs 14 and 15 of Caroline Louise's manuscript refer to the painting of garments: she recommends starting them thin and subsequently "drawing in" their folds.[30] Günther's instructions, meanwhile, reflect the wealth of variation in different parts of garments much more extensively, in that he devoted some twenty pages to this subject alone.[31]

Studies of the *Chocolate Girl* identified a wide range of approaches to the rendering of garments. The pinkish bonnet alone reveals a highly sophisticated approach. Liotard underlaid this area with pink crayons, then worked the lighter sections of the folds in white, structuring the depths of the folds partially planar, partially by drawing them in

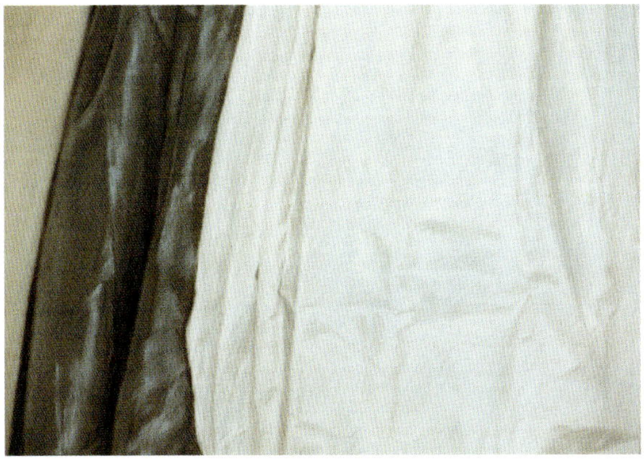

Fig. 5c Detail of the gray skirt

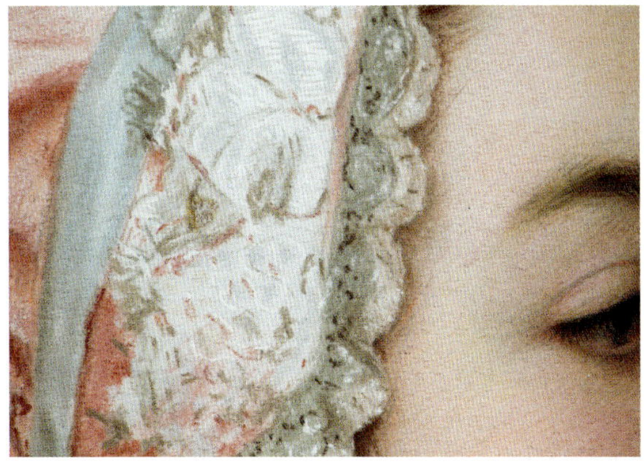

Fig. 6 Detail of the lace on the bonnet

with red-brown crayons. The wide band of lace that adorns the front of the bonnet was rendered with a white pastel crayon over a gray to pink base. To refine the patterns, which were mostly applied dry, Liotard very sparingly added a few tiny accents in liquid lead white. That is to say, he either mixed pastel crayon powder with a liquid binder[32] or used a premixed gouache pigment that he applied with a pointed brush (fig. 6).

In the girl's yellow jacket it is easy to reconstruct how the folds were built up on top of a light ocher ground tone. The artist painted the shadows on the arm, so important for the three-dimensional effect of this section, with red-brown crayons, whereby he was more concerned with imitating the special sheen of the velvet with a radiant yellow ocher than with emphasizing the three-dimensionality with light and shadow. Here it was clearly important to him to retain the lines of the yellow accents and he largely refrained from smudging the colors.

The large white apron with its pressed pleats and bottom hem was created along similar lines as Caroline Louise's notes suggest. In paragraph 15 she writes: "The white stuff is 1) quite thin, 2) very light, 3) the shadows [in] a color tending toward ocher, 4) the half-shadows shaded black, 5) not the shadows, but the highlights are drawn in."[33] And indeed, on the apron and on the white shawl one notices a thin, pale gray underlayer that corresponds to the fine, light brown lines of the folds. As already mentioned, a precise drawing in a light brown crayon, with slight corrections, also underlies the apron tie at the girl's waist. In the lower part of the apron, Liotard varied the shadow tones and placed fine hatching lines in the depths of the folds using a light blue crayon. These shading colors and their corresponding highlights, some tending toward a pure white, were partly left in their original strokes, though in places the painter also blended the colors together. This very deliberate variation in the application of color contributes greatly to the illusion of the white fabric as the most prominent motif of the painting and achieves an almost tactile effect in the juxtaposition of vertical pleats and the numerous other folds and creases that also define the fabric. In a light-dark contrast, the white apron is set off against a warm gray skirt. Delicate strokes of brown to black, almost all of them painted from the upper right to the lower left, model the contours of the skirt's folds, while light blue strokes, some of them very lightly smudged, represent the highlights on the folds and at the same time the special surface sheen (figs. 5 a, b, c).

From Caroline Louise's notes, which, as mentioned before, primarily focus on the rendering of flesh tones, we can appreciate the number of overlapping layers by which the different skin tones are produced in light and shadowed areas. Günther's introduction from 1762 also devotes considerable space to the possible ways of rendering faces.

Since, in Liotard's paintings, the various pastel pigments he used to paint faces mingle and overlap, or even blend through smudging, it is difficult to reconstruct the order in which they were applied.

Microscopic investigation of the four faces in the Dresden Liotard paintings reveals that in the *Self-Portrait* it is indeed possible to make out a bluish tone around the temples, beneath the right eye, and in the area of the eye and top of the nose, that could correspond with Caroline Louise's instructions in paragraph 26.[34] In the face of the *Chocolate Girl*, where the colors are very thick and most delicately blended, and individual strokes can only be seen in the transmitted light images, the shaded areas tend toward a brownish gray—possibly produced with the umber crayon mentioned by Caroline Louise (figs. 7 a, b, c).[35] On her forehead, just below the bonnet, we can make out fine, individual lines of shading, although some of these may also represent wisps of hair. A similarly fine texture of brush strokes is visible in the shadows next to the nostril and on the neck of the *Girl Reading a Letter*. The layers of color on the face in the *Portrait of Maurice of Saxony* are less compact and, occasionally, the pale parchment of the picture support shines through between the brown strokes in the half-shadows of the cheek. Here too, a fine texture of strokes is visible on the forehead, which was obviously crucial in the development of faces and was deliberately only partially obscured by blending the colors. In paragraph 23, Caroline Louise writes that the colors are "shaded over each other so as to avoid blotches."[36] But she does not indicate the degree to which the colors in faces are to be blended and when it is better to leave the lines, which must be drawn "very close together and thin,"[37] in their hatched pattern.

White and reddish tones predominate in the illuminated parts of the faces, which in the case of the *Chocolate Girl* seems to be made out of lead white and reddish ocher. The common color combination of lead white with vermilion and a little ocher, either as a mixture in the crayon itself or in the blend of lines in the picture, was also identified on

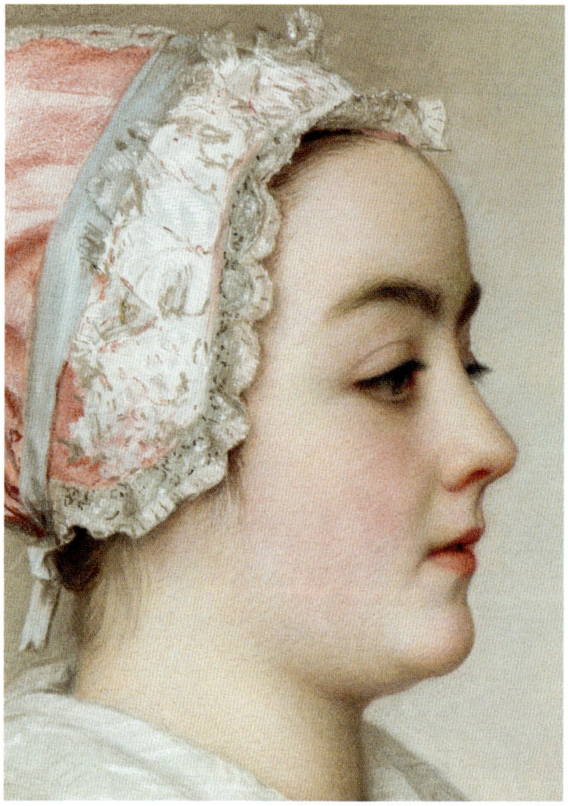

Fig. 7a Detail of the head

the neck in *Self-Portrait*, on the arm of the *Chocolate Girl*, in *Girl Reading a Letter*, and on the forehead in *Portrait of Maurice of Saxony*.

Eyes and eyebrows, nose, and mouth were obviously positioned during the sketching of each face and then completed in a combination of drawing and painting. Gray and pink crayons were used for the *Chocolate Girl's* eye. A blue-gray area can be made out in the girl's iris, edged by a thin black line. This was produced in the alternation between painting and drawing necessary to create facial accents. Whereas the eyebrows were worked into the skin tone with blackish lines in strokes that are just about visible, the underside of the nose and her mouth were painted with red pastels. Various reddish tones, blended together, surround the dark brown of the mouth opening. Liotard did not permit the girl's lips to look completely closed and even added a hint of her teeth in a light brick red (fig. 8).

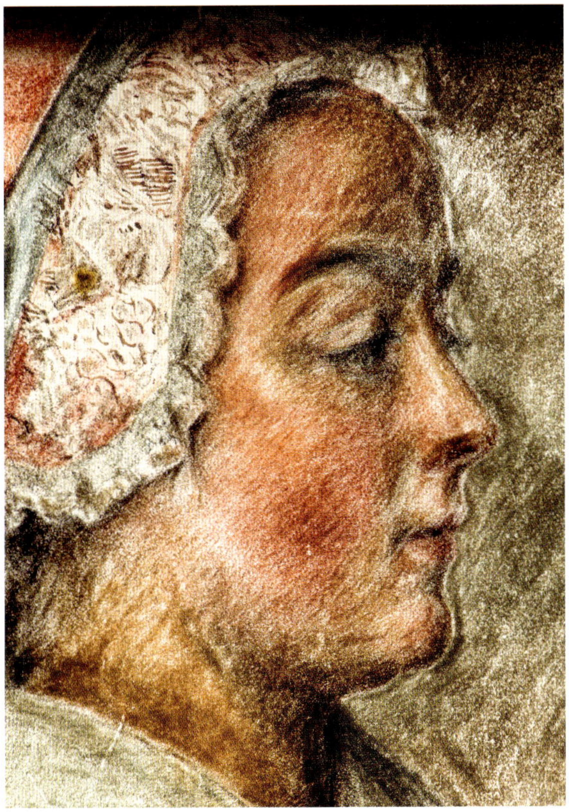

Fig. 7b Detail in backlight

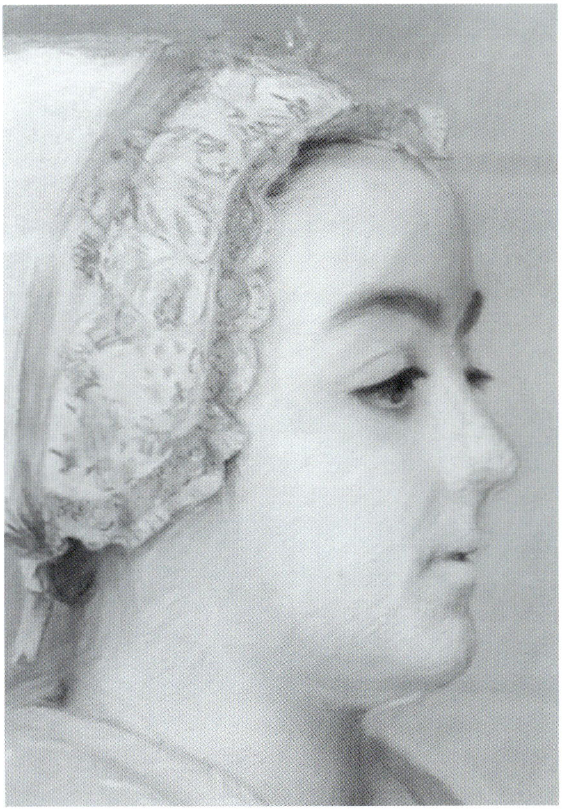

Fig. 7c Detail in infrared reflectography

The objects with which Liotard characterized his subjects' activities deserve a brief mention. In *Self-Portrait* it is no more than a brown pastel crayon—perhaps the one he used to paint the large fur cap? Liotard's representational skill is evident in the way he added a light blue line to the side of this crayon, along with two different shades of brown, and with this simple, cool reflection made it look three-dimensional.

In *Chocolate Girl*, he produced a bravura piece of painting with the tray holding the cup of chocolate, sweetmeats, and a glass of water. For the tray he used various shades of green all the way to a moss green. On this underlayer he drew the lacquer pattern and shadows, and defined the tray's edges and molding in ocher-yellow and black. The cup was evidently painted on a white ground on which he very precisely drew its colorful pattern in red and blue, using hard crayons. On the cup's silver holder and the rim of the saucer he applied a few impasto highlights in white, again using watercolor.[38] The thick chocolate drink that forms a shallow mound in the cup was rendered with a firmly applied brown and black. On close inspection, on the left edge at the back of the cup, a tiny section of the white porcelain is visible that is not covered by the cup's brown contents and serves to create the illusion of a three-dimensional object (fig. 9).

A special artistic challenge was the depiction of water in a transparent glass, and the Dresden collection includes an outstanding example of how this was mastered by Albrecht Dürer.[39] Liotard started painting his water glass with a gray-brown underlayer and structured the lower part of the glass with light-gray, pinkish, and ocher tones, and the upper part with darker brown and gray pastels. To quite precisely apply the white reflections of a

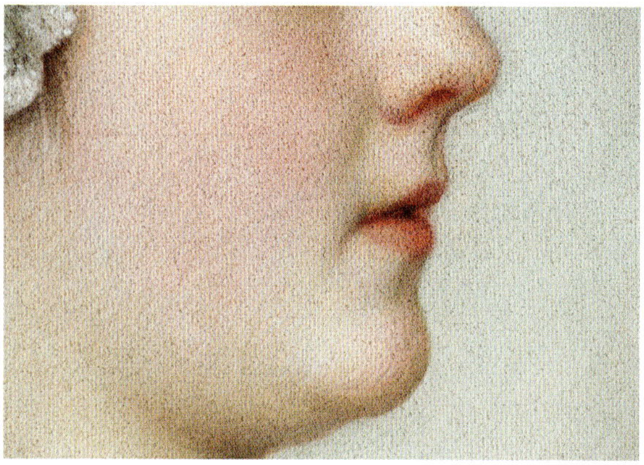

Fig. 8 Detail of the lower part of the face

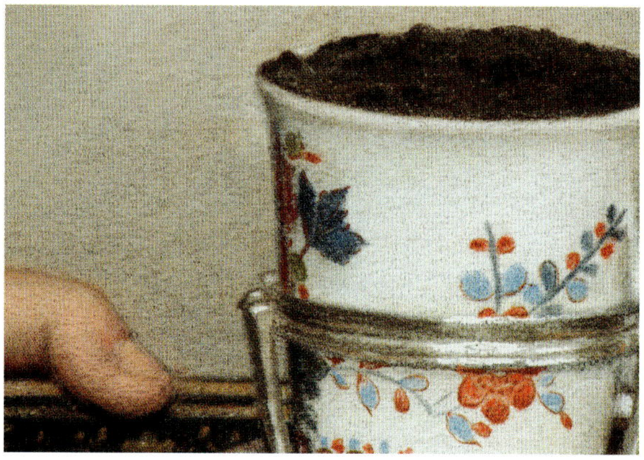

Fig. 9 Detail of the cup

window, he once again used a brush with liquid pigment.

The Protective Frame

Pastel paintings, with their highly sensitive surfaces, sometimes stabilized with fixatives,[40] need to be protected under glass as soon as they are finished.[41] Portions of the original mountings appear to have survived in the Dresden paintings. The pastel paintings were placed in slim wooden frames holding a glass sheet. Obviously, it was necessary to prevent the glass from touching the picture surface, and to ensure this, small pieces of cardboard or wood were glued into the frame's molding, or sometimes onto the edges of the picture, to serve as spacers. The frame's L-shaped molding was designed to accommodate the painting's stretchers. Thus it was possible to cover the back completely with thin wood veneer. These backings, many of which have survived on Dresden's pastels by Rosalba Carriera, were sometimes screwed to the frame and firmly glued along the edges with strips of paper. This created a hermetically sealed package that could then be fitted into a display frame. When cleaning the inside of the glass it was necessary to renew the seal, and today the various pieces of paper from earlier times are still visible on the verso of these paintings.

1 The X-ray investigation was carried out by Ivo Mohrmann and Kerstin Risse (Dresden Academy of Fine Arts), the infrared reflectography by Wolfgang Kreische, and the X-ray fluorescence by Michael Mäder (both Staatliche Kunstsammlungen Dresden). I am particularly grateful to all of them.

2 Leila Sauvage (Amsterdam) conducted the parchment tests and communicated their results to the University of York in England through Sarah Fiddyment. I am very grateful to Leila Sauvage for this support and for a number of valuable suggestions.

3 Leila Sauvage and Cécile Gombaud, "Liotard's Pastels: Techniques of an 18th-century Pastellist," in: *Studying 18th-century paintings and works of art on paper*, ed. Helen Evans and Kimberley Muir, London 2015, pp. 31–45; Leila Sauvage, "Jean-Étienne Liotard und Karoline Luise von Baden—Eine Geschichte der Pastelle," in: Christoph Frank and Wolfgang Zimmerman, *Aufgeklärter Kunstdiskurs und Höfische Sammelpraxis: Karoline Luise von Baden im europäischen Kontext*, Munich 2015, pp. 124–131; Cécile Gombaud and Leila Sauvage, "Liotard, Stoupan and the colours available to 18th-century European artists," in: *Sources on art and technology: back to basics*, 6th symposium of the ICOM-CC working group Art Technological Source Research, Amsterdam 2014, ed. by Sigrid Eyb-Green u.a., Amsterdam 2016, pp. 115–123.

4 See Christoph Schölzel, *Studie zur Pastellmalerei—Maltechnik und Restaurierung*, seminar paper, Dresden Academy of Fine Arts, Dresden 1989; Beatrix Graf, *Werkstoffe und Technik der Pastellmalerei des 18. Jahrhunderts unter besonderer Berücksichtigung der Maltechnik Jean-Étienne Liotards auf Grund der Aufzeichnungen seiner Schülerin, Markgräfin Karoline Luise von Baden*, unpublished degree thesis at the Institute for Art Technology and Conservation, State Academy of Art and Design Stuttgart, Stuttgart 1977.

5 See Graf 1977; Gombaud and Sauvage 2016, pp. 115–123.

6 Jean-Étienne Liotard, *Traité des principes et règles de la peinture*, Geneva 1781.

7 This essay presents a selection of the investigations of painting technique in the four Dresden Liotard paintings with respect to the *Chocolate Girl*. A publication of the entire study is in preparation.

8 For the parchment analyses, see note 2.

9 See the mention of parchment prices in: *Neues theoretisch-praktisches Zeichenbuch zum Selbstunterricht für alle Stände—Nebst einer Anleitung zum Colorieren der Landschaften und zur Blumen- und Pastellmahlerey*, Hof 1797, p. 45, with the added note "One has to tell the parchment maker that it is for pastel painting."

10 *Zeichenbuch* 1797, p. 45.

11 According to Jiří Vnouček (April 25, 2018), to whom Leila Sauvage thankfully pointed these out, they could be traces of bites by the ox warble fly (*Hypoderma*), a parasite that may have attacked the animal. This would mean that it was an inferior-grade parchment.

12 See Marianne Koos, *Haut, Farbe und Medialität. Oberfläche im Werk von Jean-Étienne Liotard (1702–1789)*, Paderborn 2014, pp. 10, 251.

13 Peter Nathanael Sprengel *Handwerke und Künste in Tabellen, 9. Sammlung*, Berlin 1772, p. 69.

14 Ibid.

15 See Rijksmuseum Amsterdam: reverse of the copy after a painting by Paulus Potter with a male portrait, R/L 2008, no. 374, fig. 532; *Portrait of Joseph II of Austria*, R/L 2008, no. 515; *Portrait of Archduke Maximilian Francis of Austria*, R/L 2008, no. 516.

16 See Sauvage and Gombaud 2015, pp. 38-39.

17 See Georg Christian Günther, *Praktische Anweisung zur Pastellmahlerey für Liebhaber und Mahler*, Nuremberg 1762, pp. 32–34.

18 Jean-Étienne Liotard, *The Breakfast*, Bayerische Staatsgemäldesammlungen, Munich, R/L 2008, no. 205.

19 See the talk by Elisabeth Hipp (Bayerische Staatsgemäldesammlungen, Munich) and Ulrike Fischer (Doerner-Institut, Munich) at the Liotard Study Day on January 16, 2018, in Dresden; a publication is being prepared in Munich.

20 See Günther 1762, p. 32.

21 Jan Lauts, "Jean-Étienne Liotard und seine Schülerin Markgräfin Karoline Luise von Baden," in: *Jahrbuch der Staatlichen Kunstsammlungen Baden-Württemberg* 14 (1977), p. 52; see Sauvage and Gombaud 2015, p. 38.

22 See Astrid Reuter, "Künstlerische Praxis und Kennerschaft – Karoline Luise von Baden und die Pastellmalerei," in: Christoph Frank and Wolfgang Zimmermann eds., *Aufgeklärter Kunstdiskurs und höfische Sammelpraxis: Karoline Luise von Baden im europäischen Kontext*, Munich 2015, p. 115.

23 Ibid.

24 See Günther 1762, "Vorbericht" p. 4.

25 See Schölzel 1989, pp. 20–42.

26 Lauts 1977, p. 50.

27 See R/L 2008, no. 515.

28 Lauts 1977, p. 50.

29 Ibid.

30 Ibid.

31 See Günther 1762, pp. 100–122.

32 There are as yet no findings regarding the binders used in the accents applied in liquid form in Liotard's pastels; see Graf 1977, pp. 61–62; Sauvage and Gombaud 2015, pp. 43–44.

33 Lauts 1977, p. 50.

34 Ibid., p. 52.

35 Ibid., p. 50.

36 Ibid., p. 52.

37 Ibid., p. 50.

38 See Koos 2014, p. 290.

39 See Albrecht Dürer, *Dresden Altarpiece*, right wing with Saint Sebastian, Staatliche Kunstsammlungen Dresden, gal. no. 1869.

40 In our investigations we were unable to identify fixatives on the four paintings, so this procedure has not been discussed further. For the numerous fixative possibilities in the eighteenth century, see Schölzel 1989, pp. 43–54; Sauvage/Gombaud 2015, p. 44.

41 See Günther 1762, pp. 127–30.

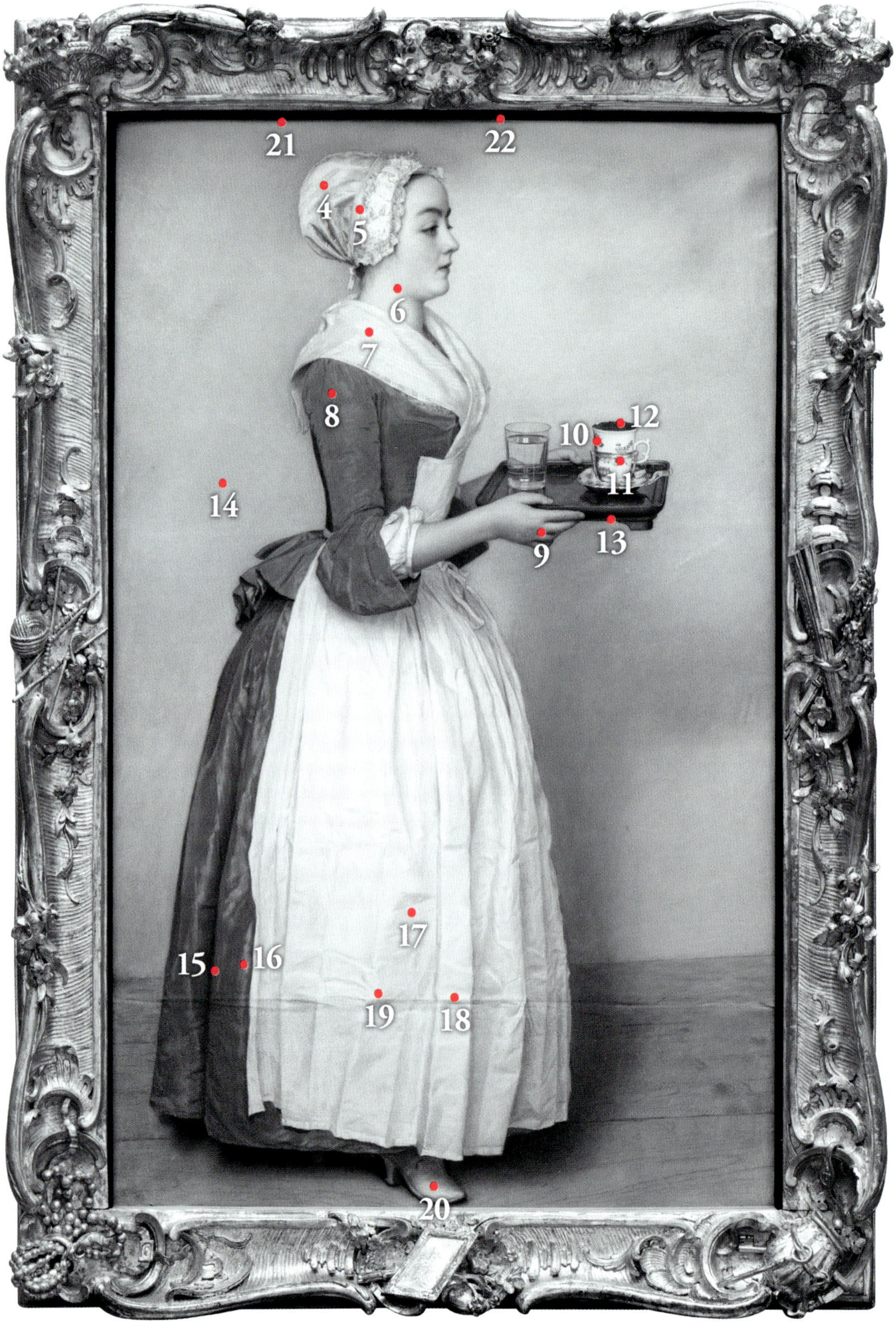
21
22
4
5
6
7
8
12
10
11
14
13
9
17
15
16
19
18
20

X-Ray Fluorescence Analysis

Responsible for the examination: Michael Mäder, January 11 & 16, 2018 (device: handheld Thermo Scientific™, Niton™ XL3t GOLDD+; mode: "Mining" for pigments, measuring time: 90 sec; measuring point ø 3mm; method: measurement in air; device attached to tripod, horizontal alignment). The examination of specifically selected 22 measuring points on the pastel, using non-destructive X-ray fluorescence analysis (RFA), yielded a number of characteristic chemical elements (main ingredients). These elements allow an interpretation of the mineral pigments used in the various colors applied by the artist.

Color	measuring points*	main chemical ingredients	pigment
White	7, 14, 17, 18, 19, 21, 22	Pb	white lead
		Ca	chalk
Skin tones	6, 9	Pb	white lead
		Fe	red ocher
Ocher/brown	8, 12	Fe	ocher
		Fe + Mn	umber
Red	4, 11	Hg + S	cinnabar
Blue	5, 10	Cu	azurite
		Fe	Prussian blue
Black	13	P	ivory black
Gray	15, 16	Pb + P	ivory black + white lead
Yellow	20	Fe	yellow ocher

* Measuring points 1–3 on the reverse side are not included here.

THE *CHOCOLATE GIRL*'S ORNAMENTAL FRAME

"The wall is covered floor to ceiling with the most beautiful pastel paintings"[1] The Function of the Frames in Dresden's Pastellkabinett

Elisabeth Schlesinger

When the former stable building and present-day Johanneum on Dresden's Jüdenhof was converted into a gallery in 1745/46, a space on the north side of the second floor was created for the exclusive display of pastels.[2] This Pastellkabinett linked the Long Corridor leading out from the elector's residence with the gallery proper. When entering his gallery from the palace, the pastels were the first thing the elector would see. Exceptionally high-quality frames that differ markedly from the gallery's otherwise uniform frames were crafted especially for these works.[3] Due to their number, their individual design, and their wall-filling arrangement, they were integral to the room's appearance—as notable as the pastels themselves.

From the outer gallery, a door led into a space of roughly 11.8 meters length, 4.7 meters width, and some 9 meters height (fig. 2, p. 91).[4] On the opposite side, a second door led into the Long Corridor. The largest continuous wall space was to the left. Discounting the wainscoting and cornice molding, the wall, roughly 6.5 meters high and 11.8 meters wide, offered a surface area of about 77 square meters.[5] The opposite wall to the right was structured by two large window openings and three floor-to-ceiling mirrors. The floor covering was in solid wood, and above the wainscoting the walls were covered in green damask wallpapers with gold moldings. Above this, towards the ceiling the wall was "ornamented and gilded in the Arabic taste."[6] The ceiling was white and the doors adorned with gilt moldings.

The room was dominated by rows and rows of paintings, hanging one above the other, further amplified by their reflections in the mirrors opposite, which seemed to multiply portraits and cabinet visitors alike.[7] In the combination of architecture, interior decor, fine art, and elaborate frames, the space represented what might be termed a Rococo *gesamtkunstwerk*.[8]

Because indications of their location are either scant or lacking altogether, it is impossible to reconstruct the original number and arrangement of the pastels.[9] Jean-Étienne Liotard's *Chocolate Girl* hung on the room's south side.[10] The first printed catalogues of the Gemäldegalerie, produced by Johann Anton Riedel and Christian Friedrich Wenzel in 1765 and 1771, list seventy-three pastels by name, yet without indicating where they were placed.[11] A note relates that the collection contained 157 works by Rosalba Carriera alone.[12] It is unclear, however, whether all the pastels were on display.

By studying the dimensions of the pastels still in the Dresden collection today and of those missing since 1945 but named in the 1765 catalogue, it is possible to detect certain patterns. The total number of 117 works falls into six different formats, but three main sizes dominate.[13] This was exploited in the arrangement of the paintings to give the wall a balanced appearance. Small, medium, and large frames could be grouped together and works

Fig 1 **Joseph Deibel** and **Matthäus Kugler**, frame for the Jean-Étienne Liotard pastel *The Chocolate Girl*, ca. 1745/46, Gemäldegalerie Alte Meister, Staatliche Kunstsammlungen Dresden

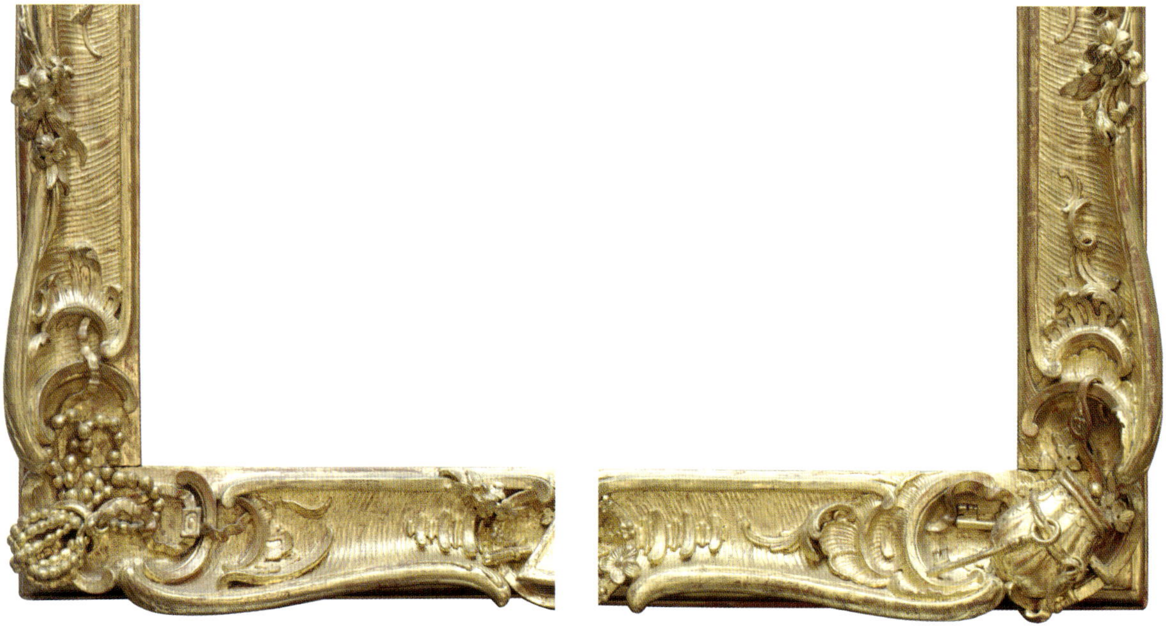

Fig. 2 Detail, bottom left and right corners

with similar motifs brought in relation to each other. Only a few pastel paintings failed to conform to the primary formats. One was the *Chocolate Girl*, which is taller than all the others. The overall surface area of the 117 pastels amounts to about 19.9 square meters. Taking into account the width of the frames and a gap of roughly 10 cm between them, some 40 square meters of wall surface were required for the hanging. According to Riedel, however, there were a total of 175 pastels in 1765,[14] so around half as many again, which means that some 60 square meters of the display surface were covered.

"An unparalleled love of decor"[15] – Form and Design of the Dresden Pastel Frames

What makes these pastel frames so special is their individuality and rich ornamentation. For each work on display a frame was made to measure, their varied decoration encompassing a broad range of typical Rococo motifs. Symmetry is rare; forms alternate or stand alone. As in the gallery frames, the rectangular format is softened by swept top edge rails and ornaments projecting beyond the frame's contours. All the pastel frames present a tall rectangular format. The frame profiles all follow a similar basic design. On the picture side, starting with the slim, smooth sight edge, a square bar marks the transition to the ornamented zone. The frame itself is essentially a concave molding, or cavetto, with a raised outer edge bordered by S-shaped or gently swept rails. Behind these ornamental elements, the back edges are either stepped or defined by a simple raised band. Each frame has individual ornamentation in the form of corner and center cartouches, often flanked by one to three C-scrolls. Flowers, ribbons, rocailles, and palmette-like forms create a soft transition to the basic frame profile.

Specific attributes are found on a number of the pastel frames. For example, the frame for gal. no. P 173 (Anton Raphael Mengs, *Friedrich Augustus III*) is decorated with a crown, scepter, electoral sword, and laurel wreath. Adorning another one (gal. no. P 164, Maurice Quentin de La Tour, *Maurice, Count of Saxony*) is a helmet. The frame for the pastel *Africa* (gal. no. P 32, Rosalba Carriera) features a small basket filled with flowers, and a similar but more opulent one can be seen on the

 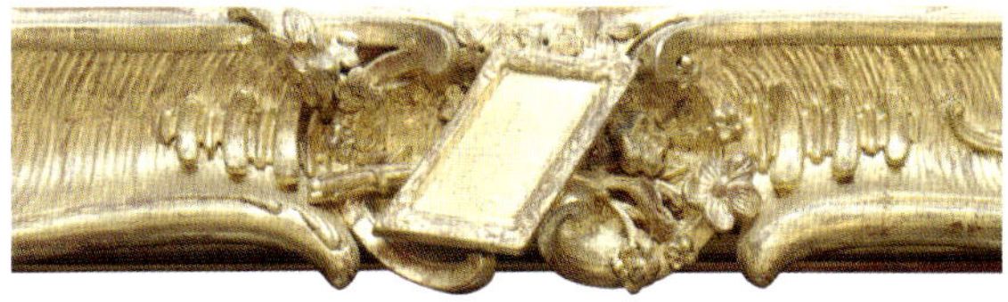

Fig. 3 Detail, center top and bottom

frame of the *Portrait of Ismael Mengs* (gal. no. P 165, Mengs). Carriera's *Virgin with Her Left Hand on Her Breast* (gal. no. P 65) is framed by a wreath of lily of the valley, a Marian symbol.[16] These attributes serve different functions by alluding to power or social position, or conveying religious or allegorical meanings. A few frames are more elaborate, even excessive (gal. nos. P 5, P 61, P 71),[17] whereas the carving on others is less virtuoso and more restrained (gal. no. P 163, La Tour, *Maria Josepha, Dauphine of France*). The corner and center ornaments sometimes project notably (gal. no. P 9, Carriera, *Louis XV of France as Dauphin*) or stay within the frame contours. The corners may be marked by a single C-shaped swept rail, by two S-shaped sweeps running towards each other, or by an outward-curved rocaille form. The carved moldings are often further defined by a pattern of grooves inscribed into the gesso. These grooves run perpendicular to the frame edge and can vary in direction and form. They are either straight (gal. no. P 159, Liotard, *Self-Portrait in Turkish Costume*), tilted in the same direction (gal. no. P 4, Carriera, *Giambattista Recanati*), or tilted in different directions in individual frame sections (gal. no. P 121, Carriera, *A Turk*). In many cases the narrow grooves are interspersed with a slightly wider band at more or less regular intervals. Further decorative elements, such as individual oval shapes, add to the range of variation (gal. no. P 160, Liotard, *Maurice, Count of Saxony*). A few frames have no grooves at all (gal. no. P 32, Carriera, *Africa*, and gal. no. P 29, Carriera, *Self-Portrait as "Winter"*). Carved into each of the top corners of the *Chocolate Girl* frame is a woven basket with a round base and wide flared rim, filled with flowers (fig. 1). The cartouche in the bottom left corner contains a detailed carving of strings of beads gathered with a narrow ribbon (fig. 2a).[18] The ends of the ribbon are secured by a rectangular clasp. In the bottom right corner is an oval purse with a metal kiss-lock closure (fig. 2b) and a decorative trim of floral shapes. Around its middle is a band holding two keys.[19] Conventional purses at the time were often "suspended from the waist by means of an attached hook or ring."[20] The *chatelaine*, a flat, teardrop-shaped hook decorated with a stylized flower can be seen above the purse.

The center ornament on the upper molding is a floral wreath (fig. 3a); six blooms linked by their stems form an oval, which is crowned by a slightly larger rose. The corresponding ornament at the bottom features a small mirror, its corners adorned with trefoil ornaments (fig. 3b). It rests atop a posy of forget-me-nots. The center cartouche on the left shows a piece of needlework; the first stitches have been cast on to four knitting needles, a ball of yarn lying next to them (fig. 4a).[21] The corresponding cartouche on the right contains a folded fan and a small bouquet tied with a ribbon (fig. 4b). The fan's guard is decorated with a row of beading. At its bottom end, accented by two circular shapes, a tiny hole can be made out for the pin that holds the fan's ribs together.[22]

Art-technological examination

The frames for the Dresden gallery and the Pastellkabinett were made by Matthäus Kugler and Joseph Deibel and their workshop. Deibel, born on January 29, 1716, in Grafendorf, Austria,[23] arrived in Dresden between 1741 and 1744 (fig. 5), where he rejoined his earlier teacher Kugler. The two worked together and Deibel became a member of the team of architects, artists, and craftsmen engaged in the creation of the new gallery. The interior of the Pastellkabinett was completed be-

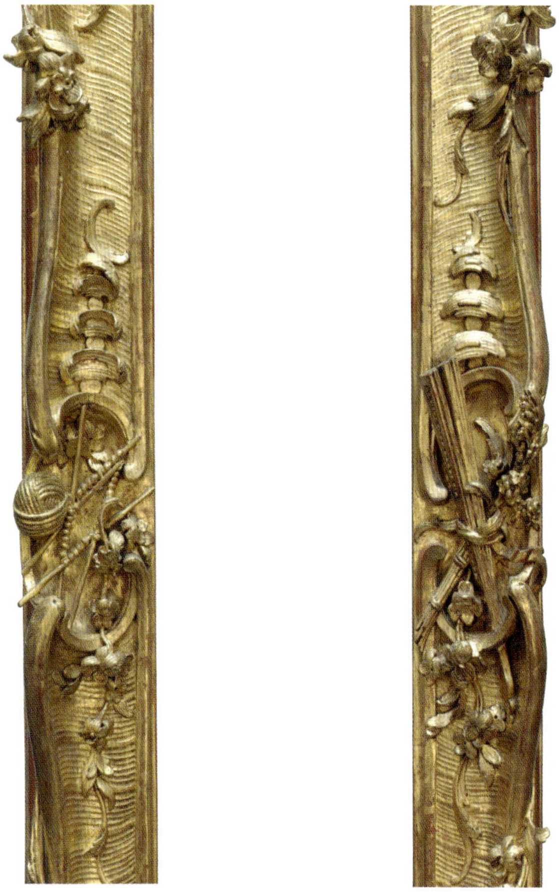

Fig. 4 Detail, center left and right

tween November 1745 and March 1746. In a list of expenditure totaling 2,200 thalers, only Kugler's name is included.[24] He is also listed as "Stall-Bildhauer" (Stable Sculptor) in all the court calendars from 1741 until his death in 1752,[25] whereas Deibel's name is never mentioned. Presumably this was because Deibel initially only worked as an ordinary sculptor in Kugler's workshop. He also worked for Count von Brühl and was repeatedly involved in building projects designed by Johann Christoph Knöffel.[26] In 1751 he was awarded the title "Hofgalleriebildhauer" (Court Gallery Sculptor) for his "demonstrated skill" in the making of frames.[27] He must have continued making the frames after Kugler's death in 1752; more than four hundred of the frames are thought to be his work.[28] As late as 1789, the now 73-year-old sculptor received a payment of 10 thalers for a frame.[29] He died in Dresden on May 18, 1792.[30]

The *Chocolate Girl's* frame was made from limewood[31] and was constructed in several layers. Its outer dimensions are 98 x 68.8 cm, the inner ones 83.3 x 53.5 cm. The frame moldings measure a maximum 8 cm wide and 9.5 cm deep. The basic frame consists of four wooden battens with vertical rabbet joints. The molding, glued to the former, is also rabbeted, but for better stability the joints are shifted 90 degrees. The projecting corner and center ornaments were applied as separate blocks of wood. The basic contour and decorative elements were all carved directly on the frame, a plane used only on the outer edge. What is striking is that the forms were worked out quite freely. The majority of the gallery frames were produced in an early assembly-line system. The profiles were prefabricated by the meter, cut to length, and glued onto the basic frame. Not so in the case of the pastel frames, which is further proof that they were individually crafted.

The surface of the wood was given a thin coating of size and between seven and ten layers of primer (a mix of size and whiting), which was sanded once dry.[32] This was followed by the carving of the gesso ground, which served to both structure the ornamented parts of the frame and redefine forms obscured in the application of the gesso. The surfaces were now sized again and then the poliment was applied. Typical of the Dresden frames is their coral-red color, derived from a mix of red and yellow bole (earth pigment). All areas that were to receive a polished gilding were given a thick coating, those that would later appear matte a thinner one. In a final step, the surface was polished and sealed. A mix of water and ethanol could then be applied and the gold leaf laid onto it. After drying, the gold surface was burnished with agate. Parts of the molding, like the gesso grooves for example, were left matte and given a coat of size to produce a darker gold tone. From the number of seams it is possible to determine that the applied sheets of gold leaf measured about 6 x 6 cm, and were therefore smaller than is customary today.[33]

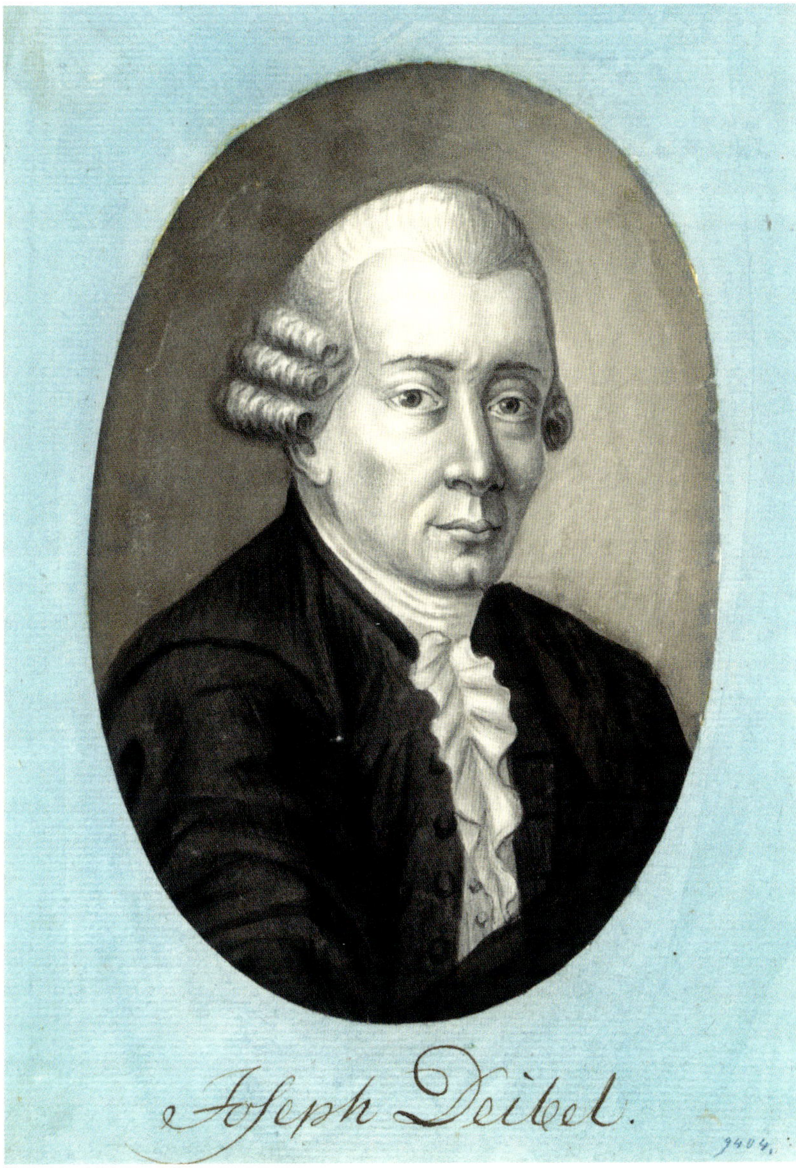

Fig. 5 **Unknown artist**, **Portrait of Joseph Deibel**, ca. 1800, brush drawing in black on oval paper, mounted on blue-tinted backing paper, 21.7 x 15.5 cm, Österreichische Nationalbibliothek, Porträtsammlung

History and Restorations

The Seven Years' War (1756–63) had a major impact on the Dresden gallery.[34] In 1759 the gallery's entire holdings were sent to Königstein for safekeeping.[35] But in that same year, the gallery curator Riedel was forced "to return by barge the best pieces among the pastels that had been taken to the fortress, since the pastels were stored where it was too damp and were suffering damage."[36] On July 12, 1760, a howitzer shell struck the gallery building and damaged the Pastellkabinett's windows.[37] In November 1760 the architect Julius Heinrich Schwarze reported that the Pastellkabinett had been bricked up for protection.[38] A short

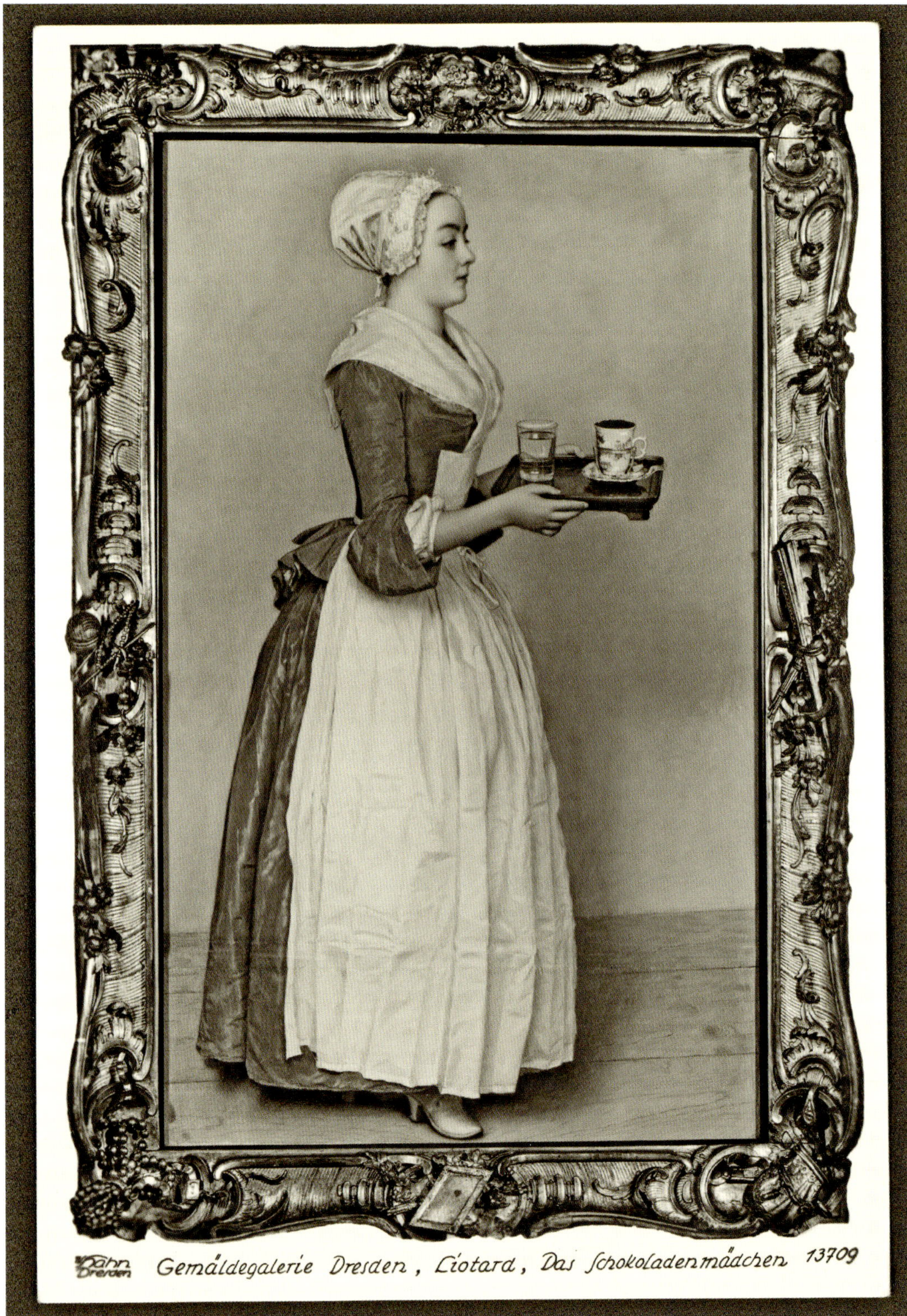
Gemäldegalerie Dresden, Liotard, Das Schokoladenmädchen 13709

time later, on Christmas Eve, Riedel confirmed in a letter to Brühl that in the event of further danger he would take all the pastels still remaining in Dresden back to Königstein.[39] In 1761 he packed 171 of them in crates with removable lids, "each screwed down carefully, and inserted with the utmost caution." However, he noted that, because of the time pressure, the packing "might not come off without damage."[40] In the end, the works were not moved at all,[41] and after the war had ended they were rehung. The Pastellkabinett remained until 1837, when the room became a restorers' workshop.[42] According to the annual report from 1839, the pastel paintings were taken down and stored leaning against the wall. Then, in 1841, they were hung on the pillars of the Outer Gallery.[43] There are but few records relating to the *Chocolate Girl*'s restoration history. The earliest mention of damage to Liotard's work is a written complaint to Minister von Lindenau by the gallery's curator Carl Schmidt from 1838: "I am, however, duty-bound to inform Your Excellency that on Saturday, the 26th of May, H. Matthäi [nephew of the gallery director Johann Friedrich Matthäi] took it upon himself to turn the Chocolate Girl by Liotard, which had been taken down and was leaning facing the wall, to show it to visitors, but put it back so clumsily that when he walked away it fell over with a loud crash and, owing to such a great upheaval, which pastel paintings cannot tolerate, a portion of the yellow of the corset, turned to dust, had fallen off and spread onto the background and the girl's white apron."[44]

In 1945 the pastel was taken to Moscow by one of the Soviet trophy brigades. Before it was returned to Dresden in 1956, the "Soviet Painting Passport" dated September 30, 1955, described its ornamental frame simply as "present."[45] As for its condition on its arrival in Moscow, it says: "Small, old, previously restored damage to the parchment as well as flaking of the pastel on the hand, the tray, between tray and blouse. Buckling and blistering of the parchment in the top corners. In the lower part of the painting the edges of a pasted strip had become detached." The use of the past tense suggests that the damage had been dealt with before the work's return.

Fig. 6 **Walter Hahn**, photograph of Jean-Étienne Liotard's *Chocolate Girl* with frame, between 1955 and 1964, Gemälderestaurierung, Staatliche Kunstsammlungen Dresden

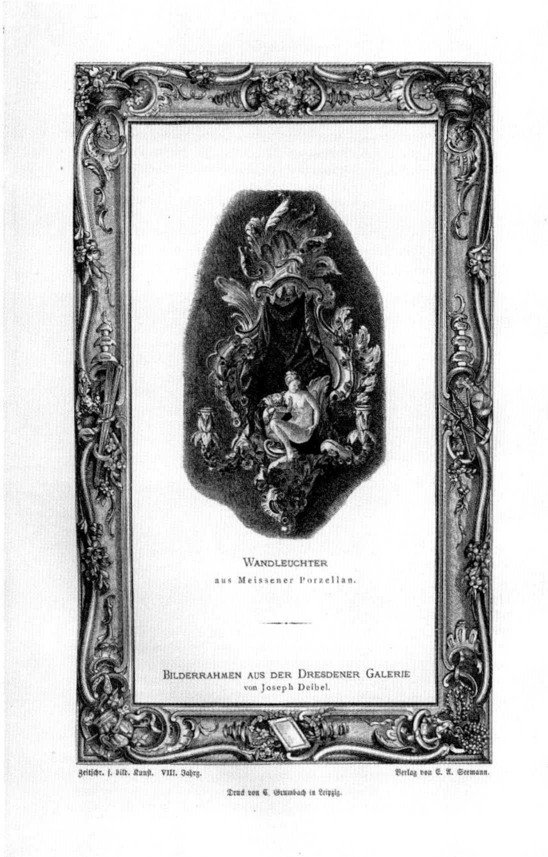

Fig. 7 **Ernst Eichler** (drawing) and **Hugo Kaeseberg** (woodcut), frame for the *Chocolate Girl*, from: *Lützows Zeitschrift für Bildende Kunst* 8 (1873)

The earliest known photo of the pastel with its frame, a print sold as a postcard, was made by the Dresden photographer Colmar Walter Hahn and must have been taken between 1955 and 1964 (fig. 6).[46] Unfortunately, the edges of the frame are not completely shown in this. Even so, it is possible to note several defects. Flowers are missing from both flower baskets, and portions of the left-hand center cartouche with the knitting needles had broken off. One of the two keys next to the purse is damaged, as is the bottom center cartouche with its mirror. A modeling clay repair is visible on the left-hand center cartouche.

In 1981, the gilder Günter Schulze worked on the frame, cleaning it and removing the modeling clay repair.[47] Missing elements were restored in wood, blemishes cemented and regilded. However, perhaps due to the lack of available illustrations at that time, the frame was not reconstructed precisely. Deviations can be detected on the basis of the earliest known illustration of the frame, an engraving from 1873 (fig. 7).[48] After restoration, the knitwork, originally with four needles, has five. The two strands originally coming away from the ball of yarn were not reconstructed at all. A small remaining piece of yarn was interpreted as part of the adjacent floral vine and restored accordingly. The key lying atop the middle of the purse is now twice as long as it was originally. Flowers in the baskets have been arranged differently and have modified shapes. Badly abraded gold sections and unsightly spots have been regilded, among them the mirror on the bottom center ornament. In June 1981, Schulze recorded: "Frame finished and hung in the gallery."[49]

The special beauty of its ornamental frame has doubtless contributed to the popularity of the *Chocolate Girl*. No other pastel frame places such emphasis on depicting objects associated with femininity, or shows a comparable symbolism and wealth of sculptural woodwork.

1 Giovanni Lodovico Bianconi, *Historische Lobschrift auf den Ritter Anton Raphael Mengs*, Zürich 1781, p. 18.

2 See Tristan Weddigen, *Die Sammlung als sichtbare Kunstgeschichte: Die Dresdner Gemäldegalerie im 18. und 19. Jahrhundert*, habilitation thesis University of Bern 2008, p. 19: "Hanging of the works in the cabinet from 1750–53, but also already in 1745–46;" see Sächsisches Hauptstaatsarchiv Dresden (HStADD), 10036 Finanzarchiv, Loc. 35823, No. 46, "Specification des Geldbetrages vom 11. August 1746."

3 Furnishing of the gallery begun in 1747. See HStADD, *Akten der Generaldirektion der Königlichen Sammlungen*, Cap. VIIa, 1a, original lost in the war 1945, copy in the archives of the Staatliche Kunstsammlungen Dresden (SKD-A), Nachlass Hans Posse (NL Posse), no. 21, Lage 7, Blatt 1b.

4 Dimensions derived from the key in Michael Keyl, "Grundriss des Galeriegebäudes," in: *Recueil d'Estampes d'après les plus célèbres Tableaux de la Galerie Royale de Dresde*, vol. 1, 1753 (1 Saxon foot = 28.319 cm).

5 Dimensions derived from the key in "Längsschnitt Obergeschoss," Landesamt für Denkmalpflege Saxony, Plansammlung, inv. no. M6. VI, Bl. 9 (1 ell = 56,638 cm). See the illustration in the essay on the Pastellkabinett by Roland Enke in this volume.

6 Bianconi 1781, pp. 18–19.

7 Ibid, p. 18.

8 See Siegfried E. Fuchs, *Der Bilderrahmen*, Recklinghausen 1985, p. 22.

9 See Weddigen 2008, reconstruction of the hangings, not including the Pastellkabinett.

10 See Bianconi 1781, p. 18, Liotard's works next to the doors; see [Johann Anton Riedel], *Verzeichniss der Gemälde, welche in der Churfürstl. Gallerie zu Dresden befindlich sind*, Dresden 1801, p. 178: "at the entrance to the right of the door."

11 Jean Antoine Riedel and Chrêtien Frederic Wenzel, *Catalogue des tableaux de la galerie electorale a dresde*, Dresden 1765; named pastels: fifty-five by Carriera, ten by A. R. Mengs, four by Liotard, two by La Tour, and two by Th. Mengs.

12 Riedel/Wenzel 1765, p. 239, note: "Tous ces portraits, de même que ceux, qui ne sont pas connu & qui composent la collection, au nombre de 157."

13 The three most common formats and matching historical paper formats: I: 505–595 x 410–490 mm (= median I and II); II: 285–340 x 230–380 mm (= quarto); III: 400–490 x 310–390 (= double folio and ledger).

14 See notes 11 and 12.

15 Christoph Schölzel, ed., *Die blendenden Rahmen*, Worms 2005, p. 26.

16 Ernst Badstübner et al., *Christliche Ikonographie in Stichworten*, Leipzig 1973, p. 252: "Maiglöckchen = Marienblumen" (Lily of the Valley = Flowers of the Virgin Mary).

17 Gal. no. P 5, Carriera, *Maria Josepha*; gal. no. P 61, Carriera, *Mary Magdalen with a Book*; gal. no. P 71, Carriera, *Gentleman in yellow waistcoat and pale-blue coat*.

18 Possibly a three-string necklace.

19 Gottlieb Siegmund Corvinus, called Amaranthes, *Nutzbares, galantes und curiöses Frauenzimmer-Lexicon*, Leipzig 1739, p. 1415: "A key

chain is a chain, provided with a hook, on which women affix their keys and . . . tend to hang them from their waist."

20 Ibid., p. 1981.

21 Knitting was not exclusively women's work. See the depiction of a man knitting socks by Annibale Carracci, as well as Simon Guillain's *Calsettaro*, 1646, engraving, no. 66 from the series *Le Arti di Bologna*; also Peter Nathanael Sprengel, *Handwerke und Künste in Tabellen*, vol. 15, Berlin 1777, pp. 188–209.

22 George Woolliscroft Rhead, *History of the Fan*, London 1910, p. 121. It took fifteen to twenty people to make a fan, an accessory doubtless too costly for a parlor maid.

23 Johann Huber, *Marktgemeinde Grafendorf bei Hartberg: Straßennamen. Herkunft und Bedeutung*, Grafendorf 2003, p. 21: his birthplace, Kleinlungitz No. 1, Grafendorf, still stands.

24 See HStADD, 10036 Finanzarchiv, Loc. 35823, No. 46. "Specification des Geldbetrages vom 11. August 1746."

25 *Königlicher Polnischer und Churfürstlich Sächsischer Hof- und Staatskalender*, 1741, p. 16; 1752, p. 24.

26 Architectural carvings and interior decor, for example: Residenzschloss, Kurländer Palais, Taschenbergpalais, and Palais Hoym, Dresden; Brühl Palace, Warsaw; Schloss Pförten (Brody, Poland).

27 HStADD, 10026 Geheimes Kabinett, Loc. 896, vol. VI, 1744–51, p. 390.

28 Heinrich Keller, *Nachrichten von allen in Dresden lebenden Künstlern*, Leipzig 1788, p. 35.

29 SKD-A, NL Posse, vol. 23, Lage 1, p. 6.

30 Julius Hübner, *Verzeichniss der Königlichen Gemälde-Gallerie zu Dresden*, Dresden 1884, note p. 472.

31 The gallery frames, by contrast, were made of pine and limewood.

32 See Johann Heinrich Zedler, ed., *Grosses vollständiges Universal Lexicon aller Wissenschafften und Künste*, vol. 47, Halle and Leipzig 1756, p. 777.

33 Wilhelm Oehmigcke, *Neue Bilder Gallerie für junge Söhne und Töchter*, vol. 7, Berlin 1800, p. 85: "Squares some two inches long and wide."

34 Woldemar von Seidlitz, "Die Schicksale der Dresdner Gemäldegalerie während des Siebenjährigen Krieges," in: *Dresdner Geschichtsblätter* 4, no. 2 (1895), pp. 184–87.

35 SKD-A, NL Posse, no. 21, Lage 7, Bl. 6.

36 Ibid.

37 Ibid.

38 Ibid., Lage 1, no page number, 127 note, Julius Heinrich Schwarze to Brühl.

39 Ibid., Lage 13, no page number, to Brühl.

40 Ibid, Lage 13, Bl. 5, to the Secretary of the Upper Chamber.

41 Seidlitz 1895, p. 186: "The pictures appear to have remained in Dresden."

42 SKD-A, NL Posse, vol. 30, Lage 5, Bl. 1.

43 Ibid., Lage 7, Bl. 6.

44 Ibid., Lage 5, no. 161.

45 Archive of the Old Masters Restoration Workshop, Soviet Painting Protocol no. 398.

46 Verso inscribed "EVP DM." Since the Deutsche Mark was issued in the GDR from 1948 to 1964, the photo must date from between the work's return in 1956 and the end of the currency being issued. I am grateful to Christoph Schölzel for providing me with the photo.

47 Archive of the Old Masters Restoration Workshop, logbook 1981, January 1 to June 5, 1981.

48 Albert von Zahn, "Barock, Rococo und Zopf," in: *Lützows Zeitschrift für Bildende Kunst* 8 (1873), pp. 1–44, illustration between pp. 38 and 39. Digital comparison of the engraving with a current photo shows virtually complete conformity with the exception of the restored carvings.

49 Archive of the Old Masters Restoration Workshop, logbook 1981, June 1, 1981.

CHOCOLATE, TEA, COFFEE

A Brief History of the Europeanization of Three Exotic Hot Beverages

Susanne Drexler

"Chocolate . . . is a brown or reddish paste, prepared from cacao alone or with the addition of various other things and spices mixed with sugar, that is cooked in milk (with the addition of several eggs), occasionaly also in wine, and drunk hot like tea or coffee, also eaten like a soup with crumbled sweetmeat. The drink prepared from it is likewise called chocolate, like the aforementioned paste."[1]

This description from Johann Georg Krünitz's *Oeconomische Encyclopädie* provides some insight into the preparation and ingredients of the "chocolate drink" in the eighteenth century. For, what Jean-Étienne Liotard's *Chocolate Girl* is about to serve an unseen recipient, is typical of chocolate consumption in the Baroque period: a hot drink composed of cacao with milk or water and laced with spices, often drunk as a breakfast pick-me-up. Up until around 1800, the idea of "chocolate" was associated with this method of preparation, not with its present-day, primarily solid form as a chocolate bar.

Along with tea and coffee, chocolate is one of the three exotic hot beverages to have reached Europe since the sixteenth century as colonial imports by various routes from China and Japan, Arabia, and Central America. Travelers and traders also brought along from there traditional preparation methods and drinking customs. In Europe, the three beverages would for the first time be brought together,[2] and for nearly three centuries were perceived as a unity and always related to each other, despite their different origins.[3] The spectacular novelty of these consumer goods brought with it enduring cultural changes;[4] they influenced trade, lifestyles, and social conventions. At the beginning of its career, chocolate was seen as a medicament and was only gradually promoted to become a luxury beverage and status symbol at Europe's princely courts. Along with the other two imports, its exclusivity did not remain limited to the precious substance itself, but was to an increasing degree also reflected in the vessels in which it was served and the rooms it was consumed in.[5]

A new European invention was the cultural blend of forms for the consumption of the three hot beverages, resulting in the design of combined coffee, tea, and chocolate services in the eighteenth century, the very first examples of which found use as diplomatic gifts. One such was the service belonging to Queen Elisabeth Farnese of Spain (fig. 1), which she received as a gift in 1738 on the occasion of the marriage of Maria Amalia of Saxony to her son Charles III.[6] Decorated with Höroldt chinoiseries (named after the porcelain painter Johann Gregorius Höroldt), the service reflects the West's enthusiasm for all things East Asian, and its exotic character was ideally suited to the consumption of the exotic hot beverages, not least because it was made of porcelain, a material that also had its origins in China. The miniature-like scenes picture exotically clad Chinese figures, promenading, drinking tea, or smoking, with Elisabeth Farnese's coat of arms at their center. The spread of the new

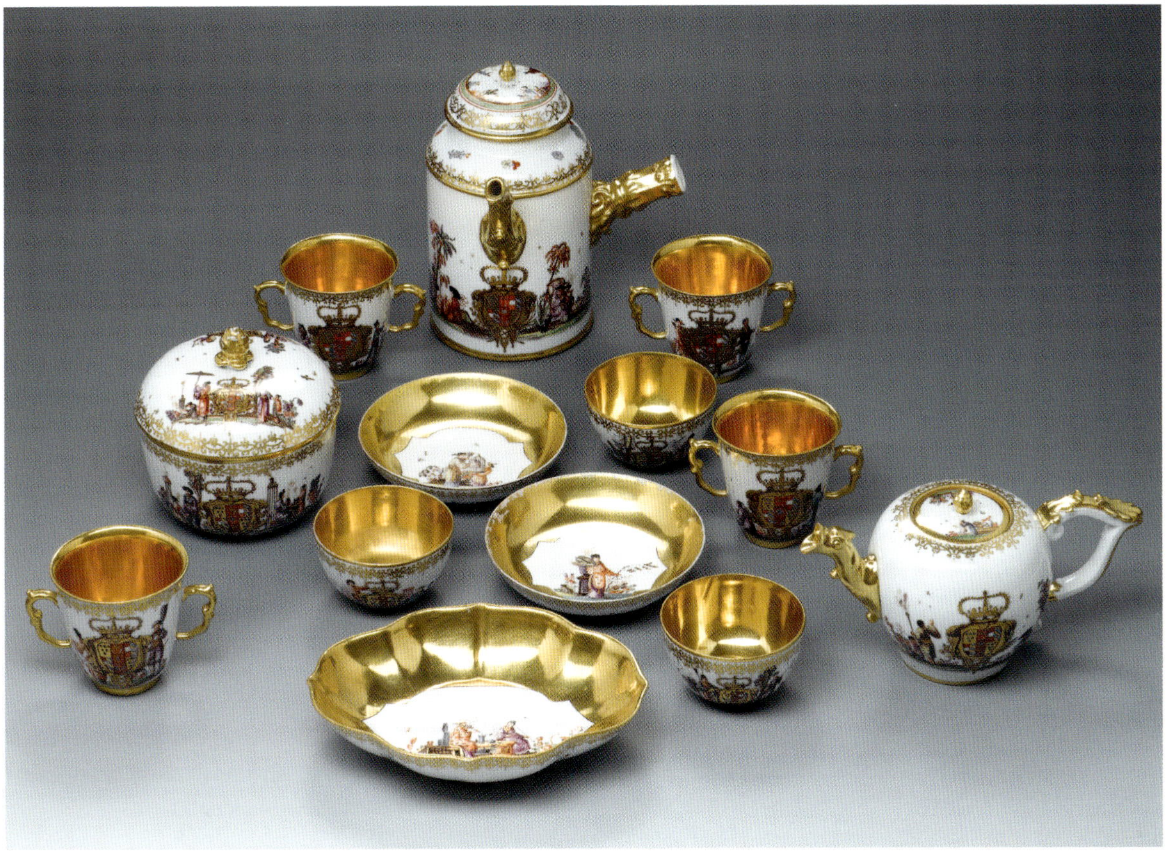

Fig. 1 **Part of a coffee, tea, and chocolate service with chinoiseries and the coat of arms of Elisabeth Farnese**; Meissen Porcelain Manufactory, ca. 1728, Porzellansammlung, Staatliche Kunstsammlungen Dresden

hot drinks was doubtless a factor in the invention of European porcelain in 1708 by Johann Friedrich Böttger in Meissen, where the first uniform services were produced[7]: for such precious beverages it was necessary to create appropriately artistic serving pieces. It was not uncommon for the drinks' different countries of origin to be featured in the decoration of such wares.

Cacao came originally from Mesoamerica, a region in Central America inhabited by various peoples with similar cultures. The high cultures of the Olmecs (1500–400 BCE), the Maya (classic period 250–900 CE, postclassic period up until final colonization by the Spanish around 1697), and the Aztecs (thirteenth century up until colonization by the Spanish in 1519–1521) were already using cacao beans to prepare a frothy drink that was mainly restricted to their aristocracies.[8] The Maya cultivated cacao in great quantities and sold the beans to neighboring peoples like the Aztecs. Based on vessels from the Andes region, one can assume that its wider distribution began around 1000 BCE. Details regarding the preparation of the cacao beverage come primarily from inscriptions and paintings on ceramics—for example, in the Maya script, a glyph resembling a fish stands for cacao—less often from the few surviving written documents from the thirteenth to sixteenth centuries. From these it is clear that shallow bowls and high-walled cups were used in the drink's consumption. Tall earthenware cups from Mexico reached Europe with the Spanish, beginning in the sixteenth century, their material associated with the medicinal effects attributed to chocolate (see cat. 28). For both the Maya and the Aztecs cacao played an important role in economic, political, and ritual life. Its close association with religion is exemplified by the deity Ek-Chuah: she was both goddess of war and patron deity of merchants and the cacao tree. The high regard for the substance is also evident from the fact that dried cacao beans were used as currency.[9]

Preparation of cacao by the Maya and Aztecs was similar; however, the former preferred to drink it warm, the latter cold. The Maya used the word *kakaw* for both the drink and the fruit. It was probably only in the sixteenth century that the new word *chocolatl* came to be used for the drink. It derives from the Aztec word *cacahuatl* (from *xococ* = bitter, and *latl* = water) and is not documented before the arrival of the Spanish in Mesoamerica. The importance of cacao for the inhabitants of Central America is still reflected in Europe centuries later in the botanical name for the cacao tree: in his botanical nomenclature Carl Linnaeus called it *Theobroma cacao* (*theos* = god, *broma* = food, i.e. "food of the gods").[10]

The Europeans' discovery of cacao coincided with the conquest of South and Central America in the sixteenth century. Christopher Columbus was probably the first to get to know it, having tried the acclaimed *xocoatl* in 1502.[11] A good fifteen years later, the conquistador Hernán Cortés laid the foundation for Spain's colonial empire, reaching the Aztec capital under Montezuma II in 1519. Bernal Diaz del Castillo, who accompanied Cortés, repeatedly describes the enjoyment of chocolate at Montezuma's court: "From time to time they brought him, in cup-shaped vessels of pure gold, a certain drink made from cacao that was said to awaken certain appetites. . . . After the prince, the guards ate and the rest of the household, then the women and female servants, bakers, and cacao cooks."[12] With the conquest of Central America, the Spaniards began to import the beans to their homeland. For the first one hundred years, consumption of chocolate remained limited mainly to Spain, which also held the trading monopoly. The first evidence of the cacao beverage in Europe dates from 1544—a group of Dominican monks from present-day Guatemala traveled with a delegation of Maya nobles to the Spanish court and brought with them numerous gifts for Prince Philipp of Spain, among them containers of chocolate.[13]

In parallel with chocolate, beginning in the last third of the sixteenth century, coffee, previously known mainly in Islamic cultures, found its way to Europe by way of travelers.[14] Despite political conflicts, such as the Turkish Wars in the sixteenth and seventeenth centuries, closer contacts were established with the oriental[15] world. The first European to mention coffee, probably having sampled it himself, was the Augsburg physician and naturalist Leonhart Rauwolf; in his printed travel report from the Orient he conveyed the first news of coffee from Aleppo in 1573/74: "Among other things they have a good drink they call *chaube* that they prize highly; it is nearly as black as ink, and in infirmity is very beneficial to the stomach."[16] Numerous descriptions of everyday life provide a sense of how widespread the beverage—which later became known in Europe as the "Turkish drink"—was in the Near East. The first small quantities of coffee presumably arrived in Europe in the mid seventeenth century by way of the traditional Levantine traders importing goods from the eastern Mediterranean.[17]

The first reports of tea reached Europe in the mid sixteenth century. In his book *Delle Navigatione et Viaggi*, published in 1559, the Venetian historian and geographer Giambattista Ramusio reported on its cultivation in China, its preparation, and beneficial properties. Tea from East Asia first arrived in Europe by way of the Dutch East India Company—along the same trading routes as porcelain—and its use slowly spread.

Even though the three beverages established a foothold in Europe at much the same time, chocolate was the first of the three stimulants to become adopted in the West, followed by tea and coffee.[18] All three could only be imported through countries with colonies. In Germany, their trade and increasing use was therefore primarily governed by France,

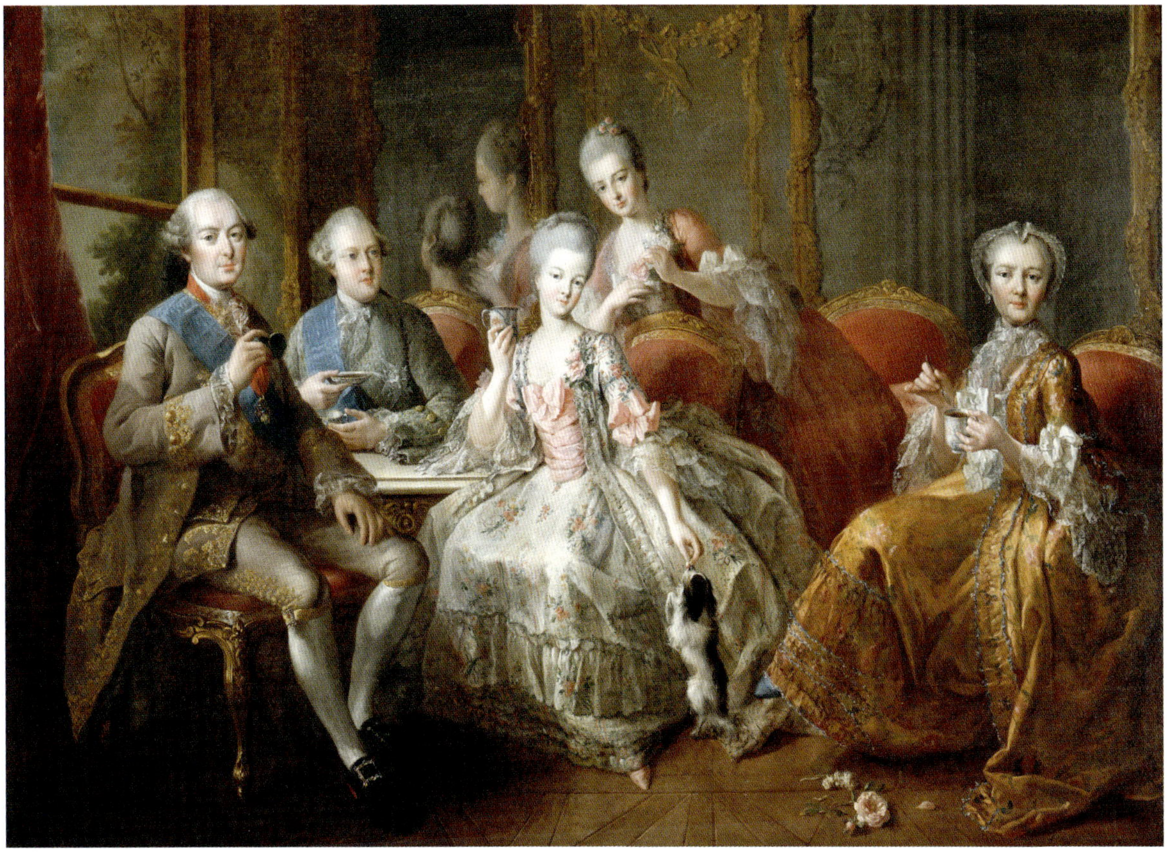

Fig. 2 **Jean-Baptiste Charpentier, La Tasse de Chocolat,** ca. 1768, oil on canvas, 177 x 255 cm, Château de Versailles et Trianon

the Netherlands, and Great Britain, in addition to Spain. Because it was distributed by way of the Catholic countries Spain and France, chocolate came to be seen as a mainly Catholic beverage, in contrast to the Protestant coffee.[19] As a luxury drink, chocolate was in fact highly popular among the higher clergy. The Catholic Church promoted the enjoyment of chocolate in Europe by recognizing it as a drink for fast days.[20] Within the Church, the question of whether chocolate should be considered a food or a beverage was hotly debated, in accordance with the dictum "liquidum non frangit jejunum" ("liquid does not break fast"). Pope Gregory XIII had already spoken in favor of chocolate in this regard.[21] This debate, which continued for nearly three hundred years, was also influenced by Cardinal Laurentius Brancati, a declared chocolate lover, who, in his treatise *De Chocolatis potu diatribe* (On the use of chocolate) from 1664, argued for its enjoyment during fast times and even included an ode to the "much vaunted drink of the gods."[22]

Today, chocolate has become an integral part of everyday life and is affordable to all social classes. However, well into the eighteenth century, it was an especially exotic beverage—and as such one of the most expensive drinks to be consumed in Europe. Up until its popularization in the nineteenth century, when industrial production of chocolate became a reality, it was largely restricted to the aristocracy. Chocolate was probably introduced to the French market by Jews fleeing the Inquisition in Spain and Portugal, who were granted asylum by King Henry IV. The well-known story that Anna of Austria, daughter of the Spanish king Philipp III, introduced chocolate to the French court on her marriage to Louis XIII in 1615 was probably invented by Jean Anthelme Brillat-Savarin in his *Physiology of Taste* from 1825, thinking of the role played by Spain in its distribution.[23] Yet the increased popularity of chocolate in French high society between 1650 and 1660 was fostered by another infanta: Maria Theresa of Spain, married to Louis XIV. In addition to numerous reports about her immoderate consumption of chocolate,[24] there are other sources that provide glimpses of the presence of chocolate at the French court and also attest to the medicinal virtues attributed to it, as in the letters of the Marquise de Sevigné, whose opinion about the effect of chocolate constantly fluctuated, and the Sun King's sister-in-law, Princess Lieselotte of the Palatinate, who could not abide the stuff: "for I can tolerate neither coffee, tea, nor chocolate, cannot imagine how people can enjoy drinking it. Tea reminds me of hay and manure, coffee of soot and lupine beans, and chocolate is too sweet for me, so I do not like any of them; chocolate gives me stomach ache."[25] In 1669, coffee also reached the court of Louis XIV in the luggage of the ambassador of Mohammed IV.

The three hot beverages not only changed drinking habits—they took the place of the alcohol until then consumed even at breakfast—but also social intercourse. In the Late Baroque and Rococo periods, chocolate was a symbol of material luxury; consumption of it was orchestrated as an element of court ceremonial. At court, chocolate was drunk mainly for breakfast, often at the so-called *levée*, the monarch's traditional morning reception of members of the high nobility, especially at absolutist courts, which provided an intimate yet elegant setting for the indulgence. The regent Philippe d'Orléans, for example, would render judicial judgments in a small circle in his bedroom over a cup of chocolate.[26] And in France the phrase *aller au chocolat* ("attend the chocolate") meant "to stand in the regent's favor."[27]

Following the example of the French court, the princely courts of Central Europe also adopted the consumption of chocolate—albeit in the German states, owing to the Thirty Years' War, somewhat later, toward the end of the seventeenth century. Chocolate arrived at the Viennese court with Emperor Charles VI, who was forced in 1712 to renounce his claim to the Spanish throne, but brought back to Austria such cultural peculiarities as chocolate. It was under him that Pietro Buonaventura Metastasio, court poet in Vienna since 1729, wrote the *Cantata alla Cioccolata*. Charles's daughter Maria Theresa, apparently unlike her husband, didn't care for chocolate. In 1775 she wrote to Countess Enzenberg: "I would like it . . . that the chocolate pleases you . . . if you wish to have more of it, you only need tell your son which kind you prefer; I know nothing about it, for I never drink it."[28] Even so, Maria Theresa had an elaborate breakfast service with pots for tea, coffee, milk, and chocolate (see cat. 34, fig. p. 70), the matching réchaud was probably used for the cacao. Today it is preserved in Vienna's Kunstkammer, together with a toiletries set that belonged to Emperor Francis I. The so-called *Nachtzeug* (night service) recalls the staged ritual of the *levée* attended by guests. The scarcely used gold service probably served mainly for display, underscoring the prominent place of these expensive drinks at court.

In Rococo painting there are a number of scenes in which chocolate is pictured as a breakfast drink, as in François Boucher's *Le Déjeuner* from 1739. And in his 1768 painting *La Tasse de Chocolat* (fig. 2) Jean-Baptiste Charpentier quite pointedly places the hot drink before the viewer as a status symbol: each member of the de Penthièvre family holds a precious cup in their hands; instead of chocolate, the second man from the right appears to be drinking coffee from a saucer, a European invention, like the handle on the chocolate cup. And a painting from 1757 by Johann Georg Ziesenis shows Charles Theodore of the Palatinate, in a morning robe in his private chamber, in front of him a *trembleuse* (cup and saucer) with a water glass and chocolate mug (see cat. 35).

At the Dresden court, the hot drinks coffee, tea, and chocolate were already being served under the elector Frederick Augustus I.[29] As early as 1674, "Indian chocolate" was listed among the valuable

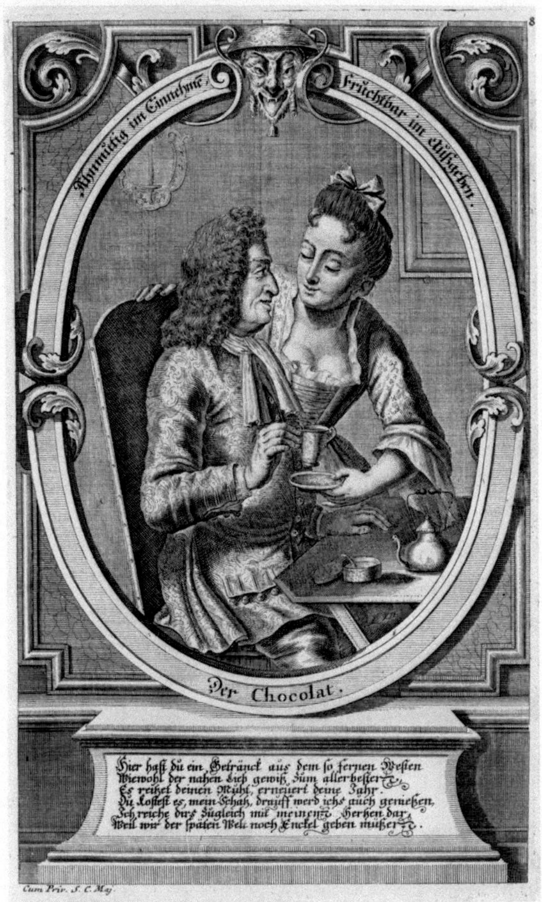

Fig. 3 **Martin Engelbrecht**, **Der Chocolat**, ca. 1740, from the series *Die Geschmacksempfindungen*, engraving, 29.3 x 18.8 cm, Kunstbibliothek, Staatliche Museen zu Berlin

items available from the elector's apothecary, Georg Fester—a fact that underscores the high value accorded to cacao.[30] Its association with Central America, here evident from the designation "Indian," is also seen in goldsmithing: the Golden Coffee Service created by Johann Melchior Dinglinger for Augustus II is the earliest example of pseudo Far-Eastern decorations suggestive of the countries origin of the three beverages considered exotic. Discreet references to chocolate are seen on the lids: beauties adorned with feathers were doubtless meant to symbolize Central America (see cat. 31). The estate of Saxony's prime minister Heinrich Count von Brühl also included chocolate: accountings include a "charge for 186 sticks and 369 bars of chocolate."[31] The precise listing is owing to the fact that Brühl had enriched himself from the state coffers, and his fortune was impounded after his death in 1763.

The spread of chocolate in the German states was accompanied by a number of treatises documenting its virtues, preparation, and effects. Particularly emphasized were its medicinal uses. Whereas tobacco had already awakened the interest of medicine in the second half of the sixteenth century, chocolate was only discovered as an elixir in the first half of the seventeenth century, coffee and tea in the second half.[32] For a long time, these colonial products appear to have been sold mainly in apothecaries; because of its high nutritional value, chocolate, especially, was considered a restorative. Dresden's court apothecary began to carry chocolate in the mid seventeenth century, and coffee from around 1685.[33]

The many written sources focus on both the positive and the negative aspects of its consumption. The first medical essay on the subject in Europe, the *Curiosos tratado de la naturaleza y calidad del chocolate,* published by the Andalusian physician Antonio Colmenero de Ledesmas in 1631, was rapidly disseminated and often quoted, if not by name, for example by the author of the *Drey curieuse Tractätgen* (cat. 29).[34] According to this, coffee was an aid to breathing, tea helped to cure headache, as well as chest and eye pain, and chocolate was recommended for the stomach and as a daily reinvigoration; at the same time, however, he warned that it could also lead to obesity. In 1694 the German physician and novelist Johann Christoph Ettner wrote about the medicinal benefits of morning consumption of chocolate: "I consider it most beneficial in the mornings, although it is also very useful in the evenings, especially to those who disregard supper; chocolate is beneficial for all ages, we are more assured in its preparation and steeping than with tea, which is why I consider a small cup of hot chocolate, having just been boiled in water, more valuable than fifty cups of tea or coffee."[35] Cornelius Bontekoe, personal physician to Frederick William of Brandenburg, called the Great Elector, was a fervent champion of the new hot beverages and introduced them to the Prussian court. In his book *Kurtze Abhandlung Von dem Menschlichen Leben, Gesundheit, Kranckheit, und Tod* (Brief treatise on human life, health, sickness, and death) from 1692, he recommended coffee and tea as alternatives to wine and beer, tea as beneficial for the stomach, mouth, and blood, and chocolate as an especially invigorating drink: "It is good for the stomach and makes a good drink, especially if one refrains from adding too much sugar."[36] But negative effects were also discussed, as suggested by the title *Von dem Missbrauch heisser und hitziger Speisen und Geträncke, sonderlich aber Des Caffes, Schockolate und Thees* (On the misuse of hot and heated foods and drinks, but especially coffee, chocolate, and tea).[37] As late as 1777, Carl Linnaeus recommended chocolate for such ailments as consumption, emaciation, and melancholy, but at the same time warned against excessive use of coffee: "Of those three beverages unknown to the ancients that have come to us from foreign lands and have now become well known through frequent use, tea, coffee, and chocolate, the former two are drunk most often; however, that does not make them preferable to or healthier than the latter, which does not affect the body so greatly . . . and is of benefit in many ailments."[38]

From the mid seventeenth to the eighteenth century there was general agreement about the special aphrodisiac effect of chocolate, about which Castillo had already reported from the court of Montezuma,[39] and this notion was linked to the "profane sphere of royal houses with respect to fantasy and desire."[40] The engraver Martin Engelbrecht illustrated this feature in the engraving *Der Chocolat* (fig. 3), from his allegorical series *Der Menschen Zung und Gurgel Weid zur Notturfft und Ergötzlichkeit vorgestellt durch die unterschiedlichen Arten der Geträncke* from the middle of the eighteenth century. An elegantly dressed lady is seductively handing a man a cup of chocolate. The caption refers to its intended effect: "Here you have a beverage from the so distant west . . . . If you drink it, my love, I will also get pleasure from it. I present it to you along with my heart, for we still have to provide grandchildren for the world to come." Ettner, too, writes that chocolate gives "potency . . . to the knights of Venus."[41] As we see in the paintings as well, the Rococo's "playfully erotic spirit"[42] is also reflected in chocolate.

What did hot cacao taste like in the eighteenth century? It certainly was not as sweet as today's chocolate. Recipes for its preparation are found in nearly all the treatises on it, as well as in housekeeping texts. The addition of sugar made chocolate more popular: in the course of their colonization in the sixteenth century, the Spanish introduced sugar cane for planting in Central America and used the product obtained from it in the preparation of a sweet chocolate drink.[43] First a cacao paste was made: the roasted, shelled cacao beans were pulverized, sometimes over a heat source (see cat. 25), and the heat turned the beans into a thick paste. To this, various flavorings were added, among them cinnamon, Mexican pepper, cloves, vanilla, almonds, lemon peel, etc. From these spiced pieces of chocolate, the drink was produced in different flavors, as described in Amaranthes' *Frauenzimmer-Lexikon* from 1715.[44] It was served as follows: "Chocolate, however, is prepared in the following manner: place 6 to 8 half ounces in a pitcher of boiling milk to make it quite good and strong; but if cooked with water use at least 15 or 16 half ounces to a pitcher, and also increase the number of eggs; beat 2 to 3 egg yolks into the milk and let everything boil up well, meanwhile frequently stirring with a spoon or whisk until everything is well blended, and when it foams and is well cooked and risen, serve it in the vessels set out for it, and slurp it in careful sips."[45] Thus, the Europeans essentially adopted the Mexican way of preparing it, but they further developed the serving pieces. To prepare it, they used a chocolate whisk (see cat. 27), a chocolate pot, usually with an opening in the lid into which the whisk was inserted, as well as a long, straight handle on the side to hold the hot pot. One of the earliest examples of such a specially shaped chocolate pot is found in the service

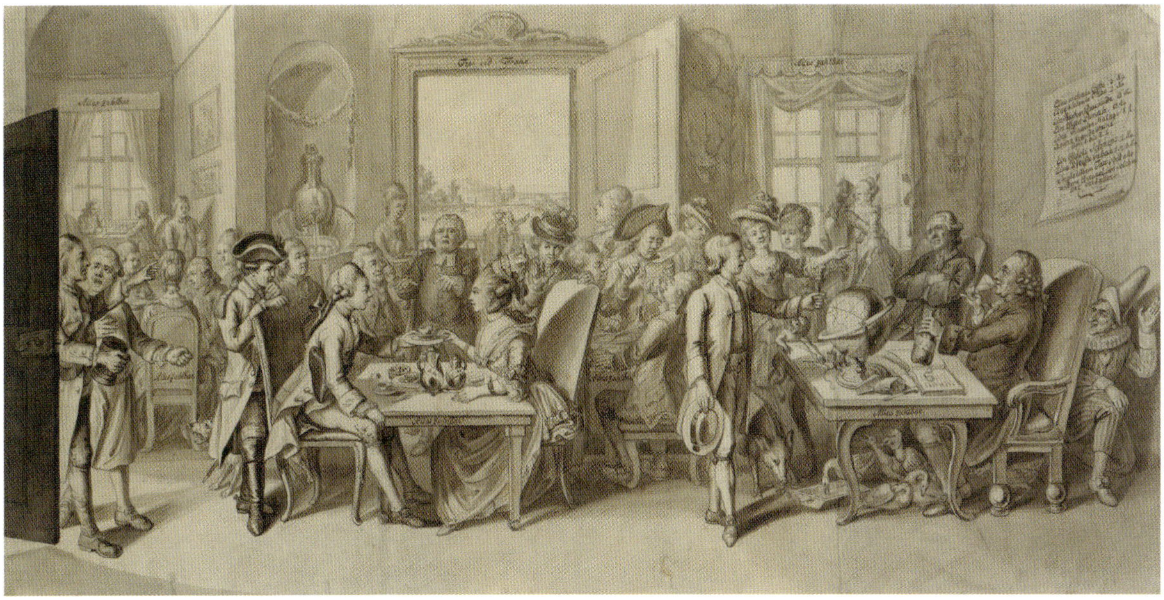

Fig. 4 **Unknown artist**, **A Public Coffeehouse**, German, ca. 1770, pen and brush in brown ink, 35.4 x 73.5 cm, Kupferstich-Kabinett, Staatliche Kunstsammlungen Dresden

made for Elisabeth Farnese—today sadly without its wooden handle. In addition, with this pot it was necessary to remove the lid to use the whisk. Whisking served both to make it frothy and to blend the ingredients, especially to prevent the cacao oil and liquid from separating. Cups were functionally adapted for this process: the Meissen manufactory was the first to add two handles to tall cups, which were held in place on a saucer and holder, generally silver, to become a *trembleuse*, like the chocolate cup in Maria Theresa's set (see cat. 34). This way, cups had a more secure footing, preventing their turning and spilling when stirring the drink. Chocolate was frequently served with a glass of water, as can be seen in the *Chocolate Girl*. For this purpose, suitable services were produced with matching water glasses and porcelain cups, as in the example by Johann Jakob Adam (see cat. 35)—the ultimate in elegant living in the eighteenth century. So as to be able to have the precious drink available at all times and take it along on journeys, compact cases and travel sets were made, usually containing a porcelain cup and saucer, a wooden whisk that could be taken apart, and tin containers for the chocolate pieces and sugar. It was a long time, however, before chocolate found favor with the bourgeois public. The coffeehouse culture, had already gained a foothold in the cities of the West by the second half of the seventeenth century. It was based on an Arab tradition adopted from the Ottomans, and also had parallels with the Chinese teahouse.[46] In Vienna, coffeehouses existed from around 1700. By 1725 it was possible to buy chocolate on the street and prepare it at home. Dresden, too, already sported coffeehouses in the eighteenth century;[47] the Saxon chronist Johann Christian Krell wrote in 1719: "The licensed public coffeehouses are also frequently visited by distinguished patrons, the best known among them is the French one on Schloss-Gasse, where in the evening especially, the most genteel cavaliers and ladies amuse themselves with coffee, chocolate, a good drop of wine, lemonade, also tobacco, and read the gazettes in any number languages."[48] Chocolate was often served in coffeehouses as well, but there were also separate chocolate parlors, especially in England, patronized by the nobility and the upper-class bourgeoisie. An anonymous German drawing from around 1770 (fig. 4) shows the interior of a public coffeehouse, emphasizing the often poor reputation of these establishments, where the elevated middle classes, who were gradually adopting the customs of the nobility, were amusing themselves in an almost dissolute manner. On the right, a price list hangs on the wall: a "mug of chocolate" costs 6 kreuzer, coffee and tea only 3 and 2 kreuzer respectively. The traveler Johann Peter Willebrand relates the cost of his stay in Vienna: "The portion of coffee with sugar and milk costs 3 kreuzer, a cup of chocolate costs 7 or 10 kreuzer; with these a very fine-grain bread called a 'Gipfel' [Kipferl] is served; for this, one pays 1 kreuzer."[49] Even in the coffeehouse, chocolate continued to be the most expensive beverage.

The fascination the three hot drinks held for Europeans in the eighteenth century went hand in hand with their predilection for all things exotic, their "Turcomania" and Orientalism. It not only brought with it exquisite new serving pieces, but in the Rococo it also served the aristocracy as a vehicle for self-representation in art. In contrast to coffee and tea, chocolate retained its exclusivity well into the nineteenth century. Only thanks to numerous new production methods in the mid century did the former luxury become affordable for the wider public. In Dresden, where a number of chocolate factories opened in the nineteenth century, Liotard's *Chocolate Girl* became the symbol of this indulgence.[50]

1 Johann Georg Krünitz, *Oeconomische Enzyklopaedie, oder allgemeines System der Land-, Haus- und Staats-Wirthschaft*, vol. 8, Berlin 1776, p. 72.

2 A fourth import from overseas was tobacco; see Stephan Blankaart, *Haustus Polychresti, Oder: Zuverläassige Gedancken Vom Thée, Coffée, Chocolate, Und Taback, Mit welchen Der grosse Nutze dieser ausländischen Wahren so wol in gesunden als krancken Tagen. . .* , Hamburg 1705.

3 For example in the treatise *Drey neue curieuse Tractätgen von dem Trancke Cafe, sinesischen The, und der Chocolata* (see cat. 29), or in the 1743 book *Curieuse Beschreibung des Thee, Coffee, und Choccolade-Trancks: wie auch des überaus herrlichen und nützlichen Chinesischen Saamens, Padian oder Anisum Stellatum Chinense . . .* , Augsburg 1743.

4 See Christian Hochmuth, *Globale Güter – lokale Aneignung: Kaffee, Tee, Schokolade und Tabak im frühneuzeitlichen Dresden*, Konstanz 2008, p. 13.

5 See Roman Sandgruber, "Genußmittel: Ihre reale und symbolische Bedeutung im neuzeitlichen Europa," in: *Jahrbuch für Wirtschaftsgeschichte* 35, no. 1 (1994), pp. 73–88, here p. 73.

6 Maureen Cassidy-Geiger, "Princes and Porcelain on the Grand Tour of Italy," in: *Fragile Diplomacy: Meissen Porcelain for European Courts ca. 1710–63*, ed. Maureen Cassidy-Geiger, New Haven, and London 2007, pp. 208–55, here pp. 215–16.

7 Maike Fabian, Sirko Möge, and Kaja Wünsche, "Lever mit Schokolade: Wie sich der Dresdner Geschmackssinn entwickelte," in: *Dresden: Ethnografische Erkundungen einer Residenzstadt*, ed. Rolf Lindner and Johannes Moser, Leipzig 2006, p. 181.

8 See Andrea Durry and Thomas Schiffer, *Kakao: Speise der Götter*, Munich 2012, pp. 23, 149–185.

9 See Annerose Menninger, *Genuss im kulturellen Wandel: Tabak, Kaffee, Tee und Schokolade in Europa (16.–19. Jahrhundert)*, Stuttgart 2004, pp. 72–84.

10 See Durry and Schiffer 2012, p. 22.

11 Ibid., p. 196.

12 Bernal Diaz del Castillo, *Geschichte der Eroberung von Mexiko*, ed. Georg Adolf Narciß, Berlin 2017, p. 212. Del Castillo also points to the importance of cacao as a currency; ibid., p. 217.

13 See Durry and Schiffer 2012, p. 221.

14 See Antoinette Schnyder-von Waldkirch, *Wie Europa den Kaffee entdeckte. Reiseberichte der Barockzeit als Quellen zur Geschichte des Kaffees*, ed. Holger Hasenkamp, vol. 1, Zürich 1988, pp. 15–36.

15 Translator's note: The term "oriental" in these essays reflects its historical meaning in the eighteenth century, referring to the regions that at the time were encompassed by the Ottoman Empire.

16 Leonharti Rauwolfen, *Aigentliche beschreibung der Raiß, so er vor diser zeit gegen Auffgang inn die Morgenländer . . .* , Lauingen 1582, p. 102.

17 Menninger 2004, p. 171.

18 Ibid., p. 222.

19 This confessional aspect is mainly associated with chocolate. See Hochmuth 2008, p. 81.

20 Wolf Mueller, *Seltsame Frucht Kakao. Geschichte des Kakaos und der Schokolade*, Hamburg 1957, p. 39.

21 See Durry and Schiffer 2012, p. 242.

22 Ibid., p. 243.

23 Bertram M. Gordon, "Chocolate in France. Evolution of a Luxury Product," in: *Chocolate: History, Culture, and Heritage*, ed. Louis Grivetti, Hoboken, NJ 2009, pp. 569–82, here pp. 569–570.

24 Ibid., p. 571.

25 Letter from December 8, 1712, to Louise, Countess of the Palatinate, in: *Briefe der Herzogin Elisabeth Charlotte von Orléans aus den Jahren 1707 bis 1715*, ed. Wilhelm Ludwig Holland, Tübingen 1871, p. 296.

26 See Günther Schiedlausky, *Tee, Kaffee, Schokolade: Ihr Eintritt in die Europäische Gesellschaft*, Munich 1961, p. 16.

27 Fabian, Möge, and Wünsche 2006, p. 187.

28 *Briefe der Kaiserin Maria Theresia*, ed. Alfred W. Fred, vol. 1, Munich and Leipzig 1914, p. 214.

29 See the essay by Holger Schuckelt in this volume.

30 Sächsisches Hauptstaatsarchiv Dresden (HStADD), Finanzarchiv 10036, Loc. 32451, Rep. 20, no. 134, n.p.

31 HStADD, Amt Dresden 10047, no. 3443, Bl. 16, "Verrechnung vom 15. Januar 1765."

32 Menninger 2004, p. 235.

33 See Hochmuth 2008, p. 91.

34 For early cacao recipes, see Grivetti 2009, pp. 99–107; Christine A. Jones, *When Chocolate was Medicine: Comenero, Wadsworth, and Dufour*, https://publicdomainreview.org/2015/01/28/when-chocolate-was-medicine-colmenero-wadsworth-and-dufour (accessed March 8, 2018).

35 Johann Christoph Ettner, *Des getreuen Eckharts Medicinischen Maul-Affens Erster Theil oder Der entlarvte Marktschreyer*, Leipzig 1719 (reprint of the Liegnitz ed. 1694), p. 197.

36 Cornelius Bontekoe, *Kurtze Abhandlung Von dem Menschlichen Leben, Gesundheit, Kranckheit, und Tod*, Bautzen 1692, p. 470.

37 Daniel Duncan, *Von dem Mißbrauch heißer und hitziger Speisen und Geträncke, sonderlich aber Des Caffes, Schockolate und Thees*, Leipzig 1707.

38 Carl Linnaeus, *Des Ritter Carl von Linné Auserlesenen Abhandlungen aus der Naturgeschichte, Physik und Arzneywissenschaft*, vol. 2, Leipzig 1777, p. 173.

39 See Hochmuth 2008, p. 60, with note 52.

40 Fabian, Möge, and Wünsche 2006, p. 179.

41 Ettner 1719, p. 197

42 Wolfgang Schivelbusch, *Das Paradies, der Geschmack und die Vernunft: eine Geschichte der Genußmittel*, Frankfurt am Main 2005, p. 99.

43 Durry and Schiffer 1012, p. 198.

44 ". . . is a certain paste made from the Indian fruit cacao and various spices such as cinnamon, cloves, vanilla, Mexican pepper, along with sugar, prepared according to the American method before the Spanish arrived there, and colored by the small green Indian almonds called *achioti*. I also readily believe it is burned in the making if one does not precisely prepare it over the *lapidem metate*," in: Gottlieb Siegmund Corvinus, called Amaranthes, *Nutzbares, galantes und cürieuses Frauenzimmer-Lexicon*, Leipzig 1715, p. 147.

45 *Curieuse Beschreibung* 1743, n.p.

46 Menninger 2004, p. 89. For the coffeehouse, see also Roman Sandgruber, "Kaffeesuppe und 'kleiner Brauner': Sozialgeschichte des Kaffeekonsums in Österreich," in: *Kaffee im Spiegel europäischer Trinksitten/Coffee in the Context of European Drinking Habits*, ed. Daniel Ball, Zürich 1991, pp. 53–67.

47 See also Ulla Heise, "Drei Jahrhunderte Kaffeekultur in Deutschland: Dresdener Aspekte im 18. Jahrhunder," in: "*Ey, wie schmeckt der Caffee Süße*": *Meissener Porzellan und Graphik*, exh. cat. Porzellansammlung, Staatliche Kunstsammlungen Dresden, Sammlung Eduscho Bremen, Dresden 1991, pp. 9–12.

48 Johann Christian Crell, *Das Fast auf dem höchsten Gipffel der Vollkommenheit Prangende Dreßden, Oder Kurtze doch deutliche Beschreibung Derer In dieser Stadt berühmten Gebäude und Merckwürdigkeiten . . .*, Leipzig 1719, pp. 24–25.

49 Johann Peter Willebrand, *Des Herrn Johann Peter Willebrand historische Berichte und Practische Anmerkungen*, Leipzig 1769, p. 338, no. 1150.

50 See Fabian, Möge, and Wünsche 2006, pp. 199–202; also *Schokoladenstadt Dresden: Süßigkeiten aus Elbflorenz*, exh. cat. Stadtmuseum Dresden (2013/14), ed. Erika Eschebach and Holger Starke, Dresden 2013.

INTERPRETATIONS OF THE *CHOCOLATE GIRL* IN ART AND EVERYDAY CULTURE

Roland Enke and Susanne Drexler

The *Chocolate Girl* as a Source of Artistic Inspiration

Jean-Étienne Liotard's pastel painting *The Chocolate Girl* was a major attraction of Dresden's Gemäldegalerie from the outset. Copied innumerable times and reproduced in the latest printmaking techniques, the motif became widely disseminated in various media from the late eighteenth century onward. Inevitably, some artists also used the motif as a starting point for their own creative endeavors. This, however, first required a certain historical distance—partly due to the fact that, by the end of the eighteenth century, both Rococo painting and the technique of pastel painting had fallen out of fashion. It was only in the second half of the nineteenth century that painting with pastels was revived by the Impressionists and subsequently the Expressionists.[1] A telling indication of the change in taste was the acquisition for the Dresden Gemäldegalerie in 1919 of the pastel *Two Dancers* (ca. 1898) by Edgar Degas. Four pastels by Rosalba Carriera were exchanged for it with Berlin's Galerie Paul Cassirer.[2]

Over the course of the twentieth century, the *Chocolate Girl* began to receive greater attention again, as, by then, it stood not so much for the Rococo style, but was seen as a motif on its own merit, released from any historical context. Whether for reasons of personal affection or even as a rejection, the motif of the *Chocolate Girl* was overpainted or cut up, reinterpreted and parodied. Since these responses have not been included in the exhibition, this essay presents a few works that might serve as examples to illustrate the *Chocolate Girl*'s potential as artistic inspiration.

One of the first noted artists to produce a response to the *Chocolatière* was the young Hermann Glöckner, known for his independently developed Constructivist style. According to the Dresden gallery's "Kopistenbuch" for the years 1912 to 1930—the ledger in which artists wishing to copy works were required to enter their name, address, the target painting, and the date—Glöckner visited the gallery almost every month between September 1921 and August 1923 in order to copy such masterpieces as Jacopo Tintoretto's *Holy Family with Saint Catherine and Honored Donor*, Sandro Botticelli's *Mary with the Child and the Boy St. John*, Gerard Ter Borch's *Lady in a Golden Dress in Front of a Bed*, and Caspar Netscher's *Seamstress*. In addition to his general interest in painting techniques, this was presumably also owing to the fact that he was only admitted to the Dresden Academy in 1923, after several unsuccessful attempts. On October 12, 1922, and March 12, 1923, Glöckner registered his desire to copy "P 161," i.e. Liotard's *Chocolate Girl*.[3] Unfortunately there is no trace of these studies in his work. Perhaps the sketches were lost when his studio was destroyed in 1945.[4] It would have been fascinating to see Glöckner's translation of the *Chocolate Girl* into geometric Constructivism.

Frequently it was postcard reproductions that triggered an artistic response. For example, beginning in the 1970s, the painter and filmmaker Strawalde

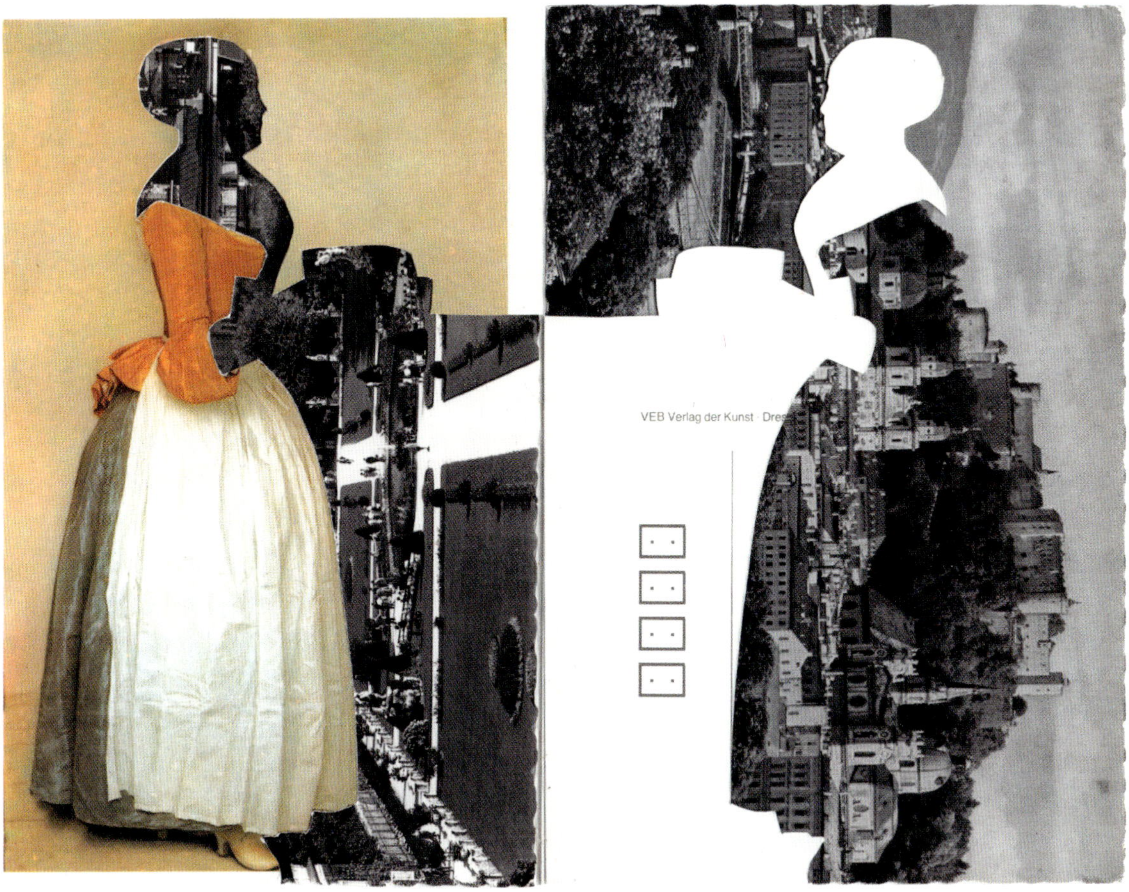

Fig. 1 **Roland Stratmann, Miracle – Post Cut 65 A**, 2014, three postcards, 15 x 21 cm, private collection

(Jürgen Böttcher) repeatedly worked with postcards of icons of art history, including, from Dresden's Gemäldegalerie, Giorgione's *Sleeping Venus*, Caspar David Friedrich's *Early Snow*, and, of course, the *Chocolate Girl*: "At first I would scribble over a few motifs that were popular in the GDR at the time and tuck them into letters to friends as greeting cards. . . . This way I made numerous variations of overpaintings . . . after all, you can overpaint anything."[5] Strawalde produced a series of some forty versions of Liotard's painting.[6] Particularly interesting is the contrast between the small format of the illustration and the often quite powerful brush strokes he used to cover the postcards. He retraced different parts of the picture, like the background, the girl's body and face, her skirt, the cup on the tray, overpainting them with varying intensities, intentions, and colors. At times he emphasized her body, at others he obliterated the entire picture. In nearly all the postcards he focused on the tray or the cup and water glass, annotating them ironically: there are numerous variations of steam rising from the hot drink in the cup, but also taking the form of a flower or plant.

Postcards are also used by the artist Roland Stratmann, who lives and works in Berlin, in his series of *PostCuts*. In this sequence, produced between 2012 and 2015, he explores "beautiful views" and their intersections, using postcards with such varied motifs as architecture, landscapes, sculptures, and paintings. Each work consists of three cards. Using a scalpel, he cuts one of them along the out-

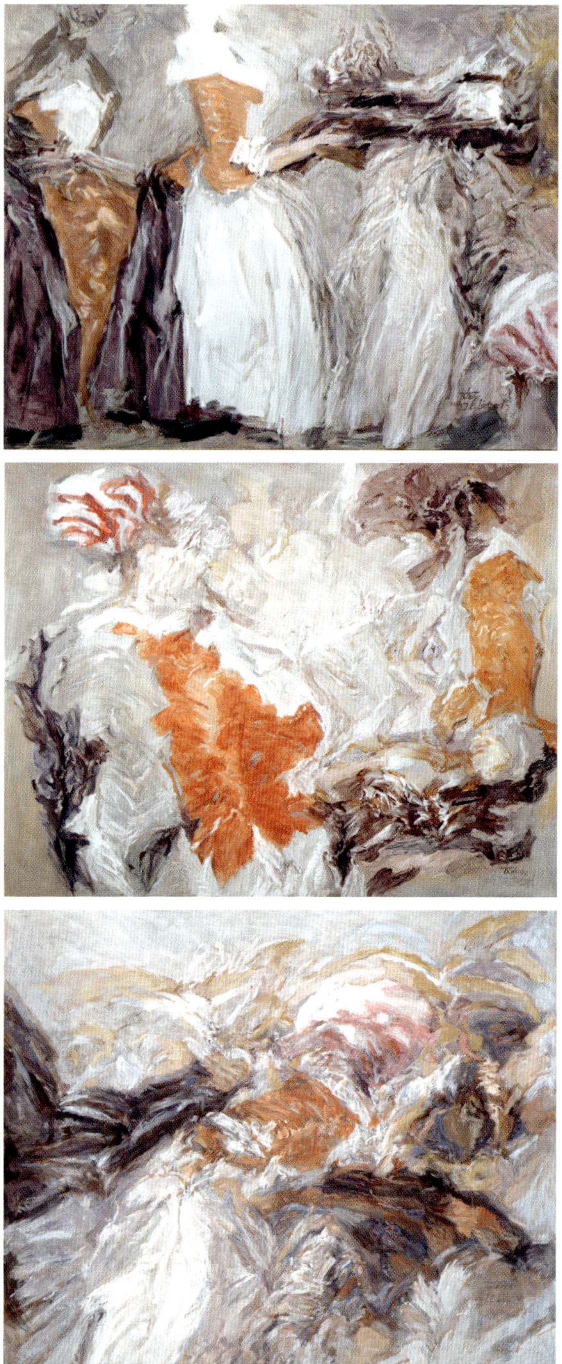

Fig. 2 **Hann Trier, Sequence after J.-E. Liotard, La tasse au chocolat: L'arrivée / Arôme et splendeur / La chute**, 1991, egg tempera on canvas, 96 x 128 cm, 96 x 128 cm, 96 x 115 cm, Albertinum/Galerie Neue Meister, Staatliche Kunstsammlungen Dresden

line of a chosen detail and, by "folding out" these mirror-image pieces onto the other two cards, creates entirely new image contexts. In his adaptation of the *Chocolate Girl*, Stratmann combined Liotard's pastel with two postcard views of the city of Salzburg: the Mirabell Gardens on the left and Hohensalzburg Fortress on the right. Following the lines of the upper body and apron of the *Chocolatière*, the two shapes complete each other in their opposites, as in a positive and negative silhouette (fig. 1).[7]

The Leipzig painter and graphic artist Matthias Klemm used the *Chocolate Girl* for an art intervention. Along with his work as an artist, and prompted by events affecting his own family, he was also engaged in political activism and campaigning for social change. Like many church congregations in the GDR in the late 1980s, Leipzig's Thomaskirche was able to offer a space for the open discussion of political and social issues. In Klemm's small black-and-white print (collage and drawing) the *Chocolatière* is sitting in a wheelchair, she alone is in color, youthful and pretty as in the original pastel.[8] Simultaneously she can still be seen on the left as the picture in its frame, yet the torn photograph and black fragment of a film negative imply the end of continuous motion. Klemm enlarged the print to more than two meters in width and put it on display in the Thomaskirche for several weeks, where it served as a prompt for a number of controversial debates: What happened to the girl? Could it happen to me? How would I deal with it? What is society's attitude toward disability?

The three-part work *Sequence after J.-E. Liotard, La tasse au chocolat* by Hann Trier is very different in form and approach. Back in the 1960s, Trier, as one of the main practitioners of abstract Art Informel, turned to the airy, French-inspired painting of the eighteenth century. For example, between 1969 and 1974, he reconstructed various ceiling paintings in Berlin's Schloss Charlottenburg—painted in 1742 by Antoine Pesne and destroyed in the Second World War—describing his appropriation of the original as a "rebirth of the Rococo in the spirit of the present."[9] In 1991, Trier also engaged with the *Chocolate Girl*, which may seem surprising at first glance. Liotard had "frozen in his painting the transitory moment of walking past,"[10] achieved through his extreme accuracy in the depiction of d etails, the neutral background, and the suppression of any hint of a narrative context. The contrast to Trier's dynamic, gestural painting, often working with a paintbrush in each hand, could hardly be greater—and that must have been precisely what attracted him to this icon of pastel painting (cat. 13). In his paraphrase, Trier attempted to free the image from being frozen in time and continued the story in three scenes (fig. 2). He retained the original coloring; especially recognizable throughout are the white of the apron and shawl, the silver-gray of the skirt, the yellow-ocher of the jacket, and the pink of the bonnet. The switch from portrait to landscape format suggests an expansion of the scene as in a film sequence. The work's title, too—*La tasse au chocolat*—shifts the focus from the *Chocolate Girl* to the chocolate drink and, furthermore, from its taste to the aroma of the cacao. Trier takes a "processual art" approach, whereby the rapid crescendo of brush strokes leads the situation to a climax. Already in the first picture of the sequence, *Arrival*, this movement, from the still almost static appearance of the girl on the left, is denoted in the duplication of the tray on the right. In *Aroma and Splendor*, the figure dissolves and becomes barely recognizable. The narrative culminates in the third picture, titled *Fall*, in which the artist has the girl tumble to the ground. Some observers may even be able to hear the shattering of the cup and water glass! In his energetic painterly style, combined with increasing abstraction, Trier speeds up the viewer's gaze.[11] In 2003, the Hann-Trier-Stiftung gifted the trilogy from the estate of the painter, who died in 1999, to the Staatliche Kunstsammlungen Dresden's Galerie Neue Meister. In honor of this acquisition, Liotard's pastel took up temporary residence in the Albertinum—a major exception—to allow direct comparison between the original and Trier's interpretation.

One of the more recent works is Slawomir Elsner's 2015 *Chocolate Girl*. Using roughly the same format as the original, he placed short, freehand hatchings this way and that across the white sheet, thus marking the girl's outline and recreating its color accents (fig. 3). Through this means of painterly engagement the artist appropriates the image, while at the same time, obscuring it, creating a blurred, even diffuse copy of the original.[12] Elsner has already produced about fifty such "faded mementos," including versions after masterpieces by Botticelli, Cranach, Titian, Michelangelo, and Velázquez. Each time, the chosen motif shifts into the background in favor of a concentration on form, color, and compositional principles. However, since Elsner has chosen well-known, often highly popular motifs, the viewer's curiosity is piqued to explore and recognize the familiar image. Even

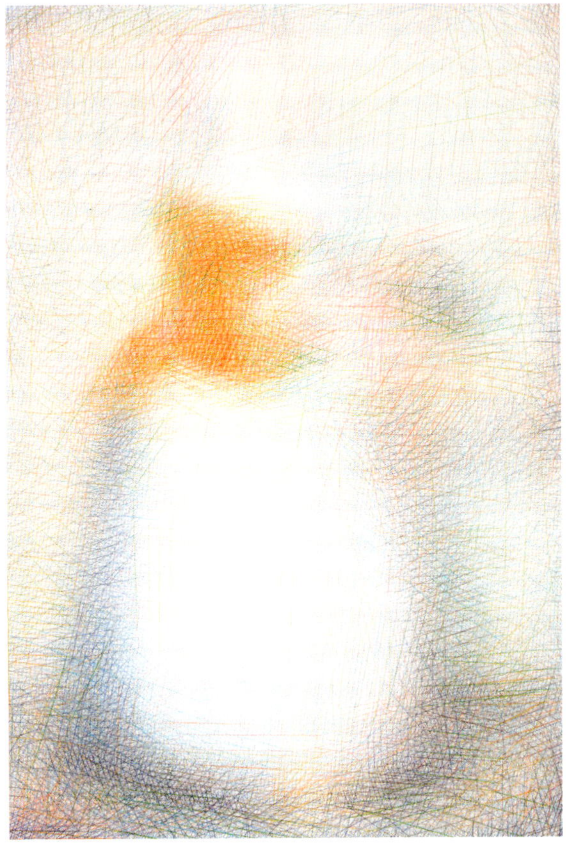

Fig. 3 Slawomir Elsner, **The Chocolate Girl (after Jean-Étienne Liotard)**, 2015, colored pencil on paper, 82.5 x 52.5 cm, private collection

in the present abstracted drawing, the *Chocolate Girl* is readily identifiable.
What becomes obvious is that most of these artists have very deliberately returned to this icon of eighteenth-century art, often using reproductions such as art postcards as their starting point. However, owing to their relatively localized availability—and despite the *Chocolatière*'s much wider fame—the motif is used as a nucleus for adaptation more often by artists working in Dresden and Saxony, the graphic art piece by Dieter Härtel (cat. 105) being a case in point. Often, as with Strawalde, Trier, and Elsner, the inspiration was a personal encounter with the original. "Here is my subject!" the artist and gallerist Holger John, active in Dresden since 1988, is said to have exclaimed; from the Gemäldegalerie he has selected the *Chocolate Girl*, along with Giorgione's *Sleeping Venus*, as his muse. He confidently draws the motif from memory using ink and paper, then supplements it with details that are sometimes purely artistic associations, sometimes relating to current political events. So far he has made around seventy such ink drawings, which convey his vibrant, humorous commentary. With these, the artist, who calls himself somewhat tongue-in-cheek Dresden's "Stadtzeichner" ("city illustrator"), chronicles the city's big and small stories in ink. Although by no means uncritical, these are not caustic caricatures, however, more like a comic strip drawn by its author with great affection, even tenderness, for his city.
Even in the works of these later artists, the *Chocolate Girl* and the city of Dresden remain closely intertwined.

Roland Enke

The *Chocolate Girl* in Folk Art and Everyday Culture

In addition to the artistic responses to Liotard's most famous pastel, countless translations and interpretations of the *Chocolate Girl* are found in the world of folk art and crafts, as well as in advertising and everyday products. Ever since the early nineteenth century, the motif has enjoyed great popularity.[13] Its appearance in folk art, mainly rooted in craft traditions, is sometimes more, sometimes less closely based on the original pastel, while in advertising and everyday culture "straightforward" reproductions predominate. Unsurprisingly, to this day, the *Chocolate Girl* is associated with the consumption of hot drinks and chocolate, still considered exotic at the time the picture was made. Particularly striking in its folk art adaptations is the variety of materials employed. One of the earliest examples is the fashion doll from around 1800, now in the Museum of Saxon Folk Art in Dresden (fig. 4). The figure, acquired by the museum's founder Oskar Seyffert, is made of colored paper, hand-carved wood, and a painted "bread dough" face; although it does not imitate the clothing of the original, it clearly recalls the characteristic pose of the painting and as such demonstrates the creative adaptation of artistic motifs in folk art.[14]
A combination of everyday porcelain and textiles are the "tea cozy dolls" that became popular in the early twentieth century: figures with porcelain bodies and large skirts that were used to keep teapots warm.[15] Often these were based on figures from Old Master paintings—and Liotard's *Chocolate Girl*.[16] The figure was also a popular motif on porcelain platters.[17] Furthermore, there are versions in lace, embroidery, and ceramics. Between the 1930s and 1960s the company Herbu (Herbert Bunzel, Leipzig) produced a series of twenty-one tin figures titled "Sonderfiguren berühmter Persönlichkeiten aus der Zeit August des Starken" (Special figures of famous personalities from the time of Augustus the Strong), showing popular Dresden figures. Along with Augustus the Strong's mistress Countess of Cosel, they also featured the *Chocolate Girl*, an unknown maidservant from Vienna. Traditional woodcarvers and toymakers in the Ore Mountains also produce *Chocolate Girl* adaptations in a wide range of forms: from incense smokers, in which the cup serves as a flue for the scented smoke, to Christmas tree ornaments and simple wooden figures in all sizes—always clearly identifiable, thanks to the tray (cat. 92, 93).

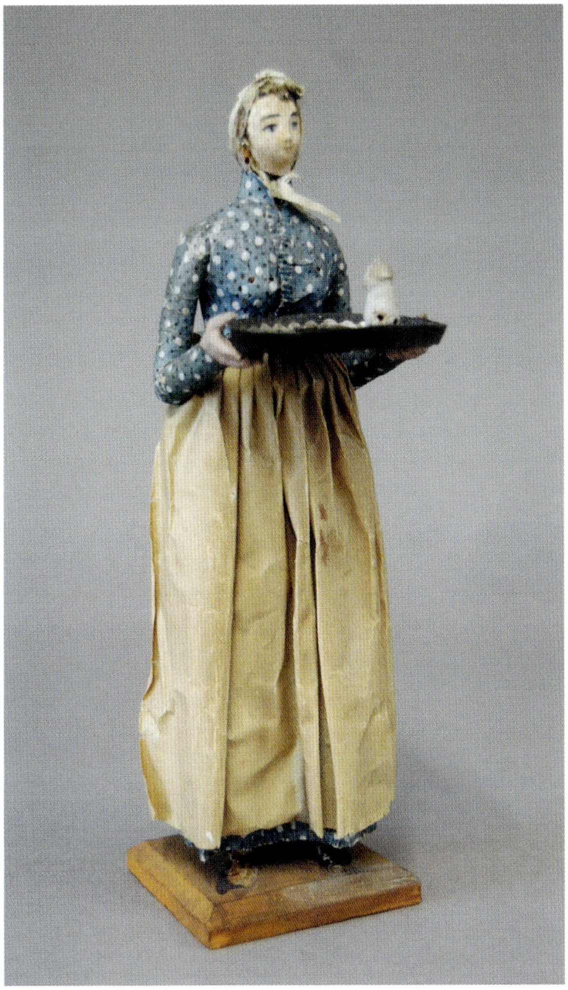

Fig. 4 **Paper Figure of a Servieng Girl**, Germany, circa 1800, paper, decorative paper, wood, "bread dough" face, Museum für Sächsische Volkskunst, Staatlich Kunstsammlungen Dresden

The Meissen porcelain manufactory were the first to produce an applied-arts *Chocolate Girl* figure in a high-quality material; the first mold was made at around 1843, and the porcelain figure is still produced in this form today (cat. 89).[18] Another adaptation is found on a damask napkin produced at around 1875 by the Grossschönau manufacturer August Ender for the Dresden department store owner Joseph Meyer: woven in beige thread on a brown background, the *Chocolate Girl*, based on a design by Karl Gotthelf Krumbholz, professor at the Dresden school of applied arts, is almost suggestive of chocolate from its coloring alone (fig. 5). To this day, the girl remains a popular motif on paper napkins.

Ever since the mid nineteenth century, the *Chocolate Girl* has been used as an emblem by chocolate manufacturers and confectioners, and there are countless adaptations on packaging, cacao tins, and as trademarks. As early as 1858, the Polish writer Józef Ignacy Kraszewski, who moved to Dresden in 1863 and later became a Saxon citizen, commented on the connection between the *Chocolate Girl* and Dresden's culinary industry: "All the confectioners have chosen her as their patron; there is no pound of caramels, no bar of chocolate, on which she is not found; you can see her made of soap, of sugar, of wood, engraved, painted, in porcelain—she haunts you like a specter, until you're strangled by this maddening little figure that you cannot get away from."[19] Here are but a few examples: Dresden's oldest chocolate factory, Jordan & Timaeus,[20] not only exhibited chocolate bars with the *Chocolatière* in relief at the Great Exhibition in London in 1851,[21] it also used the motif in 1898 on a poster for the company's seventy-fifth anniversary.[22] The girl, prominently positioned in the picture, is dressed as she is in Liotard's pastel, but instead of a tray she holds open a curtain to reveal the anniversary inscription. Another well-known Dresden chocolate factory, founded in 1838 by Carl Christian Petzold and August Ferdinand Lobeck and continued from 1860 under the name Otto Rüger,[23] also employed the motif. It not only advertised its cacao powder with the *Chocolate Girl* (see cat. 98), it even surprised the king with a living version of her: "On June 21, 1883, the Saxon king Albert . . . visited the company Otto Rüger in Dippoldiswalde. . . . His Majesty first inspected the factory's display on the second floor of the owner's house, showing the raw materials and their preparation until their final use in chocolate, icing, pastry, gingerbread, and marzipan. Then Herr Rüger's oldest daughter, dressed in the costume of Liotard's well-known *Chocolatière*, presented His Majesty a cup of the finest hot chocolate, which was graciously

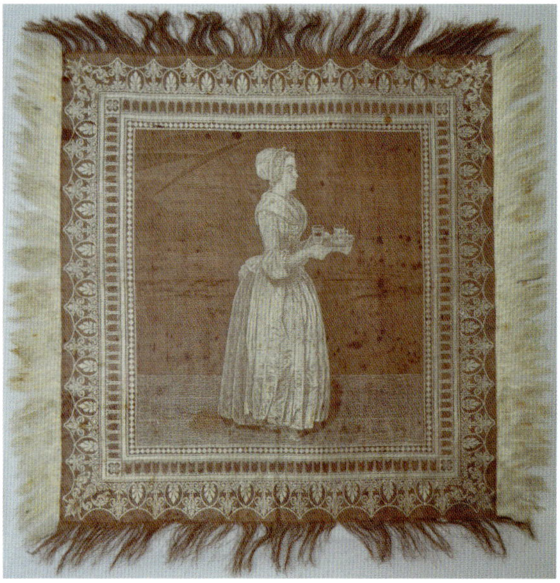

Fig. 5 **Karl Gotthelf Krumbholz** (design), **August Ender** (manufacturer), **damask napkin "Schokoladenmädchen"**, circa 1875, linen, silk, Deutsches Damast- und Frottiermuseum, Großschönau

accepted."[24] The decoration of chocolate bars with various motifs was made possible by another Dresden firm. In 1886, Anton Reiche established in Dresden-Plauen a factory that produced tins for packaging, as well as separable molds for making hollow chocolate figures and simpler ones for molding flat chocolate bars. Its offerings were published in illustrated catalogues and comprised nearly 30,000 products.[25] A copy from around 1906 lists three different types of mold featuring the *Chocolate Girl*, each with an indication of the weight of the chocolate bar that could be made with it (fig. 6).

With such widespread popularity of the motif, it is not surprising that, in 1889, for the parade celebrating the eight hundredth anniversary of the House of Wettin, the Dresden confectionery industry participated with a float featuring the *Chocolate Girl*.[26] When, in around 1900, Dresden became the German empire's market leader in the production of chocolate, its new rank as the "city of chocolate" went hand in hand with a further increase in the *Chocolate Girl*'s fame. But even companies outside of Dresden's sphere of influence used the *Chocolatière* as a trademark, such as the Stuttgart-based purveyor to the royal court of Württemberg, Waldbaur, founded in 1848, who used the picture on its chocolate wrappers.[27] Other firms went still further: in 1877, America's oldest chocolate manufacturer, Walter Baker Chocolate Co., secured the *Chocolate Girl* image as its trademark, together with the caption "La belle chocolatiere," and in its *Chocolate Recipes* of 1913 even revived the story of the servant girl Anna Baldauf as the real person behind the *Chocolate Girl*. On June 18, 1940, Baker & Co. once more renewed their trademark patent for its use in the United States.[28] The Brazilian chocolate company Sönksen also used the *Chocolatière* on its packaging (cat. 99, 100). The popularity of the motif as an advertising image for chocolates and other sweets persists to this day.

It cannot be denied that in Dresden the *Chocolate Girl* enjoys almost iconic status. A number of different factors are responsible for this, such as its early association with the "city of chocolate" and also with Dresden's coffeehouse culture. In an early drawing by Gustav Täubert it was linked to the Café Reale on Brühl's Terrace (cat. 84), and in the historic Café Robert Beyer, a coffeehouse that had been facing Dresden's Altmarkt since 1878, a tile version adorned the wall behind the counter, as is evident from a 1920s postcard (cat. 103). The motif is also found on a coffee service from the early twentieth century made by the Hof-Moschendorf porcelain manufactory (cat. 90). Here the special reference to chocolate fades into the background and the *Chocolatière* becomes a symbol for all kinds of sweet indulgences and the enjoyment of coffee in general. And at this point the exploitation of the image for marketing and tourism begins. Even in Russia it can be spotted in outlets of the coffeehouse chain Shokoladnitsa (Шоколадница).

One particular type of adaptation is the appearance of the *Chocolate Girl* as a living figure, both in the performing arts and in everyday life—and not just beginning in the twentieth century. Again we quote Kraszewski: "In the buildings that house the [paint-

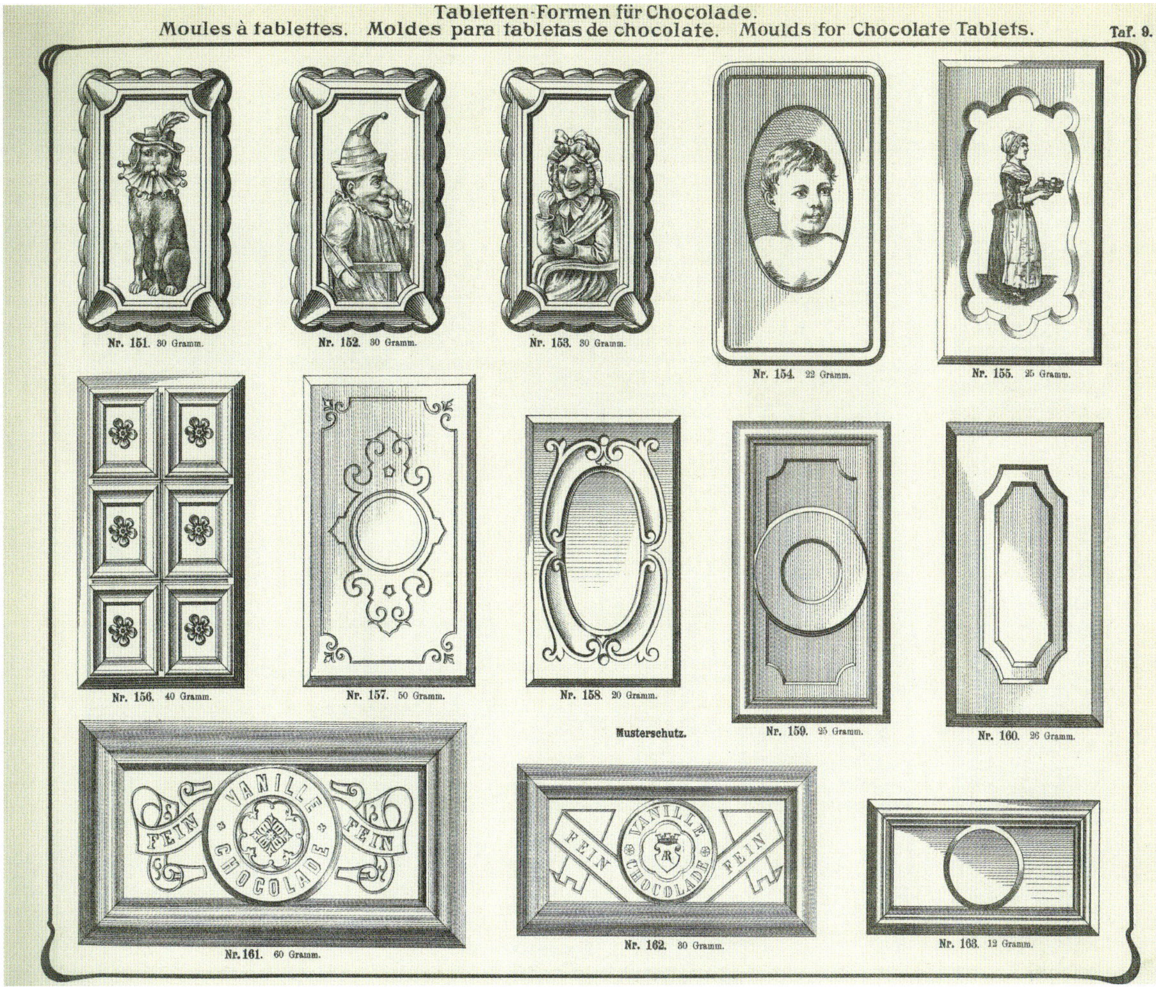

Fig. 6 **Catalogue *Schokoladenformen Anton Reiche, Tabletten-Formen für Chocolade***, circa 1906, plate 9, no. 155, Anton Reiche Museum at Stiftung Hofmühle Dresden

ing] gallery there is a by no means less interesting collection of pastels, which is, however, dominated by a certain Viennese waitress known as the 'Chocolate Girl,' who has the honor of being present in Dresden wherever you go, even as a real person in the street. Dresden's waitresses have learned—probably to please the devotees of this ideal Chocolate Girl—to match this young woman's appearance."[29] Throughout the twentieth century, the girl would materialize in the most varied contexts in everyday life: Between 1987 and 1990, East German television broadcast the program *Showkolade*, presented by Gunther Emmerlich, a mix of talk show and musical performances, in which the actress Nadja Puls from the television ballet regularly appeared as Chocolate Girl. Shortly before reunification, the play *Das Schokoladenmädchen* was performed in Dresden's Pionierpalast, as well as at the Saxonia Ensemble Dresden e.V., founded in 1970 by the VEB Messelektronik Dresden.

The popularity of the *Chocolatière* extends far beyond Dresden, however. For example, in 2002, Paul Steinmann wrote a play for the Junges Theater Konstanz about Liotard's association with the unknown girl. Commercialization of the *Chocolate Girl* has at times assumed bizarre forms: in 2001, a woman went to court in an attempt to trademark her performance as a living *Chocolatière*.[30] The figure's popularity is also linked to the numerous poster reproductions of the image, not only in cafés, such as the one in the television drama *Lindenstrasse*, but also in many people's homes. In East German art lending libraries (Artothek), for example, it was a favorite motif, along with Van Gogh's *Sunflowers*.[31] When, in preparation for this exhibition, the Gemäldegalerie Alte Meister invited the Dresden public to submit their own artworks, souvenirs, and everyday objects carrying the image of the *Chocolate Girl*, the contributions received gave a clear insight into the great variety of responses to the famous pastel, especially in the twentieth century.[32] In 2018, a Geranium variety—declared Saxony's plant of the year—was named after the *Chocolatière*.[33]

Susanne Drexler

1 See *Pastels du 16e au 21e siècle: Liotard, Degas, Klee, Scully . . .*, exh. cat. Fondation de l'Hermitage Lausanne 2018, ed. Sylvie Wuhrmann and Aurélie Caouvreur, Lausanne 2018.

2 Andreas Henning, "Rosalba Carriera e la collezione dei suoi pastelli a Dresda," in: Giuseppe Pavanello, ed., *Rosalba Carriera 1673–1757, Atti del Convegno Internazionale di Studi 2007, Verona 2009*, pp. 273–360, nos. III-31, -48, -53, -54.

3 Gemäldegalerie Alte Meister, Dresden, archive, pp. 283–84, 321–22.

4 See *Glöckner—Gemälde und Zeichnungen, 1904–1945, Werkverzeichnis der Gemälde, Zeichnungen und Photographien*, ed. Werner Schmidt, Christian Dittrich, Bernd Heise, and Sebastian Schmidt, Staatliche Kunstsammlungen Dresden, Kupferstich-Kabinett, Nachlass Hermann Glöckner, Dresden 2010.

5 Quoted from Matthias Flügge and Jutta Penndorf, *STRAWALDE Jürgen Böttcher, Maler und Regisseur*, exh. cat. Lindenau-Museum Altenburg, Nuremberg 2012, p. 230.

6 Fourteen of them are illustrated in Martin Rögener, ed., *Kunst-Postkarten übermalt von Strawalde (Jürgen Böttcher)*, Hamburg 1990, no page number [pp. 7–20].

7 http://www.rolandstratmann.de/work.php?m=2&p=papierarbeiten&s=13&1 (accessed July 18, 2018).

8 *Begegnungen—Matthias Klemm im Dialog mit Alten Meistern*, ed. Versöhnungskirche Leipzig-Gohlis, Leipzig 2014, p. 36.

9 Eberhard Roters, *Hann Trier—die Deckengemälde in Berlin, Heidelberg and Cologne*, Berlin 1981, p. 23.

10 Christoph Wagner, *Der beschleunigte Blick—Hann Trier und das prozessuale Bild*, Berlin 1999, p. 10.

11 Ibid., p. 11

12 Frank Schmidt, "Slawomir Elsner: Le Musée imaginaire," in: *Slawomir Elsner*, exh. cat. Böttchergasse Bremen, Bremen 2017, pp. 14–19, here: 14, 16.

13 For a first overview of responses to the *Chocolate Girl*, see Manfred Bachmann, "Es leben die Schokoladenmädchen! Adaption eines populären Gemäldes in Werbung und Kunsthandwerk," in: *Sachsenbummel: Magazin für Kulturgeschichte und Tourismus* 4, no. 12 (1996), pp. 18–19; also Petra Landsberg, *Wahre Geschichten um das Schokoladenmädchen*, Leipzig 2014.

14 See Manfred Bachmann, "Das Schokoladenmädchen von J. E. Liotard als Motiv der Volkskunst," in: *Dresdener Kunstblätter* 15, no. 6 (1971), pp. 181–184.

15 I am grateful to the Coburg Puppenmuseum for information about its "tea cozy dolls."

16 For the production of these dolls and their imitation of figures in paintings, see Marie Genden, "Eine moderne Kaffeegesellschaft," in: *Die Welt der Frau, Beilage zur Gartenlaube*, no. 4 (1910), pp. 51–53.

17 They are found in great numbers in auction catalogues from the early twentieth century; see, for example, *Kunst-Auktionshaus Lempertz, Cologne, no. 232, November 10–12*, 1925, lot 745.

18 Porcelain figures of the *Chocolate Girl* were also produced by the Sächsische Porzellan-Manufaktur Dresden, Freital-Potschappel, Porzellanfabrik Tettau GmbH, Reutter Porzellan GmbH (porcelain miniature).

19 Józef Ignacy Kraszewski, *Reiseblätter, übersetzt von Caesar Rymarowicz nach der Erstausgabe 1858*, Berlin 1986, pp. 323–24.

20 For the history of the chocolate company, see Hans C. Jacobs, "Die älteste Dresdner Schokoladenfabrik 'Jordan & Timaeus' (1823–1931)," in: *Schokoladenstadt Dresden. Süßigkeiten aus Elbflorenz*, exh. cat. Stadtmuseum Dresden, ed. Erika Eschebach and Holger Starke, Dresden 2013, pp. 74–77.

21 *Amtliches Verzeichnis der aus dem Deutschen Zollverein und Norddeutschland zur Industrie-Ausstellung aller Völker in London eingesandten Gegenstände . . .* , Berlin 1851, p. 206, no. 1046.

22 Illustrated in Jacobs 2013, p. 76.

23 See Holger Starke, "Vom Lever zum Schokoriegel. Dresdens Entwicklung zur Stadt der Schokolade im Industriezeitalter (1800–1990)," in: *Schokoladenstadt Dresden. Süßigkeiten aus Elbflorenz*, exh. cat. Stadtmuseum Dresden, ed. Erika Eschebach and Holger Starke, Dresden 2013, p. 55.

24 First insert in the *Dresdner Anzeiger* for June 21, 1883, vol. 153, no. 172: "Der Besuch Sr. Maiestät des Königs in Dippoldiswalde."

25 For the history of the company, see Manfred Bachmann and Monika Tinhofer, *Osterhase, Nikolaus & Zeppelin: Schokoladenformen im Spiegel alter Musterbücher*, Husum 1998, pp. 12–17, 45.

26 Illustrated in exh. cat. Dresden 2013, p. 53.

27 Examples in the Cologne Schokoladenmuseum; illustration in Andrea Durry and Thomas Schiffer, *Das Schokoladenmuseum: Geschichte und Gegenwart der Schokolade*, Cologne 2008, p. 57.

28 U.S. Patent and Trademark Office: http://tsdr.uspto.gov/documentviewer?caseId=sn71416398&docId=ORC20051101234634#docIndex=17&page=1 (accessed May 24, 2018). I am grateful to Uwe Hessel for pointing this out to me on March 24, 2018.

29 Kraszewski 1986, p. 323.

30 See *Dresdner Neueste Nachrichten*, January 16, 2001, and *Sächsische Zeitung*, January 13/14, 2001.

31 Barbara Röhner, *Von Reproduktions-Ausstellungen zum Bildverleih, Idee- und Entwicklungsgeschichte von Artotheken in der DDR*, Halle 2016, pp. 344–45.

32 Once again we would like to express our sincere thanks to all our supporters for the numerous submissions as well as to those who participated in the public day: Brigitte Beutner, Anita Bilich, Andrea Born, Gaby Donath, Dieter Härtel, Ulrike Handwerker, Barbara Hering Carola Küfner, Dieter Liebscher, Gabriele Messerschmidt, Karl-Heinz Miethe, Eberhard Münzner, Brigitte and Jochen Mütze, Manfred Pietsch, Ilka Pötter, Antje Roesner, Heidemarie Rudolf, Heinrich Seiling, László Szedlár, Ingrid Treder, Hans Waldowski, Hendrikje Wehnert, Jurij and Paul Wuschansky, Brigitte and Wolfgang Zoche, Birgit Zumpe, Ute Zacharias, as well as all those who did not wish to be named. Thanks also to the jury: Tulga Beyerle, Dr. Igor Jenzen, Dr. Stephan Koja.

33 http://www.bluehendes-sachsen.de/pflanze-des-jahres/ (accessed July 24, 2018).

THE *CHOCOLATE GIRL* – ICON AND ACQUISITION

Jean-Étienne Liotard painted his famous *Chocolate Girl* in Vienna at around 1744. The simple "parlormaid" would remain a unicum in his oeuvre, and likewise there are few preliminary works with the motif of a serving girl. A large drawing (possibly documentary?) that remained in his possession is presumably a record of it—perhaps also to be used as a model for further copies. When Liotard journeyed to Venice in the spring of 1745, Count Francesco Algarotti was able to purchase the painting directly from the artist for Dresden's newly established painting gallery. The art agent also bought a number of paintings by other contemporary artists. The Elector of Saxony and King of Poland Augustus III employed a sizable network of dealers who offered him paintings, including pastels. He was particularly interested in works by the pastel painter Rosalba Carriera, whom he greatly admired. It was she who asserted that the *Chocolate Girl* was "the most beautiful pastel ever seen." Even in the twentieth century the picture was repeatedly the subject of artistic attention.

Cat. 1
Jean-Étienne Liotard
(Geneva 1702–1789 Geneva)
The Chocolate Girl
Circa 1744
Pastel on vellum, 82.5 x 52.5 cm
Gemäldegalerie Alte Meister, Staatliche Kunstsammlungen
Dresden, gal. no. P 161

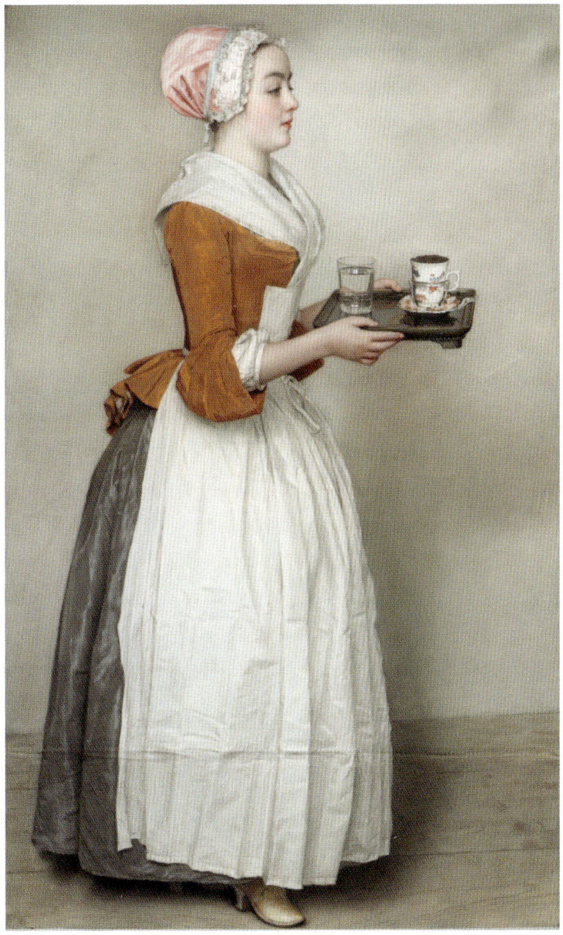

With the *Chocolate Girl*, painted at around 1744, the Genevan artist Jean-Étienne Liotard created his best-known work. The pastel depicts a young woman in profile view, walking from the left through a simple room, defined merely by a few floorboards and a blank wall. On her head she wears a pale-pink Bohemian bonnet. The shawl covering her décolletage allows a glimpse of corsage beneath her lustrous, ocher jacket. The crisp, freshly unfolded apron over her gray skirt is tied at the waist. The position of her feet in their yellow shoes leaves it unclear whether she is walking slowly or has momentarily paused. The flesh tone of her delicate face is rendered with palpable realism. The girl's pink skin and red mouth add to her flawless appearance. Her blue eyes are fixed on her mission: to serve the cup of hot chocolate and glass of water on her tray.

When Liotard arrived in Vienna in 1743 after his long sojourn in Constantinople, he came into close contact with Archduchess Maria Theresa and her husband Francis I, along with Austria's aristocracy. While the many portraits the artist produced throughout his life were clearly commissioned, for the *Chocolate Girl* there is no record of a commission nor of preliminary drawings. It is also unknown whether the portrait, unusually large for a painting on parchment, depicts an actual person or merely represents a genre piece of a "Stubenmensch" (serving person): the—from today's perspective—somewhat condescending term that appears on the sales receipt Liotard wrote for Francesco Algarotti as the art agent for Augustus III, Elector of Saxony and King of Poland. In his correspondence from Venice, Algarotti relayed Rosalba Carriera's assurance that the work was "the most beautiful pastel ever seen," while he himself referred to it as "a Holbein in pastel."

Liotard doubtless encountered servants frequently in Vienna. However, in the fine art of the eighteenth century, these people at the very bottom of the social hierarchy were rarely portrayed. One of the charms of this picture is therefore its unusual combination of the motif of a simple serving girl and its extraordinary command of the medium of pastels—especially in such a large format and on parchment. The motif, in this kind of meticulous rendering, remains unique within Liotard's oeuvre. And the painting remained equally unusual among the exhibited portraits and allegories in the pastel cabinet of Dresden's painting gallery, opened in 1748 in the former court stables.

In the nineteenth century, the *Chocolate Girl* became a highly popular motif, also as the subject of romanticizing narratives. Copied countless times in pastel, oils, or as a miniature, but also, and especially, through reproductions in print, it became well known far beyond the city limits of Dresden. To this day it is one of the best-known works in Dresden's Gemäldegalerie, second only to Raphael's *Sistine Madonna*.

RE

Literature: R/L 2008, no. 130; Riedel/Wenzel 1765, p. 243; Henning/Marx 2007, pp. 107–11; Landsberg 2014.

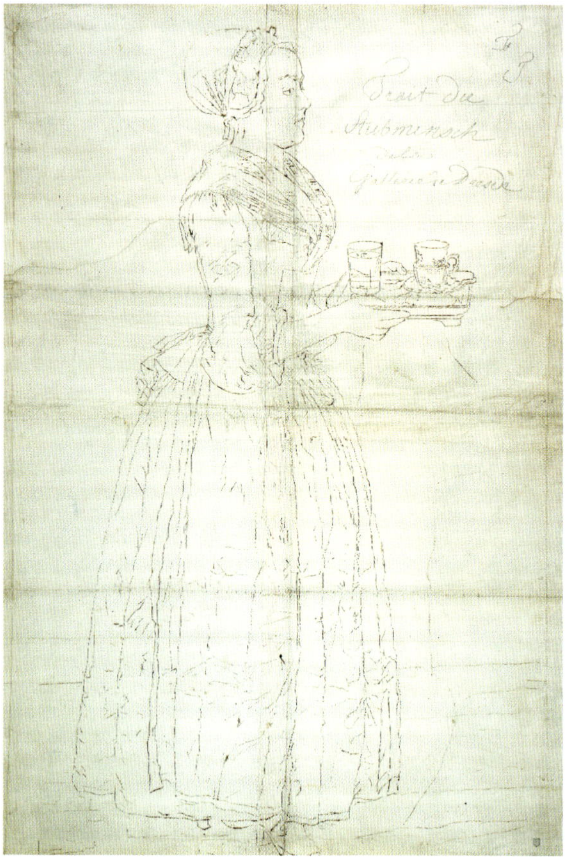

Cat. 2

Jean-Étienne Liotard

(Geneva 1702–1789 Geneva)

The Chocolate Girl

Circa 1744

Black ink on four sheets of paper, 83.8 x 58.5 cm

Inscribed in pencil upper right:

"Trait du Stubmensch de la Galerie de Dresde"

Cabinet d'arts graphiques des Musées d'art et d'histoire, Geneva, inv. no. 1935-0008

The drawing on four sheets pasted together reproduces the *Chocolate Girl* in the exact same dimensions and proportions as the original. Until recently it had been assumed that this was a preliminary drawing from which the motif was transferred onto the parchment of the Dresden painting. Yet the Geneva drawing does not exhibit either the prickings, the heavily retraced contour lines, or the pigmented verso that would confirm such a procedure. Presumably, the work is a drawing produced after the original pastel. The outlines, probably established with a quill, are composed of the tiniest, almost identical strokes—especially the horizontal lines—and suggest the use of some mechanical copying device like a pantograph. Others, like the vertical line marking the position of the shadow, were clearly made by hand. It is possible that this was a tracing from the original, the paper placed atop the glass protecting the pastel and its lines and contours copied in ink.

Since the painting already arrived in Dresden in 1745, the drawing must have been made immediately after the pastel was finished. The large sheet passed from Liotard's possession via his descendants to the Geneva collection. Perhaps the artist wished to keep this drawing in order to produce further versions of the *Chocolate Girl* at a later date, as he did with other sought-after motifs. The inscription in the upper right-hand corner was probably a later addition.

RE

Literature: R/L 2008, pp. 323–24 (no. 130); Humbert/Revilliod/Tilanus 1897, p. 154, no. 63; exh. cat. Geneva/Paris 1992, pp. 282–84, no. 98; see Frieß 1993, pp. 117–21.

Cat. 3

Jean-Étienne Liotard

(Geneva 1702–1789 Geneva)

Handmaid Presenting a Pot of Tea to an Oriental Woman Seated on a Divan

Circa 1740/42

Chalk, red chalk, and pencil on two sheets of paper, relined with Japanese paper, 20.5 x 28.5 cm

Kunst Museum Winterthur, Stiftung Oskar Reinhart, inv. no. 528

The drawing, executed in red and black chalk, crayon, and pencil shows a lady seated on a divan, a handleless teacup in her hand. A handmaid is standing next to her, holding a small tray with a metal teapot and a sugar bowl. The scene is set in a barely defined, plain, private interior. The lady is looking toward the viewer; her Turkish attire—the belted dress, black caftan, and headdress—is familiar from other Liotard works (see cat. 44). The cushions covered with arabesques and floral patterns contrast with the maid's red-and-white striped garment. Although, in her hesitant, servile pose, she seems clearly focused on the seated lady, Liotard drew the two figures on separate sheets, possibly even at different times. They were then joined to form a genre scene, the two tall-format sketches being combined into a horizontal format. In terms of composition, it is the divan that creates a sense of space. The motif of a person—usually a woman—seated on an oriental sofa is a frequent one in Liotard's oeuvre (cat. 51).

Both drawings were made during Liotard's stay in Constantinople. Of particular interest is the elegantly dressed handmaid, seen in profile facing to the left, as

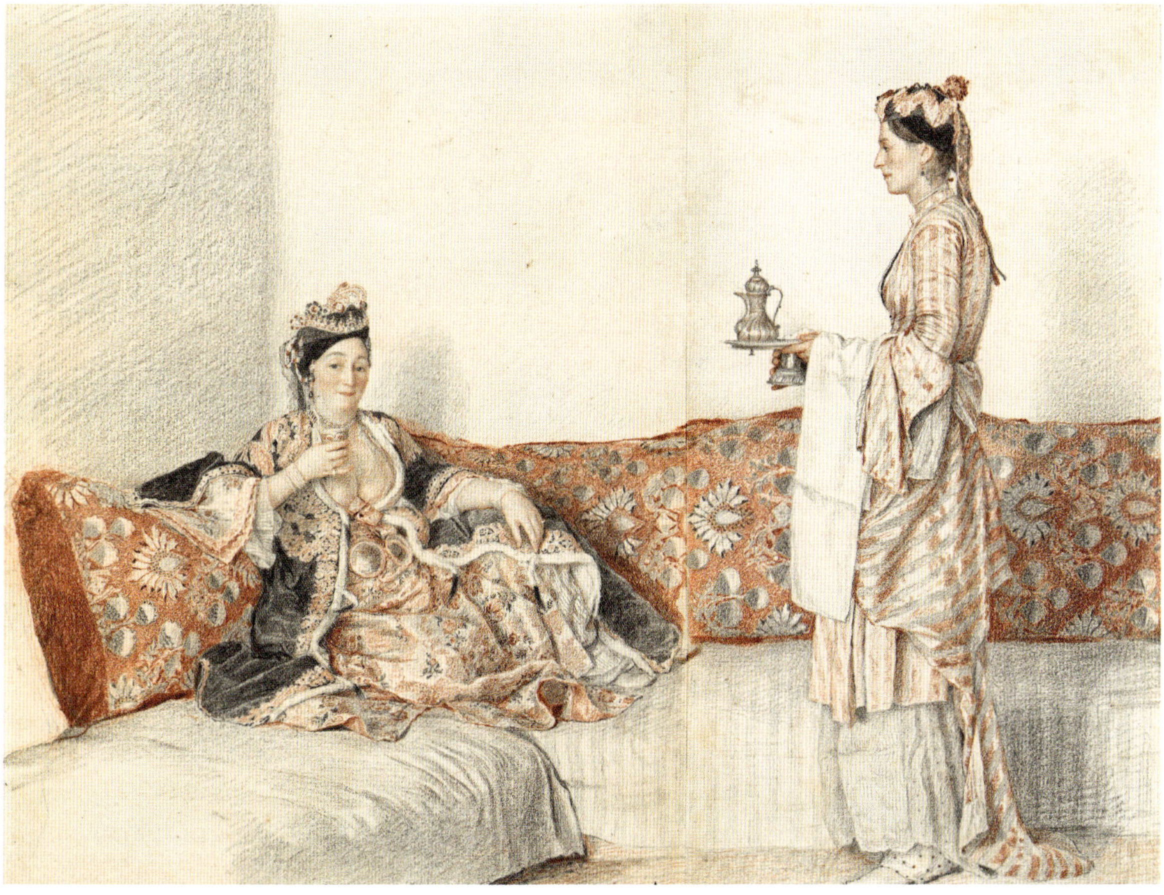

a precursor to the *Chocolate Girl*. Here the artist already focused on the most delicate details, including the chasing and light reflections on what is presumably a silver tea service. Consumption of tea imported from Asia was widespread in the Ottoman Empire in the eighteenth century.

RE

Literature: R/L 2008, no. 64; exh. cat. Geneva/Paris 1992, cat. 44; exh. cat. Edinburgh/London 2015, p. 191, cat. 22.

Cat. 4

JEAN-ÉTIENNE LIOTARD

(Geneva 1702–1789 Geneva)

Handmaid from the Levant Presenting a Teapot

1740/42

Counterproof from red and black chalk and pencil, heightened with red chalk, on paper, 22.8 x 11.5 cm

Bibliothèque nationale de France, inv. no. RCB-15719

A handmaid stands facing to the right, holding a sugar bowl in her left hand and a teapot on a silver tray in her right. A white napkin is draped across her right arm. Her red-and-white striped dress stands out against the horizontal band of floral-patterned cushions in the picture's center behind her. The fabric covering of the divan, in turn, takes up the stripes of her dress.

The present sheet is a so-called counterproof, a transfer to another sheet of paper from an original drawing with the motif reversed. In the current case, Liotard copied the motif of the handmaid from the Winterthur sheet originally composed of two drawings (cat. 3). He often used this method to quickly and simply make copies, which he used to appraise and possibly modify his composition. Normally, a counterproof was rarely made from a drawing, but more commonly from a fresh print in order to obtain an accurate mirror image of the printing plate. In this reworked counterproof, Liotard heightened the color distribution in a few places with red chalk. The *Chocolate Girl*, painted a few years later, is anticipated here, at least regarding the motif of a serving girl, her pose, and orientation.

RE

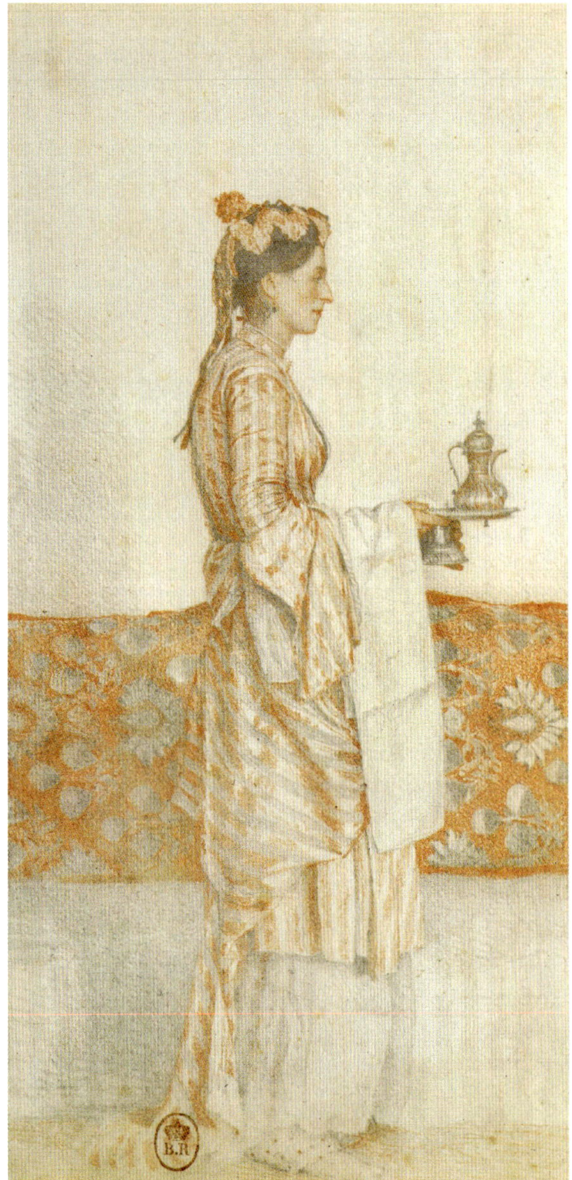

Literature: R/L 2008, p. 272 (no. 64); Humber/Revilliod/Tilanus 1897, p. 152, no. 40 (as a drawing); exh. cat. Geneva/Paris 1992, cat. 45, see cat. 44.

Cat. 5

Matthias Oesterreich

(Hamburg/Lübeck 1716–1778 Berlin)

After Pier Leone Ghezzi (Rome 1674–1755 Rome)

Bernardino Luchesini Bolognese

1751

Sheet 12 from *Recueil de quelques desseins*, Dresden 1752

Etching, 35.9 x 24.4 cm (sheet)

Inscribed in the plate, bottom right (reversed): "Matthaus Oesterreich Sculpsit Roma ad i 24. August 1751 Etat A 25"; inscribed bottom left: "Cavalliere Pietro Leone Ghezzi Disegno"; bottom right: "Matteo Oesterreich Incise. Roma 1751" and in script: "Bernardino Luchesini Bolognese / Il Disegno Originale si conserva nel Gabinetto di sua Eccelenza / Monsignore Conte de Brühl Primo Ministro di Sua Maestà / IL RÉ DI POLONIA ELTTORE DI SASSONIA"

Kupferstich-Kabinett, Staatliche Kunstsammlungen Dresden, inv. no. A 136379

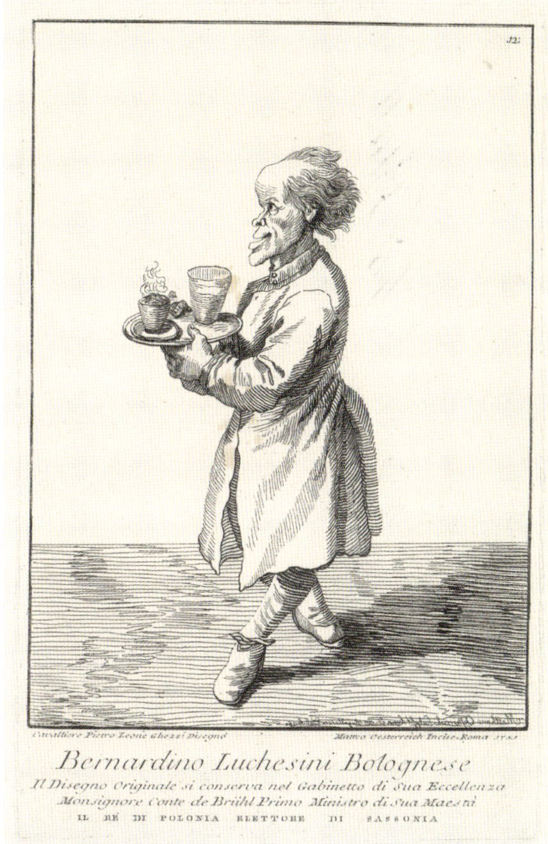

A little old man is pictured in full figure, carrying on a tray a cup with a hot drink and a glass of water. His features are benign, but clearly exaggerated as a caricature. He is walking from right to left; his left foot is placed somewhat splayed on the wooden floor, and his right leg, only partially visible, is misshapen. Walking must have been arduous for him, and balancing the drinks demanding a certain skill. Matthias Oesterreich made the etching after a drawing by Pier Leone Ghezzi (now in Ascoli Piceno). The figure, named as Bernardino Luchesini Bolognese, although this was added only in the etching, was Oesterreich's servant during his stay in Rome in 1751.

Oesterreich—a nephew of Carl Heinrich von Heineken, who arranged for his position as assistant curator at Dresden's museum of prints and drawings (now the Kupferstich-Kabinett) in 1752/53 and from 1753 at the Gemäldegalerie—had copied and etched Ghezzi's caricatures before, and published these in his book *Raccolta di XXIV caricature* in Dresden in 1751. In parallel with this, in 1752, he created the *Recueil de quelques desseins de plusieurs habiles maîtres* for the prime minister Heinrich Count von Brühl, with forty reproductions of drawings, most of which were in the Count's possession. This selection, which mainly illustrates Ghezzi's drawings, along with works by Marco Benefial and Giovanni Battista Internari, also includes this "Chocolate Man." Oesterreich reproduced him again in the collection of etchings published in Potsdam in 1766 (sheet 26). He must have known the Liotard pastel very well, since it had been in Dresden since 1745, and around 1756 he was perhaps the first to paint a copy of the *Chocolate Girl*, also for Brühl (see p. 52–53). Through this connection the exaggerated depiction of his servant takes on a special humorous note. Liotard and Ghezzi had met in Rome as early as 1737, and painted portraits of each other.

RE

Literature: Oesterreich 1766, sheet 26; exh. cat. Ascoli Piceno 1999, p. 70; Schepkowski 2009, pp. 166–180; Metze 2016, p. 66; see R/L 2008, no. 51 and p. 701, fig. 799.

Cat. 6

Anton Raphael Mengs

(Aussig 1728–1779 Rome)

Frederick Augustus II, Elector of Saxony, as Augustus III King of Poland

1745

Pastel on paper, 55.5 x 42 cm
Gemäldegalerie Alte Meister, Staatliche Kunstsammlungen Dresden, gal. no. P 173

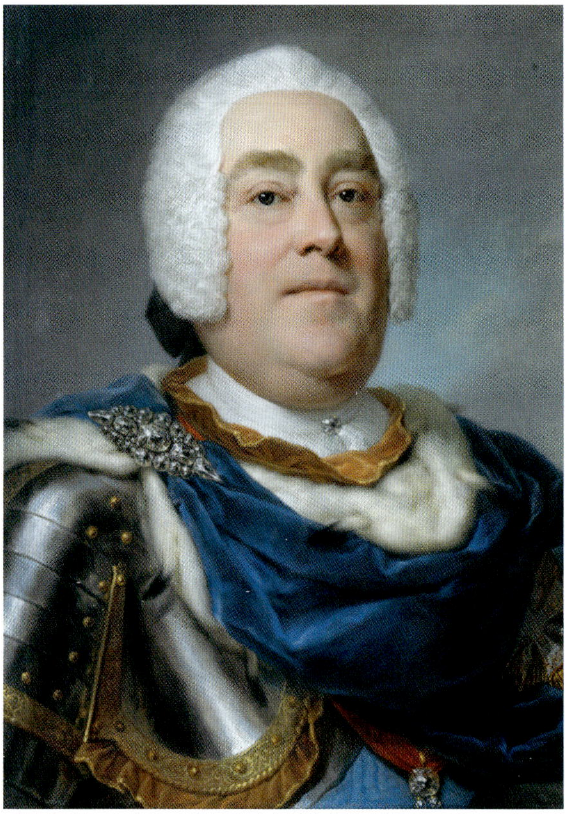

The portrait shows the Elector of Saxony Frederick Augustus II as King Augustus III of Poland, with attributes and costume indebted to the official iconography of the ruler. The view slightly from below emphasizes the monumental effect of the imposing bust portrait and leads the viewer's gaze toward the sky behind; on the other hand, it also emphasizes his double chin and fleshy face framed by the white peruke. The Elector-King's gaze is directed somewhere just above the viewer's head. He is wearing armor and a blue-lined ermine cloak fastened at the shoulder with a diamond clasp. Also visible are a small diamond brooch on his white cravat, the Order of the Golden Fleece on a red ribbon, and the star of the Polish Order of the White Eagle on his chest to the left, the blue sash partly visible, which presumably carried the order itself.

The art writer and physician Giovanni Lodovico Bianconi described in detail how Anton Raphael, aged only seventeen, portrayed the Regent in the shortest amount of time. Mengs did, however, model his portrait on a painting by the Saxon court painter Louis de Silvestre, showing Augustus in three-quarter figure. This now lost painting is known only from an engraving by Georg Friedrich Schmidt, who dates Silvestre's work to 1743. In his bust portrait, Mengs clearly limited himself to the small section showing the face and upper body. Around 1745 he again borrowed from other Silvestre pictures, effectively copying them. It is possible that Mengs wished to be seen as a potential successor to the French *peintre du roi* who had worked in Dresden for nearly thirty years.

RE

Literature: Roettgen 1999, pp. 220–21, no. 149; Riedel/Wenzel 1765, p. 242; Bianconi 1781, pp. 15–16; exh. cat. Dresden 2001, pp. 126–27, no. 16; Henning/Marx 2007, pp. 142–44; Marx 2008.

Cat. 7

Rosalba Carriera

(Venice 1673–1757 Venice)

Self-Portrait as "Winter"

1730/31

Pastel on paper, 46.5 x 34 cm

Gemäldegalerie Alte Meister, Staatliche Kunstsammlungen Dresden, gal. no. P 29

In this self-portrait from 1730, Rosalba Carriera, the best-known pastellist of her time, pictures herself as an allegory of winter. The painting was her way of seeking a meaningful representation of herself in her later years, and the artist skillfully preserves a balance between portrait and allegory. The ermine trim on her blue cloak, rendered with swift, light and dark crayon strokes, together with her headdress, symbolize the fourth season, to which she relates her advanced age of fifty-seven. She does not portray herself in idealized beauty, but with worn features and a critical, introspective gaze. She was said to have had a sharp, penetrating mind, and this is manifest in her blue eyes. Carriera initially worked as a miniaturist before concentrating on pastel painting. She attained great fame in 1720 when she was admitted to the Paris Academy on account of her skill in pastel painting. In 1730 she spent six months in Vienna, and it was there that she produced the self-portrait—possibly commissioned by the imperial court—that she sent to the Habsburg residence in 1731. Many prominent travelers sought out the painter in Venice while on their Grand Tour. Among them was the Saxon Crown Prince Frederick Augustus, who first met Carriera in 1712 and would become her most ardent admirer. He would ultimately own the most extensive collection of her pictures, a total of 157 pastels, which were displayed in Dresden's pastel cabinet, also known as "Cabinet of Rosalba." Francesco Algarotti, who purchased Liotard's *Chocolate Girl* for Augustus's collection, communicated to Dresden Carriera's verdict of it as "the most beautiful pastel ever seen."

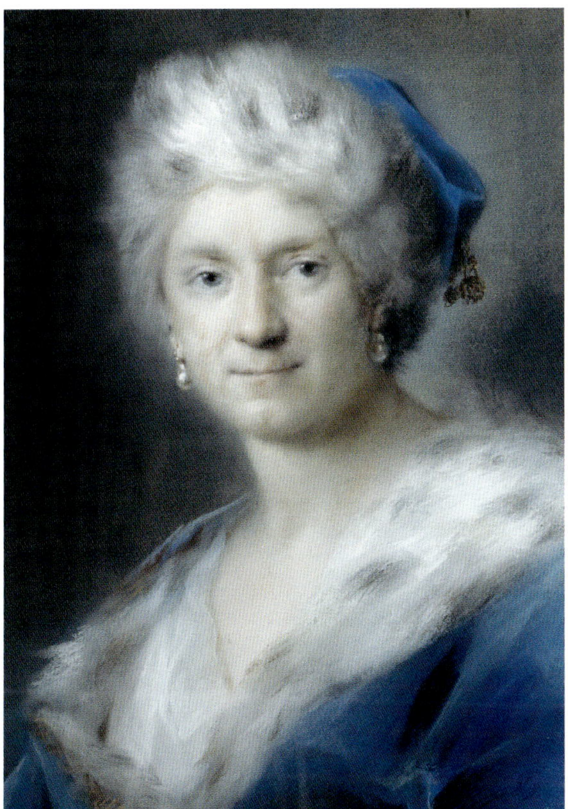

RE

Literature: Riedel/Wenzel 1765, p. 240; Sani 1988, p. 312, no. 276; Henning/Marx 2007, pp. 16–19; Sani 2008, p. 286, no. 315.

Cat. 8

Jean-Étienne Liotard

(Geneva 1702–1789 Geneva)

Il Conte Francesco Algarotti (1712–1764)

Circa 1745

Pastel on parchment, 40.5 x 31.5 cm

Museum Huis Doorn, The Netherlands, inv. no. HuD 01716

Count Francesco Algarotti, a member of a Venetian merchant family, is pictured in profile facing left, dressed in a radiant blue velvet jacket with fur trim, in front of a gray-brown background. His head is turned to gaze directly at the viewer. The white of his shirt and black of his cravat merge with the gray of his powdered peruke. Liotard presumably painted this bust of Algarotti in the spring of 1745, around the

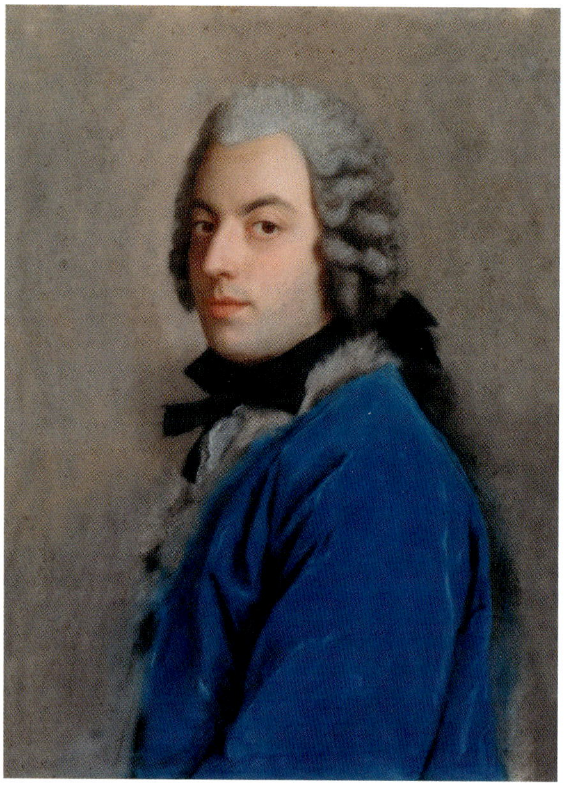

time the count acquired the *Chocolate Girl* for the Dresden gallery. A native of Venice, widely educated and acting as writer, philosopher, and advisor in all matters of art, Algarotti was a welcome conversationalist at Europe's princely courts. He enjoyed an especially close relationship with the Prussian King Frederick the Great as well as with Augustus III. He worked for the latter as his art agent, and bought in Italy any number of masterpieces for the Dresden gallery (cat. 12). It is not known why Liotard portrayed the count; perhaps he was hoping for further commissions or even a summons to the Dresden court.

In 1893 the portrait passed from the Algarotti family to the Prussian Emperor Wilhelm II, who took it with him when he fled to Huis Doorn in 1918. Since 1952 the portrait has been the property of the Dutch state. A second, slightly larger version of the portrait, which Liotard painted for himself, came by way of his descendants to Amsterdam's Rijksmuseum in 1873. Raphael Morghen made an engraving of this second painting, which served as frontispiece for the first volume of the reprinting of Algarotti's writings, published in Venice between 1791 and 1794.

RE

Literature: R/L 2008, no. 135, see no. 136; Seidel 1894, with a color heliogravure; Humbert/Revilliod/Tilanus 1897, pp. 110–11, no. 23, pp. 182–83, no. 34, 34*; Heyn 1913, pp. 282–84; exh. cat. Edinburgh/London 2015, cat. 63.

Cat. 9

Jean-Étienne Liotard

(Geneva 1702–1789 Geneva)

Receipt for payment of 120 sequins by Francesco Algarotti

1745

Handwritten on paper, 14.5 x 20.6 cm

Lowell Libson & Jonny Yarker Ltd., London

In 1742/43 Francesco Algarotti was sent to Italy by the Saxon prime minister Heinrich von Brühl to purchase works of art for the planned Dresden painting gallery. Algarotti was familiar with the Saxon Elector's taste in art and his fondness for pastel paintings, and,

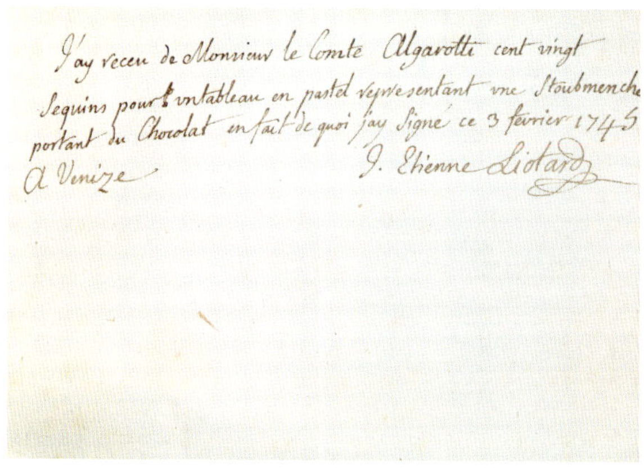

J'ay receu de Monsieur le Comte Algarotti cent vingt
Sequins pour un tableau en pastel representant une Staubmenche
portant du Chocolat en fait de quoi jay Signé ce 3 fevrier 1745
a Venize
J. Etienne Liotard

through his extensive network, he would have learned of the arrival in Venice of Jean-Étienne Liotard, possibly through the latter's twin brother Jean-Michel Liotard, who was still living in Venice at the time. This small, handwritten receipt, inscribed only in the top third of the sheet, appears to have been jotted down spontaneously. Written in French, it identifies the picture subject with the German term "Stoubmenche" (*Stubenmensch*, used synonymously for "serving girl" and "serving woman") followed by: "carrying chocolate." It confirms the receipt from Algarotti of "one hundred and twenty sequins" and is dated February 3, 1745. A sequin was equal to a Venetian gold ducat, with a gold content of ca. 3.5 grams. Considering that Rosalba Carriera charged roughly thirty sequins for a pastel, the price of 120 sequins for Liotard's work is very high. Algarotti published the details of this acquisition in his *Lettere sopra la pittura* (Letters on painting). In his correspondence, preserved in the Saxon Main State Archive in Dresden, he states the sum, which was first revealed by Wilhelm Schäfer in his gallery guide from 1864. In 1811, in his *Versuch zur Beurtheilung der Königl. Sächs. Gemähldesammlung,* von Racknitz had still spoken more vaguely of "a pastel painting" that Liotard had sold dearly for 130 sequins. This reference to his high prices, often seen as inflated, is a frequent theme in contemporary writings on Liotard's life and work.

RE

Literature: Algarotti *Opere*, 1792, vol. 8, pp. 32–33; [von Racknitz] 1811b, p. 5; Schäfer 1864, p. 289; Posse 1931, p. 29, note 7; https://neiljeffares.wordpress.com/2015/05/25/liotardiana/ (accessed August 16, 2016).

Cat. 10

Republic of Venice, Doge Marcantonio Giustinian
(1684–1688), sequin,
Venice Mint

Obverse: M•ANT•IVSTIN DVX – S•M•VENET.
Saint Mark standing on the left handing a long cross to the doge kneeling on the right.
Reverse: SIT.T:XRE•DAT.Q.TV – REGIS•ISTE•DUCA.
Christ in a mandorla.
Gold, Ø 22.0 mm, 3.52 g
Münzkabinett, Staatliche Kunstsammlungen Dresden,
inv. no. ATA724

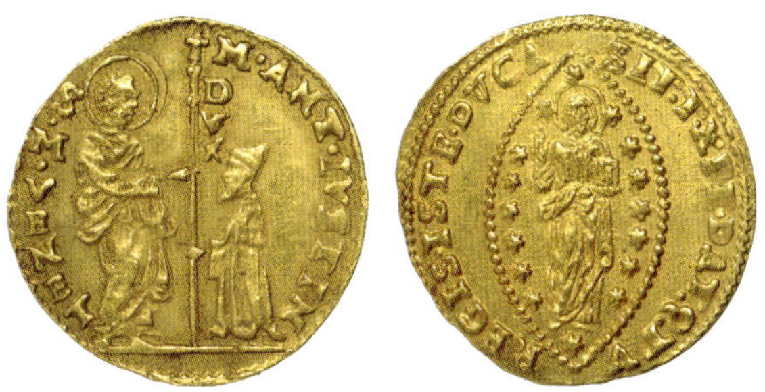

Cat. 11

Republic of Venice, Doge Alvise Mocenigo III
(1722–1732),
two sequins
(struck from the dies of the silver 1/4 ducat),
Venice Mint

Obverse: S*M*V*ALOY*MOCENI*D. Saint Mark enthroned on the left blesses the doge, kneeling before him and holding a standard adorned with a cross. In the exergue the initials V.Q (= mintmaster Vincenzo Querini) between two rosettes.
VReverse: QVAR•DVCAT•VENET. The winged Lion of Saint Mark stands facing left before a castle, resting his right paw on a book. In the exergue a large rosette between two smaller ones.
Gold, Ø 29.0 mm, 6.95 g
Münzkabinett, Staatliche Kunstsammlungen Dresden,
inv. no. ATA715

As the sales receipt (cat. 9) attests, Francesco Algarotti paid the painter Jean-Étienne Liotard 120 Venetian sequins for the pastel *The Chocolate Girl.* Sequins were gold coins first minted in Venice in 1284. The

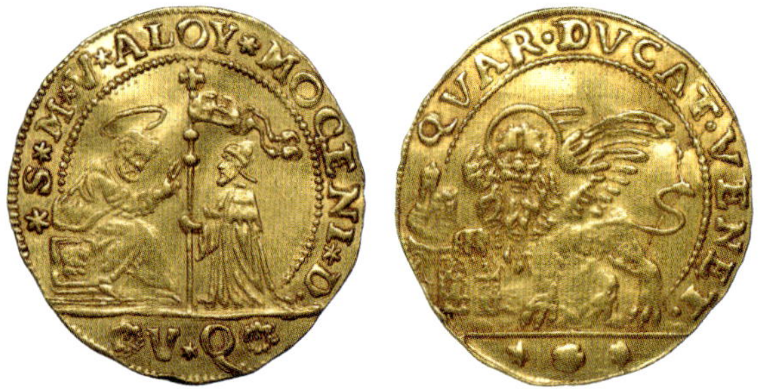

Cat. 12

Giuseppe Nogari

(Venice 1699–1763 Venice)

The Miser

Undated (before 1743)

Oil on canvas, 74.5 x 59 cm

Gemäldegalerie Alte Meister, Staatliche Kunstsammlungen Dresden, gal. no. 589

important trading and sea power issued the coins with virtually identical images and a consistent gold content and weight for more than five hundred years, until Napoleon occupied Venice in 1797 and dissolved the republic's Great Council.

The sequin's obverse shows Saint Mark handing a cross, and thus ruling authority, to the doge kneeling before him. The reverse pictures Christ standing in a mandorla. Its abbreviated inscription reads: "Sit tibi Christe datus quem tu regis iste ducatus" (To you, Christ, let this duchy be given that you rule). The double sequin takes up the obverse image with slight variations, and on the reverse presents the symbol of Venice, the Lion of Saint Mark.

The designation "ducat" derives from the word DUCATUS (duchy) appearing in the sequin's legend. The ducat was the most important, long-lived, and most stable European gold coin in the modern era. In 1559 Emperor Ferdinand I made it the main gold coin of the Holy Roman Empire. Corresponding to its Venetian predecessor, it weighed about 3.49 grams, with a gold content of 98.6 percent. Ducats were minted in Saxony from the late sixteenth century, thus in the reign of Elector Frederick Augustus II. At the Dresden court, Count Algarotti was likely reimbursed for his purchase with 120 Saxon ducats or 60 double ducats.

WH

Literature: Montenegro 2012, nos. 2063, 2434.

In dramatic chiaroscuro the painting shows an old man with gray hair and a full beard, depicted in half-length. He is wearing a brown coat with pale fur trims on the sleeves, a blue cloak across his shoulders, and a dark cap on his head. With his right hand he empties gold coins from a bag into a bowl. The thumb of his left hand reaches into the bowl with the coins and in his fingers he holds a large key. While his clothes show him to be a person of high rank, the bowl of money is generally seen as a sign of greed and stinginess. However, the title *The Miser* only appears in gallery catalogues from the mid nineteenth century onward.

Count Francesco Algarotti purchased this painting for the collections of King Augustus III directly from the artist in Venice in 1743. He also consulted the artist as an expert on other purchases and endeavored to support his career, for example by commissioning prints after Nogari's paintings. Felice Polanzani produced an engraving after Nogari's Dresden picture as early as 1744. In his role as art agent, Algarotti not only bought the *Chocolate Girl*, but among other works also the *Madonna* (Bartholomäus Sarburgh, ca. 1635, gal. no. 1892), which until the late nineteenth century was attributed to Hans Holbein the Younger. He also awarded large commissions to artist friends like Giovanni Battista Piazzetta or Giovanni Battista Tiepolo, with the aim of setting their contemporary works in competition with older art.

RE

Literature: Riedel/Wenzel 1765, G.I, p. 150; Hübner 1856, p. 134, no. 378; Posse 1931, p. 26; Liebsch 2010; Wohlfarth 2010, p. 264.

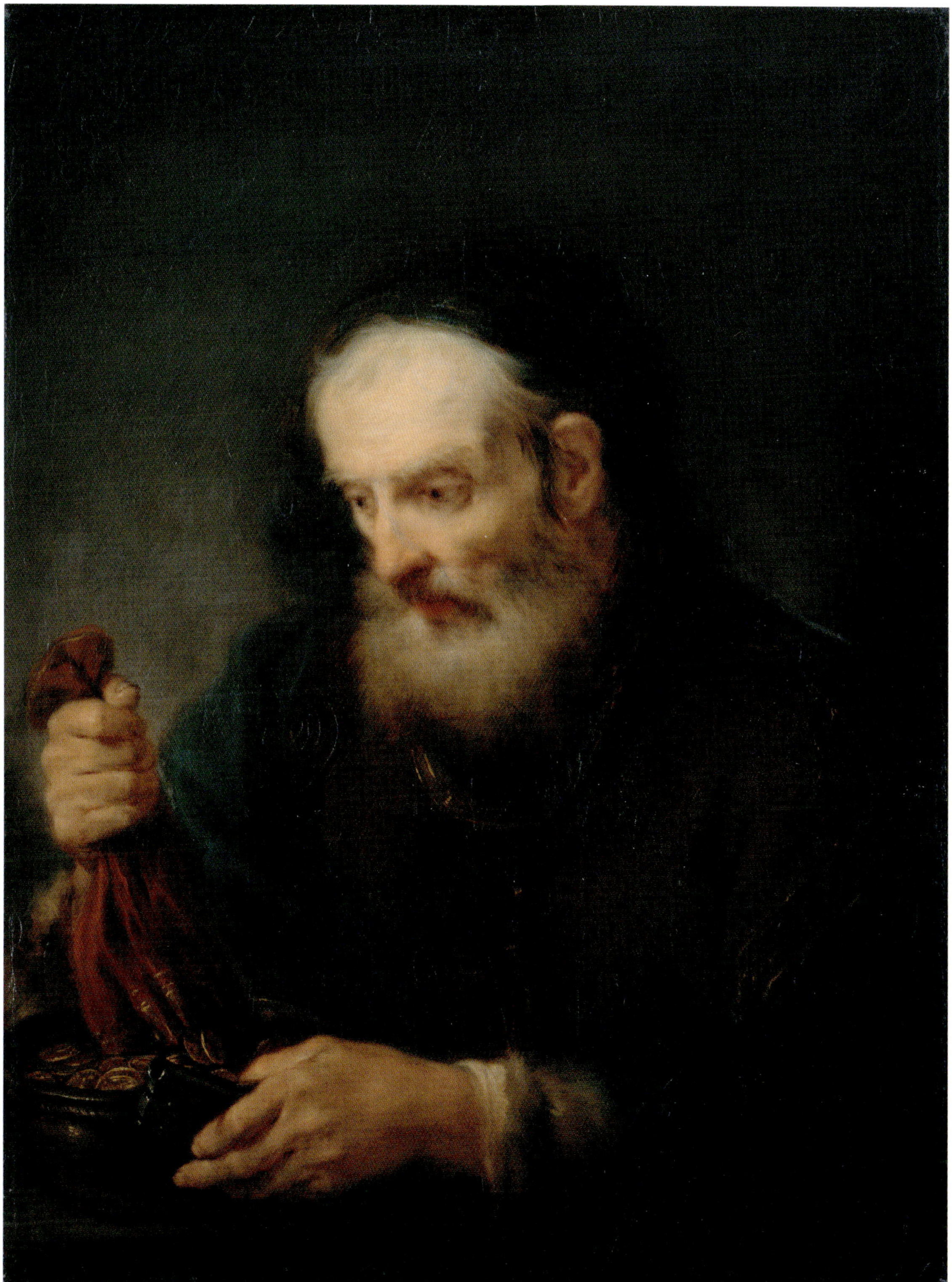

Cat. 13

Hann Trier

(Kaiserswerth 1915–1999 Castiglione della Pescaia)

Sequence after J.-E. Liotard

La tasse au chocolat: L'arrivée / Arôme et splendeur / La chute

1991

Egg tempera on canvas, 96 x 128 / 96 x 128 / 96 x 115 cm

Albertinum / Galerie Neue Meister,

Staatliche Kunstsammlungen Dresden, inv. no. 03/02

(2003 gift from the Kunststiftung Hann Trier)

The Cup of Chocolate: The Arrival / Aroma and Splendor / The Fall—these pithy titles evoke a scenic narration in three chapters. Their protagonist: the well-known *Chocolate Girl*, a jewel of exquisite pastel painting and precise rendering of objects.

Nearly 250 years after Liotard's original, this energy-filled, brightly colored work was created by the then 78-year-old Hann Trier, who felt an affinity with the Rococo, especially in his use of color. He is considered one of the most important representatives of Art Informel, which aimed to further develop Expressionism using a non-objective approach. In the early 1950s Trier began painting abstract compositions with both hands, using two brushes simultaneously and bold, dancing movements. In gestural, spontaneous brushwork he captured streaming, flowing, swirling forms on the canvas, which, in the case of *Sequence after J.-E. Liotard*, still suggest an astonishing amount of the work referenced—at least in the beginning, since the dynamism of the colors increases and accelerates from picture to picture until the forms are almost completely dissolved.

Yet the subject matter is not the only reference to the art of the Old Masters. The arrangement of the pictures into a triptych format as well as the implied simultaneous narrative are rooted in the art of the Middle Ages. Recent research has shown that even Art Informel is closely aligned with art-historical traditions, a fact that is occasionally expressed in direct pictorial homages and paraphrases. Trier's ironic picture sequence is a whimsical and sensuous approach without being obsequious, a richly contrasting transformation of a traditional picture form, in which certainties seemingly carved in stone are once again made fluid.

The triptych was presented to the Staatliche Kunstsammlungen Dresden in 2003, on the occasion of the exhibition *Hann Trier: Zwischen Alten und Neuen Meistern* in the Albertinum, where it was displayed next to works by other contemporaries such as Karl Otto Götz, Ernst Wilhelm Nay, and Wols (Alfred Otto Wolfgang Schulze)—but also in direct juxtaposition with Liotard's masterpiece.

AD

Literature: Euler-Schmidt 1995, p. 109, no. 799 (Uta Gerlach-Laxner); Wagner 1999, pp. 8–13; Wagner 2002, pp. 187–90; Bischoff 2009, pp. 116–17; Dehmer 2013, pp. 170–71.

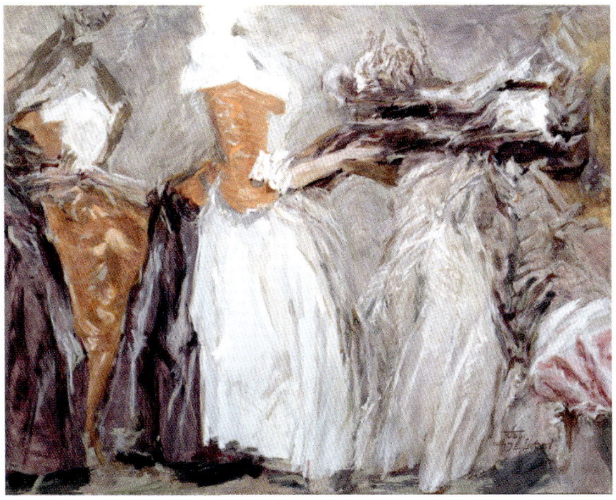

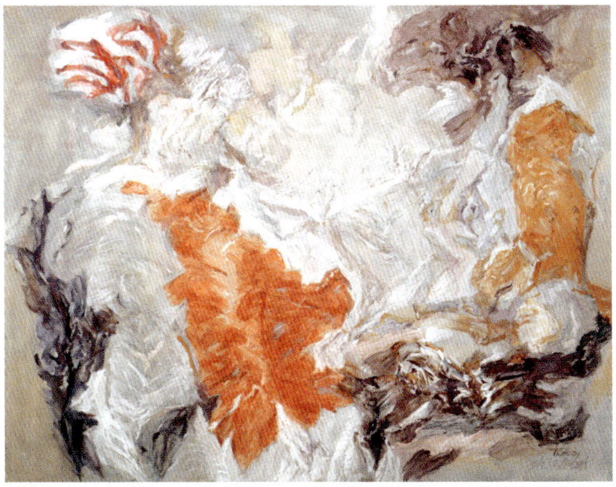

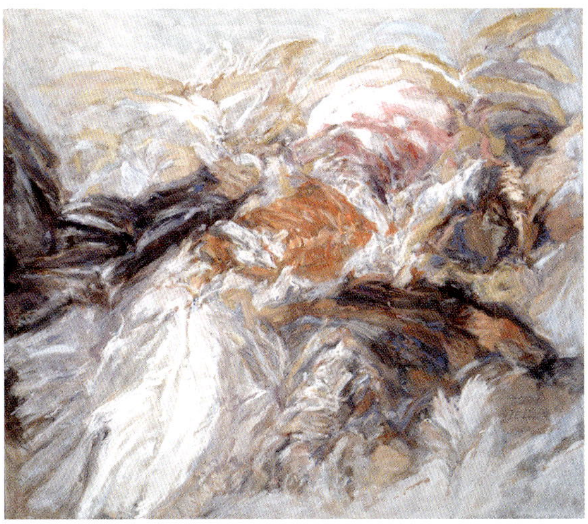

SELF-PORTRAITS AND TRAINING

Jean-Étienne Liotard produced more than twenty self-portraits at various times throughout his life, so we have a detailed record of what he looked like from the beginning of his career well into his advanced years. These self-portraits also represent all the various techniques he used—engraving, drawing, enamel, and oil and pastel painting. His self-portraits as "Turkish painter," wearing oriental costume and with a long beard, received particular attention. After his marriage in 1756 he abandoned the beard, but he continued to be known as "le peintre turc."

In the eighteenth century, Liotard's hometown of Geneva was known not only for its clockmaking. Several workshops specialized in the creation of showy enamel cases for pocket watches. Jewelers from the Huaud family in particular set the standard for quality and influenced the appearance of these miniatures until well into mid century. Liotard first learned the art of enameling and miniature painting under Daniel Gardelle in Geneva, and then, from 1723, he studied for three more years in Paris under Jean-Baptiste Massé.

Cat. 14

Jean-Étienne Liotard

(Geneva 1702–1789 Geneva)

Self-Portrait in Turkish Costume

Circa 1746

Pastel on blue paper, 60.5 x 46.5 cm

Gemäldegalerie Alte Meister,

Staatliche Kunstsammlungen Dresden,

gal. no. P 159

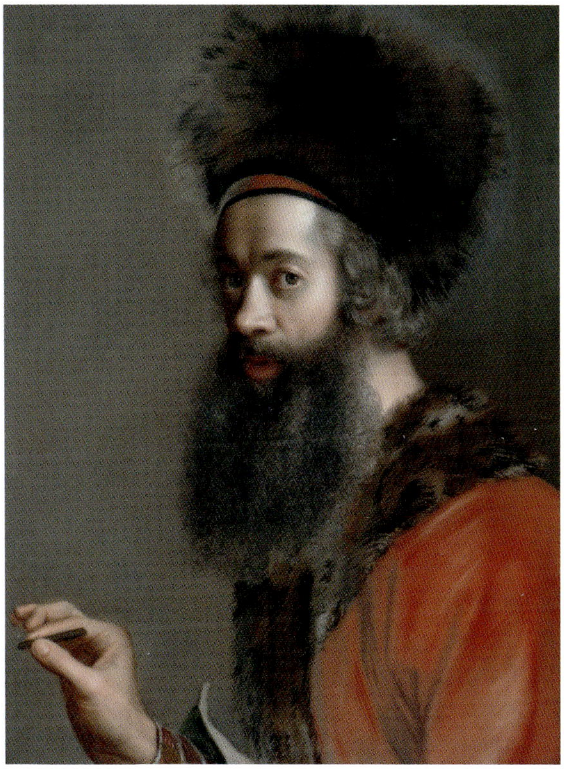

In this self-portrait Liotard pictures himself in bust format facing left; his gaze is directed toward his reflection in a mirror and thus the viewer. The pastel crayon in his right hand identifies him as a painter. His red caftan stands out in front of the green-shaded background of the blue paper. The caftan is bordered with fur, and on his head he wears a red cap with a large fur hat on top. With these items of clothing, acquired during his stays in Constantinople and Jassy between 1738 and 1742, and especially with his bushy beard, he presented himself—as in his Florentine portrait painted a short time before (see cat. 16)—as a "Turkish painter." The Dresden picture demonstrates Liotard's mastery in the realistic representation and detailed rendering of the various furs and his beard and head hair.

Throughout his life, Liotard created well over twenty self-portraits, which mainly served as displays of his skill, but also as self-presentation. While in Lyon in 1746/47 he sold this present painting, together with the portrait of his niece Mlle. Lavergne (cat. 69), to Louis François Armand de Vignerot du Plessis, Duke of Richelieu, who sent the two pictures to Dresden.

RE

Literature: R/L 2008, no. 158; Riedel/Wenzel 1765, p. 243; Henning/Marx 2007, pp. 101–05; Senlé 2008, pp. 202–03; see Williams 2012, pp. 1–5.

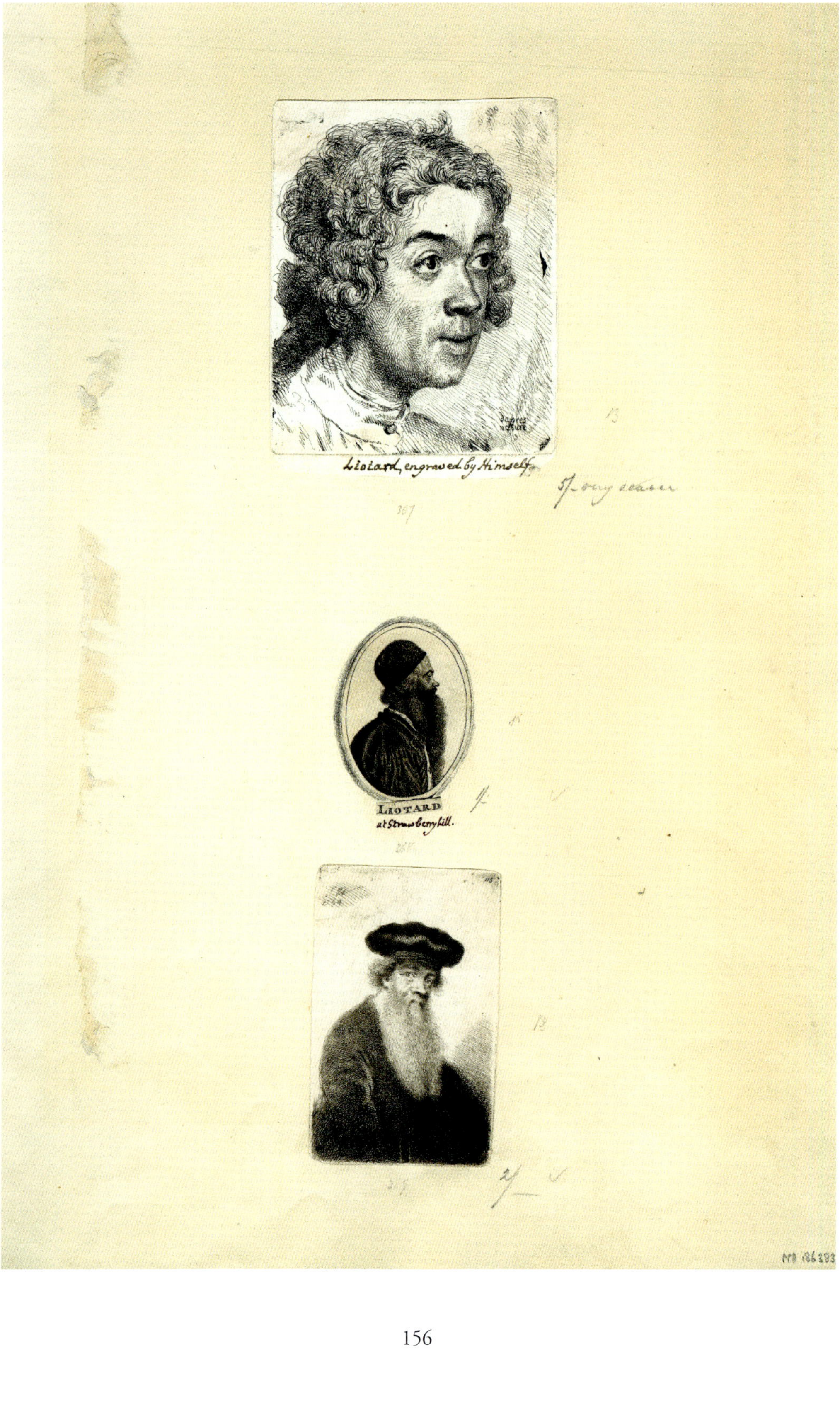
Liotard, engraved by Himself.
LIOTARD
at Strawberry hill.

Cat. 15
Horace Walpole
(London 1717–1797 London)
Three portraits of J E Liotard mounted on a sheet from an album formerly in the collection of Horace Walpole
Circa 1750–1770
40.2 x 21.5 cm
The British Museum, London, inv. no. 1852,0214.357 to 359

A: **Jean-Étienne Liotard**
(Geneva 1702–1789 Geneva)
Self-Portrait
Circa 1733 (second state)
Etching, 11.7 x 10.1, pasted onto a large album sheet
Inscribed in the plate bottom right: "d'après nature"; below this by hand on the mounting: "Liotard, engraved by Himself"

B: **James Bretherton**
(active in London second half of the eighteenth century)
Portrait of Jean-Étienne Liotard in Profile
Circa 1770
Engraving, 6.4 x 4.9 cm (oval), pasted onto a large album sheet
Inscribed on the paper: "Liotard"; below this by hand on the mounting: "at Strawberry hill"

C: **Thomas Worlidge**
(Peterborough, Cambridgeshire 1700–1766 London)
Portrait of Jean-Étienne Liotard
1754
Etching, 9.9 x 6.6 cm, pasted onto a large album sheet
Inscribed upper left: "T.W. / 1754"; upper right: "115"

Horace Walpole, 4th Earl of Orford, was a British aristocrat. He was a politician, wrote novels through which he established the genre of the "Gothic novel," theorized about English landscape gardens, and with his *Anecdotes of Painting in England* wrote the first biographical survey of painters active in England. In 1747 he acquired Strawberry Hill in Twickenham near London, which he went on to remodel to his own personal taste in the Gothic Revival style—one that would be replicated all over Europe from the eighteenth century onward. He also used the house to display his extensive collection of art treasures. He was in personal contact with a number of artists, and Jean-Étienne Liotard, too, was a guest at his estate. One sheet survives from Walpole's album of artist portraits, which he had compiled himself. Mounted on it are three small prints with portraits of Liotard—a self-portrait and two by other hands. Walpole added the handwritten inscriptions himself. The sheet attests not only to Walpole's own passion for collecting, but also to Liotard's popularity in England.

In the self-portrait, known only from a few prints, Liotard pictured himself in half-profile facing to the right (A). His head, practically filling the sheet, conveys closeness and a certain intimacy. The curls at the back of his head are tied with a ribbon; only the collar and top button of his shirt are visible. He seems to be gazing into an undefined distance. Three states of the engraving survive, the first only as a counterproof (Fondation Custodia, Paris), the third in a copy without the small mark at the level of the eyes (Bibliothèque nationale de France). According to a description that accompanies this version, it was created in 1733 when Liotard was still a pupil of Jean-Baptiste Massé in Paris. In reality, however, he was only apprenticed with him from 1723 to 1726. Comparison with his undated self-portrait in oil would suggest that this picture is from around 1731.

James Bretherton produced the oval engraving with a bust portrait of Liotard (B). It shows the Genevan artist in profile facing to the right. He is dressed in his "Turkish painter" garb, wearing his cap with a black hem and a caftan over a white shirt with a floral pattern. His curly gray hair blends into the long beard, likewise gray. Bretherton, who worked in London as an engraver, etcher, and watercolorist in the second half of the eighteenth century, drew upon a Liotard self-portrait now known from an enamel medallion from 1753 that entered the Royal Collection in London by way of Augusta, Princess of Wales. The painter presents himself looking to the left, his red cap and burgundy-red cloak glowing against a white background. The colorful flowers adorning his shirt are clearly visible. In fact, Walpole also owned an enamel of Liotard's; in a watercolor view of his cabinet of miniatures, Liotard's profile is clearly recognizable on the inside of the right door. It is possible that Walpole commissioned Bretherton to make the engraving after this enamel so as to be able to include the artist in his *Anecdotes*. Curiously, however, in there, the small oval portrait was combined with a larger portrait by the Dresden painter Christian Friedrich Zincke.

The third portrait was produced by Thomas Worlidge, an English painter and graphic artist who was greatly influenced by Rembrandt (C). It shows Liotard in half-profile turned to the right, gazing wide-eyed at the viewer. Whereas his dark coat is lost in the shadow at the bottom edge of the picture, his head with the long beard stands out against a light, unworked background. The large, dark beret is especially reminiscent of Rembrandt paintings. In Worlidge's self-portrait, also included in Walpole's *Anecdotes*, the artist depicted himself with the same headdress. Whether Liotard and Worlidge had met or were in contact with each other is not known.

RE

Literature: (A:) R/L 2008, no. 18; Humbert/Revilliod/Tilanus 1897, p. 163, no. 1; see R/L 2008, no. 17.

(B:) R/L 2008, p. 440 (no. 262), fig. 394; Vertue/Walpole, vol. 4 (1771/1780), pp. 90–91; see Walpole 1784, p.60.

(C:) R/L 2008, p. 701, fig. 813; see Vertue/Walpole, vol. 4 (1771/1780), pp. 66–67.

Cat. 16

After Jean-Étienne Liotard

(Geneva 1702–1789 Geneva)

Self-Portrait, after the painting in Florence from 1744

1762/1790

Sheet 213 of the *Raccolta di num. 220 tavole intagliate . . . ritratti . . . nella Real Galleria di Firenze*, Florence 1790

Inscribed in the picture: "Signé J. E. Liotard / de Geneve surnommé / le Peintre Turc peint / par lui meme a / Vienne 1744"; inscribed below: "Gio. Stefano Liotard Pittore / nato in Ginevra nel 1702. morto nel . . . / 213"

Engraving, colored, 29 x 18.5 cm

Cabinet d'arts graphiques des Musées d'art et d'histoire, Geneva, inv. no. Est 0330

The engraving reproduces the half-figure self-portrait that Liotard painted in 1744 in Vienna, around the time he painted the *Chocolate Girl*. This self-portrait shows the artist for the first time in the oriental attire he had acquired during his sojourns in Constantinople and Jassy: over a red cap he wears a dark-brown fur hat, and over the almost white shirt a dark green caftan. The impressive beard in the center of the portrait draws the viewer's attention while Liotard gazes out from above it. The coloring of the engraving attempts to approximate the original colors.

The Florentine pastel was the only self-portrait the artist painted on commission. Francis Stephen, Maria Theresa's husband, had ordered it, in his role as Grand Duke of Tuscany, for the famous gallery of painters' portraits in Florence's Uffizi. The collection, begun in 1664 by Cardinal Leopoldo de' Medici, remains known to this day as a unique documentation of portraiture: each of the artists represented here, among them Rosalba Carriera, along with Liotard as a non-academic artist, could be assured of great recognition. This was also the reason for the unusual inscription, which laid the foundation for the Swiss artist's lifelong presentation of himself as the "Turkish painter." The picture was widely reproduced and disseminated through various publications. The first print made from it, by Carlo Gregori, was included by Francesco Moücke in his 1762 *Museo Fiorentino*; the present, somewhat larger version in the collec-

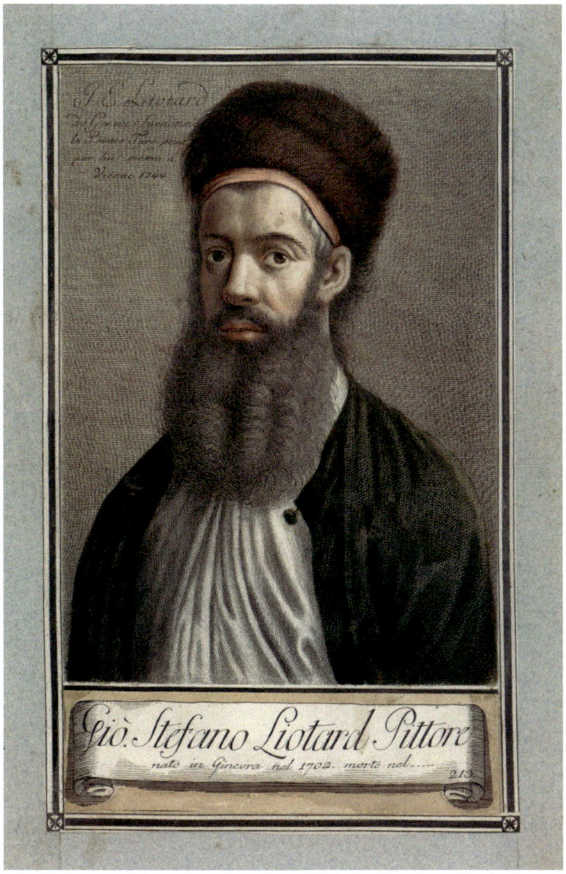

tion of 220 engravings after paintings in the Uffizi Gallery, published in 1790.

RE

Literature: R/L 2008, no. 128; Moücke 1762, pp. 273–76; Prinz 1971, pp. 14, 229–31; see Sheriff 2010, p. 97; Williams 2012, pp. 16–18; exh. cat. Karlsruhe 2015, pp. 64–65 (Astrid Reuter).

Cat. 17

Jean-Étienne Liotard

(Geneva 1702–1789 Geneva)

Self-Portrait with Hand on Chin (Large Version)

Before 1779

Mezzotint, etching and roulette (2nd state),
48.1 x 39.7 cm (image), 61 x 46 cm (sheet)
Inscribed bottom left: "No. 1"; bottom right: "Gravé par lui même"; and center: "I. E. Liotard. Effet.
Clair obscur sans sacrife"
Cabinet d'arts graphiques des Musées d'art et d'histoire, Geneva,
inv. no. E 86-0005

This self-portrait in old age shows Liotard in half-figure, facing left and seated on a chair, the back of which is visible behind him. His head is slightly tilted as he gazes pensively out at the viewer, his brow furrowed, his left hand on his beardless chin. This emphasis on the lack of his beard, which for so long had been such an important symbol of his sense of identity as an artist, has been interpreted as Liotard's reflection on the interplay of different cultural identities inherent in his work. He is wearing a cap, from which his long, gray hair emerges. The rendering of his hand and face clearly reveals the traces of old age. Liotard made two engravings from this portrait, one large version and one about half as large. The parallel hatching gives the background and clothing a lighter appearance, while his face is accentuated with short strokes and dots. The self-portrait was doubtless originally intended to be published as the first of seven illustrations in his *Traité des principes et des règles de la peinture* from 1781, to illustrate the principles discussed but also to underscore his self-understanding as an artist. As it turned out, however, Liotard never published a version of the treatise with illustrations.

Even in his advanced age, between 1765 and the late 1770s, Liotard produced at least ten self-portraits in various media that follow the present type with his hand on his chin. The print exhibited here is especially similar to a self-portrait from around 1770, executed in pastel, and a drawing from 1771, after which he probably produced the reversed engraving. A characteristic feature common to them all is the caftan with wide sleeves, rendered in blue in the pastel and the drawing, and the red cap, which he wears in nearly all of his self-portraits created after the Florence one (see cat. 16). His self-portraits appear to be not only ways to present himself, but also attempts to depict with visual precision his own body in different mediums.

SD

Literature: R/L 2008, no. 522 (large version), no. 523 (small version), see also no. 447; Schmidt-Linsenhoff 2004, pp. 173–76; Williams 2012, pp. 4, 23, 26–29, fig. 8; see also exh. cat. Edinburgh/London 2015, cat. 8; Rümelin 2018, pp. 83–84.

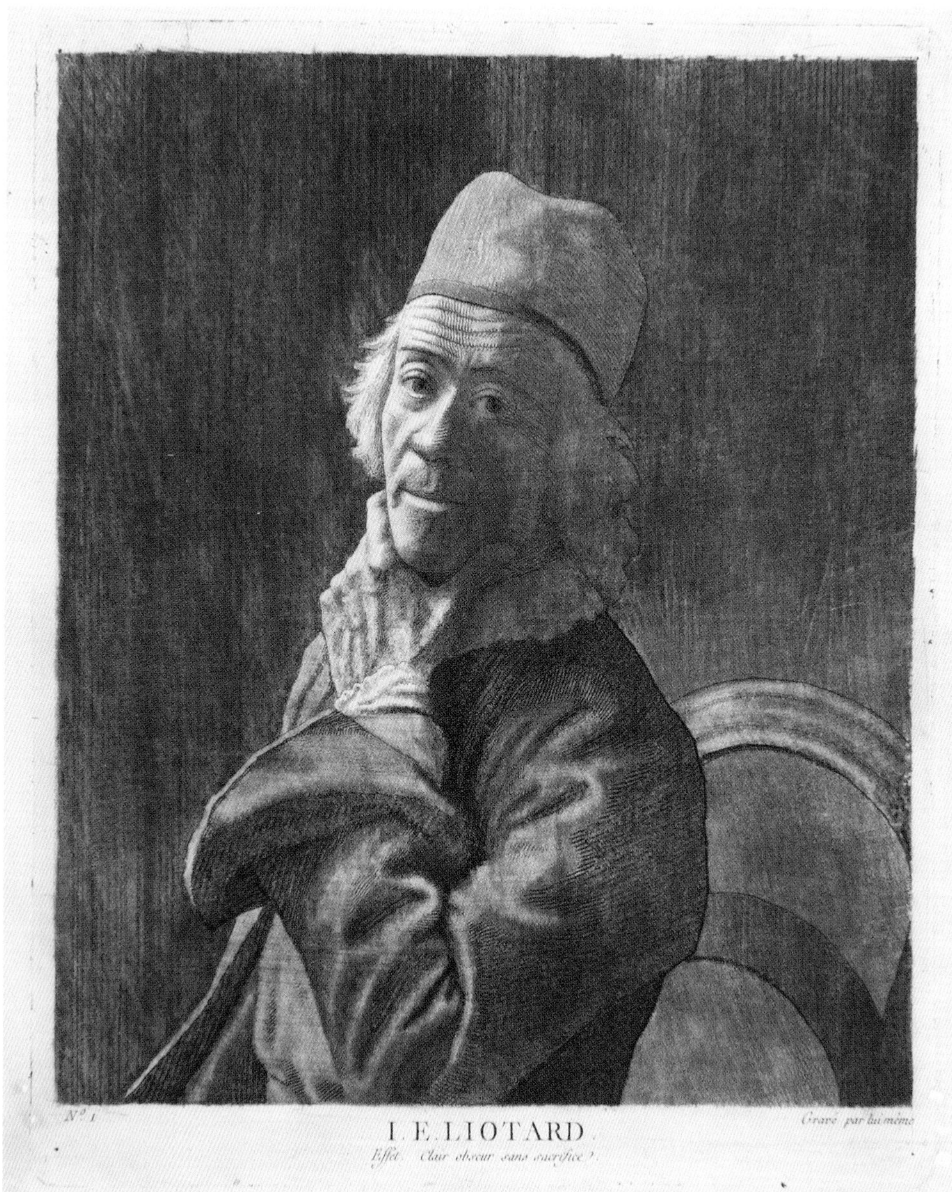

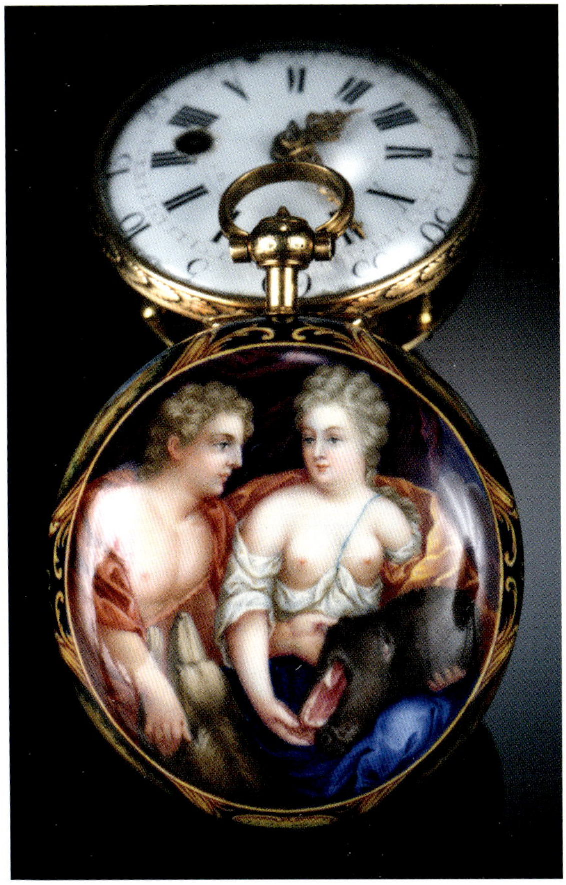

Cat. 18
Jean-Pierre Huaud
(Geneva 1655–1723 Geneva)
and **Amy Huaud**
(Geneva 1657–1724 Geneva)
John Leroux (1744–n.d.)
Enameled Gold Pocket Watch
Geneva, after 1700 /
London, late eighteenth century
Enameled gold case, enameled dial, full plate gilt movement,
diam. 4.6 cm, thickness 2.6 cm
Signed on the back plate: "J. Leroux Charing Cross London";
signed on the cartouche on the case rim:
"Frère Huaut pinx. invt"
Mathematisch-Physikalischer Salon, Staatliche
Kunstsammlungen Dresden, inv. no. D IV a 293

The watch movement produced in the late eighteenth century in London by John Leroux (member of the Clockmakers' Company from 1781 to 1808) sits in a gold case enameled in Geneva roughly one hundred years earlier by members of the Huaud family. The white enameled dial with Roman hour numerals (I–XII) and outer 5-minute divisions (5, 10 . . . 60) as well as a minute scale is protected by a glass cover.
In the course of enameling, the entire surface of the case was covered, so that the marks and punches are hidden. The painting on the case back shows Atalanta and Meleager with the head of the Calydonian Boar. Landscapes in the cartouches decorate the case edge. The inside of the case carries the coat of arms of the French noble family Galard de Brassac de Béarn.
The Huauds set the standard for Genevan enamel paintings, which was of such outstanding quality that clockmakers from of all over Europe sent cases to Geneva for painting. In this instance, the clockmaker used an already existing case. The great names among enamelists of the eighteenth century have been compiled by Catherine Cardinal: André Rouquet, Jean-Étienne Liotard, Jacques Thouron, Jean-François Soiron, Jean-Paul Hubert, Pierre Pasquier, and Nicolas-André Courtois.

PP

Literature: Baillie 1947/1972, p. 195; Schillinger 1994, p. 99 and fig. 98; Cardinal 1999, pp. 36–41.

Cat. 19

Jean-Pierre Huaud

(Geneva 1655–1723 Geneva)

and **Amy Huaud**

(Geneva 1657–1724 Geneva)

Enamel Medallion with the Caritas Romana (Cimon and Pero)

Geneva, 1700/1710

Enamel, gold, silver, partially gilt, diamonds, H. 1.0 cm, diam. 4.5 cm

Grünes Gewölbe, Staatliche Kunstsammlungen Dresden, inv. no. III 40/5

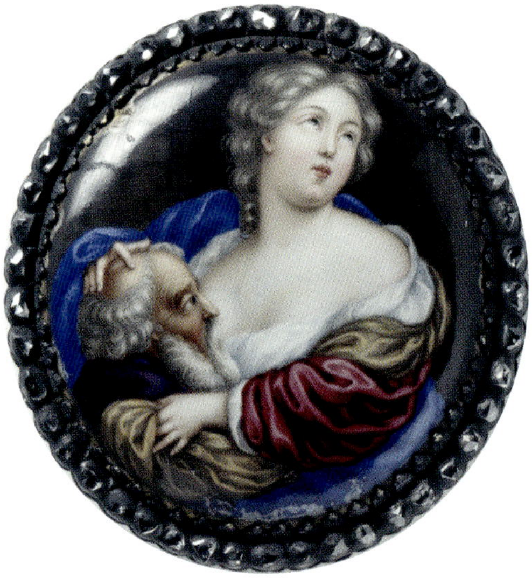

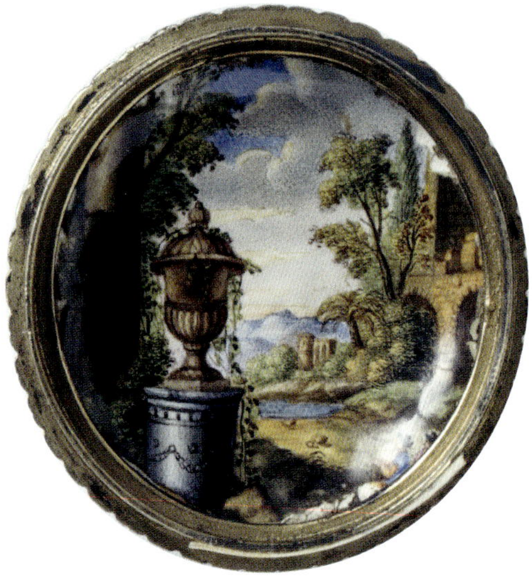

The French goldsmith Jean I Toutin had opened up new possibilities for the use of enamel in the field of jewelry-making by developing an expanded color palette and using gold as base for his enamels. Enamel miniatures thus perfected became a much sought-after commodity, thanks to their extraordinary delicacy and radiance, along with the durability of their colors. Especially in the clockmaking metropolis Geneva a number of workshops arose that furnished watchmakers with colorfully decorated cases, and by the 1670s it had become a center of enamel painting. This was in large part thanks to Pierre I Huaud, a Huguenot who had fled France in 1630 and settled in Geneva. The pocket watch decor developed by him and his sons, now known as the "Genre Huaud," established the typical look of clock cases produced in Geneva around 1700 and continued to be influential well into the eighteenth century. Whereas the fronts of the watch covers were generally reserved for mythological scenes, the backs and the oval cartouches on the outer case edges featured landscape motifs in a classical style. Enamel painters mostly relied on motifs from popular prints, adapting them to their round or oval picture formats.

The present medallion serves as an example of this. It was originally intended as a cover or back of a pocket watch, but was later transformed into the lid of a box by adding a silver-gilt setting with inset diamonds. The domed metal case was decorated with the *Caritas Romana*, a motif frequently employed by the Huaud brothers, based on an engraving by Claude Mellan after a painting by the French Baroque painter Simon Vouet. It pictures the philosopher Cimon, condemned to death by starvation, whom his daughter Pero keeps alive by breastfeeding him. The *Caritas Romana* became a symbol of Christian charity and mercy.

UW

Literature: Boeckh 1982; Kappel/Weinhold 2007, pp. 246–47, figs. 1 and 2.

Cat. 20

Jean-Pierre Huaud

(Geneva 1655–1723 Geneva)

and **Amy Huaud**

(Geneva 1657–1724 Geneva)

Enamel Medallion with the Penitent Magdalene

Berlin 1698

Enamel, gold, silver gilt, 7.2 x 5.8 cm (without frame), 9.4 x 6.5 cm (with frame)

Signed on the enamel backing: "Les freres Huaut, fac. ano 1698"

Grünes Gewölbe, Staatliche Kunstsammlungen Dresden, inv. no. III 35 c

This enamel miniature on a domed, oval-shaped gold backing shows Magdalene, her long hair caressing her shoulders, her hands crossed over her breast, her gaze directed heavenward. A thin white fabric covers her left upper arm and left breast, while at the bottom of the picture a vivid-blue cloak is wrapped around her right arm.

The inscription applied to the medallion's white back, "Les freres Huaut. fec. ano 1698," refers to Jean-Pierre and Amy, the two younger sons of the Genevan enamelist Pierre Huaud. In 1682 the brothers had joined forces, and in 1686 followed a summons from Frederick Wilhelm, Elector of Brandenburg (called the Great Elector), to come to Berlin, where they were appointed painters to the court. Among other things, they supplied the court with miniature portraits, which were popular diplomatic gifts. Alongside this, they fulfilled numerous private commissions before returning to Geneva in 1700.

The Grünes Gewölbe in Dresden holds a slightly larger copy of the medallion, dated 1712 and signed by Georg Friedrich Dinglinger, court enamelist to Augustus the Strong (inv. no. III 35 d). Apparently Dinglinger schooled himself on the work of the Huaud brothers, which was distinguished by its subtle coloring, fluid transitions, and an extraordinarily fine *pointillé*. Possibly in connection with this, the enamel picture was given a protective silver backing. The inscription "les freres huaut fec." was also added on that occasion—an indication of the high regard for the Huaud brothers' work.

UW

Literature: Menzhausen 1968, p. 95; Boeckh 1982; exh. cat. Schloss Charlottenburg 2001, pp. 78–79; exh. cat. Dresden 2008, p. 450, cat. 278.

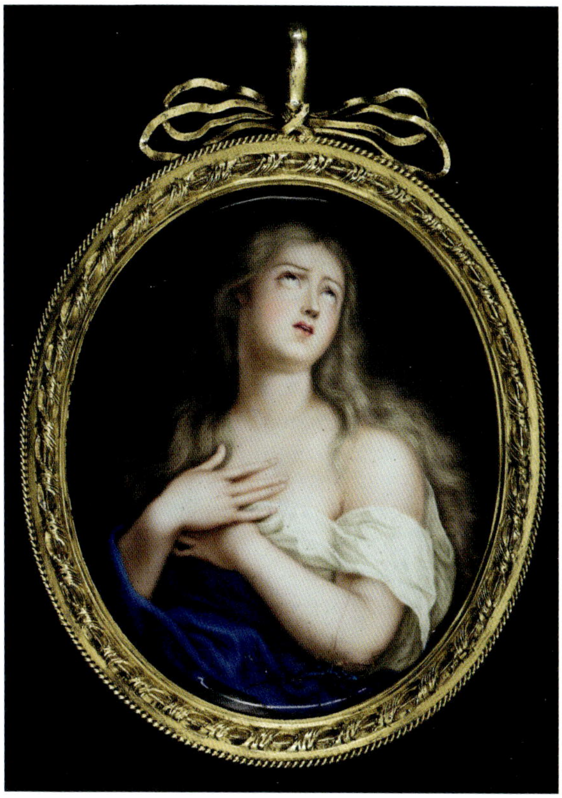

CHOCOLATE AND INDULGENCE

Cacao came to Europe from Central America as early as the sixteenth century. Together with tea from East Asia and coffee from the Near East, by the seventeenth century it was one of a trio of exotic, costly imports. Hot chocolate, made from a cacao paste, often spiced, with the addition of water or milk, was highly prized at royal courts in the eighteenth century. Special new vessels were developed for the preparation of hot drinks and their consumption. For chocolate, tall cups with handles were produced, some with a metal holder for greater stability. A whisk could be inserted into the pot to keep the ingredients from separating. The Meissen porcelain manufactory was the first in Europe to produce matching chocolate, tea, and coffee services. The frequent combination of Japanese porcelain and East Asian decor also reflects the fascination with the exotic countries from which these stimulants originated.

Cat. 21

Jean-Étienne Liotard

(Geneva 1702–1789 Geneva)

A Dutch Girl at Breakfast

Circa 1756

Oil on canvas, 46.8 x 39 cm

Rijksmuseum, Amsterdam, purchase made possible by the BankGiro Lottery, the Rembrandt Association through its National Art Fund (National Fonds Kunstbezit), Mondriaan Fund, VSBfonds, Fonds De Haseth-Möller/Rijksmuseum Fonds, LOBA Fonds/Rijksmuseum Fonds, Nan van Andel Fonds/Rijksmuseum Fonds, Marjon Ornstein Fonds/Rijksmuseum Fonds, Elles Nansink Fonds/Rijksmuseum Fonds, Rijksmuseum International Circle, and gifts from bequests and anonymous benefactors, inv. no. SK-A-5039

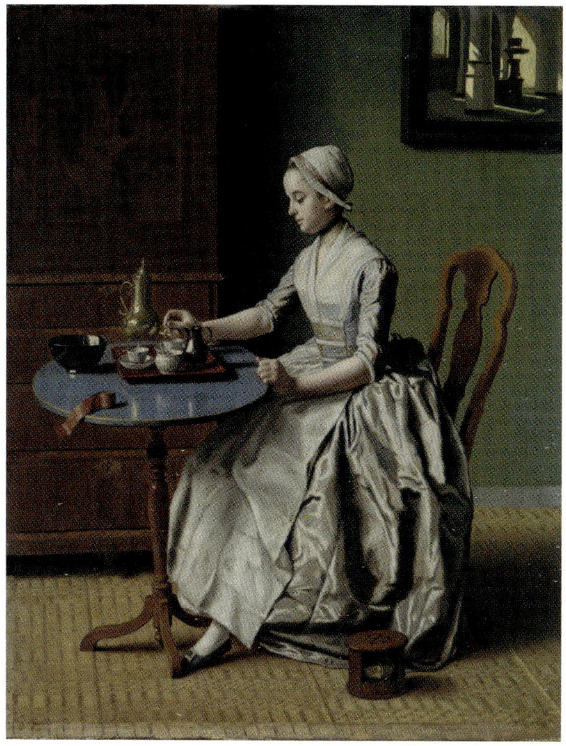

Jean-Étienne Liotard's *Dutch Girl* is one of the few works in his oeuvre picturing an everyday scene. In front of a green wall, a young woman in a silvery white dress sits at a small round table set with a lacquer tray with two cups, a sugar bowl, a milk pitcher, as well as a bowl, and a brass-colored coffee pot from which she is serving herself using a small spigot. The slight view from above allows the viewer to clearly see the utensils. Reflections from the blue of the tabletop can be seen in the folds of her dress. A wardrobe is half visible in the background, also a painting of a church interior in seventeenth-century Dutch style. These frame the girl's head, whose profile is reminiscent of both the *Chocolate Girl* and *Liseuse*. The fact that Liotard reverted to the technique of oil painting for this picture may well reflect his reception of the Dutch Masters.

Unusual for Liotard is the depiction of an interior. The influence of seventeenth-century Dutch genre scenes is palpable here, which he was able to study during his stay in Amsterdam between 1755 and 1757. It was there that in 1756 he married Marie Fargues, the daughter of an Amsterdam merchant, and assembled his collection of Old Masters with Flemish and Dutch paintings. The everyday objects on the table, including the three-footed brass pot, as well as the furniture and the young woman's clothing reflect eighteenth-century forms. Thus, in his depiction of details, Liotard, like the Dutch Masters, remained true to his time. The painting in the background has recently been identified as Hendrick van Vliet's *Interior of the Nieuwe Kerk in Delft*, which was in Liotard's collection. The whereabouts of the original are unknown.

SD

Literature: R/L 2008, no. 342; Gaba-van Dongen 2005, pp. 30–39; exh. cat. Edinburgh/London 2015, cat. 75; Godycki 2017.

Cat. 22
Jean-Étienne Liotard
(Geneva 1702–1789 Geneva)
Still Life: Tea Set
Circa 1781–83
Oil on canvas mounted on board, 37.8 x 51.6 cm
The J. Paul Getty Museum, Los Angeles, inv. no. 84.PA.57

In front of a flat, black-green background, a tea service with Chinese decor, seen slightly from above, has been left in disarray on a lacquer tray. Some of the cups are overturned, dirty, or still half full, and bits of the pastry served with the tea are scattered about the table and the tray—afternoon tea is over. This association lends the still life a narrative element. The tray, with its pattern, pierced gold edge, and shiny material—probably imitation Asian lacquer—stands out against the rough surface of the table, produced by the texture of the canvas. The lacquer tray and Chinese porcelain reflect the popularity of East Asian products, especially in courtly circles, in eighteenth-century France and Austria.

There are very few still lifes in Jean-Étienne Liotard's oeuvre; they mainly date from the last two decades of his life. A total of five depictions of such used tea sets are known, all in oil, with the objects pictured against a dark background. Lippincott sees this still life as an attempt to demonstrate the rules the artist discussed in his treatise from 1781, especially regarding the use of light. He used the contrast between white porcelain and dark background, enhanced by the porcelain's irregular arrangement, to depict reflections and effects of light and shadow.

SD

Literature: R/L 2008, no. 435; Leonhard 1985; Lippincott 1985; Roethlisberger 1985, pp. 119–20; Stevens 2015, p. 167; exh. cat. Edinburgh/London 2015, cat. 79; Etienne/Lee 2018, pp. 6–8.

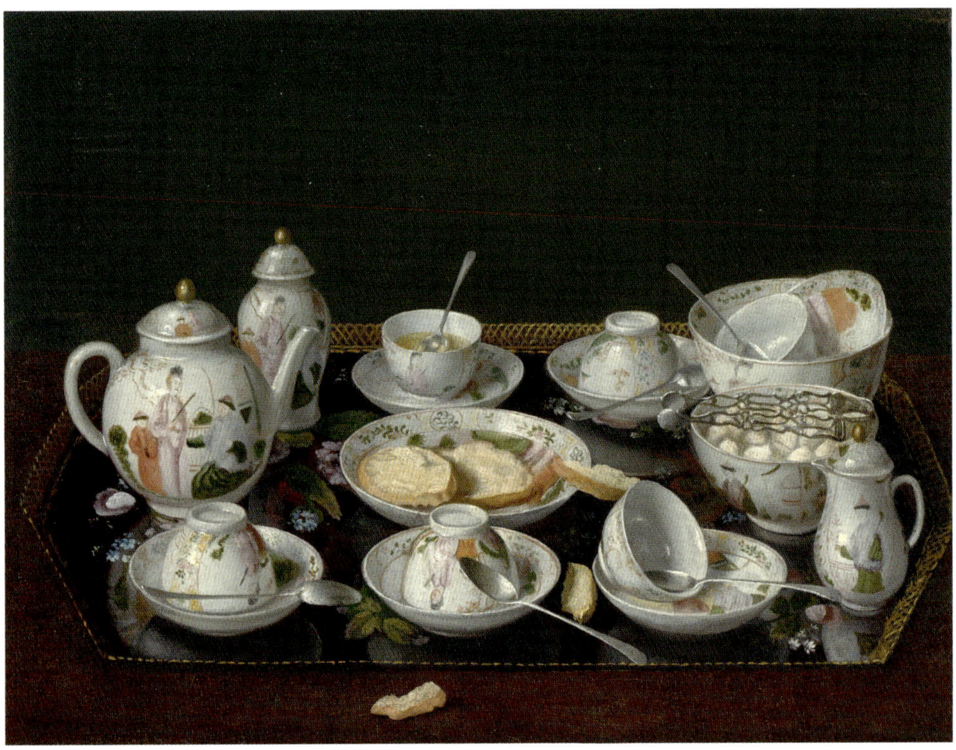

Cat. 23
Rosalba Carriera
(Venice 1673–1757 Venice)
A Turk
Undated
Pastel on paper, 56.5 x 44 cm
Gemäldegalerie Alte Meister, Staatliche Kunstsammlungen Dresden, gal. no. P 121

This bust portrait of a Turk pictures a smiling man with a mustache, wearing a richly ornamented turban-like headdress and an oriental robe elaborately decorated with floral patterns. In his right hand he holds a fine porcelain cup with a gold rim. His blue eyes and fair hair make it seem questionable whether the man is truly a Turk or only costumed as one. It is also unclear whether this is the portrait of a specific person. The light colors of the exotic dress and drinking cup stand out against the dark background.

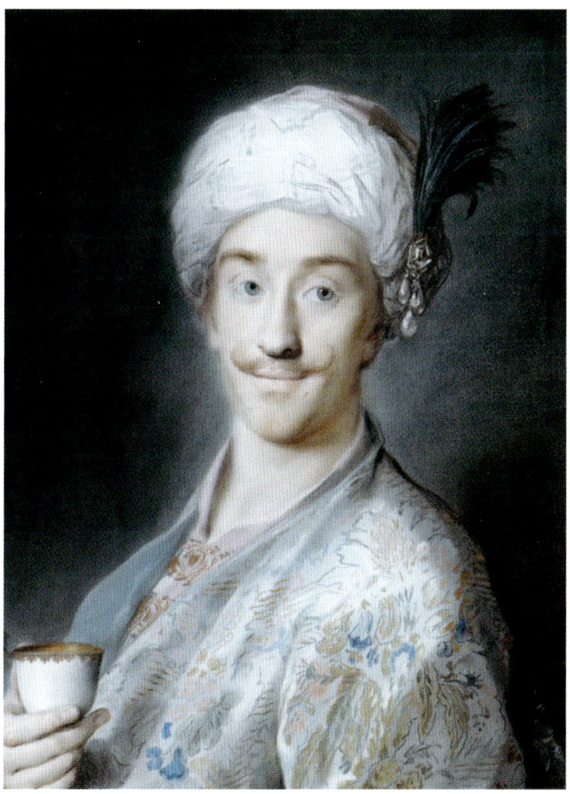

Together with the portrait of a lady in Turkish costume with a Carnival mask (1730/40, Uffizi Gallery, Florence)—probably Carriera's pupil Felicitas Sartori—the Dresden picture is part of a small group of paintings in the pastellist's oeuvre influenced by the Turkish fashion. In contrast to Liotard, whose Orientalism was greatly shaped by his travels in the Levant, Carriera rarely left her birthplace Venice, apart from a few brief sojourns in Modena, Vienna, and Paris, where, in 1721, she may have seen the Turkish embassy with the Ottoman ambassador Mehmed Said Efendi. Since the seventeenth century, Venice had been an entrepôt for coffee shipments from the Orient, a specialty that was becoming increasingly sought-after in Europe. The coffee or mocha cup in the man's hand is one of the Chinese porcelain cups without handles (Dutch *koppje*) that reached Europe on the merchant ships of the Dutch East India Company.

SD

Literature: Riedel/Wenzel 1765, p. 239 (summarily mentioned); exh. cat. Dresden/Bonn 1995, p. 332, cat. 425; Henning/Marx 2007, p. 81; Sani 2007, p. 309, no. 346.

Cat. 24
Cacao Fruit in Stone
Aztec, ca. 1250–1521
Stone, H. 11 cm, L. 27 cm, W. 11 cm
Schokoladenmuseum Köln GmbH, inv. no. 50028

This Aztec stone replica of a cacao fruit reflects the dimensions of the actual product: the fruits of the cacao tree can range between 10 and 30 centimeters and weigh between 300 and 1,000 grams. The beans are found in the fruit's sweet, juicy flesh. Between twenty and sixty cacao beans can be extracted from a single fruit, which are then roasted and ground to produce the basis for chocolate.

The cacao tree, native to tropical Central and South America, was much revered by the high cultures of the Maya and Aztecs, as reflected by the many depictions of the fruits on drinking vessels or in the *Dresden Codex* (ca. 1200–1250), which in 1739 found its way into Dresden's Royal Library, now the Sächsische

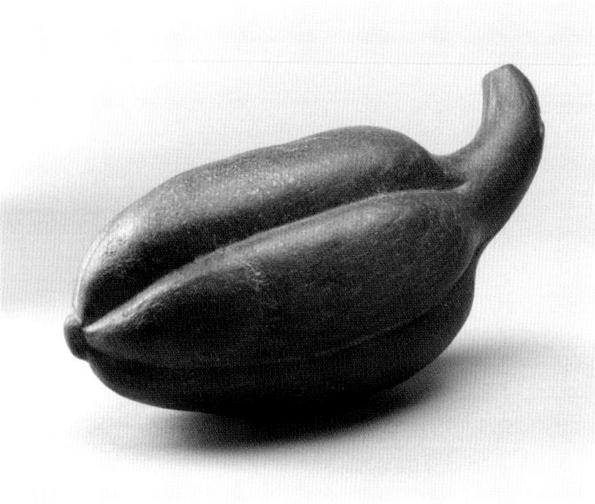

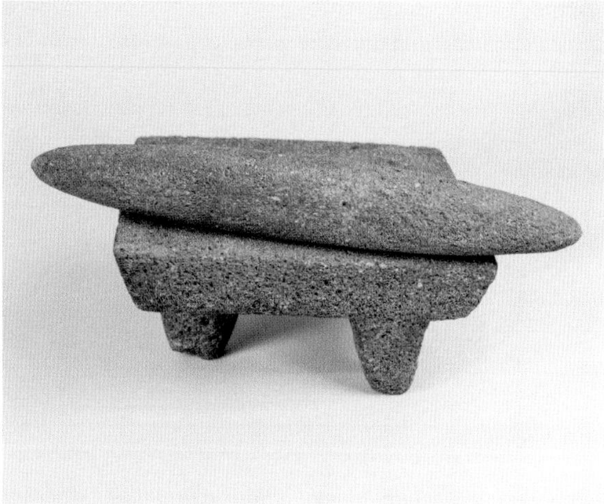

Landesbibliothek – Staats- und Universitätsbibliothek Dresden (SLUB). Also part of these depictions is the fruit rendered in stone exhibited here, whose original function and context remains unknown. The Aztecs, whose empire thrived from the thirteenth century up until it was conquered by the Spanish between 1519 and 1521, used cacao beans as currency, even though they did not cultivate the plant themselves, but procured the beans through trade with the Maya. Furthermore, chocolate was considered the drink of the gods, and was especially favored by the aristocracy. Medicinal qualities were also associated with cacao; hot chocolate was taken for stomach and intestinal complaints, or together with the bark of the kapok tree to cure infections.

SD

Literature: Grivetti 2009, pp. 99–100; Durry/Schiffer 2012, pp. 29–30.

Cat. 25

Mexican Highlands

Metate y mano (mortar and grinding stone)

1900/1910

Gray, slightly porous stone (probably volcanic), sawed and smoothed. Metate H. 9.5–11.5 cm, L. 21.7 cm, W. 17.5 cm; mano H. 4 cm, L. 32 cm, W. 4 cm

GRASSI Museum of Ethnology in Leipzig, Staatliche Kunstsammlungen Dresden, inv. no. MAm 07288 a, b

A metate is a rectangular, table-like stone with a concave work surface, on which a roller, generally of stone or later also metal, was used. The Maya and Aztecs—whose high cultures survived until the conquest of Central America by the Spanish in the sixteenth century—used this to grind corn or cacao beans and to prepare a dough-like cacao paste. This example, which comes from present-day Mexico, the original homeland of cacao, dates from the early twentieth century, but illustrates a form that was little changed for centuries and arrived in Europe from Central America along with cacao itself.

Until the end of the eighteenth century, when, in 1789, the Englishman Joseph Storrs Fry first used a steam engine to grind the beans, the preparation of chocolate paste was a very complex and arduous process. The raw beans first had to be roasted over a fire, shelled, and crushed. They were then ground into a fine paste between two stones. For pre-industrial production of chocolate, a long rolling pin on a heated stone tabletop was used, as pictured in an engraving from Diderot and d'Alembert's *Encyclopédie* of 1763.

SD

Literature: Diderot/d'Alembert 1765, "Confiseur," plate V; Mueller 1957, p. 15; Menninger 2004, pp. 76, 360–62; Durry/Schiffer 2012, pp. 167–68.

Cat. 26

Guatemala, Cobán, Kekchí peoples

Calabash

1900–1904

Interior left natural, exterior blackened, polished, carved, H. 6.4 cm, diam. 12.5–13.2 cm

GRASSI Museum of Ethnology in Leipzig, Staatliche Kunstsammlungen Dresden, inv. no. MAm 00885

This calabash from the Kekchí culture, a people belonging to the Maya and today living scattered in Guatemala, is a vessel made from the bottom half of a bottle gourd and used for drinking cacao. It was left untreated inside, but blackened on the outside, then

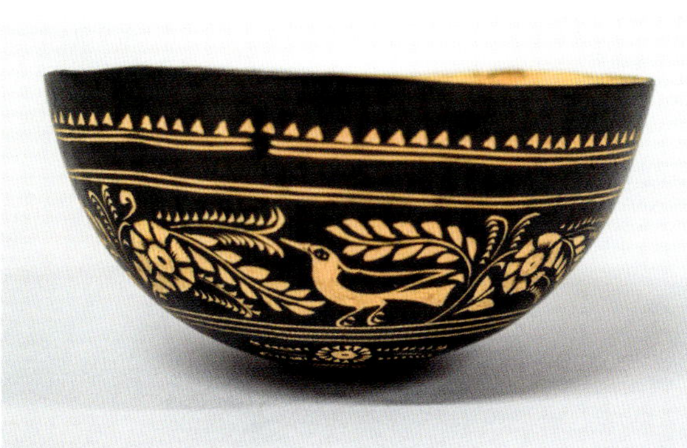

polished and decorated with carved floral ornaments and birds between finely drawn lines.

The umbrella term calabash is used for any vessel made from the shells of the bottle gourd or calabash tree. The dried, watertight shells served both for the transport and consumption of liquids, and were especially favored by nomadic peoples because of their light weight. The early cultures of the Maya and Aztecs used calabashes in addition to ceramic vessels, especially for drinking chocolate. What made them special was the shell's black lacquer work, which in the exhibited example from the twentieth century was imitated with black paint. In the late sixteenth and early seventeenth centuries these vessels, which the Spanish called *jicaras*, were brought to Europe along with cacao. Because of their perishable material, virtually no calabashes have survived. However, they are still being produced in their original form today.

SD

Literature: Norton 2006, p. 683; Durry/Schiffer 2012, p. 182.

Cat. 27

Mexico

Chocolate Whisk (Molinillo)

After 1900

Turned, sawed, and carved wood, L. 30 cm, diam. 4 cm max.

GRASSI Museum of Ethnology in Leipzig, Staatliche Kunstsammlungen Dresden, inv. no. MAm 07171

This wooden whisk from the early twentieth century is a utensil used in the preparation of hot chocolate. By twisting the handle between the hands, the serrated disks at the bottom blend the cacao with a liquid, usually water, and produce a layer of froth on the chocolate drink. Similar whisks were used as early as the sixteenth century and are documented in Spanish sources from the time. Hot chocolate was already enjoyed as a frothy drink by the Maya. No whisks are mentioned in early Maya and Aztec texts, but presumably spoons were used for the same purpose. At least of the Aztecs it is known that they often poured the drink from a certain height in order to generate froth and enhance the taste of the cacao.

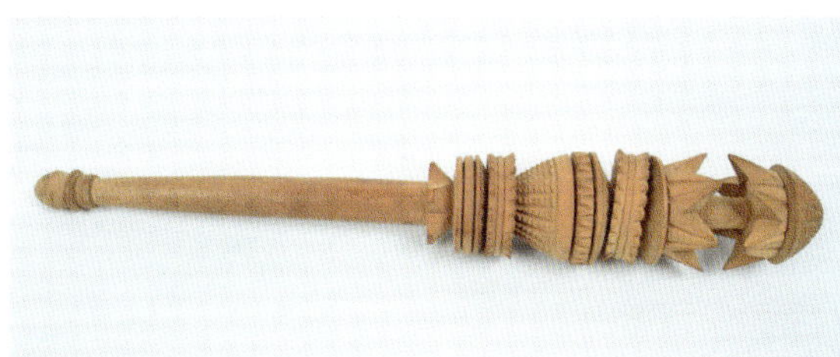

Chocolate pots with side handles produced in Europe from the seventeenth century onward often had a hole in the removable lid, into which a whisk could be inserted. Since they were usually made of wood, very few whisks from the seventeenth and eighteenth centuries survive.

SD

Literature: Mueller 1957, p. 15; Schiedlausky 1961, p. 24; Durry/Schiffer 2012, p. 180.

Cat. 28

Tonalá, Jalisco, Mexico

Chocolate Cup with Saucer

Late seventeenth to early eighteenth century

Fine-grained earthenware, stamped and incised decor, clay coating

Kunstgewerbemuseum, Staatliche Kunstsammlungen Dresden, inv. nos. 42587, 42578, 42588, 42575 (from the former Königliche Porzellan- und Gefäßsammlung, Palais-no. 76)

In the sixteenth and seventeenth centuries, earthenware from the New World conquered by the Spanish, specifically from the Mexican ceramic center Tonalá near Guadalajara, became a sought-after commodity at European princely courts. Sometimes referred to as *terra sigillata*, it was exquisitely modeled, thin-walled, covered with a red or brown luster glaze, and often with a stamped and incised decor. In Spain and Portugal, these vessels, known as *búcaros*, were thought to have medicinal properties. It is said that upper-class Spanish ladies even chewed small fragments of the vessels or ate them dissolved in water. In the 1721 inventory of the Saxon Elector's "Dutch Palace" (later the Japanese Palace), which was to be turned into a porcelain cabinet, a whole chapter is dedicated to its over four hundred pieces of "terra sigillata," whose predominantly Mexican origin was apparently unknown to contemporaries. Nevertheless, a few of these vessels were already labeled as "chocolate mugs" or "chocolate cups." For example, listed under item no. 76 are the "chocolate cups on which all manner of ornaments are impressed . . . and matching plates etc. saucers" shown here, complete with dimensions and quantities. The imprinted decor—oval incisions and lines—resembles stylized cacao beans. Whether chocolate was actually drunk from these brown ceramic mugs is not documented.

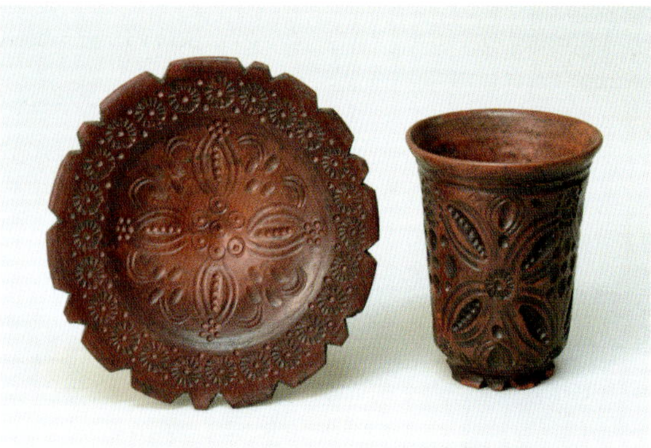

These rather unremarkable yet highly sought-after earthenware pieces were pictured in contemporary still lifes together with precious Chinese porcelain and Venetian glass. For example, in one of the most famous paintings in art history, *Las Meninas* by Diego Velézquez (1656, Prado, Madrid), a *búcaro* is being presented on a silver tray to the infanta Margaret Theresa.

The report by the French writer Marie-Catherine d'Aulnoy from her trip to Spain in 1679 offers a contemporary insight into the way chocolate was enjoyed and also mentions the ingestion of fragments of these ceramics. In Madrid she was received at the Monteleon Palace, shown around the apartments of the duchess and princess, and "accosted" with refreshments. First there were preserved dried cherries, plums, and apricots, individually wrapped in gold paper and served in large silver bowls; these were then followed by cacao: "Then I was brought *chocolat*, and each porcelain cup stood in a flat saucer of agate set in gold, the same material as the sugar bowl placed next to it. The *chocolat* was prepared in three ways, one was on ice, another was hot, and the third made with milk and eggs. . . . Some of the women drank down six cups, one after another, and there were also several who ate great pieces of the medicinal earth. I have already told you that they have a great passion for this earth."

KL

Literature: D'Aunoy 1696 (German edition), pp. 287–88; Lauterbach 2017.

Cat. 29

Drey neue Curieuse Tractätgen Von dem Trancke Café, Sinesischen Thé und der Chocolata; Budissin / In Verlegung Friedrich Arnsts / druckts Andreas Richter 1686

(Three New Curious Little Treatises on the Drinks Coffee, Chinese Tea, and Chocolate; Budissin / Published by Friedrich Arnsts / Press Andreas Richter 1686)

16.2 x 9.8 cm

Saxon State and University Library Dresden, Sign. Diaet. 444

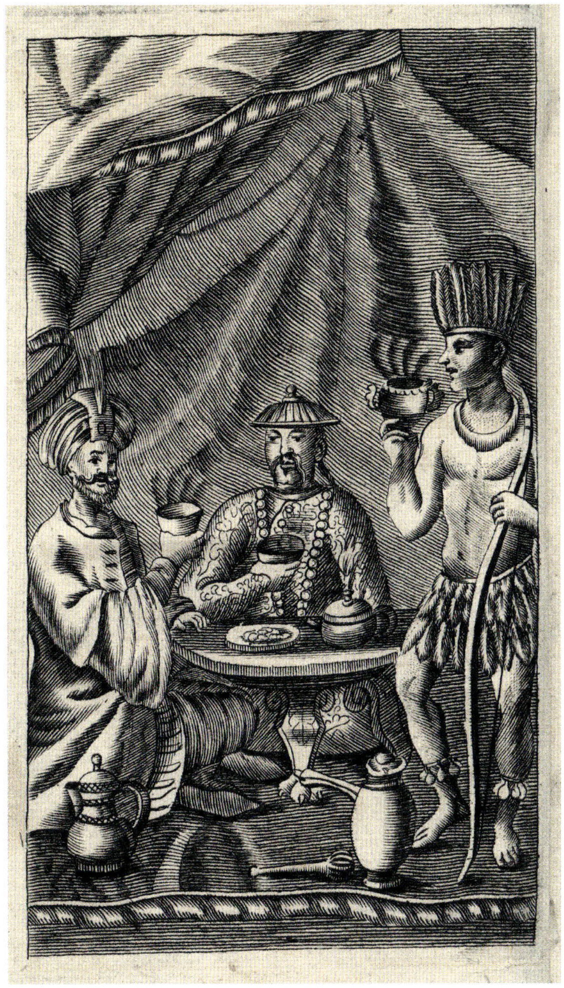

In the 1686 *Drey neue Curieuse Tractätgen* on the origin, preparation, and effects of the three exotic hot drinks that reached Europe from Arabia, Asia, and Central America in the seventeenth century, the author delves into the history of the new stimulants and their medicinal uses, the longest chapter being devoted to coffee. In addition to the title page shown here, devoted to all three drinks, the book contains allegorical illustrations for each of them, which are divided in two parts: in the upper half are personifications of each drink's country of origin—coffee (Turks, Arabs), tea (Chinese), and chocolate (American Indians)—together with the corresponding utensils for their preparation. In the lower half are botanical drawings, probably engravings after travel descriptions. The book first appeared in French in 1671 under the title *De l'Usage du Caphe, du The, et du Chocolate*, and soon became a European bestseller. By 1705 at least twelve editions had appeared in four languages in France, Germany, England, the Netherlands, and Switzerland, the first edition still anonymously. Only later, Jacob Spon, who brought out a Latin translation of the treatise in 1685, and Phillippe Sylvestre Dufour were alternately named as authors. Although Jacob Spon is documented as a historical figure—he received his doctorate in medicine in Paris in 1667—his authorship of the first edition is questionable, for he makes no mention of such a text in his report, published in 1679, of his journey to the Levant in 1675/76. By contrast, Dufour, who appears as author beginning in 1685, is undocumented, and, moreover, his life and death dates are suspiciously similar to those of Jacob Spon. It cannot be ruled out that Spon used the name as a pseudonym; Dufour might stand for "from the stove," an allusion to the hot drinks.

SD

Literature: N. N./Heise 1986, pp. [1]–[36]; Schnyder-von Waldkirch 1988, pp. 220–21.

Cat. 30
Japan
Lacquer Tray (bon)
Late eighteenth century (middle Edo Period)
Wood, black lacquer, gold decor, brushwork, relief applique,
H. 3 cm, L. 27.4 cm, W. 19.2 cm
Stiftung Schloss Friedenstein Gotha – From the collections
of the Herzog von Sachsen-Coburg und Gotha'schen Stiftung
für Kunst und Wissenschaft, inv. no. J21L

This rectangular tray with bracket feet, from the holdings of the "Chinese Cabinet" of Augustus, Duke of Saxe-Gotha-Altenburg, is decorated with a stylized landscape covering its entire surface. To the left is a temple on a steep bank, in front of it and extending to the right a choppy ocean into which a waterfall pours from an overhanging cliff. The contrast between black lacquer and gold ornaments is typical of East Asian lacquerwork. Japanese lacquers are especially famous for their sophisticated decorative techniques, as demonstrated here. Inlays of small sheets of gold, pulverized substances, or gold flakes have been added to the still-wet lacquer—either covering larger areas or to render contours—which is then polished several times and, once cured, covered with a transparent lacquer.
Both Japanese and Chinese lacquerware reached Europe by way of the Dutch East Asia trade and was highly sought-after at Western courts. Prices were correspondingly high for these works, which in the seventeenth and eighteenth centuries, along with porcelain, were a must for any royal collection of Far Eastern treasures. Maria Theresa, for example, who had a passion for East Asian artifacts, had her Chinese cabinets at Schönbrunn Palace ostentatiously decorated with lacquers and porcelains, and in Dresden's Residenzpalast Augustus III had Raymond Leplat decorate a Japanese Cabinet, which, sadly, no longer exists. The great appreciation for these two materials is also apparent in Liotard's *Chocolate Girl*, in which the chocolate drink is being served in a porcelain cup on just such a tray.

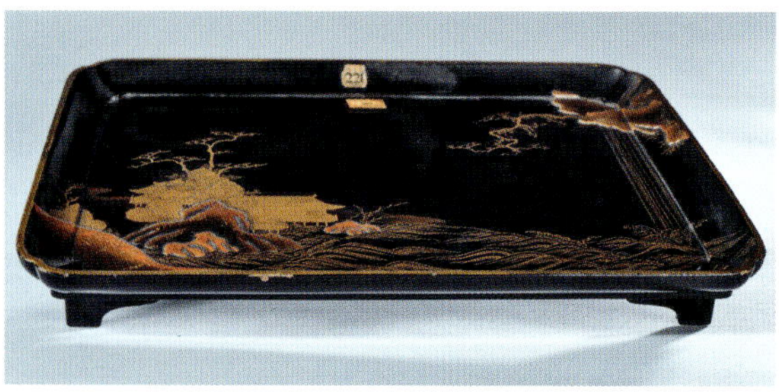

SD

Literature: Exh. cat. Versailles/Münster 2001, pp. 16–17; Bräutigam 2008, pp. 9–10, no. 144; exh. cat. Vienna 2017, pp. 300–01.

Cat. 31
Johann Melchior Dinglinger
(Biberach an der Riss 1664–1731 Dresden),
Georg Friedrich Dinglinger
(Biberach an der Riss 1666–1720 Dresden)
Two Lidded Cups with Saucers from the Golden Coffee Service
1697/1701
Enamel on gold, diamonds; cups H: 10.7 cm;
saucers diam. 10 cm
Grünes Gewölbe, Staatliche Kunstsammlungen Dresden,
inv. no. VIII 203

The two lidded cups are part of the Golden Coffee Service made for Augustus the Strong by Johann Melchior Dinglinger between 1697 and 1701. The cabinet showpiece was both extremely expensive—at a cost of 50,000 thalers—and innovative in many respects. The fact that it was made immediately after Augustus was elected King of Poland is no coincidence. At first glance the gold-enameled vessels look like porcelain, and this effect was entirely intentional. Augustus the Strong was an enthusiastic collector of objects made from the so-called "white gold" from East Asia. Yet it was not until 1708 that Johann Friedrich Böttger and Ehrenfried Walther von Tschirnhaus were able to discover the secret of its manufacture.
The "precious . . . tea or coffee service," as it is referred to in the inventory of valuables in the Grünes Gewölbe from 1725, pays homage to the exotic hot drinks, coffee, tea, and chocolate, which became all the rage at

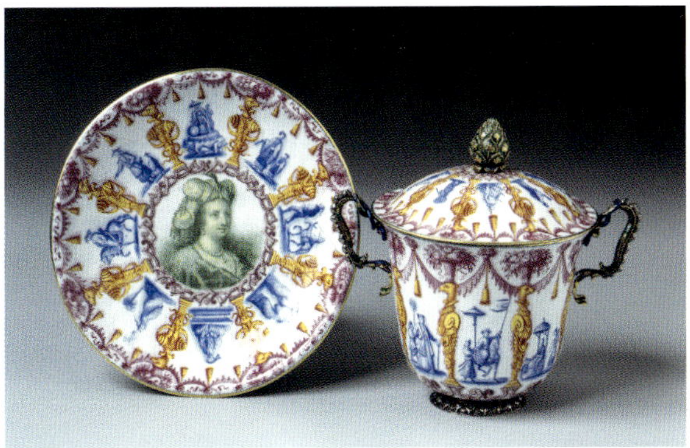

Cat. 32

Jean-Baptiste Lange

(mentioned 1706–before 1750)

Two Cups with Saucers and Teaspoons from a Travel Tea Service

Paris, 1717/18

Imari porcelain, silver; cups H. 4.2–4.3 cm, diam. 7.4–7.5 cm; holders H. 4.4 cm, diam. 7.1–7.2 cm; saucers H. 1.5–1.7 cm, diam. 13.4–13.5 cm; spoons L. 14.1–14.2 cm, W. 2.9 cm, H. 2–2.1 cm

Bundesmobilienverwaltung, Estate of Charles Alexander of Lorraine, Vienna, inv. no. MD 180510, MD 180510/006

Europe's courts around 1700. The tall lidded cup takes its cues from Chinese examples, and soon became the standard for the enjoyment of hot chocolate, often with the addition of one or two handles. The elaborate service, richly set with gems, was doubtless never meant to be used; it is purely a work of bravura goldsmithing, wholly in the service of princely self-aggrandizement.

Whereas the handleless teacups, the so-called *Koppchen*, of the Golden Coffee Service are decorated with allegorical and mythological scenes and European-style fantasy imagery, the decor of the handled cups features exotic beauties and East Asian views. These are accompanied by small, decoratively arranged Chinese figures, and thus mark the beginning of the Chinese fashion that would reach its pinnacle with the inventions of the porcelain painter Johann Gregorius Höroldt at the Meissen manufactory. The saucers picture ladies in Turkish costume in the most delicate grisaille painting, as a further aspect of the exoticism popular at the time and an allusion to the country of origin of coffee. They reference the multifigured Turkish coffee party serenaded by monkey musicians, which is hidden in the base of the ensemble's pyramid-shaped display stand. In the lids, finally, are small portraits of dark-skinned beauties adorned with feathers—probably a reference to South America, the source of chocolate.

UW

Literature: Watzdorf 1962, vol. 1, pp. 96–121; Arnold 1966; Syndram 2004; Syndram 2008, pp. 20–23 and 96–107; exh. cat. Dresden 2010, p. 163 (fig.), p. 166, cat. 7 (Claudia Banz).

These are two handleless teacups of Imari porcelain with floral decor in the colors cobalt blue, rust-red, and gold, and with openwork silver mountings on matching saucers, made by the Paris silversmith Jean-Baptiste Lange. The mountings, decorated with delicate rocailles and rows of beading, added stability to the cups, forming with the porcelain what was called a *trembleuse* (see cat. 34). Imari is a special type of highly colored porcelain from Japan's Arita region; its name is derived from the port of Imari, from which the porcelain was shipped by the Dutch East India Company. It was a popular commodity at many European courts in the seventeenth and eighteenth centuries. In this example here it has been enhanced with elaborate mountings and accessories in silver.

The travel tea service also includes two spoons, a portable stove, a teapot, a milk pitcher, a mallet and sugar cutter to break up sugarloaves, and two silver tea caddies inscribed with the names of exquisite Chinese tea varieties. The set came with a wood-veneer box, lined with red velvet and edged in silver, to transport it when traveling. It belonged to Prince Charles Alexander of Lorraine, who had presumably acquired it from the collection of his sister Anne Charlotte. Charles Alexander, a younger brother of Emperor Francis I and husband of Archduchess Maria Anna, Maria Theresa's sister, was named governor of the Netherlands in 1744. He was given 50,000 guldens from the state coffers to furnish his court in Brussels with table silver. After his death in 1780 his estate passed to his

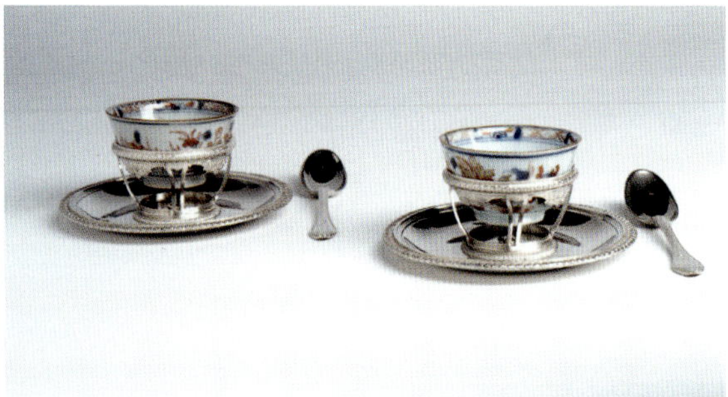

nephew, Emperor Joseph II. A large part of it was auctioned off; the remainder, including numerous mounted Imari porcelains, was sent to Vienna and added to the Hofsilber- und Tafelkammer (Court Silver and Table Rooms).

SD

Literature: Nocq 1928, p. 21; Haslinger 1993, fig. p. 88; Winkler 1996, pp. 130–32; De Ren 1998, p. 76; Pantzer 2000, pp. 17–25.

Cat. 33

Meissen Porcelain Manufactory

Two Chocolate Cups from a Tea, Coffee, and Chocolate Service for Elisabeth Farnese, Queen of Spain

1737

Hard paste porcelain with overglaze colors and gold; cups H. 6.5 cm, diam. 7 cm; saucers diam. 12 cm

Porzellansammlung, Staatliche Kunstsammlungen Dresden, inv. no. Pe 1506 e, g, l, n

In the perception of eighteenth-century Europeans, porcelain was still closely associated with the legendary country of the material's origin. Fed by travel reports and a fascination with the exquisite import wares from the Far East, the image arose of a land of abundance, where people lived in harmony, wealth, and leisure. The typical Meissen chinoiserie decor on the chocolate mugs from the service for Queen Elisabeth Farnese of Spain documents this idealization. The ensemble was one of the earliest tea, coffee, and chocolate sets and also included a special pot for the preparation of hot chocolate (fig. p. 121). The tall cups, either with one or with two handles (as in this example), were especially suited for the enjoyment of hot chocolate, which was whisked again in the cup to keep it frothy.

Matching services for the exotic hot drinks from three continents were a European invention (see cat. 34), and the Meissen manufactory with its sets dictated the fashion. Tea, coffee, and chocolate services were among the first products from Meissen, the oldest porcelain manufactory in Europe, founded in 1710. The novel material was especially well

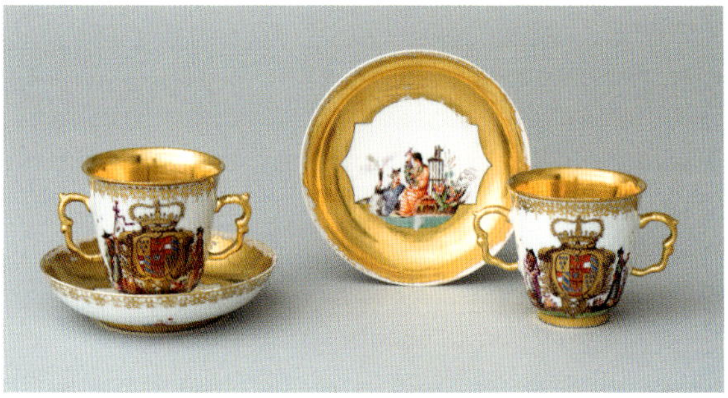

suited for serving these hot drinks, thanks to its low conductivity. Many of the vessel shapes, like the handleless cups or round teapots, were adapted from Chinese models, others—like these handled cups—were newly developed for the European market. Until late in the eighteenth century such expensive tea, coffee, and chocolate sets were mainly used as royal gifts. With its rich gilding and personalized decor in the form of the recipient's coat of arms, the service for Elisabeth Farnese is an outstanding example of this. Augustus III sent her the service in a specially made case, together with thirteen further sets, after the highly prestigious marriage of his daughter Maria Amalia to the heir to the Spanish throne in 1738.

JW

Literature: Boltz 1978; Blaauwen 2000, cat. 104 (cup); Lessmann 2006, p. 37 (bowl); Cassidy-Geiger 2007, pp. 213–15; exh. cat. Segovia 2009, pp. 52–53 (tea caddy); Weber 2010, p. 157.

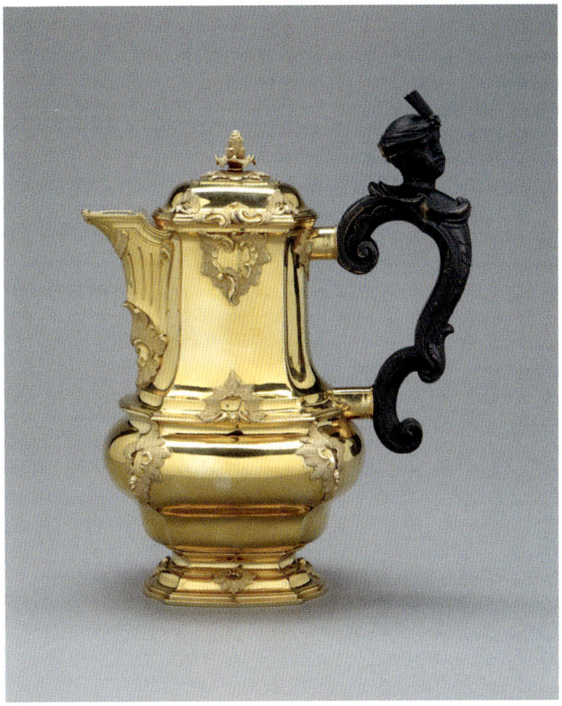

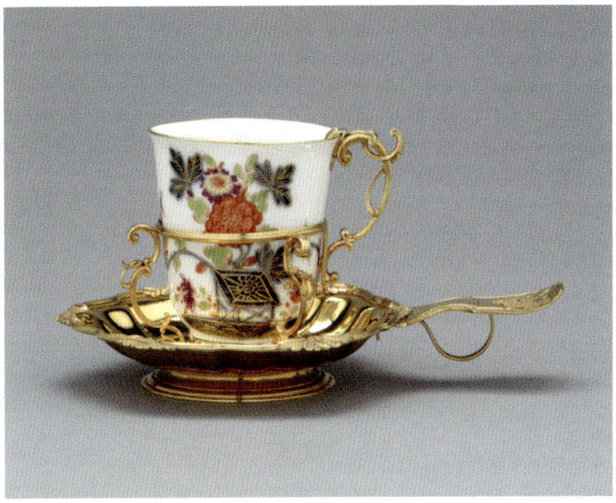

Cat. 34

Anton Matthias Domanek

(Vienna 1713–1779 Vienna)

Chocolate Pot, Chocolate Cup with Holder and Saucer (Trembleuse), and Tray from the Breakfast Service for Empress Maria Theresa

Vienna, ca. 1750

Meissen porcelain, second quarter of the eighteenth century

Gold, black-stained ebony, porcelain; chocolate pot H. 23.4 cm, chocolate cup H. 7.8 cm, saucer H. 2.7 cm, L. 18.8 cm, W. 12.4 cm, tray L. 20.8 cm, W. 17 cm

Kunsthistorisches Museum, Kunstkammer, Vienna, inv. no. KK 1260 (chocolate pot), KK 1223 (tray), KK 1213, KK 1205, and KK 1206 (trembleuse)

The vessels shown here are from Maria Theresa's Golden Breakfast Service. It was originally kept in her private apartments and used during the morning ceremony of the *levée*, attended by a select few in her bedroom. Together with the toiletries set belonging to her husband, Emperor Francis I, a total of seventy pieces were placed in the imperial treasury shortly after the Empress's death and are first listed in its inventory from 1773 (added retrospectively in 1781). Included in the set listed there as "golden night pieces" were a water kettle with stove, pitchers for tea, milk, and chocolate, a tea caddy, a lidded cup, six small cups and saucers of Japanese porcelain painted in the Imari style, and two chocolate cups of Meissen porcelain. The fact that a milk jug, a coffeepot, and a teapot are mentioned in the inventory, suggests that there was some uncertainty as to the identification of the pieces. The chocolate cups are decorated with the so-called "little table" pattern (*Tischchenmuster*), a decor in imitation of East Asian examples. The gold mountings that make them into *trembleuses* are especially intricate. The tall cups were given a handle of intertwined volutes attached to the base and clamped to the lip. Each handled cup sits in a close-fitting holder that is screwed to the saucer, which in turn is provided with a flat handle on one side, to assure stability when the chocolate was stirred.

A special feature of the exclusive service are the striking carved-ebony handles of the pitchers, each of them crowned with the small sculpted head of a turbaned Turk—a nod toward the luxurious drink's exotic origin and in keeping with the period's Turkish fashion. The limited signs of use suggest that the highly precious ensemble—in terms of its materials alone—was probably intended mainly for display purposes. Only few services in pure gold have escaped being melted down. In addition to the one shown here, the ensemble created in Augsburg for Czarina Anna Ivanovna between 1736 and 1740 has survived, though it does not include pieces specifically for chocolate (State Hermitage Museum, Saint Petersburg, inv. no. 5233).

UW

Literature: exh. cat. Schloss Schönbrunn 1980, pp. 414–15, cat. 94; exh. cat. Mannheim 2012, pp. 218–19, cat. IV 22; exh. cat. Paris 2008, p. 49, cat. 17; Weber 2013, p. 95, fig. 17; exh. cat. Vienna 2017, p. 258, cat. HM 1.3.

Cat. 35

Johann Jakob Adam

(Memmingen ca. 1720–1791 Augsburg)

Chocolate Service with Porcelain Cup with Landscape Scenes and Water Glass in a Leather Case

Augsburg, ca. 1751/1755

Meissen porcelain, third quarter of the eighteenth century; silver gilt, cut glass, faceted and gilded; hard porcelain with overglaze colors and gold; leather, wood, and velvet; porcelain cup

H. 6.8 cm, diam. 6.7 cm; glass H. 8.1, diam. 6.5 cm; tray H. 6.7 cm, L. 18.7 cm, W. 13 cm; case H. 11.6 cm, L. 21 cm, W. 13–15 cm

MAKK— Museum für Angewandte Künste Cologne, on permanent loan from a private collection, inv. no. DL 67

This chocolate service on tiny volute feet consists of two leaf-shaped saucers attached to each other to form a tray with holders for the Meissen porcelain cup and the gold-rimmed, cut-glass tumbler. The elaborate pierced rocailles of the holders served to stabilize the cups and prevent tipping. Because of this function, they have been known, probably since the nineteenth century, as *trembleuses*. The intertwined double handle on the saucer was used to carry the set. The intimate design of the service reflects the eighteenth-century practice of taking breakfast chocolate in bed. Furthermore it was customary to have a glass of water with the chocolate drink—as Philippe Sylvestre Dufour writes in the treatise attributed to him: "Some also tend to take a good gulp of fresh water before drinking it or dunking a few biscuits in the chocolate" (cat. 29). In Liotard's *Chocolate Girl*, as in his pastel *The Breakfast* (fig. p. 43), a maid serves both drinks together on a tray, albeit not combined in a single piece of crockery.

The intricate goldsmith's work by Johann Jakob Adam, who, like his father Elias Adam, specialized in settings for precious materials, dates from the heydays of Augsburg goldsmithing. Ten such *trembleuses* are known to be his work. A special feature of the set shown here is the bespoke case that served to protect it when traveling.

SD

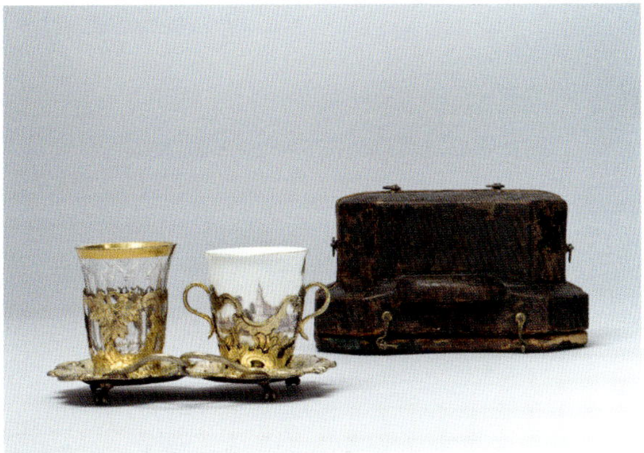

Literature: N.N./Heise 1986, p. 204; exh. cat. Munich 1994, p. 428, cat. 114; exh. cat. Dortmund 2008, p. 195, cat. 154; Weber 2008, pp. 85–86; exh. cat. Cologne 2010, p. 351, cat. 169.

Cat. 36

Meissen Porcelain Manufactory

Chocolate Service à deux

Circa 1760

Hard paste porcelain with overglaze colors and gold; chocolate pot H. 15.5 cm; tray H. 6.2 cm, L. 45.3 cm, W. 28.7 cm

Porzellansammlung, Staatliche Kunstsammlungen Dresden, inv. no. PE 2126 a–g

The increasing popularity of tea, coffee, and chocolate in Europe changed daily routines and social habits, and called for new forms of crockery. The aristocracy liked to enjoy these new hot drinks as part of their morning routine or at breakfast with an intimate circle. In the mid eighteenth century, the French porcelain manufactory in Sèvres developed so-called *déjeuners*—small services for one or two people on a matching tray—for these more private moments of the day. Elaborately combined tea, coffee, and chocolate services for larger numbers of guests, like those made in Meissen, found virtually no market in France. Developments in the fashions of the Meissen manufactory's most important export market were carefully monitored. And to appeal to the tastes of the French public, *déjeuners* were added to its offering in the second half of the eighteenth century. With its sweeping shapes, asymmetrical relief cartouches, and delicate rocailles in gold and purple, the example shown here also adopts stylistic features of the French Rococo. The shapes of the handles of the two jugs suggest that the set was designed for serving chocolate, but it may also have functioned as a coffee service.

JW

Literature: Exh. cat. Dresden 1991, cat. 83; exh. cat. Dresden 2010, cat. 170; exh. cat. Dresden 2013, p. 41; Weber 2016, pp. 89, 108.

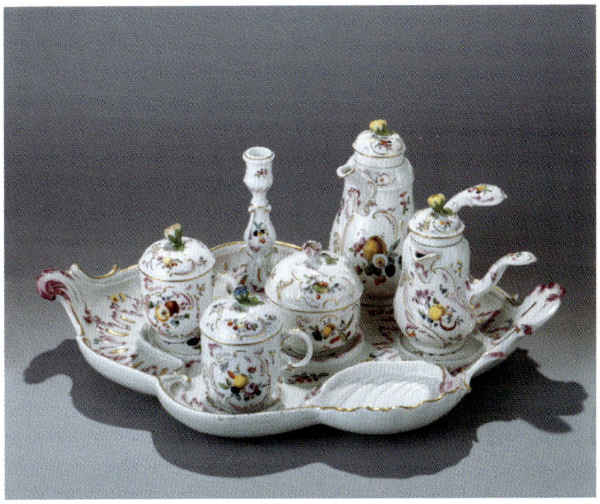

LIOTARD AND VIENNA

Jean-Étienne Liotard spent four years in Turkey and the Principality of Moldavia before arriving in Vienna in September 1743. There he gained access to one of Europe's most important courts of the time and came into close contact with the future Emperor and his wife. He made portraits of Maria Theresa and her husband Francis I as well as other members of the Habsburg family. For this he frequently resorted to drawings he had made in Constantinople, interweaving Turkish-oriental motifs with courtly ones. In social circles with access to luxury goods, anything of exotic origin met with the greatest interest. Liotard himself personified this fashion and, as self-styled "Turkish painter," attracted much attention.

During his two-year stay in Vienna, Liotard produced not only his famous self-portraits, but also the *Chocolate Girl*. He would continue to maintain close ties to the city and to the imperial family. In 1762 and 1777/78 he again paid visits to the city, each time staying for several weeks.

Cat. 37

Jean-Étienne Liotard

(Geneva 1702–1789 Geneva)

Maria Theresa in a Fur-Trimmed Gown, (1717–1780)

1743

Pastel on vellum, 62 x 49.4 cm

Oesterreichische Nationalbank, on permanent loan to Schloss Schönbrunn, Vienna, inv. no. 220002441

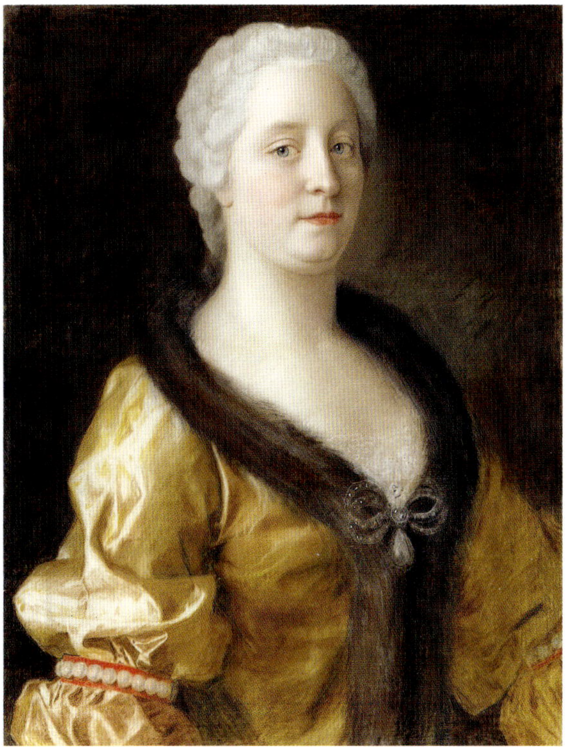

Liotard shows the Habsburg ruler Maria Theresa in regal pose and dressed with restrained splendor. Presented in half-profile and viewed from slightly below, her head turned to the right, the Empress is gazing at the viewer with a dignified expression. Her white powdered hair, face, and décolletage stand out against a dark brown background. Light entering from the left reflects on her forehead and neck as well as the right sleeve of her fur-trimmed, golden-yellow dress. The dress is pinned together above her chest by a diamond brooch. Her sleeve is ruffled just above her elbow with a red ribbon set with pearls.

After assuming ruling authority from her deceased father, Charles VI, in 1740, and having resolutely asserted herself in the War of the Austrian Succession, Maria Theresa was seen as the embodiment of Habsburg Austria. Accordingly, portraits of her were in high demand. When Liotard arrived in Vienna in 1743 he soon gained favor with the Queen of Hungary and Bohemia and her husband Francis. During his stay he produced numerous portraits of both, all based on the same two models. His various portraits of Maria Theresa, each named after its present location (for example, Weimar, Braunschweig [see cat. 43], or Schloss Ebenthal [see cat. 45] in Austria), exhibit only minimal differences in image format and pose, but greater variation in her dress and adornments, and in some cases her crown. This portrait, now on view at Schloss Schönbrunn, is not only considered to be the first of the series, but is also the only one that pictures her in a more intimate setting, without excessive jewelry or insignia of power. In his painterly approach, Liotard concentrated on a highly detailed and exact rendering of her face, while reproducing every nuance of light and dark on her monochrome dress using swift strokes.

RE

Literature: R/L 2008, no. 107, pp. 299–304; exh. cat. Vienna 2017, pp. 16, 134–35, 261, cat. HM 1.8.

Cat. 38

Martin van Meytens

(Stockholm before 1695–1770 Vienna)

Maria Theresa in Turkish Costume with Carnival Mask

Circa 1745

Oil on canvas, 97 x 76.5 cm

Schloß Schönbrunn Kultur- und Betriebsges.m.b.H, Schönbrunn Palace, Vienna, inv. no. SKB 001407

The painting shows Maria Theresa in three-quarter figure facing to the left, dressed in a sumptuous Turkish costume. The red dress above a white blouse and her ermine cloak with blue sleeves are ornamented with gold borders. Adorned with a precious hairpiece set with red gems, a multistrand pearl necklace, a long gold chain down to her waist, and a belt with large clasps, she is looking directly at the viewer, the mask she holds in her right hand

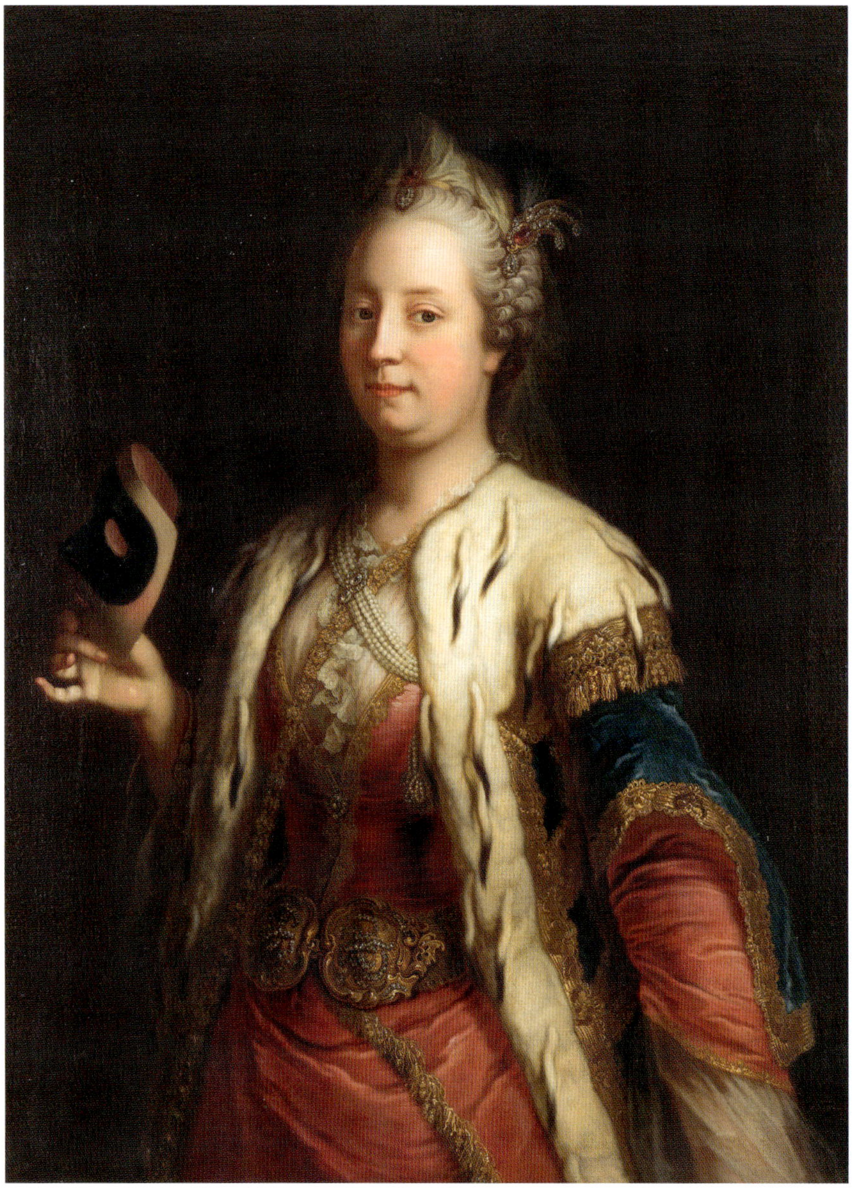

having seemingly just been removed from her face. Since its purchase on the art market in 2000 for Schloss Schönbrunn, the painting has been attributed to the Viennese court painter Martin van Meytens. Like two other versions in pastel (private collection, Austria) and oil (Schloss Nymphenburg, Munich)—neither of them painted by Liotard—it was probably based on a motif Liotard produced either in Constantinpole or Vienna, which is now missing. The dress is very similar to those in other Liotard drawings and pastels from this time. Meytens' painting not only alludes to the masked balls typical of the period and the popular Turkish fashion, it also attests to the high esteem for Liotard's pictures and to his role as a leading artist who was followed by other contemporary artists in Vienna.

RE

Literature: R/L 2008, no. 116, fig. 183; exh. cat. Schloss Schönbrunn 1980, p. 110; exh. cat. Vienna 2017, p. 17.

Cat. 39

Rosalba Carriera

(Venice 1673–1757 Venice)

Empress Wilhelmine Amalia (1673–1742), Wife of Emperor Joseph I

1730

Pastel on paper, 65.5 x 51.5 cm

Gemäldegalerie Alte Meister, Staatliche Kunstsammlungen Dresden, gal. no. P 20

After the death of her husband, Emperor Joseph I, in 1711, Empress Wilhelmine Amalia only let herself be portrayed as a widow in mourning. The black veil covering her head and shoulders, black dress, and ermine cloak, together with the background, contribute to the portrait's striking chiaroscuro. The large diamonds on her décolletage and sleeves, and the pearls on her brooch emphasize the subject's high rank. Soft surfaces like her skin or the fur cloak are rendered in pastel with equal mastery as the hard contours of the jewelry or the folds of her dress.

Wilhelmine Amalia of Brunswick-Lüneburg married the subsequent Emperor Joseph I in 1699, thus becoming Empress of the Holy Roman Empire. Her first daughter, Maria Josepha (see cat. 41), married Frederick Augustus II, later Augustus III, King of Poland (see cat. 6) in 1719, a union that consolidated the political alliance between Austria and Saxony. Wilhelmine Amalia was the sister-in-law of Elisabeth Christine of Brunswick-Wolfenbüttel, Maria Theresa's mother. This portrait was made during Carriera's stay in Vienna in 1730, at which time she also produced portraits of other members of the House of Habsburg (see cat. 40).

RE

Literature: Riedel/Wenzel 1765, p. 239; Sani 1988, p. 310, no. 259; Henning/Marx 2007, pp. 68–72.

Cat. 40

Rosalba Carriera

(Venice 1673–1757 Venice)

Archduchess Maria Theresa von Habsburg (1717–1780)

1730

Pastel on blue paper over canvas, 45 x 34.5 cm
Gemäldegalerie Alte Meister, Staatliche Kunstsammlungen Dresden, gal. no. P 153

It has only been possible to identify Maria Theresa as the subject of this painting by way of comparison with other portraits of her. Since this picture was made during Rosalba Carriera's stay in Vienna in 1730, the subsequent Empress would have been thirteen at the time. It was not uncommon in this period for the dynastic and social obligations of members of ruling families to begin in childhood; children were therefore frequently given the appearance of young adults and pictured looking older than they were. The painter Andreas Möller had already portrayed the eleven-year-old Maria Theresa three years earlier (Kunsthistorisches Museum, Vienna, 1727, inv. no. 2115, and a second version in the Gemäldegalerie Alte Meister, Dresden, 1727, inv. no. S 442). Maria Theresa's light complexion and white powdered hair contrasts with the dark background. A pink-lined ermine cloak covers her shoulders. As adornments she wears delicate flowers in her hair and large pearl earrings; her décolletage is bordered with diamonds and a clasp.

Maria Theresa was the oldest daughter of Emperor Charles VI and his wife Elisabeth Christine from the house of Brunswick-Wolfenbüttel. In 1740, after the death of her father, she took over the business of running the empire.

RE

Literature: Riedel/Wenzel 1765, p. 239, footnote: Sani 1988, pp. 310–11, no. 264; Henning/Marx 2007, pp. 70–73.

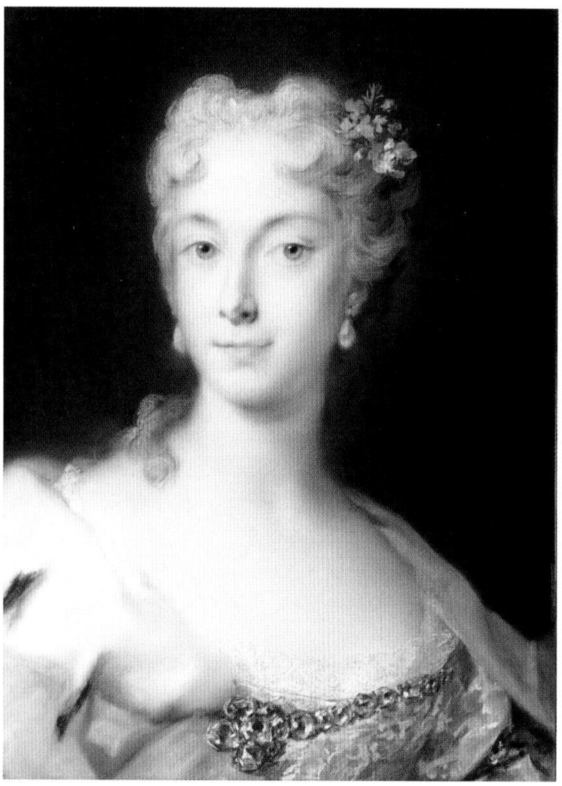

Cat. 41

Rosalba Carriera

(Venice 1673–1757 Venice)

Maria Josepha (1699–1757), Wife of Augustus III, King of Poland

1730 ?

Pastel on paper, 53.3 x 42.5 cm
Gemäldegalerie Alte Meister, Staatliche Kunstsammlungen Dresden, gal. no. P 5

Rosalba Carriera pictures Maria Josepha, daughter of Emperor Joseph I and his wife Wilhelmine Amalia (cat. 39), in front of a dark background wearing a silver dress and ermine stole. The young Habsburg princess is richly adorned with diamond and pearl jewelry in her hair, on her brooch, and on the armbands she wears on her sleeves. The radiant white of her dress, her powdered hair, and her décolletage is mitigated by her gray-blue eyes, the delicate pink of her face, and her red mouth.

Later portraits reveal that Maria Josepha was in fact no beauty, such as those by Louis de Silvestre and Anton Raphael Mengs, for example, who made no

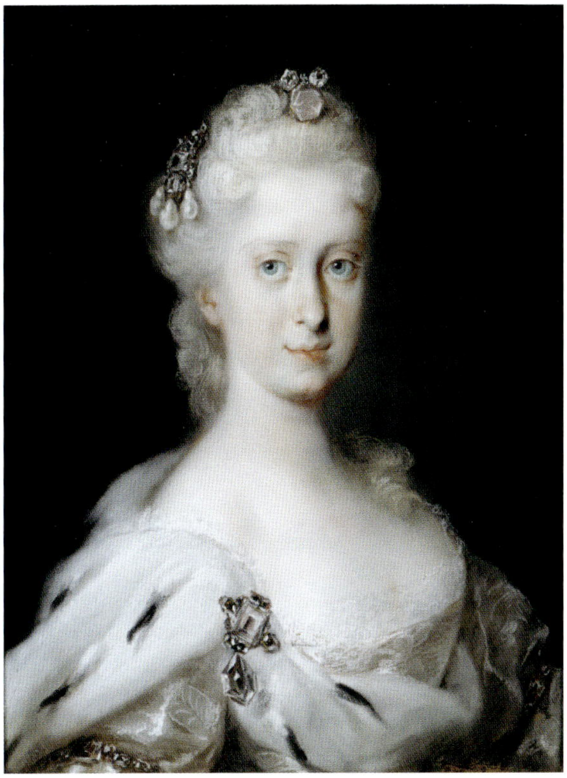

Cat. 42

Jean-Étienne Liotard

(Geneva 1702–1789 Geneva)

Maria Theresa in Turkish Costume

1743–1745

Watercolor and gouache on parchment, pasted onto cardboard, modern gilt-bronze frame, 7.3 x 5.4 cm

Musée d'art et d'histoire, Geneva, inv. no. AD 40

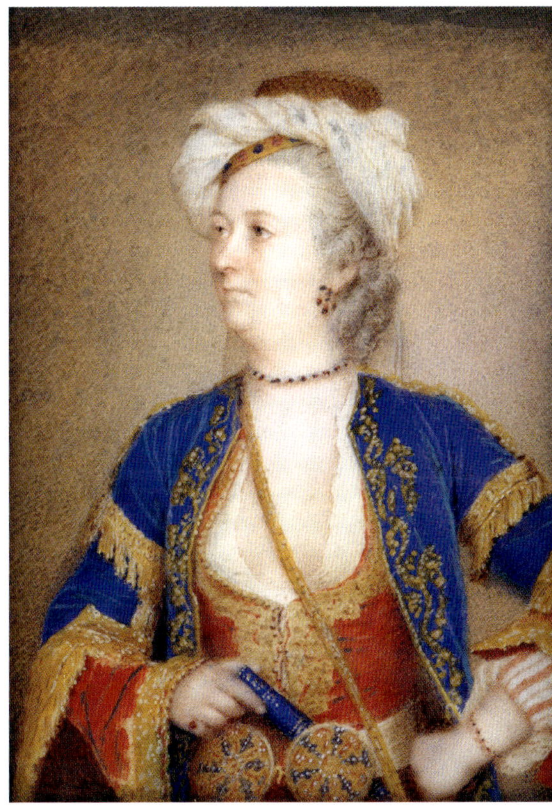

effort to disguise her protruding eyes and prominent nose. It is not known just when Carriera painted this portrait; until recently it was thought to have been made during the artist's stay in Vienna in 1730. However, in this picture Maria Josepha still appears to be youthfully idealized, and it is therefore conceivable that it was painted in connection with her marriage to Frederick Augustus of Saxony or soon afterward. The Saxon Elector Augustus the Strong had long championed this union between the Habsburg imperial house and the electorate of Saxony. In 1719, finally, he was able to stage a splendid wedding festivity. Since the crown prince had already met Rosalba Carriera in Venice in 1712, it seems plausible that he wished to have his young bride portrayed by the much-admired artist.

RE

Literature: Riedel/Wenzel 1765, p. 239; Sani 1988, p. 311, no. 266; Henning/Marx 2007, pp. 73–75; see Schnitzer 2014, pp. 51, 235, no. 7.

This minature shows the Archduchess of Austria Maria Theresa in Turkish costume against a light-brown background. The hems and sleeves of her red dress and blue caftan are decorated with gold and silver ornamental borders. She wears a white, turbanlike headdress with a yellow ribbon adorned with gemstones. Her right hand rests on the blue haft of a dagger, which is inserted into a belt with two round clasps set with blue and red stones. Her left fist is propped against her waist. Her earrings,

necklace, armband, and a ring on her little finger are set with small red gemstones.
Maria Theresa's gaze is directed at something in the far distance, yet she seems aware of her regal role. With this picture, Liotard revisits the motif of the "lady in oriental dress" (see cat. 44), which he had created during his stay in Constantinople from 1738 to 1742. But he has made small, individualizing changes: the cropping brings the Empress closer to the viewer, her gaze is directed to the right instead of the left, and her face recognizably bears the Habsburg regent's features. The portrait was made during Liotard's stay in Vienna in 1743–45. It is uncertain, however, whether he worked from an earlier study and only inserted Maria Theresa's head, or whether he was actually able to portray her in Turkish garb. What is clear, however, is that the "Turkish painter" Liotard was able to fan the flames of the Turkish craze in Vienna as well.

RE

Literature: R/L 2008, no. 223; Trivas 1938; exh. cat. Bordeaux/Geneva/Paris 1995, pp. 162–63.

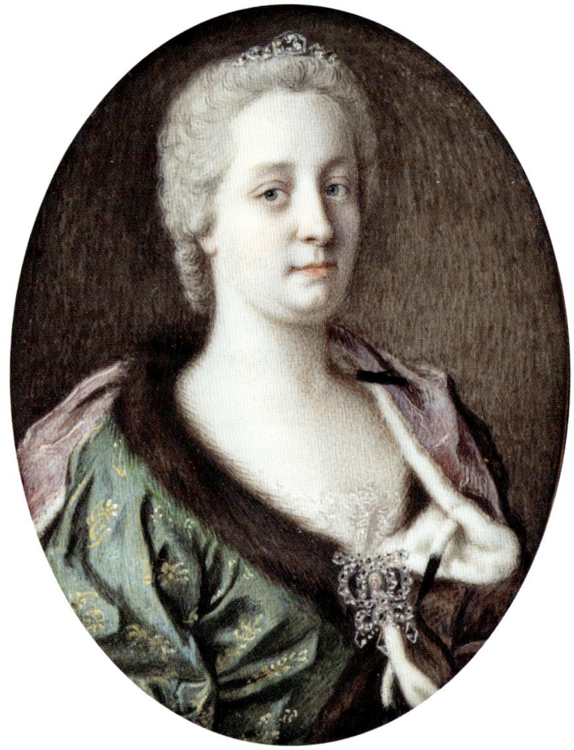

Cat. 43
Jean-Étienne Liotard
(Geneva 1702–1789 Geneva)
Portrait of Empress Maria Theresa (1717–1780)
Circa 1747
Watercolor on ivory, silver-gilt frame, probably nineteenth century, 5.8 x 4.5 cm
Inscribed on a piece of paper pasted to the back, partly illegible: "Callic. 7.5.26 / Lot 7 / Maria of Austria / wearing green / dress trimmed with fur / and ermine trimmed / cloak F. A HALL / [?]"
Private collection, Berlin

The miniature shows Maria Theresa facing right in a three-quarter view bust portrait without hands in front of a brown background. The artist's tiny brush strokes are clearly visible on the ivory. The Empress wears a green, fur-trimmed dress decorated with floral motifs. A pink-lined ermine cloak is draped around her shoulders as an insignia of her imperial rank. Her white powdered hair is crowned with a diamond diadem, and a large diamond brooch is pinned to her décolletage, which is partly covered by an undergarment of white lace. At the center of the brooch, barely recognizable, is a miniature portrait of her husband Francis I.
The painting follows the type of the Braunschweig portrait of Maria Theresa, which Liotard painted in pastel in 1745. In the ivory miniature her face seems slightly narrower. Repeats of this composition in brightly colored enamel were known, like the two rectangular versions from 1747 in Geneva (small) and Amsterdam (large), as well as a small oval one which he dated in Paris with "June 1748." The only other known version in watercolor is a smaller version in the Bayerisches Nationalmuseum, which is attributed to Liotard. The partly illegible inscription on the paper pasted to the back of the ivory of the Berlin miniature suggests that it was once in the collection of the American miniaturist Anne Hall.

RE

Literature: unpublished; see R/L 2008, no. 114 (pastel, Braunschweig, Herzog Anton Ulrich-Museum), 161 (enamel, Geneva, Musée d'art et d'histoire), 162 (enamel, Amsterdam, Rijksmuseum), 163 (enamel, Geneva, Musée Patek Philippe); see Buchheit 1911, p. 97, no. 438, plate 25.

Cat. 44

Jean-Étienne Liotard

(Geneva 1702–1789 Geneva)

Portrait of a Young Woman in Oriental Costume with Red Dress

Circa 1750

Watercolor and gouache on thick ivory, gilt frame, 9.2 x 7.2 cm

Private collection

The miniature shows a young woman in opulent oriental costume against a brown background. Her red dress and black caftan are richly decorated with intricate silver and gold borders. She wears a turban adorned with (embroidered?) flowers, gems, and a string of pearls. Her right hand rests on the blue haft of a small dagger inserted into a belt with large clasps set with green and red stones. A small necklace and a long shoulder chain, a ring with a red gemstone, and another string of pearls on her left wrist attest to the woman's wealth.

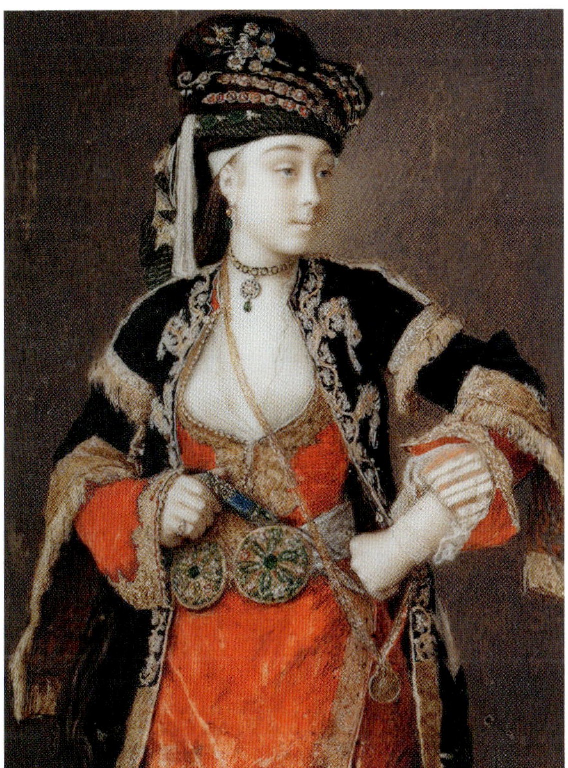

The motif, most probably developed during Liotard's sojourn in the Ottoman Empire between 1738 and 1742, was one of his most sought-after compositions and a number of versions of it exist. Based on the great similarity in size and technique—watercolor and gouache on ivory—between the five known examples, it can be assumed that they were all based on one original, which was repeatedly copied over a long period of time. Roethlisberger dates the present work to somewhere between Liotard's stays in Paris (1746–1753) and in London (1753/54). The version in Cambridge was long thought to be a portrait of Laura Tarsi, the lover of the Marquis of Granby, but there is no evidence to substantiate this claim. In addition to the above-mentioned five versions, differing only in their choice of colors, there are three further miniatures, which can be considered portraits in that we know who commissioned them: whereas the faces of "Madame Favart" and "Lady Montagu" can scarcely be distinguished from that of the *Young Woman in Oriental Costume*, Empress Maria Theresa can be clearly identified (see cat. 42).

RE

Literature: Roethlisberger 2014, p. 193, fig. 10; Hofstetter 2018, pp. 72–73, no. 30; see R/L 2008, nos. 220–22.

Cat. 45
Johann Christoph von Reinsperger
(Nuremberg 1711–1777 Vienna)
after **Jean-Étienne Liotard**
(Geneva 1702–1789 Geneva)
Portrait of Maria Theresa (1717–1789)
1744

Engraving (first state), 43.3 x 32.5 cm (sheet)
Inscribed at the bottom: "Marie Therese / Reine de Hongrie et de Boheme / Elevée au dessus de son sexe et du notre / Elle unit les vertus et de l'un et de l'autre / Sage dans ses Conseils, ferme dans ses projets / Magnanime ell fait L'amour des ses sujets. / Son Ame est sans Orgueil, son Coeur sans Artificie / Femme sans passion, Reine sans injustice; / Employant tour a tour, et joignant quelquefois / la douceur de son sexe a la fierté des Rois. / peint par J. E. Liotard, gravé par J. C. Reinsperger 1744"
Cabinet d'arts graphiques des Musées d'art et d'histoire, Geneva, inv. no. E 2002-0003

The numerous portraits that Jean-Étienne Liotard produced of Maria Theresa during his stay in Vienna from 1743 to 1745 are all based on a single model and differ in only minor details. For this engraving, Johann Christoph von Reinsperger followed the portrait of the regent that is now at Schloss Ebenthal. It pictures her as a bust portrait in half profile, her head turned to the right to face the viewer. The light face, neck, and décolletage contrast with the dark background. Her dress is trimmed with lace and gold brocade, an ermine cloak wraps around her back and shoulders. In contrast to the Ebenthal pastel, she does not wear a diamond brooch on her breast, and the lace on her right sleeve is not secured with diamonds. Only her hair is adorned with a small diadem.

The portrait in an oval frame against a masonry wall is supported by opposing volutes. An inscription between them displays Maria Theresa's name along with the titles she held in 1744. Beneath this is an eight-line encomium poem in French. There is also a matching portrait of Francis Stephen (cat. 46). Maria Theresa appears on the right in the two pendants, a position heraldically more important and normally reserved for the man. Reinsperger, who produced a number of engravings after Liotard, revised the inscriptions after the coronation in 1745, adding the imperial titles (second state, but still dated 1744), and a second time dated 1747 (third state). This also attests to the great demand for portraits of the imperial couple.

RE

Literature: R/L 2008, no. 109, p. 301, see also no. 108; Humber/Revilliod/Tilanus 1897, p. 172, no. 16 (third state).

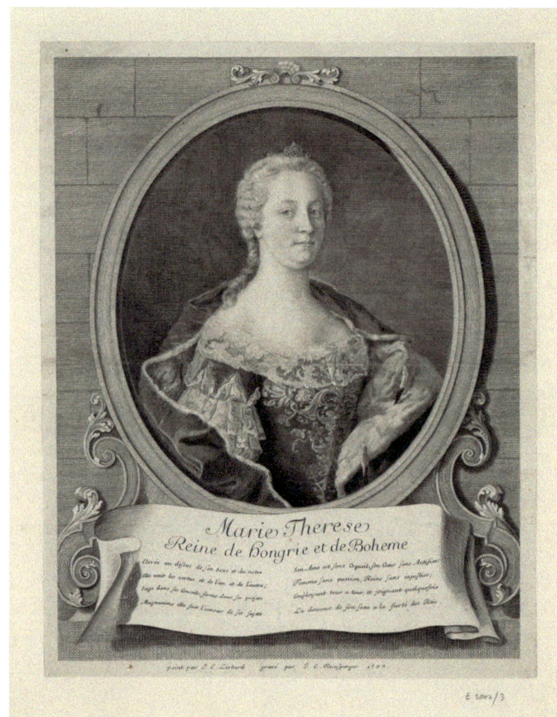

Cat. 46
Johann Christoph von Reinsperger
(Nuremberg 1711–1777 Vienna)
after **Jean-Étienne Liotard**
(Geneva 1702–1789 Geneva)
Portrait of Francis I (1708–1765)
1747

Engraving (third state), 43.3 x 32.5 cm (sheet)
Inscribed at the bottom: "François I. / Empereur des Romains / Roy de Ierusalem, Duc de Lorraine et de Bar / Grand Duc de Toscane etc. / Heros sans Vanité, Prince sans Favori / De Therese l'Appui, l'Amant et le Mari. / peint par I. E. Liotard, gravé par I. C. Reinsperger / A Paris chés l'auteur rue de la Corderie Et chés Audran Rue St. Jacques a la Ville de Paris."
Cabinet d'arts graphiques des Musées d'art et d'histoire, Geneva, inv. no. E 2002-0006

During his stay in Vienna in 1743–45 Jean-Étienne Liotard produced not only numerous portraits of Maria Theresa, but also of her husband Francis Stephen. The portrait engraving by Reinsperger was based on a now-missing pastel by Liotard—possibly the pendant to the portrait of Maria Theresa now held at Schloss Ebenthal. Francis Stephen is also pictured as a bust portrait in half-profile, his head turned to the left and his gaze directed toward the viewer. On his head he wears a long peruke. The white cravat sets off his face, bathed in light, from the dark shirt. As a member and Grand Master of the Order of the Golden Fleece, Francis wears the order's regalia, here represented by the cloak with gold-brocaded hem and the motto "JE LAI EMPRINS" on his left shoulder, as well as the long chain with the golden fleece.

As a pendant to the engraving of Maria Theresa (cat. 45), Francis I's portrait also appears in an oval frame in front of a masonry wall. The inscription between the volutes gives his name and, with "Empereur des Romains," his title as Emperor of the Holy Roman Empire, following his coronation in October 1745. In the first state, his titles were still given as Duke of Lorraine and Bar, Grand Duke of Tuscany, King of Jerusalem, and—along with Maria Theresa, his wife since 1736—co-regent of the Habsburg Hereditary Lands. After his coronation in 1745, Reinsperger revised the inscription, adding the title of Emperor (second state, but still dated 1744), and a second time dated 1747 (third state).

RE

Literature: R/L 2008, no. 110, p. 301; Humbert/Revilliod/Tilanus 1897, p. 174, no. 19*.

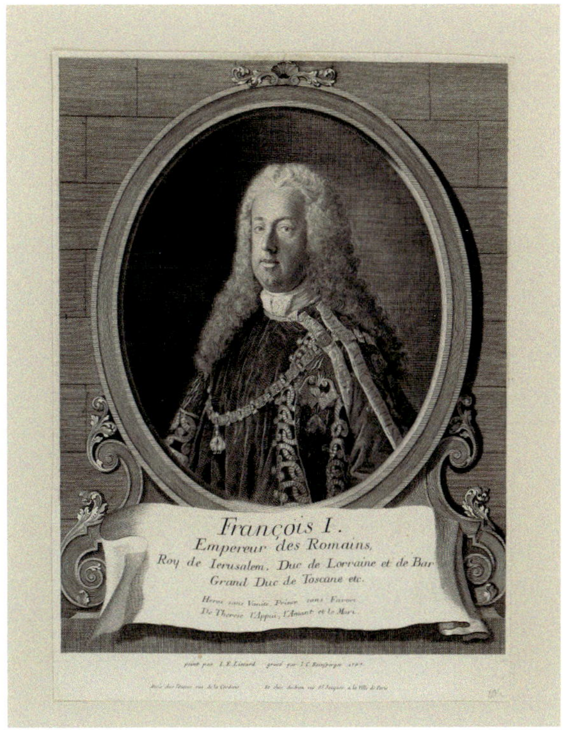

Cat. 47

Jean-Étienne Liotard

(Geneva 1702–1789 Geneva)

A Lady from Pera, Followed by a Girl, Receiving a Visitor

1738–1742

Red and black chalk, heightened with red chalk, on laid paper, 22.9 x 16.9 cm

Cabinet d'arts graphiques des Musées d'art et d'histoire, Geneva, inv. no. 1931-0006

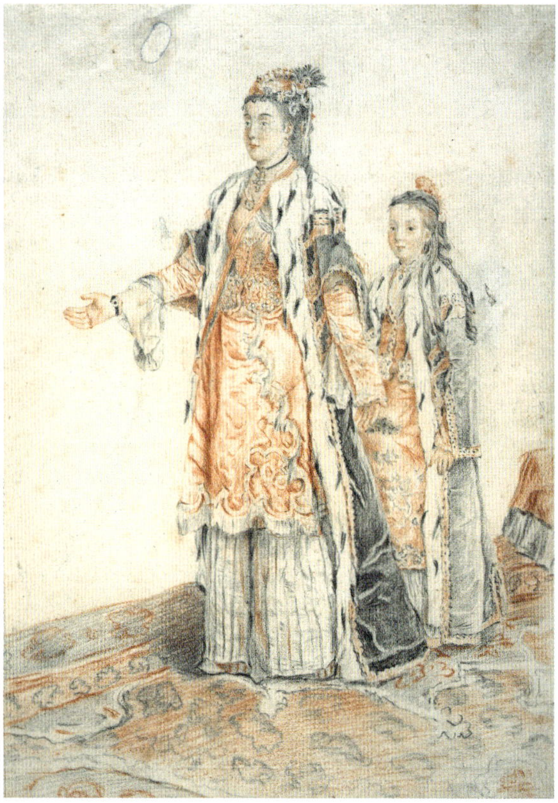

The drawing in red and black chalk pictures a lady from Pera, facing left, with her arms outspread to welcome a visitor not shown in the picture. She is dressed in a rich oriental costume: over a long striped skirt she wears a patterned dress and a long robe lined with ermine. Behind her stands a young girl in similarly elaborate attire. The two figures are depicted in an interior, standing on a carpet with a sketchily drawn oriental pattern. Behind the girl, the corner of a divan is just visible.

The picture exemplifies how Liotard re-used motifs developed earlier on and further reworked them. He reproduced this drawing of the lady from Pera in pastel, possibly even while still there (fig. p. 81). Pera (now Beyoğlu) was a part of Constantinople opposite the old Byzantine city across the Golden Horn and was the preferred residence of Western European diplomats, merchants, and travelers. From Constantinople, Liotard proceeded via Jassy to reach Vienna in 1743, where he repeatedly used the motif of the Pera lady and the girl, albeit with variants and in different media. Among these are the counterproof of an unknown drawing (cat. 48), engravings produced by Giuseppe Camerata after Liotard designs (cat. 49), and a recently discovered colored gouache on parchment.

RE

Literature: R/L 2008, nos. 70, 72, fig. 93; exh. cat. Geneva/Paris 1992, cat. 42; see Roethlisberger 2017, pp. 157–58.

Cat. 48

Jean-Étienne Liotard

(Geneva 1702–1789 Geneva)

Empress Maria Theresa with Her Daughter Maria Anna, Both in Turkish Costume

1745

Counterproof of a drawing in black and red chalk, on paper, 22 x 15 cm

Musée du Louvre, Département des Arts graphiques, Paris, inv. no. RF 1392

This counterproof of a drawing in red and black chalk—a copying technique Liotard used frequently—shows a simple scene with two figures: a lady in oriental dress opens her arms and steps toward a visitor not pictured. Behind her stands a young girl. At first glance this print greatly resembles the Genevan drawing *Lady from Pera, Followed by a Girl* (cat. 47). This, however, was not the original from which this reversed print was made. The sheet goes back to a Liotard design that is now missing.

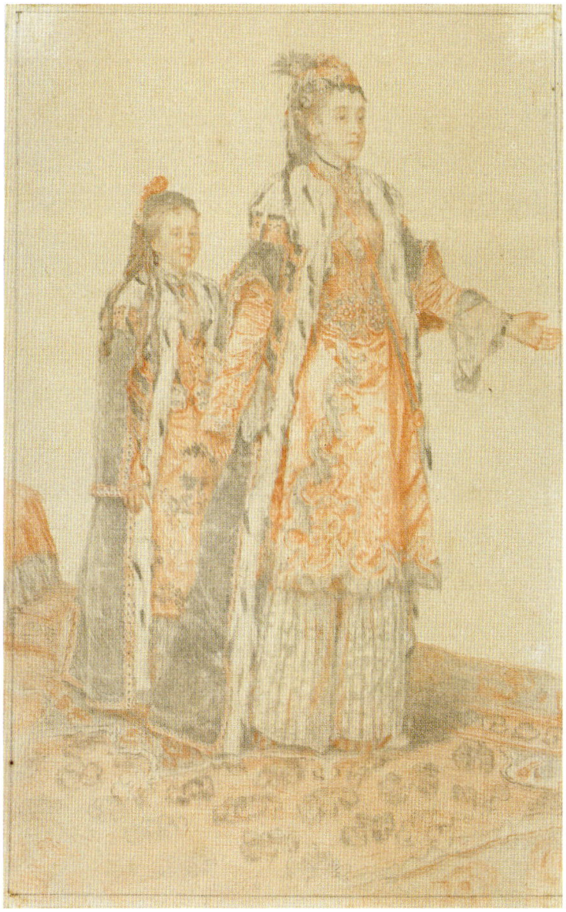

Liotard was re-using a motif captured shortly before, in Constantinople, but minimally changed the contours and especially the faces. The work is dated to 1745, that is, during his stay in Vienna. Even though the title names the figures as Maria Theresa and her then seven-year-old daughter Maria Anna, that identification is by no means assured: the inscriptions authored by Liotard make no reference to it. It is more likely that contemporaries wished to see the Empress in such pictures, which were so characteristic for Liotard. This is also confirmed by the reception of the engraving Liotard produced in that same year together with Giuseppe Camerata. This, too, was seen as a portrait of the Habsburg ruler with one of her daughters (cat. 49).

RE

Literature: R/L 2008, p. 278 (no. 72); exh. cat. Geneva/Paris 1992, cat. 43.

Cat. 49

Giuseppe Camerata

(Venice 1718–1803 Dresden)

after **Jean-Étienne Liotard**

(Geneva 1702-1789 Geneva)

A Lady from Pera Receives a Visitor

1745

Engraving (first state), 30.6 x 24 cm (sheet)

Inscribed bottom: "Une dame franque de Pera à Constantinople recevant visite. / Dessiné d'après nature à Constantinople par J. Etienne Liotard. Les visages gravéz à Vienne par lui-même, et les figures par Joseph Cameratta."; and by hand in pencil on the mounting: "The heads are those of the Empress and the Archduchess Maria Christina (Heinecken Ms. of vol. XII of his *Dictionnaire*)"

Kupferstich-Kabinett, Staatliche Kunstsammlungen Dresden, inv. no. A 66837, in the album A 744.3

The engraving depicts a lady in oriental dress, her arms spread wide, walking toward a visitor on the right not shown in the picture. It is related to the Paris counterproof (cat. 48) taken from a now-lost drawing, which was also the source for this work. The only change is that the lady and the young girl standing behind her are now looking straight at the viewer. Whereas the figures in the Paris counterproof were interpreted as Maria Theresa and her daughter Maria Anna, its caption now says "Lady from Pera with Daughter." We further learn from it that Liotard drew the motif from nature in Constantinople but engraved the faces in Vienna, and that the figures were the work of Giuseppe Camerata. The Venetian engraver produced several prints of works by Liotard. The two artists met in Vienna, where Camerata had been active since 1742. In 1751 he was summoned to the Dresden court to engrave its famous paintings for the gallery guide by Carl Heinrich von Heineken, then director of the royal collection of prints and drawings.

Underneath the image is a handwritten inscription, according to which the depicted figures are Maria

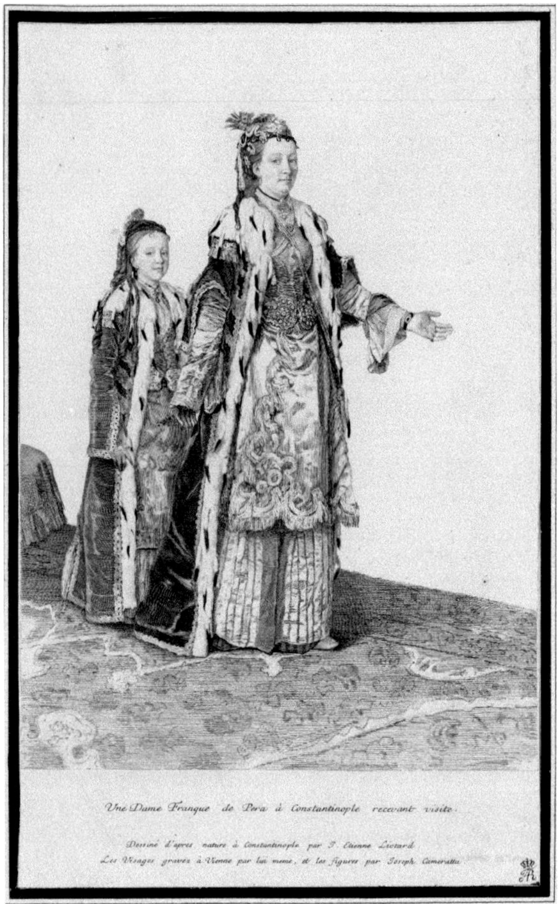

Theresa and her daughter Maria Christina. This contemporary identification, also found in an advertisement in the *Mercure de France* in 1750, was taken from Heineken's manuscript of volume 12 of his dictionary of artists, of which only the first four volumes were published until 1790. The manuscript itself has been missing since the Second World War. The Dresden print is mounted in an album created in the eighteenth century, containing a total of sixteen other prints by and after Liotard (see cat. 50) as well as works by Claude Lorrain.

RE

Literature: R/L 2008, no. 72; *Mercure de France* 1750, no. 11, p. 159; Humbert/Revilliod/Tilanus 1897, pp. 199–200, no. 100.

Cat. 50

Giuseppe Camerata

(Venice 1718–1803 Dresden)

after **Jean-Étienne Liotard**

(Geneva 1702–1789 Geneva)

A Lady from Galata with Her Servant

1745

Engraving (first state), 30.7 x 24.5 cm (sheet)

Inscribed at the bottom: "Une Dame Franque de Galata et son Esclave qui sont sur le point d'aller à Constantinople ou autre quartier turc. / L'Esclave presente à sa Maitresse un voile semblable à celui qu'elle a sur le visage et sans lequel / les Femmes Turques ne sortent jamais. / Dessiné d'après nature à Constantinople par J. Etienne Liotard. Le visage gravé à Vienne par lui-même, et les figures par Joseph Cameratta"; and by hand in pencil on the mounting: "The head is that of the Archduchess Maria Anna (Heinecken Ms. of vol. XII of his *Dictionnaire*)"

Kupferstich-Kabinett, Staatliche Kunstsammlungen Dresden, inv. no. A 66838, in album A 744.3

The engraving pictures a lady wearing oriental costume and a jeweled tiara, standing in front of a divan. Next to her stands her servant in a simple dress, her face concealed by a veil. She is handing a similar veil to her mistress, who is also about to cover up her face. According to the legend beneath the print, the lady lives in the Galata district of Constantinople, where many Europeans had settled. It goes on to discuss everyday customs in the Ottoman Empire, explaining that "Turkish women never leave the house without wearing such a veil." It is possible that, rather than a Turkish lady, Liotard was portraying a Western woman he was acquainted with. The handwritten entry in the Dresden album, taken from a lost manuscript by Carl Heinrich von Heineken, claims that she is Archduchess Maria Anna, daughter of Maria Theresa.

The engraving was based on a preliminary drawing by Liotard (Paris, Fondation Custodia) that initially showed only the two figures; a counterproof of this also exists (Paris, Louvre). Liotard then added a piece on the left, which shows part of her cloak and the sofa. Liotard's miniature technique is clear-

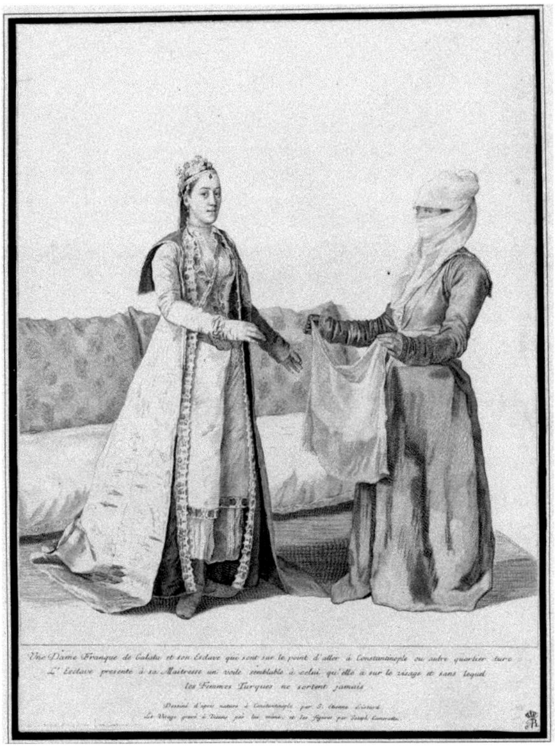

ly recognizable in the engraving, especially in the woman's face, which is composed of tiny dots. The sheet is pasted into a large-format album, on the same page as the *Lady from Pera* (cat. 49). In the eighteenth and early nineteenth centuries, prints were often kept in this manner, arranged alphabetically by artist. A few pages were left empty for future acquisitions. The prints are set off against the light mounting paper with frames in black ink.

RE

Literature: R/L 2008, no. 71; see exh. cat. Geneva/Paris 1992, cat. 55, 56.

LIOTARD AND THE ORIENT

While in Italy in 1738, Liotard joined the English aristocrats William Ponsonby and John Montagu on their journey to the Ottoman Empire, having been engaged to document their travels in pictures. By way of the Greek islands, they finally reached Constantinople. The four years that Liotard spent there, and subsequently as artist to the court in Jassy, capital of the Principality of Moldavia, would have a lasting effect on both his art and on himself as a person. From then on he would dress in a "Turkish"-style caftan and fur hat, and he grew a long beard. As he was one of the few artists who had actually been to the Ottoman Empire, his works provided an image of the "true Orient." He recorded the natives and their costumes, and also portrayed European merchants and diplomats, as well as high-ranking Ottoman dignitaries. Although he never went back there after his return to Europe, he later repeatedly drew upon motifs from this period.

Cat. 51
Jean-Étienne Liotard
(Geneva 1702–1789 Geneva)
Lady in Turkish Costume Holding a Fan
Between 1738 and 1771
Oil on copper, 16.7 x 19.5 cm
Royal Łazienki Museum, Warsaw, inv. no. Lkr 861

On a divan placed at a diagonal, a lady in a splendid costume is seated, turned slightly to the left. The composition is based on a preliminary drawing that no longer exists, but of which there is a counterproof that shows the scene reversed (cat. 52). Liotard changed the painting compared to the drawing by extending the divan on both sides and transforming the scene from a portrait format to a horizontal one. A further difference is the woman's now unornamented blue cloak, which seems quite reserved compared to the striped dress. Divan, carpet, and dress all use the same red-blue color scheme. The figure of the seated woman thus harmonizes with the voluminous forms of the cushions, which stand out against the gray-brown background. Isolated gold details are found in her

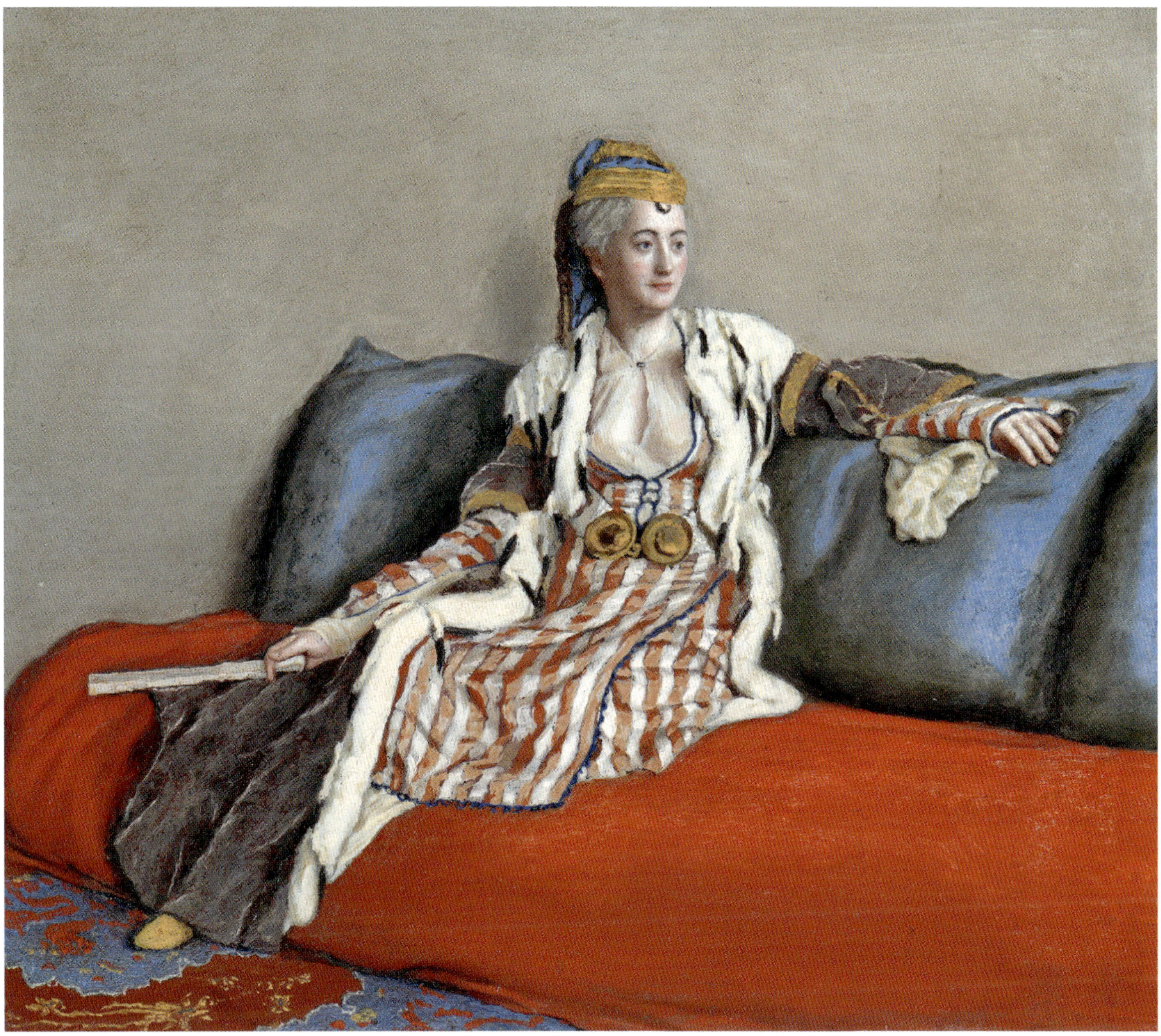

clothing, for example, the tips of her shoes peeking out from under her cloak, in the ornamental pattern of the carpet, and in the belt clasp, later also seen in some miniatures of Empress Maria Theresa (cat. 42).

This small painting on copper is the only known Liotard picture in this technique. For a long time, the woman was identified as Lady Mary Montagu, wife of the British ambassador to the Ottoman Empire Edward Wortly Montagu, who through her letters was instrumental in spreading the Turkish craze in England. But this is unlikely, since Lady Montagu had already left Constantinople in 1718, twenty years before Liotard arrived there. Accordingly, the picture appears to be a genre scene rather than a portrait. The fact that the painter later took up this Constantinople motif again and again makes a precise dating difficult.

SD

Literature: R/L 2008, no. 73; Juszczak/Małachowicz 2016, pp. 242–45, no. 62.

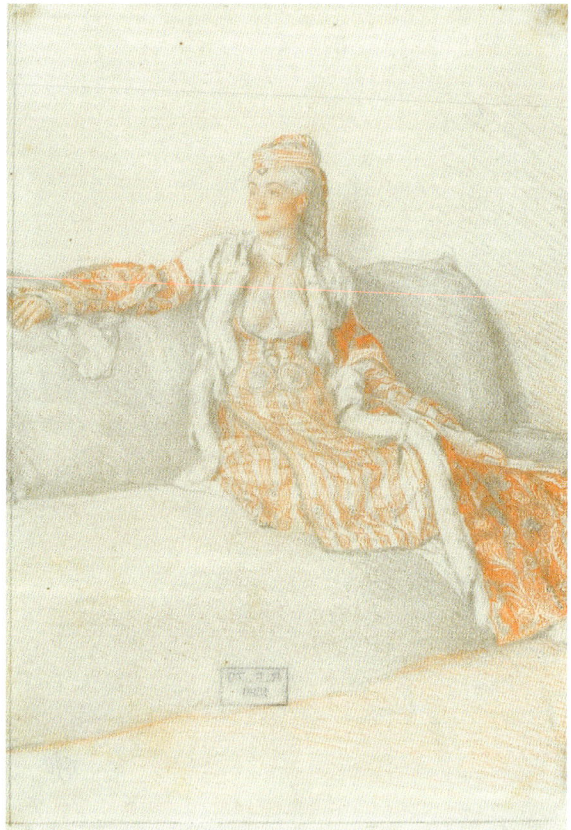

Cat. 52

Jean-Étienne Liotard

(Geneva 1702–1789 Geneva)

Lady from Constantinople on a Divan

Between 1738 and 1742

Counterproof, red and black chalk on paper, 21 x 15 cm

Musée du Louvre, Département des Arts graphiques, Paris, inv. no. RF 1390

This counterproof of a drawing shows a lady dressed in a Turkish costume seated on a divan suggested only with a few minimal strokes. Her right arm is extended along the back cushion, her left arm rests on the seat beside her, holding a folded fan. Her torso and head are turned slightly to the right, her gaze directed straight ahead along the backrest. She wears a striped dress with a wide belt held by a large clasp, an ermine-trimmed cloak with an ornamental pattern, and a headdress to which a long veil is attached. Liotard reproduced this sheet from an unknown drawing, using a procedure he often employed so as to be able to revisit motifs after works had been sold (see cat. 4, 48).

During his stay in Constantinople between 1738 and 1742, Liotard frequently drew figures in Turkish costume seated on a divan. Often they are engaged in domestic activities, playing music, or smoking, though always remaining without further narrative context. Later, mainly in the 1750s, he came back to this same motif, now also in pastel paintings. In *Lady in Turkish Costume* (cat. 51), painted on copper, he directly borrowed the composition from this sheet.

SD

Literature: R/L 2008, no. 73; exh. cat. Geneva/Paris 1992, cat. 37.

Cat. 53

Jean-Étienne Liotard

(Geneva 1702–1789 Geneva)

Portrait of Signora Maroudia Stay in Summer Dress

1738

Black and red chalk on white paper, 20.9 x 14 cm
Inscribed top center: "S.ra Maroudia la sorella di quella / davanti"; right: "le tablier de dentelles / les coliers d'or . . . / rubans rose 7 les bas rouge et broderies / d'or, les souliers brodés / d'argent 7 le bord du jupon / rouge / ce qui enveloppe la / tete est un voile / le bas est de dentelles"
Musée du Louvre, Département des Arts graphiques, Paris, inv. no. RF 1376

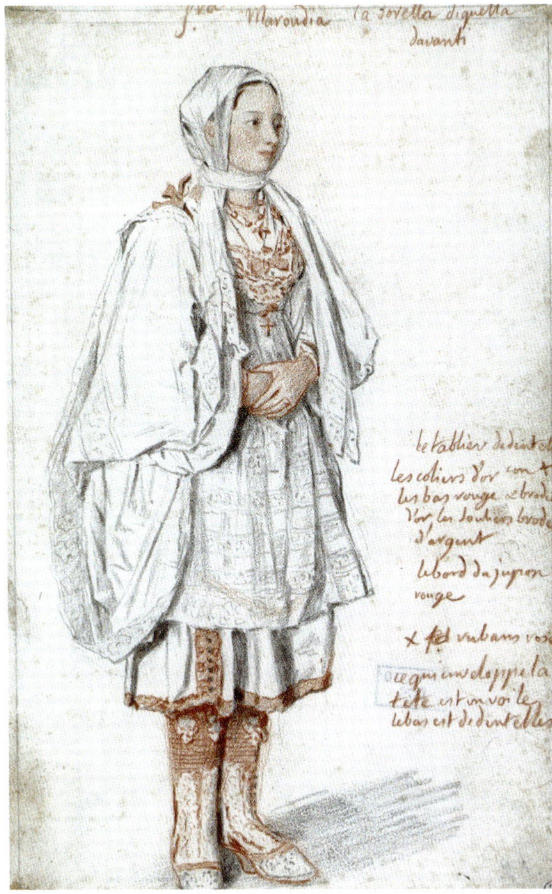

This drawing, executed in black and red chalk, was done as a full-figure study in three-quarter view. The young woman is standing facing to the left, her hands clasped in front of her waist and her gaze directed slightly downward. Liotard has carefully rendered her various layers of clothing: the patterned stockings, the straight-hemmed underskirt, the dress, cinched high just below the breast, the short cloak with bouffant sleeves, the cap, veil, and the additional necktie—indicating their patterns with swift strokes. Additional details were noted in an autograph inscription in red chalk.

In April 1738 Liotard accompanied the English noblemen William Ponsonby and John Montagu, 4th Earl of Sandwich, on their Grand Tour from Naples to Constantinople. They spent May in the Cyclades, where Liotard made a few detailed costume studies, which also have the quality of portraits inasmuch as the figures are identified by name. In addition to the Greek woman Maroudia Stay, identified on the sheet as the sister of the "previous," a reference to Marulla Stay (*Portrait of Marulla Stay*, British Museum, London, with a precise dating on the sheet), he also portrayed *Signora Lenetta Shepri* in a similar pose (Paris, Louvre). From the correspondence of the Earl of Sandwich we know that Liotard was to accompany the group to make documentary drawings. In addition to traditional costumes, he was also expected to record places of interest and local monuments. However, the painter, who left the tour in Constantinople, never pursued the latter.

SD

Literature: R/L 2008, p. 262, no. 86; Montagu 1799, p. III; exh. cat. Geneva/Paris 1992, cat. 10; See Fehlmann 2015, p. 66.

Cat. 54

Jean-Étienne Liotard

(Geneva 1702–1789 Geneva)

Bearded Turk, Standing, His Hands Crossed at His Waist

Circa 1742 (?)

Red chalk and pencil on thin paper, 21.3 x 14.3 cm
Verso: two stamps upper left: "vN" (collection of Carl Friedrich Ferdinand von Nagler, purchased for the Kupferstichkabinett 1835); and center: "Königlich Preußisches Kupferstichkabinett"; and later inscription bottom right in brown ink: "Liotard"
Kupferstichkabinett, Staatliche Museen zu Berlin, inv. no. KdZ 1625

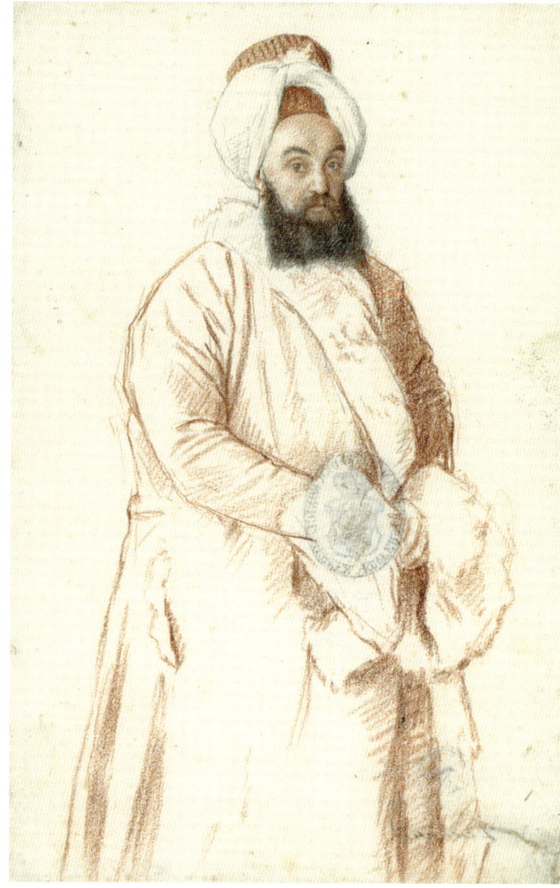

The drawing shows a man in Turkish costume as a three-quarter portrait in half-profile, his head turned to the right, looking toward the viewer. The red cap, wound with a turban-like cloth, is a *kavuk*, the sign of a nobleman in the Ottoman Empire, which comes in any number of variants. The man's face with its high forehead and wide-open eyes is meticulously captured in red chalk, while the half-length beard is rendered in tiny pencil strokes. The long cloak is only sketched; the man's hands are clasped in front of his belly. A fine, sharply drawn line in red chalk positions his right arm. A sash, draped from his right shoulder to his left hip, is outlined in pencil and textured in red chalk. He appears to be holding a cloth, though his clasped hands are merely suggested.

Liotard presumably made this portrait during his stay in Constantinople; the characteristic headgear is also found in other portraits of official figures, for example *Mehemet Aga* (cat. 62) or the convert Comte de Bonneval, later called Ahmet Paşa. The Paris Bibliothèque Nationale holds a counterproof of this drawing, on which Liotard changed the man's gaze so he now looks past the viewer. This change shows that he reworked and amended the drawing, possibly so as to be able to use the motif later on; however, there is no known pastel version. The sheet (like the following one, cat. 55), was once in the collection of Carl Ferdinand Friedrich von Nagler, Prussian postmaster general and subsequent government minister, whose important private collection was acquired for Berlin's Kupferstichkabinett in 1835.

RE

Literature: Exh. cat. Geneva/Paris 1992, p. 278, no. 35, fig. p. 82; see R/L 2008, no. 83.

Cat. 55
Jean-Étienne Liotard
(Geneva 1702–1789 Geneva)
Young Woman from Jassy
1742/43

Red and black chalk, and pencil on thin paper, 21.3 x 14.5 cm
Verso: two stamps bottom left: "vN" (collection of Carl Ferdinand Friedrich von Nagler, purchased for the Kupferstichkabinett 1835); and center: "Königlich Preußisches Kupferstichkabinett"; also later inscription bottom right in brown ink: "Liotard"
Kupferstichkabinett, Staatliche Museen zu Berlin, inv. no. KdZ 1627

Very few works survive from Liotard's time in Jassy. In this small red chalk drawing he pictures a standing woman in the country's traditional costume, in this particular case more typical of the genteel bourgeoisie than of figures at court. Her face is rendered in detail, her dark hair, eyebrows, blushed cheeks, and red lips contrasting with her pale complexion. She wears a fashionably tall, striped head covering, to which a small cloth embellished with tiny stones is attached. Her only adornments are an earring and a necklace with a medallion. The long red cloak with short sleeves worn over a close-fitting, high-waisted shirt with a broad décolletage and puffed sleeves is closed only at the neck. Her left hand is placed under her belt, which is equipped with a large round clasp; her right hand is not visible. Two pointed shoes peek out from under her skirt. A short shadow on the floor to the left anchors the woman in space. Following the personal invitation of Prince Constantine Mavrocordatos (cat. 57), Liotard spent a good ten months, from October 1742 to August 1743, at the Moldavian court in Jassy (present-day Iași, Romania). The principality was a vassal state of the Ottoman Empire. However, Mavrocordatos attempted to push through his own political and cultural reforms, as can also be seen from his appointment of Liotard as painter to the court. In addition to the latter's detailed observations of the native populace, he also came into contact with the upper classes, which he documented in drawings (cat. 56).

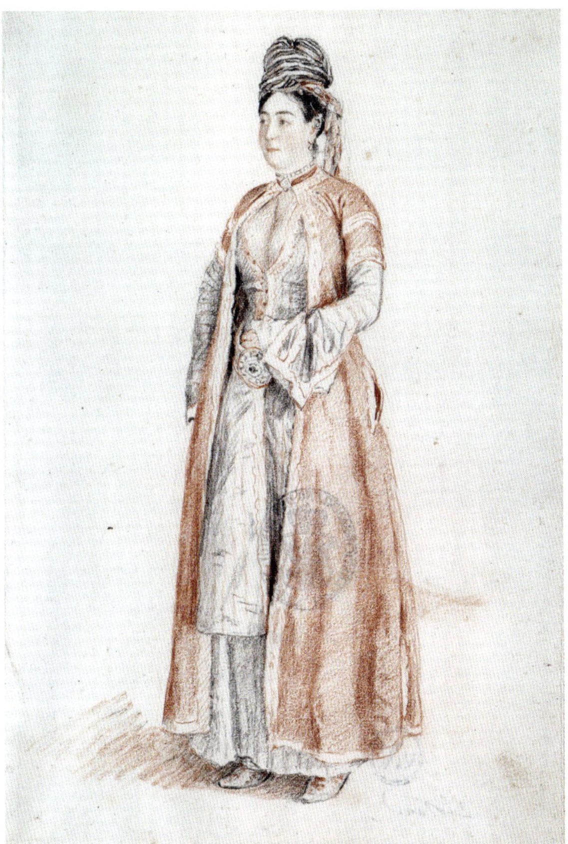

RE

Literature: R/L 2008, p. 298, no. 104; Niculescu 1982, pp. 144–45; exh. cat. Geneva/Paris 1992, p. 282, no. 86.

Cat. 56
Jean-Étienne Liotard
(Geneva 1702–1789 Geneva)
Nobleman from Jassy
1742/43

Red chalk, graphite and black chalk on paper, 22.9 x 17.8 cm
Cabinet d'arts graphiques des Musées d'art et d'histoire, Geneva, gift from the Société auxiliaire du Musée, inv. no. 1934-0035

Like the *Young Woman from Jassy* (cat. 55), this drawing from Liotard's time at the Moldavian court pictures a standing, full-figure subject in an undefined space. The

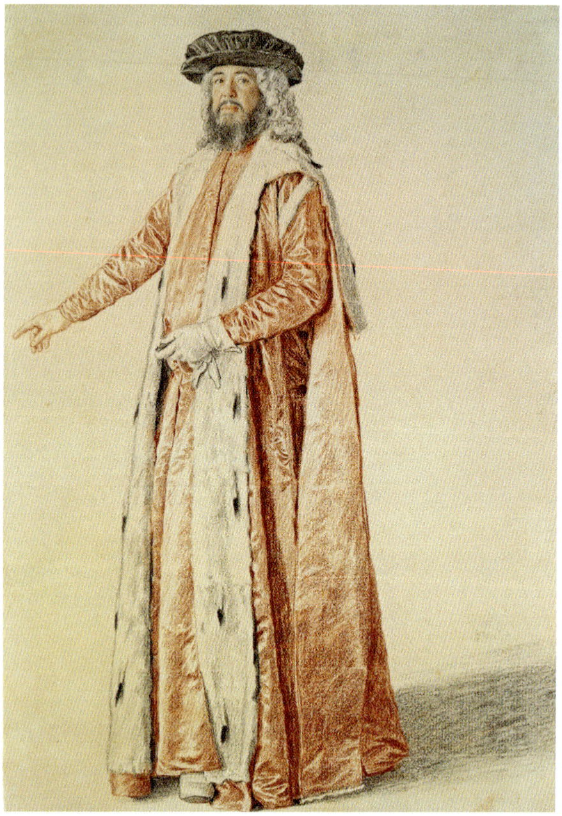

man's gaze rests attentively on the viewer; his right arm points at something behind him, his left arm rests in front of his waist. His long garment in the Turkish style, rendered mainly in red chalk, the ermine-trimmed cloak, and the white glove on his left hand show him to be a nobleman. He holds the other glove in his hand. The gray-tinged beard, executed in delicate strokes, indicates his advanced age; on top of his shoulder-length, wavy, gray hair—probably a peruke—he wears a flat, black hat. His pose and clothing are reminiscent of a scholar's. The identity of the *Nobleman from Jassy* remains unknown. However, his headdress, peruke, and gloves suggest a Western European in oriental costume. The cosmopolitan Prince engaged several such men in key positions at his court. The beard, on the other hand, would indicate that this is a portrait of a Moldavian; the expensive gloves could have been a gift to the court from the West. Niculescu saw in the subject an intellectual from Transylvania at the Prince's court. During his stay in Jassy Liotard took advantage of the opportunity to portray members of the Prince's family and various courtiers. Among the few surviving works are a drawing of Ekaterina Mavrocordato, the wife of the Moldavian Prince (now in the Kupferstichkabinett Berlin), and the two pictures shown here (see cat. 55). A portrait of Constantine Mavrocordatos, presumably painted by Liotard, can be reconstructed only from an engraving (cat. 57).

SD

Literature: R/L 2008, no. 104; Niculescu 1982, pp. 147–48; see exh. cat. Geneva/Paris 1992, cat. 72; exh. cat. Edinburgh/London 2015, cat. 18.

Cat. 57

Georg Friedrich Schmidt

(Schönerlinde near Berlin 1712–1775 Berlin)

after **Jean-Étienne Liotard** ?

(Geneva 1702–1789 Geneva)

Portrait of Constantine Mavrocordatos, Prince of Moldavia (1711–1769)

1742/43

Engraving, 30.2 x 21.8 cm

Inscribed in the print bottom right: "G. F. Schmidt Sculp. Parisiis"; in the frame: "CONSTANTINUS SCARLATI MOLDAVIAE PRINCEPS"; center, beneath the oval portrait: "Musas Augusti colit æmulus ille volentes / Per Populos dat jura, viam que affectat Olympo"

Kupferstich-Kabinett, Staatliche Kunstsammlungen Dresden, inv. no. A 24016

The portrait of Prince Constantine Mavrocordatos has been set as a half-profile into a standardized frame. From a slightly elevated standpoint he turns his head to gaze at the viewer. He still seems youthful, despite the beard. His dark fur hat and fur-trimmed caftan, furnished with shimmering ornamental braiding on his chest, stand out against a cloudy background. Mavrocordatos, born in Constantinople, came from an old noble family originally from Greece. He was elected Prince of Wallachia six times, and also four times Regent of Moldavia, to which the inscription on the oval frame refers. "Scarlati" is the family name of his second wife. His coat

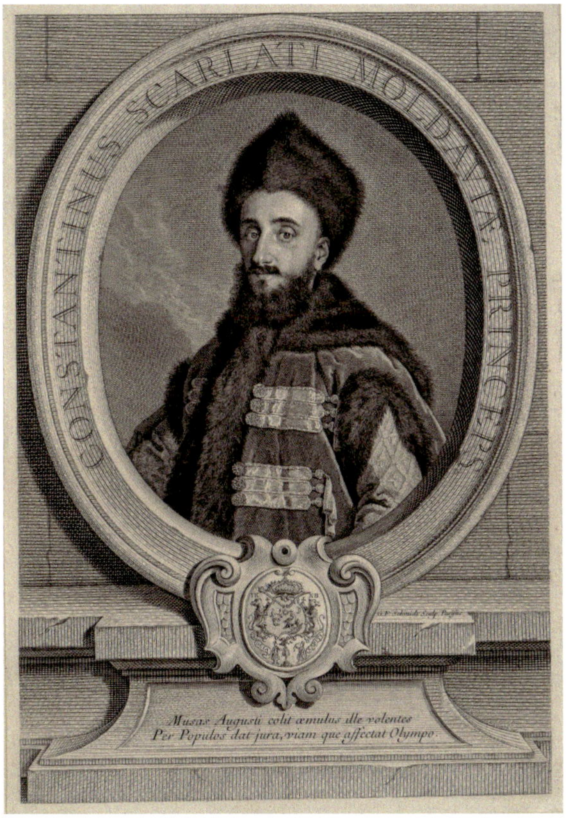

of arms, with the eagle and cross as well as sun and moon or bull's head relates to these two principalities. The inscription is taken from Virgil's *Georgica*, a didactic poem about agriculture with numerous political and cultural references.

This engraving was executed in Paris by Georg Friedrich Schmidt; early descriptions relate that it was based on a portrait of the Prince "in red chalk" by Jean-Étienne Liotard—a drawing therefore. But no preparatory drawing survives and, moreover, no other author is named in the engraving. The engraver Schmidt arrived in Paris in 1737 and worked after designs by Antoine Pesne, Nicolas Lancret, Hyacinthe Rigaud, and Maurice Quentin de La Tour. Liotard stayed in Jassy in 1742/43 at the invitation of Mavrocordatos, who reigned as Prince of Moldavia from 1741 to 1743. In July 1743, Schmidt was summoned to Berlin as engraver to the court. The Prince's portrait must have been created at around that time. Whether Liotard and Schmidt were ever in contact remains uncertain.

RE

Literature: R/L 2008, no. 12; Jacoby 1815, p. 20 (burin), no. 39; Niculescu 1982, pp. 135–37; exh. cat. Geneva/Paris 1992, p. 281, no. 79.

Cat. 58

Johann Christoph von Reinsperger
(Nuremberg 1711–1777 Vienna)
after **Jean-Étienne Liotard**
(Geneva 1702–1789 Geneva)
Roman Peasant Woman
Circa 1750
Engraving and etching,
26.2 x 20 cm (image), 40 x 27.5 (sheet)
Inscribed at the bottom: "Paisanne de la Campagne de Rome / Dessiné d'apres nature par J. E. Liotard gravé par J. C. Reinsperger"; bottom left: "A Paris chés l'Auteur rue de la Corderie"; bottom right: "Rue S. Jacq. chés la V.[e] Chereau au 2. pilliers d'Or. / Et chés Audran a la Ville des Paris"
Cabinet d'arts graphiques des Musées d'art et d'histoire, Geneva, inv. no. E 2014-0661

Reinsperger's engraving, after a drawing by Liotard that was probably made during his stay in Italy in 1737, pictures a full-figure peasant woman in traditional local costume, her hands crossed at her waist and holding a fan. The details of the drawing have been transferred precisely into the print, the facial features and hands executed in stippling technique, the rest in various cross-hatchings. The inscription "dessiné d'après nature," explicitly notes that the engraving was based on a drawing made from nature, i.e. that Liotard had seen the subject in person. This descriptor is found not only on all of Reinsperger's engravings but also on an early Liotard self-portrait (cat. 15a) and the engravings by Camerata (cat. 49, 50). It emphasizes Liotard's claim to be a "painter of truth."

Reinsperger created his engraved reproduction of the *Roman Peasant Woman* in Vienna, presumably at Liotard's request. The two were already working

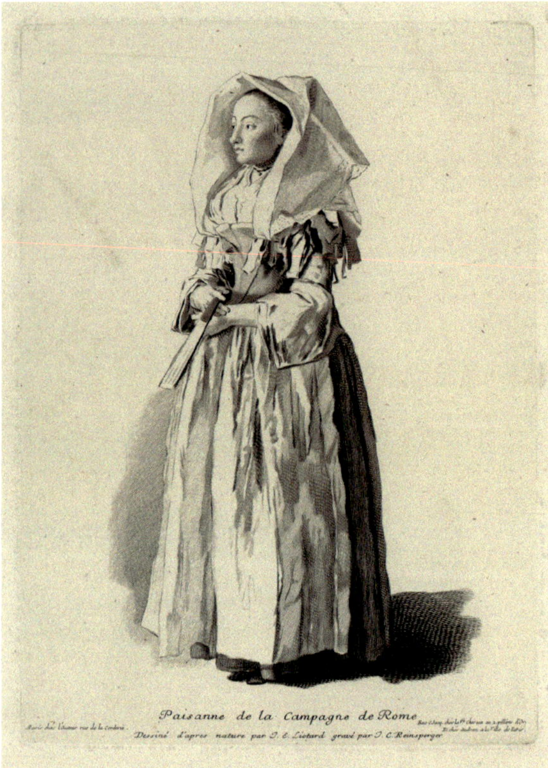

together on the portraits of Maria Theresa and Francis I (see cat. 45, 46). Reinsperger made five further engravings based on Liotard's drawings from his travels between 1737 and 1743, which were published by Liotard together with Benoît Audran and Marguerite Chéreau in Paris (cat. 59, 60, 61, 62, 63). The numerous reproductions of these mainly oriental subjects attest to the considerable interest in such themes.

SD

Literature: R/L 2008, no. 96; Humber/Revilliod/Tilanus 1897, p. 197, no. 98; see exh. cat. Geneva/Paris 1992, cat. 4.

Cat. 59

JOHANN CHRISTOPH VON REINSPERGER

(Nuremberg 1711–1777 Vienna)

after **JEAN-ÉTIENNE LIOTARD**

(Geneva 1702–1789 Geneva)

Lady from Constantinople

Circa 1750

Engraving and etching, 26 x 20 cm (image), 42.5 x 29.0 cm (sheet)

Inscribed at the bottom: "A Paris chés l'Auteur rue de la Corderie. Rue S. Jacques chés la V.e Chereau au 2. pilliers d'Or. Et chés Audran a la Ville des Paris. / Dessiné a Constantinople d'apres nature par J. E. Liotard gravé par Reinsperger"

Cabinet d'arts graphiques des Musées d'art et d'histoire, Geneva, inv. no. E 2014-0657

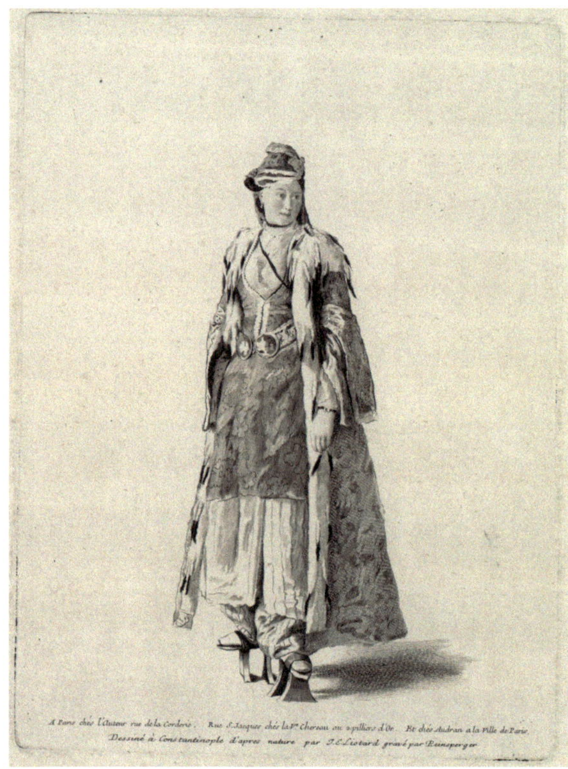

The lady from Constantinople is pictured in a standing pose wearing an elaborate Turkish costume. Over her loose-fitting, striped trousers (Turkish: *şalvar*) she wears a shirt, an embroidered dress (*entari*), and an ermine-trimmed cloak, also a tall headdress formed of multiple sheets of fabric. A ribbon running diagonally across her chest may have served to secure a purse or a vial of perfume. Particularly striking are her wooden pattens, the overshoes worn on entering a hammam, the Turkish steam bath. The shadow lends the figure spatial depth, though there is no indication of a specific setting.

The sheet is the only work in the group of engravings by Reinsperger that has no title. There is, however, a matching Liotard drawing in red and black chalk (Paris, Louvre). Liotard frequently took up the motif of a hammam visit; three paintings exist on this theme: two pastels (Geneva, Musée d'art et d'histoire; Kunst Museum Winterthur, Collection Oskar Reinhart) and one in oil (Kansas City, The Nelson-Atkins Museum of Art). In all three versions the lady is pictured with a servant, and all are distinguished by particularly vivid colors. They also all feature a water basin on the wall.

SD

Literature: R/L 2008, no. 97, see nos. 67, 68, 69; Humbert/Revilliod/Tilanus 1897, p. 197, no. 97 (as *Dame de Smyrne*); see exh. cat. Geneva/Paris 1992, cat. 28; see Koos 2014, pp. 102–06.

Cat. 60

Johann Christoph von Reinsperger
(Nuremberg 1711–1777 Vienna)
after **Jean-Étienne Liotard**
(Geneva 1702–1789 Geneva)

M. Levett, an English Merchant

Before 1755

Engraving and etching,
20 x 26 cm (image), 28.3 x 42.8 cm (sheet)
Inscribed at the bottom: "M. Levett Negociant Anglais. / Dessiné à Constantinople dapres nature par J. E. Liotard gravé par J. C. Reinsperger"; bottom left: "A Paris chés l'auteur rue de la Corderie."; bottom right: "Rue S. Jacq. chés la V.[e] Chereau au 2. pilliers d'or. / et chés Audran à la Ville des Paris."
Cabinet d'arts graphiques des Musées d'art et d'histoire, Geneva, inv. no. E 2014-0668

The portrait of the English merchant Francis Levett, who resided in Constantinople as a trade representative from 1737 to 1750, pictures him seated on a divan in a self-possessed pose. Cushions and seat are merely suggested by a few strokes. The man is dressed in a simple, long garment and wide cloak and is gazing out toward the left. His prominent moustache and the fur hat make him look like a Tatar.

Liotard portrayed Levett in oriental costume several times, also together with his wife (fig. p. 20). The drawing after which this print was made (Paris, Louvre) is therefore one of Liotard's many Constantinople portraits of Western travelers and merchants. In many cases they did not merely pose in the costume of their host country for the painting but also wore these clothes as they went about their daily

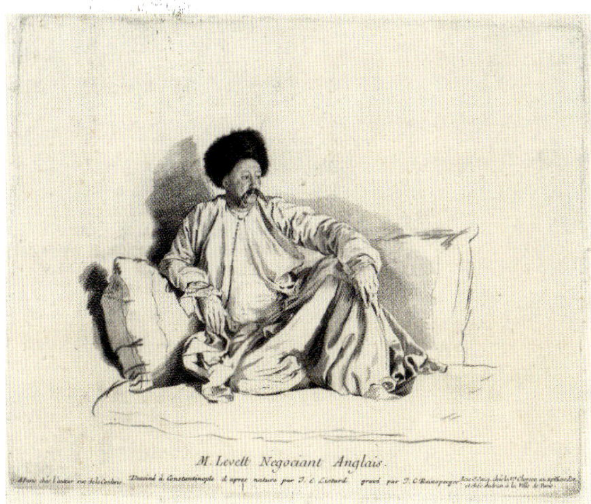

business. The English nobleman William Ponsonby, whom Liotard accompanied on his Grand Tour, and the archaeologist Richard Pococke (p. 80) were also depicted in oriental costumes.

SD

Literature: R/L 2008, no. 98; Humber/Revilliod/Tilalnus 1897, p. 200, no. 101; see exh. cat. Geneva/Paris 1992, cat. 47.

Cat. 61
Johann Christoph von Reinsperger
(Nuremberg 1711–1777 Vienna)
after **Jean-Étienne Liotard**
(Geneva 1702–1789 Geneva)
Sadig Aga (second state)
Circa 1750
Engraving and etching,
26 x 19.8 cm (image), 40.5 x 29.3 cm (sheet)
Inscribed at the bottom: "Sadig Aga Grand Tresorier des Mosqueés / A Paris chés l'Auteur rue de la Corderie. / Rue S. Jacq. chés la V.e Chereau au 2. pilliers d'Or. / Et chés Audran a la Ville des Paris. / Dessiné à Constantinople d'apres nature par J. E. Liotard gravé par Reinsperger"
Cabinet d'arts graphiques des Musées d'art et d'histoire, Geneva, inv. no. E 2014-0679

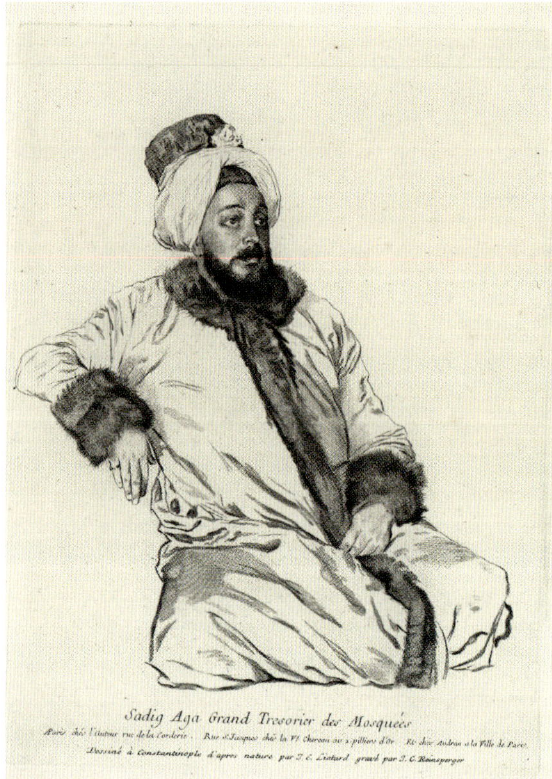

Reinsperger engraved two of Liotard's portraits of high-ranking dignitaries at the sultan's court; one is that of Sadig Aga, grand treasurer of mosques. He is shown without any spatial setting in a cross-legged seated pose, wearing a caftan with elaborate fur trim and a turban. His left arm rests in his lap, his right arm is bent as though propped against a cushion. Although no divan is visible, Liotard has implied it simply by the subject's pose.

This print is the only one from this group for which the preliminary drawing no longer exists. The beard and fur trims have been most exquisitely rendered by Reinsperger, using a variety of cross-hatchings. Sadig's pose is similar to that of the *Effendi* (cat. 64), another member of the Ottoman administration. The title "Aga" was appended to the family name and denoted a senior official or officer of rank, such as the commander of the Janissaries.

SD

Literature: R/L 2008, no. 101; Humbert/Revilliod/Tilanus 1897, p. 197, no. 94; Smentek 2010, p. 90.

Cat. 62

JOHANN CHRISTOPH VON REINSPERGER

(Nuremberg 1711–1777 Vienna)

after **JEAN-ÉTIENNE LIOTARD**

(Geneva 1702–1789 Geneva)

Mehemet Aga, Brother of Sadig Aga

Before 1755

Engraving and etching,
26 x 20 cm (image), 40 x 29 cm (sheet)

Inscribed at the bottom: "Mehemet Aga frere de Sadig. / Dessiné a Constantinople d'apres nature par J. E. Liotard gravé par J. C. Reinsperger / A Paris chés l'Auteur rue de la Corderie. Rue S. Jacques chés la Ve Chereau au pilliers d'or. et chés Audran a la Ville des Paris"

Cabinet d'arts graphiques des Musées d'art et d'histoire, Geneva, inv. no. E 2014-0683

Like his brother Sadig Aga, Mehemet Aga is pictured seated, wearing a fur-trimmed cloak, wide trousers, and a tall turban. He has a full beard and round lips and is gazing out toward the right. No shadows or background serve to anchor him in space, though he appears to be seated on the floor. For this engraving, too, a red and black chalk drawing by Liotard is preserved in the Louvre.

Along with Sadig Aga, this engraving by Reinsperger pictures another dignitary at the Ottoman court, also called the "Sublime Porte," a metonym for the administration of the Ottoman Empire. Koos notes that Liotard portrayed both Agas in a pose typical of the Ottoman-Muslim world, instead of the standing pose accustomed from depictions of Western dignitaries, and with individualized faces. Thus, unlike eighteenth-century costume books, such as *Le Recueil Ferriol*, he focused on the actual person.

SD

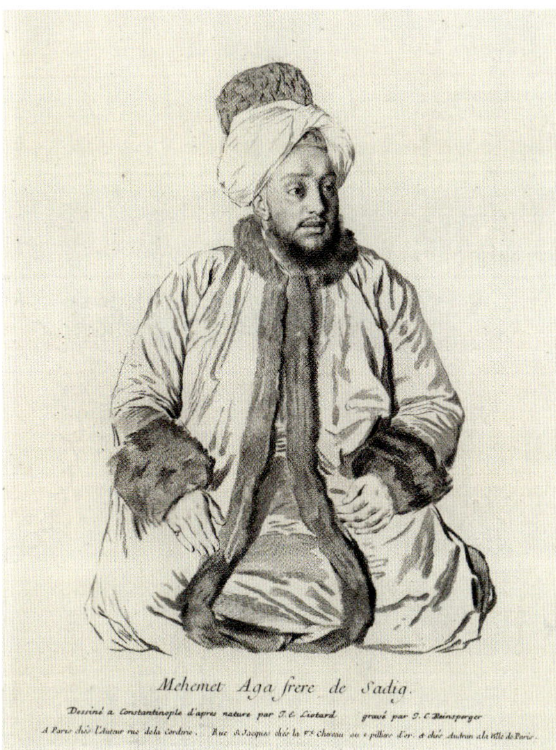

Literature: R/L 2008, no. 99; Humbert/Revilliod/Tilanus 1897, p. 197, no. 95; see exh. cat. Geneva/Paris 1992, cat. 53; Koos 2014, pp. 99–100.

Cat. 63

JOHANN CHRISTOPH VON REINSPERGER

(Nuremberg 1711–1777 Vienna)

after **JEAN-ÉTIENNE LIOTARD**

(Geneva 1702–1789 Geneva)

The Dwarf Ibrahim

Before 1755

Engraving and etching, 26 x 19.7 cm (image), 48 x 29.5 cm (sheet)

Inscribed at the bottom: "Un Nain du grand Seigneur dessiné dans le Serail. / Dessiné a Constantinople d'apres nature par J. E. Liotard gravé par J. C. Reinsperger / A Paris chés l'Auteur rue de la Corderie. Rue S. Jacques chés la Ve Chereau au 2. pillier d'or Et chés Audran a la Ville de Paris"

Cabinet d'arts graphiques des Musées d'art et d'histoire, Geneva, inv. no. E 2014-0659

The engraving after a Liotard drawing shows a "dwarf of the Grand Sultan in the seraglio" seated on the floor. He is dressed in a caftan with wide fur sleeves, which is too large for him. Like the two Agas (cat. 61, 62), he wears a tall turban. His gaze is directed toward the viewer. His large eyes, expressive eyebrows, and pointed nose give his face a particularly striking ap-

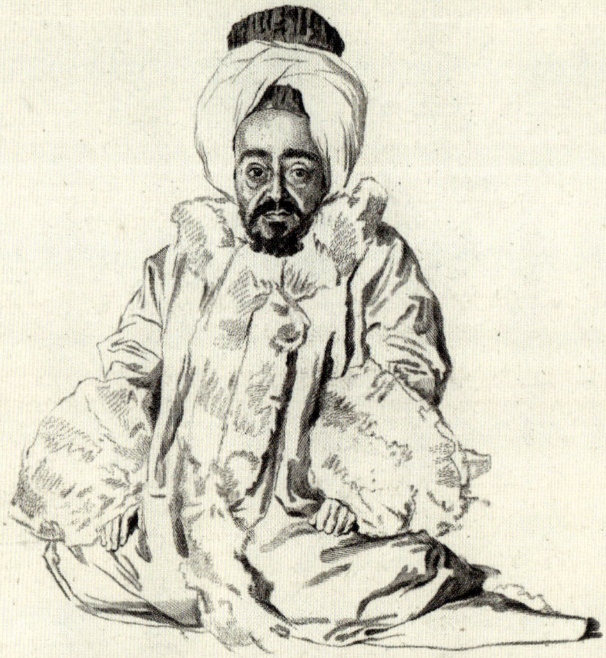

Un Nain du grand Seigneur dessiné dans le Serail.

Dessiné à Constantinople d'apres nature par J. E Liotard gravé par J. C. Reinsperger

A Paris chés l'Auteur rue de la Corderie. Rue S. Jacques chés la Ve Chereau au 2 pillier d'or Et chés Audran a la Ville de Paris

pearance. The engraving makes no mention of a specific person. Liotard's original drawing in black chalk (Louvre, Paris), however, gives the name "Ibrahim" in the artist's own hand at the bottom.

As the title indicates, the dwarf standing in the sultan's service was on the staff of the seraglio, the Ottoman palace. There, as was common at European courts too, dwarfs were valued entertainers. Reinsperger possibly chose to omit the name on the engraving as a way of providing the viewer with a general impression of the Ottoman court, rather than emphasizing the subject as an individual.

SD

Literature: R/L 2008, no. 100; Humbert/Revilliod/Tilanus 1897, p. 197, no. 99; see exh. cat. Geneva/Paris 1992, cat. 62.

Cat. 64

Jean-Étienne Liotard

(Geneva 1702–1789 Geneva)

Effendi, Smoking

1751

Black and red chalk on blue paper, squared for transfer, 57 x 42.2 cm

Inscribed by hand, bottom right: "Un effendi ami du Testerdar ou Grand Tresorie de l'empire / des a Const. Gravé par Tardieu en 1751"

Cabinet d'arts graphiques des Musées d'art et d'histoire, Geneva, inv. no. 1935-0006

The sketch shows a man in Turkish clothing and wearing a turban, seated in a cross-legged position on a divan. In his left hand he holds a long pipe that rests on the floor. The drawing is mainly executed in red chalk; Liotard merely indicates a few details with cursory strokes in black chalk, especially the folds in the clothing. The grid of lines, also drawn in red chalk, was used to transfer the motif to another sheet on a larger or smaller scale. A pastel (private collection), presumably produced in the same year, pictures the man exactly to scale; Liotard merely expanded the surrounding space. It can be assumed that Liotard made this relatively large drawing solely for the purpose of transferring it. It follows a smaller preliminary sketch of an *effendi* (private collection) produced in Constantinople before 1742. Beginning in the 1750s he used blue paper for transfers, only defining the most important contours. His return to the motif attests to Liotard's continuing interest in oriental subjects even in the 1750s.

The title identifies the subject as an *effendi*, in the Ottoman Empire a member of mid-level administration or the military. The handwritten note with the term "Testerdar" (*defterdar*, the title of the supreme treasurer directly subordinate to the sultan) points to the subject's role as a financial official. This designation, subsequently added in the bottom right corner, is identical to the title of an etching after Liotard's aforementioned Constantinople drawing (private collection), created in Paris by Pierre Alexandre Tardieu.

SD

Literature: R/L 2008, no. 204, see no. 201; exh. cat. Geneva/Paris 1992, p. 281, no. 71, see also cat. 65.

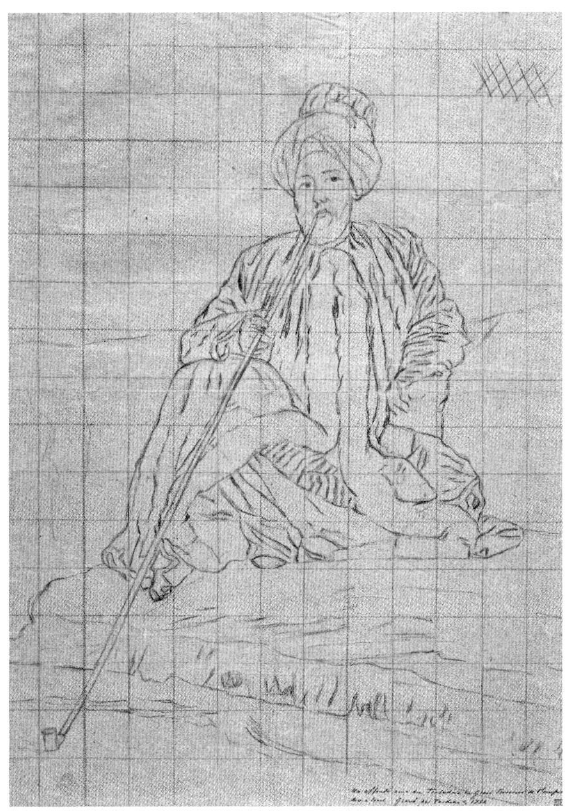

Cat. 65

Wallet

Istanbul, 1709

Leather, partially dyed, gold and silver embroidery in couching stitch, 11.1 x 17.8 cm, weight 109 g
On the back the embroidered inscription: “Constantinople 1709”; on one of the inner pockets: “سنه ١١٢٠” [the year 1120, i.e. 23 March 1708–12 March 1709]
Rüstkammer, Staatliche Kunstsammlungen Dresden, inv. no. Y 0354

Inventory of the “Turkish Tent” from 1838, sheet 83, no. 375: “A wallet of red leather, richly embroidered with gold threads, with five larger and smaller inner compartments. On the back is: Constantinople 1709, and on the fourth inner leather flap: zŵ with the year 115- embroidered in gold. Consigned from the Main State Archive to the Royal Historical Museum on April 30, 1851, with the proviso that it remain state property.”

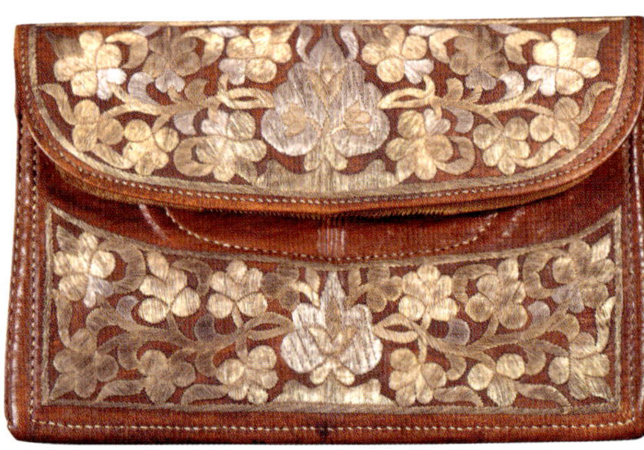

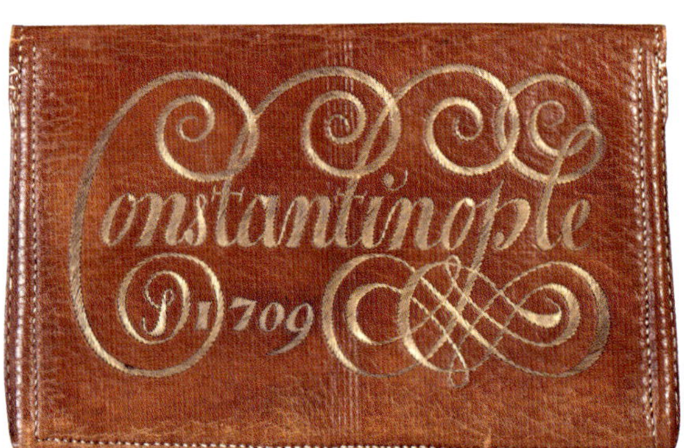

The purpose of this Ottoman leather wallet was to hold a document for transport or safekeeping. Richly embroidered on the front with stylized, intertwining floral motifs, it is dated twice. On the back, in Latin letters, is the inscription “Constantinople 1709,” and on one of the interior flaps the year 1120 in the Muslim calendar is written in Arabic letters and numerals. Given these two indications, the wallet would have been made in Istanbul between January 1 and March 12, 1709. The unusual double dating suggests that the wallet was made for either a European patron or a high Ottoman dignitary who wished to use it to deliver a document to a European diplomat. For such purposes the Ottomans used either leather wallets like this or letter bags made of precious fabrics.

On April 30, 1851, the wallet was removed from Saxony’s Main State Archives and placed in the Turkish Chamber. Whether an Ottoman document from the early eighteenth century has ever been kept in the wallet, and what precisely the history of the item was has not been possible to ascertain to date. In Dresden’s Turkish Palace a “case in leather embroidered with gold in which Turkish credentials are customarily submitted” is mentioned in 1741. It is possible that it was this wallet.

HS

Literature: Schöbel 1961, no. 18; Petrasch 1991, p. 346; Schuckelt 2010a, p. 270, cat. 249; Schuckelt 2010b, pp. 126–27.

Cat. 66

Pair of Shoes

Ottoman (?), before 1817

From the collection of Peter Ludwig Heinrich von Block
Upper material silk velvet; relief and flat embroidery in silver thread, silver purls and sequins, silver thread on ornamentally cut-out vellum, appliquéd; braiding of gold thread; leather sole; lining and insole silk velvet; L. 25.2 cm, weight 210 g
Rüstkammer, Staatliche Kunstsammlungen Dresden,
inv. no. i.0174

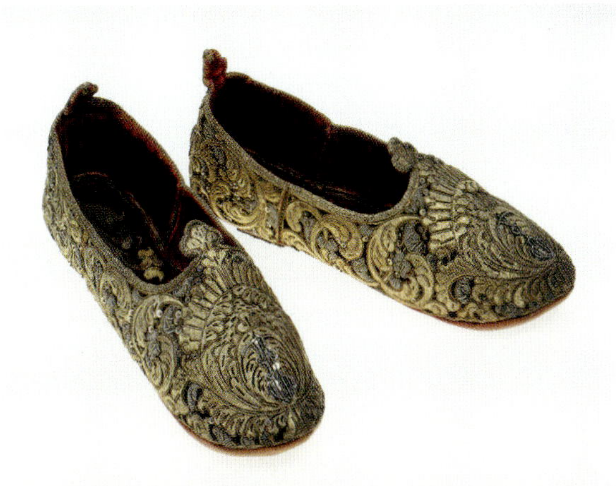

Catalogue of the Von Block Collection from 1830, p. 2, no. 42; inventory of the saddles and costumes room from 1838, p. 251, no. 95: "A pair of red velvet shoes, very richly embroidered with gold, silver, and spangles, with red morocco soles. The shoes are lined with red velvet and on the inner sole is ornamental embroidery in gold and silver. No. 42. Collection von Block."

The shoes hail from the private collection of the former curator of the Grünes Gewölbe, Baron Peter Ludwig Heinrich von Block. In 1817 he was arrested for misappropriation of artworks from the royal collections, and in 1830 his shoe collection was consigned to the armory chamber. It contained several Ottoman shoes and slippers, some of them rumored to have belonged to a sultan. The rich embroidery of the surviving pair, ornamented with rosettes, foliate vines, and palmettes, was taken as evidence that this was the pair in question. Given their relatively small size, however, these could also have been Ottoman women's shoes, which were also present in Block's collection. In a number of Liotard's pictures both men and women in oriental costume wear similar shoes.

HS

Literature: exh. cat. Dresden/Bonn 1995, p. 307, cat. 355; exh. cat. Völklingen 2005, p. 176.

Cat. 67

Horse Bridle

Consisting of headstall with noseband, chest-band, and crupper
Ottoman, before 1744

Leather straps, cast brass fittings, partially openwork and silver-gilt; bridle straps W. 2.6 cm; belly-band and crupper straps W. 4.4 cm; chest rosette diam. 10.9 cm
Rüstkammer, Staatliche Kunstsammlungen Dresden
inv. no. L 0130

Inventory of the Gute Sattelkammer from 1716, sheet 86, no. 187: "A green leather [Ao. 1755 set on yellow morocco] Turkish harness with silver-gilt fittings, consisting of a Turkish halter in green silk, worked with silver [entirely silver halter Ao. 1755]. His Excellency Lord Privy Councillor and Stablemaster Count von Brühl had the present harness placed here on April 30, 1744."

At the behest of Count Heinrich von Brühl, the harness was consigned to the Gute Sattelkammer on April 30, 1744. At that point it was still made of green morocco. Ten years later it was used in performances of the opera *Solimano* by Johann Adolph Hasse, at which time, according to a document dated February 28, 1754, it suffered considerable damage. For that reason it was restored in 1755 and its color changed, as can be seen from the amended entries in the Gute Sattelkammer inventory.
The harness is covered almost in its entirety with silver-plated cast brass fittings. Belly-band and crupper are

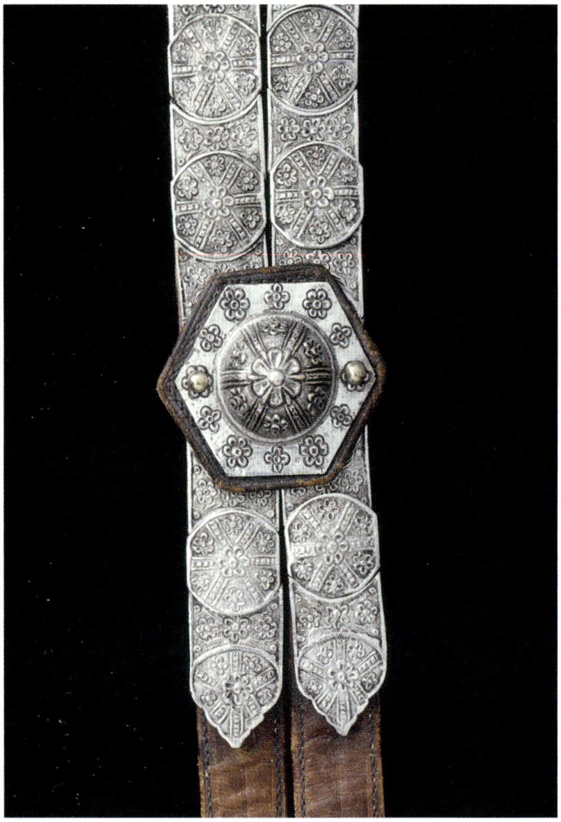

both fitted with a central, hexagonal plaque with small rosettes and a large boss. From the browband hang teardrop-shaped openwork pendants. The brass fittings are decorated with small rosettes and star-shaped double lines filled with dots. The belly-band is equipped with loops for pistol holsters.

HS

Literature: Schuckelt 2004, p. 23; Schuckelt 2010a, p. 340, cat. 328.

Cat. 68

Saddle with Stirrups and Saddle Flaps

Tatar (?), before 1744

Saddletree wood, covered with imprinted leather, brass fittings, openwork and gilt; saddle flaps painted leather; L 48 cm, W 37 cm, H 39.5 cm; saddle flaps 44.7 i.e. 43.8 x 35.5 i.e. 35.8 cm; total weight 3729 g

On the inside of the saddle flaps in black pigment سا (sā) and ١٣ (13)

Rüstkammer, Staatliche Kunstsammlungen Dresden, inv. no. L 0051

Inventory of the Gute Sattelkammer from 1821, sheet 95, no. 353: "A Polish saddle with gilt brass fittings, iron stirrups, and leather stirrup straps, the seat of red morocco, on the saddle a scarlet very defective blanket, along with side flaps of red and yellow morocco, without saddle cushion. Brought by a Tatar ambassador in the month of September 1744 as a present to the King of Poland, Augustus III."

In September 1744, King Augustus III of Poland received an ambassador from the Crimean Tatars in Warsaw. One of the gifts from the Tatar khan Selim II Girai, presented by the ambassador during his audience with the king, was this saddle with a reddish-brown leather seat. The saddletree bar, pommel, and cantle are covered in black shagreen leather. The fittings are gilt-brass and partially openwork. The saddle includes Ottoman-style box stirrups and attached leather saddle flaps. Their painted decor consists of four elongated panels with pointed arches at either end, filled with flower and various circle and arch ornaments. In black pigment on the inside are the Arabic letters "sā" and the number "13," the meaning of which remains obscure.

HS

Literature: Schuckelt 2008, p. 107; Schuckelt 2010a, p. 341, cat. 329.

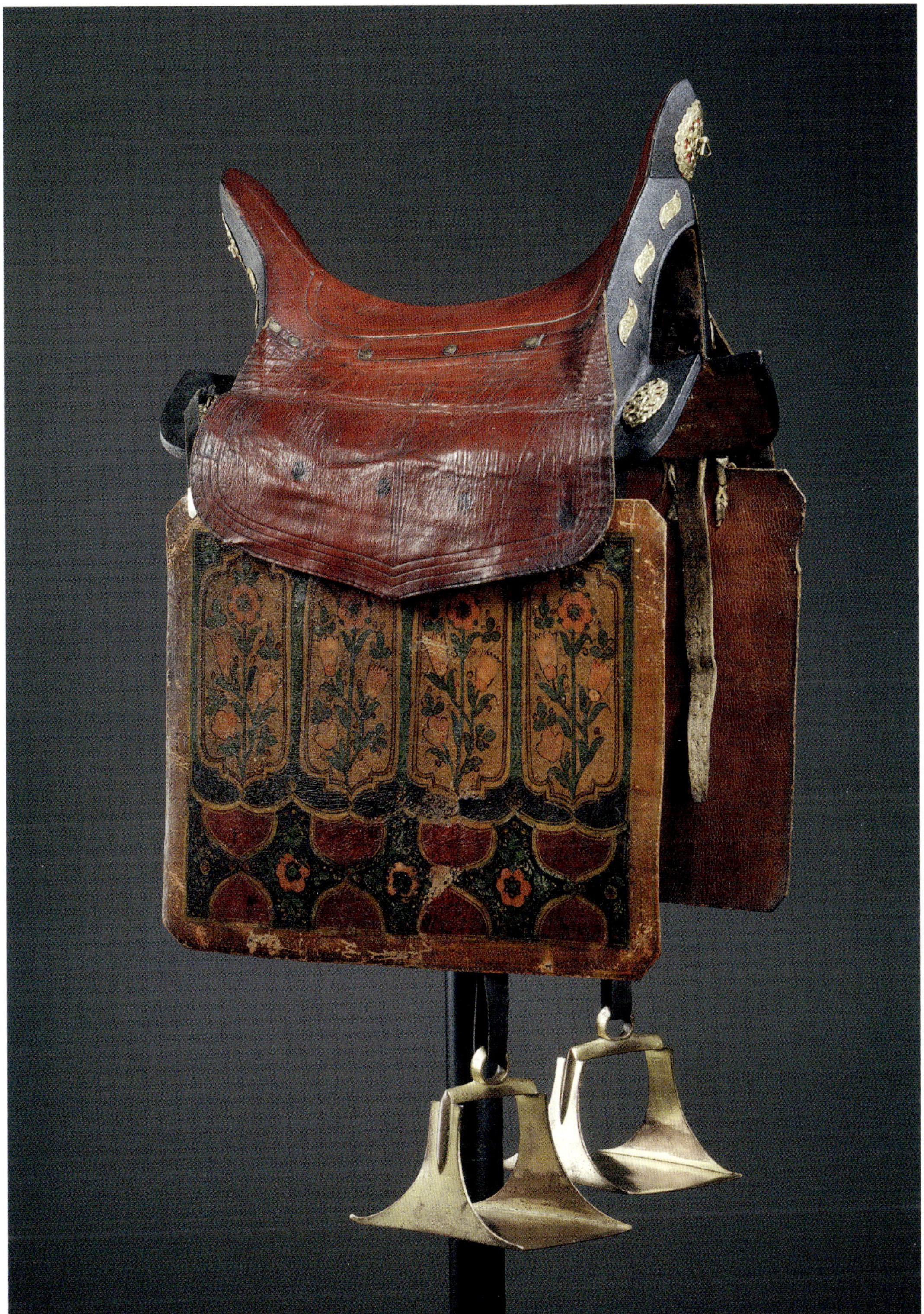

LIOTARD AND HIS ART

Jean-Étienne Liotard, along with Rosalba Carriera and Maurice Quentin de La Tour, was one of the major practitioners of pastel painting, which flourished in the Rococo period and was especially favored for portraits. In addition to pastels, his work includes oil paintings, drawings, prints, gouaches, paintings on glass, enamels, and miniatures—a technique in which he had trained in Geneva and Paris. Because of his realistic approach and his flawless, porcelain-like surfaces, he became known, even in his lifetime, as a "peintre de la verité." In his painterly style he also competed with La Tour—the two artists frequently portrayed the same figures close to the same time. All throughout his life, Liotard returned to inspiration from his travels and even in his old age he remained open to innovation; his late work increasingly features still lifes and trompe-l'oeils in pastel and oil.

Cat. 69

Jean-Étienne Liotard

(Geneva 1702–1789 Geneva)

Marianne Lavergne, the Artist's Niece (La Liseuse)

1746

Pastel on parchment, pieces added at the top and on the right side, 37.5 x 30.5 cm

Inscribed on the back of the protective frame in another hand: "Liseuse. En habit de Paysanne Lionnaise, peinte par Liotard de Genève, surnommé le peintre turc. à Lion 1746"

Gemäldegalerie Alte Meister, Staatliche Kunstsammlungen Dresden, gallery no. P 162

During a stay in 1746 with his sister Sara, who had married the Genevan merchant François Lavergne and was living in Lyon, Jean-Étienne Liotard painted his niece Marianne. The pastel pictures her in half-figure, seated on a simple chair in front of a gray-green wall. Her upper body is turned toward the viewer; her head tilted slightly to the left, she is absorbed in the letter in her left hand, the content of which remains obscure to the viewer. Her greenish-brown dress with a blue-and-white floral-patterned underbodice and three-quarter sleeves is laced with red ribbons over a white blouse, and has sometimes been described as representing the costume of a Lyonnaise peasant woman. Marianne, who was twenty-nine at the time, is portrayed as a young girl in this small pastel; yet the work is also a genre piece, as suggested by the often used titles *La Liseuse* (*The Reader*) or *La Belle Lyonnaise*.

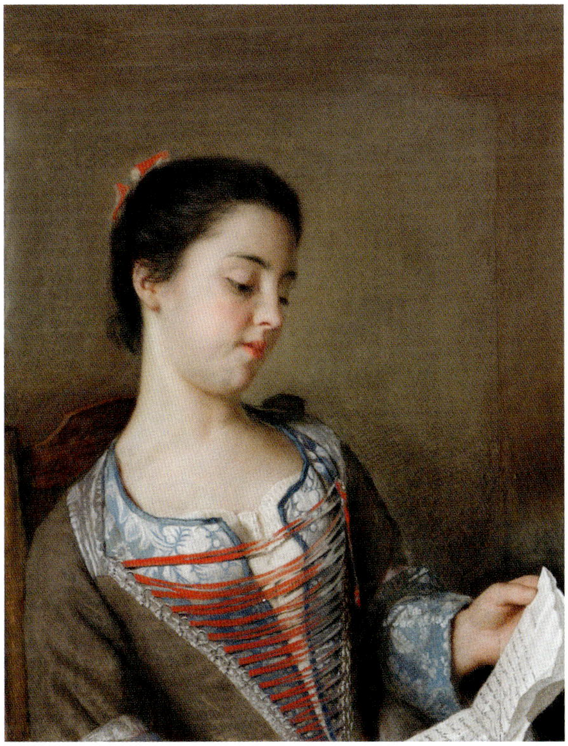

The motif is one of Liotard's most famous compositions and numerous reproductions in print exist (see cat. 70), along with copies by other hands after the version on public display in Dresden since 1748. Five copies by Liotard himself are known, the two oldest being the one in Dresden and the Amsterdam version, also dated 1746. The two paintings are very similar and in the same scale, suggesting that they are both based on the same original. The Amsterdam version has a slightly larger picture space, which also shows her right arm and the top of her skirt. It has heretofore been assumed that the picture in the Rijksmuseum is the first version, while the Dresden one had to be cut, owing to some undocumented damage, and strips of parchment pieced on. It is also possible, however, that Liotard was developing his composition on the Dresden version and that this pastel is the original.

The motif of a woman reading was a popular one in the seventeenth and eighteenth centuries. The Dresden gallery alone has a number of examples, including Johannes Vermeer's *Girl Reading a Letter at an Open Window*, two pictures by Pietro Rotari, and the small-format *Girl Reading* by Charles-François Hutin.

RE

Literature: R/L 2008, no. 160; Riedel/Wenzel 1765, p. 243; Henning/Marx 2007, pp. 111–12; see R/L 2008, no. 159 (Amsterdam), nos. 292–94.

Cat. 70

Jean Daullé

(Abbéville/Somme 1703–1763 Paris) and

Simon François Ravenet

(Paris 1706–1774 London)

after **Jean-Étienne Liotard**

(Geneva 1702–1789 Geneva)

Mademoiselle Lavergne, Niece of M. Liotard

Undated

Engraving, 42.4 x 40.1 (image), 58.4 x 42.5 cm (sheet)
Inscribed at the bottom "J. E. Liotard pinxt. – Daullé & Ravenet sculpt. / Mademoiselle Lavergne Nièce de Mr. Liotard. / à Londres chez L'Auteur dans Golden square, & chez Major Graveur de S.A:R. le Prince de Galles, à la Tête d'or dans chandois Street"
Rijksmuseum, Amsterdam, inv. no. RP-P-OB-56.955

The engraving by Jean Daullé and Simon François Ravenet reproduces—in reverse—the Liotard pastel painting of Mademoiselle Lavergne, which has been in Amsterdam's Rijksmuseum since 1873. The work is very much like the Dresden version of *La Liseuse* (see cat. 69); the most obvious difference—in addition to the greater picture space—is the thin necklace with a small crucifix pendant. As in the Amsterdam pastel, the young woman is seated on a simple wooden chair and concentrating on a letter she holds with both hands. The engraving faithfully reproduces every detail of her dress, the folds of her skirt, the floral pattern of her bodice and sleeves, and her laced corsage. But only the print also details the wood grain of the chair leg. Not included in the print are the artist's signature and date, which in the Amsterdam painting are clearly visible on the right, just above the letter.

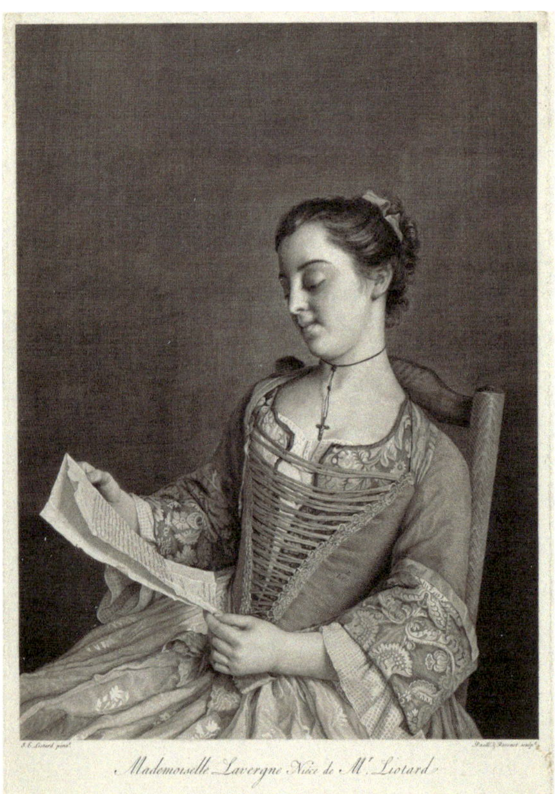

The large sheet, the only reproduction after Liotard by these two engravers, is impressive in its dimensions and the high-quality rendering of the original. The engraving was made around the time of Liotard's stays in Paris (1748–1753) and London (1753/54). It may have been started by Daullé in France and Liotard could have then taken the plate with him to London to have it finished by Ravenet, who had settled there in 1743. As indicated by the inscription, Liotard and Ravenet were marketing the print in London at their own expense.

RE

Literature: R/L 2008, pp. 363–64, no. 159, fig. 264; Humbert/Revilliod/Tilanus 1897, pp. 188–89, no. 53.

Cat. 71

Jean-Étienne Liotard

(Geneva 1702–1789 Geneva)

Maurice, Comte de Saxe, Marshal General of France (1696–1750)

Circa 1746/49

Pastel on parchment

Gemäldegalerie Alte Meister, Staatliche Kunstsammlungen Dresden, gal. no. P 160

Here Liotard shows Maurice, Count of Saxony, the extramarital son of Augustus the Strong, in his uniform as Marshal of France. Maurice joined the French service in 1720 and performed great feats for the French monarchy in numerous battles. In the half-length portrait he is pictured in the field, a tent to his right, and on his left three horsemen from his bodyguard, among them "Moors dressed as Uhlans," as Von Racknitz described them in 1811. Maurice wears the blue-and-red uniform of his cavalry regiment and across his shoulder the gold shoulder belt from which his dagger is suspended. His left hand holds the blue marshal's baton decorated with gold *fleur-de-lis*, his right rests on his helmet, which is covered with a tiger skin.

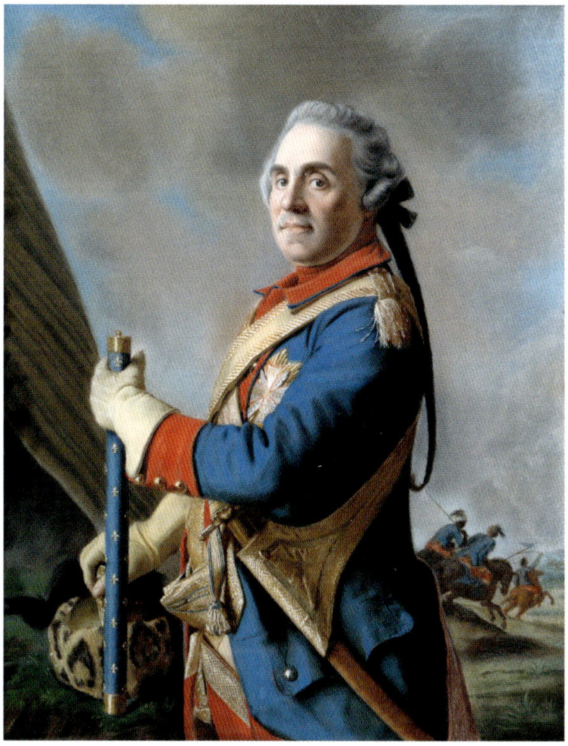

It is possible that Liotard came into contact with Maurice of Saxony through the Duc de Richelieu, who met him in Lyon in 1746/47. Soon afterward he painted this portrait, as well as a second version (Rijksmuseum, Amsterdam). Around 1850, Georg Wolff produced a lithograph of the Dresden version, while the one in Amsterdam was reproduced with slight changes in an engraving by Antoine de Marcenay in 1766.

In contemporary literature Maurice is frequently described as an especially handsome man, and his depiction by Liotard, which has the appearance of an official portrait, was criticized by some. By contrast, the portrait by La Tour pictures Maurice as a charming and gregarious figure (cat. 75). It is not known how the picture came to Dresden. One possibility is that it found its way to Saxony and into the possession of his half-brother Augustus III after the art-loving marshal's death in 1750.

RE

Literature: R/L 2008, no. 166, see also 167; Riedel/Wenzel 1765, p. 243; [von Racknitz] 1811b, pp. 4–12; Fosca 1956, p. 46; Henning/Marx 2007, pp. 105–06; Spenlé 2008, p. 203.

Cat. 72

Jean-Étienne Liotard

(Geneva 1702–1789 Geneva)

Mademoiselle Suzanne Curchod, the Future Madame Jacques Necker (1739–1794)

Circa 1760

Pastel on parchment, mounted on canvas and cardboard, 87.5 x 106 cm

Bundesmobilienverwaltung, Schönbrunn Palace, Vienna, inv. no. MD 039860/000

The writer Suzanne Curchod is shown here in one of Liotard's rare nearly full-figure portraits. She is seated on a chair, with her right hand placed on her décolletage in an introspective gesture; her left hand is resting on her knee, holding a book. The beige-brown background sets off her shimmering blue dress, which is mirrored in the color of her eyes. Her look is contemplative, her face tilted slightly upward. Liotard seems to have captured the very moment she has just stopped reading to reflect on what she has read. Next to her right elbow, on a small mahogany table in front of her, is a basket of fruit, a silver tray with a glass and carafe, bread, a folded napkin, and a long knife. In its deliberate arrangement this part of the scene seems like an independent picture within a picture. Liotard had been incorporating still life elements in his portraits since the 1740s, as for example in his *Dutch Girl at Breakfast* in the Rijksmuseum (cat. 21). That particular work, which Maria Theresa bought from Liotard for her private apartments during his second stay in Vienna in 1762, is an unusual size for a pastel—the picture support is pieced together from four parchments—a rarity in his oeuvre.

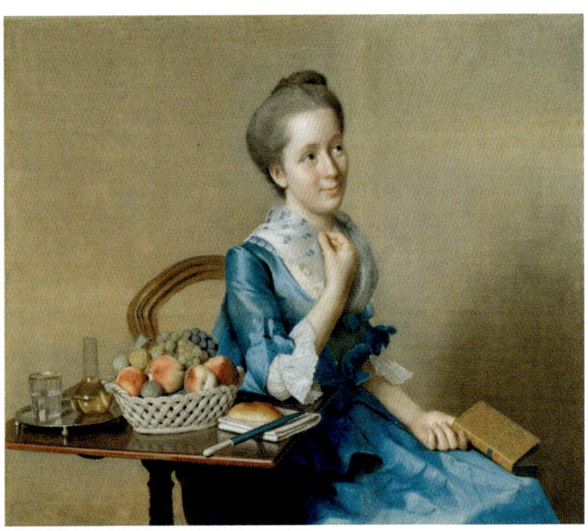

Suzanne Curchod, daughter of the pastor Louis Antoine Curchod and his wife Madeleine d'Albert de Nasse, was born in 1739 and received a humanist education in her parents' home. In 1760 she became a governess in the employ of Madame Paul Girardot de Vermenoux, first in Geneva, then in Paris, where she was not only portrayed by Liotard, but also met her future husband, Jacques Necker. In 1766 their daughter Germaine was born, who later became famous as the writer Madame de Staël.

SD

Literature: R/L 2008, no. 380; Roethlisberger 1985, pp. 109–11; exh. cat. Edinburgh/London 2015, cat. 73.

Cat. 73

Jean-Étienne Liotard

(Geneva 1702–1789 Geneva)

Still Life: A Basket of Apples

Between 1782 and 1786

Pastel on paper, 36 x 45.5 cm

Swiss private collection

This composition, reduced to a single object, pictures a woven fruit basket, in which yellow-and-red apples are piled up to form a pyramid. Against a dark-brown background, a tabletop is suggested, onto which the shadow of the basket is cast by a light source to the right. The still life as a whole is striking for its balanced colors and delicate modeling, especially of the fruit. It thus appears deceptively three-dimensional. The woven basket resembles the oval one in the portrait of Suzanne Curchod (cat. 72), there supplementing the portrait as a still life element. Liotard may have taken his inspiration here from works by the famous French painter of still lifes Jean Siméon Chardin, who also frequently used the motif of a fruit basket in his compositions. The artist would have had opportunities to see Char-

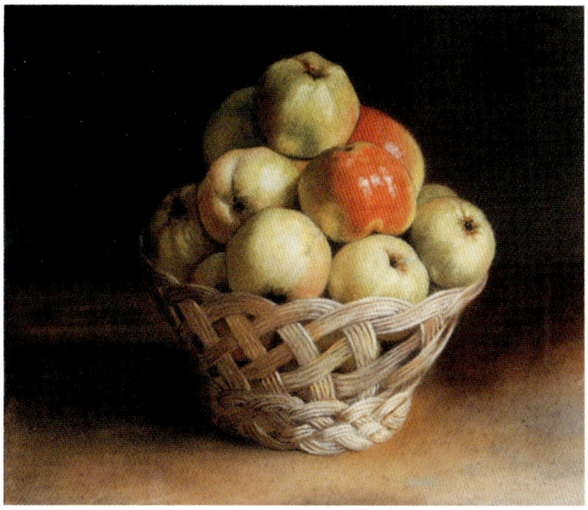

din's works during his sojourns in Paris. At the same time, the reserved, clear composition has an almost modern quality and prefigures the still lifes of a Gustave Courbet or Paul Cézanne.

Liotard only began painting still lifes and trompe-l'oeils in his later years (see cat. 74), when demand for his portraits gradually lessened, in part owing to the changing tastes of the time. The *Basket of Apples* is part of a series of pictures with apples, peaches, and apricots in horizontal format, which he produced in Geneva between 1782 and 1786, his most prolific period in this genre. Of the twelve surviving still lifes, most were executed in pastel. Created for a more intimate setting and without commissions, they remained unsold during Liotard's lifetime, probably also due to a declining demand for pastels. That he nevertheless treasured them and assigned them a high rank in his own work is evident from their frequent positive mention in his correspondence with his children.

SD

Literature: R/L 2008, no. 459, pp. 667–68; Roethlisberger 1985, pp. 112–19; exh. cat. Edinburg/London 2015, cat. 82; exh. cat. Lausanne 2018, p. 39, cat. 23.

Cat. 74

Jean-Étienne Liotard

(Geneva 1702–1789 Geneva)

Trompe-l'Oeil of a Bas-Relief with Silenus

1766–1771

Oil on wood, 22 x 28.5 cm

Private collection

A small relief appears to be hanging on a wall covered in dark-blue damask with a foliage pattern in a lighter shade of blue. It is attached with a yellow ribbon to a simple metal screw. The edges of the plaque are worn and a vertical crack runs across its right side. Depicted on it are Silenus, a mythological figure from the Dionysian retinue, a small faun, and three putti. The work by Jean-Étienne Liotard is a trompe-l'oeil, a deceptive illusion, for it is not a three-dimensional object but a two-dimensional painting. The painter was probably inspired by one of the numerous copies—here probably one in plaster—of *The Binding of the Sleeping Silenus*, a well-known work by the Flemish sculptor François Duquesnoy from the first half of the seventeenth century. Liotard took some of the figures from that relief and rearranged them into a new composition.

The same composition is also seen in an enameled and fired glass painting by Jean-Étienne Liotard in Budapest (Szépművészeti Múzeum), which, if lit from behind, could be projected onto another surface—like a modern-day transparency. After his return to Geneva

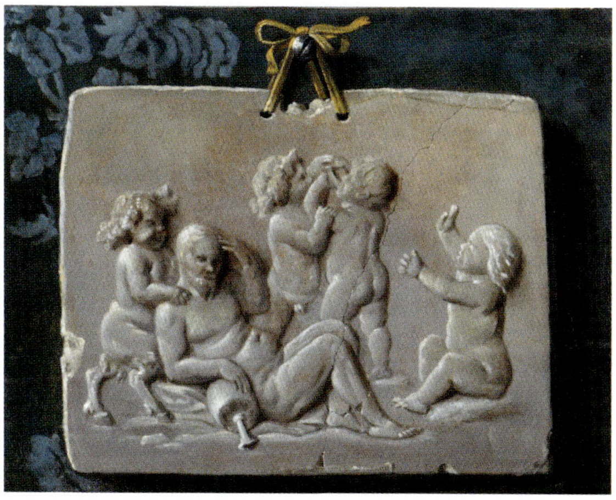

in 1757, Liotard, who was always experimenting with different techniques—such as repeating his pastel paintings in oil—turned to producing various series of pictures, which, along with still lifes, also included small, illusionistic paintings. About a dozen such pictures are documented, which he painted from the 1760s onward.

RE

Literature: unpublished; see R/L 2008, no. 477; see also Boudon-Machuel 2005, pp. 282–87, no. In 65a.

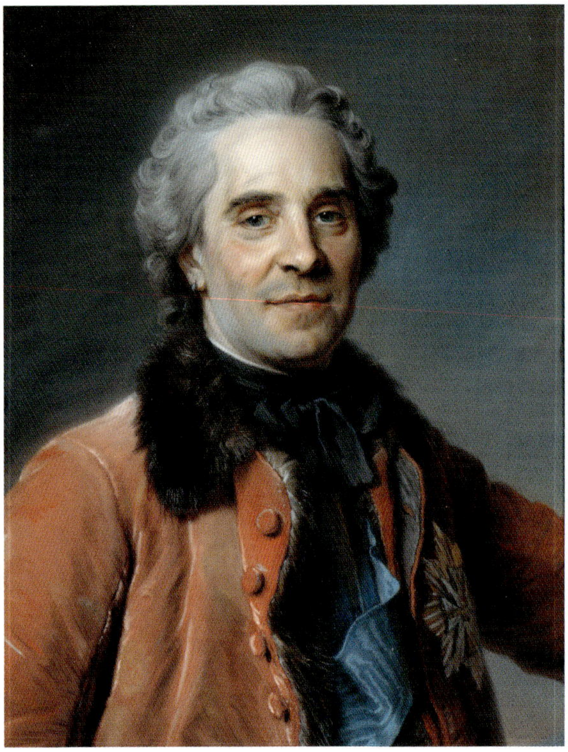

Cat. 75

Maurice Quentin de La Tour

(Saint-Quentin 1704–1788 Saint-Quentin)

Maurice Comte de Saxe (1696–1750)

1748 (?)

Pastel on paper, 59.5 x 49 cm

Gemäldegalerie Alte Meister, Staatliche Kunstsammlungen Dresden, gal. no. P 164

The pastel painter Maurice Quentin de La Tour made several portraits of his friend Maurice Count of Saxony. Whereas the first one, painted around 1747, showed him in armor, thus picturing him in his role since 1744 as Marshal of France, the aim of the Dresden portrait seems to be to endear him to the viewer as a person. The bust portrait shows Maurice wearing a red velvet jacket with fur trim above his cuirass, a black necktie, blue sash, the Polish Order of the White Eagle, and a small blue earring. His facial expression is the same as in all the pastels: he is looking directly at the viewer, his slight smile signaling openness and affability, which stands in deliberate contrast to his military rigor and determined courage. La Tour endeavored to capture the Count's many different facets, some of them contradictory. Although by then the Count was already seriously ill, La Tour idealized him as the "handsome man" he was regularly described as by contemporaries.

Maurice, a half-brother of Augustus III, was in the service of France since 1720. He won countless victories, especially during the War of the Austrian Succession from 1740 to 1747. Highly regarded as a commander by the French court, he was an important link in Saxon-French diplomacy. It was mainly thanks to his efforts that King Louis XV could be persuaded to choose Maurice's niece Maria Josepha as the new wife for the French heir apparent (see cat. 76). The portrait came to Dresden in 1753, as requested in Maurice's will. The ongoing competition between La Tour and Liotard also shows in their choice of subjects: the latter portrayed the Saxon-French commander at around the same time, possibly shortly before this picture was made (cat. 71).

RE

Literature: Riedel/Wenzel 1765, p. 243; Debrie/Salmon 2000, pp. 125–30; Henning/Marx 2007, pp. 117–20; exh. cat. Dresden 2009, pp. 211–12, no. 43.

Cat. 76

Maurice Quentin de La Tour

(Saint-Quentin 1704–1788 Saint-Quentin)

Maria Josepha, Dauphine of France (1731–1767)

1749

Pastel on paper, 60.5 x 49.5 cm
Gemäldegalerie Alte Meister, Staatliche Kunstsammlungen Dresden, gal. no. P 163

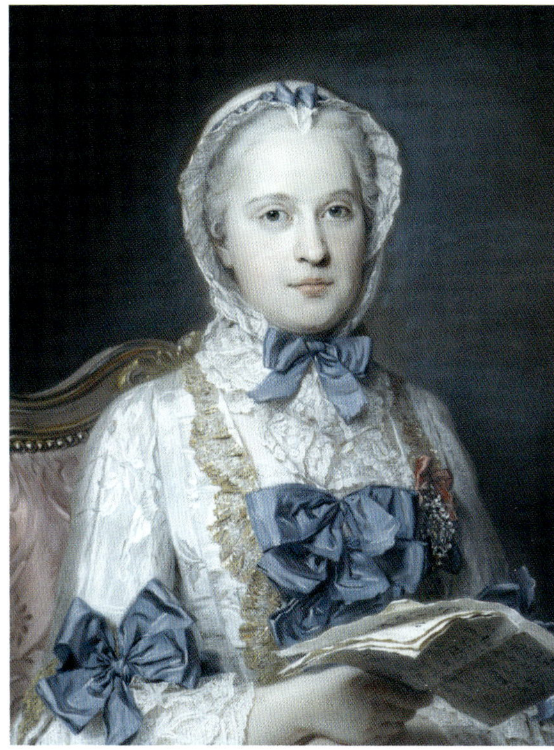

The French pastel painter Maurice Quentin de La Tour painted the Saxon princess Maria Josepha some two years after her marriage in 1747 to Louis, the Dauphin of France. The bust portrait pictures her almost frontally, with a childlike face, before a blue-gray background. She is seated in an armchair within what appears to be a private setting. Over her powdered hair she wears a bonnet tied at the neck with a blue ribbon, similar to the bows that decorate her sleeves and the décolletage of her white dress, which is trimmed with gold lace. Pinned to her chest on the left is a diamond order on a red ribbon. The sheet music in her right hand attests to her great love of music.

A dynastic tie between Saxony and France had long been desired as a political measure against the primacy of Prussia. It was mainly thanks to the influence of Maurice, Count of Saxony, who was highly regarded at the French court and a skilled diplomat (see cat. 71, 75), that Louis XV could be persuaded of the match between Maurice's niece Maria Josepha and the Dauphin. La Tour portrayed the princess on several occasions. Whether the Dresden portrait is the original painted by La Tour in 1749, as mentioned in the historical sources, or the second version by his hand, has not been verified. What is certain, however, is that it came to Dresden's pastel cabinet in 1750. Michel-Guillaume Aubert produced a reversed engraving after it. Presumably in the same year, Jean-Étienne Liotard was also able to paint a portrait of the Dauphine (now Rijksmuseum, Amsterdam).

RE

Literature: Riedel/Wenzel 1765, p. 243; Sponsel 1906, p. 167, no. 158; exh. cat. Versailles 2004, pp. 134–35, cat. 30, fig. 2; Henning/Marx 2007, pp. 114–17; see R/L 2008, no. 175; exh. cat. Dresden 2009, pp. 210–11, cat. 42.

THE DRESDEN PASTELLKABINETT

In the first half of the eighteenth century, the Dresden painting collection grew enormously with new acquisitions being made under Augustus II (the Strong) and his son Augustus III. To accommodate this, the former court stables on the Neumarkt were remodeled into a painting gallery in 1745/46. A small room on the upper floor was devoted exclusively to pastels. To have an entire gallery space just for this one painting technique was unprecedented and has remained unique to this day. The room's interior architecture, in combination with tall mirrors, the pastels themselves, and their individually designed glazed frames, formed a unified ensemble. The many paintings were hung in tightly spaced rows, one above the other. With 157 works by Rosalba Carriera alone—the best-known pastel painter at the time—the room soon became known as the "Cabinet of Rosalba." But the collection also included pictures by Jean-Étienne Liotard, Maurice Quentin de La Tour, and Anton Raphael Mengs—whose name was later immortalized in a brand of pastel crayons that were sold until the early twentieth century.

Cat. 77

Müller & Hennig, Dresden

Box with Meng's Pastel Colors

Late nineteenth century

Printed on the inside of the lid: "Nach den Originalrecepten von Raphael Mengs, von Müller & Hennig Dresden. Gegründet durch Daniel Caffee im Jahre 1785, übernommen von J. C. Richter 1810, von Hr. Werner 1854, von Müller & Hennig 1877" ("After the original recipes of Raphael Mengs, by Müller & Hennig Dresden. Founded by Daniel Caffee in 1785, succeeded in 1810 by J. C. Richter, in 1854 by Hr. Werner, and in 1877 by Müller & Hennig") Wood, pastel crayons, steel engraving; H. (closed) 2.5 cm, L. 31 cm, W. 18.5 cm

Hochschule für Bildende Künste Dresden

The pastel box from the late nineteenth century contains various chalk crayons used by past students at Dresden's Academy of Fine Arts and is now being kept in the Academy's art technology collection. The pigments manufacturer Müller & Hennig started producing these pastels in 1877, purportedly still using the original recipe of the pastel painter Anton Raphael Mengs, who had made his own pastels. The recipe was handed down by Daniel Caffee, named on the inside of the lid, a pastel painter from Mengs' circle working in Dresden, who had marketed his pastels as being based on Mengs'. His ready-made pastels became highly popular from the late eighteenth century onward, especially among amateur painters.

The pastel boxes, which came in various sizes, were decorated on the inside of the lid with a steel engraving, and the crayons, placed on cotton wool, were arranged by color. Each crayon was imprinted with a deer's head as trademark. The Müller & Hennig firm produced pastels in fifty colors, each in ten graduated shades, which were sold in different assortments. All of the firm's offerings, which, in addition to pastels, included parchment, paper, easels, and blending stumps, were recommended in Julius Ritscher's *Anleitung zur Pastellmalerei* (Introduction to pastel painting).

SD

Literature: Berger 1896/1897, p. 281; Ritscher 1901, pp. 9–14; Schölzel 1989, pp. 38–42.

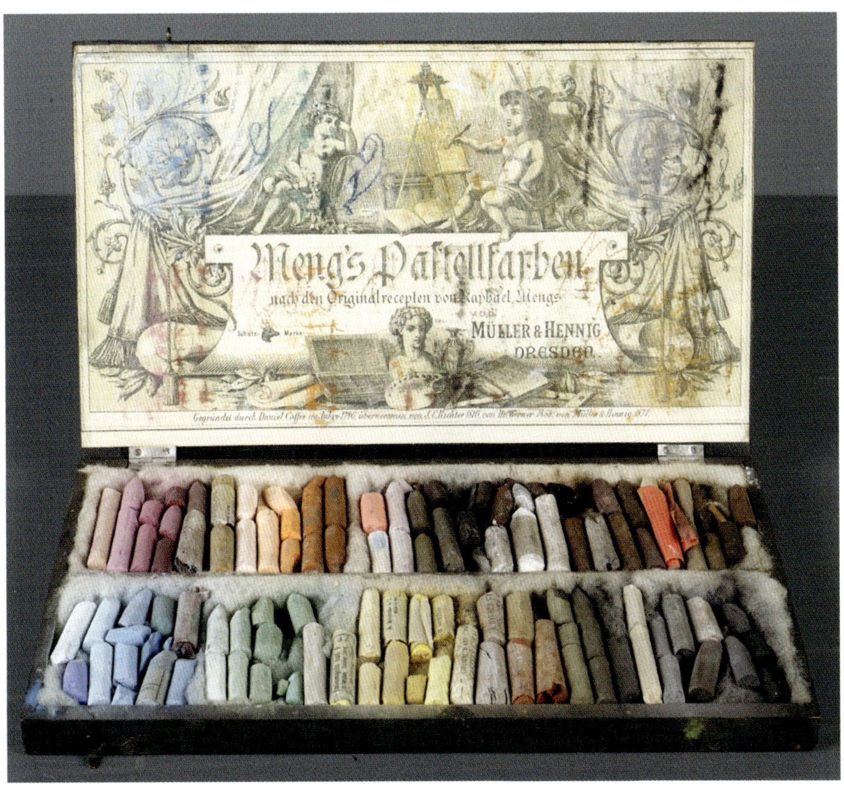

Cat. 78

Design: **Johann Christoph Knöffel**

(Oelsa 1686–1752 Dresden)

Engraving: **Michael Keyl**

(Wöhrd near Nuremberg 1722–1798 Dresden)

Plan de la galérie royale de Dresde

Before 1753

Engraving, 75 x 53 cm

From: *Recueil d'Estampes d'après le plus célébres Tableaux de la Galerie Royale de Dresde*, 1753

Kupferstich-Kabinett, Staatliche Kunstsammlungen Dresden, inv. no. A 158316

During the remodeling in 1745/46 of the former stable building into a painting gallery by Johann Christoph Knöffel, a separate room was established for the display of pastels. Located in the northeast corner of the second floor, the room was accessed by way of the Outer Gallery ("Galerie Exterieure"). Just behind the pastel cabinet was the Long Corridor, which circled the stable courtyard and connected the stable building with the palace. The long rectangular room of the pastel cabinet has two windows on the northeast side; the wall on the courtyard side is windowless. In the floor plan engraving by Michael Keyl, the "Cabinet de Pastel," labeled in the cartouche with a "C," is in the bottom left corner. The drawing was included in the front of the first volume of the *Recueil d'Estampes d'après le plus célébres Tableaux de la Galerie Royale de Dresde*, published in 1753 by Carl Heinrich von Heineken, and was followed by descriptions and engravings of the gallery's most famous paintings.

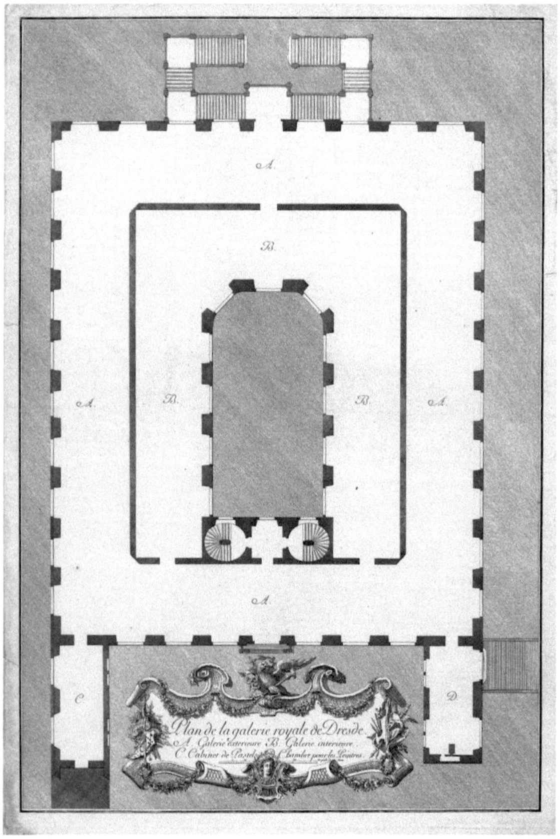

The cabinet walls were decorated in pale green, the window side featured tall mirrors, as described by Giovanni Ludovico Bianconi in 1781. The cornice above the tall windows was decorated with a long garland of gilt rocailles, which blended into the vaulted ceiling, forming a crowned "A" for Augustus at the center of each of the long walls. The 157 closely hung pastels by Rosalba Carriera gave the space its name: "Cabinet of Rosalba." The *Chocolate Girl* by Jean-Étienne Liotard was displayed on the entrance side above the door on the right.

RE

Literature: Riedel/Wenzel 1765, pp. 239–43; Bianconi 1781, pp. 17–19; Schuster 2003, pp. 10, 167–68; Henning/Marx 2007, pp. 7–12; Schuster 2009, p. 69.

The pastels listed in the following are all in the collection of the Staatliche Kunstsammlungen Dresden's Gemäldegalerie Alte Meister. As in the catalogue of the Dresden gallery produced by Karl Woermann in 187, they are arranged by artist and with their original gallery numbers, which have remained unchanged. The numbers were assigned according to the same system as those of the oil paintings, but with an additional "P" for pastel, beginning with the Italian school, here with the work by Reni (P 1), followed by Carriera and the Swiss (Liotard: P 159 to P 152) and French (La Tour: P 163 to P 164) and, finally, the German painters (Mengs: P 165 to P 177). The sequence does not reflect the way the works were displayed in the Pastellkabinett.

Guido Reni
(Calvenzano near Bologna 1686–1642 Bologna)
Saint Francis
Circa 1631 (?)
Colored chalk on paper, oval format on black,
58 x 47 cm
Gal. no. P 1

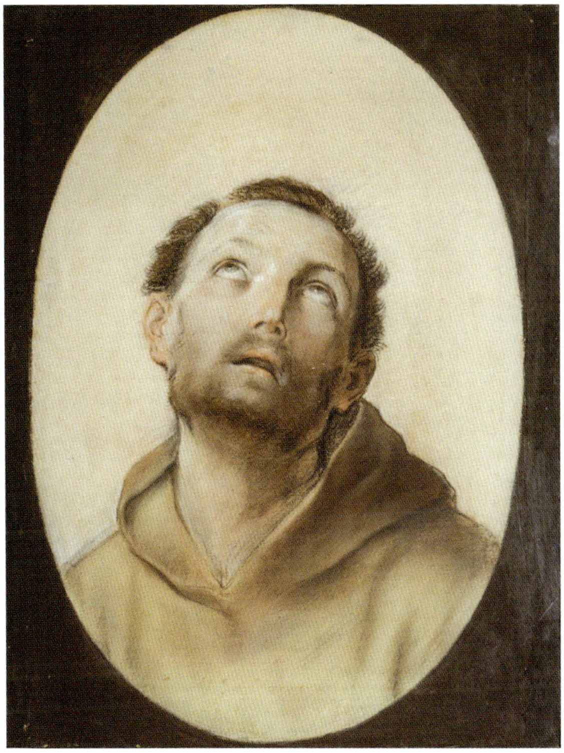

This picture of Saint Francis was a sketch for an altarpiece in the Girolamini in Naples, which the Bolognese painter Guido Reni completed in 1631. The saint's visions are alluded to by his slightly tilted head and heavenward gaze. Reni captured the contours with strong lines in black chalk while using short hatching to sculpt the face. White chalk highlights indicate the light shining from above.
The study was part of a spectacular purchase in 1746, which brought one hundred masterpieces from the ducal gallery in Modena to the Dresden collection. The picture was hung in the Inner Gallery as a pendant to Reni's other oval painting *Christ*

with the Crown of Thorns (gal. no. 323) near Raphael's *Sistine Madonna*. Strictly speaking it is a drawing in pastel, since Reni did not yet blend the individual chalk strokes in the way required by eighteenth-century pastel technique. It was not placed in the Pastellkabinett until 1835.

RE

Literature: Riedel/Wenzel 1765, p. 217, no. 261; Matthäi 1835, p. 119, no. 1; Winkler 1989, pp. 188–89; Henning/Marx 2007, pp. 13–14.

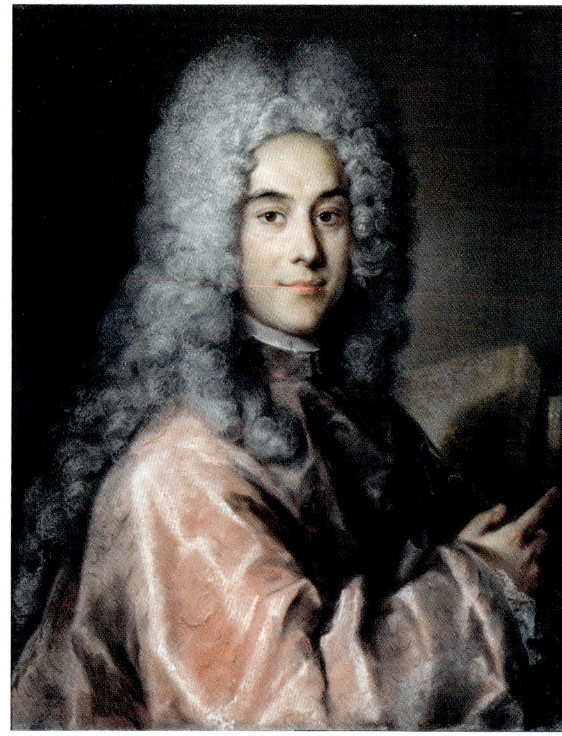

Rosalba Carriera
(Venice 1673–1757 Venice)
Princess Benedetta Ernestina Maria of Modena (1697–1777)
1723
Pastel on paper, 55.5 x 42.5 cm
Gal. no. P 3

Literature: Riedel/Wenzel 1765, p. 240; Henning/Marx 2007, pp. 35–39.

Rosalba Carriera
(Venice 1673–1757 Venice)
Giambattista Recanati (1687–1734) (?)
Circa 1710/20
Pastel on paper, 72 x 59.5 cm
Gal. no. P 4

The large-format pastel presents a stately Giambattista Recanati. A lavishly powdered, long peruke and large red cloak leave only the delicate features of his still-youthful face visible. Carriera, who was on friendly terms with Venice's patrician Recanati family, presented the philologist and poet as a scholar, or "homme de lettre." With his right hand he is pointing at the leather-bound folios behind him.

In 1735, Recanati willed his book collection, which included 216 highly valuable manuscripts, to the public library of San Marco. From his father he had inherited an extensive painting collection. He himself owned fourteen Carriera pastels, twelve of which were sold to Dresden after his death. Among them was this portrait of Recanati, which in the sales record was listed as "a Venetian procurator." The pastel titled *Man in a Dark-Gray Coat* (gal. no. P 73) is probably a later portrait of Recanati.

RE

Literature: Riedel/Wenzel 1765, p. 239; Henning/Marx 2007, pp. 24–25, 44–52.

ROSALBA CARRIERA
(Venice 1673–1757 Venice)
Louis XV of France (1710–1774) as Dauphin
1720/21
Pastel on paper, 50.5 x 38.5 cm
Gal. no. P 9

During her stay in Paris in 1720/21, Rosalba Carriera was able to paint a portrait of the then just ten-year-old king of France, who had been enthroned at the age of five. The great-grandson of Louis XIV was portrayed as a ruler, gazing confidently out of the picture, his dark eyes dominating the childlike face. The long peruke, lace cravat, orange-red coat with the Order of the Holy Spirit on a blue ribbon, and the ermine cloak, all serve as attributes of the regent. Nevertheless, Carriera managed to find a simpler form of presentation within this framework of courtly protocol.

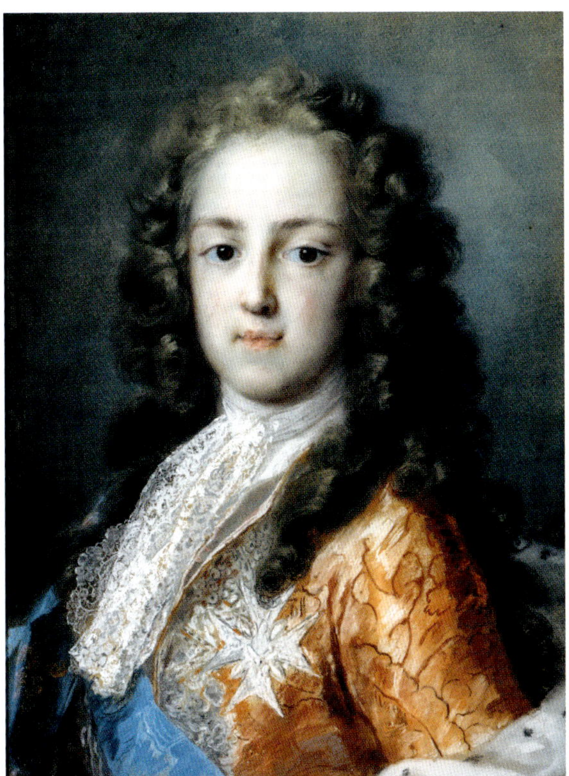

Louis is still pictured here as heir to the throne (Dauphin). It was only at the age of thirteen, in February 1723, that he took over from the Regent Philippe II, Duke of Orléans. Following the death of his first wife in 1747, Louis's only surviving son—also called Louis—married Maria Josepha of Saxony, who had been portrayed in 1749 by Maurice Quentin de La Tour (cat. 76). La Tour had also painted a portrait of Louis XV a year before, a privilege Liotard was able to enjoy a few years later, in 1750 (now Turin, Stupinigi Palace).

RE

Literature: Riedel/Wenzel 1765, p. 239; Henning/Marx 2007, pp. 30–31.

ROSALBA CARRIERA
(Venice 1673–1757 Venice)
A Venetian Woman from the House of Barbarigo (Caterina Sagredo Barbarigo)
Circa 1735–40
Pastel on paper, 42 x 33 cm
Gal. no. P 16

Literature: Riedel/Wenzel 1765, p. 240 (?); Henning/Marx 2007, pp. 90, 93.

ROSALBA CARRIERA
(Venice 1673–1757 Venice)
Enrichetta Anna Sofia d'Este, Princess of Modena (1702–1777)
1723
Pastel on paper, 53 x 41 cm
Gal. no. P 17

Literature: Riedel/Wenzel 1765, p. 240; Henning/Marx 2007, pp. 35–39.

Rosalba Carriera
(Venice 1673–1757 Venice)
Anna Amalia Giuseppa d'Este, Princess of Modena (1699–1778)
1723
Pastel on paper, 53 x 41 cm
Gal. no. P 18

Literature: Riedel/Wenzel 1765, p. 240; Henning/Marx 2007, pp. 35–39.

Rosalba Carriera
(Venice 1673–1757 Venice)
Pisana Mocenigo, née Corner (or Cornaro) (or Lucrezia Mocenigo [?])
Undated
Pastel on canvas, 52 x 41 cm
Gal. no. P 23

Literature: Riedel/Wenzel 1765, p. 240 (?); Henning/Marx 2007, pp. 22, 27–28.

Rosalba Carriera
(Venice 1673–1757 Venice)
The Dancer Barbara Campanini, known as La Barbarina (1721–1799)
1739 (?)
Pastel on blue paper over canvas, 56.5 x 46.5 cm
Gal. no. P 24

Literature: Riedel/Wenzel 1765, p. 239; Henning/Marx 2007, pp. 88–90.

Rosalba Carriera
(Venice 1673–1757 Venice)
A Tirolean Innkeeper
Circa 1728
Pastel on paper, 33 x 37 cm
Gal. no. P 28

Literature: Riedel/Wenzel 1765, p. 239, footnote; Henning/Marx 2007, pp. 51–52.

Rosalba Carriera
(Venice 1673–1757 Venice)
Africa
Undated
Pastel on blue paper, 34 x 28 cm
Gal. no. P 32

Literature: Riedel/Wenzel 1765, p. 241; Henning/Marx 2007, p. 33.

Rosalba Carriera
(Venice 1673–1757 Venice)
Transiency at the Hand of Eternity
Undated
Pastel on paper, 63.5 x 51 cm
Gal. no. P 41

Literature: Riedel/Wenzel 1765, p. 239, footnote; Henning/Marx 2007, pp. 57–58.

Rosalba Carriera
(Venice 1673–1757 Venice)
Air
1746
Pastel on paper 56 x 46 cm
Gal. no. P 50

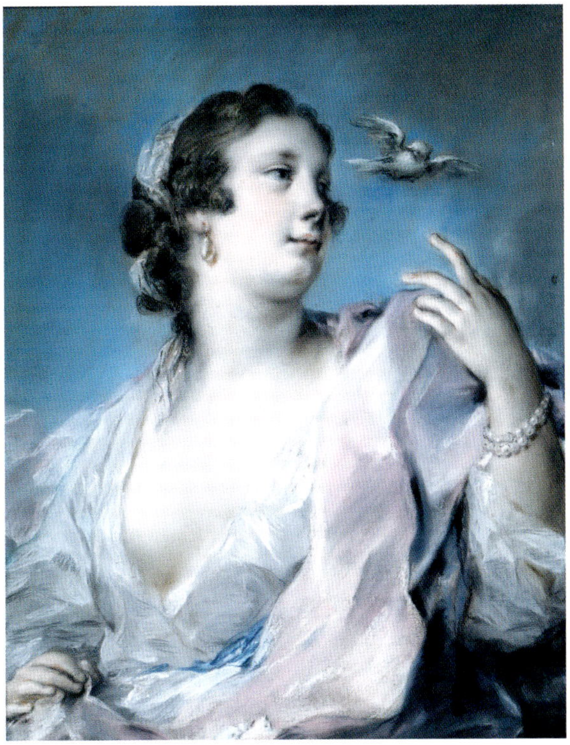

Rosalba Carriera
(Venice 1673–1757 Venice)
Water
1746
Pastel on paper, 56 x 46 cm
Gal. no. P 51

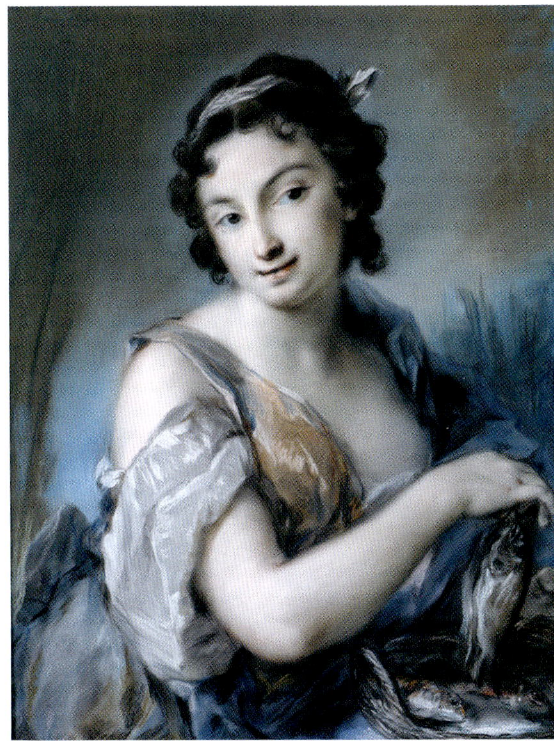

ROSALBA CARRIERA
(Venice 1673–1757 Venice)
Earth
1744
Pastel on paper 56 x 46 cm
Gal. no. P 52

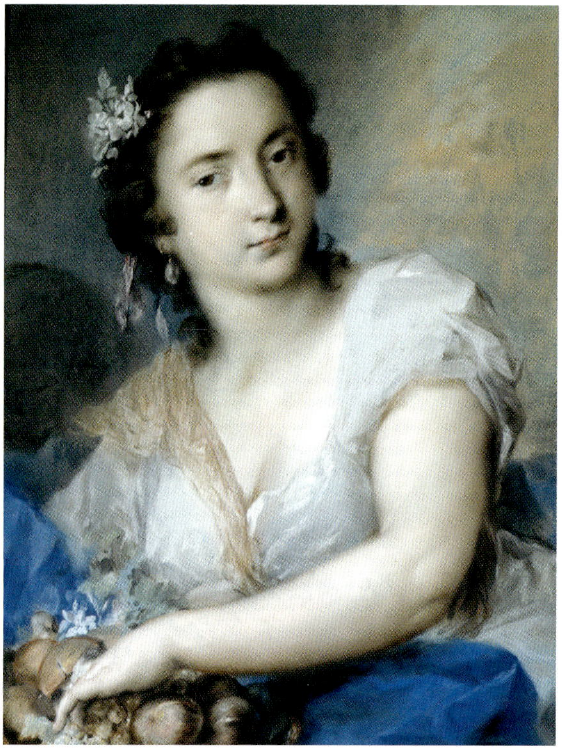

ROSALBA CARRIERA
(Venice 1673–1757 Venice)
Fire
1744
Pastel on paper, 56 x 46 cm
Gal. no. P 53

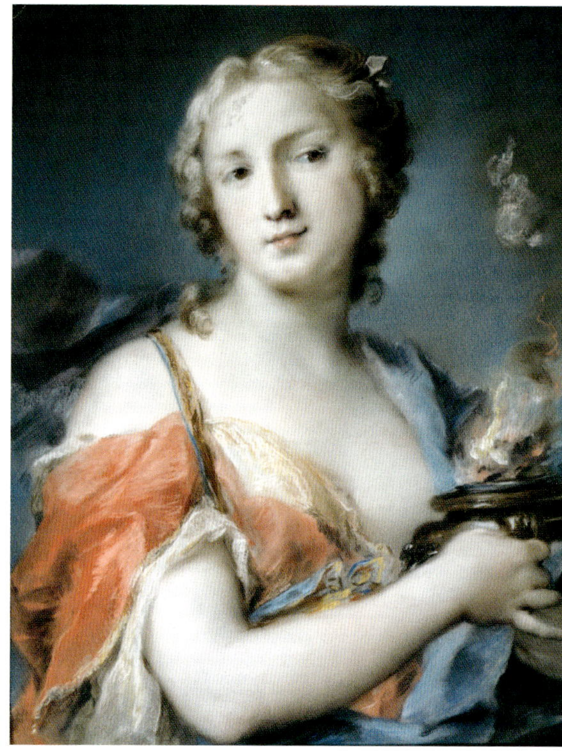

The commission for a series of the four elements in pastel for the Dresden gallery was awarded to Rosalba Carriera by Count Francesco Algarotti. The female personifications are captivating in their wealth of dynamic gestures and animated gazes. Each of the figures is furnished with a readily recognizable attribute: the allegory of *Earth* is reaching into a full basket of fruit, *Fire* is holding a brazier, *Air* is setting a bird free, and *Water* is identified by fish and reeds. Carriera received frequent commissions for allegories of the four elements and also of the four seasons. The attributes she used for the latter often resembled those of the elements, the fruit basket now representing summer or autumn. The artist executed the Dresden commission in two stages, as is evident from the slight variation in their size and coloring: she painted the personifications of *Earth* and *Fire* at around 1744; then, in 1746, those of *Air* and *Water*. This group was among Carriera's last works. In the autumn of 1746 she underwent an eye operation, which left her blind.

RE

Literature: Riedel/Wenzel 1765, p. 241; Henning/Marx 2007, pp. 94–100.

Rosalba Carriera
(Venice 1673–1757 Venice)
Christ
Undated
Pastel on paper, 30.5 x 23 cm
Gal. no. P 55

Literature: Riedel/Wenzel 1765, p. 240; Henning/Marx 2007, p. 39.

Rosalba Carriera
(Venice 1673–1757 Venice)
Mary as Mother of Sorrows
Undated
Pastel on paper, 58.5 x 48 cm
Gal. no. P 60

Literature: Riedel/Wenzel 1765, p. 241; Henning/Marx 2007, pp. 41–43.

Rosalba Carriera
(Venice 1673–1757 Venice)
Mary Magdalene with a Book
Circa 1723
Pastel on paper, 57 x 46.5 cm
Gal. no. P 61

Literature: Riedel/Wenzel 1765, p. 241; Henning/Marx 2007, pp. 39–40, 43.

Rosalba Carriera
(Venice 1673–1757 Venice)
Giambattista Recanati (1687–1734) (?)
Undated
Pastel on paper, 73 x 60.5 cm
Gal. no. P 73

Literature: Riedel/Wenzel 1765, p. 239; Henning/Marx 2007, pp. 46–52.

Rosalba Carriera
(Venice 1673–1757 Venice)
Lady in a Black Lace Dress and Pink Bow
Undated
Pastel on paper, 48.5 x 40 cm
Gal. no. P 110

Literature: Riedel/Wenzel 1765, p. 239, footnote; Henning/Marx 2007, p. 90.

Rosalba Carriera
(Venice 1673–1757 Venice)
Young Man in a Billowing Blue Cloak
Undated
Pastel on paper, 56.5 x 46.5 cm
Gal. no. P 114

Literature: Riedel/Wenzel 1765, p. 239, footnote; Henning/Marx 2007, pp. 50–51.

Rosalba Carriera
(Venice 1673–1757 Venice)
Lady in a Blue Cloak over a Light Dress
Undated
Pastel on paper, 75.5 x 64 cm
Gal. no. P 115

Literature: Riedel/Wenzel 1765, p. 239, footnote: Henning/Marx 2007, pp. 50–51.

Rosalba Carriera
(Venice 1673–1757 Venice)
The Singer Faustina Bordoni (1700–1781) with Sheet Music
Circa 1724/25
Pastel on paper, 44.5 x 33.5 cm
Gal. no. P 118

Literature: Riedel/Wenzel 1765, p. 240; Henning/Marx 2007, pp. 44–46.

Rosalba Carriera
(Venice 1673–1757 Venice)
An Officer (Man in Armor)
Undated
Pastel on canvas, 79 x 65 cm
Gal. no. P 122

Literature: Riedel/Wenzel 1765, p. 239, footnote; Henning/Marx 2007, pp. 20, 26.

Rosalba Carriera
(Venice 1673–1757 Venice)
Girl in a White Dress
Undated
Pastel on paper, 32 x 26.5 cm
Gal. no. P 131

Literature: Riedel/Wenzel 1765, p. 239, footnote; Henning/Marx 2007, pp. 72–73.

Rosalba Carriera
(Venice 1673–1757 Venice)
Diana
Undated
Pastel on paper, 30 x 26.5 cm
Gal. no. P 133

Literature: Riedel/Wenzel 1765, p. 239, footnote; Henning/Marx 2007, pp. 62–63.

Rosalba Carriera
(Venice 1673–1757 Venice)
Muse in a Pink Robe
Undated
Pastel on paper, 29 x 24.5 cm
Gal. no. P 137

Literature: Riedel/Wenzel 1765, p. 239, footnote; Henning/Marx 2007, p. 61.

Rosalba Carriera
(Venice 1673–1757 Venice)
Diana in a Blue Robe
Undated
Pastel on paper, 25.5 x 19.5 cm
Gal. no. P 140

Literature: Riedel/Wenzel 1765, p. 239, footnote: Henning/Marx 2007, pp. 62–64.

Rosalba Carriera
(Venice 1673–1757 Venice)
A Lady with a Parrot on Her Right Hand (Allegory of Eloquence)
Circa 1725/30
Pastel on paper, 54.5 x 41 cm
Gal. no. P 143

Literature: Riedel/Wenzel 1765, p. 239, footnote; Henning/Marx 2007, pp. 57, 59, 64.

Rosalba Carriera
(Venice 1673–1757 Venice)
Man in a Coffee-Brown Coat
Undated
Pastel on paper, 53.5 x 42 cm
Gal. no. P 158

Literature: Riedel/Wenzel 1765, p. 239, footnote; Henning/Marx 2007, pp. 48–49.

Anton Raphael Mengs
(Aussig 1728–1779 Rome)
Ismael Mengs, the Artist's Father (1688–1764)
1744/45
Pastel on paper, 55.5 x 42.5 cm
Gal. no. P 165

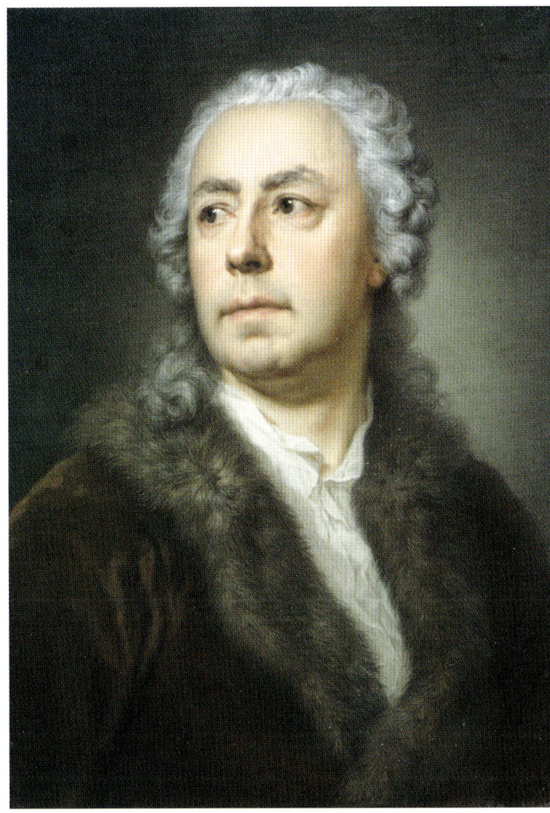

This bust portrait of his father Ismael is considered the most expressive of the series of portraits by Anton Raphael Mengs in Dresden's Pastellkabinett. The sitter's sideways gaze is not directed at the painter, which, together with the view from below, emphasizes the subject's distant nature. The muted coloring, limited to brown, ocher, and gray, underscores the man's plain appearance, which is nevertheless imbued with a courtly presence by the powdered peruke, fur trim, and the fully lit face.
Ismael Mengs was a miniature painter and enamelist to the court in Dresden from 1714. After the birth of his children he devoted himself—with great stringency—to their artistic training. Despite father and son falling out later, Bianconi reports of the reverence with which Anton Raphael Mengs viewed his father's self-portrait in oil (ca. 1720?, gal. no. 2083): "He [Anton Raphael] had never attained the level of mastery to create a head like that in oil."

RE

Literature: Riedel/Wenzel 1765, p. 242; Bianconi 1781, pp. 114, 118; Roettgen 1999, pp. 291–92, no. 223; Henning/Marx 2007, pp. 133–35.

Anton Raphael Mengs
(Aussig 1728–1779 Rome)
Self-Portrait in a Red Coat
1744/45
Pastel on paper, 55 x 42 cm
Gal. no. P 167

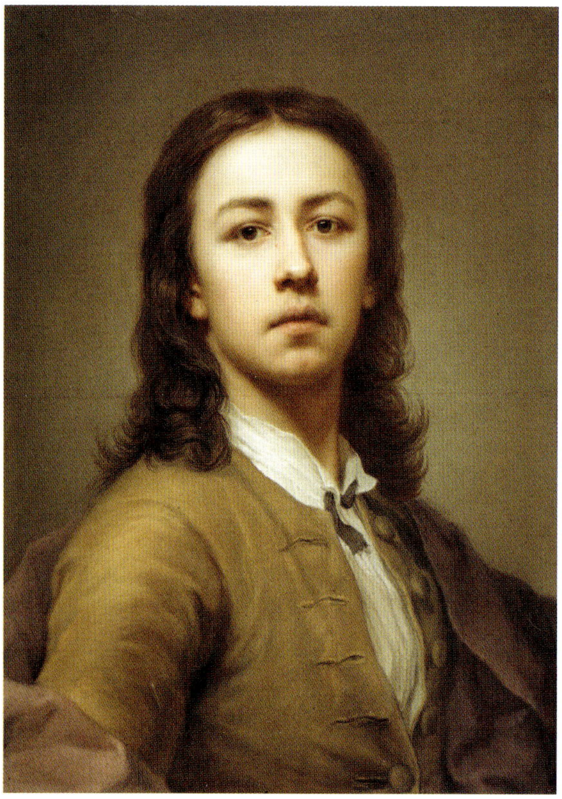

Although only seventeen years old at the time, Mengs depicts himself in this self-portrait with great confidence. Painted as a bust in half profile, his youthful face gazes straight out at the viewer. Beneath his ocher-colored jacket and the reddish cloak draped around his shoulders, he wears a white shirt with casually undone necktie. The arrangement reveals his familiarity with Baroque artists' portraits. His pose also recalls Paolo Naldini's bust of Raphael, which was placed on the Renaissance artist's tomb in the Pantheon in Rome. At the same time, Mengs asserts his own artistic independence with masterful skill.

Anton Raphael, whose father Ismael had named him with obligating intent after Antonio Allegri, called Correggio, and the famous Raphael, developed into a celebrated artist of the period between Late Baroque and Neoclassicism. After his return in 1744 from Rome, where he had traveled with his father, he created two self-portraits, of which the pendant *Self-Portrait in a Blue Coat* (gal. no. P 166) has been missing since the Second World War. Legend has it that he also portrayed King Augustus III in pastel in record time.

RE

Literature: Riedel/Wenzel 1765, p. 242; Bianconi 1781, p. 118; Roettgen 1999, pp. 335–35, no. 271; Henning/Marx 2007, pp. 131–33.

Anton Raphael Mengs
(Aussig 1728–1779 Rome)
Councilor Franz Josef von Hoffmann (1696–1763)
1745
Pastel on paper, 54 x 43 cm
Gal. no. P 169

Literature: Riedel/Wenzel 1765, p. 242; Henning/Marx 2007, pp. 137–38.

Anton Raphael Mengs
(Aussig 1728–1779 Rome)
The Singer Caterina Regina Mingotti (1722–1807)
Circa 1750
Pastel on Paper, 55.5 x 42.5 cm
Gal. no. P 170

Literature: Riedel/Wenzel 1765, p. 242; Henning/Marx 2007, pp. 138–39.

Anton Raphael Mengs
(Aussig 1728–1779 Rome)
The Singer Domenico Annibali (1705?–1779)
1744
Pastel on paper, 55.5 x 42.5 cm
Gal. no. P 171

Literature: Riedel/Wenzel 1765, p. 242; Henning/Marx 2007, pp. 139–42.

Anton Raphael Mengs
(Aussig 1728–1779 Rome)
Frederick Christian, Elector of Saxony (1722–1763)
1750/51
Pastel on paper, 55.5 x 44.5 cm
Gal. no. P 174

Literature: Henning/Marx 2007, pp. 144–45.

Anton Raphael Mengs
(Aussig 1728–1779 Rome)
Maria Antonia, Princess of Bavaria, Electress of Saxony, Wife of Frederick Christian, Elector of Saxony (1724–1780)
1751
Pastel on paper, 55.5 x 44.5 cm
Gal. no. P 175

Literature: Riedel/Wenzel 1765, p. 242; Henning/Marx 2007, pp. 145–46.

Anton Raphael Mengs
(Aussig 1728–1779 Rome)
Frederick Augustus III, Elector of Saxony, as a Child (1750–1827)
1751
Pastel on paper, 63.5 x 75.5 cm
Gal. no. P 176

Literature: [Riedel 1801], p. 180; Henning/Marx 2007, pp. 146–47.

Therese Concordia Maron, née Mengs
(Aussig 1725–1806 Rome)
The Artist's Sister, Juliane Charlotte Mengs (ca. 1730–after 1806)
Circa 1744/45 (?)
Pastel on blue paper over white paper, 41.5 x 33 cm
Gal. no. P 178

Literature: Riedel/Wenzel 1765, p. 242; Henning/Marx 2007, pp. 128–29.

Therese Concordia Maron, née Mengs
(Aussig 1725–1806 Rome)
Self-Portrait
Circa 1744/45 (?)
Pastel on blue paper over canvas, 42 x 34 cm
Gal. no. P 179

Literature: Riedel/Wenzel 1765, p. 242; Henning/Marx 2007, pp. 127–28.

Mirror
Saxony, circa 1750
Carved wood, with gold leaf gilt, mirror glass restored
88 x 61 x 7 cm
Kunstgewerbemuseum, Staatliche Kunstsammlungen Dresden, inv. no. 22739

THE *CHOCOLATE GIRL* IN PRINTMAKING

Liotard's *Chocolate Girl* is so well known to this day thanks to the long availability of the motif in reproductions. Not so much the numerous copies executed in pastel and oil since the eighteenth century, but rather the many versions in print ensured its widespread, even international, fame. Artists were utilizing the various newly emerging printmaking techniques in an attempt to reproduce the qualities of the pastel painting, so difficult to imitate, while printers, lithographic companies, and publishers eagerly took up the popular image, hoping for profitable sales with large print runs. Thus the *Chocolate Girl* has been reproduced in many different techniques of varying suitability—etching, engraving, color lithography, steel engraving, and, finally, photography—which simultaneously provides an overview of the development of printing methods from the late eighteenth to the end of the nineteenth century. In the twentieth century, the image finally became a mass-produced object in form of a postage stamp.

Cat. 79

Carl von Pechwell

(Vienna 1742–1789 Vienna)

after **Jean-Étienne Liotard**

(Geneva 1702–1789 Geneva)

The Viennese Chambermaid

Dated bottom left in the plate: "1782"

Etching, 31.8 x 19.6 cm

Inscribed at the bottom: "La Fille de Garderobbe Viennoise CC la Noblesse très illustre de Vienne / Par leurs très humble et Obeis.t Servieur Charles de Bechwill Graveur de sa Maj.té Imp. / Dans la Gallerie de S.A. S Ellett:le à Dresde se trouve la Peinture de Liotard en Bastell."

Rijksmuseum Amsterdam, gift from the Toneelmuseum, inv. no. RP-P-1955-566

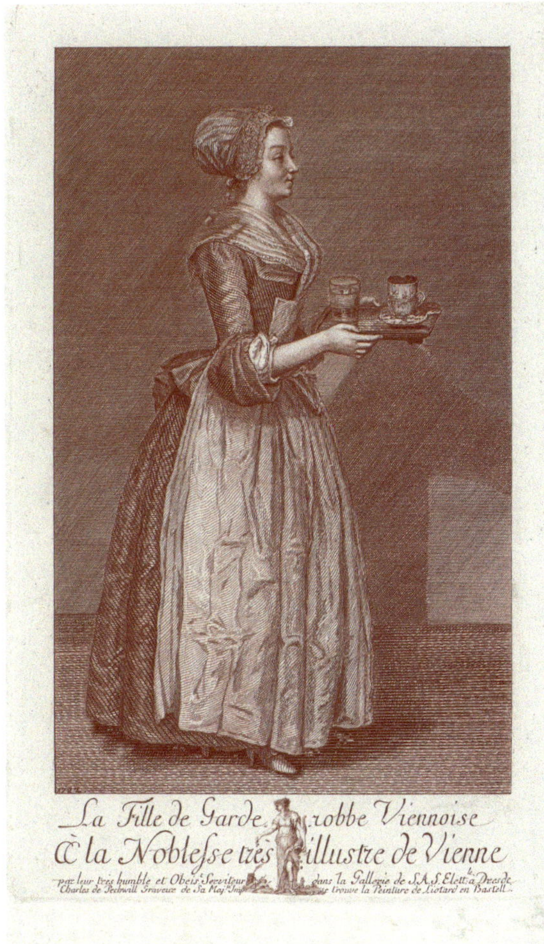

The Viennese engraver Carl von Pechwell produced the first known printed version of Jean-Étienne Liotard's *Chocolate Girl* in 1782. In the sepia-colored etching, considerably smaller than the original, the background and floor are indicated through parallel hatching in different directions, while the maidservant was drawn freehand in dots and various cross-hatchings. The technique was not yet capable of reproducing the fine, powdery surface of the pastel. As a result, her face appears older, and the shadow on the back wall seems somewhat simplified.

In the image caption, Pechwell (Pechwill) identifies himself as engraver to His Imperial Majesty, and provides a description of the picture: "The Viennese Chambermaid who works for Vienna's most distinguished artistocracy." It further mentions the Dresden collection where the painting is to be found and its author. A small allegorical figure with a cornucopia stands for good fortune and wealth granted to the arts. Presumably, Pechwell worked from the original pastel in Dresden's painting gallery, which was then in the Johanneum. He also reproduced another work from the gallery as an engraving, the *Penitent Magdalene* by Pompeo Girolamo Batoni, from the period around 1742 (lost in the war).

RE

Literature: R/L 2008, p. 331; Humbert/Revilliod/Tilanus 1897, p. 193, no. 72.

Cat. 80

Augusta von Buttlar

(Pillnitz near Dresden 1796–1857 Florence)

The Chocolate Girl after the Painting by Jean-Étienne Liotard

1837

Pencil on paper, 18.8 x 14.6 cm (sheet), 21.8 x 19.6 (album)
Inscribed bottom left: "D'après Liotard / Gallerie de Dresden"; bottom right: signed with ligature monogram and dated "1837"
Kupferstich-Kabinett, Staatliche Kunstsammlungen Dresden, inv. no. Ca 46/22

The portrait and miniature painter Augusta von Buttlar reproduced Liotard's *Chocolate Girl* in a small pencil study in 1837. She captured the proportions exactly, with confidently drawn outlines. She also reproduced the texture of the clothing with its folds and highlights with soft pencil hatching. In her drawing Buttlar has the girl gazing downward, whereas in Liotard she looks straight ahead, apparently focused on something in front of her. Certain details, like the shawl concealing the corsage that in the original is partly visible, the missing pastry on the silver saucer, the shadow,

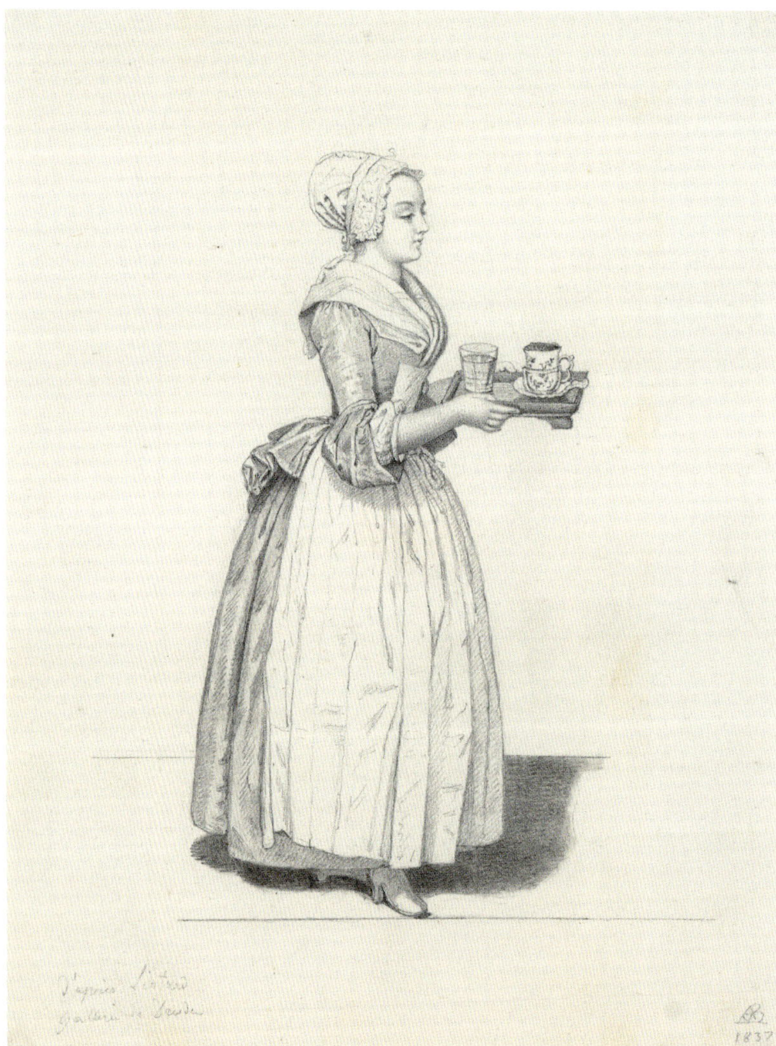

which only shows on the floor but not the wall, and the way the floor has been leveled to a horizontal, attest to the artist's free treatment of the original, which she did not copy exactly.

Augusta von Buttlar was a niece of the early Romantic writer and poet brothers August Wilhelm and Friedrich Schlegel. Starting in 1810 she studied under Friedrich Matthäi, a teacher and director of the Dresden Academy, and acquired further training during study sojourns in Paris, Vienna, London, and Florence. The album, which Buttlar willed in 1848, along with two others, to the Dresden Kupferstich-Kabinett, contains a total of thirty-six drawings. These were produced between 1836 and 1838, mainly after paintings from the Dresden gallery, but also from Berlin's Royal Museum and a "Collection of Count Dohna." The motifs are mainly children, madonnas, and portraits from the Italian Renaissance and Baroque, or Dutch genre scenes. In 1827 Buttlar converted to Catholicism; her fondness for depictions of emotionally charged gazes and religious themes places her artistically in the vicinity of the Nazarenes. As demonstrated by her copy of the *Chocolate Girl*, she also devoted herself to the gallery's best-known paintings.

RE

Literature: exh. cat. Dresden 2017, pp. 238–41 (Petra Kuhlmann-Hodick).

Cat. 81

Alphonse Léon Noël

(Paris 1807–1884 Paris)

after **Jean-Étienne Liotard**

(Geneva 1702–1789 Geneva)

La belle chocolatière de Vienne

Undated [1837?]

Lithograph, Imprimerie Lemercier, Paris, 30 x 21.5 cm (image), 57 x 39 cm (sheet)

Inscribed at the bottom: "D'après le tableau original qui se trouve dans la Galerie de Dresde par Liotard. / Lith. de Lemercier / LA BELLE CHOCOLATIÈRE DE VIENNE. / London published by Ch. Tilt 86 Fleet Street. / Paris, publié par Rittner et Goupil b.ard Montmartre, No. 12. / New York, published by Bailly Ward and Co."

Cabinet d'arts graphiques des Musées d'art et d'histoire, Geneva, inv. no. E 2014-0769

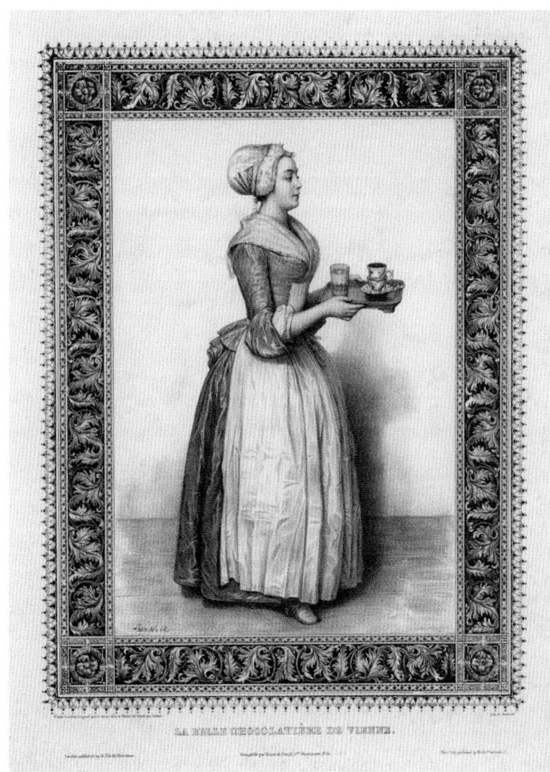

With his version of the *Chocolate Girl*, Alphonse Léon Noël created one of the earliest lithographs of the

Liotard painting. The new technique enabled him to reproduce the soft, powdery surface of the pastel—albeit still in black and white—as a close notion of the original. An elaborate, historicizing frame of sculpturally rendered foliage scrolls surrounds the picture. The sheet, signed by Noël in the stone, was widely distributed, even beyond France's borders. It appeared in licensed editions produced by the printing houses of Charles Tilt (London), Rittner and Goupil (Paris), and Bailly Ward (New York City).
After studying painting at the École des Beaux-Arts in Paris, Noël turned to the graphic arts. He soon came to be known as a highly skilled lithographer. A major part of his graphic oeuvre consists of portraits, but he also worked after other originals. His reproduction of Liotard's *Chocolatière* was published by the Lemercier printing house, which was established in 1830 and distinguished at the Paris industrial exhibition of 1839 as one of the most important firms in the field. The publisher Rose-Joseph Lemercier worked closely with painters and contemporary artists. At the same time, he made use of industrial production methods, allowing him to make prints cost-effectively in large numbers. In 1843, the cost of a print was one Reichstaler. This lithograph must have been made in or shortly before 1837, for in that year Jean-François Benard became a partner in the firm, which was henceforth called "Lith. Lemercier, Benard et Cie."

RE

Literature: R/L 2008, p. 331; Exposition 1839, p. 147; Weigel 1843, p. 120, no. 2949; Humbert/Revilliod/Tilanus 1897, p. 194, no. 81; Rosen 1988, pp. 1–16, 32–68.

Cat. 82
James Posselwhite
(unknown 1798–1884 London)
after **Jean-Étienne Liotard**
(Geneva 1702–1789 Geneva)
La Belle Chocolatière
1842
Etching, engraving, stipple technique, 40.7 x 29 cm
Inscribed in pencil, bottom left: "Liotard pinx";
bottom right: "Posselwhite sculp."
Kupferstich-Kabinett, Staatliche Kunstsammlungen Dresden, inv. no. A 114432

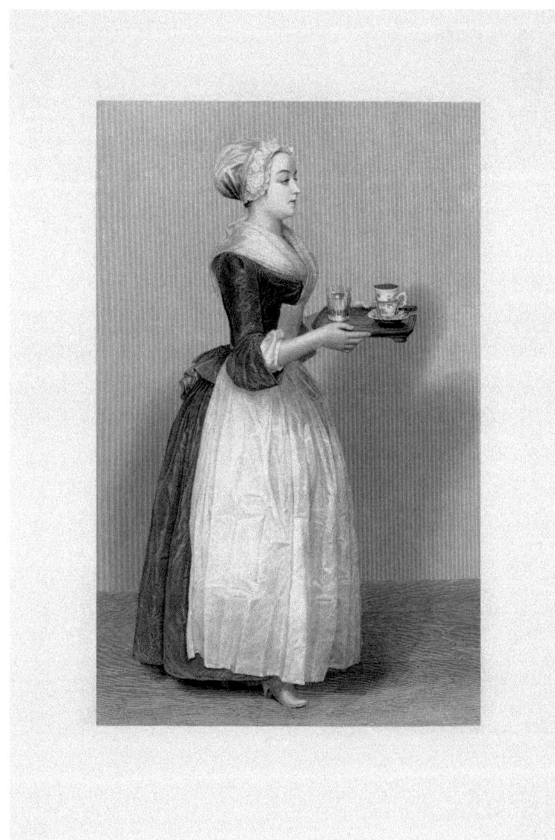

In his version of the *Chocolate Girl*, the English engraver James Posselwhite endeavored to translate the qualities of the pastel into print by way of stipple engraving. While the background is formed by straight and diagonal lines, and the dress, bonnet, tray, and floor in wavy and contour hatching, the lighter areas of the original pastel, like the girl's face, arm, her shawl, and especially the white apron, are rendered with tiny dots. These are made by piercing small holes into the metal plate with a stippling tool or burin. The technique is particularly suitable for the depiction of soft textures like skin or fabric.

In contemporary literature this reproduction technique was known as "English manner," as in the late eighteenth and early nineteenth centuries it was particularly popular in England. Posselwhite is known for his countless portraits of rulers, aristocrats, and historical figures. He was moreover credited by his contemporaries with having "engraved in the English manner many souvenirs of beloved works." Among them, in addition to Liotard's *Chocolatière*, were *La Curieuse (The Nosy Maid)* and *L'Ecouteuse (The Eavesdropper)* after Vincent Vidal from the nineteenth century—two dishonest maidservants hoping to learn their employers' secrets—as well as female allegories.

RE

Literature: R/L 2008, p. 331, fig. 225; Beraldi 1891, pp. 32–33; Humbert/Revilliod/Tilanus 1897, p. 194, no. 74.

Cat. 83

ALBERT HENRY PAYNE

(London 1812–1902 Leipzig)

after **JEAN-ÉTIENNE LIOTARD**

(Geneva 1702–1789 Geneva)

Dresdener Gallerie: The Chocolate Girl / Das Chokoladen Mädchen

From: Adolph Görling and A. H. Payne, *Der Kunstverein. Neue Serie: Stahlstich-Sammlung der vorzüglichsten Gemälde der Dresdener Gallerie*, Leipzig and Dresden [1848–1851], Frontispiece

Circa 1850

Steel engraving, hand-colored, 25.7 x 20.5 cm

Inscribed bottom left: "Liotard pinx."; bottom right: "A. H. Payne sc."

Collection Petra Landsberg, Dresden

The *Chocolate Girl* appears without frame and in an undefined space, the floor and background forming a circle. The fine lines of the engraving permitted the rendering of many details. In the mid nineteenth century, inexpensive steel engraving replaced copper engraving as a widespread reproduction technique. The present example was subsequently watercolored, presumably still in the nineteenth century.

Around 1850 there was a flurry of publications about the Dresden gallery, not published by its directors but by independent authors. Between 1848 and 1851, Albert Henry Payne, an English steel engraver, painter, illustrator, and publisher who had been active in Leipzig since 1839 and in 1845 had co-founded the Englische Kunstanstalt, created a series of steel engravings after masterworks from the Dresden gallery, which he then collated and published as a book in

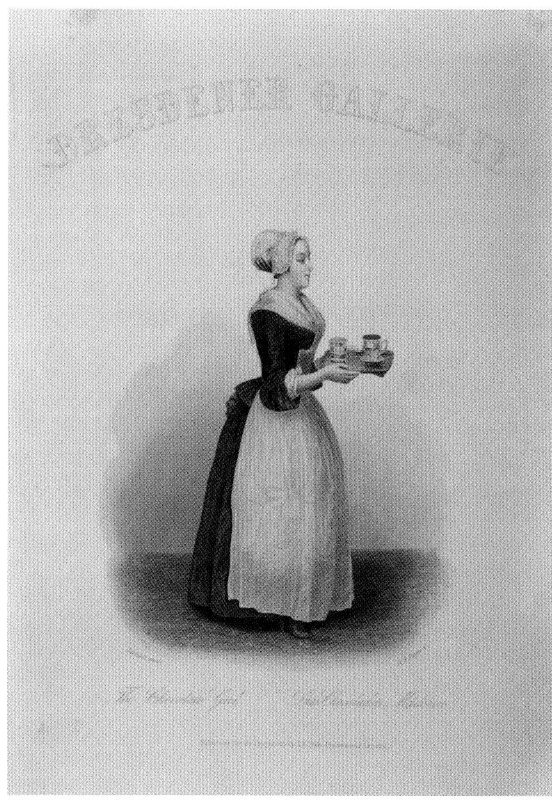

1851. For this edition he chose Liotard's *Chocolate Girl* as the frontispiece and thus as representative of the gallery. Payne also used the engraving, captioned in both English and German, for an English edition, titled *Payne's Royal Dresden Gallery*. The picture appeared in editions in other languages too, for example with the Polish title *Kawiarka* (Coffee Girl), and later also in smaller formats. The short descriptive texts were written by the art writer and journalist Adolph Görling.

RE

Literature: Görling 1851, p. 328; Humbert/Revilliod/Tilanus 1897, p. 193, nos. 70, 71.

Cat. 84

JOHANN ANTON WILLIARD (?)
(Ettlingen 1807–1898 Dresden)
after GUSTAV TÄUBERT
(Dresden 1817–1913 Dresden)

Café Reale (The Brühlsche Terrasse in Dresden looking west from the Jungfernbastei toward Café Reale, Brühlsche Galerie, Katholische Hofkirche, first Semperoper [Hoftheater] and Augustus Bridge)

Circa 1860

Lithograph, printed by Ferdinand Franke sen. (active ca. 1850–1880), 17 x 23.5 cm (image), 23.7 x 31.2 cm (sheet)
Inscribed top center: "Dresden"; bottom left: "Lith. v. Williard Druck v. Ferd. Franke sen. Dresden"; bottom right: "Naturzeichnung u. Verlag v. Gustav Täubert, Dresden"
Städtische Galerie Dresden – Kunstsammlung, Museen der Stadt Dresden, inv. no. 1978/k 394

Set within a wide ornamental frame, this print shows a view of the Brühlsche Terrasse in Dresden. From the Jungfernbastei it takes in the Café Reale and the Brühlsche Galerie. Well-dressed pedestrians enliven the foreground. A tree to the left directs the view. The ornamental frame is filled with arabesques and plant scrolls and edged by an outer border reminsicent of branchwork. The picture is crowned at the top by a cartouche displaying the name "Café réale." Two bouquet-topped mirrors are set into the frame's ornamentation to the left and right, each containting a drawing of Liotard's *Chocolate Girl* facing the city view in the center. The artist has treated his model freely in that he robbed the girl of her calm poise: her forward movement is clearly visible, the ties of her apron fluttering, her head slightly bent, as though watching her step so as not to spill anything on her tray. She also lacks the shawl of the original. The sheet illustrates the popular connection between the *Chocolate Girl* and Dresden's coffeehouse culture.

The lithograph, after a drawing by Gustav Täubert, was probably transferred to the stone by Johann Anton Williard, who had owned a lithography firm in Dresden since 1840. The inscription and the figure of the *Chocolate Girl* refer to the building on the left: the

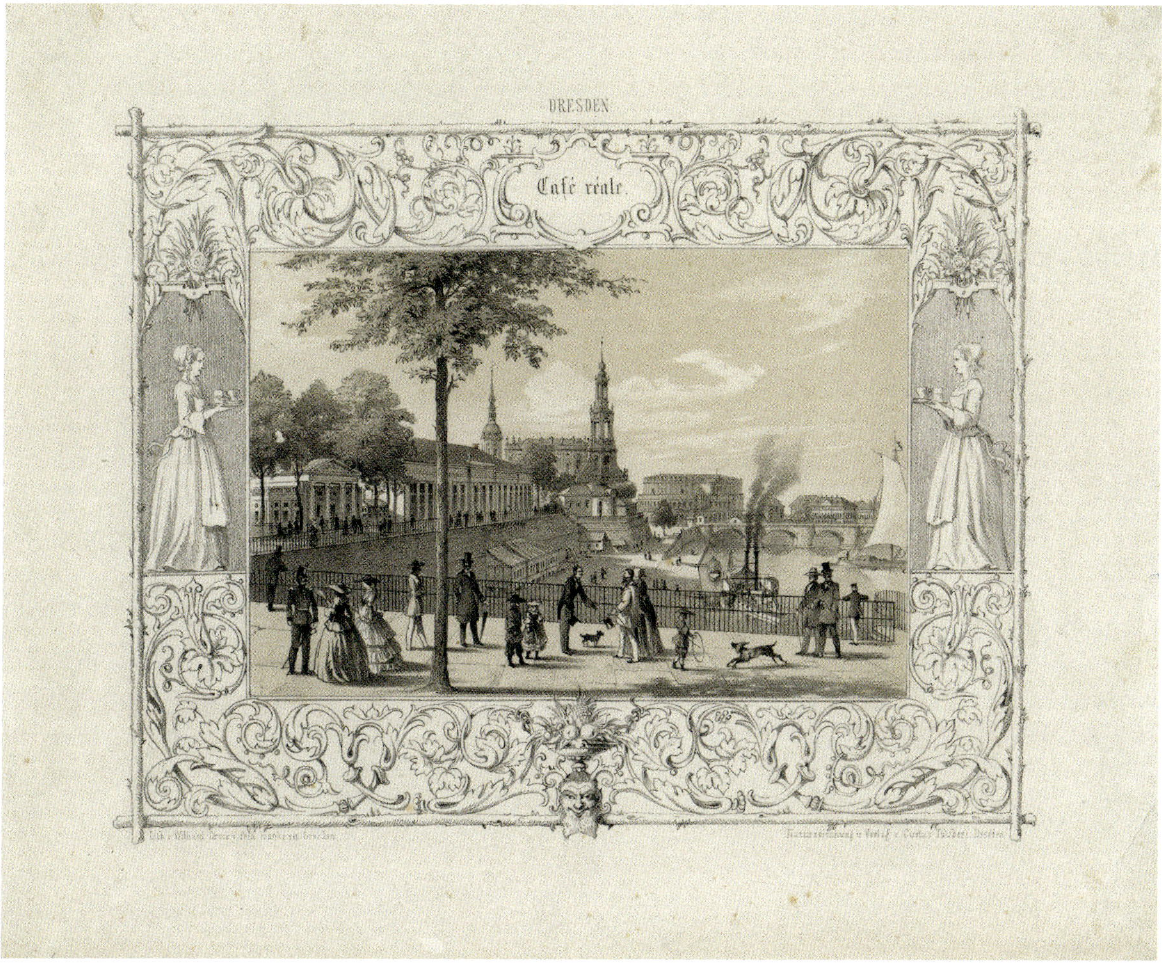

Café Reale was a favorite meeting place for artists and intellectuals in the nineteenth century. The Neoclassical structure in the form of a temple with a projecting portico comprised of four tall columns was built in 1843 by Otto von Wolframsdorf. For a long time it was operated by the Italian Giovanni Ercole Samuel Torniamenti, and for that reason was also often referred to as Café Torniamenti. In 1886 it was demolished to make way for Dresden's new art academy building.

SD

Literature: Zumpe 1991, p. 172; *Stadtlexikon Dresden* 1994, p. 84.

Cat. 85

François-Eugène Burney

(Mailley, Haute-Saône 1845–1907 Paris)

after **Jean-Étienne Liotard**

(Geneva 1702–1789 Geneva)

La Chocolatière de Vienne

1885

Engraving, Chine-collé, 54.2 x 36.1 cm

Inscribed at the bottom:

"D'APRES LA PASTEL DE JEANÉTIENNE LIOTARD, GRAVÉ PAR E. BURNEY / SOCIÉTÉ DE PUBLICATIONS D'ART_(Déposé), La chocolatière de Vienne (MUSÉE DE DRESDE), IMP. CH. WITTMANN_PARIS"

Kupferstich-Kabinett, Staatliche Kunstsammlungen Dresden, inv. no. A 1903-940

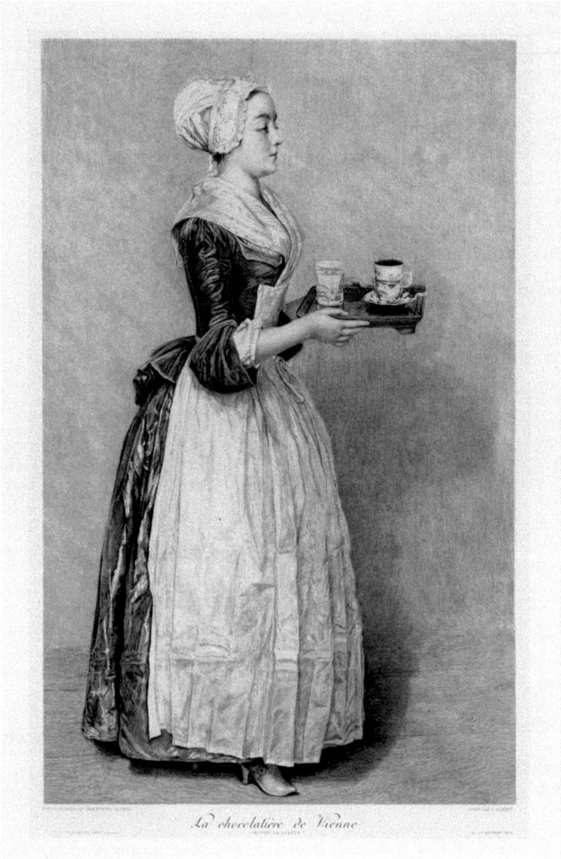

This engraving after the *Chocolate Girl* was produced by François-Eugène Burney in the special technique of *Chine-collé*. In this, a very thin sheet paper—originally paper imported from China was used—is placed between the printing plate and the picture support, which during printing adheres (French: *coller*) to the print. With this method, and by combining different kinds of paper, the image can be imbued with greater vibrancy and depth. In the case of the *Chocolate Girl* this meant that the pastel's characteristic appearance could be reproduced more faithfully. Burney also formed the background, the fabrics, the girl's face, and the tray with its cup and water glass, using a profusion of dashes and dots, as well as by leaving small areas unworked, thus adding to the picture's vibrant impression.

He had learned this printing technique from his teacher Claude Ferdinand Gaillard, with whom he studied in Paris from 1860. After initially producing engravings of other works, he then began creating graphic art with his own motifs, which he exhibited to great acclaim at the World's Fairs in 1889 and 1900. He presented his *Chocolate Girl* at the Paris Salon in 1886, and soon afterward received high praise for it from the art writer and future curator of the Louvre, Henry de Chennevières: "Reproduced about twenty times, but generally interpreted unskillfully, this fine work has now found its ultimate form, since a publisher of great taste had it engraved by the very faithful pupil of our poor Gaillard, M. Burney. We marvel at the confident and delicate engraving, which was necessary to translate this lovely powdery pastel [into print]."

RE

Literature: R/L 2008, p. 331; Chennevières 1888, p. 228; Humbert/Revilliod/Tilanus 1897, p. 194, no. 75.

Cat. 86

Emil Leopold Hodermann

(Drössnitz, Thuringia 1831–after 1897 Dresden)

after **Jean-Étienne Liotard**

(Geneva 1702–1789 Geneva)

The Chocolate Girl

Before 1887

Chromolithograph, 64 x 50.3 cm

Kupferstich-Kabinett, Staatliche Kunstsammlungen Dresden, inv. no. A 1883-85

This color-print version of the *Chocolate Girl* was made by the lithographer and printer Emil Leopold Hodermann. The image is reversed and, furthermore, the bottom quarter with the floor is missing, thereby losing the delicate elegance of the original, which, despite the girl's feet being visible, leaves it uncertain whether she has paused or is in motion. The reproduction of the pastel's coloring, on the other hand, is very successful. At the 1875 Trade and Industry Exhibition in Dresden, Hodermann's portrait of King Albert, which he produced from fifteen separate color lithographs and without retouching, was singled out for praise. It was in this technique, used from around 1870 to mass-produce pictures for numerous purposes, that Hodermann also reproduced Liotard's painting. The large undated sheet is first mentioned in the gallery cat-

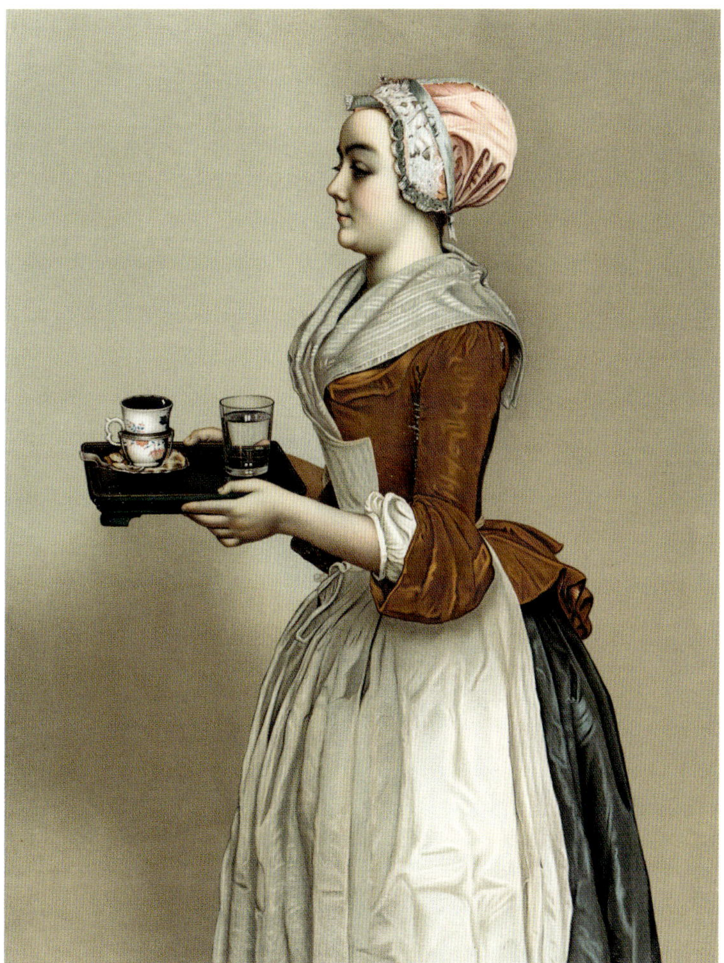

alogue from 1887, and the *Chocolate Girl* was the only picture from the gallery that he reproduced in print. Hodermann's company, the Chromolithografische Anstalt in Dresden, had been publishing color lithographs since 1873. Along with city views, he reproduced paintings and portraits. Even before 1875 he had already been awarded the Austrian Grand Gold Medal for Science and Art as well as Saxony's Grand Gold Medal "virtuti et ingenio."

RE

Literature: Uhland [1875], p. 148; Woermann 1887, full edition, p. 781; Humbert/Revilliod/Tilanus 1897, p. 195, no. 84; Döring 2013, pp. 14–28.

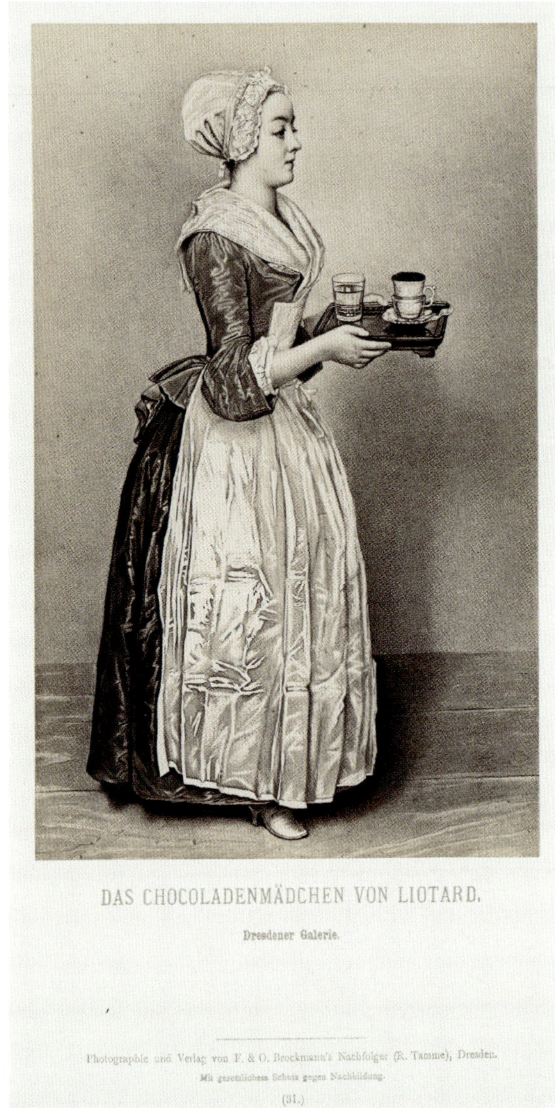

Cat. 87

Friedrich Christian Ferdinand Brockmann

(Güstrow 1809–1886 Dresden?)

Heinrich Friedrich Rudolf Tamme

(Gronau 1835–1910 Dresden)

The Chocolate Girl after Jean-Étienne Liotard

Circa 1887

Photograph, mounted, 20 x 13.6 cm

Inscribed on the mount: "Das Chocoladenmädchen von Liotard. Dresdener Galerie" Gemäldegalerie Alte Meister, Bibliothek, Staatliche Kunstsammlungen DresdenSig. KB 100 Dresd/ AM o. J. Dresd

In the second half of the nineteenth century, photography evolved as a new visual medium that would soon replace all other means of image reproduction and was quickly adopted for reproducing artworks too. This early photograph of the *Chocolate Girl* still gives a rough sense of the pastel's details; for example, the thin strip of parchment in the lower part of the picture that is pasted over the two larger pieces is barely perceptible. The photo comes from the portfolio *Königliche Gemäldegalerie Dresden* from around 1887, containing thirty photographs.

Friedrich Brockmann had trained as a portrait painter in Düsseldorf and Paris before settling in Dresden and devoting himself to photography from 1854. Together with his wife Ottilie he ran the photographic studio and publishing company F. & O. Brockmann. Their son-in-law Rudolf Tamme took over in 1869 and continued under the name F. & O. Brockmann's Nachfolger, Photographische Kunstverlagshandlung, Inhaber H. F. Rud. Tamme. Like other photographic publishers, too, such as Bruckmann in Munich or Alinari in Florence, it offered individual prints in various sizes and on different paper, or collated in portfolios. A leader in the field of photographic prints was Franz Seraph Hanfstaengl in Munich, who, starting in 1835, had initially produced lithographs of masterworks in the Dresden gallery, before starting to photograph the paintings from the 1880s onward. Another important competitor was the French photographer Adolphe Braun. Both had versions of the *Chocolate Girl* in their publishing repertoire.

RE

Literature: Starke 2018.

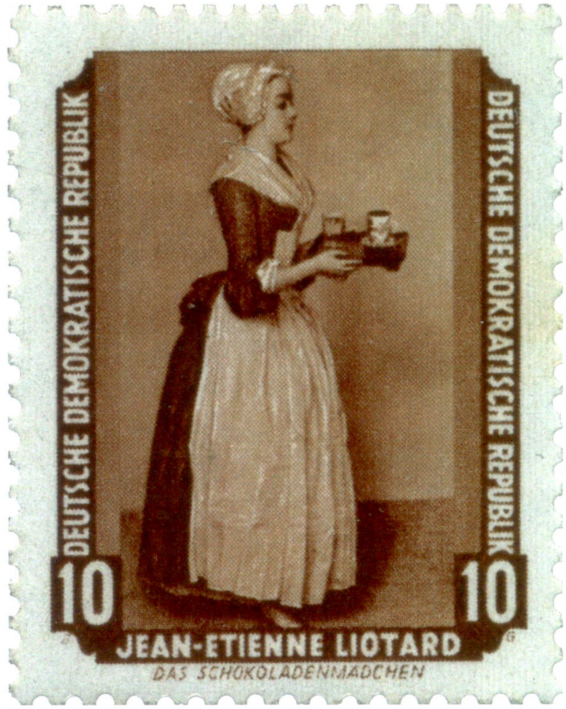

Cat. 88

Erich Gruner

(Leipzig 1881–1966 Leipzig)

German Democratic Republic

10-pfennig stamp

Special issue: Art treasures of the Dresden Gallery rescued and returned by the USSR

1955

Gravure printing, 3.2 x 2.7 cm

Private collection Dresden/Berlin

The German Democratic Republic's Ministry for Post and Telecommunications commemorated the return of the Dresden Gemäldegalerie paintings from the Soviet Union in 1955/56 with a special issue of postage stamps. To mark the important occasion, the Leipzig graphic artist and illustrator Erich Gruner was commissioned to design the stamps. In three series (1955, 1957, 1959) he created a total of seventeen different-colored postage stamps, each picturing an important work from the Dresden collection. The reddish-brown stamp with Liotard's *Chocolate Girl* was part of the first series from 1955 and was printed in an edition of 4 million. Its postage value was 10 pfennigs. Also in this series were Albrecht Dürer's *Portrait of a Young Man* (5 pfennigs), Johannes Vermeer's *Girl Reading a Letter at an Open Window* (40 pfennigs), and Raphael's *Sistine Madonna* (70 pfennigs). Erich Gruner, who for a time was director of Leipzig's school of applied arts, had already made a name for himself in 1917 with his design of the Leipziger Messe logo. The iconic double M, visible from afar, still welcomes visitors to the city today.

JMG

Literature: Mittelstädt 1955, p. 230; Fischer/Skupin/Gudenschwager 1986, pp. 233–35, no. 265; Boesch 1996, pp. 193–94; Schimpfermann 2006, pp. 38–39.

THE *CHOCOLATE GIRL* IN FOLK ART AND EVERYDAY OBJECTS

The *Chocolate Girl* motif can now be seen everywhere: on packaging, brochures, posters—especially in the confectionery and chocolate industry. It also appears in everyday culture and in folk art, as a Christmas tree ornament in wood or porcelain, or as an incense smoker. The first translations of Liotard's most famous pastel in other materials began to appear in the nineteenth century and, by the end of the century, it also emerged as an advertising device. The girl was often reproduced accurately, but sometimes small details were changed or her appearance distorted with ironic intent. Beginning in 1850, waitresses in Dresden coffeehouses came to be costumed like the graceful young Viennese woman, a convention that persists to this day. Such borrowings helped to make the *Chocolate Girl* a familiar figure in Dresden and beyond.

Cat. 89

Meissen Porcelain Manufactory

Chocolate Girl with Cup

Original model: circa 1843; production: circa 1920;

form no. V 86

Porcelain with polychrome decor and gold trim; H. 39 cm

Staatliche Porzellan-Manufaktur Meissen GmbH (MEISSEN©), inv. no. 00321

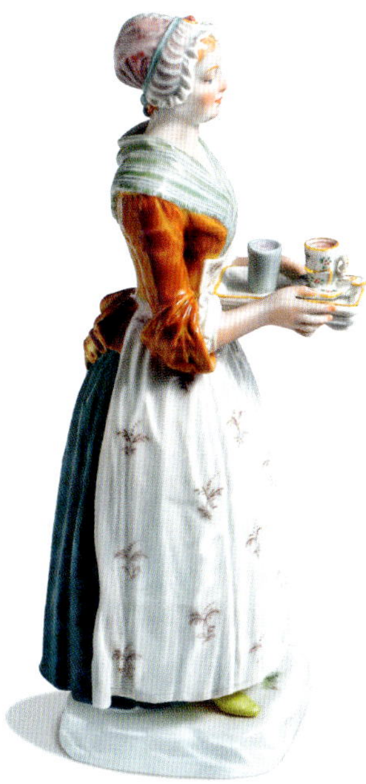

This figure in Meissen porcelain was based on Liotard's *Chocolate Girl*. She stands on a rectangular base, which made it possible to include her feet in the sculpture and still ensure stability. Whereas her skirt and bodice reflect the colors of the pastel, the white elements are delicately painted with dark-pink ferns on the apron, green stripes on the shawl, and additional red dots on her bonnet. The water glass and chocolate cup on the tray are removable. The first model of the *Chocolate Girl* in porcelain was developed in 1843. The example shown here was made at around 1920. While the figure always remained the same, there has been a wealth of variation in the painting: The apron is usually ornamented with different floral decorations, the shawl with a striped pattern. The decor of the cup also varies. The Meissen Porcelain Manufactory, known since the eighteenth century for its figural pieces, especially those made by Johann Joachim Kändler, was aiming to appeal to nineteenth-century tastes with figural representations of famous motifs like the *Chocolate Girl*, partly also in its endeavor to compete with the porcelain manufactories in Sèvres and Berlin.

SD

Literature: Humbert/Revilliod/Tilanus 1897, p. 196, no. 91; Finger 2010.

Cat. 90

Porcelain Manufactory Hof-Moschendorf

Pieces from the "Chocolate Girl" Coffee Service

Circa 1905–1920

Porcelain, white and red with transfer print; coffeepot H. 24.5 cm; milk pitcher H. 14 cm; sugar bowl H. 13 cm; coffee cup H. 5.5 cm; saucer diam. 15 cm

Private collection, Dresden

This porcelain coffee service comprises a coffeepot, milk pitcher, sugar bowl, coffee cups, and saucers with straight, angular handles and double-loop handles on the lids. Its main colors are cream-white with a rust-red base, handles, and lids. Images of Liotard's *Chocolate Girl* have been applied by way of transfer prints, so that the lower part of her skirt

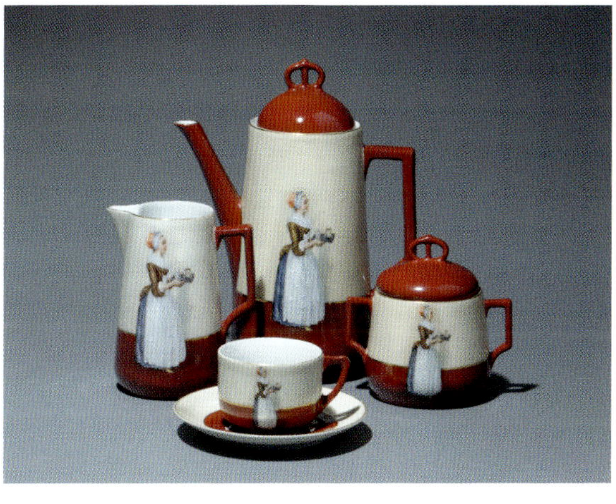

is set against the red base and the rest of the image in front of the cream-colored background. The images on the coffeepot and pitcher are larger, those on the sugar bowl and the cups considerably smaller.

The service was produced by Bavaria's Moschendorf porcelain manufactory. The mark on the bottom with the ligature monogram "P M" crowned and surrounded by a laurel wreath was registered as a trademark in 1905, but was used in parallel with others. The manufactory was founded in 1878 in Moschendorf (now part of Hof) by Hermann Kühnert and Magnus Tischer. It operated until 1957, producing mainly everyday porcelain. Its use of the *Chocolate Girl* attests to the popularity of the motif at the time.

SD

Literature: Danckert 1992, p. 232; Mey 2002, pp. 23–58, 70, 104–06.

Cat. 91

Weimar Porzellan GmbH

Chocolate Girl Tealight Holder

Early twenty-first century

Biscuit porcelain, lithophane, diam. 9 cm

Collection Petra Landsberg, Dresden

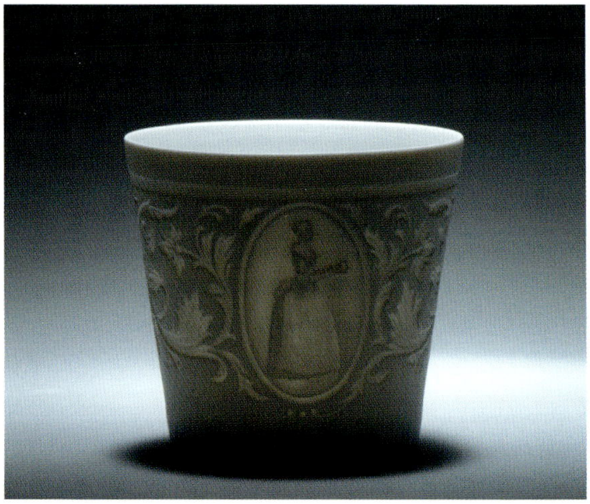

The tealight holder features an image of the *Chocolate Girl* set within an oval frame surrounded by arabesques and foliage scrolls. The cup is made of white biscuit porcelain, a thin, unglazed porcelain with a matte, translucent appearance. The decor was applied in the lithophane technique often used with this material, whereby a plaster relief of the decorative elements is pressed into the soft porcelain, leaving an imprint of the patterns or images. When lit from behind, the patterns stand out due to the different thicknesses of the material, creating subtle transitions between light and shadow. The lithophane technique was already in use in the mid nineteenth century, especially for window decorations and lampshades. The first patent for it was issued in Paris in 1827. The Weimar porcelain manufactory in Blankenhain, established in 1790 by the manufacturer and ceramist Christian Andreas Wilhelm Speck, is one of the oldest porcelain manufactories in Germany, and to this day still produces traditionally made lithophanes, the name of which is derived from the Greek λίθος/*lithos* (stone) and φαίνειν/*phainein* (make visible, illuminate). The use of the *Chocolate Girl* on this tealight holder documents its widespread use as a decorative motif.

SD

Literature: Danckert 1992, pp. 64–65, 347–48.

Cat. 92

Walter Werner, Seiffen

Chocolate Girl

Undated (second half of the twentieth century)

Wood, polychromy, H. 8 cm

Collection Petra Landsberg, Dresden

Cat. 93

Erzgebirgische Hennig Miniaturen

Chocolate Girl

Undated

Wood, polychromy, textile, H. 5.5 cm

Collection Petra Landsberg, Dresden

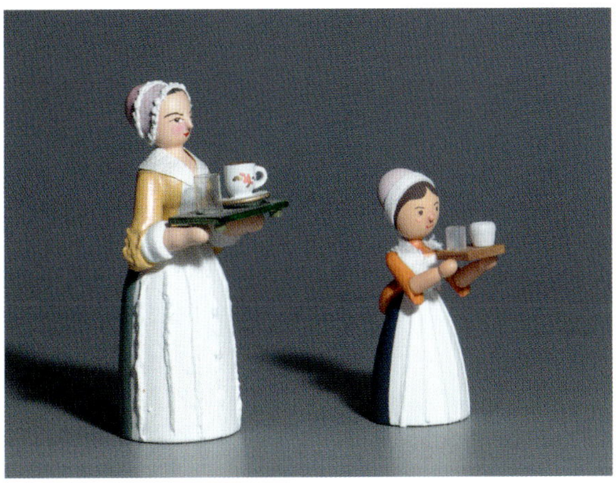

In these two small wooden figures the *Chocolate Girl* is interpreted in three dimensions. Her clothes and bonnet, as well as the two objects on her tray, are based on the original pastel, but greatly simplified in form. In contrast to the painting, the figure stands on the cone-shaped skirt; her feet are not included. This is also owing to the way these wooden figures from Seiffen are made: the basic shapes are produced on a lathe and finishing touches are then added by carving. The technique forces a concentration on the most essential features. The drapery folds, peplum, and lace were still included on the larger figure, rendered to suggest the texture of the materials. On the smaller figure, the attached piece of fabric serves the same end. Both are polychromed, as is typical of Seiffen crafts, and the details of her face, excluding the nose, are delicately painted.

Following the decline in mining in the Ore Mountains at the end of the eighteenth century, woodworking, especially toy making—for which a special vocational school was established—developed in the town of Seiffen as a new source of livelihood. It was at this school that Walter Werner studied, the maker of the larger figure. In 1957 he set up a small workshop producing traditional local crafts. In addition to the famous Seiffen Christmas figures, he also made models of historical figures and well-known motifs like the *Chocolate Girl*. The second figure was made at Hartmut Hennig's workshop near Seiffen, who had specialized as early as 1952 in a variety of miniature figures, which are still being produced today.

SD

Literature: Bachmann 1968, pp. 179–83; Werner 2017, pp. 214–22.

Kat. 94

WPS

The Chocolate Girl

Undated (twentieth century)

Tin, flat figure, H. 5.5 cm

On the top of the stand: "W P S/1745"

Collection Petra Landsberg, Dresden

This figure of the *Chocolate Girl* is cast in tin. The unpainted version shown here is delicately executed, the tray with cup and glass being a thin projection, as is the narrow ribbon hanging down from her bonnet. Instead of shoes, a small stand is attached to the bottom of her skirt.

Small tin figures of people and animals have been made since Greco-Roman antiquity. Their first known appearance as toys dates from the sixteenth century. The main production center was Nuremberg. From the second half of the eighteenth century they became widespread, even forming entire scenarios. The flat figures were cast in slate molds, then engraved and painted according to current fashion, often by the

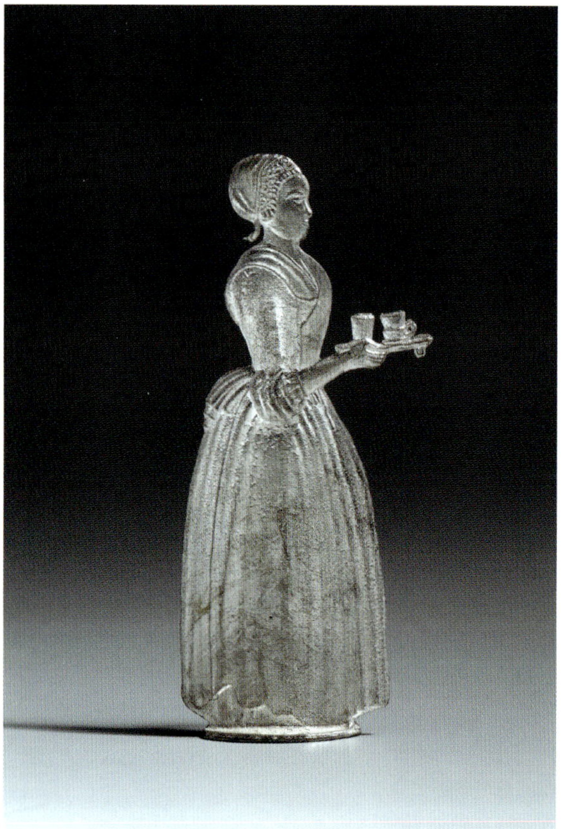

collectors themselves. The design of these toys was always influenced by the tastes of the time, following national preferences and political events, as evidenced by the production of a wide variety of tin soldiers. Tin figures of the *Chocolate Girl* can be bought to this day, for example from Berliner Zinnfiguren, founded by Werner Scholtz in Berlin-Charlottenburg in 1934.

SD

Literature: Ortmann 1973; Mory/Pichelkastner/Höfler 1977, p. 300; Landsberg 2014, pp. 76–77.

Cat. 95

Schilkin Likörfabrik, Berlin

Bottle Cover for Cacao Liqueur

Circa 2008

Plastic, H. 26 cm

Brigitte and Jochen Mütze, Moritzburg

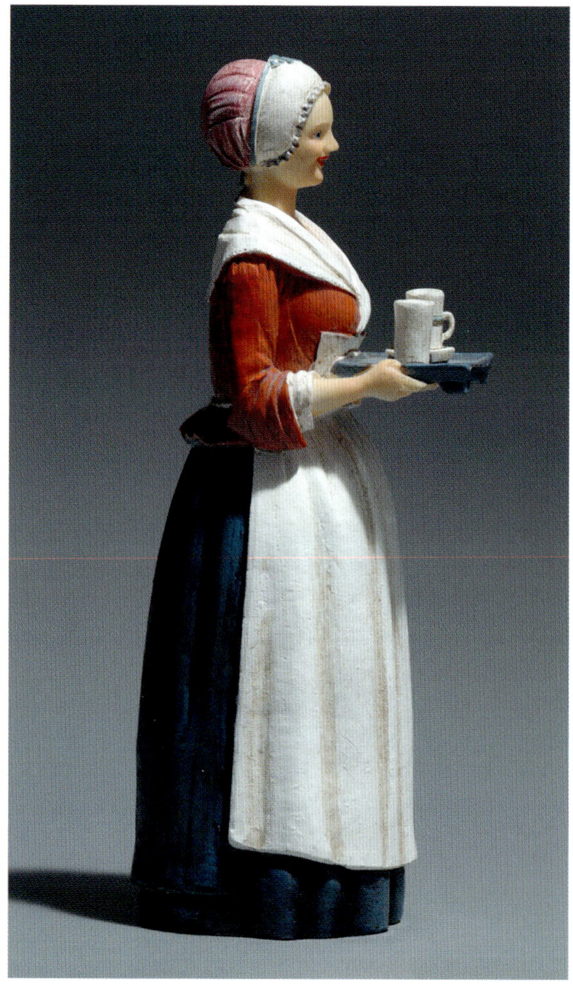

This figural bottle cover is based on Dresden's *Chocolate Girl* in pose and clothing, though the colors are more intense than in the Liotard original. The bodice is now a bright red and the skirt a dark blue. The delicate facial expression of the original pastel has also been changed; the girl is now smiling and looking at the viewer.

The bottle cover produced by the Berlin liqueur and spirits manufacturer Schilkin can be opened at the bottom to hide a 200-ml bottle beneath the figure's skirt. Originally this held a cacao liqueur—in keeping with the *Chocolate Girl* motif. The company was established in 1932 by the former purveyor to the Saint Petersburg court Apollon Fyodorovich Schilkin, who had emigrated to Berlin in 1921. The business is still active today and continues to market its chocolate-cream liqueur under the name "Chocolatière" and with Liotard's *Chocolate Girl* on the label.

SD

Literature: Biermann 2007.

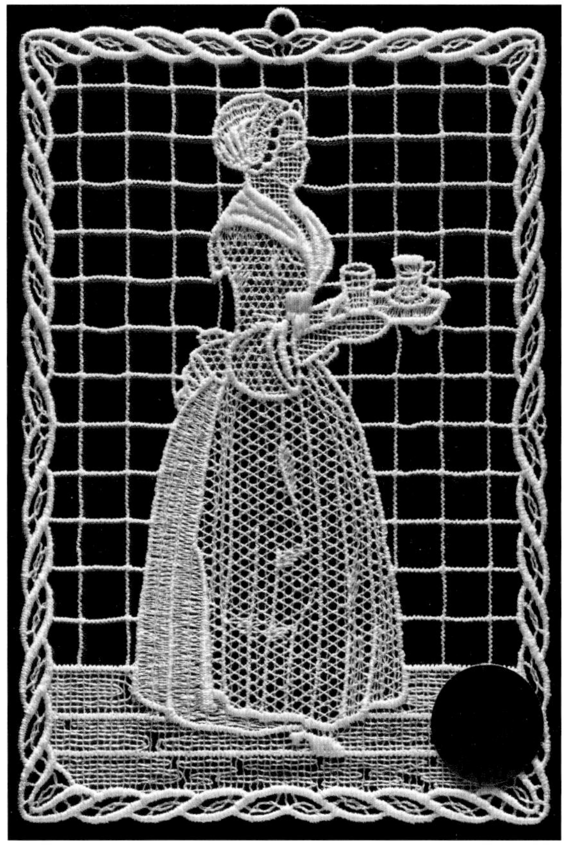

Cat. 96

Plauen Lace

Window hanging:
The Chocolate Girl

Undated

White thread, Plauen lace, 21.7 x 15.1 cm

Collection Petra Landsberg, Dresden

This depiction of the *Chocolate Girl* is in the form of a window decoration in delicate white lace. The design precisely follows the original painting; the space surrounding the figure is indicated by a grid of fine threads and the Rococo frame by twisted threads. A small loop is attached at the top for hanging the piece in a window. The different fabrics and surfaces were rendered in different embroidery techniques. The piece is made from a type of machine-made lace known as chemical lace. The motif is machine-embroidered on a fabric that is then chemically removed.

The delicate embroidery thus takes on the appearance of lace. This invention from the industrial age, developed simultaneously in Plauen and St. Gallen in the nineteenth century, made it possible to manufacture inexpensive lace. Today such window decorations are produced in countless different forms and colors. Genuine "Plauen Lace" continues to be the trademark for the regional products from Plauen and the Vogtland region to this day.

SD

Literature: Exh. cat. Berlin 1976, no page number; Landsberg 2014, p. 84.

Cat. 97

Helmut Erich Brühl

(Dresden 1910–2000 Dresden)

The Chocolate Girl

Undated

Intarsia, various types of wood, 41.3 x 25.8 cm

Antje Roesner, Dresden

Liotard's *Chocolate Girl* served Helmut Erich Brühl as inspiration for this work in intarsia. Using various woods, some of them dyed, he sought to reproduce in inlay work the original coloring of the girl's clothing and bonnet. The floor, background, and frame are the same color, but differentiated by the direction of the wood grain. For the green he presumably used dyed maple veneer or a turquoise-green variant of lignum vitae.

Intarsia was mainly employed in furniture-making from the fourteenth to the nineteenth century. Brühl, a trained cabinetmaker, had already used the technique in his journeyman's piece, a desk with integrated chessboard. From around 1955 he began making pieces of decorative art alongside his work as a joiner and cabinetmaker. In his choice of motifs he remained committed to his native city of Dresden: in addition to the *Chocolate Girl*, he also made intarsia pictures of the Frauenkirche and of the famous bronze sculpture of a bowman, made by Ernst Moritz Geyger and situated on the bank of the Elbe. Brühl willed the present piece to his granddaughter Antje Roesner.

SD

Literature: Krauss 1974, pp. 22–25, 71–75; Brüggemann 1988, pp. 10–13.

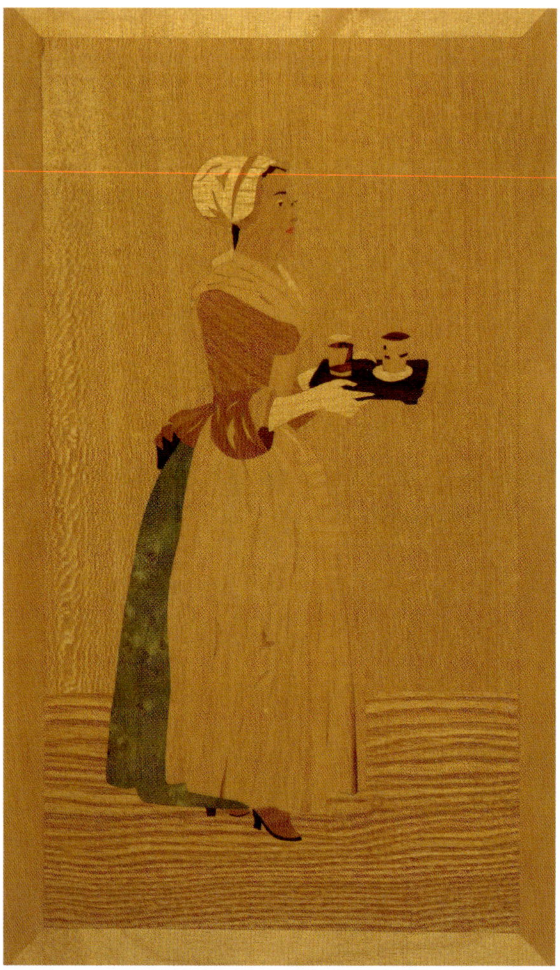

Cat. 98

Otto Rüger Schokoladenfabrik Dresden-Lockwitzgrund

Cacao Tin

Circa 1900

Metal, H. 9 cm, W. 5.7 cm, D. 5.7 cm

Collection Petra Landsberg, Dresden

This square cacao tin features a different motif on each side, all set within arched ornamental cartouches in Art Nouveau style against a dark purple background. Liotard's *Chocolate Girl* is shown on the front of the tin—but reversed and only down to the level of her knees, as if seen in a mirror. Above her, following the arched line of the cartouche frame, the name "Kakao Rüger" is written against the yellow background. On the opposite side, the name of the manufacturer is given in greater detail as: "Otto Rüger Kakao- und Schokoladen-Fabriken Dresden-Lockwitzgrund und Bodenbach i. Böhmen." The other two sides feature, respectively, a picture of a cacao plantation with dark-skinned workers and a plantation owner, and an image of a trading ship entering a harbor. Both thus re-

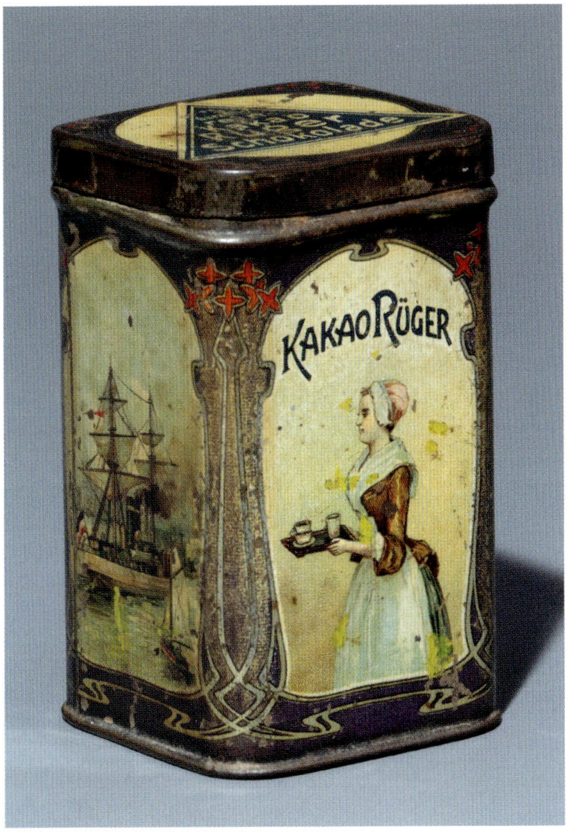

Cat. 99

Sönksen S. A.

Commemorative Booklet for the Company's Seventieth Anniversary

Print on paper, 32.3 x 23.5 cm

Inscribed: "70 anos / Sönksen / Edição comemorativa / de Sönksen Chocolates S/A. / Magazine das Nações Ediçao da Editora & Publicidado Roman Ltda. / São Paulo Santos Rio de Janeiro Buenos Aires Los Angeles, California Ano 11, August 1959, Ediçao especial"

Private collection, Brazil

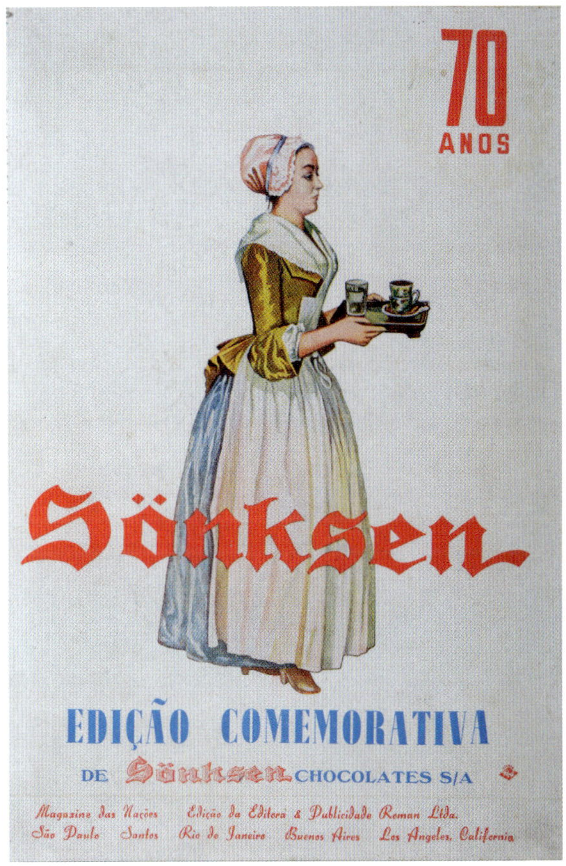

call the exotic origins of cacao. In a blue triangle on the lid we read the slogan "Garantie rein Kakao Rüger Schokolade."

In the nineteenth century, Dresden developed into a center for the chocolate industry. New production methods made the former luxury item into an everyday commodity. The Dresden chocolate factory Otto Rüger, founded in 1838 by August Ferdinand Lobeck and Carl Christian Petzold, was taken over in 1860 by Otto Rüger, who also operated a confectionery store. He marketed his cacao powder in storage tins decorated with the motif of the *Chocolate Girl*.

SD

Literature: Rüger/Rüger 1975; Fabian/Möge/Wünsche 2006, pp. 189–94; Starke 2013, pp. 55, 63, Landsberg 2014, p. 99.

Cat. 100

Sönksen S. A.

Oval tin "Azedinhas – Sortidas"

Mid twentieth century

Tin plate, H. 2.5 cm, L. 8.2 cm, W. 6.5 cm

Private collection, Brazil

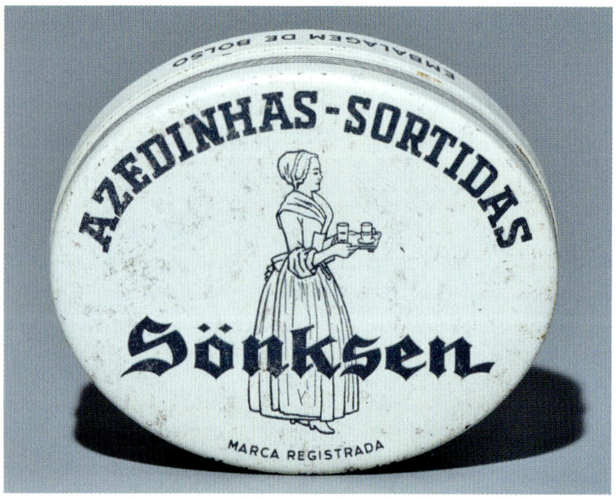

These two objects from the Brazilian confectionery company Sönksen are examples of the wide reach, even beyond Europe, of the *Chocolate Girl*'s appeal and popularity as an advertising motif. The cover of the booklet commemorating the firm's seventieth anniversary shows a picture of Liotard's *Chocolatière* without any background and with the firm's name printed in red letters across her skirt. Her image also appears several times inside the booklet and stands for the highest quality and perfection in the field of chocolate and sweets. A *Chocolate Girl* rendered in black outlines also adorns the lid of the small, white oval tin, again with the brand name printed across her skirt. Curving around the upper edge are the words "Azedinhas – Sortida," i.e. "assorted [fruit] pastilles." Red and green versions of this tin were also produced, as well as round and tall ones. Sönksen furthermore reproduced the *Chocolate Girl* on small coffee cups, here wearing a green skirt against a yellow background.

The booklet documents the firm's history in great detail. Presumably the first confectionery company in São Paulo, it was founded in 1889 by Alfredo Richter under the name La Bonbonniere. Family connections in Germany brought the confectioner Christian Sönksen and his brother August from northern Germany to Brazil, where they took over the firm in 1910. Along with the chocolate now also being produced, they expanded the range of boiled sweets, and added gingerbread as well. Until it went into administration in 1983, the firm was using the *Chocolate Girl* as its logo thanks to a personal connection: the brothers' grandmother, Johanna Grollmuss, born in Dresden, had probably brought a copy of the picture to Brazil, which is how the Sönksen brothers came to know the image and began to use it in their marketing (see cat. nos. 98, 101).

SD

Literature: Nascimento 2018.

Cat. 101

Nestlé S. A.

Cacao Tin

Circa 2000

Tin plate, painted in brown, gold, and white,

H. 14.4 cm, W. 12.1 cm, D. 8.1 cm

Collection Petra Landsberg, Dresden

This hexagonal brown tin with gold vertical stripes features on the broad side a white label with the text in gold: "Nestlé. Feine heiße Schokolade." Above the lettering is a tall cup with saucer, spoon, and two bars of chocolate. The narrow sides feature a reproduction of the *Chocolate Girl* in sepia tones, captioned with "'Das Schokoladenmädchen' 1745 Gemäldegalerie Dresden." Here, however, the *Chocolate Girl* is not part of the firm's logo. Printed on the lid are the company name and the tin's contents.

Like many other companies, the food and drinks conglomerate Nestlé, founded in 1866 and, since its acquisition in 1929 of the Swiss chocolate manufacturers Peter, Cailler and Kohler, also a major force in the confectionery industry, made use of

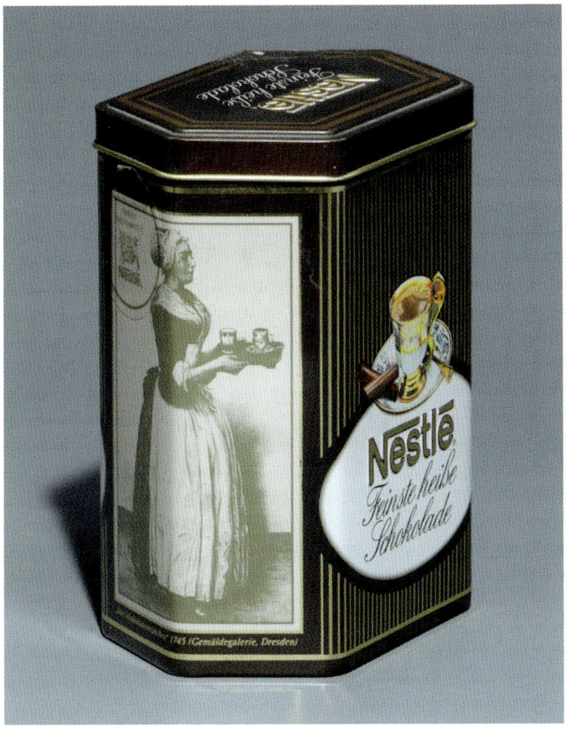

Dresden's *Chocolate Girl* as an advertising motif to promote its cacao powder, although, in contrast to the chocolate firm Otto Rüger (cat. 98), only temporarily.
Overall, Liotard's *Belle Chocolatière* can look back on widespread, even global success as an advertising icon. The American Walter Baker Company used her as its logo from 1877 onward and the Brazilian Sönksen firm (cat. 99, 100) from the beginning of the twentieth century. The motif has also been used in slightly altered form: from 1881 it decorated the cacao tins of the English Rowntree brand in the form of a serving girl adapted from Liotard, but with a long braid, and from 1900 the Dutch companies De Jong and Van Houten pictured her dressed in national costume, while the Droste confectionery firm used a picture of a nurse reminiscent of the *Chocolate Girl*—all of them carrying cups of chocolate on a tray.

SD

Literature: Heer 1991, pp. 118–58.

Cat. 102

Bäckerei Scholze GmbH

Stollen packaging "Original Dresdner Stollen"

Dresden, undated (twenty-first century)

Cardboard, H. 5 cm, L. 24 cm, W. 12 cm

Collection Petra Landsberg, Dresden

This stollen packaging by the Dresden-based bakery Scholze features Liotard's *Chocolate Girl* in half-figure in front of a blue background. In the center is an image of a partly sliced stollen on a wooden board, grouped around it are famous Dresden landmarks, such as the Frauenkirche and the Semperoper. The delicate rocaille ornament curving around the right-hand side of the box recalls the original frame of the Liotard pastel. The lettering on the box is in both German and Cyrillic, as in the early 2000s the bakery was also producing stollen for the Russian market.
The *Chocolate Girl* is here again being used as an advertising motif, in this case for traditional stollen, an indication of how closely the image is associated with Dresden's culinary indulgences. In its present form, Dresden stollen dates back to the late fifteenth century, when butter, dried fruit, and sugar were first added to plain fasting bread, thereby giving it its typical sweet taste. To this day it is being produced by the various Dresden bakeries, often family businesses, each using their own individual recipe.

JMG

Literature: Rudoph 2013, p. 115, Landsberg 2014, pp. 105–06.

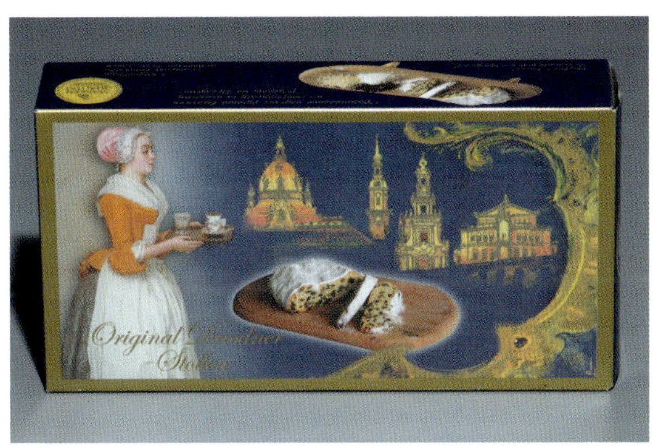

Cat. 103

Postcard Café Robert Beyer

After 1919

Print on paper, 8.9 x 13.9 cm

Inscribed at the bottom: "Ehrhard Schmorl, Rob. Beyer's Konditorei, Dresden-A. Buffett- und Eingangsseite der Gasträume im 1. Stock"

Private collection, Dresden

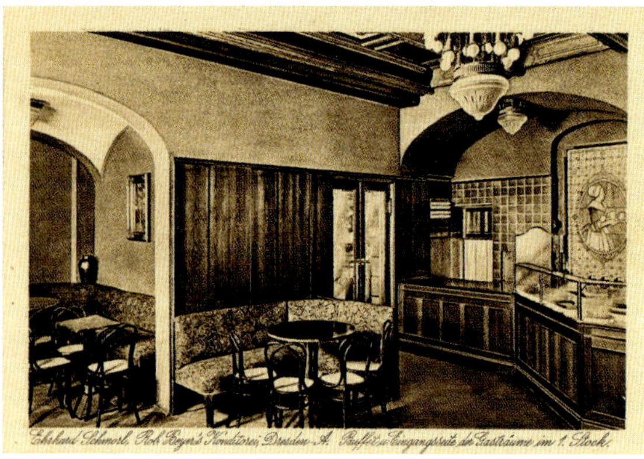

This photographic print shows the interior of the Dresden café Robert Beyer after its refurbishment in 1919. The rooms on the second floor featured panelled ceilings and walls. The cake and service counter is visible on the right; the wall behind it is faced with plain tiles on the left and on the right with a tile version of the *Chocolate Girl.* She is pictured as a half-figure in an oval cartouche. The building was destroyed in the Second World War and no record exists of the picture's coloring.

The café's name dates back to the confectioner Robert Beyer, who in 1870/71 had opened a small shop at Marienstrasse 28. In 1878 he moved his confectionery store to Wilsdruffer Strasse 20, not far from Dresden's Altmarkt. In 1916 Ehrhard Schmorl leased the store and expanded it. The choice of the *Chocolate Girl* as interior decor for a café was made again nearly a century later: in the 1960s, Krista Grunicke designed a collage for an ice cream parlour on Neustädter Markt, consisting of twenty-two pictures of the *Chocolate Girl* combined with Dresden landmarks, which continued to adorn the café until the early 1990s.

SD

Literature: Them 2011, pp. 49–52; Landsberg 2014, p. 87.

Cat. 104

Verlag Junge Welt

Druckerei Franz Maecker

Paper Theater – Sheet of pictures "Ein Fest im Dresdner Zwinger"

East Berlin, 1984

Color screen print on paper, 29.5 x 42 cm

Collection Petra Landsberg, Dresden

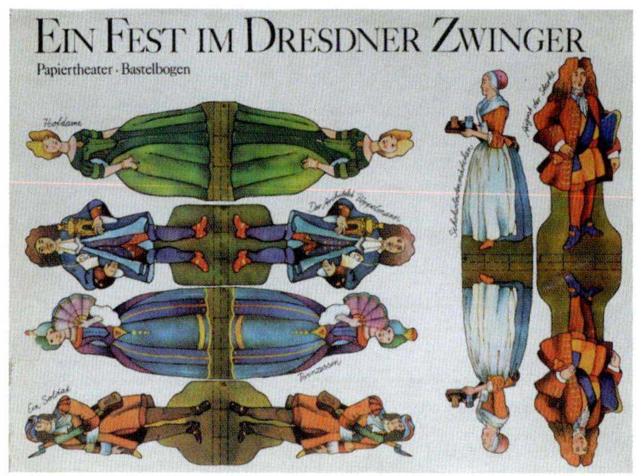

The sheet *Ein Fest im Dresdner Zwinger* features six colored figures and a Zwinger backdrop to be cut out. Along with such historical figures as Augustus the Strong and the architect Matthäus Daniel Pöppelmann, the *Chocolate Girl* appears as a coequal. These three are joined by a nameless lady-in-waiting, a princess, and a soldier. Although created in Vienna, here the *Chocolatière* is deliberately placed in the context of eighteenth-century festivities at the Saxon court. Though the pairing suggests otherwise, Liotard painted the pastel only after the death of Augustus II, who died in 1733.

Inexpensive paper theaters already enjoyed great popularity and wide distribution in the nineteenth century. The range of subjects was virtually unlimited. The sheets frequently pictured figural groupings or genre scenes that could be both informative and edifying. The small town of Neuruppin in Brandenburg was an early center for the production of such sheets. During the GDR era, the Berlin-based publisher of children's books Junge Welt continued the tradition of Neuruppin theater cut-out sheets.

JMG

Literature: Riedel 1984, pp. 3–4; Rockel 1995, pp. 6–7; Links 2010, pp. 261–62; Landsberg 2014, p. 57.

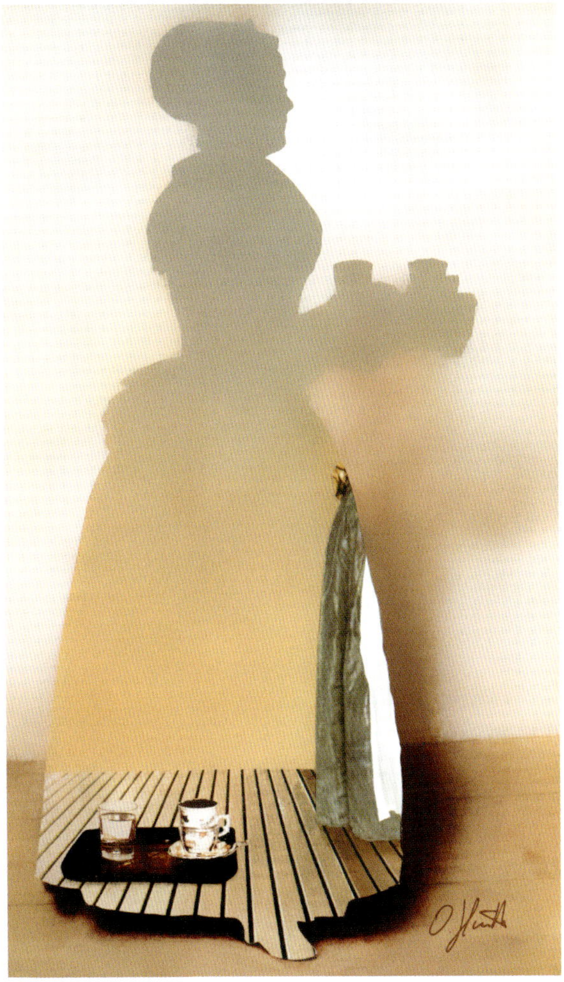

Cat. 105

Dieter Härtel

(born Görlitz 1952)

Out of the Frame

2010 (collage 1986)

Mixed technique / collage, direct print on canvas, 36 x 23 cm

Hand-signed

Private collection, Dresden

Against a light, marbled background, the silhouette of Liotard's *Chocolate Girl* is outlined, casting a shadow on the wall just as in the original pastel. Within this outline are further echoes of the picture: the tray with the water glass and cup has been set down on the floorboards; within the outline of her skirt the back of the original skirt can be seen in color—the girl has left her tray behind and has stepped out of her own shadow and thus her expected role.

The original collage was made in 1986 from a paper reproduction of the *Chocolate Girl*. Härtel cut out its outline and added a suitable background and floorboards. He then pasted in the skirt and tray, slightly retouched. In the 1980s, inspired by such Surrealist artists as René Magritte, Max Ernst, and Adolf Hoffmeister, Härtel began adapting versions of the works of Old Masters to ironically question and dismantle our accustomed ways of seeing. In the 2000s he digitized a slide of the collage—which no longer exists in original—reworked it using image processing software, and printed an edition of twenty copies in a 100 x 60 cm format. The copy shown here is a special print in a smaller size.

SD

Literature: Nowak 1986.

JEAN-ÉTIENNE LIOTARD

Biography

1702–1723
Liotard is born on December 22, a son of the French Huguenot and merchant Antoine Liotard and his wife Anne Sauvage, in Calvinist Geneva.
Training together with his twin brother Jean-Michel as a miniature and enamel painter, presumably under Daniel Gerdelle in Geneva.

1723–1735
Sojourn in Paris. Liotard studies for three years under the miniature painter and engraver Jean-Baptiste Massé. Paints his first self-portrait in around 1731.

1735–1737
Journeys to Naples with Louis Philogène Brûlart, Marquis de Puysieux, the French ambassador in Naples. Stays in Rome and Florence.

1738–1742
Journeys with William Ponsonby, later 2nd Earl of Bessborough, and John Montagu, 4th Earl of Sandwich, by way of the Greek islands to Constantinople (Istanbul), where he stays for four years.
In addition to costume studies, he produces drawings and paintings of political dignitaries of the Ottoman Empire and Europeans residing on the Bosporus, wearing Turkish clothing.

1742–1743
At the invitation of Prince Constantine Mavrocordatos of Moldavia, Liotard spends ten months at his court in Jassy. From this time on he adopts "Turkish" clothing and grows a long beard.

1743–1744
Visits Vienna for the first time. Close association with Maria Theresa and her husband Francis Stephen of Lorraine, later Holy Roman Emperor as Francis I. On commission from the latter he paints his *Self-Portrait* for the Uffizi. Liotard paints the *Chocolate Girl*.

1745–1746
Travels to Venice to see his brother Jean-Michel. Becomes acquainted with Count Francesco Algarotti, who purchases *The Chocolate Girl* for the Saxon elector Frederick Augustus II.
Proceeds to Frankfurt for the coronation of Francis I, and from there to Darmstadt. Portrait of *Princess Caroline Louise of Hesse-Darmstadt* at her easel.

1746–1748
Returns to Geneva. Travels to Basel and Lyon.
Portrait of his niece Marie Anne Lavergne, *La Liseuse*.

1748–1753
Sojourns in Paris. Maurice of Saxony arranges access to the French court at Versailles. Portraits of the royal family. Although he is never accepted into the Académie Royale, starting in 1749 he calls himself "Peintre ordinaire du roi", and under this title exhibits at the Salon de l'Academie de Saint-Luc. Engravings are made after his oriental drawings.

1753–1754
Sojourn in London. William Ponsonby arranges portrait commissions, among them from the royal family.

1755–1756
Sojourn in the Netherlands (Delft, The Hague, and Amsterdam). Paints portraits of the royal house of Orange-Nassau. Acquires the greater part of his collection of Dutch art of the seventeenth century.
On August 13, 1756 marries Marie Fargues, the daughter of a French Huguenot merchant in Amsterdam.

1757
Returns to Geneva. Paints a number of portraits of Genevan patricians, including the art collector and council member François Tronchin. Liotard's first son Jean–Étienne (1758) and first daughter Marie-Jeanne (1761) are born.

1762
Second visit to Vienna. Liotard produces eleven color drawings of Maria Theresa's children and pastel portraits of the imperial pair.

1763–1770
Birth of his daughter Marie-Thérèse (1763), whose godmother is Maria Theresa, and of Jean-Daniel (1764) and Marie-Anne Françoise (1767).
Liotard paints his only landscape.

1770–1771
Lyon and Paris. Portraits of Jean-Jacques Rousseau and Marie-Antoinette.

1771–1773
Second visit to the Netherlands. Liotard is awarded only few commissions.

1773–1774
Second stay in London. Again commissions through the Earl of Bessborough. Exhibits at the Royal Academy of Arts.

1774
Returns to Geneva.

1777–1778
Third visit to Vienna.
Emperor Joseph II visits Liotard in his studio under the pseudonym Duke of Falkenstein.

1781
Liotard publishes his *Traité des principes et des règles de la peinture.*

1782
Liotard's wife dies. He paints mainly still lifes and trompe-l'oeils.

1789
Liotard dies on 12 June.
His estate remains in the family for nearly one hundred years. In 1873 and 1885 the Rijksmuseum in Amsterdam makes purchases from it, and in 1934 the Musée d'art et d'histoire in Geneva acquires the majority of the remaining works.

BIBLIOGRAPHY

A.S. 1884
A.S., "Ad. Brauns Photographien nach Gemälden der Dresdener Galerie," in: *Kunstchronik* 19 (1884), Cols. 331–332.

Algarotti Opere
Francesco Algarotti, *Opere, Edizione Novissima*, 8 vols., Venice 1791–1794.

Alpatow 1966
Michail W. Alpatow, *Die Dresdner Galerie Alte Meister*, Dresden 1966.

Amtliches Verzeichnis 1851
Amtliches Verzeichnis der aus dem Deutschen Zollverein und Norddeutschland zur Industrie-Ausstellung aller Völker in London eingesandten Gegenstände . . ., Berlin 1851.

Arnold 1966
Ulli Arnold, *Dinglingers Tafelgeschirr*, Leipzig 1966.

Avcıoğlu 2011
Nebahat Avcıoğlu, *Turquerie and the politics of representation, 1728–1876*, Farnham 2011.

Bachmann 1968
Manfred Bachmann, *Zur Geschichte der Seiffener Volkskunst, Sonderdruck aus Abhandlungen und Berichte des Staatlichen Museums für Völkerkunde Dresden*, vol. 28, Berlin 1968.

Bachmann 1971
Manfred Bachmann, "Das Schokoladenmädchen von J. E. Liotard als Motiv der Volkskunst," in: *Dresdener Kunstblätter* 15, no. 6 (1971), pp. 180–185.

Bachmann 1996
Manfred Bachmann, "Es leben die Schokoladenmädchen! Adaption eines populären Gemäldes in Werbung und Kunsthandwerk," in: *Sachsenbummel. Magazin für Kulturgeschichte und Tourismus* 4, no. 12 (1996), pp. 18–19.

Bachmann/Tinhofer 1998
Manfred Bachmann and Monika Tinhofer, *Osterhase, Nikolaus & Zeppelin. Schokoladenformen im Spiegel alter Musterbücher*, Husum 1998.

Bader 2013
Lena Bader, *Bild-Prozesse im 19. Jahrhundert. Der Holbein-Streit und die Ursprünge der Kunstgeschichte*, diss. Humboldt-Universität Berlin 2010, Paderborn 2013.

Badstübner 1973
Ernst Badstübner et al., *Christliche Ikonographie in Stichworten*, Leipzig 1973.

Baillie 1947/1972
Granville Hugh Baillie, *Watchmakers and Clockmakers of the World*, London 1947 (reprint 1972).

Bauer 1985
Roger Bauer, "'Luxus' in Österreich: Joseph von Sonnenfels zwischen Jean-Jacques Rousseau und Adam Smith," in: *Österreich im Europa der Aufklärung. Kontinuität und Zäsur in Europa zur Zeit Maria Theresias und Josephs II.*, Internationales *Symposium Wien 20.–23.10.1980*, Vienna 1985, pp. 319–334.

Beerli 1955
Frieda Beerli, *Jean-Étienne Liotard. Die Kinder der Kaiserin. Zwölf farbige Bildnisse der Kinder Maria Theresias*, Wiesbaden 1955.

Beraldi 1891
Henri Béraldi, *Les Graveurs du XIXe siècle*, vol. 11, Paris 1891.

Berger 1896/1897
Ernst Berger, "Pastellfarben," in: *Deutsche Kunst* 1, no. 24 (1896/97), pp. 280–281.

Bianconi 1781
Giovanni Lodovico Bianconi, *Historische Lobschrift auf den Ritter Anton Raphael Mengs nebst einem Verzeichniße seiner Werke*, Zürich 1781.

Biermann 2007
Dietmar Biermann, "Der Zarenwodka kommt aus Berlin," in: *Lebensmittel Zeitung* 2007, no. 15, Länder Report Berlin-Brandenburg, p. 52.

Bischoff 2009
Ulrich Bischoff, "Hann Trier," in: *Defiance & Melancholy. German Painting from the Dresden Albertinum / Galerie Neue Meister*, exh. cat. Art Museum Meilahti, Helsinki City Art Museum, Helsinki 2009.

Blaauwen 2000
Abraham L. den Blaauwen, *Meissen porcelain in the Rijksmuseum*, Catalogues of the Decorative Arts in the Rijksmuseum, vol. 4, Amsterdam 2000.

Blankaart 1705
Stephan Blankaart, *Haustus Polychresti, Oder: Zuverlässige Gedancken Vom Thée, Coffée, Chocolate, Und Taback, Mit welchen Der grosse Nutze dieser ausländischen Wahren so wol in gesunden als krancken Tagen . . .*, Hamburg 1705.

Boeckh 1982
Hans Boeckh, *Emailmalerei auf Genfer Taschenuhren vom 17. bis zum beginnenden 19. Jahrhundert*, Freiburg im Breisgau 1982.

Boesch 1996
Christiane Boesch, "Gruner, Erich," in: *Die Leipziger Kunstgewerbeschule. Eine Dokumentation zu Geschichte und Wirkung der Kunstgewerbeschule der Stadt Leipzig und ihrer Vorgänger- und Nachfolgeeinrichtungen*, exh. cat. Museum für Kunsthandwerk/ Grassimuseum Leipzig, ed. Ute Camphausen, Leipzig 1996, pp. 193–194.

Boltz 1978
Claus Boltz, "Ein Beitrag zum grünen Watteau-Service für Neapel," in: *Keramos* 79 (1978), pp. 5–25.

Bontekoe 1692
Cornelius Bontekoe, *Kurtze Abhandlung Von dem Menschlichen Leben, Gesundheit, Kranckheit, und Tod*, Bautzen 1692.

Boudon-Machuel 2005
Marion Boudon-Machuel, *François du Quesnoy 1597–1643*, Paris 2005.

Bourguignon d'Anville 1721
Jean-Baptiste Bourguignon d'Anville, "Mémoire où il est question de la Peinture des Turcs & des Persans, de la façon dont les Turcs meublent leur apartemens, & principalement de la richesse des apartemens du Sérail du grand-Seigneur," in: *Le Nouveau Mércure*, April 1721, pp. 25–51.

Braun & Cie 1887
Ad. Braun & Cie, *Catalogue général des photographies inaltérables au charbon et héliogravures*, Paris and Dornach 1887.

Braunfels 1986
Wolfgang Braunfels, *François Cuvilliés. Der Baumeister der galanten Architektur des Rokoko*, Munich 1986.

Bräutigam 2008
Herbert Bräutigam, *Schätze japanischer Lackkunst auf Schloß Friedenstein, Schloßmuseum Gotha*, Gotha 2008.

Brüggemann 1988
Erich Brüggemann, *Kunst und Technik der Intarsien. Werkzeug und Material – Anregungen und Beispiele*, Munich 1988.

Buchheit 1911
Hans Buchheit, *Katalog der Miniaturbilder im Bayerischen Nationalmuseum*, Munich 1911.

Cardinal 1999
Catherine Cardinal, *Splendeurs de l'émail. Montres et horloges du XVIe au XXe siècle, Institut L'homme et le temps*, La Chaux-de-Fonds 1999.

Cassidy-Geiger 2007
Maureen Cassidy-Geiger, "Princes and Porcelain on the Grand Tour of Italy," in: *Fragile diplomacy, Meissen porcelain for European Courts ca. 1710–63*, ed. Maureen Cassidy-Geiger, New Haven und London 2007, pp. 208–255.

Cassirer/Helbing 1926
Erwin Hensler, ed., *Ludwig Schnorr von Carolsfeld. Auktionskatalog Paul Cassirer und Hugo Helbing: Aus Königlich Sächsischem Besitz im Auftrag des Hauses Wettin Albertinische Linie e.V. Mit einem Anhang von Kunstgegenständen aus Gräflich Brühlschem Besitz und anderem Besitz*, Berlin 1926.
Catalogue 1790
Catalogue Des Médailles Et Monnoies Antiques Du Cabinet De Feu Monsieur Quintus Icilius, Potsdam 1790.
Chennevières 1888
Henry de Chennevières, "Liotard," in: *L'art* 14 (1888), pp. 225–230.
Christoph 1908
Paul Christoph, ed., *Maria Theresia. Geheimer Briefwechsel mit Marie Antoinette*, Vienna und Munich 1908.
Ciancio 1999
Valentina Ciancio, "Signor Conte Rotari, dilettante di pittura« am Dresdener Hof – Archiv Nachforschungen," in: Gregor J.M. Weber, *Pietro Graf Rotari in Dresden. Ein italienischer Maler am Hof König Augusts III., Ausstellungs- und Bestandskatalog, Gemäldegalerie Alte Meister, Staatliche Kunstsammlungen Dresden*, Emsdetten and Dresden 1999.
Ciancio 2009
Valentina Ciancio, "Francesco Algarotti und die Galerie der modernen Maler am Hof von Dresden (1742–1746)," in: Hans Schumacher and Brunhilde Wehinger, eds., *Francesco Algarotti. Ein philosophischer Hofmann im Jahrhundert der Aufklärung*, Hannover 2009, pp. 151–159.
Corvinus 1715
Gottlieb Siegmund Corvinus, called Amaranthes, *Nutzbares, galantes und cürieuses Frauenzimmer-Lexicon*, Leipzig 1715.
Corvinus 1739
Gottlieb Siegmund Corvinus, called Amaranthes, *Nutzbares, galantes und curiöses Frauenzimmer-Lexicon*, Leipzig 1739.
Crell 1719
Johann Christian Crell, *Das Fast auf dem höchsten Gipffel der Vollkommenheit Prangende Dreßden, Oder Kurtze doch deutliche Beschreibung Derer In dieser Stadt berühmten Gebäude und Merckwürdigkeiten* . . . , Leipzig 1719.
Curieuse Beschreibung 1743
Curieuse Beschreibung des Thee, Coffee, und Choccolade-Trancks: wie auch des überaus herrlichen und nützlichen Chinesischen Saamens, Padian oder Anisum Stellatum Chinense . . . , Augsburg 1743.
D'Aunoy 1696
Marie Catherine D'Aunoy, *Der Gräfin D'Aunoy Beschreibung ihrer Reise nach Spanien*, Leipzig 1696.
Danckert 1992
Ludwig Danckert, *Handbuch des Europäischen Porzellans*, Munich 1992.
De Ren 1998
Leo de Ren, "Das Tafelsilber des Prinzen Karl Alexander von Lothringen," in: Ilsebill Barta-Fliedl, Andreas Gugler, and Peter Parenzan, eds., *Tafeln bei Hofe. Zur Geschichte der fürstlichen Tafelkultur. Eine Publikationsreihe der Museen des Mobiliendepots, Sammlungsband 4*, Hamburg 1998, pp. 73–80.
De Sacken 1876
Jean Gustave de Sacken, "Korrespondenzen zum Ankauf der Bildergalerie der Grafen Brühl," in: *Sbornik imperatorskago russkago istoričeskago obščestva* 17 (1876).
Debrie/Salmon 2000
Christine Debrie and Xavier Salmon, *Maurice-Quentin de La Tour, prince des pastellistes*, Paris 2000.
Degiorgio/Fiorentino 2004
Stephen Degiorgio and Emmanuel Fiorentino, *Antoine de Favray (1706–1798), A French Artist in Rome, Malta and Constantinople*, Valletta 2004.
Dehmer 2013
Andreas Dehmer, "'Wunderwelt der alten Bilder.' Kunsterfahrungen Neuer Meister in der Dresdner Gemäldegalerie," in: *Constable, Delacroix, Friedrich, Goya. Die Erschütterung der Sinne*, exh. cat. Albertinum, Staatliche Kunstsammlungen Dresden, ed. Ulrich Bischoff and Luc Tuymans, Dresden 2013, pp. 164–173.
Del Castillo 2017
Bernal Diaz del Castillo, *Geschichte der Eroberung von Mexiko*, ed. Georg Adolf Narciß, Berlin 2017.
[Demiani] 1817
[Karl Friedrich Demiani], *Catalogue explicatif des tableaux de la Galerie Royale de Dresde*, Dresden 1817.
Denk 2017
Claudia Denk, "At any Price! Jean-Etienne Liotard's self-marketing strategy and the extravagance de son prix," in: Andreas Tacke et al., eds., *Kunstmärkte zwischen Stadt und Hof. Prozesse der Preisbildung in der europäischen Vormoderne*, Petersberg 2017, pp. 120–134.
Diderot/d'Alembert 1765
Denis Diderot and Jean Baptiste le Rond d'Alembert, *Encyclopédie ou Dictionnaire raisonné des Sciences, des Arts et des Métiers*, vol. III., Planches, Paris 1765.
Döring 2013
Jürgen Döring, *Als Kitsch noch Kunst war. Farbendruck im 19. Jahrhundert*, exh. cat. Museum für Kunst und Gewerbe, Hamburg, Berlin and Munich 2013.
Dresdner Anzeiger 1883
"Der Besuch Sr. Maiestät des Königs in Dippoldiswalde," *Dresdner Anzeiger* 153, no 172, 21 June 1883, first insert.
Duncan 1707
Daniel Duncan, *Von dem Mißbrauch heißer und hitziger Speisen und Geträncke, sonderlich aber Des Caffes, Schockolate und Thees*, Leipzig 1707.
Düriegl 1985
Günter Düriegl, "Wien – eine Residenzstadt im Übergang von der adeligen Metropole zur bürgerlichen Urbanität," in: *Österreich im Europa der Aufklärung. Kontinuität und Zäsur in Europa zur Zeit Maria Theresias und Josephs II., Internationales Symposium Wien 20.–23.10.1980*, Vienna 1985, pp. 305–317.
Durry/Schiffer 2008
Andrea Durry and Thomas Schiffer, *Das Schokoladenmuseum: Geschichte und Gegenwart der Schokolade*, Cologne 2008.
Durry/Schiffer 2012
Andrea Durry and Thomas Schiffer, *Kakao: Speise der Götter*, München 2012.
Enke 2018
Roland Enke, "Schloss Weesenstein als Auslagerungsort für die Werke der Dresdner Gemäldegalerie," in: *Bombensicher! Kunstversteck Weesenstein 1945*, exh. cat. Schloss Weesenstein, Staatliche Schlösser, Burgen und Gärten Sachsen GmbH, ed. Birgit Finger and Robert Hänel, Dresden 2018, pp. 60–74.
Etienne 2017
Noémie Etienne, *The restoration of paintings in Paris, 1750–1815*, Los Angeles 2017.
Etienne/Lee 2018
Noémie Etienne and Chonja Lee, "Lüster, Lack und Liotard. Techniken und Texturen zwischen Asien und Europa: die glänzende Oberfläche à l'imitation de la Chine ist ein medienübergreifendes Phänomen," in: *Kunst + Architektur in der Schweiz* 69, no. 1 (2018), pp. 4–11.
Ettner 1719
Johann Christoph Ettner, *Des getreuen Eckharts Medicinischen Maul-Affens Erster Theil oder Der entlarvte Marktschreyer*, Leipzig 1719 (reprint of the Liegnitz 1694 ed.).
Euler-Schmidt 1995
Michael Euler-Schmidt, ed., *Hann Trier. Werkverzeichnis der Gemälde 1990–1995*, Cologne 1995.
Exh. cat. Ascoli Piceno 1999
Pier Leone Ghezzi. Settecento alla moda, exh. cat. Palazzo dei Capitani, Ascoli Piceno, ed. Anna Lo Bianco, Venice 1999.
Exh. cat. Berlin 1976
Plauener Spitze, exh. cat. Staatlicher Kunsthandel der DDR, Berlin 1976.
Exh. cat. Bordeaux/Geneva/Paris 1995
L'age d'or du petit portrait, exh. cat. Musée des Arts décoratifs, Bordeaux; Musée de l'Horlogerie, Geneva; Musée du Louvre, Paris, ed. Anne de Margerie, Paris 1995.
Exh. cat. Cologne 2010
Meissen. Barockes Porzellan, exh. cat. Museum für Angewandte Kunst, Cologne, ed. Patricia Brattig, Stuttgart 2010.
Exh. cat. Dortmund 2008
Kirchengold & Tafelsilber. Die Sammlung von Silberarbeiten im Museum für Kunst und Kulturgeschichte Dortmund, exh. cat. Museum für Kunst und Kulturgeschichte, Dortmund, ed. Brigitte Buberl, Berlin and Munich 2008.
Exh. cat. Dresden 1991
"Ey! wie schmeckt der Coffee süße." Meissener Porzellan und Graphik, exh. cat. Porzellansammlung, Staatliche Kunstsammlungen Dresden, ed. Klaus-Peter Arnold, Ulla Heise, and Michael Ropers, Dresden 1991.
Exh. cat. Dresden 2001
Mengs. Die Erfindung des Klassizismus, exh. cat. Staatliche Kunstsammlungen Dresden, Residenzschloss, ed. Steffi Roettgen, Munich 2001.
Exh. cat. Dresden 2008
Goldener Drache – Weißer Adler. Kunst im Dienste der Macht am Kaiserhof in China und am sächsisch-polnischen Hof (1644–1795), exh. cat. Staatliche Kunstsammlungen Dresden, Residenzschloss, ed. Cordula Bischoff and Anne Henning, Munich 2008.

Exh. cat. Dresden 2009
Sehnsucht und Wirklichkeit. Wunschbilder: Malerei für Dresden im 18. Jahrhundert, exh. cat. Gemäldegalerie Alte Meister, Staatliche Kunstsammlungen Dresden, ed. Harald Marx, Dresden 2009.
Exh. cat. Dresden 2010
Triumph der blauen Schwerter. Meissener Porzellan für Adel und Bürgertum 1710–1815, exh. cat. Porzellansammlung, Staatliche Kunstsammlungen Dresden, ed. Ulrich Pietsch and Claudia Banz, Leipzig 2010.
Exh. cat. Dresden 2013
Schokoladenstadt Dresden. Süßigkeiten aus Elbflorenz, exh. cat. Stadtmuseum Dresden, ed. Erika Eschebach and Holger Starke, Dresden 2013.
Exh. cat. Dresden 2017
Miniatur-Geschichten. Die Sammlung indischer Malerei im Dresdner Kupferstich-Kabinett, exh. cat. Kupferstich-Kabinett, Staatliche Kunstsammlungen Dresden, ed. Monica Juneja and Petra Kuhlmann-Hodick, Dresden 2017.
Exh. cat. Dresden/Bonn 1995
Im Lichte des Halbmonds. Das Abendland und der türkische Orient, exh. cat. Albertinum, Staatliche Kunstsammlungen Dresden; Kunst- und Ausstellungshalle der Bundesrepublik Deutschland Bonn, Dresden 1995.
Exh. cat. Edinburgh/London 2015
Jean-Etienne Liotard, 1702–1789, exh. cat. Scottish National Gallery, Edinburgh; Royal Academy of Arts, London, London 2015.
Exh. cat. Geneva/Paris 1992
Dessins de Liotard. Suivi du catalogue de l'œuvre dessiné, exh. cat. Musée d'art et d'histoire, Geneva; Musée du Louvre, Paris, ed. Anne de Herdt, Paris 1992.
Exh. cat. Karlsruhe 2015
Die Meistersammlerin Karoline Luise von Baden, exh. cat. Staatliche Kunsthalle Karlsruhe, ed. Holger Jacob-Friesen and Pia Müller-Tamm, Berlin und Munich 2015.
Exh. cat. Lausanne 2018
Pastels du 16e au 21e siècle. Liotard, Degas, Klee, Scully . . ., exh. cat. Fondation de l'Hermitage, Lausanne, ed. Sylvie Wuhrmann and Aurélie Couvreur, Lausanne 2018.
Exh. cat. London 2003
Below stairs. 400 years of servants' portraits, exh. cat. National Portrait Gallery, London, ed. Giles Waterhouse, Anne French, and Matthew Craske, London 2003.
Exh. cat. Mannheim 2012
Sammeln! Die Kunstkammer des Kaisers in Wien, exh. Reiss-Engelhorn-Museen, Mannheim, ed. Sabine Haag and Alfried Wieczorek, Munich etc. 2012.
Exh. cat. München 1994
Silber und Gold. Augsburger Goldschmiedekunst für die Höfe Europas, exh. cat. Bayerisches Nationalmuseum, Munich, ed. Reinhold Baumstark and Helmut Seling, catalogue by Lorenz Seelig, Munich 1994.
Exh. cat. Paris 2008
Marie-Antoinette, exh. cat. Galeries nationales du Grand Palais, Paris, ed. Pierre Arizzoli-Clémentel and Xavier Salmon, Paris 2008.
Exh. cat. Schloss Charlottenburg 2001
Preußen 1701. Eine europäische Geschichte, exh. cat. Schloss Charlottenburg, Berlin, ed. Deutsches Historisches Museum and the Stiftung Preußische Schlösser und Gärten, Berlin-Brandenburg, Berlin 2001.
Exh. cat. Schloss Schönbrunn 1980
Maria Theresia und ihre Zeit. Zur 200. Wiederkehr des Todestages, exh. cat. Schloß Schönbrunn, im Auftrag der österreichischen Bundesregierung veranstaltet vom Bundesministerium für Wissenschaft und Forschung, Salzburg 1980.
Exh. cat. Segovia 2009
La porcelana de Meissen en la Colección Britzke. 1709–1765. Das Meissner Porzellan der Britzke-Sammlung, exh. cat. Obra Social y Cultural de Caja, Segovia, ed. Carmen de Aréchaga y Rodríguez-Pascual, Segovia 2009.
Exh. cat. Versailles 2004
Xavier Salmon, Le voleurs d'âmes – Maurice Quentin de La Tour, exh. cat. Musée national des châteaux de Versailles et de Trianon, Versailles 2004.
Exh. cat. Versailles/Münster 2001
Japanische Lacke. Die Sammlung der Königin Marie-Antoinette, exh. cat. Musée national des châteaux de Versailles et de Trianon; Museum für Lackkunst, Münster, ed. Monika Kopplin, Munich 2001.
Exh. cat. Vienna 2017
Maria Theresia 1717–1780: Strategin – Mutter – Reformerin, exh. cat. Schloss Hof, Schloss Niederweiden, Hofmobiliendepot – Möbel Museum, Vienna, Kaiserliche Wagenburg, Vienna, ed. Elfriede Iby et al., Vienna 2017.
Exh. cat. Völklingen 2005
Schätze aus 1001 Nacht. Faszination Morgenland, exh. cat. Völklinger Hütte, ed. Meinrad Maria Grewenig, Annweiler 2005.
Exh. cat. Zürich 1978
Jean-Etienne Liotard. Genf 1702–1789. Sammlung des Musée d'Art et d'Histoire, Geneva, exh. cat. Kunsthaus Zürich, ed. Felix Baumann and Romy Storrer, Zürich 1978.
Exposition 1839
Exposition des produits de l'industrie française en 1839, Rapport du Jury Central, vol. 3, Paris 1839.
Faber 1846
Friedrich Faber, *Conversations-Lexicon für Bildende Kunst*, vol. 3, Leipzig 1846.
Fabian/Möge/Wünsche 2006
Maike Fabian, Sirko Möge, and Katja Wünsche, "Lever mit Schokolade. Wie sich der Dresdner Geschmackssinn entwickelte," in: *Dresden. Ethnografische Erkundungen einer Residenzstadt*, ed. Rolf Lindner and Johannes Moser, Leipzig 2006, pp. 177–201.
Fehlmann 2015
Marc Fehlmann, "Orientalism," in: *Jean-Etienne Liotard, 1702–1789*, exh. cat. Scottish National Gallery, Edinburgh; Royal Academy of Arts, London, London 2015, pp. 65–71.
Ferriol 1714
Charles de Ferriol, ed., *Recueil de cent estampes représentant les diverses nations du Levant, tirées d'après nature en 1707 et 1708 par les ordres de M. de Ferriol, ambassadeur du Roy à la Porte et gravées en 1712 et 1713 par les soins de Le Hay*, Paris 1714.
Finger 2010
Birgit Finger, "Kunst oder Kommerz? Meissener Porzellan im 19. Jahrhundert," in: *Kunst oder Kommerz? Meissener Porzellan im 19. Jahrhundert, Ausstellungskatalog anlässlich der Jubiläumsausstellung "300 Jahre Mythos Manufaktur Meissen: Die Albrechtsburg als Porzellanschloss,"* ed. Staatliche Schlösser, Burgen, Gärten Sachsen, Dresden 2010, pp. 10–18.
Fischer/Skupin/Gudenschwager 1986
Peter Fischer, Frithjof Skupin, and Wolfgang Gudenschwager, eds., *DDR-Universalkatalog*, Berlin 1986.
Flügge/Penndorf 2012
Matthias Flügge and Jutta Penndorf, *STRAWALDE Jürgen Böttcher, Maler und Regisseur*, exh. cat. Lindenau-Museum, Altenburg 2012, Nuremberg 2012.
Forberg 2015
Corinna Forberg, *Die Rezeption indischer Miniaturen in der europäischen Kunst des 17. und 18. Jahrhunderts*, Petersberg 2015.
Fosca 1956
François Fosca, *La Vie, les voyages et le œuvres de Liotard, citoyen de Genève, dit le peintre turc*, Lausanne and Paris 1956.
Frank/Zimmermann 2015
Christoph Frank and Wolfgang Zimmermann, eds., *Aufgeklärter Kunstdiskurs und höfische Sammelpraxis. Karoline Luise von Baden im europäischen Kontext*, Munich 2015.
Fred 1914
Briefe der Kaiserin Maria Theresia, ed. Alfred W. Fred, vol. 1, Munich and Leipzig 1914.
Frieß 1993
Peter Frieß, *Kunst und Maschine. 500 Jahre Maschinenlinien in Bild und Skulptur*, Munich 1993.
Fuchs 1985
Siegfried E. Fuchs, *Der Bilderrahmen*, Recklinghausen 1985.
Gaba-van Dongen 2005
Alexandra Gaba-van Dongen, "Zwischen Wirklichkeit und Fantasie: Gebrauchsgegenstände auf holländischen Gemälden des siebzehnten Jahrhunderts," in: *Der Zauber des Alltäglichen. Holländische Malerei von Adriaen Brouwer bis Johannes Vermeer*, exh. cat. Museum Boijmans Van Beuningen, Rotterdam; Städelsches Kunstinstitut and Städtische Galerie, Ostfildern-Ruit 2005, pp. 30–39.
Gebhardt 1984
Heinz Gebhardt, *Franz Hanfstaengl, Von der Lithographie zur Photographie*, exh. cat. Münchner Stadtmuseum 1984, Munich 1984.
Genden 1910
Marie Genden, "Eine moderne Kaffeegesellschaft," in: *Die Welt der Frau*, enclosure in *Gartenlaube* 4 (1910), pp. 51-53.
Gerlach-Laxner 1990
Uta Gerlach-Laxner, "Werkverzeichnis der Gemälde," in: Sabine Fehlemann, ed., *Hann Trier, Monographie und Werkverzeichnis*, Cologne 1990, pp. 305–461.
Glöckner 2010
Glöckner – Gemälde und Zeichnungen. 1904–1945. Werkverzeichnis der Gemälde, Zeichnungen und Photographien, ed. Werner Schmidt, Christian Dittrich, Bernd Heise, and Sebastian Schmidt, Staatliche Kunstsammlungen Dresden, Kupferstich-Kabinett, Nachlass Hermann Glöckner, Dresden 2010.

Godycki 2017
Albert Godycki, "Jean Etienne Liotard and seventeenth-century Dutch painting," in: *The Burlington Magazine* 159, no. 1367 (2017), pp. 117–121.

Gombaud/Sauvage 2016
Cécile Gombaud and Leila Sauvage, "Liotard, Stoupan and the colours available to 18th-century European artists," in: *Sources on art technology: back to basics; 6th symposium of the ICOM-CC working group Art Technological source Research, Amsterdam 2014*, ed. Sigrid Eyb-Green et al., London 2016, pp. 115–123.

Gordon 2009
Bertram M. Gordon, "Chocolate in France. Evolution of a Luxury Product," in: *Chocolate: History, Culture, and Heritage*, ed. Louis Grivetti, Hoboken, N.J., 2009, pp. 569–582.

Görling 1851
Adolph Görling, *Die vorzüglichsten Gemälde der Dresdener Gallerie*, Leipzig and Dresden 1851.

Görling 1872
Adolph Görling, *Deutschlands Kunstschätze, eine Sammlung der hervorragendsten Gemälde der Berliner, Dresdener, Münchener, Wiener, Casseler und Braunschweiger Galerien, . . . mit biographischen Notizen von Alfred Woltmann und Bruno Meyer*, vol. 4, Leipzig 1872.

Graf 1977
Beatrix Graf, Werkstoffe und Technik der Pastellmalerei des 18. Jahrhunderts unter besonderer Berücksichtigung der Maltechnik Jean-Etienne Liotards auf Grund der Aufzeichnungen seiner Schülerin, Markgräfin Karoline Luise von Baden, unpublished graduate thesis, Institut für Technologie der Malerei, Staatliche Akademie der Bildenden Künste, Stuttgart 1977.

Graf 2006
Roland Graf, *Adeliger Luxus und städtische Armut. Eine soziokulturelle Studie zur Geschichte der Schokolade in Mitteleuropa vom 16. bis zum 18. Jahrhundert*, Vienna 2006.

Grivetti 2009
Louis Evan Grivetti, "From Bean to Beverage. Historical Chocolate Recipes," in: *Chocolate: History, Culture, and Heritage*, ed. Louis Grivetti, Hoboken, N.J., 2009, pp. 99–114.

Grossegger 1987
Elisabeth Grossegger, *Theater, Feste und Feiern zur Zeit Maria Theresias 1742–1776. Nach den Tagebucheintragungen des Fürsten Johann Joseph Khevenhüller-Metsch, Obersthofmeister der Kaiserin*, Vienna 1987.

Günther 1762
Georg Christoph Günther, *Praktische Anweisung zur Pastellmahlerey für Liebhaber und Mahler*, Nuremberg 1762.

Hafner 1700
Philipp Hafner, *Songes Hannswurstiques oder auf gut Chinesisch:Es* könnte einem nicht närrscher traumen, Vienna 1700.

Hanway 1753
Jonas Hanway, *An historical Account of the British Trade over the Caspian Sea, with a Journal of Travels*, vol. 2, London 1753.

Hasche 1783
Johann Christian Hasche, *Umständliche Beschreibung Dresdens mit allen seinen inneren und äußeren Merkwürdigkeiten historisch und architektonisch*, 2 vol., Leipzig 1783.

Haslinger 1993
Ingrid Haslinger, *Küche und Tafelkultur am kaiserlichen Hofe zu Wien. Zur Geschichte von Hofküche, Hofzuckerbäckerei und Hofsilber- und Tafelkammer*, Bern 1993.

Haslinger 1998
Ingrid Haslinger, "Die Wiener Silberkammer zur Zeit Maria Theresias," in: Ilsebill Barta-Fliedl, Andreas Gugler, and Peter Parenzan, eds., *Tafeln bei Hofe. Zur Geschichte der fürstlichen Tafelkultur*, Hamburg 1998.

Hauptmann 2015
William Hauptmann, "Painting in Dry-colours," in: *Jean-Etienne Liotard, 1702–1789*, exh. cat. Scottish National Gallery, Edinburgh; Royal Academy of Arts, London, London 2015, pp. 22–25.

Heer 1991
Jean Heer, *Nestlé. Hundertfünfundzwanzig Jahre von 1866 bis 1991*, Vevey 1991.

Heinz 1979
Gerhard Heinz, "Bemerkungen zur Geschichte der Malerei zur Zeit Maria Theresias," in: Walter Koschatzky, ed., *Maria Theresia und ihre Zeit*, Salzburg and Vienna 1979, pp. 277-293.

Heise 1991
Ulla Heise, "Drei Jahrhunderte Kaffeekultur in Deutschland. Dresdener Aspekte im 18. Jahrhundert," in: »Ey! wie schmeckt der Coffee süße«. Meissener Porzellan und Graphik, exh. cat. Porzellansammlung, Staatliche Kunstsammlungen Dresden, Sammlung Eduscho Bremen, ed. Klaus-Peter Arnold, Ulla Heise, and Michael Ropers, Dresden 1991, pp. 9–12.

Henning 2009
Andreas Henning, "Rosalba Carriera e la collezione dei suoi pastelli a Dresda," in: Giuseppe Pavanello, ed., *Rosalba Carriera 1673–1757, Atti del Convegno Internazionale di Studi 2007*, Verona 2009, pp. 273–360.

Henning/Marx 2007
Andreas Henning and Harald Marx, *"Das Kabinett der Rosalba" – Rosalba Carriera und die Pastelle der Dresdener Gemäldegalerie Alte Meister, Staatliche Kunstsammlungen Dresden*, Munich and Berlin 2007.

Hensler 1926
Erwin Hensler, ed., *Ludwig Schnorr von Carolsfeld. Auktionskatalog Paul Cassirer und Hugo Helbing: Aus Königlich Sächsischem Besitz im Auftrag des Hauses Wettin Albertinische Linie e.V. Mit einem Anhang von Kunstgegenständen aus Gräflich Brühlschem Besitz und anderem Besitz*, Berlin 1926.

Heß 1999
Helmut Heß, *Der Kunstverlag Franz Hanfstaengl und die frühe fotografische Kunstreproduktion. Das Kunstwerk und sein Abbild*, diss. LMU München 1993, Munich 1999.

Heyn 1913
Konrad Heyn, "Graf Francesco Algarotti und seine Beziehungen zur Dresdner Gemäldegalerie," in: *Neues Archiv für Sächsische Geschichte und Altertumskunde* 34 (1913), pp. 272–298.

Hilscher 2000
Elisabeth Theresia Hilscher, *Mit Leier und Schwert. Die Habsburger und die Musik*, Graz etc. 2000.

Hochmuth 2008
Christian Hochmuth, *Globale Güter – lokale Aneignung. Kaffee, Tee, Schokolade und Tabak im frühneuzeitlichen Dresden*, Konstanz 2008.

Hofstetter 2018
Bodo Hofstetter, *Portraitminiaturen. Hundert Bildnisse aus der Sammlung JRKV*, Potsdam 2018.

Holland 1871
Briefe der Herzogin Elisabeth Charlotte von Orléans aus den Jahren 1707 bis 1715, ed. Wilhelm Ludwig Holland, Tübingen 1871.

Holleczek 2002
Andreas Holleczek, *Jean-Etienne Liotard. Erkenntnisvermögen und künstlerischer Anspruch*, diss. Freie Universität Berlin 2000, Frankfurt am Main 2002.

Huber 2003
Johann Huber, *Marktgemeinde Grafendorf bei Hartberg. Straßennamen. Herkunft und Bedeutung*, Grafendorf 2003.

Hübner 1856
Julius Hübner, *Verzeichniss der Königlichen Gemälde-Gallerie zu Dresden*, Dresden 1856.

Hübner 1884
Julius Hübner, *Verzeichniss der Königlichen Gemälde-Gallerie zu Dresden*, Dresden 1884.

Hübner [1900]
Julius Hübner, *Die Dresdener Galerie, Photographien nach den Original-Gemälden*, vol. 2, Berlin [1900].

Humbert/Revilliod/Tilanus 1897
Edouard Humbert, Alphonse Revilliod, and Jan Willem Reinier Tilanus, *La vie et les œuvres de Jean-Étienne Liotard (1702–1789), Étude Biographique et Iconographique*, Amsterdam 1897.

Impey/Jörg 2004
Oliver Impey and Christiaan Jörg, *Japanese export lacquer, 1580–1850*, Amsterdam 2004.

Jacobs 2013
Hans C. Jacobs, "Die älteste Dresdner Schokoladenfabrik 'Jordan & Timaeus' (1823–1931)," in: *Schokoladenstadt Dresden. Süßigkeiten aus Elbflorenz*, exh. cat. Stadtmuseum Dresden, ed. Erika Eschebach and Holger Starke, Dresden 2013, pp. 74–77.

Jacoby 1815
Ludwig David Jacoby, *Schmidt's Werke, oder beschreibendes Verzeichniss sämtlicher Kupferstiche und Radirungen, welche der berühmte Künstler George Friederich Schmidt . . . verfertigt hat*, Berlin 1815.

Jeffares 2006
Neil Jeffares, *Dictionary of Pastellists before 1800*, London 2006. Online version http://www.pastellists.com.

Jeffares 2015
Neil Jeffares, "Liotard and the Medium of Pastel," in: *Jean-Etienne Liotard, 1702–1789*, exh. cat. Scottish National Gallery, Edinburgh; Royal Academy of Arts, London, London 2015, pp. 26–33.

Jones 2015
Christine A. Jones, "When Chocolate was Medicine: Colmenero, Wadsworth, and Dufour," in: https://publicdomainreview.org/2015/01/28/when-chocolate-was-medicine-colmenero-wadsworth-and-dufour.

Juszczak/Małachowicz 2016
Dorota Juszczak and Hanna Małachowicz, eds., *The Stanisław August Collection of Paintings at the Royal Łazienki, Catalogue*, Warsaw 2016.
Kappel/Weinhold 2007
Jutta Kappel and Ulrike Weinhold, *Das Neue Grüne Gewölbe. Führer durch die ständige Ausstellung*, München und Berlin 2007.
Kauffmann 1994
Kai Kauffmann, *"Es ist nur ein Wien!" – Stadtbeschreibungen von Wien 1700 bis 1873. Geschichte eines literarischen Genres*, Vienna etc. 1994.
Keller 1788
Heinrich Keller, *Nachrichten von allen in Dresden lebenden Künstlern*, Leipzig 1788.
Klemm 2014
Begegnungen – Matthias Klemm im Dialog mit Alten Meistern, ed. Versöhnungskirche Leipzig-Gohlis, Leipzig 2014.
Kleuthgen 2015
Christina Kleuthgen, "From science to art. The evolution of linear perspective in eighteenth-century Chinese art," in: Petra ten-Doesschate Chu, ed., *Qing encounters. Artistic exchanges between China and the West*, Los Angeles 2015, pp. 173–189.
Koch 2016
Ute Christina Koch, *Maecenas in Sachsen.* Höfische Repräsentationsmechanismen von Favoriten am Beispiel von Heinrich Graf von Brühl, diss. Technische Universität Dresden 2010, pp. 188–197; http://nbn-resolving.de/urn:nb-n:de:bsz:14-qucosa-193760 (accessed 25 May 2018).
Koos 2008
Marianne Koos, "La jouissance du détail: Liotards Bartlocke", in: *Kritische Berichte* 36 (2008), no. 3, pp. 19–27.
Koos 2014
Marianne Koos, *Haut, Farbe und Medialität. Oberfläche im Werk von Jean-Étienne Liotard (1702–1789)*, Paderborn 2014.
Krapf 2006
Michael Krapf, "Das Zeitalter Maria Theresias. Eine erfolgreiche Spurensuche," in: Michael Krapf und Cornelia Reiter, eds., *Das Zeitalter Maria Theresias. Meisterwerke des Barock, Österreichische Galerie Belvedere, Akademie der bildenden Künste Wien*, exh. cat. Musée national d'histoire et d'art de Luxembourg, Vienna 2006.
Kraszewski 1986
Józef Ignacy Kraszewski, *Reiseblätter*, trans. Caesar Rymarowicz from the 1st ed. 1858, Berlin 1986.
Krauss 1974
Friedrich Krauss, *Intarsien. Herkunft, Herstellung, Verwendung*, Leipzig 1974.
Krellig 2017
Heiner Krellig, "Francesco Algarotti as an agent acquiring works of art for the German courts at Berlin, Dresden and Kassel," in: Andreas Tacke et al., eds., *Kunstmärkte zwischen Stadt und Hof. Prozesse der Preisbildung in der europäischen Vormoderne*, Petersberg 2017, pp. 263–278.
Krünitz 1776
Johann Georg Krünitz, *Oeconomische Enzyklopaedie, oder allgemeines System der Land-, Haus- und Staats-Wirthschaft*, vol. 8, Berlin 1776.
Kudriaffsky 1880
Euphemia von Kudriaffsky, *Die historische Küche. Ein Culturbild*, Vienna 1880.
Kuhlmann-Hodick 2017
Petra Kuhlmann-Hodick, "Introduction," in: Petra Kuhlmann-Hodick, ed., *Indian paintings. The collection of the Dresden Kupferstich-Kabinett*, Dresden 2017, pp. 22–23.
[Kurz] 1770
[Joseph von Kurz], *Ein Neues Pantomimisches Singspiel . . . , oder Die versoffenen Köche und die verliebten Stubenmädel*, Wien 1770.
Laing 1992
Alastair Laing, Review of *Dessins de Liotard. Suivi du catalogue de l'œuvre dessiné*, ed. Anne de Herdt, Paris 1992, in: *The Burlington Magazine* 134 (1992), pp. 749–750.
Landsberg 2014
Petra Landsberg, *Wahre Geschichten um das Schokoladenmädchen*, Leipzig 2014.
Lauterbach 2017
Katrin Lauterbach, "Terra Sigillata und ihr Heilaspekt. Mexikanische Búcaros im Inventar des Japanischen Palais 1721," in: *Dresdener Kunstblätter* 61, no. 2 (2017), pp. 30–41.
Lauts 1977
Jan Lauts, "Jean-Etienne Liotard und seine Schülerin Markgräfin Karoline Luise von Baden," in: *Jahrbuch der Staatlichen Kunstsammlungen Baden-Württemberg* 14 (1977), pp. 43–70.
Le Blanc 1747
Jean-Bernard Le Blanc, *Lettre sur l'exposition des ouvrages de peinture, sculpture, etc. de l'Année 1747. Et en général sur l'utilité de ces sortes d'Expositions* [Paris 1747].
Leeflang 2011
Huigen Leeflang, "A Self-Portrait by Jean-Etienne Liotard from the Artist's Family Holdings," in: *The Rijksmuseum Bulletin* 59 (2011), pp 204-207.
Lempertz 1925
Kunst-Auktionshaus Lempertz Köln, Nr. 232, 10. bis 12. November 1925.
Leonhard 1985
Mark Leonhard, "Notes on the Restoration of Jean-Etienne Liotards's Tea Set," in: *The J. Paul Getty Museum Journal* 13 (1985), pp. 131–132.
Lessmann 2006
Johanna Lessmann, *Porzellan. Glanzstücke der Sammlung des Museums für Kunst und Gewerbe Hamburg*, Hamburg 2006.
Lewerken 1998/99
Heinz-Werner Lewerken, "Zur Geschichte der Dresdner Gewehrgalerie," in: *Jahrbuch der Staatlichen Kunstsammlungen Dresden* 27 (1998/99), pp. 93–98.
Liebsch 2006/2007
Thomas Liebsch, "Das Schicksal der Gemäldegalerie König Augusts III. von Polen im Jagdschloss Hubertusburg im Siebenjährigen Krieg," in: *Jahrbuch der Staatlichen Kunstsammlungen Dresden* 33 (2006/07), pp. 42–57.
Liebsch 2010
Thomas Liebsch, "'… una piccola e scelta raccolta di quadri moderni' – Francesco Algarottis Gemäldeauftrag für Dresden an zeitgenössische Maler in Venedig," in: Barbara Marx and Andreas Henning, eds., *Venedig – Dresden. Begegnung zweier Kulturstädte*, Italien-Zentrum der TU Dresden, Staatliche Kunstsammlungen Dresden, Leipzig 2010, pp. 217–239.
Lindau 1820
Wilhelm Adolf Lindau, *Neues Gemählde von Dresden in Hinsicht auf Geschichte, Kultur, Kunst und Gewerbe*, 2nd ed., Dresden 1820.
Links 2010
Christoph Links, *Das Schicksal der DDR-Verlage. Die Privatisierung und ihre Konsequenzen*, Freiburg 2010.
Linné 1777
Carl von Linné, *Des Ritter Carl von Linné Auserlesenen Abhandlungen aus der Naturgeschichte, Physik und Arzneywissenschaft*, vol. 2, Leipzig 1777.
Liotard 1781
Jean-Étienne Liotard, *Traité des principes et règles de la peinture*, Geneva 1781.
Lippincott 1985
Louise Lippincott, "Liotard's 'China Painting,'" in: *The J. Paul Getty Museum Journal* 13 (1985), pp. 121–130.
Liu 2015
Lihong Liu, "Shadows in Chinese art. An intercultural perspective," in: Petra ten-Doesschate Chu, ed., *Qing encounters. Artistic exchanges between China and the West*, Los Angeles 2015, pp. 190–213.
Marx 2002
Harald Marx, "'Das ganze Colorit ist belebt und verschmolzen.' Jean-Etienne Liotard zum 300. Geburtstag," in: *Dresdener Kunstblätter* 46, no. 6 (2002), pp. 194–202.
Marx 2008
Harald Marx, "Einige Betrachtungen zum Verhältnis zwischen dem jungen Anton Raphael Mengs und Louis de Silvestre," in: Uta Neidhardt, ed., *Festschrift für Anneliese Mayer-Meintschel, Staatliche Kunstsammlungen Dresden*, Dresden 2008, pp. 16–27.
Marx 2010
Barbara Marx, "Diplomaten, Agenten, Abenteurer im Dienst der Künste – Kunstbeziehungen zwischen Dresden und Venedig," in: Barbara Marx and Andreas Henning, eds., *Venedig – Dresden. Begegnung zweier Kulturstädte*, Italien-Zentrum der TU Dresden, Staatliche Kunstsammlungen Dresden, Leipzig 2010, pp. 10–67.
[Matthäi] 1833
[Friedrich Matthäi], *Neues Sach- und Ortsverzeichniss der Königlich Sächsischen Gemälde-Gallerie zu Dresden*, Dresden 1833.
Matthäi 1835
Friedrich Matthäi, *Verzeichniss der Königlich Sächsischen Gemälde-Galerie zu Dresden*, Dresden 1835.
[Matthäi] 1848
[Friedrich Matthäi], *Catalog der königlichen Gemälde-Galerie zu Dresden*, Dresden 1848.
Mellenthin/Peters 2017
Paul Mellenthin and Dorothea Peters, "Das photographische Museum," in: *Adolphe Braun. Ein europäisches Photographie-Unternehmen und die Bildkünste im 19. Jahrhundert*, exh. cat. Münchner Stadtmuseum, ed. Ulrich Pohlmann and Paul Mellenthin, Munich 2017, pp. 297–310.

Menninger 2004
Annerose Menninger, *Genuss im kulturellen Wandel. Tabak, Kaffee, Tee und Schokolade in Europa (16. – 19. Jahrhundert)*, Stuttgart 2004.
Menz 2007
Cäsar Menz, "Zu Jean-Etienne Liotards Selbstbildnissen," in: *Liber Veritatis. Mélanges en l'honneur du Professeur Marcel G. Roethlisberger*, ed. Leila el-Wakil, Patrick-André Guerretta, Paul Lang, et al., Milan 2007, pp. 191–199.
Menzhausen 1968
Joachim Menzhausen, *Das Grüne Gewölbe*, Leipzig 1968.
Mercure 1750
Mercure de France 1750, no. 11.
Metze 2016
Gudula Metze, "(Fast) römische Druckgrafik aus Dresden. Die radierten Karikaturen von Matthias Oesterreich nach Pier Leone Ghezzi und ihre Vorlagen," in: *Begegnungen mit Rom*, exh. cat. Kupferstich-Kabinett, Staatliche Kunstsammlungen Dresden, ed. Gudula Metze and Iris Yvonne Wagner, Dresden 2016, pp. 55-75.
Mey 2002
Ellen Mey, *Porzellan aus Hof und Oberkotzau, 47. Bericht des Nordoberfränkischen Vereins für Natur-, Geschichts- und Landeskunde e.V. Hof*, Hof 2002.
Mittelstädt 1955
Kuno Mittelstädt, "Meisterwerke der Dresdner Galerie," in: *Sammler-Express. Fachzeitung für Philatelie und andere Sammelgebiete* 9, no. 21 (1955), p. 330.
Montagu 1799
Earl of Sandwich (John Montagu), *A Voyage performed by the late Earl of Sandwich round the Mediterranean in the Years 1738 and 1739*, London 1799.
Montenegro 2012
Eupremio Montenegro, *I dogi e le loro monete*, Turin 2012.
Mory/Pichelkastner/Höfler 1977
Ludwig Mory, Eleonore Pichelkastner, and Bernd Höfler, *Bruckmann's Zinn-Lexikon*, Munich 1977.
Moser 1755
Friedrich Carl von Moser, *Deutsches Hofrecht*, vol. 2, Frankfurt and Leipzig 1755.
Moücke 1762
Francesco Moücke, *Serie di Ritratti degli eccellenti pittori dipinti di propria mano che esistono nell'imperial Galleria di Firenze*, vol. 4, Florence 1762.
Mourey 2011
Marie-Thérèse Mourey, "Tanz und Ballettkultur unter Maria Theresia," in: Pierre Béhar, Marie-Thérèse Mourey, and Herbert Schneider, eds., *Maria Theresias Kulturwelt*, Hildesheim, Zürich, and New York 2011, pp. 171–191.
Mraz 1979
Gerda und Gottfried Mraz, *Maria Theresia. Ihr Leben und ihre Zeit in Bildern und Dokumenten*, Munich 1979.
Mueller 1957
Wolf Mueller, *Seltsame Frucht Kakao. Geschichte des Kakaos und der Schokolade*, Hamburg 1957.
N.N./Heise 1986
N.N. and Ulla Heise, *Drey neue curieuse Tractätgen Von dem Trancke Cafe, Sinesischen The und der Chokolata, mit einem Nachwort von Ulla Heise* (reprint of the Bautzen 1686 ed.), Leipzig 1986.
Nascimento 2018
Douglas Nascimento, "Sönksen – A fantástica fábrica de chocolates," in: *Sao Paulo Antiqua*, http://www.saopauloantiga.com.br/sonksen/.
Nicolai 1783
Friedrich Nicolai, *Beschreibung einer Reise durch Deutschland und die Schweiz im Jahre 1781*, Berlin and Stettin 1783.
Niculescu 1982
Remus Niculescu, "Jean-Etienne Liotard à Jassy, 1742–1743," in: *Genava* 30 (1982), pp. 127–166.
Nocq 1928
Henry Nocq, *Le Poinçon de Paris. Repertoire des maîtres-orfèvres de la juridiction de Paris depuis le Moyen-Age jusqu'à la fin du XVIIIe siècle*, vol. III, Paris 1928.
Norton 2006
Marcy Norton, "Tasting Empire: Chocolate and the European Internalization of Mesoamerican Aesthetics," in: *The American Historical Review* 111, no. 3 (2006), pp. 660–691.
Nowak 1986
Erika Nowak, "Es sind nicht in allen Muscheln Perlen," in: *Das Magazin* 1986, no. 1, pp. 42–43.
Nugent 1756, quoted from Schmidt 1921
Thomas Nugent, *The grand tour*, London 1756, quoted from Otto Eduard Schmidt, *Minister Graf Brühl und Karl Heinrich von Heinecken*, Leipzig and Berlin 1921.
Oehmigcke 1800
Wilhelm Oehmigcke, *Neue Bilder Gallerie für junge Söhne und Töchter*, vol. 7, Berlin 1800.
Oesterreich 1766
Matteo Oesterreich, *Raccolta de vari disegni dell Cavalliero Pietro Leone Ghezzi Romano è di Giovann Battista Internari Romano e di alcuni altri Maestri incise in rame da Matteo Oesterreich Hambourghese*, Potsdam 1766.
Oesterreich 1784
Matthias Oesterreich, *Verzeichnis der Gemäldesammlung des verstorbenen Obristen Quintus Icilius*, Potsdam 1784.
Ortmann 1973
Erwin Ortmann, *Zinnfiguren einst und jetzt*, Leipzig 1973.
Pantzer 2000
Peter Pantzer, "Die Habsburgische Sammlung von frühem Imari-Porzellan," in: *Imari-Porzellan am Hofe der Kaiserin Maria Theresias*, exh. cat. Hetjens-Museum Düsseldorf, Deutsches Keramikmuseum Düsseldorf, ed. Peter Pantzer and Bernd Hakenjos, Düsseldorf 2000, pp. 17–37.
Perini/Bianconi 1998
Giovanna Perini, "Giovanni Ludovico Bianconi: un bolognese in Germania," in: *Giovanni Ludovico Bianconi, Scritti tedeschi*, ed. Giovanna Perini, Bologna 1998, pp. 7-140.
Petrasch 1991
Ernst Petrasch, ed., *Die Karlsruher Türkenbeute, die »Türckische Kammer« des Markgrafen Ludwig Wilhelm von Baden-Baden, die »Türckischen Curiositaeten« der Markgrafen von Baden-Durlach*, ed. Badisches Landesmuseum Karlsruhe, Munich 1991.
Pezzl 1787
Johann Pezzl, *Skizze von Wien, Viertes Heft*, Vienna and Leipzig 1787.
Pietsch 1996
Ulrich Pietsch, *Johann Gregorius Höroldt und die Meissener Porzellan-Malerei*, exh. cat. Porzellansammlung, Staatliche Kunstsammlungen Dresden, Dresden 1996.
Posse 1931
Hans Posse, "Die Briefe des Grafen Francesco Algarotti an den sächsischen Hof und seine Bilderkäufe für die Dresdner Gemäldegalerie 1743-1747," in: *Jahrbuch der Preußischen Kunstsammlungen* 52 (1931), supplement, pp. 1-73.
Prinz 1971
Wolfram Prinz, *Geschichte der Sammlung mit Regesten zur Tätigkeit der Agenten und Dokumentaranhang, Die Sammlung der Selbstbildnisse in den Uffizien*, vol. 1, ed. Ulrich Middeldorf and Ugo Procacci, Berlin 1971.
[von Racknitz] 1811a
[Johann Friedrich von Racknitz], *Skizze einer Geschichte der Künste*, Dresden 1811.
[von Racknitz] 1811b
[Johann Friedrich von Racknitz], *Versuche zur Beurtheilung der Königl. Sächs. Gemähldesammlung und deren Meister*, Dresden 1811.
[Rautenstrauch] 1781
[Johann Rautenstrauch], Über die Stubenmädchen in Wien, 4th ed., Vienna 1781.
Rauwolfen 1582
Leonharti Rauwolfen, *Aigentliche beschreibung der Raiß, so er vor diser zeit gegen Auffgang inn die Morgenländer . . .*, Lauingen 1582.
Ravagnan 1836
Girolamo Ravagnan, "Carriera (Rosalba)," in: *Biografia degli italiani illustri nelle scienze lettere ed arti del secolo XXVIII, e de' contemporanei*, ed. Emilio de Tipaldo, vol. 3, Venice 1836.
Recueil d'Estampes 1753
Recueil d'Estampes d'après les plus célèbres Tableaux de la Galerie Royale de Dresde, Contenant Cinquante Pieces Avec Une Description De Chaque Tableau En François Et En Italien, vol. 1, Dresden 1753.
Reichler 1978
Claude Reichler, "Liotard avec Variations. Les autoportraits de Jean-Etienne Liotard," in: *Genava* 16 (1978), pp. 221–228.
Reuter 2015
Astrid Reuter, "Künstlerische Praxis und Kennerschaft – Karoline Luise von Baden und die Pastellmalerei," in: Christoph Frank and Wolfgang Zimmermann, eds., *Aufgeklärter Kunstdiskurs und höfische Sammelpraxis: Karoline Luise von Baden im europäischen Kontext*, Munich 2015, pp. 112–123.
[Riedel 1801]
[Johann Anton Riedel], *Verzeichniss der Gemälde, welche in der Churfürstl. Gallerie zu Dresden befindlich sind*, Dresden 1801.
Riedel 1804
Johann Anton Riedel, *Catalogue des tableaux de la Galerie électorale à Dresde*, Dresden 1804.

Riedel 1984
Lisa Riedel, *Zur Geschichte des Neuruppiner Bilderbogen*, ed. Heimatmuseum Neuruppin, Neuruppin 1984.
Riedel/Wenzel 1765
Jean Antoine Riedel and Chrêtien Frederic Wenzel, *Catalogue des Tableaux de la Galerie Electorale à Dresde*, Dresden 1765.
Riedel/Wenzel 1771
Johann Anton Riedel and Christian Friedrich Wenzel, *Verzeichniß der Gemälde in der Churfürstl. Gallerie in Dresden*, Leipzig 1771.
Ritscher 1901
Julius Ritscher, *Anleitung zur Pastellmalerei, neu bearbeitet von A. v. Broecker*, 4th ed., Dresden 1901.
R/L 2008
Marcel Roethlisberger and Renée Loche, *Liotard. Catalogue, Sources et Correspondance*, 2 vols., Doornspijk 2008.
Rockel 1995
Irina Rockel, "Zur Neuerwerbung des Heimatmuseums Neuruppin," in: *Was ist der Ruhm der TIMES gegen die zivilisatorische Aufgabe des Ruppiner Bilderbogens?* Die Bilderbogen-Sammlung Dietrich Hecht, ed. Kulturstiftung der Länder, Potsdam 1995, pp. 6–7.
Roethlisberger 1985
Marcel Roethlisberger, "Jean-Etienne Liotard as a Painter of Still Lifes," in: *The J. Paul Getty Museum Journal* 13 (1985), pp. 109–120.
Roethlisberger 2001
Marcel G. Roethlisberger, "Le 'Traité' de Liotard," in: Jürg Albrecht and Michael Egli, eds., *Horizonte: Beiträge zu Kunst und Kunstwissenschaft: 50 Jahre Schweizerisches Institut für Kunstwissenschaft*, Ostfildern-Ruit 2001, pp. 65–72.
Roethlisberger 2014
Marcel Roethlisberger, "Liotard mis à jour," in: *Zeitschrift für schweizerische Archäologie und Kunstgeschichte* 71, nos. 2–3 (2014), pp. 187–200.
Roethlisberger 2017
Marcel Roethlisberger, "Jean-Etienne Liotard (Genève, 1702–1789): nouvelles découvertes," in: *Zeitschrift für Archäologie und Kunstgeschichte* 74, no. 2 (2017), pp. 157–161.
Roethlisberger/Loche 1978
Marcel Roethlisberger and Renée Loche, *L'opera completa di Liotard*, Milan 1978.
Roettgen 1999
Steffi Roettgen, *Anton Raphael Mengs (1728–1779), Das malerische und zeichnerische Werk*, 2 vols., Munich 1999.
Rögener 1990
Martin Rögener, ed., *Kunst-Postkarten übermalt von Strawalde (Jürgen Böttcher)*, Hamburg 1990.
Röhner 2016
Barbara Röhner, *Von Reproduktions-Ausstellungen zum Bildverleih. Idee- und Entwicklungsgeschichte von Artotheken in der DDR*, Halle 2016.
Rosen 1988
Jeffrey Howard Rosen, *Lemercier et Compagnie: Photolithography and the Industrialization of Print Production in France 1837–1859*, diss. Northwestern University 1988.
Roters 1981
Eberhard Roters, *Hann Trier – die Deckengemälde in Berlin, Heidelberg und Köln*, Berlin 1981.
Rudolph 2013
Andrea Rudolph, "Süsser Winter, Schokolade und Süßwaren zwischen Advent und Ostern," in: *Schokoladenstadt Dresden. Süßigkeiten aus Elbflorenz*, exh. cat. Stadtmuseum Dresden, ed. Erika Eschebach and Holger Starke, Dresden 2013, pp. 111–127.
R-u-ff 1781
R-u-ff, *Gedanken über die Kleidertracht in Wien, und mir gutscheinende Kleiderordnung*, Vienna 1781.
Rüger/Rüger 1975
Conrad Alfred Rüger and Conrad Georg Frank Rüger, eds., *Otto Rüger, ein Leben für die Schokoladenindustrie*, Waiblingen 1975.
Rümelin 2018
Christian Rümelin, "Jean-Etienne Liotard als Radierer," in: *Von der Genauigkeit des Sehens. Festschrift zum 75. Geburtstag von Anne Röver-Kann*, ed. Rebecca Duckwitz and Christien Melzer, Bremen 2018, pp. 83–88.
Sandgruber 1991
Roman Sandgruber, "Kaffeesuppe und 'kleiner Brauner.' Sozialgeschichte des Kaffeekonsums in Österreich," in: *Kaffee im Spiegel europäischer Trinksitten/Coffee in the Context of European Drinking Habits*, ed. Daniel Ball, Zürich 1991.
Sandgruber 1994
Roman Sandgruber, "Genußmittel. Ihre reale und symbolische Bedeutung im neuzeitlichen Europa," in: *Jahrbuch für Wirtschaftsgeschichte* 35, no. 1 (1994), pp. 73–88.
Sani 1988
Bernardina Sani, *Rosalba Carriera*, Turin 1988.
Sani 2007
Bernardina Sani, *Rosalba Carriera 1673–1757. Maestra del pastello nell' Europa ancien régime*, Turin etc. 2007.
Sani 2008
Bernardina Sani, *Rosalba Carriera*, Turin etc. 2008.
Sani 2010
Bernardina Sani, "Il Gabinetto della Rosalba della Gemäldegalerie di Dresda florilegio della pittura a pastello euopea tra Rococo e Illuminismo," in: Barbara Marx and Andreas Henning, eds., *Venedig – Dresden. Begegnung zweier Kulturstädte*, Italien-Zentrum der TU Dresden, Staatliche Kunstsammlungen Dresden, Leipzig 2010, pp. 201–216.
Sauvage 2015
Leila Sauvage, "Jean-Etienne Liotard und Karoline Luise von Baden – Eine Geschichte der Pastelle," in: Christoph Frank and Wolfgang Zimmermann, eds., *Aufgeklärter Kunstdiskurs und höfische Sammelpraxis. Karoline Luise von Baden im europäischen Kontext*, Munich 2015, pp. 124–131.
Sauvage/Gombaud 2015
Leila Sauvage and Cécile Gombaud, "Liotard's Pastels: Techniques of an 18th-Century Pastellist," in: *Studying 18th-Century Paintings and Works of Art on Paper*, ed. Helen Evans and Kimberley Muir, London 2015, pp. 31–45.
Schäfer 1860
Wilhelm Schäfer, *Die Königliche Gemälde-Gallerie im Neuen Museum zu Dresden*, vol. 1, Dresden 1860.
Schäfer 1864
Wilhelm Schäfer, *Führer in der königlichen Gemälde-Gallerie zu Dresden*, Dresden 1864.
Schepkowski 2009
Nina Simone Schepkowski, *Johann Ernst Gotzkowsky, Kunstagent und Gemäldesammler im friderizianischen Berlin*, Berlin 2009.
Schiedlausky 1961
Günther Schiedlausky, *Tee, Kaffee, Schokolade: Ihr Eintritt in die Europäische Gesellschaft*, Munich 1961.
Schillinger 1994
Klaus Schillinger, ed., *Kostbare Instrumente und Uhren aus dem Mathematisch-Physikalischen Salon Dresden*, Leipzig 1994.
Schimpfermann 2006
Helmut Schimpfermann, "Unsterblich durch Doppel – M. Erich Gruner zum 125. Geburtstag," in: *Deutsche Briefmarken-Zeitung (DBZ). Sammler Express* 81, no. 23 (2006), pp. 38–39.
Schivelbusch 2005
Wolfgang Schivelbusch, *Das Paradies, der Geschmack und die Vernunft: eine Geschichte der Genußmittel*, Frankfurt am Main 2005.
Schmidt 2017
Frank Schmidt, "Slawomir Elsner. Le Musée imaginaire," in: *Slawomir Elsner*, exh. cat. Böttchergasse Bremen, Bremen 2017.
Schmidt-Linsenhoff 2004
Viktoria Schmidt-Linsenhoff, "Liotards Bart. Transkulturelle Maskeraden der Männlichkeit," in: *Männlichkeit im Blick. Visuelle Inszenierungen in der Kunst seit der Frühen Neuzeit*, ed. Mechthild Fend and Marianne Koos, Cologne etc. 2004, pp. 161–180.
Schnitzer 1995
Claudia Schnitzer, "Zwischen Kampf und Spiel – Orientrezeption im höfischen Fest," in: *Im Lichte des Halbmonds, Das Abendland und der türkische Orient*, exh. cat. Staatliche Kunstsammlungen Dresden, Albertinum; Kunst- und Ausstellungshalle der Bundesrepublik Deutschland, Bonn, Dresden 1995, pp. 227–234.
Schnitzer 2014
Claudia Schnitzer, *Constellatio Felix. Die Planetenfeste Augusts des Starken anlässlich der Vermählung seines Sohnes Friedrich August mit der Kaisertochter Maria Josepha 1719 in Dresden, Bestandskatalog Kupferstich-Kabinett der Staatlichen Kunstsammlungen Dresden*, Dresden 2014.
Schnyder-von Waldkirch 1988
Antoinette Schnyder-von Waldkirch, *Wie Europa den Kaffee entdeckte. Reiseberichte der Barockzeit als Quellen zur Geschichte des Kaffees*, Veröffentlichungen des Jacobs-Suchard-Museums zur Kulturgeschichte des Kaffees, vol. 1, ed. Holger Hasenkamp, Zürich 1988.

Schöbel 1961
Johannes Schöbel, *Orientalica*, Dresden 1961.
Schölzel 1989
Christoph Schölzel, *Studie zur Pastellmalerei. Maltechnik und Restaurierung*, term paper Hochschule für bildende Künste Dresden, Abt. Restaurierung, 2 vols., 1989.
Schölzel 2005
Christoph Schölzel, ed., *Die blendenden Rahmen*, Worms 2005.
Schuckelt 2000
Holger Schuckelt, "'Folget Das Türckische Serail.' Das Wachsfigurenkabinett Augusts des Starken, Kammertürken und Türkenkammer am Dresdner Hof," in: *Eine gute Figur machen. Kostüm und Fest am Dresdner Hof*, exh. cat. Kupferstich-kabinett, Staatliche Kunstsammlungen Dresden, ed. Claudia Schnitzer and Petra Hölscher, Dresden 2000, pp. 69–83.
Schuckelt 2004
Holger Schuckelt, "Reitzeuge und Reitzubehör der Osmanen in der Dresdner Rüstkammer," in: *Jahrbuch der Staatlichen Kunstsammlungen Dresden* 29 (2001), Dresden 2004, pp. 15–30.
Schuckelt 2008
Holger Schuckelt, "Relations between Saxony and the Crimean Tatars in the 17th and early 18th Centuries," in: *Caucasus, Crimea and the Volga-Ural Region: Islamic Art & Architecture in the European Periphery, Tagungsband*, ed. Barbara Kellner-Heinkele, Joachim Gierlichs, and Brigitte Heuer, Wiesbaden 2008, pp. 93–108.
Schuckelt 2010a
Holger Schuckelt, *Die Türckische Cammer – Sammlung Orientalischer Kunst in der kurfürstlich-sächsischen Rüstkammer Dresden*, Staatliche Kunstsammlungen Dresden, Dresden 2010.
Schuckelt 2010b
Holger Schuckelt, *Türckische Cammer – Orientalische Pracht in der Rüstkammer Dresden, Meisterwerke*, Berlin and Munich 2010.
Schuster 2003
Martin Schuster, *Zur Entstehung des Dresdener Galeriewerkes*, unpublished master's thesis, Technische Universität Dresden 2003.
Schuster 2009
Martin Schuster, "Das Dresdener Galeriewerk. Die Publikation zur neuen Bildergalerie im umgebauten Stallgebäude," in: *Dresdener Kunstblätter* 52, no. 1 (2009), pp. 65–78.
Schutzschrift 1781
Schutzschrift der gekränkten Stubenmädchen in Wien, 2nd ed., Vienna 1781.
Seidel 1894
Paul Seidel, "Pastellbildnis des Grafen Francesco Algarotti von Jean-Etienne Liotard," in: *Jahrbuch der Königlich-Preußischen Kunstsammlungen* 15, no. 2 (1894), pp. 122–124.
Seidlitz 1895
Woldemar von Seidlitz, "Die Schicksale der Dresdner Gemäldegalerie während des siebenjährigen Krieges," in: *Dresdner Geschichtsblätter* 4, no. 2 (1895), pp. 184–187.
Sheriff 2010
Mary D. Sheriff, "The Dislocations of Jean-Etienne Liotard, Called the Turkish Painter," in: *Cultural Contact and the Making of European Art since the Age of Exploration*, ed. Mary D. Sheriff, Chapel Hill 2010, pp. 97–121.
Sloboda 2014
Stacey Sloboda, *Chinoiserie. Commerce and critical ornament in eighteenth-century Britain*, Manchester and New York 2014.
Smentek 2010
Kristen Smentek, "Looking East. Jean-Étienne Liotard, the Turkish Painter," in: *Ars Orientalis* 39 (2010), pp. 84–112.
Spenlé 2008
Virginie Spenlé, *Die Dresdener Gemäldegalerie und Frankreich. Der "bon goût" im Sachsen des 18. Jahrhunderts*, Beucha 2008.
Sponsel 1906
Jean Louis Sponsel, *Fürsten-Bildnisse aus dem Hause Wettin*, ed. Königlich Sächsischer Altertumsverein, Dresden 1906.
Sprengel 1772
Peter Nathaniel Sprengel, *Handwerke und Künste in Tabellen, 9. Sammlung*, Berlin 1772.
Sprengel 1777
Peter Nathaniel Sprengel, *Handwerke und Künste in Tabellen, 15. Sammlung*, Berlin 1777.
Stadtlexikon Dresden 1994
Stadtlexikon Dresden A-Z, ed. Folke Stimmel et al., Basel 1994.
Starke 2013
Holger Starke, "Vom Lever zum Schokoriegel. Dresdens Entwicklung zur Stadt der Schokolade im Industriezeitalter (1800–1990)," in: *Schokoladenstadt Dresden. Süßigkeiten aus Elbflorenz*, exh. cat. Stadtmuseum Dresden, ed. Erika Eschebach and Holger Starke, Dresden 2013, pp. 45–73.
Starke 2018
Holger Starke, *F. & O. Brockmann, Frühe photographische Arbeiten aus Dresden*, http://photo.dresden.de/de/04/c_99.php (accessed 16 May 2018).
Stekl 1975
Hannes Stekl, "Hausrechtliche Abhängigkeit in der industriellen Gesellschaft," in: *Wiener Geschichtsblätter, Verein für Geschichte der Stadt Wien* 30 (1975), pp. 301–313.
Stekl 1985
Hannes Stekl, "Unterschichten und Obrigkeit im Wien des ausgehenden 18. Jahrhunderts," in: Österreich im Europa der Aufklärung. Kontinuität und Zäsur in Europa zur Zeit Maria Theresias und Josephs II., *Internationales Symposium Wien 20.–23.10.1980*, Vienna 1985, pp. 291–304.
Stevens 2015
Maryanne Stevens, "Still-life, Trompe l'oeil and Genre Painting," in: *Jean-Etienne Liotard, 1702–1789*, exh. cat. Scottish National Gallery, Edinburgh; Royal Academy of Arts, London 2015, pp. 162–181.
Stollberg-Rilinger 2017
Barbara Stollberg-Rilinger, *Maria Theresia. Die Kaiserin in ihrer Zeit*, München 2017.
Stubenmägdchen 1778
Die Stubenmägdchen – Eine Satyre in drey Gesprächen [Munich ca. 1778].
Syndram 2004
Dirk Syndram, *Das Goldene Kaffeezeug Augusts des Starken. Johann Melchior Dinglingers erstes Meisterwerk im Grünen Gewölbe*, Leipzig 2004.
Syndram 2008
Dirk Syndram, *Juwelenkunst des Barock. Johann Melchior Dinglinger im Grünen Gewölbe*, Munich 2008.
Teuber 1896
Otto Teuber, *Die Theater Wiens*, Vienna 1896.
Them 2011
Andreas Them, *Kaffeehausgeschichten aus dem alten Dresden*, Dresden 2011.
Theresia M. 1781
Dem Verfasser des Büchels über die Stubenmädchen, Etwas auf die Nase, von Theresia M., einem Stubenmädchen in Wien, Vienna 1781.
Trauth 2009
Nina Trauth, *Maske und Person, Orientalismus im Porträt des Barock*, Berlin and Munich 2009.
Trivas 1936
N. S. Trivas, "Les portraits de Liotard par lui-même," in: *Revue de l'art ancien et moderne* 70 (1936), pp. 153–162.
Trivas 1938
N. S. Trivas, "Une miniature de J.-E. Liotard: Portrait de Marie-Thérèse D'Autriche en costume oriental," in: *Genava* 16 (1938), pp. 169–170.
Uhland [1875]
Wilhelm Heinrich Uhland, *Officieller Bericht über die Sächsische Gewerbe-& Industrie-Ausstellung zu Dresden 1875*, Leipzig [1875].
Vertue/Walpole
George Vertue and Horace Walpole, *Anecdotes of Painting in England*, 4 vols., Strawberry Hill 1762–1780.
Verzeichniß 1790
Verzeichniß der zum Nachlaß des verstorbenen Königl. Preuß. Obristen Herrn von Quintus gehörigen und zum Verkauf stehenden Gemählde, Antiquen alten Münzen, Berlin 1790.
Vivian 1971
Frances Vivian, *Il console Smith - mercante e collezionista*, Vicenza 1971.
Vocelka 2002
Karl Vocelka, *Geschichte Österreichs. Kultur – Gesellschaft – Politik*, Graz, Vienna, Cologne 2002.
Vocelka 2017
Karl Vocelka, "Aufbruch in neue Zeiten. Der Reformeifer Maria Theresias," in: *Maria Theresia 1717–1780: Strategin – Mutter – Reformerin*, exh. cat. Schloss Hof, Schloss Niederweiden, Hofmobiliendepot – Möbel Museum Wien, Kaiserliche Wagenburg Wien, ed. Elfriede Iby et al., Vienna 2017, pp. 45–56.
Vocelka/Heller 1997
Karl Vocelka and Lynne Heller, *Die Lebenswelt der Habsburger. Kultur- und Mentalitätsgeschichte einer Familie*, Graz etc. 1997.

Wagner 1999
Christoph Wagner, *Der beschleunigte Blick – Hann Trier und das prozessuale Bild*, Berlin 1999.

Wagner 2002
Christoph Wagner, "Hann Trier und die 'Alten Meister,'" in: *Informel – Begegnung und Wandel*, ed. Heinz Althöfer, Dortmund 2002, pp. 187–209.

Walpole 1784
Horace Walpole, *A description of the villa of Mr. Horace Walpole*, Strawberry Hill 1784.

Walther 1975
Angelo Walther, "Zu den Werken der Rosalba Carriera in der Dresdener Gemäldegalerie," in: *Beiträge und Berichte der Staatlichen Kunstsammlungen Dresden* 1972–75, Dresden 1975, pp. 69–90.

Watelet 1754
Claude-Henri Watelet, "Dessein," in: Denis Diderot and Jean Baptiste le Rond d'Alembert, *Encyclopédie ou Dictionnaire raisonné des Sciences, des Arts et des Métiers*, vol. 4, Paris 1754, pp. 889–891.

Watzdorf 1962
Erna von Watzdorf, *Johann Melchior Dinglinger. Der Goldschmied des deutschen Barock*, vol. 1, Berlin 1962.

Weber 1999
Gregor J. M. Weber, "Die Gemälde Pietro Graf Rotaris für den sächsischen Hof," in: Gregor J.M. Weber, *Pietro Graf Rotari in Dresden. Ein italienischer Maler am Hof König Augusts III.*, exh. and coll. catalogue, Gemäldegalerie Alte Meister, Staatliche Kunstsammlungen Dresden, Emsdetten und Dresden 1999, pp. 17–53.

Weber 2000
Gregor J.M. Weber, "Alles getürkt. Die lebensgroßen Figurenbilder im Türkischen Palais Dresdens," in: *Eine gute Figur machen. Kostüm und Fest am Dresdner Hof*, exh. cat. Kupferstich-Kabinett, Staatliche Kunstsammlungen Dresden, ed. Claudia Schnitzer and Petra Hölscher, Dresden 2000, pp. 85–99.

Weber 2008
Julia Weber, ". . . zu ihrer Ergötzung und Erquickung." Geschirre für Tee, Kaffee und Schokolade im 18. Jahrhundert," in: *Kirchengold & Tafelsilber. Die Sammlung von Silberarbeiten im Museum für Kunst und Kulturgeschichte Dortmund*, exh. cat. Museum für Kunst und Kulturgeschichte, Dortmund, ed. Brigitte Buberl, Munich and Berlin 2008, pp. 82–93.

Weber 2010
Julia Weber, ". . . daß andere Nationen darüber erstaunen müssen. . . .' Sächsisches Porzellan in der europäischen Diplomatie," in: *Triumph der blauen Schwerter. Meissener Porzellan für Adel und Bürgertum 1710–1815*, exh. cat. Porzellansammlung, Staatliche Kunstsammlungen Dresden, ed. Ulrich Pietsch and Claudia Banz, Leipzig 2010.

Weber 2013
Julia Weber, *Meißener Porzellane mit Dekoren nach ostasiatischen Vorbildern. Stiftung Ernst Schneider in Schloss Lustheim*, vol. 2, Munich 2013.

Weber 2016
Julia Weber, "Boundless Rivalry: Meissen's Counteroffensive after the Seven Years' War," in: *The French Porcelain Society Journal* 6 (2016), pp. 83–116.

Weddigen 2004
Tristan Weddigen, "Der visuelle Diskurs des Inventars – Geschmackliche und kunstgeschichtliche Argumentationsmuster in der Dresdener Gemäldegalerie im 18. Jahrhundert," in: *Jahrbuch der Staatlichen Kunstsammlungen Dresden* 31 (2004), pp. 97–104.

Weddigen 2008
Tristan Weddigen, *Die Sammlung als sichtbare Kunstgeschichte. Die Dresdner Gemäldegalerie im 18. und 19. Jahrhundert*, habilitation thesis Universität Bern, Bern 2008.

Weigel 1843
Rudolf Weigel, *Kunstlager-Catalog, 2. Abt.*, Leipzig 1843.

Werner 2017
Walter Werner, *Seiffen in acht Jahrhunderten. Figuren von Walter Werner erzählen Seiffens Geschichte*, Chemnitz 2017.

Willebrand 1769
Johann Peter Willebrand, *Des Herrn Johann Peter Willebrand historische Berichte und Practische Anmerkungen*, Leipzig 1769.

Williams 2012
Hannah Williams, "A Phenomenology of Vision: the Self-Portraits of Jean-Étienne Liotard," in: *RIHA Journal* 34 (20 January 2012), URL: http://www.riha-journal.org/articles/2012/2012-jan-mar/williams-phenomenology-of-vision.

Winkler 1989
Johannes Winkler, ed., *Der Verkauf an Dresden, Dresden und Modena aus der Geschichte zweier Galerien*, Modena 1989.

Winkler 1996
Hubert Chryspolitus Winkler, *Ehemalige Hofsilber & Tafelkammer. Silber – Bronzen – Porzellan - Glas*, ed. Ilsebil Barta-Fliedl and Peter Pernzan, Vienna etc. 1996.

Witt-Dörring 2011
Christian Witt-Dörring, "Die Möbel am Hofe Maria Theresias," in: Pierre Béhar, Marie-Thérèse Mourey, and Herbert Schneider, eds., *Maria Theresias Kulturwelt*, Hildesheim etc. 2011, pp. 247–253.

Woermann 1887, Große Ausgabe
Karl Woermann, *Katalog der Königlichen Gemäldegalerie zu Dresden, Große Ausgabe*, Dresden 1887.

Woermann 1892, Große Ausgabe
Karl Woermann, *Katalog der Königlichen Gemäldegalerie zu Dresden, Große Ausgabe*, Dresden 1892.

Wohlfarth 2010
Katrin Wohlfarth, "Die Gemäldeerwerbungen von August III. in Venedig. Die venezianischen Kunstagenten Antonio Maria Zanetti d. Ä. und Giovanni Pietro Minelli," in: Barbara Marx and Andreas Henning, eds., *Venedig – Dresden. Begegnung zweier Kulturstädte*, Italien – Zentrum der TU Dresden, Staatliche Kunstsammlungen Dresden, Leipzig 2010, pp. 262–315.

Woolliscroft Rhead 1910
George Woolliscroft Rhead, *History of the fan*, London 1910.

Zahn 1873
Albert von Zahn, "Barock, Rococo und Zopf," in: *Lützows Zeitschrift für Bildende Kunst* 8 (1873), pp. 1–44.

Zedler 1756
Johann Heinrich Zedler, ed., *Grosses vollständiges Universal Lexicon aller Wissenschafften und Künste*, vol. 47, Halle and Leipzig 1756.

Zeichenbuch 1797
Neues theoretisch-praktisches Zeichenbuch zum Selbstunterricht für alle Stände. Nebst einer Anleitung zum Colorieren der Landschaften und zur Blumen- und Pastellmahlerey, Hof 1797.

Zumpe 1991
Manfred Zumpe, *Die Brühlsche Terrasse in Dresden*, Berlin 1991.

INDEX

Bold numbers refer to images of the named persons.

PHOTO CREDITS

If not otherwise indicated Gemäldegalerie Alte Meister, Staatliche Kunstsammlungen Dresden, Elke Estel/Hans-Peter Klut

© **akg-images**, p. 95
Amsterdam © Rijksmuseum, Steaske Rebers: pp. 25, 165, 212, 233
Berlin© bpk / Kupferstichkabinett, Staatliche Museen zu Berlin, Dietmar Katz: p. 196, Jörg P. Anders: p. 197
© bpk / Kunstbibliothek, Staatliche Museen zu Berlin, Knud Petersen: p. 125
© Roland Stratmann: p. 131
Cologne © Lempertz / Helmut Buchen: p. 35 left
Museum für angewandte Kunst © Rheinisches Bildarchiv, Marion Mennicken, rba_d013613: p. 177 left
© Schokoladenmuseum GmbH, p. 16 left
Doorn © Museum Huis Doorn NL, pp. 47, 148
Dresden © Albertinum/Galerie Neue Meister, SKD, Elke Estel/Peter Klut: pp. 132, 153
© Anton Reiche Museum Dresden, Stiftung Hofmühle Dresden, p. 137
© Dieter Härtel: p. 255
© Gemäldegalerie Alte Meister, SKD, Herbert Boswank: Cover, pp. 5, 6, 7, 35 right, 41, 69 left, 111, 112 right and left, 113 right and left, 114, 141; Andreas Diesend, pp. 54, 242; Jürgen Karpinski: pp. 17, 155
© Gemälderestaurierung, SKD, Wolfgang Kreische, Christoph Schölzel: pp. 99, 100, 101, 102, 103, 104, 105, 106, 211; Elisabeth Schlesinger, Wolfgang Kreische: p. 116
© SES – GRASSI Museum für Völkerkunde zu Leipzig, SKD, Melanie Meier: pp. 168 right, 169 right and left
© Grünes Gewölbe, SKD, Jürgen Lösel: p. 163; Jürgen Karpinski: pp. 162, 173
© Hochschule für Bildende Künste Dresden, Kerstin Riße: p. 219
© Kunstgewerbemuseum, SKD, Katrin Lauterbach: p. 170
© Kupferstich-Kabinett, SKD, Andreas Diesend: pp. 73 left and right, 91, 145, 190, 191, 199, 220, 234, 236, 237, 240, 241; Herbert Boswank: pp. 60, 61, 62, 63, 72, 127
© Landesamt für Denkmalpflege Sachsen (Reproduction: Wolfgang Junius), pp. 92, 93
© Mathematisch-Physikalischer Salon, SKD, Jürgen Karpinski: p. 161
© Münzkabinett, SKD, Roger Paul: pp. 149, 150
© Museum für Sächsische Volkskunst, SKD, Melanie Meier: p. 135
© Porzellansammlung, SKD, Werner Lieberknecht: p. 121; Adrian Sauer: p. 174 right; Klaus Täufert: p. 177 right
© Rüstkammer, SKD, Hans-Peter Klut: pp. 206 top and bottom, 207, 208; Elke Estel/Hans-Peter Klut: p. 209
© Sebastian Schobbert, courtesy Galerie Gebr. Lehmann, Dresden, p. 133
© SLUB Dresden, Digitale Sammlungen, Diaet. 444, p. 171; Deutsche Fotothek, Regine Richter: pp. 59, 64; Deutsche Fotothek, p. 117
© Städtische Galerie Dresden – Kunstsammlung, Museen der Stadt Dresden, p. 239
Florence © bpk / Scala – courtesy of the Ministero Beni e Att. Culturali (Galleria degli Uffizi), p. 48
Geneva © Musées d'art et d'histoire, Ville de Genève, Bettina Jacot-Descombes: p. 80; Yves Siza: p. 81; Musées d'art et d'histoire, Ville de Genève, Cabinet d'arts graphiques, pp. 82, 83, 159, 186, 200 right and left, 201, 202, 203, 204, 235; Maurice Aeschimann: p. 183 right, Bettina Jacot-Descombes: pp. 37 right and left, 44 right, 84, 85, 142; André Longchamp: pp. 160, 187, 205; Nathalie Sabato: pp. 77, 188; Jean Marc Yersin: p. 198
Gotha © Stiftung Schloss Friedenstein Gotha – Aus den Sammlungen der Herzog von Sachsen-Coburg und Gotha'schen Stiftung für Kunst und Wissenschaft, pp. 69 right, 172
Großschönau © Deutsches Damast- und Frottiermuseum, inv. no. 56-594, p. 136
London © The Trustees of the British Museum, p. 156
© bpk / The Trustees of the British Museum, p. 44 left
© Lowell Libson & and Jonny Yarker Ltd., pp. 45, 148 right
© Tate London 2018, p. 51
Los Angeles © The J. Paul Getty Museum, pp. 71, 166
Meissen © MEISSEN®, p. 245 left
Munich © bpk / Bayerische Staatsgemäldesammlungen, Alte Pinakothek, Sammlung HypoVereinsbank, Member of UniCredit, p. 43
Paris © bpk / RMN – Grand Palais, Musée du Louvre, Michèle Bellot: p. 79 right and left, 195; Thierry Le Mage: p. 194; René-Gabriel Ojéda: p. 20; Michel Urtado: p. 189
© bpk / RMN – Grand Palais, Château de Versailles et Trianon, Gérard Blot: p. 123
© Bibliothèque nationale de France, p. 144
© Sylvie Lhermite-King: p. 34
© **Private collection**, Holger Vonderlind: pp. 184, 185; André Longchamp: p. 215 bottom; Reproduktion Steffi Reh: pp. 243, 254 left
© Private collection, Europe, p. 24
© Swiss private collection, p. 215 top
Vienna © ALBERTINA, Vienna, pp. 26, 65
© Bundesmobilienverwaltung, Silberkammer-Hofburg Wien, Edgar Knaack: p. 174
© KHM-Museumsverband, pp. 31, 33, 70, 175 top and bottom
© Österreichisches Staatsarchiv, Kriegsarchiv, HKR 1771, 98-136 (fol. 8v), p. 32
© Österreichische Nationalbibliothek (ÖNB) Wien: PORT_00079549_01, pp. 115
© Schloß Schönbrunn Kultur- und Betriebsgesellschaft, Sammlung: Bundesmobilienverwaltung, Objektstandort: Schloss Schönbrunn, Edgar Knaack: pp. 12, 30, 214
© Schloß Schönbrunn Kultur- und Betriebsges.mbH, Johannes Wagner: Sammlung Oesterreichische Nationalbank, p. 29, 179
© Schloß Schönbrunn Kultur- und Betriebsges.mbH, Alexander Eugen Koller: p. 180
© Wien Museum, p. 49
Warsaw © Royal Łazienki Museum, p. 193
Washington © Courtesy National Gallery of Art, p. 23
Winterthur © Schweizerisches Institut für Kunstwissenschaft, Zürich, Philipp Hitz: p. 143

In the event that certain illustrations are not properly credited, we request that the rights holders make themselves known. Legitimate claims will be compensated in line with customary agreements.

AUTHORS

AD	Andreas Dehmer
SD	Susanne Drexler
RE	Roland Enke
JMG	Jan-Markus Göttsch
WH	Wilhelm Hollstein
KL	Katrin Lauterbach
PP	Peter Plassmeyer
HS	Holger Schuckelt
JW	Julia Weber
UW	Ulrike Weinhold

Cover illustration: Jean-Étienne Liotard, *The Chocolate Girl*, pastel on vellum, circa 1744, Gemäldegalerie Alte Meister, Staatliche Kunstsammlungen Dresden, gal. no. P 161 (detail)

Sponsored by

COLOPHON

"The most beautiful pastel ever seen."
The Chocolate Girl by Jean-Étienne Liotard
Gemäldegalerie Alte Meister, Semperbau of the Zwinger
Staatliche Kunstsammlungen Dresden
Exhibition September 28, 2018 – January 6, 2019
Curators: Roland Enke, Stephan Koja, in cooperation with Susanne Drexler

Catalogue

Editors:
Staatliche Kunstsammlungen Dresden, Roland Enke, Stephan Koja
P.O. 12 05 51
D-01006 Dresden
phone: 0049-351-4914-0
Besucherservice@skd.museum
www.skd.museum
Editorial staff: Roland Enke, Susanne Drexler
Picture editing: Susanne Drexler, Steffi Reh
Intern: Jan-Markus Göttsch
Publication department: Antje Harnisch

Hirmer Verlag GmbH
Nymphenburgerstrasse 84
D-80636 München
Publishing project management: Jürgen Kleidt
Editing: Markus Kersting
Translation: Russell Stockman
Translation editing: Betti Moser
Design and layout: Peter Baldinger, Vienna
Lithography: ReproMayer GmbH, Reutlingen
Printing and binding: Printer Trento S.r.L.,
Via alle Ròste, 12
38100 Trento TN, Italien
Printed in Italy

Bibliographic information published by the Deutsche Nationalbibliothek
The Deutsche Nationalbibliothek lists this publication in the Deutsche Nationalbibliografie; detailed bibliographic data is available on the Internet at http://www.dnb.de.

ISBN 978-3-7774-3136-9 (English edition)
ISBN 978-3-7774-3134-5 (German edition)

www.hirmerpublishers.com

Main Sponsor

Medienpartner